Visual Basic® Graphics Programming, Second Edition:
Hands-on Applications and Advanced Color Development

D1500440

Visual Basic® Graphics Programming, Second Edition:
Hands-on Applications and Advanced Color Development

Rod Stephens

Wiley Computer Publishing

John Wiley & Sons, Inc.

NEW YORK · CHICHESTER · WEINHEIM · BRISBANE · SINGAPORE · TORONTO

Publisher: Robert Ipsen
Editor: Carol A. Long
Managing Editor: Angela Murphy
Electronic Products, Associate Editor: Mike Sosa
Composition: Benchmark Productions Inc., Boston

Designations used by companies to distinguish their products are often claimed as trademarks. In all instances where John Wiley & Sons, Inc., is aware of a claim, the product names appear in initial capital or ALL CAPITAL LETTERS. Readers, however, should contact the appropriate companies for more complete information regarding trademarks and registration.

This book is printed on acid-free paper. ∞

Published by John Wiley & Sons, Inc.

Published simultaneously in Canada.

This publication is designed to provide accurate and authoritative information in regard to the subject matter covered. It is sold with the understanding that the publisher is not engaged in professional services. If professional advice or other expert assistance is required, the services of a competent professional person should be sought.

Library of Congress Cataloging-in-Publication Data:

Stephens, Rod
   Visual Basic graphics programming : hands-on applications and advanced color development / Rod Stephens.—2nd ed.
      p. cm.
   "Wiley computer publishing."
   Includes bibliographical references and index.
   ISBN 0–471–35599–2 (pbk. : CD-ROM : alk. paper)
   1. Computer graphics. 2. Microsoft Visual BASIC. I. Title.
T385.S756 1999
006.6'76521--dc21   99–043686
                                                                         CIP

Printed in the United States of America.

10 9 8 7 6 5 4 3 2

CONTENTS

A picture is worth a thousand words.

Graphics are cool. Sure, pouring a huge pile of paperwork into a computer and producing a neatly sorted and summarized report has its rewards, but nothing beats a good picture for pure impact. The same data that makes up a drab report can make a bright, eye-catching, animated three-dimensional chart that reveals trends that are completely hidden in a text format. Graphics can make data easier to understand, can make a dull report more interesting, and are just plain fun.

In this day of powerful personal computers, sophisticated graphics are necessary if your application is to stand out from the crowd. The ever-growing World Wide Web has raised user expectations to the point where sophisticated graphics are an absolute requirement for acceptability. Not long ago, a checkbook application had to balance a checkbook. Today, if the program does not have a conservative marble desktop, color-coded entries, three-dimensional graphs, and transactions carried out by little animated dollar symbols, it is barely acceptable. Cash register noises and the stock market closing bell may also be required, but they are beyond the scope of this book.

As users' graphical expectations have grown, Visual Basic's graphics capabilities have not. Visual Basic makes it easy to build forms and dialogs, but it gives you very little help in creating any but the simplest graphics. To add even simple charts or graphs to your application, you have to buy third-party add-on products or the Visual Basic Professional Edition.

You have even fewer options for providing sophisticated imaging, animation, or two- or three-dimensional graphics. Visual Basic provides no tools for creating three-dimensional images. The few third-party tools available focus on the display of graphs, surfaces, and other data representations rather than more general three-dimensional graphics. The two most promising exceptions, OpenGL and DirectX, are cumbersome at best and incredibly painful at worst.

Visual Basic Graphics Programming provides everything you need to add advanced graphics to your applications. This book explains how to use Visual Basic controls to create impressive graphic effects without buying expensive add-on products. It shows how to integrate imaging, animation, and two- and three-dimensional graphics into an application. Finally, *Visual Basic Graphics Programming* provides a large collection of example programs and ready-to-use functions that you can easily add to your own programs.

What This Package Includes

This book and CD package provides you with:

- A broad, in-depth introduction to graphic programming in Visual Basic. After reading the book and running the example programs, you will be able to use sophisticated graphics in your Visual Basic projects.

- Two hundred forty complete, ready-to-run example programs that allow you to explore the graphic techniques described in the text. You can use these programs to get a better understanding of how the graphical algorithms work. You can also modify these programs to form the basis of your own applications.

- Tools and functions for implementing graphics in your programs. The example programs contain routines for manipulating color images, overlaying one image on another, building scrolled windows, and performing a variety of other common graphics tasks. You can extract these tools and plug them into your programs.

Intended Audience

This book covers advanced Visual Basic programming topics. It does not teach Visual Basic itself. If you have a good understanding of the fundamentals of Visual Basic, you will be able to concentrate on the graphic algorithms without becoming bogged down in the details of the Visual Basic language. If you do not know how to place controls on a form, write an event handler, or run a Visual Basic program, you might want to brush up on your Visual Basic a bit.

This book does review the fundamentals of graphic programming in Visual Basic (using picture box controls, drawing lines, handling Paint and Resize events, and so forth), so do not worry if you have not had much experience with graphics.

Even if you have not yet mastered Visual Basic, you will be able to understand the graphic algorithms and run the example programs. With occasional references to your Visual Basic manuals, you will be able to modify the example programs to build applications of your own. By the time you have finished exploring all of the examples in this book, you will have become an experienced Visual Basic programmer.

Equipment and Version Compatibility

To read the book and understand the algorithms, you need no special equipment. To run and modify the example programs, you need a computer that is reasonably able to run Visual Basic. Naturally, you need a compact disk drive to load the programs from the CD-ROM.

All the example programs have been tested in Visual Basic 6.0 SP3 under Windows NT. They should run with little or no modification in other operating systems and with later versions of Visual Basic.

Most of the programs should also run with little trouble in Visual Basic 5. To open a Visual Basic 6 program in Visual Basic 5, first edit the program's .vbp file using an editor such as Notepad. Find any lines that say "Retained=0" and remove them. Save the file and open the program in Visual Basic 5.

Many examples will also run in Visual Basic 4, though translating them is harder. Open the project files in an editor, and cut and paste the code into a Visual Basic 4 project. You will need to add any necessary controls yourself. If you are running in a 16-bit environment such as Windows 3.1, you will need to translate any API functions the program needs into their 16-bit equivalents.

The OldSrc directory on the CD-ROM contains Visual Basic 4 source code from the previous edition of this book. Many of the examples still work and they may help you get started if you are using Visual Basic 4. They are provided "as-is" without any real support, however. Use them if you can; ignore them if you are using a later version of Visual Basic.

Few of the examples will port easily to earlier versions of Visual Basic. If you have an older version of Visual Basic, you should seriously consider upgrading to a more recent version. At least look at the Visual Basic 5 Control Creation Edition (CCE).

The Visual Basic 5 CCE lets you build programs and ActiveX controls much as Visual Basic 5 does. It will not let you create a compiled executable (.exe), but it will let you build a compiled ActiveX control (.ocx). Best of all, the CCE is available free on Microsoft's Web site. As of this writing, it is at http://msdn.microsoft.com/vbasic/downloads/cce. Microsoft often changes their links, however, so you may have to search to find the CCE's current location.

The example programs run at different speeds on different computers with different configurations. A 450MHz Pentium with 132Mb of memory will run much faster than a 486-based computer with 16Mb of memory (if such a computer can run Visual Basic anymore). You will quickly learn the limits of your hardware.

Chapter Overview

Visual Basic Graphics Programming is divided into five sections. Each covers a major topic in graphic programming.

Part One: Working with Windows

Part One describes beginning, intermediate, and advanced Visual Basic Windows programming. The techniques described in these chapters are used throughout the rest of the book.

Chapter 1, Visual Basics, covers the fundamentals of graphic programming in Visual Basic. If you are an experienced Visual Basic programmer, some of this material may be familiar to you. This chapter includes discussions of Visual Basic coordinates and scaling, custom coordinate systems, controls that can contain graphics, graphic methods and events, graphic properties, and the simple use of color. These topics form the foundation of any graphic program in Visual Basic.

Chapter 2, Using the API, discuses the use of the Windows Application Programming Interface (API). The API provides many powerful functions you can use to extend your graphic capabilities. This chapter explains generally how to use the API and discusses the complexities of passing parameters to API functions. It then describes some API functions, like Polygon and FloodFill, which are particularly useful in graphics programming. This chapter also discusses metafiles, which are files that allow a program to store graphic commands for later use.

Chapter 3, Advanced Color, explains how to deal with bitmaps and color on your system. It explains different color modes available to you and tells how you can change your system's color mode. It also tells how to manipulate device-independent bitmaps (DIBs) and device-dependent bitmaps.

Chapter 3 also talks about the color palettes used by the more restrictive color modes. The chapter explains how palettes are supposed to work, but the support for color palettes seems to be slowly slipping away. What was reasonable in Visual Basic 4 became harder in Visual Basic 5 and 6. At the same time, the reason for color palettes (high memory prices) has been fading. Color palettes still exist, but they are extremely confusing and not really necessary with today's memory prices.

Chapter 4, Advanced Text, deals with advanced text issues. You may not often think of it this way, but text is graphic, too. This chapter deals with such issues as text color, size, proportion, positioning, and orientation. It explains how to use the CreateFont API function to print text at an angle and how to make text follow a circular or curving path.

Chapter 5, Printing, discusses printing in Visual Basic. It explains printing fundamentals, low- and high-resolution printing, text wrapping across lines and pages, and print preview.

Part Two: Image Processing

Part Two covers techniques for manipulating bitmapped images. Using the information presented in these chapters, you will be able to add simple and not-so-simple images to your programs.

Chapter 6, Point Processes, explains methods for manipulating images one pixel at a time. Using these techniques you can adjust such image attributes as color balance, brightness, and contrast.

Chapter 7, Area Processes, covers procedures that modify images using the pixels in an area. It shows how to use filters to soften, sharpen, or emphasize edges in an image. It also describes morphing operations you can use to resize, rotate, warp, and otherwise deform an image.

Part Three: Animation

The chapters in Part Three explain how you can add animation to your Visual Basic programs.

Chapter 8, Bitmap Animation, explains animation basics. It shows how to use a series of bitmaps to provide the illusion of motion. It explains several different methods for timing images to provide the smoothest animation possible.

Chapter 9, Advanced Animation, describes several different ways a program can control an animation sequence. It tells how to use techniques such as simulation, scripting, and sprites to determine how animation should proceed. It also explains methods for generating animation sequences, including tweening and morphing.

Part Four: Two-Dimensional Graphics

The chapters in Part Four cover a variety of two-dimensional topics.

Chapter 10, Fractals and Tilings, describes fractal and tiling programs you can use to create extremely intricate pictures with remarkably little code.

Chapter 11, Drawing Curves, shows how to draw several useful types of curves. It explains such topics as working with parametric curves and using curves to smoothly fit a set of data values.

Chapter 12, Two-Dimensional Transformations, introduces homogeneous coordinates and two-dimensional transformations. These allow a program to perform a wide variety of graphical operations on objects in a simple, consistent manner. It is important that you understand these techniques before moving on to the three-dimensional technique described later.

Part Five: Three-Dimensional Graphics

Part Five takes graphics into the third dimension. It explains a progression of topics that display three-dimensional objects with increasing levels of realism. The chapters in Part Five start with simple wireframe images and lead you through the steps of creating photo-realistic ray traced images.

Chapter 13, Three-Dimensional Transformations, extends the concepts described in Chapter 12 into the third dimension. It explains how to translate, scale, and rotate three-dimensional objects. It also shows how to project them so you can display them on your computer's two-dimensional screen.

Chapter 14, Surfaces, explains how a program can display three-dimensional. It shows how to take advantage of the special structure of a surface to remove hidden parts of the image quickly and easily.

Chapter 15, Hidden Surface Removal, tells how to remove hidden surfaces in more general three-dimensional scenes. It covers the relatively simple backface removal algorithm that works for convex solids and the more involved depth-sort algorithm that works in general circumstances.

Chapter 16, Shading Models, explains how to shade the surfaces that make up an object. Using a simplified model of the physics of light, a program can greatly increase the realism of the objects it displays.

Chapter 17, Ray Tracing, shows how to create ray traced images that display reflective, shadowed, transparent, and textured objects. The programs described in this chapter produce images of almost photographic quality.

Part Six: Beyond Three Dimensions

Part Six covers two major topics. Chapter 18, Higher-Dimensional Transformations, shows methods for viewing higher-dimensional data. It explains how to use animation to display four-dimensional surfaces. It also extends the transformations covered in previous chapters to higher dimensions.

Chapter 19, Mathematical Tools, describes some useful mathematical formulas. It summarizes the standard transformation matrices in two, three, and four dimensions.

Changes in the Second Edition

By far the biggest change in this edition is the way it handles color in the programs that support it. The first edition dealt almost exclusively with 8-bit, 256-color mode. As memory prices have continued to fall, this mode has become less important. Now it is relatively inexpensive to add more memory to a computer and run in 24-bit color mode.

The Second Edition takes advantage of this change and uses 24-bit color almost exclusively. It includes instructions for using other color modes, but 24-bit color is so much simpler that you should consider using it if you need to write advanced color applications.

Other changes in the Second Edition include:

- A scrolled window control
- Routines that quickly load and save the pixel values of images in a variety of advanced colors modes
- Detailed discussion of text metrics so that you can determine exactly where text is positioned, normally or rotated
- Expanded coverage of the Rich Text Box control, including a Rich Text editor
- Printing routines to wrap text across lines and pages, preview printouts, and generate a high-resolution printout of a form automatically
- Multipage print previews
- New, faster methods for timing bitmap animations
- Bitmap image morphing
- High-degree polynomial curve fitting
- New Z-order algorithm for hidden line removal in surfaces
- Shaded fractal valley surface
- Shading and ray tracing with multiple light sources
- Gouraud and Phong shading
- Ray tracing speed improvements
- Checkerboard object
- Textured and environment mapped objects
- Formulas for calculating such values as the distance between a point and a line or between two lines
- Derivation of Platonic solid vertices

How to Use This Book

The chapters later in the book cover topics that are generally more complicated than those covered at the beginning. While the later concepts are more advanced, they do not necessarily require all of the preceding chapters.

Chapters 1, 2, and 3 discuss topics used throughout much of the rest of the book, so you should probably at least skim them first. After that, things spread out quite a bit.

The longest chain of dependent chapters starts with Chapter 12. This chapter introduces two-dimensional transformations. Chapter 13 extends those transformations into the third dimension. Chapter 18 further extends the transformations into even higher dimensions, and Chapter 19 contains a summary of two-, three-, and four-dimensional transformations.

Chapters 14 through 17 use the transformations explained in Chapter 13 to generate increasingly more sophisticated three-dimensional images, finishing with ray tracing.

Figure I.1 shows the dependencies between the chapters graphically. Before reading a chapter, you should read or at least skim the chapters to its left in the figure. For example, before you read Chapter 9, read Chapters 1, 2, 3, and 8.

Why Visual Basic?

One the most common complaints about Visual Basic is that it is slow. Even with the compiler introduced in Visual Basic 5, Delphi, Pascal, C, C++, and many other compiled languages are faster, more flexible, and more powerful than Visual Basic. With this in mind,

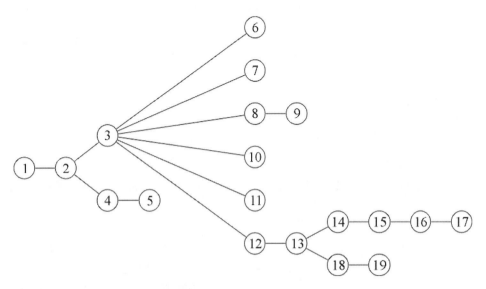

Figure I.1   Chapter dependencies.

it is natural to ask, "Why should I write complex graphics programs in Visual Basic? Wouldn't it be better to write complex applications in C? Or at least to build graphic algorithms in C and make them available to Visual Basic programs through libraries?"

Writing graphics programs in Visual Basic makes sense for several reasons.

First, Visual Basic provides a powerful environment for developing graphical user interfaces. Building a complete application in C or C++ is much more difficult and dangerous. If your program does not handle all the details of Windows programming correctly, your application, the development environment, and possibly all of Windows will come crashing down around your ears.

Second, building a C library for use by Visual Basic involves many of the same dangers as writing a Windows application in C. While the mechanics are simple, the details can be tricky. If your library and the Visual Basic program do not cooperate in just the right way, you will again crash your program, probably the Visual Basic environment, and maybe Windows as well.

Third, many graphics algorithms are efficient enough that they give good performance even in a slower language like Visual Basic. With personal computers increasing in power every year, many graphics techniques give perfectly acceptable results. You might be able to make some algorithms run a little faster using a C library, but the Visual Basic version is fast enough in most cases.

Fourth, if Visual Basic was your first programming language, there is no need for you to wait until you have mastered Pascal or C before you study graphic algorithms. While some techniques are a bit easier to handle in other languages, others are much harder. Using Visual Basic will also save you the expense of buying a new compiler.

Finally, by writing graphic applications in *any* programming language, you will learn more about graphic programming in general. As you study the example programs, you will learn techniques that you can use in other applications. Once you have mastered a graphic technique in Visual Basic, it will be much easier for you to reimplement it in Pascal or C if you find it absolutely necessary.

Using the CD

Table I.1 lists the contents of the CD-ROM that accompanies this book.

Table I.1 CD-ROM Contents

DIRECTORY	CONTENTS
Src	Source code and data files for most of the graphic techniques discussed in the book
Pictures	Pictures you can use with many of the example programs
Images	Images generated by the programs
Figs	Color images of many of the figures printed in this book
OldSrc	Source code for the example programs from the book's first edition

Within the Src directory, code is separated into subdirectories by chapter. For example, the source code for Chapter 7 is in the Src\Ch7 directory.

The OldSrc directory is similarly divided, although the chapters refer to the chapters in the book's first edition, so the subdirectories do not exactly match those in the Src directory. For example, the first edition's Chapter 7 covered two-dimensional transformations, and this edition's Chapter 12 covers that material. That means the OldSrc\Ch7 directory contains material similar to the Src\Ch12 subdirectory.

You can load the example programs from the Visual Basic environment using the File menu's Open Project command. You can select the files directly from the CD-ROM, or you can copy them onto your hard disk.

Read-Only Default

Note that files are always marked read-only on a CD-ROM. If you copy the files to your hard disk, they are marked read-only by default. If you want to modify one of the files, you must make sure it is not marked read-only.

You can do this with the File Manager. First copy the file onto your hard disk. Next select the file or files you want to unmark and invoke the File menu's Properties command. Uncheck the Read Only check box and press the OK button.

When you run the example programs, keep in mind that they are for demonstration purposes only. They are intended to help you understand particular graphic concepts, and they do not spend a great deal of time validating data and trapping errors. If you enter invalid data, the programs may crash.

Invalid "Retained" Keyword

The programs on the CD-ROM are saved in Visual Basic 6 format. If you try to run them in Visual Basic 5, you will get an error message complaining about an invalid "Retained" keyword. To fix this problem, edit the program's .vbp file using an editor such as Notepad. Find any lines that say "Retained=0" and remove them. Save the file and open the program in Visual Basic 5.

Web Resources

For updates, bug fixes, and to see what other readers are doing with graphics in Visual Basic, visit the book's Web page at www.vb-helper.com/vbgp.htm. If you generate particularly interesting images, let me know at RodStephens@vb-helper.com. If your images are interesting enough, I may post them on the book's Web page.

Working with Windows

Visual Basic provides enough graphic tools to produce any kind of graphic image. It gives you routines for drawing text, lines, circles, and other shapes. It also provides methods that allow you to examine and modify the individual pixels that make up an image.

While Visual Basic's methods give you complete control over an image, some of these methods are slow or cumbersome. For example, you can read and write every pixel in an image individually, but for large images, that can take a very long time. You could also draw text one pixel at a time using your own customized font, but it would be incredibly difficult. The Windows Application Programming Interface (API) provides many functions that make operations such as these faster and easier.

The chapters in Part One explain the fundamental graphic tools provided by Visual Basic. They also describe some of the more useful API graphic functions. These techniques form the building block that the later chapters use to produce graphics.

CHAPTER 1

Visual Basics

Visual Basic provides all the tools you need to generate any type of graphic image. It supplies routines for drawing text, lines, rectangles, circles, ellipses, and a host of other graphic shapes. The Point and PSet methods allow you to specify the exact value for every pixel in an image, giving you absolute control over the result. This chapter explains these fundamental tools that Visual Basic gives you for producing graphics.

The chapter begins by describing graphic coordinate systems in Visual Basic. There are many coordinate systems you can use to make graphic programming easier. Depending on your application, you may find it most convenient to measure distances in pixels, twips, millimeters, inches, or even a custom scale you design.

The sections that follow describe the methods that are most useful for drawing graphics in Visual Basic. Using these methods, you can display points, lines, circles, and other simple graphic objects that you can use to build more complicated pictures.

Next, the chapter discusses graphic events and properties that help you manage graphic operations. The chapter finishes with an introduction to the simple color system used by many Visual Basic applications.

Visual Basic Coordinate Systems

The three most important types of object for drawing in Visual Basic are the form, picture box, and printer. These objects support a wide variety of drawing commands that you can use to produce graphics. Forms, picture boxes, and printer objects provide almost exactly the same graphic operations, so most of the things you can do with one you can do with the others. For example, all three objects use scale properties to define their drawing coordinates, and all three use the Line statement to draw lines.

To make referring to these objects easier, this book sometimes calls them *drawing objects*. A drawing object is any object such as a form, picture box, or printer that accepts the standard Visual Basic drawing commands. In later chapters, you will see that these objects also support the same nonstandard drawing operations provided by API functions.

Whenever you want to draw something, you must determine where the drawing will be displayed. To do that, you need to understand how Visual Basic measures drawing coordinates. Each point on a form, picture box, or printer object has an X and a Y coordinate. By default, the X coordinate represents the distance from the left edge of the drawing area to the point, and the Y coordinate represents the distance from the top edge of the drawing area to the point. Figure 1.1 shows how the X and Y coordinates of a point relate to the drawing area.

Visual Basic provides several standard coordinate systems for your convenience. You select one of these systems by setting the drawing object's ScaleMode property.

The many different scales available in Visual Basic support flexibility in your graphic programming. You select one of these scales by setting the drawing object's ScaleMode property to one of the values in Table 1.1. The units in this list are specified in *logical inches*. A logical inch is an inch as it is theoretically displayed on a printer. Its length on your actual monitor or printer depends on your hardware and is probably not exactly one real inch.

In all of these scale modes, the upper left corner of the drawing area has coordinates (0, 0), and other coordinate values increase to the left and down.

By default, Visual Basic uses the vbTwips ScaleMode. This coordinate system gives sufficient precision for many applications, but sometimes another system is more convenient. If you want to draw a grid with lines every half inch, you may find it easier to work in inches.

Many advanced graphic techniques described in later chapters use Windows Application Programming Interface (API) functions. These functions always measure coordinates in pixels. If you use API functions in a drawing area, you may want to set the drawing area's ScaleMode to vbPixels. Then you will not need to convert back and forth between pixels for the API functions and whatever other scale you use for Visual Basic drawing commands. It is also usually easier to work with pixels when a program needs exact control over every pixel.

The vbCharacters coordinate system is the only one in which the horizontal and vertical units are not the same length. The coordinate values are roughly the size of a 12-point character, so they make aligning 12-point text in rows and columns easier. For example,

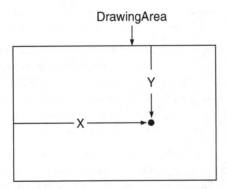

Figure 1.1 The default Visual Basic coordinate system.

Table 1.1   ScaleMode Property Values

SCALEMODE	MEANING
vbTwips	There are 1440 twips per logical inch (20 twips per point).
vbPoints	There are 72 printer's points per logical inch.
vbPixels	The pixel is the smallest unit of display on your screen (a single dot).
vbCharacters	Characters measure 12 points (240 twips) per unit vertically and 6 points (120 twips) per unit horizontally.
vbInches	Measurements are in logical inches.
vbMillimeters	There are roughly 254 millimeters per logical inch.
vbCentimeters	There are roughly 2.54 centimeters per logical inch.

the first character would be at position (0, 0), the next at (1, 0), and so forth. In practice, this may not be terribly useful because many programs use proportional fonts. Different characters have different widths, so they do not line up nicely in rows and columns.

Another value for the ScaleMode property is vbUser. This value indicates a custom coordinate system defined by the application. Generally, a program does not set Scale-Mode to this value. Visual Basic sets ScaleMode to vbUser when the program installs a custom coordinate system as described in the following section.

One last standard coordinate system worth mentioning here is vbHimetric. There are 100 himetric units per millimeter. The value vbHimetric is not included in Table 1.1 because you cannot select it as a ScaleMode value. Some functions return lengths in himetric units, however, so it is worth knowing what they are. You can use the ScaleX and ScaleY methods described shortly to convert from these units into something more useful.

Custom Coordinates

In addition to the standard coordinate systems listed in the previous section, a program can define its own coordinate system. A drawing object's ScaleLeft and ScaleTop properties define the coordinates of the leftmost and topmost points in the drawing area. The ScaleWidth and ScaleHeight properties determine how wide and how tall the drawing object is in custom units. For example, if you set ScaleWidth to 100, the X coordinates of the points in the drawing area will range from ScaleLeft to ScaleLeft + 100.

Suppose you want to draw a bar chart like the one shown in Figure 1.2. This chart represents seven data items with values between 50 and 100. You could use these custom coordinates to simplify the drawing of the chart:

```
ScaleLeft:    0
ScaleWidth:   9
ScaleTop:     110
ScaleHeight: -120
```

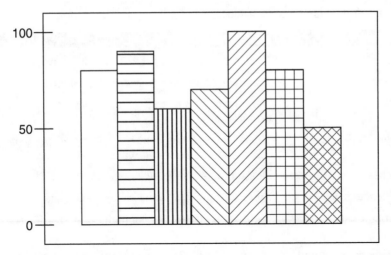

Figure 1.2 A bar chart.

Then the X coordinates on the drawing object range from 0 to 0 + 9 = 9, and the Y coordinates range from 110 to 110 + (-120) = -10. Because Y coordinates are measured from the top down, this means that the topmost point in the drawing area has a Y coordinate of 110, and the bottommost point in the drawing area has a Y coordinate of -10.

This arrangement is more in keeping with intuition: Larger Y coordinates are at the top of the drawing area, and smaller Y coordinates are at the bottom. This also makes drawing the bar chart easy. For the Kth data value, the program simply draws a box with X coordinates ranging from K to K + 1, and Y coordinates ranging from 0 to the value of the Kth data item.

Example program Bars uses this method to draw a bar chart like the one shown in Figure 1.2. When the program starts, it stores some random values in the DataValue array. When the form is resized, including when it is first created, the program redefines its coordinate system to match the data values. It clears its form and redraws the bar chart using the following code. (Do not worry too much about the drawing commands just yet. They are described later in this chapter. For now, just concentrate on the scale commands and the coordinates used to draw the bars.)

```
Option Explicit

Private Const NUM_VALUES = 7
Private DataValue(1 To NUM_VALUES) As Integer

' Create some random data.
Private Sub Form_Load()
Dim i As Integer

    Randomize
    For i = 1 To NUM_VALUES
        DataValue(i) = Rnd * 100
```

```
        Next i
End Sub


' Draw the bar chart.
Private Sub Form_Paint()
Dim i As Integer

    ' Define the custom coordinate system.
    ScaleLeft = 0
    ScaleWidth = NUM_VALUES + 2
    ScaleTop = 110
    ScaleHeight = -120

    ' Clear the form.
    Cls

    ' Draw the bar chart.
    For i = 1 To NUM_VALUES
        ' Pick a new fill style.
        FillStyle = i Mod 8

        ' Draw a box with i <= X <= i + 1 and
        ' 0 <= Y <= Data(i).
        Line (i, 0)-(i + 1, DataValue(i)), , B
    Next i
End Sub
```

To make creating custom coordinate systems easier, Visual Basic provides a Scale method. This routine takes as parameters the coordinates you want to give the upper-left and lower-right corners of the drawing area. For example, to create a custom coordinate system with the upper-left corner at (0, 0) and the lower-right corner at (100, 10), a program could use the single statement:

```
Scale (0, 0)-(100, 10)
```

This method is usually easier to understand than the ScaleLeft, ScaleTop, ScaleWidth, and ScaleHeight properties. Unfortunately, recent versions of Visual Basic do not allow the coordinates of the lower-right point to be smaller than the coordinates of the upper-left point. For example, if you execute the statement Scale (0, 100)-(100, 0), Visual Basic switches the Y coordinate arguments and treats the statement as if it were Scale (0, 0)-(100, 100).

This means you cannot use the Scale method to define the more intuitive coordinate systems where small Y values are near the bottom of the drawing object and larger values are near the top. You must use the ScaleLeft, ScaleTop, ScaleWidth, and ScaleHeight properties individually instead.

However, you can write a subroutine similar to the SetScale method to make defining the coordinate system easier. The SetTheScale routine shown in the following code sets a drawing object's Scale properties. The first parameter is the form, picture box, or printer object that should have the new coordinate system.

```
' Set the object's Scale properties.
Private Sub SetTheScale(ByVal obj As Object, _
    ByVal upper_left_x As Single, ByVal upper_left_y As Single, _
    ByVal lower_right_x As Single, ByVal lower_right_y As Single)

    obj.ScaleLeft = upper_left_x
    obj.ScaleTop = upper_left_y
    obj.ScaleWidth = lower_right_x - upper_left_x
    obj.ScaleHeight = lower_right_y - upper_left_y
End Sub
```

Example program Bars2 is similar to program Bars except it uses the SetTheScale subroutine to define its coordinate system as shown in the following code.

```
' Define the custom coordinate system.
SetTheScale Me, 0, 110, NUM_VALUES + 2, -10
```

Coordinate Overflow

Eventually, all coordinate systems must be converted into pixels for output to the computer's screen. No matter which ScaleMode you use, Visual Basic internally performs its calculations in pixels. These internally calculated coordinates are stored in signed integers, so they must lie between -32,768 and 32,767. If they do not, Visual Basic generates an overflow error.

Because it is the transformed coordinates that might overflow, the range of coordinates you can use depends on the coordinate system you are using. If you measure distances in pixels, you can use coordinate values between -32,768 and 32,767. If you use twips, you can use much larger coordinates because a large number of twips translates into a smaller number of pixels.

A typical computer screen might have 15 twips per pixel. In that case, you can use twip coordinate values up to 15 times as large as you can use pixel values. In other words, you can use coordinates between -491,520 and 491,505.

Similarly, a typical screen might display 96 pixels per inch. In that case, you can measure coordinates in inches between about -341.3 and 341.3 inches.

If your program generates overflow errors while drawing, you should determine whether your coordinate values are too large.

Scale Conversions

Drawing objects provide two functions, ScaleX and ScaleY, for translating between different scale modes. These functions take as parameters a coordinate value or length, the value's current coordinate system, and the desired coordinate system. For example, the following code converts 120 twips into pixels.

```
dist_pixels = ScaleX(120, vbTwips, vbPixels)
```

These functions are provided by a drawing object. This code does not specify an object, so Visual Basic uses the current form. This is equivalent to the following statement.

```
dist_pixels = Me.ScaleX(120, vbTwips, vbPixels)
```

Usually, it does not matter what object a program uses to convert from one coordinate system to another. Converting from inches to twips gives the same result no matter what object performs the conversion. There are 1440 twips per logical inch whether the drawing object is a form, picture box, or printer.

However, when an object has a custom coordinate system, using the correct properties is very important. If either of the ScaleMode values is vbUser, the object uses its own custom coordinates in the conversion. For example, suppose you want to draw a box five pixels square on a form that uses a custom coordinate system. You can use the form's ScaleX and ScaleY functions to convert the value five pixels into the form's coordinate system. Note that the form may scale differently in the X and Y directions, so its ScaleX and ScaleY functions may return different results.

Example program Bars3 uses the following code to draw a red box five pixels square. Once again, ignore the details of drawing the box for now. Focus instead on the use of the ScaleX and ScaleY functions.

```
Dim wid As Single
Dim hgt As Single
      :
    ' Draw a 5 by 5 pixel box at position
    ' (NUM_VALUES / 2 + 1, 50).
    wid = ScaleX(5, vbPixels, ScaleMode)
    hgt = ScaleY(5, vbPixels, ScaleMode)
    Line (NUM_VALUES / 2 + 1, 50)-Step(wid, hgt), vbRed, BF
```

Size and Positioning

The ScaleLeft, ScaleTop, ScaleWidth, and ScaleHeight properties determine the coordinates Visual Basic uses within a drawing object. The Top, Left, Width, and Height properties determine the object's size and position within its parent.

For a form or printer object, these properties are always measured in twips. For a picture box or other control, they are measured in the units used by the form or control that contains the object. For example, if a picture box is contained within another picture box with ScaleMode set to vbPixels, you must specify the position and size of the inner picture box using pixels. Figure 1.3 shows how these properties determine an object's position.

For forms, the Width and Height properties include the space taken up by borders and the form's title bar. Figure 1.4 shows the relationship between the Width, ScaleWidth, Height, and ScaleHeight properties for a form.

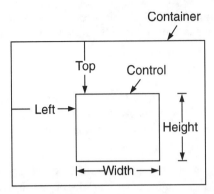

Figure 1.3 The Left, Top, Width, and Height properties determine an object's size and position.

Interior Sizing

For both forms and controls, the difference between Width and Height, on one hand, and ScaleWidth and ScaleHeight on the other can cause some confusion. For example, suppose you want to draw a picture on a form using custom coordinates with $0 <= X <= 100$ and $0 <= Y <= 100$. Suppose also that you want the picture to be one inch square.

If you set both the Width and Height to 1440 twips (1 inch), the actual drawing area will be somewhat smaller because the form must use some of its 1 square inch for borders. Even more of the form's height is removed for its title bar. That makes the drawing area slightly wider than it is tall. If you now define the custom coordinates $0 <= X <= 100$ and $0 <= Y <= 100$, your picture appears slightly flattened. Squares are a little too short and wide to be square.

The easiest way to deal with this mess is to use the form itself to figure out how large the borders and title bar will be. When you are ready to size the form, compute the difference between the Width and ScaleWidth properties. That is the amount used by the form for its side borders. Similarly, compute the difference between the form's Height

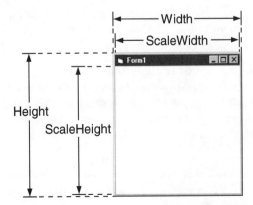

Figure 1.4 The relationship between Width, ScaleWidth and between Height and Scale-Height.

and ScaleHeight properties. Because you must specify the form's height and width in twips, you should calculate these values in twips.

Then when you resize the form, add these amounts to the desired width and height to allow room for the borders and title bar. The following Visual Basic code shows how to size a form so that its interior drawing area is 1 logical inch square.

```
Dim extra_wid As Single
Dim extra_hgt As Single

    extra_wid = Width - ScaleWidth
    extra_hgt = Height - ScaleHeight
    Me.Width = 1440 + extra_wid
    Me.Height = 1440 + extra_hgt
```

Example program Insize demonstrates this code. When it starts, the program creates two forms. It sets the Width and Height of the first to 1 inch. It uses code similar to the previous code to set the interior width and height of the second form to 1 inch. The program draws a grid in both forms, so you can see that the drawing area in the first is not square.

When you use this method, you must be sure that you use the correct units of measurement. A form's Width and Height are always specified in twips. Its ScaleWidth and ScaleHeight may be defined in some other units, including a custom coordinate system. In that case, you must convert the ScaleWidth and ScaleHeight into twips as shown in the following code.

```
extra_wid = Width - ScaleX(ScaleWidth, ScaleMode, vbTwips)
extra_hgt = Height - ScaleY(ScaleHeight, ScaleMode, vbTwips)
```

This fails if the resizing causes the form to rearrange its menus. If the form is wide, it may be able to display all of its menus in one row within its title bar. If you make the form too narrow, it may need to display the title bar on multiple rows. In that case, the title bar height increases and the amount allowed by the program will not be enough to hold the larger title bar.

You must also allow room for borders on picture boxes that have them. Suppose you want to create a picture box with an interior area 1500 twips tall and 2500 twips wide. Suppose the form that contains the picture box has defined a custom scale. To correctly size the picture box, you must convert its size into the form's custom coordinate system, allowing room for its border.

Example program BoxSize, shown in Figure 1.5, uses the following code to display two picture boxes. The first includes extra room for its borders while the second does not. The program draws a diamond shape in each picture box, so you can see that the second picture box is not big enough to hold its desired drawing area.

```
' Size the picture boxes and draw a diamond in each.
Private Sub Form_Load()
Dim wid As Single
Dim hgt As Single
```

```
Dim extra_wid As Single
Dim extra_hgt As Single

    ' Convert the desired width and height from
    ' twips into the form's custom coordinates.
    wid = Me.ScaleX(2500, 1, 0)
    hgt = Me.ScaleY(1500, 1, 0)

    WrongPict.Width = wid
    WrongPict.Height = hgt
    WrongPict.Line (0, 750)-(1250, 0)
    WrongPict.Line -(2500, 750)
    WrongPict.Line -(1250, 1500)
    WrongPict.Line -(0, 750)

    With RightPict
        extra_wid = .Width - Me.ScaleX( _
            .ScaleWidth, .ScaleMode, Me.ScaleMode)
        extra_hgt = .Height - Me.ScaleY( _
            .ScaleHeight, .ScaleMode, Me.ScaleMode)
        .Width = wid + extra_wid
        .Height = hgt + extra_hgt
    End With
    RightPict.Line (0, 750)-(1250, 0)
    RightPict.Line -(2500, 750)
    RightPict.Line -(1250, 1500)
    RightPict.Line -(0, 750)
End Sub
```

This method for using a custom coordinate system works well as long as you do not
need to locate points too close to the right or bottom edges of the drawing object. Points
very close to the right and bottom edges will fall just outside the drawing object's inte-

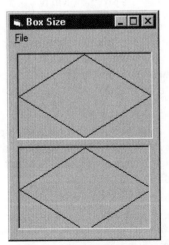

Figure 1.5 Program BoxSize shows the right and wrong way to size a picture box.

rior. If you look very closely at Figure 1.5, you will see that one pixel was cropped off the right and bottom corners of the first diamond in the program BoxSize.

To prevent this problem, you can make your coordinate system slightly larger to provide a small margin around whatever you are drawing. For example, you can add one pixel's worth of room when you calculate Width and Height. In the code above, you would set the values of extra_wid and extra_hgt as shown here:

```
extra_wid = .Width - _
    Me.ScaleX(ScaleWidth, .ScaleMode, Me.ScaleMode) + _
    Me.ScaleX(1, vbPixels, Me.ScaleMode)
extra_hgt = .Height - _
    Me.ScaleY(.ScaleHeight, .ScaleMode, Me.ScaleMode) + _
    Me.ScaleY(1, vbPixels, Me.ScaleMode)
```

The Move Method

Forms and controls provide a Move method that allows you to set the Top, Left, Width, and Height properties all at once. The syntax for the Move method is:

object.**Move** *left, top, width, height*

Here, *object* is the object you want to move, and *left*, *top*, *width*, and *height* are the new values you want to set for the Left, Top, Width, and Height properties. Not only does this method save you a little coding, it is also quite a bit faster. Each time you change one of these four properties, Visual Basic must move or resize the control and redraw it. If you change all four of these values separately, Visual Basic redraws the control four times. If you use the Move method, Visual Basic redraws the control only once. In tests, using the Move method works almost four times as fast as changing the four properties individually.

Only the Move method's first argument, *left*, is required. You can leave other arguments off if you do not need to change them. For example, you can specify only the *left* and *top* values to move the control without resizing it.

Graphic Container Controls

Three kinds of objects—forms, picture boxes, and printer objects—can supply most of your graphic needs. Forms are the largest unit in a typical Visual Basic user interface. You can draw directly on a form, and forms can contain other controls. A form can have different kinds of "window decoration," including a title bar, system menu, buttons, and resizable borders.

As with forms, you can draw directly on a picture box. You can also place other controls within a picture box. While you can draw directly on a form, it is more common to place one or more picture boxes on the form and then draw on those. This approach takes a bit more memory but provides extra flexibility. If you decide to move a drawing to another part of the form, for example, you can simply move the picture box to a new position. In contrast, to move a drawing that you have drawn directly on a form, you would need to modify the drawing source code.

Printer objects represent printers attached to your computer. By drawing to a printer object and then telling the object you are finished, you can print text and graphics.

Forms, picture boxes, and printers all provide the graphic methods shown in Table 1.2.

Forms and picture boxes also provide a Cls method that clears the drawing area. These methods are described in detail in the following sections.

Line Method

The Line method allows you to draw line segments using the following syntax:

```
Line Step(x1, y1)-Step(x2, y2), color, BF
```

Step	If you include the first Step keyword, the coordinates of the line's starting point are relative to the end of your last drawing command. If you just finished drawing a line that ended at (100, 100), and you now specify $x1 = 10$ and $y1 = 50$, this line starts at (110, 150).
(x1, y1)	The coordinate of the point at which the line should start. If you omit this point, the line starts where the previous drawing command ended.
Step	If you include the second Step keyword, the coordinates of the line's ending point are relative to the line's starting point.
(x2, y2)	The coordinate of the point at which the line should end.
color	The color the line should have.
B	If you include the B flag, the Line method draws a box with corners at the start and end points.
F	If you include the F flag, the Line command fills the box with corners at the start and end points, using the same color used to draw the box. If you use the F flag, you must also include the B flag.

A common reason to omit the line's starting point is to draw a sequence of connected line segments like this:

Table 1.2   Graphic Methods for Objects

METHOD	PURPOSE
Line	Draws a line, rectangle, or filled box
Circle	Draws a circle or ellipse, or an arc of a circle or ellipse
PaintPicture	Copies a picture from one control to another
PSet	Sets the color of a specified point
Point	Returns the color of a specified point
Print	Displays text

```
Line (0, 0)-(100, 100)
Line -(200, 400)
Line -(300, 300)
Line -(400, 500)
```

The Line method honors custom coordinates, so it places the line's end points where they belong in the current coordinate system.

Circle Method

The Circle method draws circles, ellipses, and sections of circles and ellipses. It uses the syntax:

Circle Step(x, y), radius, color, start, end, aspect

Step	If you include the Step keyword, the X and Y coordinates of the circle's center are relative to the end of your last drawing command.
(x, y)	The coordinates where you want the center of the circle.
radius	The radius of the circle.
color	The color of the circle.
start, end	The starting and ending angles for drawing an arc or pie slice.
aspect	The aspect ratio (height divided by width) for drawing ellipses.

The angles used by the Circle method are measured counterclockwise in radians where a horizontal line to the right lies along the angle 0. Figure 1.6 shows how Visual Basic measures angles.

You can convert from radians to degrees using the following formulas.

```
radians = degrees / 180 * 3.14159265
degrees = radians * 180 / 3.14159265
```

The Circle method has several interesting features. If you set *start* to a negative number, Circle draws a line from the center of the circle to the starting point and then treats *start* as a positive angle. Similarly, if *end* is negative, the Circle method draws a line from the center to the end position and treats *end* as a positive angle. Using these features, you can draw pie slices. The commands below draw the pie slice shown in Figure 1.7.

```
Const PI = 3.14159265
Circle (50, 50), 30, , -π / 6, -π * 0.75
```

Figure 1.6   Measuring angles in Visual Basic.

Figure 1.7   Output from the statement Circle (50, 50), 30, , -π / 6, -π * 0.75.

Unfortunately –0 = 0, so the Circle method cannot tell whether it should draw a radius when an angle is 0. You can make Circle draw a radius by specifying the equivalent angle –π.

The Circle method also requires that its angles lie between –2 * π and 2 * π. If you specify an angle outside this range, Visual Basic generates an error.

The PieSlice subroutine shown in the following code makes drawing pie slices easier. While either angle is greater than 2 * π, that routine subtracts 2 * π from the angle. Then, while either angle is less than or equal to 0, the routine adds 2 * π to that angle. This ensures that both angles are positive, between 0 and 2 * π, and not exactly 0. The routine then uses Circle as usual to draw the pie slice.

```
' Draw a pie slice.
Public Sub PieSlice(ByVal obj As Object, _
    ByVal X As Single, ByVal Y As Single, ByVal radius As Single, _
    ByVal start_angle As Single, ByVal end_angle As Single)

    ' Make both angles <= 2 * π.
    Do While start_angle > 2 * π
        start_angle = start_angle - 2 * π
    Loop
    Do While end_angle > 2 * π
        end_angle = end_angle - 2 * π
    Loop

    ' Make both angles strictly positive.
    Do While start_angle <= 0
        start_angle = start_angle + 2 * π
    Loop
    Do While end_angle <= 0
        end_angle = end_angle + 2 * π
    Loop

    ' Draw the slice
    obj.Circle (X, Y), radius, obj.ForeColor, -start_angle, -end_angle
End Sub
```

Example program Pie, shown in Figure 1.8, uses the Circle method and subroutine PieSlice to draw pie slices. Enter negative values in the text boxes on the left to make the Circle method draw pie slices. Enter positive values in the right text boxes, and the PieSlice subroutine will convert them into negative values as necessary.

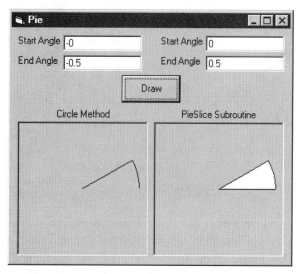

Figure 1.8 Example program Pie uses the PieSlice subroutine to make drawing pie slices easier.

The Circle method can also draw ellipses. If you set the method's *aspect* parameter to a value other than 1.0, Visual Basic draws an ellipse with that height/width ratio. Circle draws an ellipse with major (longer) axis of length 2 * radius, and it adjusts the minor (shorter) axis to give the ellipse the correct aspect ratio. Figure 1.9 shows a circle surrounding an ellipse with aspect ratio 2.0. These shapes were drawn with the following commands.

```
Circle (50, 50), 20
Circle (50, 50), 20, , , , 2.0
```

One drawback to the Circle method is that it does not honor custom coordinate systems. If you omit the *aspect* parameter or set it to 1.0, the Circle method draws a circle with a width equal to 2 * *radius*. It then gives the circle the same height on the screen. This result may not agree with your custom coordinate system.

For instance, suppose you have a square form and you have defined a custom coordinate system with the command Scale (0, 0)-(200, 100). If you then draw a circle with radius 20, you expect the circle's width and height to be 40 units in the custom coordinate system. Because the custom coordinate system contains 200 units horizontally and only 100 units vertically, you expect the circle to be taller than it is wide.

The Circle method, however, makes the circle 40 units wide and then adjusts the circle's height so that it is round on the screen. If the Circle method honored the custom coordinate system, the box and circle drawn with the following commands would have the same height and width. Because it does not, these commands produce a round circle inside a taller rectangle with the same width.

```
Line (80, 30)-(120, 70), , B
Circle (100, 50), 20
```

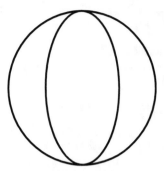

Figure 1.9 A circle and an ellipse with aspect ratio 2.

There are a couple of ways you can make ellipses more easily using custom coordinates. The EllipseWithSegments subroutine shown in the following code draws an ellipse using short line segments. It uses the sine and cosine functions, multiplied by the ellipse's half width and height, to draw the ellipse. Because the Line method does honor custom coordinates, the result is an ellipse in the drawing object's coordinate system.

```
' Draw an ellipse using line segments.
Private Sub EllipseWithSegments(ByVal obj As Object, _
    ByVal xmin As Single, ByVal ymin As Single, _
    ByVal xmax As Single, ByVal ymax As Single)
Const π = 3.14159265
Dim theta As Single
Dim cx As Single
Dim cy As Single
Dim radius_x As Single
Dim radius_y As Single
Dim X As Single
Dim Y As Single

    ' Find the center.
    cx = (xmin + xmax) / 2
    cy = (ymin + ymax) / 2

    ' Find the X and Y half-widths.
    radius_x = (xmax - xmin) / 2
    radius_y = (ymax - ymin) / 2

    ' Draw the ellipse.
    obj.CurrentX = cx + radius_x
    obj.CurrentY = cy
    For theta = 0 To 2 * π Step π / 10
        X = cx + radius_x * Cos(theta)
        Y = cy + radius_y * Sin(theta)
        obj.Line -(X, Y)
    Next theta
    obj.Line -(cx + radius_x, cy)
End Sub
```

The ScaledCircle subroutine shown in the following code uses the Circle method to draw an ellipse using custom coordinates. It converts the desired ellipse's width and height into twips so that it can study the ellipse's dimensions as they should appear on the screen, not in the custom coordinate system. It uses these values to calculate the ellipse's aspect ratio.

Next, if the ellipse's width is greater than its height, the routine sets the ellipse's radius to half of its width converted back into the custom coordinate system. This gives the ellipse the proper width. The aspect ratio makes the ellipse adjust its height properly.

If the ellipse's height is greater than its width, the routine sets the ellipse's radius to half of its width converted back into the custom coordinate system, multiplied by the aspect ratio. This gives half the height of the ellipse converted into the drawing object's horizontal scale mode. This value and the aspect ratio make the Circle method provide the necessary ellipse.

Finally, the subroutine calls the Circle method to draw the ellipse.

```
' Draw a circle stretched to obey the object's
' scale mode.
Private Sub ScaledCircle(ByVal obj As Object, _
    ByVal xmin As Single, ByVal ymin As Single, _
    ByVal xmax As Single, ByVal ymax As Single)
Dim cx As Single
Dim cy As Single
Dim wid As Single
Dim hgt As Single
Dim aspect As Single
Dim radius As Single

    ' Find the center.
    cx = (xmin + xmax) / 2
    cy = (ymin + ymax) / 2

    ' Get the ellipse's size in twips.
    wid = obj.ScaleX(xmax - xmin, obj.ScaleMode, vbTwips)
    hgt = obj.ScaleY(ymax - ymin, obj.ScaleMode, vbTwips)
    aspect = hgt / wid

    ' See which dimension is larger.
    If wid > hgt Then
        ' The major axis is horizontal.
        ' Get the radius in custom coordinates.
        radius = obj.ScaleX(wid / 2, vbTwips, obj.ScaleMode)
    Else
        ' The major axis is vertical.
        ' Get the radius in custom coordinates.
        radius = aspect * obj.ScaleX(wid / 2, vbTwips, obj.ScaleMode)
    End If

    ' Draw the circle.
    obj.Circle (cx, cy), radius, , , , aspect
End Sub
```

The EllipseWithSegments and ScaledCircle subroutines both take X and Y coordinate values that bound the ellipse as parameters. This is much easier to understand than the center, radius, and aspect ratio values required by the Circle method.

The sines and cosines used by subroutine EllipseWithSegments are a bit easier to understand than the seemingly arbitrary way in which ScaledCircle sets its radius. Depending on the number of segments EllipseWithSegments draws, however, ScaledCircle may be faster and produce a smoother result.

Example program Ellipses, shown in Figure 1.10, demonstrates the EllipseWithSegments and ScaledCircle subroutines.

The problem with the Circle method is that it has been asked to do too many things at once. Because it can draw circles, ellipses, arcs, and pie slices, it is quite confusing to use in all but the simplest cases.

PaintPicture Method

The PaintPicture method copies images from a form or picture box onto a form, picture box, or printer. PaintPicture has this syntax:

```
PaintPicture source, dx, dy, dwidth, dheight, sx, sy, swidth, sheight, opcode
```

source	The Picture or Image property of the source form or picture box.
dx, *dy*	The destination X and Y coordinates.
dwidth, *dheight*	The width and height of the destination area. If the source and destination are different sizes, the image is stretched or shrunk to fit.
sx, *sy*	The source X and Y coordinates.
swidth, *sheight*	The width and height of the part of the source image to copy.
opcode	The method by which the source is copied.

The *source* parameter must specify a valid image. If you load a form or picture box with a bitmap or other graphic file, that control's Picture property holds a valid image. If you set a

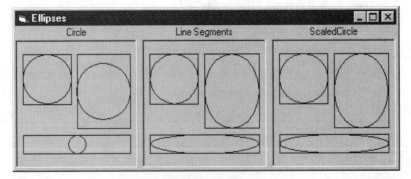

Figure 1.10 Example program Ellipses compares the Circle method with the Ellipse-WithSegments and ScaledCircle subroutines.

form or picture box's AutoRedraw property to true, that control's Image property holds a valid copy of whatever the control displays. If a program tries to use the PaintPicture method with an invalid *source* parameter, Visual Basic generates an Invalid picture error.

The Picture and Image properties are often a source of great confusion. When AutoRedraw is True, the Image property is a permanent copy of the control's surface in memory. The Picture property is used for repainting the control when it is cleared. To make a control's visible contents a permanent part of the background, the program should set the control's Picture property equal to its Image property. The following code shows how a program might draw a line on one picture box, make it a permanent part of its background image, and then copy it to a second picture box.

```
' Set AutoRedraw = True so we can use the Image property.
picFrom.AutoRedraw = True

' Draw a line.
picFrom.Line (0, 0)-(1440, 1440)

' Make the a line permanent part of the picture.
picFrom.Picture = picFrom.Image

' Copy the image from picFrom to picTo.
picTo.PaintPicture picFrom.Picture, 0, 0
```

PaintPicture's *opcode* parameter tells PaintPicture how to merge the pixels in the source image with those in the destination image. The bits that define the pixels are combined according to different bitwise Boolean operations depending on the value of *opcode*. Visual Basic has defined constants for the most commonly used opcodes.

vbBlackness	Make all output black.
vbDstInvert	NOT Destination.
vbMergeCopy	Pattern AND Source.
vbMergePaint	(NOT Source) OR Destination.
vbNotSrcCopy	NOT Source.
vbNotSrcErase	NOT (Source OR Destination).
vbPatCopy	Pattern.
vbPatInvert	Destination XOR Pattern.
vbPatPaint	((NOT Source) OR Pattern) OR Destination.
vbSrcAnd	Source AND Destination.
vbSrcCopy	Source.
vbSrcErase	(NOT Destination) AND Source.
vbSrcInvert	Source XOR Destination.
vbSrcPaint	Source OR Destination.
vbWhiteness	Make all output white.

These operations can be very confusing, particularly because the Boolean operations used by Visual Basic do not behave exactly as you might expect. For instance, the color produced by combining the colors &HFFFFFF and &H0000FF with the vbSrcInvert opcode is not necessarily &HFFFF00. The way these operations work depends on whether the system is using palettes and the state of the system color palette. This extremely confusing topic is discussed further in Chapter 3.

One of the most useful opcodes is vbSrcCopy. This simply copies the source image into the destination without modification.

The vbSrcInvert opcode is also useful because it is easily reversible. If you copy the same source image into a destination twice using vbSrcInvert, you are left with the original destination image. The second PaintPicture operation undoes the inversion performed by the first.

You can achieve another reversible combination by copying the source to the destination using vbSrcInvert and then copying the source to the destination again using vbDestInvert. This produces an effect similar to that which is produced by vbSrcInvert alone, but the destination is inverted twice. This approach restores parts of the destination that correspond to blank parts of the source image to their original colors. You can reverse this process by again copying the source to the destination using vbSrcInvert followed by vbDestInvert.

Using a series of calls to PaintPicture, you can overlay a source image onto a destination image. Create a mask image that is black over the parts of the source image that you want to copy and white over the rest. Next, copy the mask onto the destination image using the vbMergePaint opcode. This blanks out the portions of the destination corresponding to black parts of the mask. Finally, copy the source image onto the destination using the vbSrcAnd opcode.

Where the destination image is white, including the areas blanked by the mask, the source image appears. In places where the source image is white, the destination image remains unchanged. In places where neither the source nor the destination is white, the two images combine bitwise.

The best way to learn about opcodes is to experiment with them yourself. Example program PaintPic, shown in Figure 1.11, lets you experiment with different opcodes. Click on a source image and select an opcode from the list. When you click the Copy button, the program uses PaintPicture to copy the source image to the destination image with the opcode you selected. The destination images are three different sizes so you can see how PaintPicture stretches and shrinks an image.

In Figure 1.11, the program used vbSrcCopy to copy the checkerboard image to the destination images. It then used the black rose mask image with the vbMergePaint opcode to block out space for the rose image. Finally, it copied the rose image using the vbSrcAnd opcode to overlay the rose on the checkerboard.

PSet Method

The PSet method allows you to set the color of a single pixel at a specific position. PSet has this syntax:

```
PSet Step (x, y), color
```

Step   If you include the Step keyword, the X and Y coordinates are relative to
                  the end of your last drawing command.

x, y   The coordinates of the point you want to color.

color   The color for the point.

Because PSet sets a single pixel, it is easiest to use when the drawing object's Scale-
Mode is vbPixels. Then the coordinates you send to PSet exactly match those drawn on
the screen. If you use some other ScaleMode, such as vbTwips, you need to compute the
location of the pixel you want to draw. If you are not careful, you may have trouble setting each pixel exactly once.

For example, the following code sets every pixel in the picture box picBlack to the color
black.

```
Dim X As Single
Dim Y As Single

    ' Make all the pixels black.
    For X = 0 To picMirror.ScaleWidth
        For Y = 0 To picMirror.ScaleHeight
            picBlack.PSet (X, Y), vbBlack
        Next Y
    Next X
```

This code works as you would expect if the control's ScaleMode is vbPixels. If the control's ScaleMode is vbTwips, however, the code takes far longer than it should. Because
twips are relatively small, there are several twips per pixel. A typical monitor might display 72 pixels per logical inch. There are 1440 twips per logical inch, so the monitor has
20 twips per pixel. As X moves from 0 to picBlack.ScaleWidth, it sets the color of each
pixel 20 times, so the code takes roughly 20 times as long as it should.

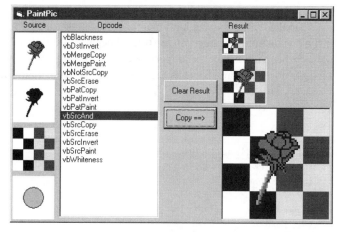

Figure 1.11   Example program PaintPic demonstrates PaintPicture opcodes.

Point Method

The Point method returns the color of the pixel at the specified coordinates. Its syntax is:

Point *(x, y)*

x, y   The coordinates of the point.

The PSet and Point methods complement each other: one gets the color of a pixel, and the other sets the color of a pixel. Like the PSet method, the Point method is easiest to use when the drawing object's ScaleMode is vbPixels.

You could use the PSet and Point methods to make the right half of a picture box named picMirror display a reflected image of its left half using the following code:

```
Dim X As Single
Dim Y As Single
Dim wid As Single
Dim hgt As Single

    ' Work in pixels.
    picMirror.ScaleMode = vbPixels

    ' Get the image's dimensions.
    wid = picMirror.ScaleWidth
    hgt = picMirror.ScaleHeight

    ' Mirror.
    For X = 0 To wid / 2
        For Y = 0 To hgt
            picMirror.PSet (wid - X, Y), picMirror.Point(X, Y)
        Next Y
    Next X
```

Note that you can achieve the same effect more efficiently using the PaintPicture method. If you give PaintPicture a negative width for the source image, the routine stretches the image by a factor of -1 to make it fit in the destination image. This makes a mirror image of the source appear in the destination. Because you are using a negative width, you must also specify the upper-right corner rather than the upper-left corner as the start of the source image. The following code does the same thing as the previous code using PaintPicture.

```
Dim wid As Single
Dim hgt As Single

    ' Get the area's dimensions.
    wid = PaintPict.ScaleWidth / 2
    hgt = PaintPict.ScaleHeight

    ' Mirror the area.
    picMirror.PaintPicture picMirror, _
```

```
wid + 1, 0, wid, hgt, _
wid - 1, 0, -wid, hgt, vbSrcCopy
```

Example program Mirror demonstrates both of these methods for creating a mirror image. It creates a third image using the Point and PSet methods, as shown in Figure 1.12, updating the image as it progresses. You can see from the program that the Paint-Picture version is much faster than the other methods. In general, using special-purpose routines such as PaintPicture is faster than building routines yourself using the Point and PSet methods. For example, it is much faster to draw a line using the Line method than to plot the points in the line one at a time using PSet.

The two Point/PSet techniques used by program Mirror take similar amounts of time, although they raise an interesting user interface design issue. Users generally perceive an interface element as more responsive if it presents itself all at once rather than showing itself in pieces as it is built. That means the version that does not refresh to show its progress may be perceived as faster even if the two methods take about the same amount of time.

On the other hand, if a picture takes more than a few seconds to draw, the user may become impatient or not realize that the program is working. In that case, it is better to provide some feedback by allowing the user to watch the picture under construction.

Print Method

The Print method displays text on a drawing object. Its syntax is quite simple:

Print *output list*

The *output list* is a series of data items to be printed. If you separate two items with a semicolon, the Print method displays the second immediately after the first. If you separate two items with a comma, the Print method displays the second at the picture's next *print zone*. Print zones start every 14 columns, where the width of a column is the average width of a character on the drawing object.

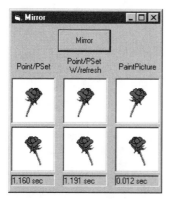

Figure 1.12   Example program Mirror compares three different methods for creating a mirror image.

You can also include the two special items **Spc(n)** and **Tab(n)** in the output list. Spc(n) makes the Print method display n spaces. Keep in mind that, in most fonts, different characters have different widths, and the space character is often quite thin. Tab(n) makes the Print method move to the nth print zone.

The Print method begins displaying text with the upper-left corner of the text at the coordinates (CurrentX, CurrentY). A drawing object's CurrentX and CurrentY properties indicate the end point of the last drawing operation. When the Print statement finishes, it sets CurrentX to 0, and CurrentY so the next line of text appears below the current one.

The following code draws an X at position (1440, 720). It then sets (CurrentX, CurrentY) to this position and prints the text Line 1. After displaying Line 1, the Print statement sets CurrentX to 0 and CurrentY to position the next line of text under the first.

The program then displays Line 2. Because a comma comes next in the Print statement's output list, the Print method advances to the next print zone before displaying Zone 2. Another comma follows, so Print moves to the next print zone before printing Zone 3. Because this line ends in a semicolon, the Print command does not advance CurrentX and CurrentY. These values are left alone, so the next text appears immediately after Zone 3.

Finally, the code displays the text Line 3. Example program Print, shown in Figure 1.13, demonstrates this code.

```
Const X = 1440
Const Y = 720

    AutoRedraw = True
    Line (X - 100, Y - 100)-Step(100, 100)
    Line (X + 100, Y - 100)-Step(-100, 100)

    CurrentX = X
    CurrentY = Y

    Print "Line 1"
    Print "Line 2", "Zone 2", "Zone 3";
    Print "Line 3"
```

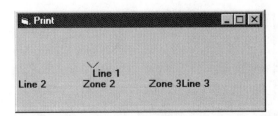

Figure 1.13   Example program Print displays text with the Print method.

Scrolled Windows

Sometimes your program may need to display more information than can fit on a single form. In that case, you might like to display the information in a scrolled window. Unfortunately Visual Basic does not have a scrolled window control, so this is not easy, but you can use Visual Basic's controls to build a scrolling window yourself.

Place a PictureBox named picOuter on a form. Inside picOuter, place another Picture-Box named picInner. Make sure picInner is contained inside picOuter and not just sitting on top of it. Next, place horizontal and vertical scroll bars next to picOuter.

Now put whatever information you want to scroll inside picInner. For example, to display a large image, set picInner's Picture property to the image. Set picInner's AutoSize property to True so that the control resizes to fit the image.

Because it is contained in picOuter, picInner is clipped if it extends beyond the edges of picOuter. When the user changes the scroll bar values, the program should adjust picInner's Left and Top properties. That makes different parts of picInner visible inside picOuter, so the image appears to scroll.

Example program Scroll, shown in Figure 1.14, displays a large image in a scrolled window.

Example program Scroll manages its scrolled window with the following code. The most interesting part of the program is the ArrangeControls subroutine. ArrangeControls determines how big picInner is and how much space is available on the form, subtracting room for picOuter's borders. It compares the space required with the space available to see which scroll bars it needs. Notice that any scroll bar it uses reduces the space available. That means using one scroll bar may require the use of the other.

```
Option Explicit

Private Sub Form_Load()
    picInner.AutoSize = True
    picInner.Move 0, 0
End Sub
```

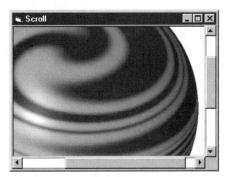

Figure 1.14 Example program Scroll displays a large image in a scrolled window.

```vb
Private Sub Form_Resize()
    ArrangeControls
End Sub

' Arrange the scroll bars.
Private Sub ArrangeControls()
Dim border_width As Single
Dim got_wid As Single
Dim got_hgt As Single
Dim need_wid As Single
Dim need_hgt As Single
Dim need_hbar As Boolean
Dim need_vbar As Boolean
    ' See how much room we have and need.
    border_width = picOuter.Width - picOuter.ScaleWidth
    got_wid = ScaleWidth - border_width
    got_hgt = ScaleHeight - border_width
    need_wid = picInner.Width
    need_hgt = picInner.Height

    ' See if we need the horizontal scroll bar.
    If need_wid > got_wid Then
        need_hbar = True
        got_hgt = got_hgt - hbarMarble.Height
    End If

    ' See if we need the vertical scroll bar.
    If need_hgt > got_hgt Then
        need_vbar = True
        got_wid = got_wid - vbarMarble.Width

        ' See if we now need the horizontal scroll bar.
        If (Not need_hbar) And need_wid > got_wid Then
            need_hbar = True
            got_hgt = got_hgt - hbarMarble.Height
        End If
    End If

    ' Arrange the controls.
    picOuter.Move 0, 0, got_wid + border_width, got_hgt + border_width
    If need_hbar Then
        hbarMarble.Move 0, got_hgt + border_width, _
            got_wid + border_width
        hbarMarble.Min = 0
        hbarMarble.Max = picInner.ScaleWidth - got_wid
        hbarMarble.SmallChange = got_wid / 5
        hbarMarble.LargeChange = got_wid
        hbarMarble.Visible = True
    Else
        hbarMarble.Value = 0
        hbarMarble.Visible = False
```

```
        End If
        If need_vbar Then
            vbarMarble.Move got_wid + border_width, 0, _
                vbarMarble.Width, got_hgt + border_width
            vbarMarble.Min = 0
            vbarMarble.Max = picInner.ScaleHeight - got_hgt
            vbarMarble.SmallChange = got_hgt / 5
            vbarMarble.LargeChange = got_hgt
            vbarMarble.Visible = True
        Else
            vbarMarble.Value = 0
            vbarMarble.Visible = False
        End If
End Sub

' Reposition picInner.
Private Sub hbarMarble_Change()
    picInner.Left = -hbarMarble.Value
End Sub

' Reposition picInner.
Private Sub hbarMarble_Scroll()
    picInner.Left = -hbarMarble.Value
End Sub

' Reposition picInner.
Private Sub vbarMarble_Change()
    picInner.Top = -vbarMarble.Value
End Sub

' Reposition picInner.
Private Sub vbarMarble_Scroll()
    picInner.Top = -vbarMarble.Value
End Sub
```

Once it knows which scroll bars it needs, the program positions picOuter and the scroll bars. It then sets the scroll bar properties. It sets each scroll bar's Min property to 0. Remember that the program adjusts picInner's Top and Left property values when the user changes the scroll bar values. When the scroll bars have the value 0, the program sets picInner's Top or Left property to 0. That positions the control in the upper-left corner of picOuter so that the upper-left corner of picInner is visible.

ArrangeControls sets the scroll bar's Max property to the difference between the space needed and the space available. When the program adjusts picInner's Top or Left properties by this amount, the farthest parts of picInner's image are visible.

The program sets the scroll bar's SmallChange values to one fifth of the available space. When the user clicks on a scroll bar's arrows, the program adjusts the position of the image by one fifth of the size of the visible area. This value was chosen somewhat arbitrarily; you could pick a different value.

Finally, ArrangeControls sets the scroll bar's LargeChange property to the amount of visible space. When the user clicks between a scroll bar thumb and a scroll bar arrow, this is the amount by which the value is changed. Setting LargeChange to the amount of visible space makes the control move the image by the amount visible.

Scrolled Window Controls

The method described in the previous section is effective, but it is hardly convenient. You need to write quite a bit of code to make it work. If you wanted to put two scrolled windows on the same form, you would need to repeat all of the code for a new set of picture boxes and scroll bars.

In Visual Basic 5 and later versions, you can create an ActiveX control that implements the scrolled window functionality. The control contains the picture boxes, scroll bars, and the code that manages them. You simply place the scrolled window control on a form and put controls inside it. The control does the rest.

Example program TestSwin, shown in Figure 1.15, demonstrates this approach. The program's form contains four scrolled window controls, each containing a picture. The controls manage each picture separately.

Building ActiveX controls is outside the scope of this book. For detailed information, see the book *Custom Controls Library* by Rod Stephens, 1998, John Wiley & Sons.

When to Draw

If you place drawing commands in a form's Load event procedure, you may be surprised to find that the form is blank when it appears. The reason is the program draws to the form before the form actually exists on the screen. When the form is finally ready to appear, Visual Basic creates the form blank. Because your drawing commands have already been executed, they do not draw anything on the screen.

There are two general strategies for making graphics appear in a form or picture box: setting AutoRedraw and using the Paint event.

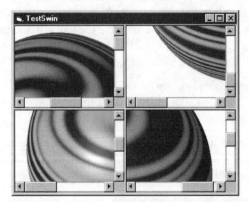

Figure 1.15   Example program TestSwin demonstrates the ScrolledWindow ActiveX control.

AutoRedraw Property

First, you can set the AutoRedraw property of the object to true. In this case, Visual Basic allocates a piece of memory to represent the object's screen image. Whenever you perform a drawing command, Visual Basic executes the command in this memory. Visual Basic uses this memory to update the contents of the form or picture box whenever necessary.

When the object is first displayed, Visual Basic uses this memory to draw the object. Later, if the object is covered up by another form and is then exposed, Visual Basic uses the memory to redisplay the newly exposed pieces of the object.

When you set AutoRedraw to true, you can execute drawing commands at any time, and Visual Basic stores them in memory. Many programs execute drawing commands during a form's Load event procedure or the Load event procedure of the parent form if the object is a picture box. In this case, the program should set AutoRedraw to true so the drawing is displayed.

Paint Events

If you do not set the AutoRedraw property to true, Visual Basic generates a Paint event any time part of the object needs to be updated. When Visual Basic first creates a drawing object, it generates a Paint event. Whenever another form covers part of a drawing object and then the object is uncovered, Visual Basic generates another Paint event.

If you set a form or picture box's AutoRedraw property to false, you should redraw the picture inside the Paint event procedure. Then, whenever Visual Basic needs to redraw the picture, it executes your drawing commands.

When you set the AutoRedraw property to false, Visual Basic does not need to allocate memory to store the object's screen image, so it saves some memory. On the other hand, it forces your program to execute the drawing commands every time the object receives a Paint event. If those commands take a long time, the picture redraw will occur slowly. In that case, you may want to set AutoRedraw to true so that Visual Basic can handle the details of redrawing the picture quickly.

Example program Auto, shown in Figure 1.16, contains two picture boxes. The first has AutoRedraw set to true. The second draws in its Paint event handler. When you run the program, click on other forms so that they cover part of the picture boxes. Then click on the picture boxes to expose the covered parts. The picture box with AutoRedraw set to true redraws almost instantly. The picture box on the right takes much longer to redraw whenever it is exposed.

Redrawing During Resize Events

In many programs, redrawing forms when they are resized is important. When the user makes a form larger, more information can be displayed. When the user makes a form smaller, the images you want to display may no longer fit on the form. You can rearrange a form and redraw the pictures when the form receives a Resize event.

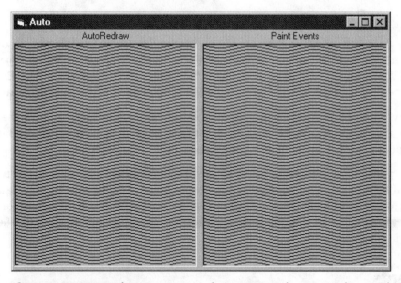

Figure 1.16 Example program Auto demonstrates the AutoRedraw and Paint event handler drawing strategies.

When a form is enlarged, it receives both a Resize event and a Paint event. You already need to redraw the form for the Paint event. It would be nice to avoid drawing the form twice, so you might skip the drawing in the Resize event. You could recalculate drawing parameters during the Resize event and then wait until the Paint event to perform the actual drawing.

Unfortunately, when a form shrinks, it receives only a Resize event. Because no new part of the image has been exposed, the form does not receive a Paint event. If your program waits for a corresponding Paint event, it may never redraw the form. Table 1.3 shows occurrences that cause Resize or Paint events. It is not too difficult to write a program that handles all of these situations correctly.

First, you need to redraw the form any time it receives a Paint event. Doing so handles redrawing the form for every occurrence in this list except when the form is shrunk in size or minimized.

Table 1.3 Occurrences That Cause Resize or Paint Events

WHEN THE FORM IS:	THESE EVENTS ARE GENERATED:
Created	Resize, Paint
Exposed	Paint
Shrunk	Resize
Enlarged	Resize, Paint
Minimized	Resize
Restored	Resize, Paint

To determine whether the form has shrunk, you can keep track of its width and height. When you receive a Resize event, compare the new and old widths and heights to see if either dimension has gotten larger. If so, the Resize event will be followed by a Paint event, so you do not need to redraw the form yet. Otherwise, the form has shrunk. If you want to rearrange the form to take into account its new size, you should do so.

Finally, in most applications, there is no reason to redraw the form or even recompute its drawing parameters when the form is minimized. Because the user cannot see the form anyway, any effort you spend at this point is wasted. When the form is restored, its size will probably be the same as it was before the form was minimized, so you would only have to recompute the drawing parameters again.

You can check whether a form is minimized using the form's WindowState property. If, during a Resize event, the form's WindowState has the value vbMinimized, the form is minimized and you can exit the event handler.

The following code shows Paint and Resize events that manage these interactions. This code assumes the two subroutines CalculateParameters and DrawForm compute the drawing parameters and redraw the form.

```
Private Sub Form_Paint()
    ' Always redraw when we get a Paint event.
    DrawForm
End Sub

Private Sub Form_Resize()
Static wid As Single
Static hgt As Single

    ' If we're minimized, do nothing.
    If WindowState = vbMinimized Then Exit Sub

    ' If the size has changed, recalculate the
    ' drawing parameters. This will not happen if
    ' we are being restored after being minimized.
    If Width <> wid Or Height <> hgt Then CalculateParameters

    ' If we are shrinking, redraw now. If we are not shrinking,
    ' leave the drawing to the Paint event handler.
    If Not ((Width >= wid) And (Height >= hgt)) Then DrawForm

    ' Save the new width and height.
    wid = Width
    hgt = Height
End Sub
```

Example program Resize, shown in Figure 1.17 uses this code to draw a smiley face. Whenever the form is resized, the program recalculates drawing parameters so that the face is as large as possible. The form contains two labels that tell you how many times it has calculated the drawing parameters and redrawn the picture.

Figure 1.17   Example program Resize calculates and draws only when necessary.

Controlling Controls

Visual Basic allows you to create a wide variety of controls quickly and easily. Controls range in complexity from the Line control, which simply displays a line on a form, to the RichTextBox control, which has all the power of a full-featured text editor.

Many of these controls are designed to display data, such as text, that is not drawing oriented. Even so, this is basically graphic in nature. For example, it is easy to think of a Label control as a container for text. However, a Label control occupies space on the screen, can obscure other label controls placed behind it, and has many graphic properties, including font type, font size, and foreground color. While Label controls are most often used to display text in a fairly boring fashion, they provide a rich assortment of graphic features.

Example program Font, shown in Figure 1.18, contains a label using a font named Bremen with a three-dimensional border and a white background. The sections that follow explain how you can use graphic properties to determine the appearance of controls on the screen.

Figure 1.18   Example program Font demonstrates some of a label's many graphic properties.

Text Properties

Many Visual Basic controls can display text. The main purpose of text boxes and labels is to display text, but many other controls use text as well. Command buttons, check boxes, and many others display text in a caption. Forms display text in a title bar. Even picture boxes can display text created with the Print method.

A control's Font property determines how the control displays text. The Font property is actually an object that contains several properties of its own. The properties you can access in a Font object are Name, Size, Bold, Italic, StrikeThrough, Underline, and Weight.

Font Name Property

A Font object's Name property determines which typeface the control uses. You can find out what typefaces are available on a computer or printer at run time by examining the object's Fonts property. For example, the following code adds the names of the available screen fonts to a list control named ScreenList.

```
Dim i As Integer

    For i = 0 To Screen.FontCount - 1
        ScreenList.AddItem Screen.Fonts(i)
    Next i
```

Example program ListFont, shown in Figure 1.19, uses similar code to list the fonts available on your screen and printer. It compares the two lists and highlights fonts that appear in one list but not the other.

If a control's font is not available, the font mapper picks a different font for you. This can happen, for example, if you write a program and then give it to other people to use

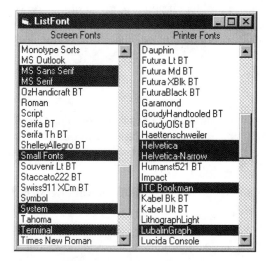

Figure 1.19 Example program ListFont lists the fonts available on the computer and printer.

on their computers. Sometimes the font selected by the system will make your controls look strange or line up incorrectly.

One way to avoid this problem is to use a font that you are reasonably sure will be available on the system running the program. If you pick one of the standard fonts that is shipped with Windows, you will be fairly safe. Some of the most common fonts are Arial, Courier New, MS Sans Serif, and Times New Roman.

Font Size Property

A Font object's Size property determines the size of the text. A font's size is measured in *printer's points* with 72 points to an inch. However, just because you ask for a font in a certain size does not mean the system will give it to you. The system can provide different fonts only in certain fixed sizes. When you set a Font object's Size property, your program gets the fixed size closest to the one you specified.

Some fonts, such as TrueType fonts, are designed to be scaled. They contain mathematical instructions for drawing characters at a wide variety of different sizes. The system can scale these fonts easily so that it can produce them at many different sizes. Arial, Courier New, and Times New Roman are TrueType fonts.

Other fonts are provided in bitmap formats to be displayed only at specific sizes. If you request one of these fonts in a nonstandard size, the system may scale the font. These fonts tend to look somewhat rough when they are displayed at nonstandard sizes. MS Sans Serif is one such font.

Even if the font you are using is scalable, you may not get exactly the size you request. The system usually gives you a font that is within one printer's point of the size you want. Keep in mind that a point is only 1/72 of an inch. If you ask for 73 point and get 72.75 point instead, the system has adjusted your font by only 1/4 of a point, or about 0.003 inches.

This resizing of fonts can be a bigger problem if you are not careful when you change typefaces and sizes. Suppose you have a label in 18 point MS Sans Serif and you want it in 21 point Arial. You could execute the following code:

```
Label1.Font.Size = 21
Label1.Font.Name = "Arial"
```

When Visual Basic executes the first command, it tries to make the label use 21-point MS Sans Serif. Unfortunately, MS Sans Serif does not have a 21-point size. The nearest available size is 19.5 point, so Visual Basic sets the font size to 19.5. Now when you set the font name to Arial, the label displays in 19.5-point Arial.

This problem does not occur if you execute the two statements in reverse order.

```
Label1.Font.Name = "Arial"
Label1.Font.Size = 21
```

The first statement sets the label's font to 18-point Arial. Arial happens to have an 18-point size, but it really does not matter because the second statement immediately changes the font's size to 21 point. Now the label uses 21-point Arial, which is what you wanted. To avoid problems, always set a font's name before you set its size.

The exception to this rule is when you use very small point sizes. Many fonts are hard to read at sizes smaller than 8 point. If you try to use a font in a size smaller than 8 point, and that size is not supported by that font, Windows may automatically switch typefaces for you and pick a font that is more legible. For example, if you try to use the Arial font at a size smaller than 8 point, Windows may switch to a font called Small Fonts. This font is legible (barely) down to around 5.25 points.

Other Font Properties

The Font object's Bold, Italic, StrikeThrough, and Underline properties are all Boolean properties. They determine whether text is **bold**, *italicized*, ~~struck through~~, or underlined. You can mix these properties to make combined styles like ***bold, italic, and underlined***.

The Weight property is another way to specify whether text is bold. If you set the Weight to the default value 400, the text is not bold. If you set Weight to 700, the text is bold. If you set Weight to any other value, Visual Basic changes the Weight to either 400 or 700, whichever is closer to the value you specified. You can make your code easier to read by using the Bold property instead of Weight.

Example program ShowFont, shown in Figure 1.20, displays samples of the fonts available on your screen. Check the Bold, Italic, StrikeThrough, and Underline boxes to determine the font's properties. Enter the font's size and click on one of the font names to see a sample of that font.

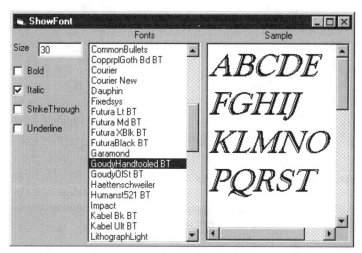

Figure 1.20 Example program ShowFont displays samples of fonts.

TextWidth and TextHeight Methods

While not exactly text properties, the TextWidth and TextHeight methods are extremely useful for managing text placement. The form, picture box, and printer objects all support the TextWidth and TextHeight functions.

TextWidth takes as a parameter a string that you might want to display. It returns the width of the string in the drawing object's current scale mode. For example, TextWidth for a form using a ScaleMode of vbTwips returns the width of its input string in twips as it would appear displayed on the form using the form's current font. Similarly, the TextHeight method returns the height of a string.

These methods are extremely useful for positioning text because many fonts have characters of variable width. That means you cannot calculate the width of a string by multiplying a simple character width by the number of characters in the string. For instance, in 12-point Arial, the width of the string "WIDTH" is 750 twips, while the width of the string "width" is only 540 twips. The characters in the first string are wider than those in the second.

Although not all types of controls have TextWidth and TextHeight methods, you can use the methods provided by a control's parent form to perform necessary calculations. For example, you might want to know how large a button's caption is, but the command button control does not provide TextWidth and TextHeight functions. You can use the button's parent form to calculate the caption's size.

First set the parent form's Font property so that it matches the Font property of the control. Then use the form's TextWidth and TextHeight functions to find the string's size. The TextWidthAndHeight subroutine shown in the following code uses this method to compute the height and width of a string.

```
Private Sub TextWidthAndHeight(ByVal ctl As Control, _

    ByVal txt As String, ByRef wid As Single, ByRef hgt As Single)
Dim frm As Form

    Set frm = ctl.Parent
    Set frm.Font = ctl.Font
    wid = frm.TextWidth(txt)
    hgt = frm.TextHeight(txt)
End Sub
```

Other Graphic Properties

Controls have many other properties that modify their graphic appearance. Some of the more important of these are described in the following sections.

ForeColor Property

The ForeColor property specifies the foreground color of an object. For controls such as labels and text boxes, this is the color of the text. For graphic methods like Line and Circle, this is the color of the line or circle.

BackColor Property

BackColor specifies the background color of an object. If you change the BackColor property of a form or picture box, all graphics are erased and the drawing object is filled with the new color whether or not AutoRedraw is true.

BackStyle Property

The label control displays its background only if its BackStyle property is set to vbBSSolid. If BackStyle is vbTransparent, whatever lies behind the label shows through.

FillColor Property

The FillColor property specifies the color used to fill closed shapes such as rectangles, circles, and pie slices. If the FillStyle property is vbFSTransparent (the default value), this property is ignored.

AutoSize Property

AutoSize determines whether a picture box adjusts its Width and Height to fit the picture it contains. If this value is true when you load a bitmap into a picture box, the picture box shrinks or expands to fit the bitmap exactly.

CurrentX and CurrentY Properties

The CurrentX and CurrentY properties give the coordinates of the next point for use in graphic output. When you execute a graphic method like Line or PSet, Visual Basic sets these properties to indicate the last point drawn. You can use this point as the start of the next drawing operation. This method is commonly used to draw a sequence of connected lines like this:

```
' This sets (CurrentX, CurrentY) to (100, 100).
Line (100, 100)

' Subsequent lines start at (CurrentX, CurrentY) and then
' update (CurrentX, CurrentY) to the end of the next line.
Line -(200, 300)
Line -(300, 200)
Line -(400, 250)
    etc.
```

DrawMode Property

The DrawMode property is the mode in which lines are drawn and shapes are filled. Two useful DrawModes are:

vbCopyPen	Draws in the normal drawing color, overwriting whatever is underneath. This is the default value for DrawMode.
vbInvert	Inverts the colors over which you are drawing. This has the useful property that drawing the same thing twice using mode vbInvert restores the underlying image to its original form.

You can use vbInvert mode and a form's MouseDown, MouseMove, and MouseUp event procedures to create rubber-band effects. In the MouseDown event procedure, set both end points of the rubber band line to the current mouse position. Then draw a line between those points using vbInvert mode. Initially, these are the same points, so you will not see much.

In the MouseMove procedure, draw a line in vbInvert mode between the rubber band line's current end points. Drawing the same line twice in vbInvert drawing mode erases the line, so this erases the previous line between those points. Update the final end-point coordinates for the line so that the line ends at the new mouse position. Finally, draw the new line in vbInvert mode.

In the MouseUp event, redraw the most recent line once more to erase it. You can then take whatever action you need to process the line selected by the user. For example, you might draw the line again using drawing mode vbSrcCopy to make the line permanent.

Example program RubrLine uses this technique to draw rubber-band lines. Click and drag the mouse to create a rubber-band line. When you release the mouse to finish the line, the program draws the line permanently on the form.

DrawStyle Property

The DrawStyle property determines the style in which lines are drawn. You can set DrawStyle as follows:

vbSolid	Draws solid lines.
vbDash	Draws dashed lines.
vbDot	Draws dotted lines.
vbDashDot	Draws alternating dashes and dots.
vbDashDotDot	Draws in a dash-dot-dot pattern.
vbInvisible	Draws lines invisibly. This is handy, for instance, if you want to fill a box without making its borders visible.
vbInsideSolid	Draws the line inside the position you specify. This is most noticeable if you draw a box with a large DrawWidth. In that case vbSolid draws the box's border half inside and half outside the box you specify, while vbInsideSolid draws the border entirely within the box.

Example program StyleBox, shown in Figure 1.21, demonstrates each of these drawing styles.

Many applications combine DrawMode vbInvert with DrawStyle vbDot to produce dotted rubber-banding effects. Example program RubrBox, shown in Figure 1.22, uses this technique to let you to select a rectangle using the mouse. Click and drag to select a rectangle using a dotted rubber-band box. When you release the mouse, the program fills the box you selected with a random color.

DrawWidth Property

DrawWidth specifies how thick lines, circles, and points are drawn.

Unfortunately, Visual Basic does not honor the DrawStyle property unless DrawWidth is 1. That means you cannot use DrawStyle to draw a thick dotted line.

If you make DrawWidth greater than 1, Visual Basic treats vbDash, vbDot, vbDashDot, and vbDashDotDot as if they were vbSolid. It draws vbSolid and vbInvisible as you would expect, and it draws vbInsideSolid as if DrawWidth were 1. Figure 1.23 shows program StyleBox modified so DrawWidth is 5.

FillStyle Property

FillStyle determines how a box or circle is filled. This property can take the following values.

vbFSSolid	Fills the object with the color specified by FillColor.
vbFSTransparent	Does not fill the object.
vbHorizontalLine	Fills the object with horizontal lines.
vbVerticalLine	Fills the object with vertical lines.
vbUpwardDiagonal	Fills the object with lines slanting upward from right to left.
vbDownwardDiagonal	Fills the object with lines slanting downward from right to left.
vbCross	Fills the object with vertical and horizontal lines.
vbDiagonalCross	Fills the object with lines slanting both upward and downward from right to left.

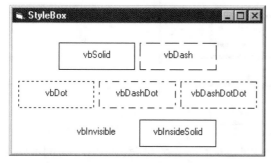

Figure 1.21   Example program StyleBox demonstrates Visual Basic's drawing styles.

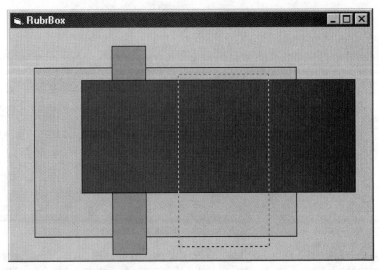

Figure 1.22 Example program RubrBox lets you select rectangles with a dotted rubber-band box.

Notice that there is some inconsistency in the names of these values. Visual Basic has other constants, vbTransparent and vbSolid, so the first two values have an extra FS at the beginning of their names to differentiate them from those other values. If you want to draw a transparent shape and the shape is filled, you probably have used vbTransparent, which has a value of 0, instead of vbFSTransparent, which has a value of 1.

Example program Fills, shown in Figure 1.24, displays rectangles filled in each of these styles.

The effects of vbUpwardDiagonal and vbDownwardDiagonal may seem strange. You would probably think of upward diagonal as meaning a slant upward from left to right, rather than from right to left. The Visual Basic interpretations make sense if you think about the standard pixel coordinate system. Here X increases from left to right, and Y increases from top to bottom. Then a line slanting upward from right to left on the screen has increasing Y values as X values increase.

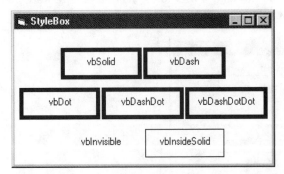

Figure 1.23 Visual Basic does not honor the DrawStyle property when DrawWidth is greater than 1.

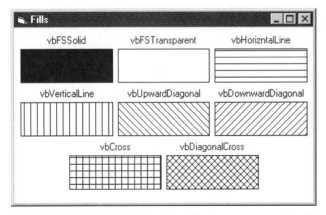

Figure 1.24   Example program Fills demonstrates the FillStyle property.

Example program Styles, shown in Figure 1.25, lets you experiment with different graphic properties. Enter a value for DrawWidth and use the option buttons to select the type of object to draw: DrawStyle, FillStyle, FillColor, and ForeColor. Then click and drag to create objects using the properties you selected.

ClipControls Property

ClipControls is an important but confusing property of forms, picture boxes, and frames. When ClipControls is true and a form receives a Paint event, Visual Basic creates a clipping region around any non-graphic controls on the form. Any graphics you draw on the form within the clipping region are ignored, so those controls are not covered by your graphics.

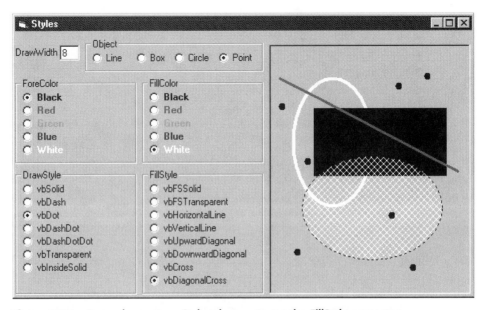

Figure 1.25   Example program Styles demonstrates the FillStyle property.

Some lightweight controls, such as image and label controls, do not become part of the clipping region. As a result, graphics you draw on top of those controls covers them. When you are through with the Paint event, Visual Basic refreshes these controls so that they are no longer covered by your graphics.

When ClipControls is false and a form receives a Paint event, Visual Basic does not create a clipping region. Instead, it lets you draw over any controls on the form. When the Paint event finishes, Visual Basic refreshes any controls that would not have been part of the clipping region, like image controls or labels. As a result, those kinds of controls will appear on top of your graphics, but other controls will not.

Creating and using a clipping region can be time consuming, especially if you have a lot of controls on your form. If you know that you will not draw graphics on top of controls like text boxes, which are not automatically refreshed by Visual Basic after Paint events, you should set ClipControls to false so that your program can run faster.

If you might draw graphics over text controls, you can still set ClipControls to false to make your program faster. After you have finished drawing on the form, execute the Refresh method for any controls that Visual Basic does not automatically refresh for you.

Example program ClipCtls, shown in Figure 1.26, displays three picture box controls, each containing a label, a text box, and an image control. The first picture box has Clip-Controls set to true. During Paint events, the graphics obscure the label and image control. The clipping region prevents the graphics from covering the text box. When the Paint event is complete, Visual Basic refreshes the label and image controls so that the graphics do not cover any of the controls.

ClipControls is false in the second picture box. During Paint events, the graphics obscure all of the controls. When the Paint event is complete, Visual Basic refreshes the label and image controls, but the text control remains covered by the graphics.

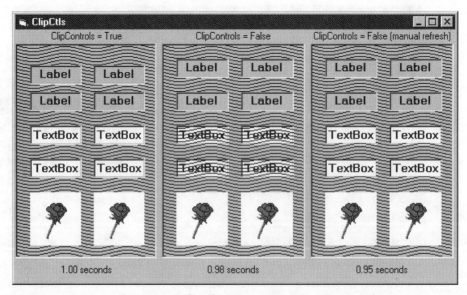

Figure 1.26 Example program ClipCtls demonstrates the ClipControls property.

In the third picture box, ClipControls is set to false, so graphics during Paint events cover all the controls. After drawing the graphics, code in the Paint event handler explicitly executes the text box's Refresh method, so the text box is redrawn. Then, after the Paint event is complete, Visual Basic automatically refreshes the label and image controls so that the graphics lie behind all the controls. If you look closely at the text box, however, you will see that the form's graphics cover parts of the control's border.

While the first picture box takes a little longer to redraw than the others, the difference is usually so small that it may not be worth the added complications. You may want to leave ClipControls true until you are certain you have performance problems and this small improvement is worth the extra effort.

Picture Property

The Picture property of a form, image, or picture box specifies the picture that should be displayed by the object. This picture becomes the background that is displayed whenever all other graphics are erased. For instance, a form's Cls method erases all other graphics from the form so that only the background picture is displayed.

Image Property

The Image property of a form or picture box is a persistent bitmap stored in memory that contains the object's current contents. If you set AutoRedraw to true, Visual Basic uses this bitmap to redraw the object when it is exposed. If you set AutoRedraw to false, the Image property still exists, but Visual Basic does not use it to redraw the object. You must do any necessary redrawing in the object's Paint event procedure.

You can use the Image property to set the value of an object's Picture property. For example, the following code sets the Picture property of one picture box equal to the Image property of another. The first will display as a permanent part of its background whatever the second is currently displaying.

```
picTo.Picture = picFrom.Image
```

Example program ImagePic, shown in Figure 1.27, displays two picture boxes. Click and drag the mouse on either picture box to draw on it. Click the Copy button to copy the left picture box's Image property into the right picture box's Picture property. That makes whatever the left picture box is displaying become the permanent background for the right picture box.

When you click the left Clear button, the left picture box clears. When you click the right Clear button, the right picture box clears to display whatever is stored in its Picture property.

For example, draw on the left picture box and click the Copy button. That copies the picture into the right picture box. Now draw on top of that image in the right picture box. If you now click the right Clear button, the new drawing is erased, leaving the original image from the left picture box.

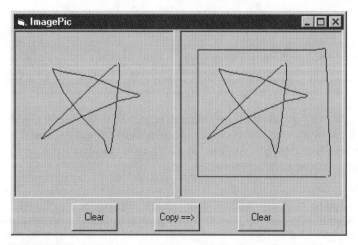

Figure 1.27 Example program ImagePic demonstrates the Picture and Image properties.

Icon Property

A form's Icon property contains the icon that is displayed when the form is minimized. Usually you set a form's icon by selecting a .ico file at design time or by loading an icon using the LoadPicture function.

The LoadPicture and SavePicture Functions

As you might guess from their names, LoadPicture and SavePicture load and save pictures to and from files. You can use LoadPicture to load a picture into a form, picture box, or image control, as in:

```
picSmile.Picture = LoadPicture("grin.bmp")
```

In older versions of Visual Basic, LoadPicture could load images stored in the file formats bitmap (.bmp), device-independent bitmap (.dib), icon (.ico), run-length encoded (.rle), or Windows metafile with placeable header (.wmf). Newer versions of Visual Basic can also read images stored in Graphics Interchange Format (.gif) and Joint Photographic Electronic Group (.jpeg or .jpg) formats.

You can use SavePicture to save the contents of a form, picture box, or image control to a file, as shown in the following code:

```
SavePicture Pict.Image, "MYPICT.BMP"
```

When you load an image at design time, it is stored in the form's data in its original format. When it is displayed at run time, it is converted into an appropriate format for display. For example, if you load a compressed JPEG file onto a form, the form stores the compressed data. That makes the program smaller than it would have been had you loaded the image from a bitmap. On the other hand, the program will take longer to display the image because it must decompress it at run time.

Example program Viewer uses the LoadPicture function to quickly view graphic files. The program's form contains DriveList, DirectoryList, and FileList controls that let you search your computer's files. When you click on a file in the FileList, the program uses LoadPicture to display the file.

Example program Thumbs uses LoadPicture to display thumbnails of the files in a directory. It also uses DriveList, DirectoryList, and FileList controls to let you search your computer's files. When you select a directory and press F5, the program examines the files in its FileList control. For each file, the program uses LoadPicture to load the file into a hidden picture box. It then uses the PaintPicture method to copy the image at a reduced size into a visible thumbnail picture box.

The Thumbs program is useful for managing directories full of graphic files. One other way the program helps is by allowing you to delete a file. If you click on a thumbnail and press the Delete key, the program moves the file into the system's wastebasket.

Graphical Controls

The image, label, line, and shape controls are special objects that provide simple graphic features with low overhead. To keep their use of system resources low, these objects have fewer properties and methods than most other controls. They also do not have an hWnd property, which you need if you want to use the API functions described in Chapter 2. If you have simple drawing needs, however, these objects can help keep your use of system resources down and still save you the trouble of drawing your own graphics in Paint event handlers.

These objects are in some sense not true controls. They do not use all the resources that other controls do. In particular, they are not drawn on their own windows. Instead they are drawn directly on the form or control that contains them. That saves resources, but it also means they cannot be placed above other controls. For example, a label control cannot lie on top of a text box within the same container. If you really need to place a label over a text box, you can place the label inside a borderless picture box and place the picture box on top of the text box.

The following sections describe the graphic controls in more detail.

Image Control

The image control is a lightweight version of the picture box control. It uses fewer system resources and repaints more quickly than a picture box control, but it has only some of the picture box's properties, methods, and events. In particular, the image control does not have Line, Circle, PaintPicture, PSet, Point, or Print methods. Because they have such limited capabilities, image controls are usually used either to display pictures or to hold pictures that are copied into a picture box for further manipulation.

Image controls have one important property that picture boxes do not: Stretch. If Stretch is true, the picture you load into the image control stretches to fill the control. If Stretch is false, the control resizes to fit the picture.

Example program FastView, shown in Figure 1.28, uses an image control and the Load-Picture function to display the contents of a graphic file. Use the drive, directory, and file list boxes to select the file you want to display. When you click on the name of a file, the program uses the LoadPicture function to load the file into the image control.

Label Control

You can use the label control to display text instead of using the Print method. You can use the font properties described earlier to change the label's appearance.

If you set a label control's AutoSize property to true, the control resizes to fit the text it contains. If you later change the text within the control by setting its Caption property to a new string value, Visual Basic resizes the control to fit the new text.

Line Control

A line control draws a line on the form or picture box that contains it. You can use line controls to display a few lines without going to the trouble of drawing them using the Line method during the Paint event.

The properties that determine a Line control's position are X1, Y1, X2, and Y2. The line connects the points (X1, Y1) and (X2, Y2).

You can use the Line's BorderStyle and BorderWidth properties to determine how the line is displayed. These properties are similar to DrawStyle and DrawWidth described earlier. You can also use the BorderColor property to specify the color the line should have. This property is similar to ForeColor described earlier.

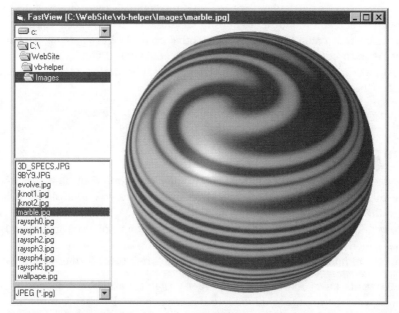

Figure 1.28 Example program FastView uses LoadPicture to quickly display image files.

Shape Control

You can use a shape control to display a rectangle, square, oval, circle, rounded rectangle, or rounded square without needing to draw it yourself during Paint events. You can determine the control's shape by setting its Shape property to one of the following values:

- vbShapeRectangle
- vbShapeSquare
- vbShapeOval
- vbShapeCircle
- vbShapeRoundedRectangle
- vbShapeRoundedSquare

Example program Shapes, shown in Figure 1.29, displays each of these different shapes.

As is the case with the Line control, you can use a Shape control's BorderStyle and BorderWidth properties to determine how the shape's border is displayed. You can also use the control's BorderColor property to specify the color of the shape's border.

Color

Many Visual Basic controls have color properties that determine the control's foreground, background, or fill colors. Color can be one of the most confusing topics in computer graphics. Chapter 3 discusses color in more detail. This section describes only simple color concepts that you can use in much of your Visual Basic programming.

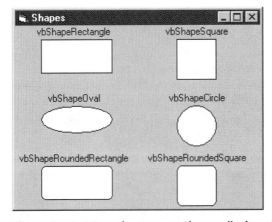

Figure 1.29 Example program Shapes displays the different shape control types.

RGB Colors

Visual Basic represents a color as a long integer that is a combination of red, green, and blue components. The red, green, and blue values all have a numeric range between 0 and 255. If all three of these values are 0, the color contains no red, green, or blue, so the color is black. If all three of these values are 255, the color contains as much red, green, and blue as possible, and the color is white.

The RGB function provided by Visual Basic combines red, green, and blue values and produces the long integer representing the combined color. The RGB function has this syntax:

RGB *(red, green, blue)*

red, green, blue   The amounts of red, green, and blue you want the color to have.

The RGB function computes the color value using the formula:

```
color = blue * &HFF00& + green * &HFF& + red
```

Using this information, you can decompose a color from its long integer representation into its red, green, and blue components, as shown in the following code:

```
r = color And &HFF&
g = (color And &HFF00&) \ &H100&
b = (color And &HFF0000) \ &H10000
```

You can specify a color by either using the RGB function or giving its numeric value. Hexadecimal makes specifying numeric values easier because each of a color's components occupies exactly two hexadecimal digits. If the color has red, green, and blue components of RR, GG, and BB in hexadecimal, you can represent the color as &HBBG-GRR. For example, if a color has a red value of &H80, a green value of &H00, and a blue value of &HFF, the color value is &HFF0080.

Visual Basic also has several predefined constants that give the values for some of the most commonly used colors. These values are shown in Table 1.4.

You should use these color constants whenever possible. Your code will be easier to understand, and Visual Basic is more likely to be able to supply the exact colors you want. If your computer is set up to use color palettes, it can display only a limited number of colors at once. If you try to use too many different colors, you may exceed that number and you will not get exactly the colors you want. By using standard colors as much as possible, you reduce the total number of colors you need.

System Colors

You can use the RGB method to specify colors between 0 and &HFFFFFF. Values &H80000000 and larger represent system-defined colors instead of RGB values. These colors include such things as the color of menu bars and the title bar for active windows.

Table 1.4 Predefined Constants and Values for Common Colors

CONSTANT	VALUE
vbBlack	&H0
vbRed	&HFF
vbGreen	&HFF00
vbYellow	&HFFFF
vbBlue	&HFF0000
vbMagenta	&HFF00FF
vbCyan	&HFFFF00
vbWhite	&HFFFFFF

You can use system-defined colors to give your application a look and feel similar to that provided by other Windows applications. If you use these colors and the user changes the computer's system colors, your application automatically uses the new colors selected by the user. Visual Basic defines the constants shown in Table 1.5 for using system-defined colors.

Table 1.5 Constants for Using System-Defined Colors

CONSTANT	VALUE	COLOR FOR:
vbScroll bars	&H80000000	Scroll bars
vbDesktop	&H80000001	Desktop
vbActiveTitleBar	&H80000002	Background of the active window's title bar
vbInactiveTitleBar	&H80000003	Background of inactive windows' title bars
vbMenuBar	&H80000004	Menu background
vbWindowBackground	&H80000005	Window background
vbWindowFrame	&H80000006	Window frame
vbMenuText	&H80000007	Text in menus
vbWindowText	&H80000008	Text in windows
vbTitleBarText	&H80000009	Title bar caption, size box, and scroll arrow text
vbActiveBorder	&H8000000A	Borders on the active window
vbInactiveBorder	&H8000000B	Borders on inactive windows
vbApplicationWorkspace	&H8000000C	MDI application background
vbHighlight	&H8000000D	Background of selected items
vbHighlightText	&H8000000E	Text of selected items
vbButtonFace	&H8000000F	Command button face shading
		Continues

Table 1.5 Constants for Using System-Defined Colors *(Continued)*

CONSTANT	VALUE	COLOR FOR:
vbButtonShadow	&H80000010	Command button edge shading
vbGrayText	&H80000011	Disabled text
vbButtonText	&H80000012	Command button text
vbInactiveCaptionText	&H80000013	Inactive caption text
vb3DHighlight	&H80000014	3D object highlight
vb3DDKShadow	&H80000015	3D object darkest shadow
vb3DLight	&H80000016	3D object lightest color after vb3DHighlight
vbInfoText	&H80000017	ToolTips text
vbInfoBackground	&H80000018	ToolTips background

Example program SysColor, shown in Figure 1.30, displays the system-defined colors currently set on your system.

Decomposing Colors

For a color stored in an RGB format, you can use the method described earlier to break the color into its red, green, and blue components. Some objects, however, use system color indexes instead of RGB colors. For example, a label control's BackColor property might have the value &H8000000F.

In cases like this, you can remove the leftmost digit from this number and use the result as the input to the GetSysColor API function. This function returns the true color associated with a system color index. You can now use the method described earlier to break the color into its components.

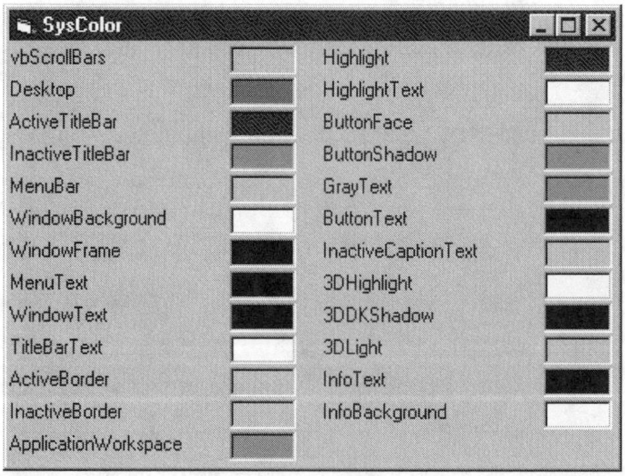

Figure 1.30 Example program SysColor displays the system-defined colors.

There is one final special case for colors. If you use the Point method to obtain a pixel's color and that pixel does not exist, Point returns -1 (&HFFFFFFFF). For example, if a form's ScaleMode property is vbPixels, then Point(-10, -10) returns -1 because the location (-10, -10) is off the form.

The BreakColor subroutine shown in the following code combines these facts to separate a color into its components. The routine can handle normal RGB colors, system color indexes, and the noncolor value -1. If the color has value -1, BreakColor leaves its color component parameters unchanged. Depending on your application, you might want it to set the components to default values such as 0 or 255.

```
Private Declare Function GetSysColor Lib "user32" _
    (ByVal nIndex As Long) As Long

' Break a color into its components.
Private Sub BreakColor(ByVal color As Long, _
    ByRef r As Long, ByRef g As Long, ByRef b As Long)

    If color = &HFFFFFFFF Then Exit Sub

    If color And &H80000000 Then _
        color = GetSysColor(color And &HFFFFFF)

    r = color And &HFF&
    g = (color And &HFF00&) \ &H100&
    b = (color And &HFF0000) \ &H10000
End Sub
```

QBColor

Visual Basic also defines a group of 16 colors that make up the standard VGA color palette. The codes for these colors are used by some other versions of Basic like Microsoft Visual Basic for MS-DOS. You can use the QBColor function to convert these color codes into RGB values that you can use in Visual Basic like this:

```
color = QBColor(code)
```

Table 1.6 shows the color codes in the VGA palette and the color represented by each.

Example program QBColor, shown in Figure 1.31, displays the VGA colors palette.

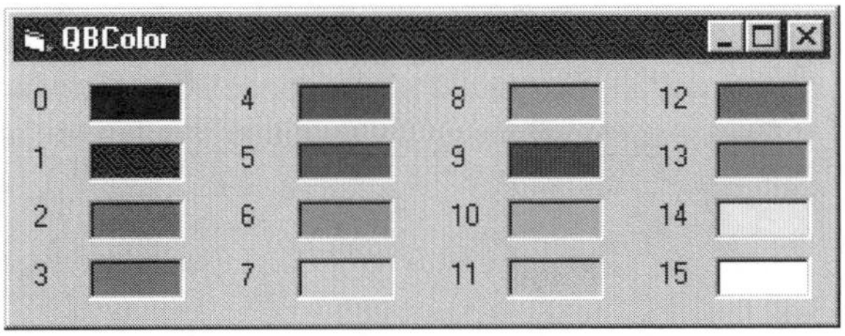

Figure 1.31   Example program QBColor displays the colors in the VGA palette.

Table 1.6 Color Codes in the VGA Palette

VALUE	COLOR	VALUE	COLOR
0	Black	8	Gray
1	Blue	9	Light Blue
2	Green	10	Light Green
3	Cyan	11	Light Cyan
4	Red	12	Light Red
5	Magenta	13	Light Magenta
6	Yellow	14	Light Yellow
7	White	15	Bright White

Summary

Theoretically a program can perform any graphic operation using only Visual Basic's methods. If absolutely necessary, a program can use Point and PSet to read and write every pixel in an image individually. While the API functions described in the following chapter provide faster and more powerful graphic operations, they are also much more complicated. To avoid unnecessary complications, always try to build graphic programs using Visual Basic methods first. Only after you are sure Visual Basic's tools are inadequate should you bother with API functions.

CHAPTER 2

Using the API

Windows programming has long been a difficult task. If you do not get every detail just right, your program can crash spectacularly, sometimes bringing down the operating system as well. If you do not manage system resources properly, your program might "leak," using more and more resources over time. Eventually, your program might use so many resources that other programs will be unable to run and your system will grind to a halt.

By freeing you from most of the worries of Windows programming, Visual Basic protects you from these dangers. It allows you to program quickly and safely while ignoring many of the details of Windows programming.

Unfortunately, this added safety comes at the price of reduced flexibility and sometimes performance. Visual Basic makes it unnecessary to use many dangerous but powerful tools in the Windows Application Programming Interface (API). Sometimes, however, you may want to use those tools.

This chapter explains how you can use Windows API functions in your Visual Basic programs. It explains generally how to use the API and discusses the complexities of passing parameters to API functions. Later chapters have more to say about using particular functions.

The Genie

Using the API directly is like letting a genie out of a bottle—you gain access to tremendous power but at a substantial risk. Once you have finished, putting the genie back in the bottle may not be easy.

If you pass the wrong arguments to an API function, your program may generate a General Protection Fault (GPF). This will crash the program, probably the Visual Basic development environment, and possibly Windows as well. You will lose any work you have done since the last time you saved your files.

To avoid losing work, you should save often when you are working with API routines. You should certainly save files just before you run a program, especially if you are testing a new API call. You can make this process easier by activating the Visual Basic development environment's autosave feature.

To do this, select Options from the Tools menu. In the Options dialog box, select the Environment tab. In Visual Basic 6, look in the "When a program starts" frame. To save your work automatically each time you run a program, click the Save Changes option button. If you want to be prompted to save changes before running a program, click the Prompt To Save Changes option. Earlier versions of Visual Basic have similar options.

Using the API

There are four steps to using the API:

1. Identify the routine you want to use.
2. Define any data structures you need to pass to the routine using a Type statement.
3. Declare the routine using a Declare statement.
4. Call the routine.

These steps are covered in the following sections.

Identifying the Routine

The MSDN help that comes with Visual Basic 6 includes help on API functions. Set the HTML help application's Active Subset to (Entire Collection). Then the help will list entries for API functions.

Some older versions of Visual Basic come with the normal help file Win31wh.hlp. This file contains help about many API functions. Look for this file in the Visual Basic directory's Winapi subdirectory.

Microsoft's Knowledge Base is another good source of information on API functions. It contains many articles explaining how to use API functions to perform tasks that are difficult or impossible using Visual Basic alone. You can search the Knowledge Base at Microsoft's Web site.

You can also gather information on API functions from books on the API. Many of these books were written for C programmers; but with a little practice, you will be able to translate between C declarations and Visual Basic declarations.

Defining Data Structures

Many API routines take special data structures as parameters. You can use the GetObject function, for example, to fill in the fields that describe a bitmap in a BITMAP data structure. In C, this structure is defined as:

```
typedef struct tagBITMAP {
    int     bmType;
    int     bmWidth;
    int     bmHeight;
    int     bmWidthBytes;
    BYTE    bmPlanes;
    BYTE    bmBitsPixel;
    void FAR*    bmBits;
} BITMAP;
```

To use the GetObject function, you must pass it a BITMAP data structure. You can define this structure in Visual Basic using a Type statement like this:

```
Type BITMAP
    bmType As Integer
    bmWidth As Integer
    bmHeight As Integer
    bmWidthBytes As Integer
    bmPlanes As String * 1
    bmBitsPixel As String * 1
    bmBits As Long
End Type
```

Visual Basic comes with the file Win32api.txt that contains declarations for types, constants, and functions useful when you are working with the API. For example, this file contains the definition of the BITMAP data type.

By default, Win32api.txt is installed in the Program Files\Microsoft Visual Studio\Common\Tools\Winapi directory. If you cannot find it there, search your Visual Basic CD-ROM for files that match the pattern *api*.

If you want, you can include this file directly into your Visual Basic project, and all of the API types, constants, and functions will be defined for you. Unfortunately, this file is large (653KB on my computer), so it makes your program quite large. Instead of including the entire file, you can cut and paste the declarations you need into your project.

You can also use the API Viewer application that comes with Visual Basic to copy the definitions you need. The API Viewer, shown in Figure 2.1, is the program Apiload.exe and should be in the same directory as the file Win32api.txt.

Select the File menu's Load Text File command and load Win32api.txt. Pick Types from the API Type combo box to see a list of the data type declarations. Select the data types you need and click the Add button to build a list of items for copying into your program.

When the list is complete, click the Copy button. The API Viewer copies the selected declarations into the clipboard. You can now open a module in Visual Basic and press CTRL-V to paste the declarations from the clipboard into your project.

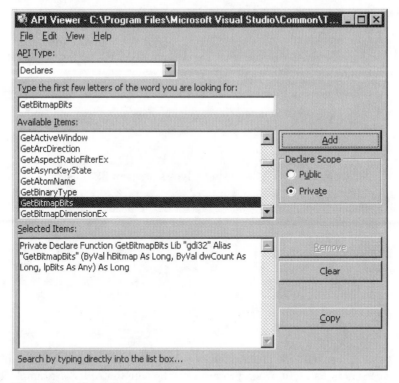

Figure 2.1 The API Viewer.

Declaring the Routine

Because API routines are not part of Visual Basic, you must use a Declare statement to tell Visual Basic where to find them. The syntax for a Declare statement is:

```
Declare Sub name Lib "lib" [Alias "alias"] (arguments)
```

```
Declare Function name Lib "lib" [Alias "alias"] (arguments) As type
```

Definitions for terms used in the statement are as follows:

name. The name by which you want to call the function in your program. This is useful if the name as it appears in the library is a reserved word in Visual Basic (such as Open) or if it begins with an underscore (Visual Basic does not allow function names to begin with an underscore). You can also use an alias to make programming easier. For example, you might make SizeBitmap the alias for the SetBitmapDimensionEx function to save some typing.

lib. The location of the library. For system libraries, this is the name of the library (such as gdi32 or kernel32). The API functions are all in system libraries. For non-system libraries, *lib* is the path to the library, such as C:\Winstuff\Bitmaps.dll.

alias. The name by which the subroutine or function is defined in the library.

arguments. The arguments expected by the API function. These may include data types defined by Type statements as described in the previous section.

type. The type returned by the API function.

For example, you could declare the CreateCompatibleBitmap function like this:

```
Private Declare Function CreateCompatibleBitmap _
    Lib "gdi32" Alias "CreateCompatibleBitmap" ( _
    ByVal hdc As Long, ByVal nWidth As Long, _
    ByVal nHeight As Long) As Long
```

This function is in the gdi32 system library. It takes as parameters three long integers—hDC, nWidth, and nHeight—passed by value. It returns a long integer.

You can use the API Viewer to copy subroutine and function declarations. Choose Declares from the API Type combo box to see a list of the function declarations available. Select the declarations you need and click the Add button to build a list of items for copying into your program. Click the Copy button to copy the declarations to the clipboard. Finally, use CTRL-V to paste the declarations from the clipboard into your Visual Basic project.

Argument Passing

By default, Visual Basic passes all variables by reference. That means Visual Basic passes the memory addresses of arguments rather than the argument values themselves. If you use the ByVal keyword in a Declare statement, or if you place ByVal in front of an argument when you call a routine, Visual Basic passes the argument by value rather than by reference.

Some API routines take arguments passed by value, and some take arguments passed by reference. Some routines even take some arguments by value and others by reference. When you call an API routine, you must be sure the arguments you pass to the routine exactly match the arguments the routine expects. Otherwise, you will be lucky if the routine merely fails to work properly. At worst, the routine will generate a General Protection Fault and crash your program, possibly taking Visual Basic and even Windows along for the ride. By using the ByVal keyword properly in Declare statements, you can ensure that Visual Basic passes arguments correctly.

The following sections explain some specific argument passing details.

Strings

Strings are a special case in argument passing. Internally, Visual Basic handles a string as the address of a data structure that contains the character data. Most API routines expect to receive the address of the character data rather than the address of the address of a data structure.

To tell Visual Basic to convert strings into addresses of character data, you should pass strings by value. Visual Basic does not actually pass the text value of the string. It passes the address of the characters.

For example, the C code syntax for the GetModuleHandle API function is:

```
HMODULE GetModuleHandle(lpszModuleName)

LPCSTR lpszModuleName;      /* The name of the module */
```

This function takes as a parameter an LPCSTR holding the name of a module. LPCSTR is a fancy name for a C string—an array of characters that ends with an ASCII 0 (NULL) character. To translate a Visual Basic string into an LPCSTR, you use the ByVal keyword. The Visual Basic declaration for the GetModuleHandle function is:

```
Private Declare Function GetModuleHandle Lib "kernel32" _
    Alias "GetModuleHandleA" (ByVal lpModuleName As String) _
    As Long
```

NULL Values

Strings have one more important special case. If you declare a string variable and pass it into an API routine without initializing it, the string is passed as NULL rather than as an empty string. When the string is passed as NULL, the API routine receives 0 as the address of the character data. When it receives an empty string, the function receives an address that points to a string that contains only the ASCII value 0. The difference is small but important.

Many API routines understand the value NULL and take special action when they see it. The CreateCaret function, for example, takes as one of its parameters the bitmap it should use to create a new system caret. If this parameter is NULL, the function creates a solid caret.

While you can use an uninitialized string to pass NULL to an API routine, this could be very confusing. The API routine call will not indicate that the string is uninitialized, and if you later accidentally give the string a value, the routine may no longer work properly.

Better methods for passing NULL to an API routine include passing the value ByVal 0&, the value ByVal Nothing, or the constant vbNullString.

API Functions That Modify Strings

Some API routines modify the contents of the string you pass them. The API routine will not allocate more space for the string, however, so you must make sure the string is large enough to hold all of the function's output before you call the function. One way to do this is to give the string a fixed size in its declaration.

```
Dim txt As String * 256
```

This line of code makes the string 256 characters long, which is long enough for most API routines.

Another method for sizing a string is to fill it with some characters using the String command. The following code fills the variable txt with 256 ASCII 0 (NULL) characters.

```
Dim txt As String
    txt = String(256, 0)
```

You can also initialize a string to a sequence of spaces using the Space$ function.

```
Dim txt As String
    txt = Space$(256)
```

All of these methods create a 256-character string that you can pass into an API routine.

Arrays

You can pass a single element in an array just as you would pass any other single item. For example, the following code uses the MoveTo and LineTo API functions to connect the points with coordinates stored in the ptx and pty arrays.

```
Private Type POINTAPI
    x As Long
    y As Long
End Type

Private Declare Function MoveToEx Lib "gdi32" _
    Alias "MoveToEx" (ByVal hdc As Long, _
    ByVal x As Long, ByVal y As Long, lpPoint As POINTAPI) _
    As Long
Private Declare Function LineTo Lib "gdi32" _
    Alias "LineTo" (ByVal hdc As Long, _
    ByVal x As Long, ByVal y As Long) As Long

Private ptx(0 to 10) As Long
Private pty(0 to 10) As Long

' (Initialize the arrays, etc.)
    :
Sub DrawLines()
Dim pt As POINTAPI
Dim i As Integer

    MoveToEx hDC, ptx(0), pty(0), pt
    For i = 1 To 10
        LineTo hDC, ptx(i), pty(i)
    Next i
End Sub
```

The values ptx(i) and pty(i) are passed into the LineTo routine just like any other long integers.

Many API functions expect the address of an array as a parameter. Because the first element in an array is at the beginning, you can pass the address of an entire array by passing the address of the first element. Simply use the first element, omitting the ByVal keyword.

For instance, the Polygon function draws a polygon connecting a series of points with coordinates stored in an array. The following code passes the Points array to the Polygon function by passing the first element Points(1).

```
' Define the POINTAPI type.
Type POINTAPI
    x As Long
    y As Long
End Type

Private Declare Function Polygon Lib "gdi32" _
    Alias "Polygon" (ByVal hdc As Long, _
    lpPoint As POINTAPI, ByVal nCount As Long) As Long

Private Points(1 to 10) As POINT

' (Initialize the Points array, etc.)
    :
Sub DrawPoly()
    Polygon hDC, Points(1), 10
End Sub
```

Handles

Many API routines use *handles* to represent objects. These handles refer to windows (HWND), device contexts (HDC), bitmaps (HBITMAP), and so forth. A handle is nothing more than an integer used to represent an object. When an API routine uses a handle, you should declare it as ByVal Long.

Handles are not memory addresses, and you should never try to do anything directly with a handle. They are just numbers, and they have no meaning outside the functions that know how to deal with them.

Many handles can change over time, so you should not store them in another variable for later use. Instead, get the value of the handle again each time you need to use it.

The most important handles you use when dealing with API routines are window handles and device context handles. Forms, picture boxes, frames, text boxes, and many other controls have window handles given by their hWnd properties. A window handle represents the window that contains the form or control.

Forms, picture boxes, and printers also have device context handles given by their hDC properties. The hDC is a handle to the device representing the form, picture box, or printer.

Properties

Visual Basic properties are not typical variables, and you cannot always treat them like other variables when you work with API routines. You must always pass properties to API routines by value rather than by reference. If an API routine takes an argument by value, you can use the property directly. For example, the hWnd and hDC handles are usually passed by value. In the Polygon function mentioned earlier, the device context handle is passed by value, so you can use a form's hDC property directly for that argument.

```
Polygon MyForm.hDC, Points(1), 10
```

If an API function expects a value passed by reference, you must use an intermediate variable to pass the property value to the function. For example, the GetClassName function returns a window's class name. The Visual Basic declaration for this function is:

```
Private Declare Function GetClassName Lib "user32" _
    Alias "GetClassNameA" (ByVal hwnd As Long, _
    ByVal lpClassName As String, ByVal nMaxCount As Long) _
    As Long
```

While the string argument is declared ByVal, this actually passes to the function the address of the string's character data. Because this value is passed by reference, the following code does not correctly set a form's Caption to the form's class name.

```
Private Sub Form_Load()
Dim length As Long

    ' This does not work!
    length = GetClassName(hWnd, Caption, Len(Caption))
End Sub
```

Instead, you need to use an intermediate variable to retrieve the class name and then assign it to the form's Caption property.

```
Private Sub Form_Load()
Dim length As Long
Dim txt As String * 256

    ' This version works.
    length = GetClassName(hWnd, txt, Len(txt))
    Caption = Left$(txt, length)
End Sub
```

Translating C into Visual Basic

The API Viewer and the file Win32api.txt declare API types, constants, and functions for use by Visual Basic programs. The MSDN help and most other sources of API information describe API routines using C language syntax. To understand how to use these functions, it helps to be able to translate from C syntax into Visual Basic syntax. Table 2.1 shows C language declarations and their Visual Basic equivalents. Note that in 32-bit operating systems, the API functions assume integers are actually long integers. If you are working on a 32-bit operating system and a C language API declaration calls for an integer, use a long integer instead.

Calling the Routine

Once you have defined any constants and data structures you need and you have declared the API function, you can call it as you would any Visual Basic function. The following code shows everything needed to determine the number of colors loaded into a form's color table if the computer is using color palettes.

Table 2.1 C Language Declarations and Visual Basic Equivalents

OBJECT	C DECLARATION	VISUAL BASIC EQUIVALENT
Integer	**BOOL** *var*; **int** *var*;	**ByVal** *var* **As Long**
Pointer to integer	**int** **var*;	*var* **As Integer**
Unsigned integer	**UINT** var;	**ByVal** var **As Integer**
Long	**DWORD** var; **LONG** var; **WORD** var;	**ByVal** var **As Long**
Pointer to Long	**LPDWORD** var;	var **As Long**
Byte	**BYTE** var;	**ByVal** var **As Byte**
Color reference	**COLORREF** var;	**ByVal** var **As Long**
Pointer to void (anything)	**void** **var*;	var **As Any**
Single character	**char** var;	**ByVal** var **As Byte**
Pointer to character	**char** **var*;	var **As Byte**
Pointer to NULL-terminated string	**LPSTR** var; **LPCSTR** var;	**ByVal** var **As String**
Handle	**HBITMAP** var; **HWND** var; etc.	**ByVal** var **As Integer**
Pointer to user-defined data type	**BITMAP** **var*; **PALETTE** **var*; etc.	*var* **As BITMAP**, *var* **As PALETTE**, etc.

```
Option Explicit

Private Declare Function GetDeviceCaps Lib "gdi32" ( _
    ByVal hdc As Long, ByVal nIndex As Long) As Long
Private Const NUMCOLORS = 24

Private Sub Form_Load()
Dim num_colors As Long

    num_colors = Str$(GetDeviceCaps(hdc, NUMCOLORS))
    If num_colors < 0 Then
        MsgBox "This computer is not using color palettes."
    Else
        MsgBox "There are " & Format$(num_colors) & _
            " colors in the form's color table."
    End If
End Sub
```

Useful API Functions

There are two reasons you might want to use an API function: It does something Visual Basic cannot do, or it does something faster than Visual Basic can do it. For example, the Polyline API function can draw a series of connected lines much faster than Visual Basic's Line method can. Unfortunately, API routines define screen coordinates in a slightly different way from Visual Basic. The next section describes ways you can deal with this problem. The sections that follow describe a few API functions that are useful in graphics programming. Some of these functions are used extensively in later parts of the book, and they are described in more detail there.

Drawing

Visual Basic's drawing methods are fairly good at what they do. They allow you to draw simple shapes quickly and easily. The Point and PSet methods give you complete control over every pixel in an image.

Visual Basic's ScaleMode properties also let you work in one of several different coordinate systems, including custom coordinate systems you define yourself. When you use API functions, you can work in only one coordinate system: pixels. This limitation can be extremely inconvenient. Your application may not translate naturally into pixels. In addition, not all computer monitors have the same number of pixels per inch vertically and horizontally. As a result, writing a program that produces the same results on all computer screens can be difficult.

One way to work around this problem is to convert your coordinates from whatever unit is convenient into pixels using the ScaleX and ScaleY methods. The following code illustrates this approach:

```
pixel_x = pic.ScaleX(x - pic.ScaleLeft, _
    pic.ScaleMode, vbPixels)
pixel_y = pic.ScaleY(y - pic.ScaleTop, -
    pic.ScaleMode, vbPixels)
```

If you need to convert lots of coordinates many times, you can make this code a bit faster by storing the values of ScaleLeft and ScaleTop and by precomputing some scaling factors.

```
Dim scale_left As Single
Dim scale_top As Single
Dim pix_per_unit_x As Single
Dim pix_per_unit_y As Single

    ' Prepare for translation.
    scale_left = pic.ScaleX(pic.ScaleLeft, _
        pic.ScaleMode, vbPixels)
```

```
scale_top = pic.ScaleY(pic.ScaleTop, _
    pic.ScaleMode, vbPixels)
pix_per_unit_x = pic.ScaleX(1, pic.ScaleMode, vbPixels)
pix_per_unit_y = pic.ScaleY(1, pic.ScaleMode, vbPixels)

' Translate coordinates into pixels.
pixel_x = x * pix_per_unit_x - scale_left
pixel_y = y * pix_per_unit_y - scale_top
```

Even with these changes, this method can be time consuming. It can also result in small rounding errors that make objects drawn using Visual Basic methods and objects drawn using API functions fail to line up perfectly.

Example program Scale, shown in Figure 2.2, uses the Visual Basic Line method to draw an X on a form. It then converts the coordinates of the lines' endpoints into pixels and uses the Rectangle API function to draw a box around the X. If you look closely, you will see that the lower endpoints of the X do not fall exactly on the bottom edge of the rectangle.

Despite these drawbacks, API functions sometimes have advantages over Visual Basic's drawing routines. In fact, because the API functions work only in pixels, they avoid the computations Visual Basic performs to deal with custom coordinate systems. This difference can make the API routines much faster than their Visual Basic counterparts.

For instance, Visual Basic's Line method is great for drawing a few dozen lines; but if you need to draw thousands of connected lines all at once, the Polyline API function is much faster. Example program Lines, shown in Figure 2.3, uses the Line method and the Polyline function to draw lines connecting 221 points 100 times. In one test on a 133MHz Pentium, the Polyline function took roughly 1.5 seconds; the Visual Basic Line method needed about 4 seconds. Of course, most programs do not need to draw this many connected line segments. You will have to decide whether the increase in speed is worth the extra trouble for your application.

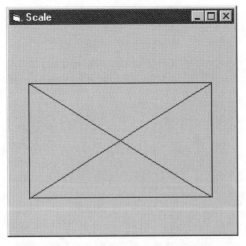

Figure 2.2 Visual Basic coordinates do not always translate perfectly into pixels.

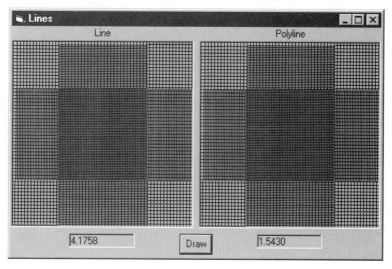

Figure 2.3 Example program Lines compares the speeds of Visual Basic's Line statement and the Polyline API function.

MoveToEx and LineTo Functions

The MoveToEx function sets the current X and Y positions for future drawing using LineTo. It returns the coordinates of the previous current position in a POINTAPI parameter. Usually a program does not need these coordinates.

LineTo draws a line from the current position to the position specified. This function returns a non-zero value if it is successful and zero if there is an error.

MoveToEx and LineTo do not change the values of Visual Basic's CurrentX and CurrentY properties. Note, however, that the Visual Basic Line method resets the current position used by the LineTo function. To prevent unnecessary confusion, you should avoid mixing the MoveToEx and LineTo functions with Visual Basic's Line method.

The following code shows declarations for the MoveToEx and LineTo functions. The final argument to the MoveToEx function is normally the address of a POINTAPI data structure. It is declared here as type Any, so the program can use the value vbNullString for that argument. The MoveToEx function understands that it should not return the current drawing location when this parameter is null.

```
Private Declare Function MoveToEx Lib "gdi32" _
    Alias "MoveToEx" (ByVal hdc As Long, _
    ByVal x As Long, ByVal y As Long, lpPoint As Any) _
    As Long
Private Declare Function LineTo Lib "gdi32" _
    Alias "LineTo" (ByVal hdc As Long, _
    ByVal x As Long, ByVal y As Long) As Long
```

Example program LineTo, shown in Figure 2.4, compares the MoveToEx and LineTo functions with the Visual Basic's Line method. It fills two picture boxes with small line segments, one using the Line method and one using the MoveToEx and LineTo functions. In one set of tests on a 133MHz Pentium, drawing the lines using the Line method took more than three times as long.

Polygons and Polylines

The Polyline, Polygon, PolyPolyline, and PolyPolygon functions let you draw many line segments all at once. The following code shows the Visual Basic declarations for these functions.

```
Private Type POINTAPI
    x As Long
    y As Long
End Type

Private Declare Function Polyline Lib "gdi32" _
    Alias "Polyline" (ByVal hdc As Long, _
    lpPoint As POINTAPI, ByVal nCount As Long) As Long

Private Declare Function Polygon Lib "gdi32" _
    Alias "Polygon" (ByVal hdc As Long, _
    lpPoint As POINTAPI, ByVal nCount As Long) As Long

Private Declare Function PolyPolyline Lib "gdi32" _
    Alias "PolyPolyline" (ByVal hdc As Long, _
    lppt As POINTAPI, lpdwPolyPoints As Long, _
    ByVal cCount As Long) As Long
```

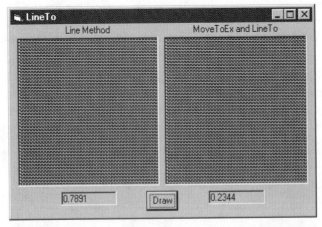

Figure 2.4 Example program LineTo compares the speeds of Visual Basic's Line statement and the LineTo API function.

```
Private Declare Function PolyPolygon Lib "gdi32" _
    Alias "PolyPolygon" (ByVal hdc As Long, _
    lpPoint As POINTAPI, lpPolyCounts As Long, _
    ByVal nCount As Long) As Long
```

The Polyline function draws a sequence of line segments connecting the points in the lpPoints array. The nCount parameter gives the number of points in lpPoints. Be certain this number is correct. If this number is too large, the Polyline API function will try to read beyond the end of the lpPoints array, and it may crash your program.

The Polygon function is similar to Polyline except it connects the first and last points to form a closed polygon. The function fills the polygon using the current FillStyle and FillColor.

The PolyPolyline function draws a group of polylines. Its second parameter, lppt, is an array of POINTAPI data structures that define all the points for all of the polylines. The first polyline's points comes first, the second polyline's points come next, and so forth. The function's third parameter, lpdwPolyPoints, is an array of long integers giving the number of points in each polyline. The value lpdwPolyPoints(1) is the number of points in the first polyline, lpdwPolyPoints(2) is the number of points in the second polyline, and so forth. The PolyPolyline function's final parameter, cCount, is the number of poly-lines. This tells the function how many entries are in the lpdwPolyPoints array. The number of entries in that array tells the function which entries to combine in the lppt array to produce the polylines.

The PolyPolygon function is similar to PolyPolyline except it connects the first and last point in each polyline to form a closed polygon. The function fills the polygons using the current FillStyle and FillColor.

Example program Polyline is shown in Figure 2.5.

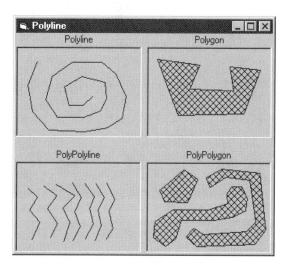

Figure 2.5   Program Polyline demonstrates the Polyline, Polygon, PolyPolyline, and Poly-Polygon API functions.

Rectangle and RoundRect Functions

The Rectangle and RoundRect functions draw rectangles and rounded rectangles similar to those produced by the Visual Basic Shape control.

```
Private Declare Function Rectangle Lib "gdi32" _
    Alias "Rectangle" (ByVal hdc As Long, _
    ByVal X1 As Long, ByVal Y1 As Long, _
    ByVal X2 As Long, ByVal Y2 As Long) As Long

Private Declare Function RoundRect Lib "gdi32" _
    Alias "RoundRect" (ByVal hdc As Long, -
    ByVal X1 As Long, ByVal Y1 As Long, _
    ByVal X2 As Long, ByVal Y2 As Long, _
    ByVal nWidth As Long, ByVal nHeight As Long) As Long
```

The Rectangle function draws a rectangle with opposite corners at coordinates (X1, Y1) and (X2, Y2). The RoundRect function draws a similar rectangle with the corners rounded to follow a quarter of an ellipse. The nWidth and nHeight arguments specify the width and height of the ellipses that are used in rounding the corners. Figure 2.6 shows how these parameters determine the shape of the rounded rectangle.

Example program Rect, shown in Figure 2.7, demonstrates the Rectangle and RoundRect functions. Whenever the program's form is resized, including when it is first created, the program draws several rectangles and rounded rectangles.

Curve Functions

The Ellipse, Arc, Chord, and Pie functions draw pieces of ellipses in different styles.

```
Private Declare Function Ellipse Lib "gdi32" _
    Alias "Ellipse" (ByVal hdc As Long, _
```

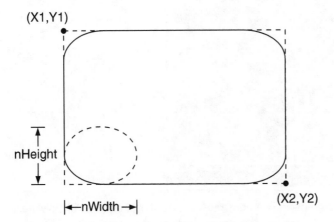

Figure 2.6 A rounded rectangle drawn by RoundRect.

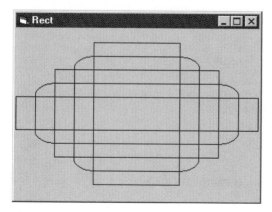

Figure 2.7   Example program Rect demonstrates the RoundRect API function.

```
        ByVal X1 As Long, ByVal Y1 As Long, _
        ByVal X2 As Long, ByVal Y2 As Long) As Long

  Private Declare Function Arc Lib "gdi32" _
      Alias "Arc" (ByVal hdc As Long, _
      ByVal X1 As Long, ByVal Y1 As Long, _
      ByVal X2 As Long, ByVal Y2 As Long, _
      ByVal X3 As Long, ByVal Y3 As Long, _
      ByVal X4 As Long, ByVal Y4 As Long) As Long

  Private Declare Function Chord Lib "gdi32" _
      Alias "Chord" (ByVal hdc As Long, _
      ByVal X1 As Long, ByVal Y1 As Long, _
      ByVal X2 As Long, ByVal Y2 As Long, _
      ByVal X3 As Long, ByVal Y3 As Long, _
      ByVal X4 As Long, ByVal Y4 As Long) As Long

  Private Declare Function Pie Lib "gdi32" _
      Alias "Pie" (ByVal hdc As Long, _
      ByVal X1 As Long, ByVal Y1 As Long, _
      ByVal X2 As Long, ByVal Y2 As Long, _
      ByVal X3 As Long, ByVal Y3 As Long, _
      ByVal X4 As Long, ByVal Y4 As Long) As Long
```

The Ellipse function draws an ellipse bounded by a rectangle with opposite corners at (X1, Y1) and (X2, Y2). This is much easier to understand than Visual Basic's Circle function with its aspect parameter. Figure 2.8 shows how these coordinates determine the shape of the ellipse.

The Arc function draws an arc of an ellipse. The ellipse is bounded by the rectangle with corners (X1, Y1) and (X2, Y2) as in the Ellipse function. The arc begins where the line connecting the center of the ellipse and the point (X3, Y3) intersects the ellipse. The arc ends where the line connecting the center of the ellipse and the point (X4, Y4) intersects the ellipse. Figure 2.9 shows how these parameters define the arc. Note that the points (X3, Y3) and (X4, Y4) do not need to lie on or within the ellipse.

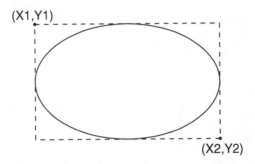

Figure 2.8 An ellipse defined by the Ellipse API function.

The Chord function draws an arc of an ellipse much as the Arc function does. It then draws a line connecting the endpoints of the arc. The chord is filled using the current FillStyle and FillColor. Figure 2.10 shows how the Chord function's parameters determine the shape of the chord.

The Pie function is similar to the Chord function, except it draws lines from the center of the ellipse to the endpoints of the arc rather than connecting the endpoints. It fills the resulting pie slice using the current FillStyle and FillColor. Figure 2.11 shows how the Pie function draws a pie slice.

Example program Curves, shown in Figure 2.12, demonstrates these four functions. Whenever you resize the form, and when the form is initially created, the program draws an example ellipse, arc, chord, and pie slice.

Drawing Attributes

Visual Basic provides various properties, like DrawMode and FillStyle, that determine the graphic characteristics of the items you draw. You can set DrawStyle to vbDot, for example, to make Visual Basic draw with dotted lines.

In a similar manner, the Windows API uses *pens* and *brushes* to specify how lines should be drawn and shapes filled. To use a pen, you first create it using the CreatePen or CreatePenIndirect function. Next, you use the SelectObject function to make future graphic

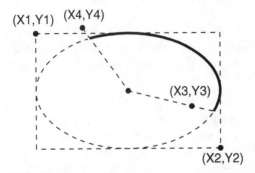

Figure 2.9 An arc drawn by the Arc API function.

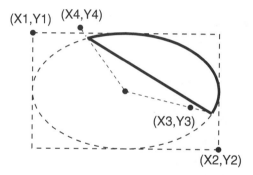

Figure 2.10 A chord defined by the Chord API function.

operations use the pen. When you are finished using the pen, you should reselect the original pen using SelectObject and then use the DeleteObject function to free the system resources used by the pen you created. If you do not invoke DeleteObject, Windows may eventually run out of resources and none of your programs will be able to get anything done.

You use a brush in a similar manner. First you create it using one of the functions CreateBrushIndirect, CreateHatchBrush, CreatePatternBrush, or CreateSolidBrush. Then you make the brush active using SelectObject. When you are finished with the brush, you should reselect the original brush using SelectObject and then use DeleteObject to free the system resources used by the brush you created.

Visual Basic's DrawWidth, DrawStyle, FillStyle, and FillColor properties perform almost exactly the same functions as Windows pens and brushes, so you will rarely need to use the API functions directly. It is much simpler to use the Visual Basic properties.

Background Attributes

One way the pen and brush API functions differ from Visual Basic's properties is in the way a drawing object's background interacts with a filled pattern. When you use only Visual Basic, areas inside a filled area are cleared and replaced by the fill pattern selected by the FillStyle property. The brush API functions allow this behavior too, but they also allow you to keep the background unchanged where the pattern is blank.

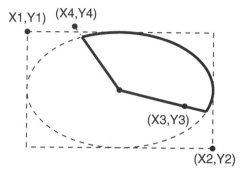

Figure 2.11 A pie slice drawn by the Pie API function.

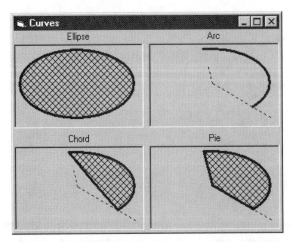

Figure 2.12 Program Curves demonstrates the Ellipse, Arc, Chord, and Pie API functions.

The SetBkMode API function determines whether the area behind a fill pattern is erased or preserved during a fill operation. If this function's second parameter is the constant TRANSPARENT, the area behind the fill pattern is preserved. If this parameter is OPAQUE, the area behind the fill pattern is erased.

Normally, the area behind the pattern is set through use of the drawing object's Back-Color property. You can change this color using the SetBkColor API function. You can use Visual Basic's FillColor property to change the color of the pattern itself.

```
Private Const OPAQUE = 2
Private Const TRANSPARENT = 1

Private Declare Function SetBkColor Lib "gdi32" ( _
    ByVal hdc As Long, ByVal crColor As Long) As Long

Private Declare Function SetBkMode Lib "gdi32" ( _
    ByVal hdc As Long, ByVal nBkMode As Long) As Long
```

Example program BkMode, shown in Figure 2.13, demonstrates the SetBkMode and SetBkColor API functions. The program fills its form with a checkerboard pattern. It then draws two ellipses. For the first ellipse, the program sets the background mode to TRANSPARENT. For the second, it sets the background mode to OPAQUE and the background color to white.

Fill Modes

When you draw polygons using the Polygon or PolyPolygon API functions, there are two ways the function can fill them: WINDING and ALTERNATE. You can use the SetPolyFillMode API function to determine which method to use. The following code shows how to declare this function in Visual Basic.

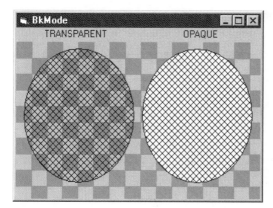

Figure 2.13   Program BkMode shows how to use API functions to control pattern fills.

```
Private Declare Function SetPolyFillMode Lib "gdi32" _
    Alias "SetPolyFillMode" (ByVal hdc As Long, _
    ByVal nPolyFillMode As Long) As Long
```

When the fill mode is ALTERNATE, the system fills every other section in the polygon along each horizontal scan line. To see how this works, trace a horizontal line from the left edge of the screen until it reaches a segment in a polygon. The system begins filling at that point. When it reaches another segment, the system stops filling. If it later hits a third segment, it starts filling again, and so on until it reaches the right side of the screen.

When the fill mode is WINDING, the system uses the direction in which the polygons' segments were drawn to decide which parts of the shape to fill. Start with a counter initialized to zero and trace a scan line from the left side of the screen as before. This time, whenever you meet one of the polygon's segments, add one to the counter if that segment was drawn in the clockwise direction and subtract one if the segment was drawn in the counterclockwise direction. Then, if the counter is not zero, start filling. If the counter is zero, stop filling.

Example program FillMode, shown in Figure 2.14, uses the PolyPolygon function to draw a star and a rectangle several times. The program draws its top three pictures with fill mode ALTERNATE and its bottom three with fill mode WINDING. The two pictures on the left show a star drawn in the counterclockwise direction. The middle pictures contain a star and a rectangle, both drawn counterclockwise. In the pictures on the right, the rectangle is drawn in the clockwise direction.

When you are drawing only a single polygon, the difference between the two styles is relatively easy to understand. The WINDING fill mode fills all of the polygon while the ALTERNATE mode may result in some unfilled sections. When more than one polygon is involved, things can become confusing. In that case, it may be easiest to write a program and try drawing the polygons clockwise and counterclockwise using the different fill modes until you get the result you want.

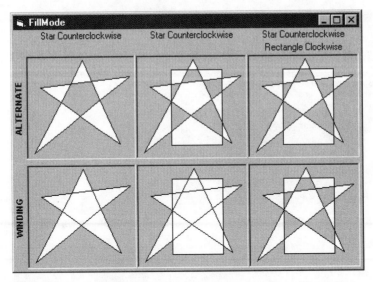

Figure 2.14   Program FillMode demonstrates polygon fill modes.

FloodFill

The FloodFill function fills an area of the screen using the current brush. The fill begins at the point (X, Y) and continues in all directions until the function encounters a pixel with the color crColor. At that point, the function stops filling in that direction. The following code shows how to declare the FloodFill function in Visual Basic.

```
Private Declare Function FloodFill Lib "gdi32" _
    Alias "FloodFill" (ByVal hdc As Long, _
    ByVal x As Long, ByVal y As Long, _
    ByVal crColor As Long) As Long
```

Example program Flood, shown in Figure 2.15, demonstrates the FloodFill API function. When you click on the form, the program fills the area you clicked using a random color.

The ExtFloodFill function is similar to FloodFill except it takes an extra parameter that determines how the fill progresses. If you set the wFillType parameter to FLOODFILL-BORDER, the fill stops when it finds a pixel with color crColor (exactly as before). If you set wFillType to FLOODFILLSURFACE, the fill continues as long as the function finds pixels that do have the specified color rather than as long as they do not have that color. This approach can be useful when you want to fill an object that has a single color but that has a multicolored boundary.

```
Private Const FLOODFILLBORDER = 0
Private Const FLOODFILLSURFACE = 1

Private Declare Function ExtFloodFill Lib "gdi32" _
    Alias "ExtFloodFill" (ByVal hdc As Long, _
```

Figure 2.15   Program Flood demonstrates the FloodFill API function.

```
ByVal x As Long, ByVal y As Long, _
ByVal crColor As Long, ByVal wFillType As Long) As Long
```

Figure 2.16 shows two shapes that you could fill using FloodFill. The shape on the left is filled with more than one color (light gray and white), but its border is a single color (black). You could fill this shape using FloodFill or using ExtFloodFill with wFillType set to FLOODFILLBORDER and crColor set to black.

The shape on the right is filled with a single color (light gray) and is surrounded by a border with more than one color (dark gray and white). You could fill this shape using ExtFloodFill specifying FLOODFILLSURFACE for wFillType and light gray for crColor.

The FloodFill and ExtFloodFill functions fill areas using the color and pattern specified by the drawing object's FillStyle and FillColor properties.

Figure 2.16   Objects to be filled through use of FloodFill.

Metafiles

A Windows metafile (.wmf file) contains a series of graphics instructions that describe an image. While a bitmap (.bmp) file stores an image as a collection of pixel values, a metafile stores instructions for drawing an image using lines, rectangles, ellipses, and so forth. This approach makes metafiles more compact than bitmap files for many types of images.

Many other applications, like drawing packages, can load and save Windows metafiles. You can use this fact to import images drawn by your programs into a drawing package. Many of the illustrations in this book started as metafiles created by a program. I loaded the metafiles into a drawing program, scaled, edited, and added captions to them and then saved the results in a different format for publication.

Like other API routines, metafile functions work only in pixels. You must measure distances in pixels when you are drawing into a metafile. Similarly, when you play a metafile back into a form or picture box, you draw the image using pixels whether you normally measure distances in pixels, twips, or some other unit.

You can create a new metafile using the CreateMetaFile function. This function takes as a parameter the name of the file you want to create. If you set this parameter to vbNullString, the function creates a metafile in memory rather than in a file. This approach can be useful if you want to draw the same image in several different places in your program. You can create a memory metafile and play it back into several different forms or picture boxes without creating the file on your hard disk.

Most programs that import metafiles expect the metafile to include information about how large it should be. If you do not include this information, an application importing the metafile may make its picture extremely small. Metafiles contain instructions for drawing rather than bitmapped images, so you can probably resize the image to make it bigger.

You can make an imported image start at a more reasonable size using the SetWindow-ExtEx API function. This routine includes information about the drawing's size in the metafile, so the importing program can give the image a reasonable size.

The CreateMetaFile function returns a device context handle (hDC) for the new metafile. You can use this handle as the device context parameter for many API drawing routines including Arc, Chord, Ellipse, FloodFill, LineTo, MoveToEx, Pie, Rectangle, and RoundRect.

After you place drawing commands in the metafile using the API drawing routines, close the metafile using the CloseMetaFile function. This function returns a handle to the newly created metafile. This is different from the handle to the file's device context that is returned by the CreateMetaFile function. You use the device context handle to draw into the metafile. You use the metafile handle to play the metafile back if you like.

You can obtain a handle to an existing metafile using the GetMetaFile function. For example, if you previously created a metafile, you can use GetMetaFile to open the file to display it later.

Once you have a handle to a metafile, obtained from either CloseMetaFile or Get-MetaFile, you can play the file's drawing commands back into a form or picture box using the PlayMetaFile function. Pass the function the device context of the form or picture box and the metafile handle. You can use PlayMetaFile repeatedly to draw the image into several different forms or picture boxes if you like.

Finally, when you have finished using the metafile, use the DeleteMetaFile function to free the resources used by the metafile. Note that this function does not actually delete the metafile if it is stored on disk. If you want to use a metafile stored on disk again, you can use the GetMetaFile function to reload it. If you want to remove the metafile physically from the disk, use Visual Basic's Kill statement.

The following code shows the Visual Basic declarations for these metafile functions.

```
Private Declare Function CreateMetaFile Lib "gdi32" _
    Alias "CreateMetaFileA" (ByVal lpString As String) As Long
Private Declare Function CloseMetaFile Lib "gdi32" _
    Alias "CloseMetaFile" (ByVal hMF As Long) As Long
Private Declare Function GetMetaFile Lib "gdi32" _
    Alias "GetMetaFileA" (ByVal lpFileName As String) As Long
Private Declare Function PlayMetaFile Lib "gdi32" _
    Alias "PlayMetaFile" (ByVal hdc As Long, _
    ByVal hMF As Long) As Long
Private Declare Function DeleteMetaFile Lib "gdi32" _
    Alias "DeleteMetaFile" (ByVal hMF As Long) As Long
Private Declare Function SetWindowExtEx Lib "gdi32" ( _
    ByVal hdc As Long, ByVal nX As Long, ByVal nY As Long, _
    lpSize As SIZE) As Long
Private Type SIZE
    cx As Long
    cy As Long
End Type
```

Example program Meta, shown in Figure 2.17, allows you to save and restore metafiles from disk. Click and drag the mouse to draw on the form. Select Save As from the File

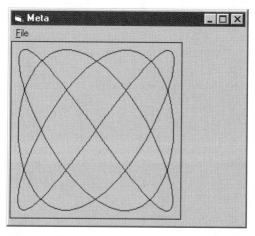

Figure 2.17   Program Meta saves and restores metafiles.

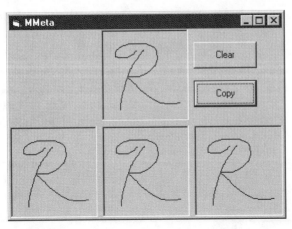

Figure 2.18 Program MMeta uses a memory metafile to copy a drawing several times.

menu to save your drawing to a metafile. Select the Load command from the File menu to load a metafile. The Ch2 directory on the CD-ROM contains some metafiles you can load.

If you have access to a drawing program that can import metafiles, try creating a metafile and importing it into that application. Depending on your application, you may be able to stretch, shrink, rotate, and otherwise manipulate the file.

Example program MMeta, shown in Figure 2.18, uses a memory metafile to copy an image from one picture box into several others. Click and drag the mouse in the upper picture box to draw. When you click the Copy button, the program creates a memory metafile holding your drawing. It then plays the metafile back into each of the other picture boxes.

Summary

You should respect the API but not fear it. It can be an unpredictable nightmare when used recklessly, but it is a powerful tool when used carefully. Save your work often when you use API functions. Wrap API function calls in Visual Basic subroutines that you can call safely. Once you have them working properly, they will allow you to take advantage of features normally hidden from you and extend the boundaries of what you can achieve with Visual Basic.

CHAPTER 3

Advanced Color

C hapter 1 describes the fundamentals of color in Visual Basic. Methods like PSet and Line take a parameter that indicates the color they should use. You can control the colors of other drawing operations using a drawing object's ForeColor, BackColor, and FillColor properties.

While these techniques allow a program to select one of the computer's available colors, they do not determine which colors are available. This chapter covers advanced color topics. It explains how to determine which colors are available on a computer and how to take best advantage of them.

The chapter begins with a discussion of the different color modes available to modern computers. This section explains how you can make your system use different color models.

Color Models

Color is almost synonymous with memory. To display many colors, a computer needs a lot of memory. For example, suppose you need your computer to display only 16 different colors at one time. Then you can make a table listing the 16 colors. To specify a pixel's color, you can give its index in this table.

You can use the values 0 through 15 to indicate each pixel's index. Because you can specify the values 0 through 15 using only 4 bits, you can represent each pixel with only 4 bits. The number of bits used to represent each pixel is called the model's *color depth* or *color resolution*.

If your monitor displays 640 pixels horizontally and 480 pixels vertically, you need a total of 640 * 480 * 4 = 1,228,800 bits = 153,600 bytes or roughly 150KB of memory to determine the colors of every pixel.

Not too long ago, memory was quite expensive, and this 16-color configuration was common. As memory prices dropped, more sophisticated color models became more popular. One model that is still popular uses a table of 256 color entries. The model uses 8 bits to store the index of each pixel in the table. If your monitor is 640 by 480 pixels, graphic memory uses $640 * 480 * 1 = 307,200$ bytes or 300KB of memory.

Recently, even more memory-intensive color models became common. Many computers can use 16 or 24 bits to describe each pixel's value, and some even use 32 bits. These models do not use color tables. Instead, the bits for each pixel describe the pixel's color directly. In 24-bit color, for example, 8 bits are used to describe each of the pixel's red, green, and blue color components.

This is almost exactly the same way Visual Basic's RGB function works. Suppose you want a pixel to have color components r, g, and b. The value RGB(r, g, b) is a long integer containing the bits in the values r, g, and b.

You can represent a value between 0 and 255 using two hexadecimal digits. For instance, the value 0 is &H00, and the value 255 is &HFF. That makes it easy to represent a color's numeric value using hexadecimal. If a pixel's component values are RR, GG, and BB in hexadecimal, the pixel's numeric value is &HBBGGRR. In fact, this is the value given by the RGB function.

As models such as 16-bit and 24-bit have become more popular, monitor resolution has also increased. If you have the right hardware and enough memory, you may be able to display 32-bit color on a monitor that is 1600 by 1200 pixels in size for a total memory requirement of $1600 * 1200 * 4 = 7,680,000$ bytes, or more than 7MB.

Currently the two most popular color modes are 8-bit and 24-bit. This book concentrates mostly on 24-bit color because it is easier to program than the other models. It is also likely to become even more common in the future. It provides enough colors to create images of photographic quality, and it stores information in a format that is easy to use.

The gradual decrease in memory prices has left us with a morass of color models, most of which are confusing and hard to use. Because of the simplicity and popularity of 24-bit color, I strongly encourage you to set your computer to 24-bit color mode and use the others as little as possible.

Table 3.1 summarizes the most common color models. The third column shows the amount of memory needed to display a 600 by 800 pixel screen in each color model.

To make your computer use a certain color model, right-click on an empty part of the desktop and select the Properties command. In the resulting dialog, click the Settings tab. The dialog should be similar to the one shown in Figure 3.1. The dialog's exact appearance depends on your operating system.

Using this dialog, you can select the system's color model and monitor resolution. If the dialog includes a Test button on your system, you should test the new configuration before you click the OK or Apply buttons. Testing lets you determine whether your hardware can really support the color model. If you somehow select a mode that your hardware cannot support, you may be stuck with a black monitor.

Table 3.1   Color Models

BITS PER PIXEL	COLORS	MEMORY (KB)	NOTES
1	2	59	Black and white
2	4	117	
4	16	234	VGA colors
8	256	468	
15	32,768	938	One bit out of 16 is ignored
16	65,536	938	Sometimes called "high color"
24	16,777,216	1405	Sometimes called "true color"
32	16,777,216	1875	One byte in four is ignored

Depending on your hardware, operating system, and the exact options you select, the changes you make could take effect immediately. Sometimes the changes seem to take effect when the system is in a slightly ambiguous state. Some programs will work normally,

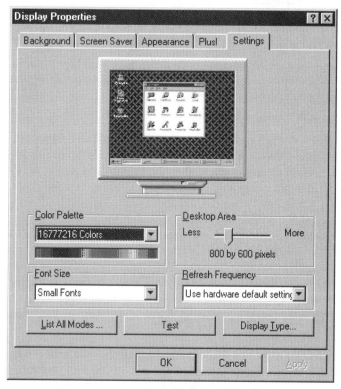

Figure 3.1   Selecting the system color model.

others may be slower than normal, and still others may not work at all. To avoid problems, you should always shut your computer down and restart it after changing the color depth.

The sections that follow explain some methods you can use to manipulate images using different color models.

Bitmaps

Visual Basic's Point function lets you determine the color of any pixel on a form or picture box. Conversely, the PSet command lets you set the color of any pixel. These commands are easy to use, but they are quite slow. A complex imaging program might need to examine and modify every pixel in a picture. Using these commands is tedious for all but the smallest pictures.

You can greatly improve the performance of your program by using API functions to process images. While the bitmap API functions are faster than Visual Basic's method, they are also much more complicated.

The following sections briefly describe ways you can use API functions make image manipulation faster. Later chapters use these functions more extensively.

Device-Dependent Bitmaps

A device-dependent bitmap is an image that is ready for display at a particular color resolution. You could display a device-dependent bitmap directly on a form or picture box.

The Windows API includes several functions for manipulating device-dependent bitmaps. The GetObject API function describes an object currently selected by a drawing object. For example, you can use GetObject to retrieve information about the bitmap, pen, brush, font, or logical color palette used by a picture box.

The following code shows the Visual Basic declaration for the GetObject API function. Visual Basic has its own GetObject function, so the declaration gives this function the name GetObjectAPI to avoid ambiguity. In the gdi32 library, the function is known as GetObjectA. The Visual Basic program refers to the function as GetObjectAPI.

```
Private Declare Function GetObjectAPI Lib "gdi32" _
    Alias "GetObjectA" (ByVal hObject As Long, _
    ByVal nCount As Long, lpObject As Any) As Long
```

The function's hObject parameter should be the handle of a bitmap, pen, brush, font, or logical palette. If you set a form or picture box's AutoRedraw property to true, Visual Basic stores a handle to the object's persistent bitmap in its Image property, and you can use that to retrieve bitmap information.

The lpObject parameter is a pointer to the data structure that will hold the information about the object. The nCount parameter gives the size of the lpObject data structure. For example, the following code gets information about the picCanvas control's bitmap.

```
' Define the BITMAP data structure.
Private Type BITMAP
    bmType As Long
    bmWidth As Long
    bmHeight As Long
    bmWidthBytes As Long
    bmPlanes As Integer
    bmBitsPixel As Integer
    bmBits As Long
End Type
    :
Dim bm As BITMAP

    ' Load the bm data structure with
    ' information about the bitmap.
    GetObjectAPI picCanvas.Image, Len(bm), bm
```

The fields in the BITMAP data structure contain the following information about the bitmap.

bmType	Zero for logical bitmaps
bmWidth, bmHeight	The size of the bitmap in pixels
bmWidthBytes	How many bytes are in each scanline of the bitmap
bmBitsPixel	How many bits are used to represent each pixel's color value
bmPlanes	The number of color planes used by the bitmap
bmBits	An array of data representing the pixels' values

The value bmWidthBytes is the product of bmBitsPixel and bmWidth rounded up to the nearest even number. When you deal directly with bitmap structures, it is important to remember the extra bytes added by this rounding. If you do not allow space for them, you program will probably crash, possibly bringing down the Visual Basic development environment with it.

The GetObject function does not fill in the bmBits field for bitmaps. After you use GetObject to see how large the bitmap is, you can allocate an array to hold the pixel values and then get those values using the GetBitmapBits function. The following code shows the declaration of the GetBitmapBits function.

```
Private Declare Function GetBitmapBits Lib "gdi32" _
    Alias "GetBitmapBits" (ByVal hBitmap As Long, _
    ByVal dwCount As Long, lpBits As Any) As Long
```

GetBitmapBits fills an array with the pixel values that make up a bitmap. Its dwCount parameter tells the function how many bytes it should copy into the array specified by lpBits. The bits are copied into the array one row at a time from top to bottom and left to right.

The SetBitmapBits function does the opposite of GetBitmapBits. This function copies data from an array into a bitmap. The following code shows its declaration.

```
Private Declare Function SetBitmapBits Lib "gdi32" _
    Alias "SetBitmapBits" (ByVal hBitmap As Long, _
    ByVal dwCount As Long, lpBits As Any) As Long
```

You can use GetBitmapBits to transfer pixel data from a bitmap into an array. You can then manipulate the data in the array and use SetBitmapBits to transfer the data back into the bitmap when you are finished. If you need to modify many of the values in the array, this is much faster than using Visual Basic's Point and PSet routines.

Unfortunately, the API documentation says that GetBitmapBits and SetBitmapBits are obsolete and are included for compatibility with 16-bit applications. These functions are still provided in Windows NT, an operating system that cannot run 16-bit applications, so it seems there is no big hurry to remove these functions from use. They are also faster and easier to use than the device-independent bitmap (DIB) routines that are designed to replace them. Later sections have more to say about DIB functions. If these functions really do become extinct in later versions of the Windows operating systems, look at this book's Web page (www.vb-helper.com/vbgp.htm) for updates.

The following code uses GetObject to obtain information about the bitmap contained in the picture box picSource. It uses the bitmap's width in bytes and its height to create an array large enough to hold the bitmap's pixel data. It then calls GetBitmapBits to copy the pixel data into the array. After manipulating the data in the array, in this case giving each pixel the color value 0, the code uses SetBitmapBits to copy the pixels back into the bitmap.

```
Dim bm As BITMAP
Dim bytes() As Byte
Dim i As Integer
Dim j As Integer
Dim wid As Integer
Dim hgt As Integer

    ' Get the basic bitmap information to see how big it is.
    GetObject picSource.Image, Len(bm), bm

    ' Get the pixels.
    wid = bm.bmWidthBytes
    hgt = bm.bmHeight
    ReDim bytes(1 To wid, 1 To hgt)
    GetBitmapBits picSource.Image, wid * hgt, bytes(1, 1)

    ' Set all bits to color 0.
    For i = 1 To hgt
        For j = 1 To wid
            bytes(i, j) = 0
        Next j
    Next i

    ' Update the bitmap.
    SetBitmapBits hbm, wid * hgt, bytes(1, 1)
```

This example is relatively simple because it sets each byte in the array to 0. Doing anything more complex is much harder. The main difficulty lies in mapping the bytes in the array to the colors of the pixels in the image. Depending on how your computer is configured, bitmaps on your system may use 1, 4, 8, 15, 16, 24, 32, or some other number of bits per pixel. These different color depths lead to different arrangements of bits in the array.

As if this were not confusing enough, Windows handles different color depths in fundamentally different ways. If an image uses eight or fewer bits per pixel, the bits correspond to indexes in a color table. If an image uses more than eight bits per pixel, the bits give the red, green, and blue components of the pixel's color directly.

Each pixel in a 15-bit image corresponds to two bytes in the array. The least significant five bits contain the pixel's blue component. The next five bits contain the pixel's green component. The last five bits contain the pixel's red component. The final bit is unused.

Images that use 16-bit color are similar to 15-bit images except they use six bits to represent the pixels' green components instead of just five. Unfortunately, the bmBitsPixel field in the BITMAP data structure filled in by the GetObject API function contains the value 16 for both 15- and 16-bit images. That means you cannot easily tell whether an image uses 15- or 16-bit color.

One way to solve this problem is to draw a white pixel on the image using PSet. Then use GetBitmapBits to read the pixel's bit value and see if the leftmost of the 16 bits is set. If it is, the color is using all 16 bits, and this is a 16-bit image. If the leftmost bit is not set, this is a 15-bit image.

For 24-bit images, each pixel corresponds to three bytes that contain the pixel's red, green, and blue color components. The one-to-one mapping of bytes to color components makes 24-bit images relatively easy to manipulate.

The 32-bit systems I have encountered assign four bytes for each pixel, but they actually use only three. The first three bytes give the pixel's color components, and the fourth byte is ignored. Using four bytes per pixel aligns each pixel's bytes on a four-byte boundary, and that simplifies the hardware.

By now you have probably decided that working with all of these different color depths is extremely confusing. To make things easier, you can store pixel information using the RGBTriplet data type shown in the following code. Then you can manage the pixels' red, green, and blue color components separately and intuitively no matter what color model you use.

```
Public Type RGBTriplet
    rgbBlue As Byte
    rgbGreen As Byte
    rgbRed As Byte
End Type
```

Now you can write routines to transfer pixel values between an array of RGBTriplets and a bitmap. For example, the following code copies the bits representing a 15-bit image's pixel data from the array bytes into the array of RGBTriplets names pixels.

```
For Y = 0 To hgt - 1
    For X = 0 To wid - 1
        With pixels(X, Y)
            ' Get the combined 2 bytes for this pixel.
            two_bytes = bytes(X * 2, Y) + _
                bytes(X * 2 + 1, Y) * 256&

            ' Separate the pixel's components.
            .rgbBlue = two_bytes Mod 32
            two_bytes = two_bytes \ 32
            .rgbGreen = two_bytes Mod 32
            two_bytes = two_bytes \ 32
            .rgbRed = two_bytes
        End With
    Next X
Next Y
```

Transferring data for a 24-bit image is easier because each color component is represented by its own byte. In fact, the bytes in a row of the bytes array correspond exactly to the bytes in a row of pixels array. The only annoying detail is the bytes array may contain some extra bytes at the end to make each row have an even number of bytes. If it were not for this fact, you could make GetBitmapBits copy its data directly into the pixels array.

Instead, you can use the CopyMemory API function to copy the rows of data directly into the pixels array. Using CopyMemory is much faster than looping through the array copying the bytes one at a time.

```
For Y = 0 To hgt - 1
    CopyMemory pixels(0, Y), bytes(0, Y), wid * 3
Next Y
```

Transferring the pixel values in and out of an RGBTriplet array takes a little longer than working with them directly in the array filled by GetBitmapBits, but it is much simpler, particularly for the stranger color models. Using the original array, you need to search for a pixel's bits and assemble them into red, green, and blue color components in one of several different ways, depending on the image's color depth. Using the array of RGB-Triplet values, you can access any pixel's color components quickly and easily.

Example program CopyDDB, shown in Figure 3.2, demonstrates this approach. The code is not included here because it is quite long. You can find the complete source code on the CD-ROM.

When you click the Copy button, the program copies a source picture into two picture boxes. It draws some colored boxes on the resulting image to show that it can manipulate pixel values using the RGBTriplets.

The program uses Point and PSet to copy the image into the first picture box. The program uses an array of RGBTriplet values to copy the image into the second picture box. In one test, Point and PSet took more than 20 times longer than using the RGBTriplet array.

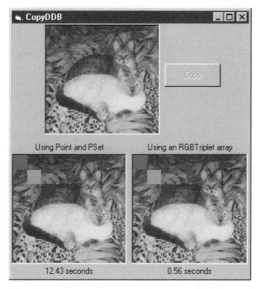

Figure 3.2   Program CopyDDB uses an array of RGBTriplet values to manipulate a bitmap.

When a program does not need to examine and modify many pixels in an image, the differences in speed are not as dramatic. Drawing lines or circles using Visual Basic's Line and Circle methods is faster than individually setting the pixels needed to draw these shapes using GetBitmapBits and SetBitmapBits.

Device-Independent Bitmaps

In an attempt to bring order to chaos, Microsoft created device-independent bitmaps (DIBs). A DIB is basically a data structure that contains the pixel information needed to produce an image at a certain color depth. For example, an 8-bit color depth DIB contains a color table listing the 256 colors used by the image. Keeping the color information in the DIB makes it somewhat easier to display the image at different color resolutions.

Despite its name, a DIB is really not very device independent. As is the case with device-dependent bitmaps, DIBs of different color depths are different. A DIB with 1-, 4-, or 8-bit color includes a color table. DIBs that use more than 8 bits per pixel contain the pixels' color component values instead. While DIBs make some operations easier, they do not solve every color problem.

A DIB is described by a BITMAPINFO data structure. The first part of this structure is a BITMAPINFOHEADER data structure that defines certain characteristics of the DIB.

The second part of the BITMAPINFO structure contains the color table used by the DIB. A DIB with a color depth of eight or less includes entries here. A DIB with a higher color resolution does not have a color table. Because the largest color table a program might need holds 256 entries, you can declare the BITMAPINFO data type to include 256 color table entries. The DIB functions will not use all of these entries if the image does not need them, but that does little harm. You will just allocate a little more memory than necessary.

The following code shows the Visual Basic definition of the BITMAPINFO and BITMAP-INFOHEADER data structures.

```
Public Type BITMAPINFO
    bmiHeader As BITMAPINFOHEADER
    bmiColors(0 To 255) As RGBQUAD
End Type

Public Type BITMAPINFOHEADER
    biSize As Long              ' Size of BITMAPINFOHEADER
    biWidth As Long             ' Width of bitmap.
    biHeight As Long            ' Height of bitmap.
    biPlanes As Integer         ' Must be 1.
    biBitCount As Integer       ' Number of bits per pixel.
    biCompression As Long       ' BI_RGB for no compression.
    biSizeImage As Long         ' Size. Can be 0 if BI_RGB.
    biXPelsPerMeter As Long     ' Resolution of target device.
    biYPelsPerMeter As Long     ' Resolution of target device.
    biClrUsed As Long           ' # colors in color table.
    biClrImportant As Long      ' # required colors.
End Type

Public Type RGBQUAD
    rgbBlue As Byte
    rgbGreen As Byte
    rgbRed As Byte
    rgbReserved As Byte
End Type
```

The general steps for loading a DIB from a picture box are:

1. Use the CreateCompatibleDC API function to create a device context (DC) in memory that is compatible with the picture box.

2. Use the CreateCompatibleBitmap API function to create a bitmap in memory that is compatible with the picture box.

3. Use the SelectObject API function to select the new bitmap into the new device context.

4. If the picture box has a color depth of eight or less, it uses a color palette. Use the SelectPalette and RealizePalette API functions to select the palette into the new device context.

5. Use BitBlt to copy the image from the picture box into the new device context. This puts a copy of the picture box's image in the new bitmap in memory.

6. Use SelectObject to deselect the new bitmap from the new device context. The GetDIBits API function requires that the bitmap it uses not be selected in any device context.

7. Initialize the biSize, biWidth, biHeight, biPlanes, biBitCount, and biCompression fields in a BITMAPINFO data structure to describe the new DIB.

8. Create an array that is big enough to hold the image's pixel information.

9. Use the GetDIBits API function to finally copy the image's pixel information into the array.

10. Use the DeleteObject API function to delete the new device context and bitmap.

At this point the program has copied the pixel information from the picture box into a byte array. You can now rearrange the information to make working with it easier. For example, the previous section shows how to copy the pixel data for a device-dependent bitmap into an array of RGBTriplets for easier manipulation. You can perform a similar operation with the DIB pixel information.

Looking at the previous list of steps, you may have noticed that working with DIBs is much more complicated than working with device-dependent bitmaps. Working with DIBs is also generally slower.

There are two main reasons DIBs are useful. First, they are the newer technology and support for them will probably improve. Later versions of Windows may someday include faster DIB routines that are easier to use.

Second, a program can load a DIB at a color resolution different from its current one. In step 7, the program sets the BITMAPINFOHEADER's biBitCount field to indicate the number of bits per pixel the DIB should have. This need not be the same as the picture box's number of bits per pixel. For instance, the program could load a 24-bit image into an 8-bit DIB and then display it at its new resolution.

Thankfully, displaying a DIB is much easier than loading one. The program simply uses the StretchDIBits API function to copy the DIB into the picture box.

Example program CopyDIB, shown in Figure 3.3, shows how to load and display DIBs. The original image on the left is loaded at your computer's full resolution. Select a color resolution from the combo box and click the Copy button. The program converts the image into a DIB of the color resolution you selected. It draws some colored squares to show that it can manipulate the image's pixels. It then displays the results in the picture box on the right. In Figure 3.3, the program has downgraded an image from 24-bit color to 4-bit color.

Color Palettes

The previous sections explain how to manipulate device-dependent and device-independent bitmaps. For images that use more than 8 bits per pixel, the pixels map directly into color components. While the arithmetic involved in translating from bits to pixel components may be confusing for some color models, using 8 bits or fewer per pixel can be even more complicated.

If you have the right hardware and enough memory, use 24-bit color. If you do not have enough memory, buy some more. Then you can skim the rest of this chapter just so that you know how much pain and trouble you are avoiding.

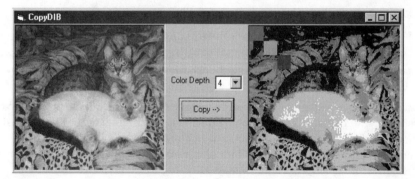

Figure 3.3   Program CopyDIB uses an array of RGBTriplet values to manipulate a DIB.

If memory on your system is scarce, you may need to use color palettes. The rest of this chapter explains color palettes and how you can manage them. The rest of the example programs described in this chapter were designed to work with 256 color palettes. If your computer uses some other color model, the programs may not work normally. Some present an error message and refuse to run.

Ideally, your program could specify a pixel and a color, and your computer would make the pixel that color. This is the way it works in color models with more than 8 bits per pixel.

Some, but not all, systems that use fewer bits per pixel can still produce a wide range of colors, but they can display only a limited number of colors at one time. EGA systems use two bits to specify each of the red, green, and blue components of a color in hardware. Because they use a total of six bits to store the colors, EGA systems can distinguish only $2^6 = 64$ different colors. In other words, an EGA system can produce only 64 distinct colors.

VGA and Super-VGA displays use six bits to store each of the red, green, and blue components of a color. Because they use a total of 18 bits to define colors to the hardware, these displays can distinguish up to $2^{18} = 262,144$ different colors.

Even with all of these colors, an 8-bit per pixel VGA system can display only 256 different colors at one time. To keep track of the colors that are in use at any given moment, the system uses a *system color palette*. This palette lists all the colors that the system is prepared to display. For a VGA system, the palette contains 256 entries, each containing an 18-bit color value. To each pixel on the screen, the system assigns an index into the system palette. To find out the color of a pixel, you can look up the pixel's value in the palette. Figure 3.4 shows how the color palette maps pixels to colors.

When the system is told to make a pixel a particular color, the system assigns the pixel the index of the color in the palette. If the requested color is not in the palette and the palette is not full, the system adds it.

Things become complicated if the color is not in the palette and the palette is full. In that case, the system must either replace an entry in the palette or use the closest available

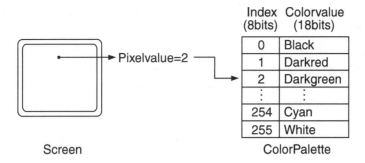

Figure 3.4 Mapping palette entries to color values.

color for the pixel. In either case, some of the colors displayed on the screen may not be exactly the colors you want.

In an attempt to improve this situation, Windows provides *logical palettes* in addition to the system palette. Images such as those in forms and picture boxes can all have their own logical palette. When an image receives the input focus, Windows copies entries from the image's logical palette into the system palette in a process known as *realizing* the palette. The logical palette that is mapped into the system palette first is called the *foreground palette*.

If the logical palette contains more colors than the system palette, Windows matches the extra colors in the logical palette to the entries in the system palette that are closest. For example, suppose a logical palette contains 300 entries, but the system palette contains only 256. The system palette fills before all of the logical palette's colors have been added.

Suppose the system palette becomes full, and the next color in the logical palette is dark pink. This color may be mapped to pure red if that is the closest match in this system palette. Any pixels that are dark pink in the image are seen as red on the display.

If the logical palette holds fewer entries than the system palette, Windows fills the remaining system palette entries with colors requested by other programs. The palettes of these other programs are called *background palettes*. Windows continues to add colors to the system palette until all the background palettes are satisfied or the system palette is full.

Finally, Windows matches any remaining colors to whatever values in the system palette are closest. As a result, background images can look strange. If the foreground palette fills the system palette with shades of blue, for example, a picture that uses reds and oranges will not map closely into the system palette.

To make an already confusing situation almost incomprehensible, recent versions of Visual Basic have intruded into the domain of color palettes. Visual Basic forms now have Palette and PaletteMode properties that are supposed to help referee palette use within your application.

The Palette property is a picture that contains the palette the form should use. This need not be the palette required by the images displayed on the form, so it can produce some very unsatisfying results.

The PaletteMode property determines how the form manages its palette. If this property's value is 2 - Custom, the control uses the palette of the image specified in its Palette property.

If PaletteMode is 0 - Halftone, the form uses a halftone palette. That allows the form to display several different images that would like to use different palettes. The results are a bit grainy, but they are better than the garbage you might get if one picture has total control of the system palette.

If PaletteMode is 1 - Use ZOrder, the form uses the palette of the control it contains that is on top of the other controls. This setting is particularly useful when the form must display a single image.

The Palette and PaletteMode properties have still not really solved the problems you may face working with palettes. They make it easier to do simple things, but they make performing more advanced tasks even more confusing. They help you determine which image has control of the system palette, but they do not help you determine what colors are in the palette.

This would be an excellent time to reevaluate your decision to not buy more memory and move to 24-bit color.

Static Colors

To make it easier for programs to share the same system palette, Windows reserves several static entries in the system color table. These entries are filled with commonly used colors, such as red, blue, and dark green. These colors include the 16 colors in the Windows 3.0 VGA color palette, plus 4 others. Table 3.2 shows the 20 static colors in the system palette.

If your program uses only these static colors, you are almost guaranteed to get exactly the colors you want. If you run many programs that all use the static colors, they can share the same system palette without conflict. Only when you run several applications that use non-static colors will you have color palette conflicts.

These static colors are also useful as a last resort for mapping background palette colors. For example, suppose the foreground palette contains only shades of green. If a background palette contains dark pink, Windows can match the color more closely to the static color red than to one of the shades of green defined by the foreground palette.

Inverting Static Colors

The ordering of the static colors in the system palette is not accidental. If your program sets DrawMode to vbInvert and draws on top of a color, Visual Basic inverts each of the bits representing the color in the system color palette.

You can also compute a color's inverted index by subtracting the index from 255. For instance, the previous list shows that the system palette index of the static color green

Table 3.2   Static Colors

SYSTEM PALETTE INDEX	VISUAL BASIC CONSTANT	VALUE	COLOR
0	vbBlack	&H0	Black
1		&H80	Dark red
2		&H8000	Dark green
3		&H8080	Dark yellow
4		&H800000	Dark blue
5		&H800080	Dark magenta
6		&H808000	Dark cyan
7		&HC0C0C0	Light gray
8		&HC0DCC0	Money green
9		&HF0CAA6	Sky blue
246		&HF0FBFF	Cream
247		&HA4A0A0	Medium gray
248		&H808080	Dark gray
249	vbRed	&HFF	Red
250	vbGreen	&HFF00	Green
251	vbYellow	&HFFFF	Yellow
252	vbBlue	&HFF0000	Blue
253	vbMagenta	&HFF00FF	Magenta
254	vbCyan	&HFFFF00	Cyan
255	vbWhite	&HFFFFFF	White

is 250, or &HFA in hexadecimal. If you invert the bits in the value &HFA, you get &H05. If you subtract 250 from 255, you get 5, the same value.

Because the inverted value for 250 is 5, if you draw in invert mode on a form with a green (system palette entry 250) background, you produce the color at position 5 in the system color palette, which is dark magenta.

The static colors are arranged so that inverting one of them produces a color that contrasts sharply with the original color. Green is a very bright color, and dark magenta is a very dark color. As you can see from the list, inverted values of bright colors are dark colors and vice versa. As a result, when you draw in invert mode, the results should be visible, no matter how cluttered the screen is.

On the other hand, the system cannot guarantee that the inverted value of a non-static color will contrast well with the original color. For instance, the system palette may happen to contain the color &HD0FFD0 (pale green) in entry 10 and the almost identical color &HDOFFD1 in entry 245. Because the inverted value for 10 is 245, lines drawn in invert mode over either of these colors will be very difficult to see. In fact, these colors are so similar that your screen may display them identically or your eyes may not be able to tell the difference. Whether inverted non-static colors provide a good contrast depends on the colors in the system palette and the order in which they are loaded.

Colors in Visual Basic

There are several ways you can specify a color in Visual Basic. One of the best methods is to use a constant such as vbCyan. These colors are part of the static colors, so they should always be available, and using constants with meaningful names makes your code easier to understand.

You can also use the RGB function to calculate the value of a color based on its component values. If a pixel's color components are R, G, and B, then:

```
RGB(R, G, B) = R + G * 256 + B * 256 * 256
```

For instance, RGB(&HFF, &HFF, &H00) = &H00FFFF, which is yellow.

When you specify a color using these sorts of RGB values, Visual Basic matches the color to the closest one available in the current logical palette. This may not always be a very close match to the color you want.

If your program executes a command that fills an area, Visual Basic tries to fill the area with a color in the logical palette. If the picture box uses the default Visual Basic palette, only the system static colors are available. If there is no exact match for the color your program specifies, the system uses a combination of two static colors in a pattern to approximate that color. Using this type of color patterning to approximate another color is called *dithering*.

For example, suppose a program executes the following command.

```
Line (0, 0)-(50, 50), RGB(255, 127, 127), BF
```

Visual Basic tries to draw a box filled with the color salmon pink. Because pink is not a static color, the system approximates pink by filling the box with red covered by a pattern of white dots. Over a large area, this gives a reasonable approximation of the color pink.

By using only static colors, Visual Basic increases the chances that your program can find the colors it needs and that the display will look the same no matter what foreground palette is currently realized. On the other hand, Visual Basic does not use the exact colors your program requests unless you happen to use only static colors.

Example program Rainbow demonstrates the difference between Visual Basic's default color behavior and the use of a palette. Use the scrollbars to set the red, green, and blue color components for the color you want to see.

The picture box on the left uses Visual Basic's default, static colors. The program fills this box using the RGB function so colors are dithered to approximate the color you specify.

The picture box on the right contains a bitmap that defines a rainbow selection of different colors. When the program fills this box, Visual Basic selects the color in the picture box's palette that is closest to the specified color. While these colors are not dithered, they usually do not match the color you request exactly.

Example program Custom, shown in Figure 3.5, displays colors using static colors and a customized color palette. Whenever you select a new color value, the program modifies the right picture box's color palette so that it can display exactly the color you select. In Figure 3.5, Visual Basic has dithered using white dots on dark gray to produce a slightly lighter shade of gray in the left picture box.

Logical Palette Indexes

There are two ways you can specify a color in a logical palette. First, you can specify the index of the color. To do this, add &H1000000 to the index of the color you want and pass the result to the Visual Basic drawing routine. For instance, the following code fills a box using the color in position 72 in the logical palette:

```
Line (0, 0)-(50, 50), 72 + &H1000000, BF
```

Visual Basic automatically translates the color value 72 + &H1000000 into whatever value is in position 72 in the logical palette.

Example program LogIndex, shown in Figure 3.6, uses this technique to display the colors in a logical palette. Choose an image file by selecting Open from the File menu. The program loads the image into the left picture box. It then uses the following statements to make the right picture box use the same palette as the left picture box.

```
picPalette.Picture = picPalette.Image
picPalette.Picture.hPal = picBitmap.Picture.hPal
```

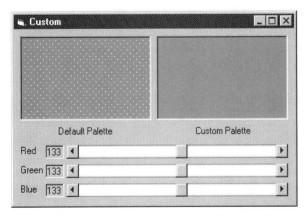

Figure 3.5 Example program Custom displays colors using static colors and a customized palette.

Figure 3.6 Example program LogIndex displays the colors used in a picture's logical palette.

The program then uses the following code to fill the right picture box with rectangles containing each of the colors in its logical palette. The program defines the constant PALETTE_INDEX = &H1000000 to make the code a little easier to understand.

```
Option Explicit

Private Const PALETTE_INDEX = &H1000000

' Fill picture box Pal with its logical palette
' colors using palette indexes.
Private Sub FillPicture()
Dim i As Integer
Dim j As Integer
Dim dx As Single
Dim dy As Single
Dim clr As Long

    dx = picPalette.ScaleWidth / 16
    dy = picPalette.ScaleHeight / 16
    clr = 0
    For i = 0 To 16
        For j = 0 To 16
            picPalette.Line (j * dx, i * dy)-Step(dx, dy), _
                clr + PALETTE_INDEX, BF
            clr = clr + 1
        Next j
    Next i
End Sub
```

Palette-Relative RGB Values

The second method for specifying palette colors is to use a *palette-relative RGB value*. To do this, pass to a drawing routine the normal RGB value of the color you want, plus &H2000000. The system maps your color to the closest value in the logical color map. This method is similar to using ordinary RGB values, except Visual Basic does not dither to approximate colors. When it cannot match a color exactly, the program uses the closest color available in the color palette.

When you fill a rectangle, circle, or other shape using a palette-relative RGB value, Visual Basic does not dither the area, even if dithering might produce a better result. For example, suppose you are using the default, static color palette and you want to fill a circle using the color salmon pink. If you specify the color as RGB (255, 127, 127), Visual Basic dithers the area using red with white dots to produce a reasonable approximation of pink.

If you specify the color as &H2000000 + RGB(255, 127, 127), Visual Basic fills the area completely with the color in the logical palette that most closely matches the color you requested. In the default palette, that color is red. Depending on your application, the dithered pink may look better than solid red. When you specify palette-relative RGB values, you assume the responsibility for ensuring that the colors in your palette produce a satisfactory result.

Example program Relative, shown in Figure 3.7, demonstrates palette-relative RGB values using the system static colors. The program fills the picture box on the left with various shades of red, green, and blue specified using the RGB function. Because this picture box uses the default static palette, Visual Basic dithers to produce approximations of the colors.

The program fills the picture box on the right with the same colors using palette-relative RGB values. Visual Basic selects the colors in the static palette that match the specified colors most closely. The result is not as grainy as the dithered version, but the colors form large blocky regions.

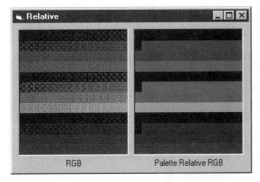

Figure 3.7 Example program Relative displays dithered and palette-relative colors.

Programming with Palettes

Palette indexes and palette-relative colors give you a great deal of control over how colors are used in an image. The easiest way to gain control is to load an image that contains the palette you want to use. Then you can erase the image's pixels and draw using the colors defined by the image's palette.

Example program PalDraw, shown in Figure 3.8, lets you use all the colors available in an image's palette. Select Open from the program's File menu and select a bitmap file. The program loads that file and its color palette.

Click on the ForeColor and FillColor boxes to select colors from the image's color palette. Click the Clear button to erase the picture using the FillColor you have selected. Use the program's combo boxes to determine the program's other drawing attributes. Then click and drag on the picture to draw shapes using the colors you have selected.

Getting Palette Information

There are several API functions that provide information for working with color palettes. The GetDeviceCaps function returns data about your computer's display. This information includes the display type (plotter, raster screen, and so forth), the size of the display, and whether the device can rotate text 90 degrees. Take a look at the online help for a complete list of this function's abilities.

GetDeviceCaps takes as parameters a device context and a flag indicating the kind of information you want to retrieve. If you use the RASTERCAPS flag, the function returns a long integer containing the sum of several possible values. One of the more important values when you want to manipulate palettes is RC_PALETTE. If this flag is set, the device is using palettes. If it is not, you may as well not bother with palettes because the device will not support them. You can use the following code to see if a display device supports palettes and end your program if it does not.

```
Const RASTERCAPS = 38       ' Raster device capabilities.
Const RC_PALETTE = &H100    ' Has palettes.
```

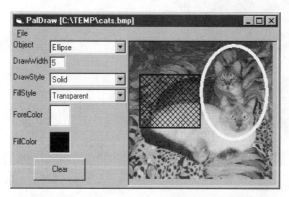

Figure 3.8 Example program PalDraw lets you draw using the colors in an image's palette.

```
' If the device does not support palettes, quit.
If Not GetDeviceCaps(hDC, RASTERCAPS) And RC_PALETTE Then
    MsgBox "This device is not using palettes."
    End
End If
```

GetDeviceCaps returns the size of the system palette if you pass it the flag SIZEPALETTE. It returns the number of reserved static colors in the system palette if you use the flag NUMRESERVED. Half of the static colors lie in the first system palette entries, and half lie in the last. These numbers can be useful when you work with palettes.

```
Const SIZEPALETTE = 104  ' Size of system palette.
Const NUMRESERVED = 106  ' # reserved entries in palette.

' See how big the system palette is.
SysPalSize = GetDeviceCaps(hDC, SIZEPALETTE)

' See how many static colors there are.
NumStaticColors = GetDeviceCaps(hDC, NUMRESERVED)
```

Example program DevInfo uses GetDeviceCaps to display many of the capabilities of your computer's display. Keep in mind that Visual Basic may be able to provide a feature even though GetDeviceCaps indicates the hardware cannot. For example, in the unlikely event that your hardware cannot draw circles, Visual Basic may be able to draw circles itself.

Palette Handles in Visual Basic

So far, this chapter has described ways you can use the entries in a logical palette, but it has not explained how you can create or modify such a palette. The Windows API provides several functions for manipulating palettes. Many of these functions take as a parameter a handle to a palette object. To make working with these functions easier, Visual Basic gives you a way to access the palette handle for forms, image controls, and picture boxes that have them.

Each of these objects has a Picture property. This property is actually a reference to a Picture object that has its own properties and methods. One of those properties is hPal, a handle to the logical palette used by the object. You can use Windows API routines and this handle to manipulate the palette.

It is important to know, however, that objects do not always have pictures or logical palettes. If you create a picture box and draw on it using methods like Circle and Line, the drawing object's Picture property still has the value zero. Because the Picture property does not contain a reference to a Picture object, you cannot use that object's hPal property. If you try to access the hPal property for the nonexistent Picture object, you get the rather enigmatic run-time error '-2147483640 (80000008)': OLE Automation error.

You can give a drawing object a valid Picture property by setting AutoRedraw to True, drawing on the object, and then setting its Picture property equal to its Image property as in the following code.

```
picCanvas.AutoRedraw = True
picCanvas.Line (0, 0)-(1440, 1440), B
picCanvas.AutoRedraw = picCanvas.Picture
```

You can also set a drawing object's Picture property directly from a file using the Load-Picture statement.

An object can also have a valid Picture property and still not have a logical palette. If an object uses only static colors, the system does not bother to create a palette for the object. Later, when you draw on the object, the system knows that a picture without a palette needs to use only the static colors. While this sort of object has a valid Picture property, the value of the hPal property is zero. You can examine this value without causing an error, but you cannot use it as a parameter to API functions that manipulate palettes.

Resizing Palettes

Once you have assigned a picture with a palette to a Picture object, you can use the Picture's hPal property to manipulate the palette.

As you might guess from its name, the ResizePalette function allows you to change a logical palette's size. If you use this function to make a palette larger, the new entries are initially set to black. ResizePalette takes as parameters a handle to the logical palette and the number of entries you want the palette to have. The function returns zero if there is an error and a nonzero value otherwise.

```
Private Declare Function ResizePalette Lib "gdi32" _
    Alias "ResizePalette" (ByVal hPalette As Long, _
    ByVal nNumEntries As Long) As Long
```

Examining Palette Entries

You can use the GetPaletteEntries function to find out exactly what color values are loaded in a logical palette. This function takes as parameters a handle to the palette, the index of the first entry in the palette that you want to examine, the number of palette entries you want to examine, and an array of PALETTEENTRY structures. The function fills in the peRed, peGreen, and peBlue fields in the PALETTEENTRY structures to indicate the red, green, and blue components of the colors. The function returns the number of palette entries for which it retrieved information.

```
Private Type PALETTEENTRY
    peRed As Byte
    peGreen As Byte
    peBlue As Byte
    peFlags As Byte
End Type

Private Declare Function GetPaletteEntries Lib "gdi32" _
    Alias "GetPaletteEntries" (ByVal hPalette As Long, _
```

```
ByVal wStartIndex As Long, ByVal wNumEntries As Long, _
    lpPaletteEntries As PALETTEENTRY) As Long
```

Example program GetEntry, shown in Figure 3.9, uses the following code to retrieve the definitions of the colors in the logical palette used by a picture. It displays the colors' red, green, and blue components in the text box txtColors.

```
' Display a list of the colors in the logical palette.
Private Sub ShowEntries()
Dim num_entries As Integer
Dim palentry(0 To 255) As PALETTEENTRY
Dim i As Integer
Dim txt As String

    If picCanvas.Picture = 0 Then
        txtColors.Text = "No picture loaded."
        Exit Sub
    ElseIf picCanvas.Picture.hPal = 0 Then
        txtColors.Text = "Default palette."
        Exit Sub
    End If

    num_entries = GetPaletteEntries( _
        picCanvas.Picture.hPal, 0, 256, palentry(0))

    txt = "  #  Red Green Blue" & vbCrLf
    For i = 0 To num_entries - 1
        txt = txt & _
            Format$(i, "@@@") & ":" & _
            Format$(palentry(i).peRed, "@@@@") & _
            Format$(palentry(i).peGreen, "@@@@@@") & _
            Format$(palentry(i).peBlue, "@@@@@") & _
```

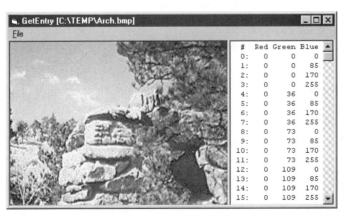

Figure 3.9 Example program GetEntry shows the color components of a picture's color palette.

```
            vbCrLf
    Next i

        txtColors.Text = txt
End Sub
```

Working with the System Palette

Much as the GetPaletteEntries function retrieves information about a logical palette, the GetSystemPaletteEntries function returns information about the colors in the system palette. The main difference between these functions is that GetSystemPaletteEntries takes as a parameter a device context instead of a palette handle. For this parameter, you can use the hDC property of a form or picture box.

```
Private Declare Function GetSystemPaletteEntries Lib "gdi32" _
    Alias "GetSystemPaletteEntries" (ByVal hdc As Long, _
    ByVal wStartIndex As Long, ByVal wNumEntries As Long, _
    lpPaletteEntries As PALETTEENTRY) As Long
```

Remember that the system palette includes static colors, colors loaded from the foreground palette, and usually colors loaded from background palettes. The colors are also not necessarily arranged the same way in the system palette as they are in the foreground and background palettes. In general, the system palette does not match any logical palette exactly.

Changing Palette Entries

You can use the SetPaletteEntries function to change the values of the colors in a logical palette. This function is similar in form to the GetPaletteEntries function, except the array of PALETTEENTRY structures is used to define the color values rather than to return them. SetPaletteEntries returns the number of entries successfully set or zero if there is a problem.

```
Private Declare Function SetPaletteEntries Lib "gdi32" _
    Alias "SetPaletteEntries" (ByVal hPalette As Long, _
    ByVal wStartIndex As Long, ByVal wNumEntries As Long, _
    lpPaletteEntries As PALETTEENTRY) As Long
```

The final field in the PALETTEENTRY structure, the peFlags field, determines how the color is mapped into the system palette. This field can have one of four values. If peFlags is zero, the color is added to the system palette normally. If the color is already in the system palette, the new logical palette entry is mapped to the existing entry, so the color does not take up more space in the system palette. If the color is not already present, it is placed in a new system palette entry. If the system palette is full, the color is mapped to the closest color already available.

If you set the peFlags field to PC_NOCOLLAPSE (4), the new color is not mapped to an existing color, even if the color is already in the system palette. Instead, the color is placed in a new system palette entry. If the system palette is full, it is mapped to the closest available color.

If peFlags is PC_RESERVED (1), the color is mapped much as it is when peFlags is PC_NOCOLLAPSE. The color is also marked as reserved for your program's use only, so colors used by other logical palettes will not map to this entry. This is useful if you expect to change the value of the color frequently. In that case, the system might spend a lot of time remapping the colors of other applications whenever you change the value of this color. By setting peFlags to PC_RESERVED, you guarantee that other applications will not use the color, and you minimize the remapping.

Finally, if you set peFlags to PC_EXPLICIT (2), the system maps the color directly to the corresponding system palette entry. For example, it maps the first logical palette entry to the first system palette entry. In this case, the logical palette entry always holds the value of the corresponding system palette entry. You cannot change the value of the color in the logical palette to make the system palette entry change. Instead, the logical color value changes to reflect the value of the corresponding system palette entry.

Changing a Logical Palette While It Is in Use

If you make a change to a logical palette while the palette is in use, you must call the function RealizePalette to make the changes take effect. This function takes as a parameter the device context of the object using the palette. The function remaps the entries in the logical palette into the system palette and returns the number of entries that were mapped to new positions.

```
Private Declare Function RealizePalette Lib "gdi32" _
    Alias "RealizePalette" (ByVal hdc As Long) As Long
```

Program PalWatch

The following code maps all the palette entries in the picture box picCanvas to the colors in the system palette. First, the routine resizes the control's logical palette to make it big enough to hold the entire system palette. It then fills in an array of PALETTE-ENTRY structures, setting the peFlags field of each to PC_EXPLICIT. It also gives each entry a different peRed value so that the colors do not all map to the same position. Finally, the routine uses SetPaletteEntries to update the logical palette.

```
' Load the Pict palette with PC_EXPLICIT entries
' so they match the system palette.
Private Sub LoadSystemPalette()
Dim palentry(0 To 255) As PALETTEENTRY
Dim i As Integer

    ' Make the logical palette as big as possible.
```

```
        LogicalPalette = picCanvas.Picture.hPal
        If ResizePalette(LogicalPalette, SysPalSize) = 0 Then
            MsgBox "Error resizing the palette."
            End
        End If

        ' Flag all palette entries as PC_EXPLICIT.
        ' Set peRed to the system palette indexes.
        For i = 0 To SysPalSize - 1
            palentry(i).peRed = i
            palentry(i).peFlags = PC_EXPLICIT
        Next i

        ' Update the palette (ignore return value).
        i = SetPaletteEntries(LogicalPalette, 0, _
            SysPalSize, palentry(0))
    End Sub
```

Example program PalWatch, shown in Figure 3.10 together with the Viewer program, uses this subroutine to display the values in the system color palette. It uses the LoadSystemPalette subroutine to copy the system palette colors into the picCanvas control's logical palette.

PalWatch then uses palette-indexed colors to draw boxes using each of the colors in the logical palette. Because these colors match those in the system palette, the picture box shows the colors in the system palette. The program covers the static colors with a diagonal hatch pattern. If you click on one of the colors, the program displays the color's red, green, and blue components in its menu bar.

When you run other programs, their logical color palettes may require changes to the system color palette. If you leave PalWatch running, it automatically updates to display the new system palette colors.

PalWatch can be particularly useful when you are writing programs that manipulate palettes. Unless a program draws with all the colors in its logical palette, you will not be

Figure 3.10 Example program PalWatch displays the current system palette colors.

able to see which colors it has loaded into the system palette. For example, an image may define 200 colors in its logical color palette but display only 100 of them. PalWatch lets you see the other colors even if they are not displayed.

Learning the System Palette Mapping

The system palette is maintained by the *palette manager*, and you have little control over how it does its job. The way colors are added to the system palette depends on the colors that are already there, the flags set for the colors (for example, PC_NOCOLLAPSE), and the other applications that are running. In general, it is difficult for you to force your logical palette entries into the system palette in any particular positions. It's even hard to determine after the fact where your logical palette entries were placed. Both of these tasks are possible, however.

You can determine the location of your logical colors by using the PSet method and the GetBitmapBits API function. GetBitmapBits lets you examine the system palette indexes of the pixels that make up an image. The function takes as parameters a handle to a bitmap, the number of bytes of information you want to retrieve, and an array of bytes.

If you set the AutoRedraw property of a form or picture box to true, that object's Image property gives a handle to the object's persistent bitmap. You can use that handle in calls to GetBitmapBits. The function places the system palette indexes of the pixels in the byte array and returns the number of bytes it fetched. If the function fails, it returns the value zero.

Using GetBitmapBits, you can determine how your logical palette has been mapped into the system palette. For each color in the logical palette, use the PSet method to set the color of the pixel in the upper-left corner of the image. Specify the color of the pixel using its logical palette index.

Then use GetBitmapBits to retrieve the system palette index of that pixel. This tells you how your logical palette index mapped into the system palette. The following code uses this technique to show where each logical palette entry is mapped.

```
' Display a list of the colors in the logical
' palette and how they map to the system palette.
Private Sub ShowEntries()
Dim num_entries As Long
Dim palentry(0 To 255) As PALETTEENTRY
Dim pixel As Byte
Dim orig_color As Long
Dim i As Integer
Dim txt As String

    If picCanvas.Picture = 0 Then
        txtPositions.Text = "No picture loaded."
        Exit Sub
    ElseIf picCanvas.Picture.hPal = 0 Then
        txtPositions.Text = "Default palette."
```

```
        Exit Sub
    End If

    num_entries = GetPaletteEntries( _
        picCanvas.Picture.hPal, 0, 256, palentry(0))

    ' Save the color of pixel (0, 0).
    orig_color = picCanvas.Point(0, 0)

    txt = "Log Sys  Red Green Blue" & vbCrLf
    For i = 0 To num_entries - 1
        ' See to what system entry each logical
        ' palette entry is mapped.
        picCanvas.PSet (0, 0), i + PALETTE_INDEX

        GetBitmapBits picCanvas.Image, 1, pixel

        ' Add the information to the string.
        txt = txt & _
            Format$(i, "@@@") & _
            Format$(pixel, "@@@@") & _
            Format$(palentry(i).peRed, "@@@@@") & _
            Format$(palentry(i).peGreen, "@@@@@@") & _
            Format$(palentry(i).peBlue, "@@@@@") & _
            vbCrLf
    Next i

    ' Restore pixel (0, 0) to its original color.
    picCanvas.PSet (0, 0), orig_color

    txtPositions.Text = txt
End Sub
```

Example program SysMap, shown in Figure 3.11, uses this subroutine to display the mapping between a logical palette and the system palette. Select Open from the File menu to load an image. For each of the colors in the image's logical palette, the program displays the color's logical and system palette indexes and its red, green, and blue components.

Specifying System Palette Placement

Although you cannot tell the system where to place a color in the system palette, you can use the palette mapping rules to make colors land in the positions you want. Start by using SetPaletteEntries to map the static colors to their normal locations. Use the GetSystemPaletteEntries function to determine the color values the system static colors should have. Map the first half of the static colors into the beginning of the color palette. Map the remaining static colors into the end of the color palette.

Initially, make all the non-static palette entries black and set their flags to PC_NO-COLLAPSE. These entries would normally map to the static color black, which always

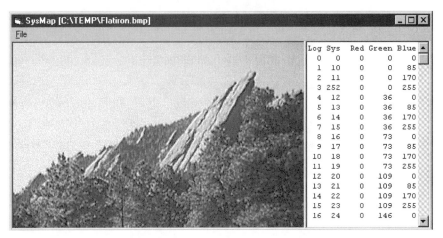

Figure 3.11   Example program SysMap displays the mapping between an image's logical color palette and the system color palette.

has index 0 in the system palette. Because these entries are flagged PC_NOCOLLAPSE, they are placed at the next available system palette entries starting after the first block of static colors.

Now use SetPaletteEntries again to redefine the non-static colors so that they have the final values you want. Be sure to keep their flags set to PC_NOCOLLAPSE.

You can use this method to make each logical palette entry for an image map to the corresponding system palette entry. First, load an image and realize its palette. This step makes the system load the logical palette into the system palette in some unknown order. Next, use GetSystemPaletteEntries to retrieve the system palette entries. Then use the previous technique to copy the colors in the system palette into the logical palette. When you are finished, the colors in the logical palette correspond to those in the system palette.

Subroutine LoadLogicalPalette, shown in the following code, uses this method to load the logical palette for picture box ImagePict into the system palette. It first realizes the palette for ImagePict so that the system palette contains the colors in the logical palette. The routine next uses GetSystemPaletteEntries to identify the colors loaded in the system palette. It then reloads the static colors into the system palette, turning all the other colors black. Finally, it updates the non-static colors in the logical palette so that they match those in the system palette.

```
' Load the picHidden palette so its entries
' match the system entries.
Private Sub LoadLogicalPalette()
Dim palentry(0 To 255) As PALETTEENTRY
Dim blanked(0 To 255) As PALETTEENTRY
Dim i As Integer

    ' Make picVisible and picSwatch use the same
```

```
    ' palette as picHidden.
    picVisible.Picture = picHidden.Picture
    picSwatch.Picture = picHidden.Picture
    LogicalPalette = picHidden.Picture.hPal

    ' Draw the image at the correct scale.
    DrawImage

    ' Make sure picVisible has the foreground palette.
    RealizePalette picVisible.hdc

    ' Give the system a chance to catch up.
    DoEvents

    ' Make the logical palette as big as possible.
    If ResizePalette(LogicalPalette, SysPalSize) = 0 Then
        MsgBox "Error resizing logical palette."
        Exit Sub
    End If

    ' Get the system palette entries.
    GetSystemPaletteEntries picHidden.hdc, 0, _
        SysPalSize, palentry(0)

    ' Blank the non-static colors.
    For i = 0 To StaticColor1
        blanked(i) = palentry(i)
        blanked(i).peFlags = PC_NOCOLLAPSE
    Next i
    For i = StaticColor1 + 1 To StaticColor2 - 1
        With blanked(i)
            .peRed = i
            .peGreen = 0
            .peBlue = 0
            .peFlags = PC_NOCOLLAPSE
        End With
    Next i
    For i = StaticColor2 To 255
        blanked(i) = palentry(i)
        blanked(i).peFlags = PC_NOCOLLAPSE
    Next i
    SetPaletteEntries LogicalPalette, 0, _
        SysPalSize, blanked(0)

    ' Insert the non-static colors.
    For i = StaticColor1 + 1 To StaticColor2 - 1
        palentry(i).peFlags = PC_NOCOLLAPSE
    Next i
    SetPaletteEntries LogicalPalette, StaticColor1 + 1, _
        StaticColor2 - StaticColor1 - 1, _
        palentry(StaticColor1 + 1)
```

```
        ' Realize the new palette values.
        RealizePalette picVisible.hdc

        ' Select the color that was selected before.
        SelectColor SelectedI, SelectedJ
    End Sub
```

Summary

Color palettes served an important purpose when memory was expensive and programmers were cheap. Now, when many desktop computers have 32MB or more of memory, the small memory savings palettes provide is not worth the extra confusion.

Support for palettes also seems to be slipping. With each release of Visual Basic, performing simple tasks with palettes becomes easier while performing more interesting tasks becomes harder. With so many other graphics programming topics to pursue, palettes are a headache you can live without. Buy a little extra memory and use 24-bit color. Then move on to more interesting topics such as fractals and ray tracing.

Advanced Text

P lacing simple text on a screen is easy with Visual Basic. You can use labels to display text and text boxes to allow the user to change text. Using the controls' ForeColor and BackColor properties, you can determine the color of the text. These controls also have a Font property that determines the appearance of the text. The Font property is actually an object with properties you use to specify, for example, the font's name and size and whether it is **bold**, underlined, or *italicized*.

Instead of using labels or text boxes, you can also draw text directly on a form, picture box, or printer using the Print command. Like labels and text boxes, these drawing objects have ForeColor, BackColor, and Font properties that determine the appearance of the text.

This chapter describes several ways you can use more advanced text features. Using a few Visual Basic tricks and a couple of API functions, you can create text written at an angle, text that is stretched or compressed, and text that uses more than one color or style. Figure 4.1 shows a few of the possibilities.

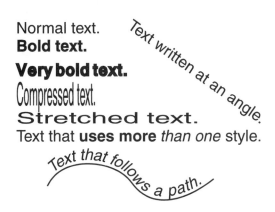

Figure 4.1 Advanced text display.

The following sections describe ways you can use advanced text features to display text that you want the user to see but not modify. These techniques give you the equivalent of label controls that display multiple colors and fonts.

The first section explains how you can use Visual Basic methods to create labels using more than one color or font. Later sections show how to use API functions to perform more powerful font operations.

Multiple Colors and Fonts

Label controls have a single Font property, so they can display text using only one font at a time. Labels also have a single ForeColor property, so all of the text contained in a label must be displayed in the same color.

When you draw text directly on a form or picture box using the Print method, however, Visual Basic uses whatever values the form or picture box's Font object has at the time. If you draw some text, modify the Font object, and then draw more text, the two pieces of text are displayed in different styles. Similarly, you can change a form or picture box's ForeColor property to produce text of different colors.

There is one drawback to this approach: You must draw the text yourself instead of using label controls. That means you must keep the screen up–to–date whenever it is obscured by another window and then exposed.

One approach is to redraw the text whenever your program receives a Paint event. This may make your program more complicated and it may be quite slow if the text you are redrawing is very complicated.

Another approach to keeping the display up–to–date is to set the form or picture box's AutoRedraw property to true. This is easier and quicker than responding to Paint events, but it makes your program use extra memory at run time.

The RandomStyles subroutine shown in the following code draws a text string on a form. For each word in the string, RandomStyles uses randomly chosen color, size, bold, and italic attributes.

```
' Draw a string on the form using randomly chosen
' ForeColor, size, bold, and italic values. Start
' the text at Y position min_y and keep it
' between the margins min_x and max_x.
Private Sub RandomStyles(txt As String, _
    min_size As Integer, max_size As Integer, _
    min_x As Single, max_x As Single, min_y As Single)
Dim length As Integer
Dim pos1 As Integer
Dim pos2 As Integer
Dim new_word As String
Dim clr As Long
Dim y As Integer
Dim font_names As Collection
```

```
    ' Erase the form.
    Cls

    CurrentX = min_x
    y = 0

    ' Make the list of font names.
    Set font_names = New Collection
    font_names.Add "Times New Roman"
    font_names.Add "Courier New"
    font_names.Add "Arial"
    font_names.Add "MS Sans Serif"

    ' Break the string into words.
    length = Len(txt)
    pos1 = 1
    Do
        ' Get the next word.
        pos2 = InStr(pos1, txt, " ")
        If pos2 = 0 Then
            new_word = Mid$(txt, pos1)
        Else
            new_word = Mid$(txt, pos1, pos2 - pos1)
        End If
        pos1 = pos2 + 1

        ' Randomly select a ForeColor.
        clr = QBColor(Int(16 * Rnd))
        If clr = BackColor Then clr = vbBlack
        ForeColor = clr

        ' Randomly pick Font properties.
        ' (The Underline and Strikethrough
        ' properties make things too cluttered.)
        Font.Name = font_names(Int(font_names.Count * _
            Rnd + 1))
        Font.Size = Int((max_size - min_size + 1) * _
            Rnd + min_size)
        Font.Bold = (Int(2 * Rnd) = 1)
        Font.Italic = (Int(2 * Rnd) = 1)

        ' If the word won't fit, start a new line.
        If CurrentX + TextWidth(new_word) > max_x Then
            CurrentX = min_x
            y = y + 1.25 * max_size
        End If

        ' Display the text.
        CurrentY = y + max_size - Font.Size
        Print new_word; " ";
    Loop While pos2 > 0
End Sub
```

This code demonstrates a couple of useful techniques. First, just before the routine displays a new word, it checks to see if that word will fit on the current line of text. If the value of CurrentX plus the width of the new word in the current font is greater than the right margin max_x, the routine starts a new line of text.

```
If CurrentX + TextWidth(new_word) > max_x Then
    CurrentX = min_x
    y = y + 1.25 * max_size
End If
```

RandomStyles also uses a technique for making the baselines of the words line up correctly. The CurrentX and CurrentY properties of a form determine where the upper-left corner of printed text appears. If you print words with different font sizes one after another, their tops line up at the Y coordinate value given by CurrentY. Text generally looks better if the words' baselines rather than their tops line up.

To make the words line up properly, RandomStyles keeps track of the Y value where each word's baseline should fall. It then computes a new value for CurrentY based on each word's font size with the following code:

```
CurrentY = y + max_size - Font.Size
```

Example program Styles, shown in Figure 4.2, uses subroutine RandomStyles to draw text directly on a form using randomly selected colors and font styles. The form's AutoRedraw property is set to true, so the display is kept up–to–date automatically. Whenever its form is resized, the program redraws the text using new random colors, sizes, and bold and italic attributes.

Notice that some of the words in Figure 4.2 look better than others. The word "styles" at the end of the third line, for example, appears somewhat jagged. This can happen when Visual Basic must scale a font to fit the point size requested by the program. Some fonts are not designed to scale, and they produce good results only at certain fixed sizes. Stretching the font to another size produces a jagged result.

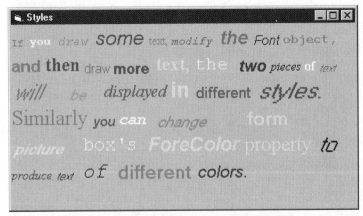

Figure 4.2 Program Styles displays text with randomly selected fonts.

The font used to draw the word styles in Figure 4.2 is MS Sans Serif. It does not scale well, and it gives poor results at many font sizes.

TrueType fonts are designed to be scaled so that they produce good results at most sizes. TrueType fonts that are present on most Windows systems include Arial, Courier New, and Times New Roman.

The section "CreateFont Function" later in this chapter explains how the font mapper selects fonts and gives further insights into using fonts at different scales.

Text Metrics

If you look very closely at Figure 4.2, you will see that the words' baselines (the line where the characters sit) do not all line up exactly. On the last line, for example, the baseline of the word "colors" is slightly above the baseline of the word "different." As it draws text using different fonts, program Styles uses its current font size to align the bottom of the text. Unfortunately, not all fonts position their baselines the same distance from the bottom of the font.

Figure 4.3 shows some important features of a character's geometry. Each character occupies a certain area called its *cell*. *Internal leading* is the space at the top of the cell. Usually the internal leading space is empty, though certain special features such as accent marks may occupy this space.

The character's *ascent* is the distance from the top of the character's cell to the font's baseline. The character's *descent* is the distance from the font's baseline to the bottom of the character cell. The font's height is the sum of its ascent and its descent.

The GetTextMetrics API function returns several useful pieces of information about a font, including its internal leading, ascent, descent, and height values. This function takes as its first parameter the handle of a device context for which it should retrieve information. For example, if this is the device context handle of a form, GetTextMetrics returns information about the font currently selected by the form.

The GetTextMetrics function's second parameter is a TEXTMETRIC data structure. The function fills this structure with information about the font.

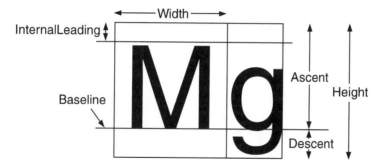

Figure 4.3   Anatomy of a character.

```
Private Type TEXTMETRIC
    tmHeight As Long
    tmAscent As Long
    tmDescent As Long
    tmInternalLeading As Long
    tmExternalLeading As Long
    tmAveCharWidth As Long
    tmMaxCharWidth As Long
    tmWeight As Long
    tmOverhang As Long
    tmDigitizedAspectX As Long
    tmDigitizedAspectY As Long
    tmFirstChar As Byte
    tmLastChar As Byte
    tmDefaultChar As Byte
    tmBreakChar As Byte
    tmItalic As Byte
    tmUnderlined As Byte
    tmStruckOut As Byte
    tmPitchAndFamily As Byte
    tmCharSet As Byte
End Type

Private Declare Function GetTextMetrics Lib "gdi32" _
    Alias "GetTextMetricsA" (ByVal hdc As Long, _
    lpMetrics As TEXTMETRIC) As Long
```

Example program FMetrics, shown in Figure 4.4, uses GetTextMetrics to learn about a font's internal leading, ascent, descent, and height values. It draws some text with these values displayed graphically.

Once you know how to use the GetTextMetrics function, you can modify the Styles program described earlier so that it displays text in different fonts aligned on their baselines. Example program Styles2, shown in Figure 4.5, uses this method to display text using randomly selected fonts.

The main difference between programs Styles and Styles2 comes just before the program prints text. Program Styles2 adjusts the text's Y coordinate using the current font's ascent. The value y + max_size gives the Y coordinate where the font's base should be. Subtracting the font's ascent value places font's baseline at this Y coordinate.

```
' Get the font's metrics.
GetTextMetrics hdc, text_metrics
ascent = ScaleY(text_metrics.tmAscent, vbPixels, ScaleMode)

' Display the text.
CurrentY = y + max_size - ascent
Print new_word; " ";
```

Figure 4.4 Example program FMetrics uses the GetTextMetrics API function to obtain detailed information about a font's geometry.

CreateFont Function

Using a drawing object's Font property, you can make the object display text using one of the standard fonts available on your system. You can also use the CreateFont API function to build customized versions of many fonts. These fonts can be unusually tall and thin, unusually short and wide, or rotated at an angle.

With 14 arguments, CreateFont is one of the more complicated API functions. Its Visual Basic declaration is:

```
Private Declare Function CreateFont Lib "gdi32" _
    Alias "CreateFontA" ( _
    ByVal Height As Long, _
    ByVal Width As Long, _
```

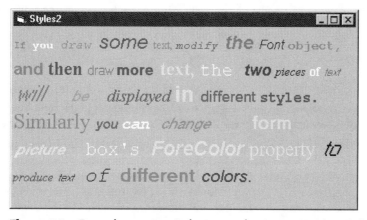

Figure 4.5 Example program Styles2 uses the GetTextMetrics API function to align the baselines of text in different fonts.

```
           ByVal Escapement As Long, _
           ByVal Orientation As Long, _
           ByVal Weight As Long, _
           ByVal Italic As Long, _
           ByVal Underline As Long, _
           ByVal StrikeOut As Long, _
           ByVal CharacterSet As Long, _
           ByVal OutputPrecision As Long, _
           ByVal ClipPrecision As Long, _
           ByVal Quality As Long, _
           ByVal PitchAndFamily As Long, _
           ByVal Face As String) As Long
```

The function's parameters are described shortly.

CreateFont returns the handle of a *logical font* that describes the font you specified using the parameters. The operating system's *font mapper* selects a *physical font* that matches your logical font as closely as possible. How close the match is depends on the parameters you specify in CreateFont and on the fonts available on your system.

After you have obtained a logical font handle, you can use the SelectObject API function to make a form or picture box use the font.

Usually, a program specifies at least the Height and Face parameters to define the size and name of the font. You can set the values of many of the other parameters to zero to make the font mapper use default values. All the CreateFont parameters are described in the following sections.

Height

The Height parameter gives the height for the font in logical units. If this parameter is greater than zero, it specifies the cell height of the font. Keep in mind that the cell height includes internal leading space that is usually empty. If Height is less than zero, it specifies the character height of the font. The character height does not include the internal leading space. If the Height parameter is zero, the font mapper uses a default value.

Width

The Width parameter specifies the average width of characters in the font. Set Width to zero to make the font mapper pick a default width that matches the Height parameter.

Escapement

The font's escapement is the angle of slope of the text in tenths of degrees measured counterclockwise from horizontal. Figure 4.6 shows how to measure the escapement of rotated text.

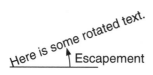

Figure 4.6   Measuring escapement for rotated text.

Orientation

The Orientation parameter specifies the orientation angle of the characters in tenths of degrees. Windows assumes that Escapement and Orientation are the same, so it ignores Orientation.

Weight

The Weight parameter specifies the weight of the font. You can specify one of the values listed in Table 4.1. The result depends on the font. Many fonts honor only FW_NORMAL and FW_BOLD weights, and other values are mapped to one of those. If you set the weight to FW_DONTCARE (0), the font mapper uses a default weight. Note that some of the values are duplicates. For instance, FW_NORMAL and FW_REGULAR both have value 400, so they produce the same result.

Table 4.1   Font Weight Constants

CONSTANT	VALUE
FW_DONTCARE	0
FW_THIN	100
FW_EXTRALIGHT	200
FW_ULTRALIGHT	200
FW_LIGHT	300
FW_NORMAL	400
FW_REGULAR	400
FW_MEDIUM	500
FW_SEMIBOLD	600
FW_DEMIBOLD	600
FW_BOLD	700
FW_EXTRABOLD	800
FW_ULTRABOLD	800
FW_BLACK	900
FW_HEAVY	900

Italic, Underline, StrikeOut

If the values for Italic, Underline, and StrikeOut are nonzero, the font is, respectively, *italic*, underlined, or ~~stricken out~~.

CharacterSet

The CharacterSet parameter specifies one of the character sets listed in Table 4.2. Usually, you should set this to ANSI_CHARSET. If you specify the value DEFAULT_CHARSET, the font mapper uses the name and size parameters to select the logical font. If the specified font name does not exist, the font mapper may substitute any other font, with sometimes unexpected results.

Table 4.2   Character Set Values

CONSTANT	VALUE
ANSI_CHARSET	0
DEFAULT_CHARSET	1
SYMBOL_CHARSET	2
OEM_CHARSET	255
ARABIC_CHARSET	178*
BALTIC_CHARSET	186*
CHINESEBIG5_CHARSET	136
EASTEUROPE_CHARSET	238*
GB2312_CHARSET	134
GREEK_CHARSET	161*
HANGEUL_CHARSET	129
HANGUL_CHARSET	129
HEBREW_CHARSET	177*
JOHAB_CHARSET	130*
MAC_CHARSET	77*
RUSSIAN_CHARSET	204*
SHIFTJIS_CHARSET	128
THAI_CHARSET	222*
TURKISH_CHARSET	162*
VIETNAMESE_CHARSET	163*

* Not available in all versions of Windows.

OutputPrecision

OutputPrecision specifies how closely the selected font must match the height, width, escapement, character orientation, pitch, and face you specify. Table 4.3 lists output precision values.

You can use OUT_DEVICE_PRECIS, OUT_RASTER_PRECIS, and OUT_TT_PRECIS to control how the font mapper selects a font when more than one font matches your specifications. For example, suppose you specify the font Helvetica and your system contains both a raster font and a TrueType font named Helvetica. If you set OutputPrecision to OUT_TT_PRECIS, the font mapper selects the TrueType font.

If you specify OUT_TT_ONLY_PRECIS, the font mapper always selects a TrueType font, even if a device or raster font matches the font you specified. In that case, the TrueType font selected may not match your selections very closely.

ClipPrecision

The clipping precision parameter determines how characters that are partially outside the clipping region are clipped. Table 4.4 lists possible values.

When you use fonts with a nonzero escapement, you should add CLIP_LH_ANGLES to the ClipPrecision using the Or operator. For example, to have text clipped one character at a time, you would specify ClipPrecision as CLIP_LH_ANGLES Or CLIP_CHARACTER_PRECIS.

Using CLIP_LH_ANGLES makes different kinds of fonts measure rotations in the same direction. If you do not use CLIP_LH_ANGLES, device fonts will measure rotation counterclockwise, but other fonts may measure rotation clockwise or counterclockwise.

Table 4.3 Font Output Precision Values

CONSTANT	VALUE
OUT_DEFAULT_PRECIS	0
OUT_DEVICE_PRECIS	5
OUT_OUTLINE_PRECIS	8
OUT_RASTER_PRECIS	6
OUT_STRING_PRECIS	1
OUT_STROKE_PRECIS	3
OUT_TT_ONLY_PRECIS	7
OUT_TT_PRECIS	4

Table 4.4   Font Clipping Precision Values

CONSTANT	VALUE
CLIP_DEFAULT_PRECIS	0
CLIP_CHARACTER_PRECIS	1
CLIP_STROKE_PRECIS	2
CLIP_EMBEDDED	128
CLIP_LH_ANGLES	16
CLIP_TT_ALWAYS	32

Quality

The Quality parameter tells the font mapper how hard it should try to match the logical font you specify with the physical font eventually displayed. Table 4.5 lists values you can give this parameter and their meanings.

PitchAndFamily

The PitchAndFamily parameter specifies the pitch and family of the font combined using the Or operator. These values tell the font mapper generally what kind of font to use if it cannot find the exact font you specify.

Pitch indicates whether the font's characters all have the same cell size. Fonts in which all characters have the same cell size are called *fixed pitch fonts* or *monospaced fonts*. Fonts that use different cell sizes for different characters are called *proportionally spaced fonts*. Table 4.6 lists values that you can use for a font's pitch.

Table 4.5   Font Quality Values

CONSTANT	VALUE	MEANING
DEFAULT_QUALITY	0	The font's appearance is not too important.
DRAFT_QUALITY	1	The font's appearance is more important than with DEFAULT_QUALITY but less important than with PROOF_QUALITY. The font mapper will scale raster fonts to the size you specify if necessary. It will also create **bold**, *italic*, <u>underline</u>, and ~~stricken out~~ fonts if needed.
PROOF_QUALITY	2	The font's character quality is more important than an exact match of the logical font attributes. The font mapper will not scale raster fonts if they do not match the size you specify. Instead, it will pick the font with the closest size. The font mapper will construct **bold**, *italic*, <u>underline</u>, and ~~strikeout~~ fonts if necessary.

Table 4.6   Font Pitch Values

CONSTANT	VALUE	EXAMPLE
DEFAULT_PITCH	0	(Depends on the font)
FIXED_PITCH	1	abcdefghijklmnopqrstuvwxyz
VARIABLE_PITCH	2	abcdefghijklmnopqrstuvwxyz

A font's family indicates generally what sort of appearance the font should have. Table 4.7 lists the values you can give for the font's family.

You can also set the second bit in the PitchAndFamily parameter to indicate that the font mapper should select a TrueType font. Do this by adding 4 to the value using the Or operator. For example, to specify a TrueType font with variable stroke widths, no serifs, and variable pitch, you could set PitchAndFamily to VARIABLE_PITCH Or FF_SWISS Or 4.

Face

Face specifies the typeface name of the font, such as Times New Roman. This is generally what you think of when you think of a font.

Although the CreateFont function can create fonts for use in forms, picture boxes, and printers, the fonts available on your monitor may not be the same as those available on your printer. You cannot always use the same font face names to display text on the monitor and the printer.

Standard Fonts

Table 4.8 lists 13 standard TrueType fonts included in the Windows family of operating systems. You cannot be certain that these fonts will be present on all computers, but chances are good that any computer running Windows will have them. If you use these fonts in your programs, you increase the odds that your program will run correctly on other computers.

Table 4.7   Font Family Values

CONSTANT	VALUE	MEANING	EXAMPLES
FF_DECORATIVE	80	Novelty fonts.	GoudyHandtooled BT Staccato222 BT
FF_DONTCARE	0	Don't care or don't know.	(Depends on the font.)
FF_MODERN	48	Constant width strokes, with or without serifs.	Courier New
FF_ROMAN	16	Variable width strokes with serifs.	Times New Roman Serifa BT
FF_SCRIPT	64	Designed to look like handwriting.	ShelleyAllegro BT
FF_SWISS	32	Variable width strokes, no serifs.	AmerType Md BT

Table 4.8 Standard Windows Fonts

FONT FAMILY	FONT NAME
Arial	Arial
	Arial Bold
	Arial Italic
	Arial Bold Italic
Courier New	Courier New
	Courier New Bold
	Courier New Italic
	Courier New Bold Italic
Symbol	Symbol (ABCDEFabcdef)
Times New Roman	Times New Roman
	Times New Roman Bold
	Times New Roman Italic
	Times New Roman Bold Italic

Programming with CreateFont

Once you have used CreateFont to obtain a logical font handle, you can select that font into a form, picture box, or printer using the SelectObject function. This function returns the handle of the font that was previously in use. When you are done using the new font, you should reselect the original font using SelectObject. Then delete the font you created, using the DeleteObject function to free system resources.

The following code shows how you would write text at a -45 degree angle starting at the upper-left corner of a form.

```
Private Sub Form_Load()
Const txt = "This text is written at a -45 degree angle."

Dim newfont As Long
Dim oldfont As Long

    AutoRedraw = True

    ' Create the logical font.
    newfont = CreateFont(20, 0, -450, 0, _
        FW_NORMAL, False, False, False, _
        ANSI_CHARSET, OUT_DEFAULT_PRECIS, _
        CLIP_CHARACTER_PRECIS, PROOF_QUALITY, _
        VARIABLE_PITCH Or FF_ROMAN Or 4, _
        "TimesNewRoman")

    ' Select the new font.
    oldfont = SelectObject(hdc, newfont)
```

```
    ' Display the text.
    CurrentX = 240
    CurrentY = 30
    Print txt

    ' Reselect the old font.
    newfont = SelectObject(hdc, oldfont)

    ' Delete the new font to free resources.
    DeleteObject newfont
End Sub
```

Example program MkFonts, shown in Figure 4.7, uses CreateFont to make and display several different versions of the Times New Roman font.

In the column on the left, the program displays text in weights ranging from 0 to 900. On the computer that produced the output shown in Figure 4.7, this font has only FW_NORMAL, FW_DEMIBOLD, and FW_BOLD values. All the other font weights are mapped to one of these.

In the second column, MkFonts draws characters that are five points wide and have heights ranging from 15 to 55. The third column shows fonts with height 15 and widths ranging from 3 to 18.

The program then displays 10 strings with different escapements starting at the same point. The strings begin with several space characters, so they do not overlap.

Curved Text

With a little extra work, you can display text that follows a curve. The CurveText subroutine, shown in the following code, uses CreateFont to display text along a path defined by a series of points.

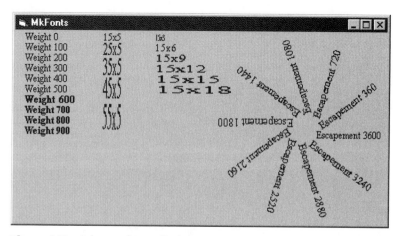

Figure 4.7   Advanced text display.

As CurveText considers each segment in the curved path, it creates a font appropriately rotated to lie along the segment. It determines the width of the next character using that font. If there is room to display the character, the subroutine does so. It continues displaying characters on the segment until no more will fit.

When there is not enough room to display another character, the routine adds the next segment to the first. It continues adding segments until their combined length is long enough to hold the next character. At that point, it displays the character. The subroutine continues until it runs out of either path segments or characters to display.

When CurveText moves from one segment to the next, the orientation of the characters changes, too. For that reason, text usually looks best when displayed along a smoothly curving path. If the path makes sudden changes in direction, the text displayed may contain gaps or overlaps.

Because rotated fonts tend to be rougher than original fonts, rotated text also looks better if the font is relatively large and bold.

```
Private Sub CurveText(txt As String, numpts As Integer, _
        ptx() As Single, pty() As Single, above As Boolean, _
        nHeight As Long, nWidth As Long, fnWeight As Long, _
        fbItalic As Long, fbUnderline As Long, _
        fbStrikeOut As Long, fbCharSet As Long, _
        fbOutputPrecision As Long, fbClipPrecision As Long, _
        fbQuality As Long, fbPitchAndFamily As Long, _
        lpszFace As String)
Dim newfont As Long
Dim oldfont As Long
Dim theta As Single
Dim escapement As Long
Dim ch As String
Dim chnum As Integer
Dim needed As Single
Dim avail As Single
Dim newavail As Single
Dim pt As Integer
Dim x1 As Single
Dim y1 As Single
Dim x2 As Single
Dim y2 As Single
Dim dx As Single
Dim dy As Single

    avail = 0
    chnum = 1

    x1 = ptx(1)
    y1 = pty(1)
    For pt = 2 To numpts
```

```
' See how long the new segment is.
x2 = ptx(pt)
y2 = pty(pt)
dx = x2 - x1
dy = y2 - y1
newavail = Sqr(dx * dx + dy * dy)
avail = avail + newavail

' Create a font along the segment.
If dx > -0.1 And dx < 0.1 Then
    If dy > 0 Then
        theta = PI_OVER_2
    Else
        theta = -PI_OVER_2
    End If
Else
    theta = Atn(dy / dx)
    If dx < 0 Then theta = theta - PI
End If
escapement = -theta * 180# / PI * 10#
newfont = CreateFont(nHeight, nWidth, escapement, 0, _
    fnWeight, fbItalic, fbUnderline, fbStrikeOut, _
    fbCharSet, fbOutputPrecision, fbClipPrecision, _
    fbQuality, fbPitchAndFamily, lpszFace)
oldfont = SelectObject(hdc, newfont)

' Output characters until no more fit.
Do
    ' See how big the next character is.
    ' (Add a little to prevent characters
    ' from becoming too close together.)
    ch = Mid$(txt, chnum, 1)
    needed = TextWidth(ch) * 1.2

    ' If it's too big, get another segment.
    If needed > avail Then Exit Do

    ' See where the character belongs
    ' along the segment.
    CurrentX = x2 - dx / newavail * avail
    CurrentY = y2 - dy / newavail * avail
    If above Then
        ' Place text above the segment.
        CurrentX = CurrentX + dy * nHeight / newavail
        CurrentY = CurrentY - dx * nHeight / newavail
    End If

    ' Display the character.
    Print ch;
```

```
        ' Move on to the next character.
            avail = avail - needed
            chnum = chnum + 1
            If chnum > Len(txt) Then Exit Sub
        Loop
        x1 = x2
        y1 = y2
    Next pt
End Sub
```

Example program Spiral, shown in Figure 4.8, uses the CurveText subroutine to draw text along a spiral path.

You can write similar subroutines for printing text along other curves. For example, you could write routines to draw text along a circle or sine wave. Example program CurveTxt, shown in Figure 4.9, uses the CurveText subroutine to draw text along several curves. It also uses the CircleText subroutine to draw text along circular paths.

Notice that text printed by program CurveTxt on the insides of curves looks somewhat crowded, and text printed on the outsides of curves looks more widely spaced. This may be a problem when a path curves too suddenly. In that case, there may be large gaps between characters, or characters may overlap. The sharp curves in the rectangle cause large gaps between adjacent characters.

Notice also that the text generally looks a bit jagged. Characters look a bit rough when they are tilted and displayed on a computer monitor. Most look much better when they are rotated by an angle that is a multiple of 45 degrees, and they look best of all when rotated by a multiple of 90 degrees.

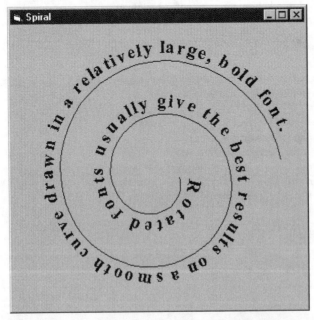

Figure 4.8 Example program Spiral draws text along curves and circles.

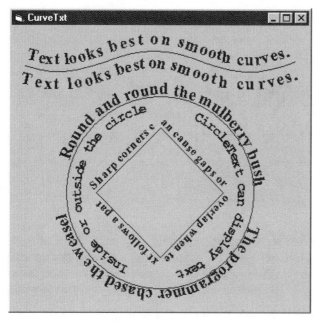

Figure 4.9 Example program CurveTxt draws text along curves and circles.

Printers usually have a much higher resolution than a typical computer screen, so rotated fonts look much smoother when drawn directly on a printer.

Centering Rotated Text

Centering normal text is relatively easy. You can use the TextWidth and TextHeight functions to see how much room the string will occupy. Then you can subtract half of these values from coordinates of the string's desired center position. The following code shows how a program might center a string on a form.

```
Private Sub Form_Load()
    CurrentX = ScaleWidth / 2 - TextWidth("Some Text") / 2
    CurrentY = ScaleHeight / 2 - TextHeight("Some Text") / 2
    Print "Some Text"
    Line (0, 0)-(ScaleWidth, ScaleHeight)
    Line (0, ScaleHeight)-(ScaleWidth, 0)
End Sub
```

The situation is much more complicated when the text is rotated. The TextWidth and TextHeight functions return the dimensions of the text as if it were not rotated; they do not return the dimensions of the rotated text. TextHeight can become confused when you use SelectObject to select a customized font, making its value completely useless.

Figure 4.10 shows the geometry of a rotated string. This picture seems intimidating, but it is manageable when considered in small pieces.

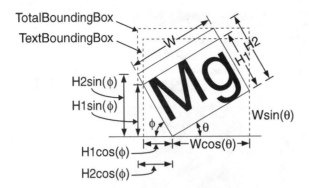

Figure 4.10 The geometry of rotated text.

The figure shows a rotated string with its bounding box and the internal leading space above the characters. You can learn the string's height without the internal leading space (H1) and total height (H2) using the GetTextMetrics API function described earlier in this chapter. The TextWidth function correctly returns the string's width (W).

The text has been rotated through the angle θ. The angle ϕ is 90 degrees minus θ. Trigonometry gives the other distances marked on the figure.

Example program CentText, shown in Figure 4.11, uses the geometry shown in Figure 4.10 to display text centered in a picture box.

The heart of the program is the CenterText subroutine. CenterText takes as parameters the string to draw, the picture box to hold it, the coordinates where the string should be centered, and parameters describing the font the routine should use.

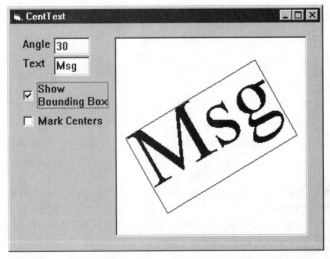

Figure 4.11 Example program CentText displays rotated text centered in a picture box.

CenterText begins by creating the rotated font and installing it in the picture box as described earlier in this chapter. It then uses the GetTextMetrics API function to get information about the font's dimensions. It uses the results to determine the height of the text with and without its internal leading space. It uses TextWidth to determine the string's width.

CenterText then uses the geometry shown in Figure 4.10 to find the dimensions of the bounding boxes that surround the rotated text. The values total_bound_wid and total_bound_hgt give the dimensions of the box including the internal leading space. The values text_bound_wid and text_bound_hgt give the dimensions of the bounding box that does not include the internal leading space.

The routine then calculates the starting point for the text in small steps. It begins with the point (x1, y1) at the desired center position. It subtracts half of the width and height of the text bounding box. That moves (x1, y1) to the upper-left corner of the text bounding box.

The program then adds $W * Sin(\theta)$ to y1. That moves the point (x1, y1) to the upper-left corner of the text. In Figure 4.10, this is right next to the upper-left corner of the letter M.

Next CenterText subtracts the differences in the widths and heights of the two bounding boxes from the coordinates. That moves the point (x1, y1) to the upper-left corner of the outer bounding box. This is the position where the program must start printing to properly center the string.

The following code fragment shows the most important parts of subroutine CenterText. The routine is rather long, so only its parts that deal with positioning the rotated text are shown here. You can find the entire routine in the CentText program on the CD-ROM.

```
    :
' Get the font metrics.
GetTextMetrics pic.hdc, text_metrics
internal_leading = _
    pic.ScaleY(text_metrics.tmInternalLeading, _
    vbPixels, pic.ScaleMode)
total_hgt = _
    pic.ScaleY(text_metrics.tmHeight, _
    vbPixels, pic.ScaleMode)
text_hgt = total_hgt - internal_leading
text_wid = pic.TextWidth(txt)

' Get the bounding box geometry.
theta = nEscapement / 10 / 180 * PI
phi = PI / 2 - theta
text_bound_wid = text_hgt * Cos(phi) + _
    text_wid * Cos(theta)
text_bound_hgt = text_hgt * Sin(phi) + _
    text_wid * Sin(theta)
total_bound_wid = total_hgt * Cos(phi) + _
    text_wid * Cos(theta)
total_bound_hgt = total_hgt * Sin(phi) + _
    text_wid * Sin(theta)
```

```
' Find the desired center point.
x1 = xmid
y1 = ymid

' Subtract half the height and width of the text
' bounding box. This puts (x1, y2) in the upper
' left corner of the text bounding box.
x1 = x1 - text_bound_wid / 2
y1 = y1 - text_bound_hgt / 2

' The start position's X coordinate belongs at
' the left edge of the text bounding box, so
' x1 is correct. Move the Y coordinate down to
' its start position.
y1 = y1 + text_wid * Sin(theta)
    :
' Move (x1, y1) to the start corner of the
' outer bounding box.
x1 = x1 - (total_bound_wid - text_bound_wid)
y1 = y1 - (total_bound_hgt - text_bound_hgt)

' Display the text.
pic.CurrentX = x1
pic.CurrentY = y1
pic.Print txt
    :
```

Editable Text

The previous sections explain how you can display text in different colors, sizes, and styles, giving you the equivalent of a multifont label. Unfortunately, the user cannot easily interact with this text, so you cannot use these techniques to make multifont text boxes. You could write a complex set of event handlers to allow the user to change the text, but this would be much more difficult than using a text box.

Recent versions of Visual Basic come with the RichTextBox control. This control is similar to a text box, but it is much more powerful. A rich text box can display text using multiple colors, fonts, point sizes, and styles. It also includes a collection of useful text-processing features that allow paragraph alignment, indentation, hanging indentation, bullets, and so forth.

To change the formatting of text in a rich text box, the text must first be selected. The user can select text as usual by clicking and dragging over the text. Programmatically, you can select text by setting the SelStart and SelLength properties to indicate where the selected text begins and how long it is.

Once text is selected, you can use the rich text box's other properties to modify it. For example, you could use the following code to make the first 10 characters in a rich text box named rchStatements turn **bold**.

```
rchStatements.SelStart = 0
rchStatements.SelLength = 10
rchStatements.SelBold = True
```

The following are some of the rich text box properties that you can change to modify the selected text:

SelBold. Determines whether the selected text is bold.

SelCharOffset. Determines whether the selected text is in a normal, superscript, or subscript position. If SelCharOffset is 0, the text is in a normal position. If SelCharOffset > 0, the text is raised by SelCharOffset twips. If SelCharOffset < 0, the text is lowered by SelCharOffset twips. Unfortunately, the control does not allow extra room for raised or lowered characters, so they may be partially obscured by the previous and following lines.

SelColor. The selected text's color.

SelFontName. The selected text's font name.

SelFontSize. The selected text's font size.

SelItalic. Determines whether the selected text is *italicized*.

SelStrikethru. Determines whether the selected text is ~~stricken through~~.

SelUnderline. Determines whether the selected text is underlined.

Rich text boxes also have several paragraph-formatting properties. The units used by the BulletIndent, SelHangingIndent, SelIndent, and SelRightIndent properties are determined by the ScaleMode property of the form containing the rich text box.

BulletIndent. Determines the amount by which text is indented when SelBullet is true.

SelAlignment. Sets paragraph alignment:

> RtfLeft. Paragraphs are left justified.
>
> RtfRight. Paragraphs are right justified.
>
> RtfCenter. Paragraphs are centered.
>
> Null. The selected text contains paragraphs with more than one alignment.

SelBullet. Determines whether paragraphs are bulleted. If SelBullet is Null, the selected text contains both bulleted and non-bulleted paragraphs.

SelHangingIndent. Specifies the distance between the left edge of the first and subsequent lines in paragraphs. If the selected text contains paragraphs with different hanging indent values, SelHangingIndent is zero.

SelIndent. Specifies the distance between the left edge of the rich text box and the left edge of the text. If the selected text contains paragraphs with different indent values, SelIndent is zero.

SelRightIndent. Specifies the distance between the right edge of the rich text box and the left edge of the text. If the selected text contains paragraphs with different right indent values, SelRightIndent is zero.

The rich text box also includes several methods that perform more general word processing functions like searching for text and loading and saving the text together with its formatting information. The following list describes these methods.

Find. Searches the text for a string.

GetLineFromChar. Returns the number of the line containing a specified character position.

LoadFile. Loads the rich text box from a text or RTF format file.

SaveFile. Saves the contents of the rich text box in a text or RTF format file.

SelPrint. Sends the selected text to a printer.

Span. Selects text forward or backward until it finds one of a set of characters. This is useful for selecting words or sentences.

UpTo. Moves the insertion point forward or backward to one of a set of characters. This is useful for moving to a new word or sentence.

The rich text box provides three properties for getting and setting its text value.

Text. Returns or sets the control's text without any formatting.

RTFText. Returns or sets the control's text including rich text formatting codes.

SelRTF. Returns or sets the control's selected text, including rich text formatting codes.

Example program Rich, shown in Figure 4.12, uses these properties to combine text in two rich text boxes. When you click the Combine button, the program copies the Text property from the upper controls into the rich text box on the lower left.

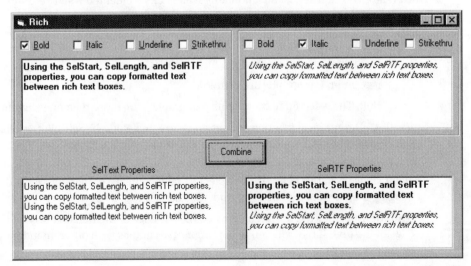

Figure 4.12 Example program Rich shows how to combine formatted text in rich text boxes.

The program then uses the SelStart and SelLength properties of the upper two controls to select all their text. Similarly, it sets the lower-right control's SelStart and SelLength properties to select its text. The program sets the lower-right control's SelRTF property equal to the same property in the upper-left control. This copies the text from the upper-left control into the lower-right control with its formatting codes.

Next, the program sets the lower-right control's SelStart and SelLength properties to the end of the control's text. It sets the control's SelText property to vbCrLf to add a carriage return to the text.

Once again, the control sets the lower-right control's SelStart and SelLength properties to the end of the control's text. Finally, it sets the control's SelRTF property to the SelRTF value of the control in the upper right. That finishes combining the text of the two upper controls.

The following code shows how program Rich combines the text in its input controls.

```
' Combine the values in the rchInput controls.
Private Sub cmdCombine_Click()
Dim sel_start(0 To 1) As Integer
Dim sel_length(0 To 1) As Integer
Dim i As Integer

    ' Combine text only.
    rchOutput(0).Text = rchInput(0).Text & _
        vbCrLf & rchInput(1).Text

    ' Save the current SelStart and SelLength values.
    For i = 0 To 1
        sel_start(i) = rchInput(i).SelStart
        sel_length(i) = rchInput(i).SelLength
        rchInput(i).SelStart = 0
        rchInput(i).SelLength = Len(rchInput(i).Text)
    Next i

    ' Combine the text only.
    rchOutput(0).Text = rchInput(0).Text & _
        vbCrLf & rchInput(1).Text

    ' Combine the rich text values.
    ' Copy the first control's text with RTF codes.
    rchOutput(1).SelStart = 0
    rchOutput(1).SelLength = Len(rchOutput(1).Text)
    rchOutput(1).SelRTF = rchInput(0).SelRTF

    ' Add vbCrLf to the end.
    rchOutput(1).SelStart = Len(rchOutput(1).Text)
    rchOutput(1).SelLength = 0
    rchOutput(1).SelText = vbCrLf
```

```
' Add the second control's text with RTF codes.
rchOutput(1).SelStart = Len(rchOutput(1).Text)
rchOutput(1).SelLength = 0
rchOutput(1).SelRTF = rchInput(1).SelRTF

' Restore the SetStart and SelLength values.
For i = 0 To 1
    rchInput(i).SelStart = sel_start(i)
    rchInput(i).SelLength = sel_length(i)
Next i
rchOutput(1).SelLength = 0
End Sub
```

Example program RichEdit, shown in Figure 4.13, uses a rich text box to build a simple but powerful text editor.

Program RichEdit provides menu commands that give access to many of the rich text box's features. When the user selects one of these commands, the program toggles the value of the corresponding rich text box property. For example, the following code shows how the program toggles the bold status of the selected text when the user invokes the Bold menu item. Similar event handlers handle the program's other menu items.

```
Private Sub mnuFontBold_Click()
    rchText.SelBold = Not rchText.SelBold
    rchText_SelChange
End Sub
```

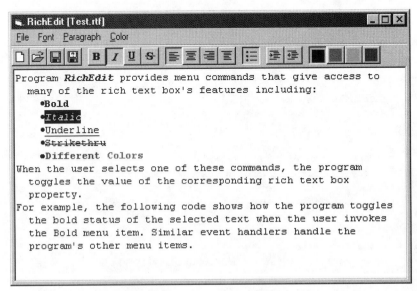

Figure 4.13   Example program RichEdit uses the Rich text box control to build a text editor.

The program also uses a toolbar to let the user select commands using buttons. The buttons invoke the corresponding menu items. For instance, the following code fragment shows how the program responds when the user clicks the bold toolbar button. The rest of the ButtonClick event handler is similar.

```
' Execute a command.
Private Sub tbrButtons_ButtonClick( _
    ByVal Button As ComctlLib.Button)

    Select Case Button.Key
            :
        Case "Bold"
            mnuFontBold_Click
            :
    End Select
End Sub
```

When the user changes the selection in the rich text box, the control's SelChange event handler executes. It examines the control's properties to determine which menu items should be checked and which toolbar buttons should be depressed. The following code fragment shows how the program handles the selected text's bold property. The rest of the subroutine handles other button presses in a similar way.

```
' Set the menu item and button states for the
' selected text.
Private Sub rchText_SelChange()
        :
    If rchText.SelBold Then
        tbrButtons.Buttons("Bold").value = tbrPressed
        mnuFontBold.Checked = True
    Else
        tbrButtons.Buttons("Bold").value = tbrUnpressed
        mnuFontBold.Checked = False
    End If
        :

    tbrButtons.Refresh
End Sub
```

Summary

Visual Basic's normal text handling methods are good enough in most circumstances. Labels let a program display static text. Using multiple labels, a program can display static text using multiple fonts and colors.

To display more complex text, a program can use the CreateFont API function. This function is very complicated, however, so you should use normal Visual Basic methods if possible.

The TextBox control allows a program to display text that the user can change. Unfortunately a TextBox can use only one font and color at a time. For more complex editable text, the program can use the RichTextBox control. This control is more complicated than a TextBox control, but it is far simpler than the CreateFont API function.

CHAPTER 5

Printing

So far this book has explained how to use Visual Basic to draw lines, circles, text, and other simple objects on a computer screen. It has shown how to save images in bitmap files and Windows metafiles. It has said little about displaying things on a printer.

There are several ways you can send output to a printer. The PrintForm method is by far the easiest, but it produces the poorest quality and can be very slow. Using graphic output methods like Line and Circle, you can send graphics directly to a printer. This approach requires much more programming, but it produces better output, and your printer will usually print more quickly. With only a little extra work, you can also provide a print preview feature to let users see what a printout will look like before printing it.

This chapter discusses these methods for creating printed output. It explains ways you can make high-resolution printing easier, and it describes a couple of useful printing routines for producing high-quality output with little additional programming.

Before continuing, however, a word of caution. There are many different kinds of printers, each requiring its own device drivers and operating system support. Different combinations of printer, device driver, operating system, and Visual Basic version can produce different, sometimes disastrous, results.

Printer Objects

When you print in Visual Basic, you work with an object named Printer. Initially, this object represents your system's default printer, but you can make the Printer object represent a different printer if you like.

The Printers collection holds a list of all of the printers available on your system. You can use the items in this collection to print to a different printer or to select a different printer. For example, to make the Printer object represent the first printer in the Printers collection, you could use the statement:

```
Set Printer = Printers(0)
```

The following code displays a list of the printers in the Printers collection.

```
Dim pr As Printer
Dim txt As String

    For Each pr In Printers
        txt = txt & pr.DeviceName & vbCrLf
    Next pr
    MsgBox txt
```

Example program Printers, shown in Figure 5.1, uses similar code to list the device names, ports, and drivers for the printers on your system.

When you run the Printers program, you may be surprised to find more printers than you expected. Several objects including fax software and graphic subsystems can appear as printers to the operating system. Generally, if an object looks enough like a printer to appear in the Printers collection, you should be able to treat it like a printer. You can draw on it, tell it to print a page, and so forth.

Many of these non-printer objects take special actions when you print to them. For instance, you can make the Printer object represent fax software and then use the PrintForm method to send graphics to the Printer object. The fax software might then present a dialog box in which you would enter the name of the person who should receive the fax, the person's phone number, and the style of cover page you want to use. When you finish entering this information, the software would fax the image created by the PrintForm command.

Selecting a Printer

The Common Dialog Control that comes with Visual Basic makes it easy for a user to select a printer. When you invoke the control's ShowPrinter method, it presents a dialog that allows the user to select a printer. By pressing the dialog's Properties button, the user can modify many of the selected printer's properties. For example, this button lets the user set the printer's paper size and orientation.

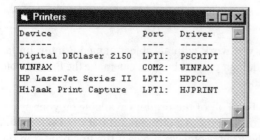

Figure 5.1   Example program Printers lists the printer devices available on the system.

An easy way to use the control is to set its CancelError property to True. Then if the user cancels the printer dialog, the program receives an error. To avoid crashing, the program should use an On Error statement to trap the error.

If the user presses the dialog's OK button, the program does not receive an error. The dialog automatically updates the program's Printer object to indicate the newly selected printer. The program can examine the dialog control's properties to learn about other values specified by the user. For instance, the program can learn whether the user checked the Print to file box.

A program can set the dialog's Flags property to modify the dialog's appearance. For example, if you set the cdlPDHidePrintToFile flag, the dialog hides its Print to file check box.

Example program PickPtr, shown in Figure 5.2, uses the following code to display a printer selection dialog. If the user cancels, the program does nothing. If the user accepts the dialog, the program prints the name of the selected printer on that printer.

```
' Let the user select a printer.
Private Sub cmdPickPrinter_Click()
    dlgPrinter.CancelError = True

    On Error Resume Next
    dlgPrinter.ShowPrinter
    If Err.Number = cdlCancel Then
        ' The user canceled. Do nothing.
        Exit Sub
    ElseIf Err.Number <> 0 Then
        ' Unexpected error. Report it.
```

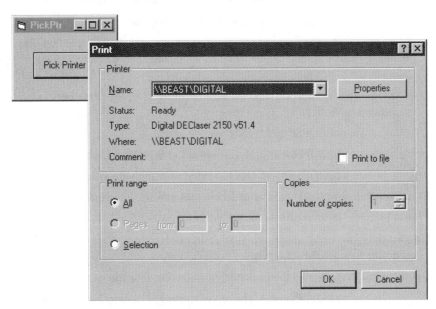

Figure 5.2 Example program PickPtr lets the user select a printer.

```
                    MsgBox "Error " & Format$(Err.Number) & _
                        " selecting printer." & vbCrLf & _
                        Err.Description
                Exit Sub
            End If
            On Error GoTo 0

            ' Print to the newly selected Printer object.
            Printer.Print "Selected printer: " & Printer.DeviceName
            Printer.EndDoc
        End Sub
```

Unfortunately, the Common Dialog Control's printer selection capabilities vary greatly with different combinations of printer, device driver, operating system, and Visual Basic version. You may need to use some trial and error to determine which capabilities work for you.

Printer Properties

The Printer object has several attributes that you should understand to get the most out of your printer. Several of the most useful properties for controlling printer characteristics are listed below. The exact effects of many of these properties depend on your physical printer and the printer's device driver.

ColorMode. Determines whether a color printer prints in color or monochrome. ColorMode can have these values:

> vbPRCMMonochrome. Output is printed in monochrome.

> vbPRCMColor. Output is printed in color.

Copies. The number of copies to be printed. On many printers, it is faster to allow the printer to print multiple copies than to send the same output to the printer several times.

Duplex. For printers that can do two-sided printing, Duplex determines whether pages are printed on both sides. This property can have these values:

> vbPRDPSimplex. Single-sided printing.

> vbPRDPHorizontal. Double-sided printing with horizontal page turn.

> vbPRDPVertical. Double-sided printing with vertical page turn.

FontCount. Returns the number of fonts available on the printer.

Fonts. Lists the fonts available on the printer.

Height. Sets the height of the paper. You can use Height and Width instead of one of the predefined values for PaperSize.

Orientation. Determines the paper orientation. Orientation can have the values:

> vbPRORPortrait. The top of the page is along the short edge of the paper (normal).

vbPRORLandscape. The top of the page is along the long edge of the paper (sideways).

Page. Returns the current page number. Visual Basic resets this count when you finish printing using the EndDoc method.

PaperBin. Determines the default bin from which paper feeds. For printers with the corresponding paper bins, you can use the following values. The values vbPRBN-Manual and vbPRBNEnvManual are particularly useful when the user must insert a special form or envelope before the program prints.

vbPRBNUpper. Use the upper bin.

vbPRBNLower. Use the lower bin.

vbPRBNMiddle. Use the middle bin.

vbPRBNManual. Wait for manual insertion of each sheet.

vbPRBNEnvelope. Use the envelope feeder.

vbPRBNEnvManual. Wait for manual insertion in the envelope feeder.

vbPRBNAuto. Use the current default bin.

vbPRBNTractor. Use the tractor feeder.

vbPRBNSmallFmt. Use the small bin.

vbPRBNLargeFmt. Use the large bin.

vbPRBNLargeCapacity. Use the large-capacity bin.

vbPRBNCassette. Use the paper cassette cartridge.

PaperSize. Tells the printer the paper's size if you do not use the Width and Height properties. This property can take dozens of different values ranging from Folio to German Legal Fanfold. Read the online help for a complete list of possible values. Some of the more useful values include:

vbPRPSLetter. Letter, 8 1/2 x 11 inches.

vbPRPSLegal. Legal, 8 1/2 x 14 inches.

vbPRPSEnv10. Envelope #10, 4 1/8 x 9 1/2 inches.

vbPRPSEnvPersonal. Personal envelope, 3 5/8 x 6 1/2 inches.

PrintQuality. Determines the printer's resolution. You can specify a resolution in dots per inch (DPI) or you can use one of the values:

vbPRPQDraft. Draft resolution.

vbPRPQLow. Low resolution.

vbPRPQMedium. Medium resolution.

vbPRPQHigh. High resolution.

TrackDefault. Determines whether the Printer object stays the same when you change the default printer using the Windows Control Panel. Normally, TrackDefault is true and the Printer object changes to indicate the new printer the user selects using the Control Panel. If TrackDefault is false, the Printer object continues to indicate the same printer, even if the user changes the default printer.

Width. Sets the width of the paper. You can use Height and Width instead of one of the predefined values for PaperSize.

Zoom. Determines the percentage by which output is scaled up or down.

Printer Control Methods

The Printer object has several methods you need to use to control printing. Some of the most important are NewPage, EndDoc, and KillDoc. NewPage starts a new page, resetting CurrentX and CurrentY to the upper-left corner of the new page.

EndDoc finishes the current print job and sends it to the physical printer. If your program exits without calling EndDoc or KillDoc, the system implicitly sends an EndDoc command. Until you execute EndDoc, output to the printer is buffered and does not appear.

When printing a typical long document, you would execute the NewPage method several times to create the document's pages. You would use EndDoc once when the document was finished.

The Printer object's KillDoc method cancels the current print job.

If you use EndDoc immediately after NewPage, Visual Basic does not print an extra blank page at the end. As a result, you can use NewPage after every page without worrying about whether you are at the end of the document.

In fact, the NewPage method will not print a page that is blank even if you want it to. If you want to display a blank page, use the Print method to display a space character on the page and then use NewPage as in the following code.

```
Printer.Print "Hello"    ' Put something on page 1.
Printer.NewPage          ' Print page 1.
Printer.Print " "        ' Put a space character on page 2.
Printer.NewPage          ' Print the blank page 2.
Printer.EndDoc           ' End the document.
```

The PrintForm Method

The PrintForm method is by far the easiest way to print. Simply invoke a form object's PrintForm method, and the form sends an image of itself, including any controls it contains to the printer. If the form's AutoRedraw property is set to true, the printout also includes any graphics you have drawn on the form. While this method is extremely simple, it has a couple of drawbacks.

First, PrintForm can display graphics drawn on the form only if AutoRedraw is true. This means your program must use more memory than it might otherwise need if you want to print those graphics.

Second, the image is a bit-by-bit copy of whatever the form looks like on your screen. Your monitor probably has a much lower resolution than your printer does. A typical computer monitor has a resolution of 96 pixels per inch. Many printers have resolutions of 300 dots per inch. When the 96-pixels-per-inch picture is stretched to a reasonable size at 300 dots per inch, it appears rough and grainy.

Another problem with the PrintForm method is that it usually sends far more data to the printer than necessary. Suppose you have a 400-by-400 pixel form with the word "Hello" displayed in the middle. The PrintForm method sends your printer information describing all of the form's 160,000 pixels, even though only a few contain interesting data. Sending the printer only the text "Hello," together with some information about the text's position and font characteristics, is much faster.

Some applications have more subtle problems with PrintForm. If the form contains a scrolling region, like a text box with scrollbars, PrintForm displays only the portion of the region that is visible at the time it is invoked. If the user resizes the form or if there is an unknown amount of information in the scrolling region, it may be difficult to tell if all of the information is visible.

Despite these drawbacks, the PrintForm method is simple and powerful. With a single line of code, you can print almost anything. For that reason, it is still useful, particularly in the early stages of program development. In the project's later stages, when form layouts are final, you can go back and write printing routines that take advantage of the printer's higher resolution.

High-Resolution Printing

Printer objects provide most of the same graphic properties and methods provided by forms and picture boxes. Printer objects have the properties CurrentX, CurrentY, Draw-Mode, DrawStyle, DrawWidth, FillColor, FillStyle, Font, FontBold, FontCount, FontItalic, FontName, FontSize, FontStrikethru, FontTransparent, FontUnderline, ForeColor, Scale-Height, ScaleLeft, ScaleMode, ScaleTop, ScaleWidth, TwipsPerPixelX, and TwipsPerPixelY. Printer objects also provide the methods Circle, Line, PaintPicture, Print, PSet, Scale, ScaleX, ScaleY, TextHeight, and TextWidth.

Printer objects even have device contexts and support API drawing functions such as Polygon and Polyline. However, the API functions print nothing unless your program uses some Visual Basic method to print something first. If you do not want the Visual Basic method to modify the printout, use the following statement:

```
Printer.Print ""
```

Although this statement does nothing visible, it initializes the printer so that the API functions can work properly.

Example program PolyPrnt uses the Polyline, Polygon, PolyPolyline, and PolyPolygon API functions to print several shapes. It uses Visual Basic's Line method to draw four boxes on the printout, so it does not need to print a blank string to initialize the printer.

Using Visual Basic and API drawing methods, you can print anything you can display on a form or picture box at the printer's full resolution. To produce high-quality output, however, there are still a couple of details you must be prepared to handle.

Printing Text

Using the Printer object's CurrentX and CurrentY properties and its Print method, you can print text. The Print command knows nothing about margins, however. If you print a very long string using the Print statement, the text will extend off the right side of the printed page and be truncated. If you want text to wrap when it reaches the printer's right margin, you must write code to control the positioning of each word.

The simplest way to wrap text is to examine the string one word at a time. For each word, use the Printer object's TextWidth function to see how wide the word will be on the printer. If that width added to CurrentX is greater than the right margin, start a new line.

Similarly, when the program starts a new line, it should check the Printer object's CurrentY property to see if there is room for the next line of text. If there is no more room on the page, the program can use the NewPage method to start a new page.

After examining the new word, possibly starting a new line or page, the program should use the Print statement to display the word.

Example program WordWrap uses this technique to print text. The program also supports simple paragraph formatting. When it finds a carriage return and line feed combination, it starts a new paragraph by skipping some extra vertical space and indenting the paragraph's first word.

Program WordWrap uses the PrintWrappedText subroutine, shown in the following code, to print text on an object. This routine repeatedly searches the text for carriage return and line feed pairs to see where the first paragraph ends. It removes the paragraph from the text and increases CurrentX to indent the paragraph.

It then repeatedly searches the paragraph for a space character to see where the first word ends. It removes the word from the paragraph.

The routine adds the word's length to the Printer object's CurrentX property to see if there is room for the word. If there is no more room on the line, the program starts a new line and determines whether there is room for the new line on the current page. If there is no more room on the page, then PrintWrappedText starts a new page.

```
' Print a string on a Printer or PictureBox,
' wrapped within the margins.
Private Sub PrintWrappedText(ByVal txt As String, _
    ByVal indent As Single, _
    ByVal left_margin As Single, _
    ByVal top_margin As Single, _
    ByVal right_margin As Single, _
```

```
      ByVal bottom_margin As Single)
Dim next_paragraph As String
Dim next_word As String
Dim pos As Integer

   ' Start at the top of the page.
   Printer.CurrentY = top_margin

   ' Repeat until the text is all printed.
   Do While Len(txt) > 0
      ' Get the next paragraph.
      pos = InStr(txt, vbCrLf)
      If pos = 0 Then
         ' Use the rest of the text.
         next_paragraph = Trim$(txt)
         txt = ""
      Else
         ' Get the paragraph.
         next_paragraph = Trim$(Left$(txt, pos - 1))
         txt = Mid$(txt, pos + Len(vbCrLf))
      End If

      ' Indent the paragraph.
      Printer.CurrentX = left_margin + indent

      ' Print the paragraph.
      Do While Len(next_paragraph) > 0
         ' Get the next word.
         pos = InStr(next_paragraph, " ")
         If pos = 0 Then
            ' Use the rest of the paragraph.
            next_word = next_paragraph
            next_paragraph = ""
         Else
            ' Get the word.
            next_word = Left$(next_paragraph, pos - 1)
            next_paragraph = _
               Trim$(Mid$(next_paragraph, pos + 1))
         End If

         ' See if there is room for this word.
         If Printer.CurrentX + _
            Printer.TextWidth(next_word) > right_margin _
         Then
            ' It won't fit. Start a new line.
            Printer.Print
            Printer.CurrentX = left_margin

            ' See if we have room for a new line.
            If Printer.CurrentY + _
```

```
                    Printer.TextHeight(next_word) _
                    > bottom_margin _
            Then
                ' Start a new page.
                Printer.NewPage
                Printer.CurrentX = left_margin
                Printer.CurrentY = top_margin
            End If
        End If

        ' Now print the word. The ; makes the
        ' Printer not move to the next line.
        Printer.Print next_word & " ";
    Loop

        ' Finish the paragraph by ending the line.
        Printer.Print
    Loop
End Sub
```

Print Preview

Modern high-quality applications allow the user to preview a printout before printing it. You can provide a print preview by drawing all the printout's commands into a picture box and then displaying it to the user.

Unfortunately, producing high-resolution printouts usually requires a lot of code. Generating a print preview requires that you duplicate all of that code. This gives you even more code to program and debug. If you later make changes to the printout code, you have to be sure to make exactly the same changes to the preview code, or the print preview will not look like the final printout.

One solution to this potential source of errors is to create a single printing routine that generates both the preview and the final printed output. This routine takes as a parameter a reference to the object on which it should print.

To display a print preview, the program passes this routine a reference to a picture box. To produce a printout, the program passes it a reference to the Printer object. After the routine finishes, the program executes the printer's EndDoc method to send the printout to the physical printer.

Example program ObjPrint, shown in Figure 5.3, uses this technique to draw a diamond on its form or on the printer. Select the File menu's Print command to print the diamond.

The following code shows how program ObjPrint works. The DrawPicture subroutine draws a diamond shape onto the object it is passed as a parameter.

The form's Paint event handler clears the form and then uses DrawPicture to display the diamond on the form.

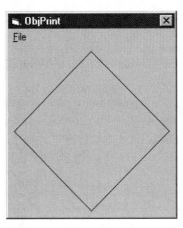

Figure 5.3   Example program ObjPrint displays a rectangle on its form or on the Printer object.

Subroutine mnuFilePrint_Click is invoked when you select Print from the program's File menu. That procedure uses DrawPicture to display the diamond on the printer. It then calls the printer's EndDoc method to finish printing the document.

```
' Draw a diamond on the form or printer.
Private Sub DrawPicture(obj As Object)
    obj.CurrentX = 1540
    obj.CurrentY = 100
    obj.Line -Step(1440, 1440)
    obj.Line -Step(-1440, 1440)
    obj.Line -Step(-1440, -1440)
    obj.Line -Step(1440, -1440)
End Sub

' Draw the picture on the form.
Private Sub Form_Paint()
    Cls
    DrawPicture Me
End Sub

' Draw the picture on the Printer object.
Private Sub mnuFilePrint_Click()
    MousePointer = vbHourglass
    DoEvents

    DrawPicture Printer
    Printer.EndDoc

    MousePointer = vbDefault
End Sub
```

Displaying a print preview at multiple scales is only slightly harder. Use the previous methods to generate a preview image in a picture box with Visible property set to False.

Then use the PaintPicture method to copy the result into a visible picture box for the user to see. By changing the size of the visible picture box and using PaintPicture to stretch the preview image to fit, you can generate previews at different scales. Example program HiRes, described at the end of this chapter, demonstrates this technique.

Previewing text is slightly harder because the fonts provided by your printer and your screen are probably different. Even if you select the same font name and size on your preview picture box and on the printer, you are unlikely to get identical results. For example, in one test using 20 point Arial, the system gave the preview picture box 20.25 point Arial and it gave the printer 19.92 point Arial. This made the preview look slightly different from the final printed result.

These effects are most noticeable for very long text when differences between the picture box and the printer can accumulate. The final pages in multipage documents may look quite different when previewed and printed. The following section discusses multipage print preview and explains a method for making previews agree more closely with printed results.

Multipage Print Preview

Generating a print preview for multiple pages of output is conceptually simple. The program uses the techniques described in the previous section to generate previews for each of the pages. If each page's output is independent of the others, that is easy. When each page's output depends on the output of the previous pages, however, this can be tricky.

For example, the WordWrap program, described earlier in this chapter, prints a large amount of text. When the text extends past the right margin, the program starts a new line. When the text extends beyond the bottom margin, the program begins a new page. It is not obvious where a page begins unless you have already printed the previous pages. That makes printing or previewing an arbitrary page difficult.

One solution is to modify the printing subroutine so that it produces output for pages within a specified range. The routine can still use the Printer object's CurrentX and CurrentY methods to position text. It can also use the Print method to print blank strings. It should not use Print to display text, however, unless it is on one of the selected pages. For other pages, it should use the TextWidth function to calculate the width of the text and then add that value to the printer's CurrentX property.

Similarly, the routine should not invoke the Printer object's NewPage method unless it has just finished printing one of the selected pages. For other pages, it should simply reset the printer's CurrentX and CurrentY properties to start a new page.

Note that the printing routine can follow these same steps while generating output on a picture box. Then the program can use the techniques described in the previous section to provide a print preview of arbitrary pages of output.

As is mentioned in the previous section, differences in the font selected by the preview picture box and the printer can make a big difference in previewed and printed results for long documents. To keep the two as similar as possible, the output routine can use the Printer object for positioning. Only when it must generate printed output does it use the actual object (picture box or printer) on which it is printing.

The following code shows a modified version of the PrintWrappedText subroutine used by the WordWrap program described earlier. It takes as input the object on which it should print, the number of the page it should print, the text, and the margins it should use. It breaks the text into words much as program WordWrap does.

As it examines the output words, the routine adjusts the Printer object's CurrentX and CurrentY properties. Only when it reaches the specified page does the routine actually print anything on the output object.

```
' Print a string on a Printer or PictureBox,
' wrapped within the margins.
Private Sub PrintWrappedText(ByVal ptr As Object, _
    ByVal target_page As Integer, ByVal txt As String, _
    ByVal indent As Single, ByVal left_margin As Single, _
    ByVal top_margin As Single, _
    ByVal right_margin As Single, _
    ByVal bottom_margin As Single)

Dim next_paragraph As String
Dim next_word As String
Dim pos As Integer
Dim current_page As Integer

    ' Start at the top of the page.
    Printer.CurrentY = top_margin

    ' Keep track of the page we are on.
    current_page = 1

    ' Repeat until the text is all printed.
    Do While Len(txt) > 0
        ' Get the next paragraph.
        pos = InStr(txt, vbCrLf)
        If pos = 0 Then
            ' Use the rest of the text.
            next_paragraph = Trim$(txt)
            txt = ""
        Else
            ' Get the paragraph.
            next_paragraph = Trim$(Left$(txt, pos - 1))
            txt = Mid$(txt, pos + Len(vbCrLf))
        End If

        ' Indent the paragraph.
        Printer.CurrentX = left_margin + indent

        ' Print the paragraph.
        Do While Len(next_paragraph) > 0
```

```
        ' Get the next word.
        pos = InStr(next_paragraph, " ")
        If pos = 0 Then
            ' Use the rest of the paragraph.
            next_word = next_paragraph
            next_paragraph = ""
        Else
            ' Get the word.
            next_word = Left$(next_paragraph, pos - 1)
            next_paragraph = _
                Trim$(Mid$(next_paragraph, pos + 1))
        End If

        ' See if there is room for this word.
        If Printer.CurrentX + _
            Printer.TextWidth(next_word) _
                > right_margin _
        Then
            ' It won't fit. Start a new line.
            Printer.Print
            Printer.CurrentX = left_margin

            ' See if we have room for a new line.
            If Printer.CurrentY + _
                Printer.TextHeight(next_word) _
                > bottom_margin _
            Then
                ' Start a new page.
                current_page = current_page + 1
                If current_page > target_page _
                    Then Exit Sub
                Printer.CurrentX = left_margin
                Printer.CurrentY = top_margin
            End If
        End If

        ' Now print the word. The ; makes the
        ' Printer not move to the next line.
        If current_page = target_page Then
            ' Print the word.
            If ptr Is Printer Then
                ' This is the printer. Print.
                ptr.Print next_word & " ";
            Else
                ' This is not the printer. Go to
                ' the printer's position and print.
                ptr.CurrentX = Printer.CurrentX
                ptr.CurrentY = Printer.CurrentY
                ptr.Print next_word & " ";
```

```
                        ' Skip space for the word.
                        Printer.CurrentX = Printer.CurrentX + _
                            Printer.TextWidth(next_word & " ")
                    End If
                Else
                    ' Skip space for the word.
                    Printer.CurrentX = Printer.CurrentX + _
                        Printer.TextWidth(next_word & " ")
                End If
            Loop

            ' Finish the paragraph by ending the line.
            Printer.Print
        Loop

        ' See if we got to the desired page yet.
        If current_page < target_page Then
            MsgBox "This page does not exist."
        End If
    End Sub
```

Example program PrvPages, shown in Figure 5.4, uses this code to produce previews of pages in a multipage document. Enter the number of the page you want to see and click the Preview button to see a print preview. The preview form uses techniques described in Chapter 1, Visual Basics, to display the preview in a scrolled window. Enter a page number and click the Print button to print the page.

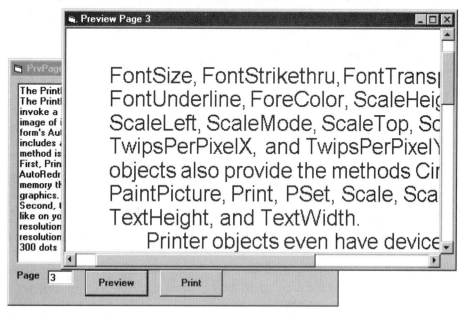

Figure 5.4   Example program PrvPages displays print previews of pages in a long document.

Printer Scale Properties

The DrawPicture routine in program ObjPrint draws a diamond 1 inch tall and 1 inch wide on the form, picture box, or printer it is passed. As is mentioned in Chapter 1, Visual Basics, it is often convenient to work in a coordinate system other than inches. You might want to measure your graphics in centimeters, pixels, or some customized coordinate system with an unequal number of units per inch in the X and Y directions. You might also want to move the origin of the coordinate system to some place other than the upper-left corner of the drawing area.

You can perform all of these steps using a form or picture box's scaling properties ScaleLeft, ScaleTop, ScaleWidth, and ScaleHeight. If you do, however, you cannot simply pass the Printer object into a drawing routine and expect the printed output to match what is displayed on the form. Unless the Printer object's scale properties match those of the form, the printed output will be incorrect.

Unfortunately, the Printer's size and scale properties do not work the same way they do for a form or picture box. The Printer's Height and Width properties are determined by the paper the printer is using, and you cannot simply change them to match the output. Printers also do not print over the entire page. The printable area generally does not go all the way to the edges of the paper. Figure 5.5 shows how the dimensions of the paper relate to the printer's size and scale properties.

Because you cannot easily change the size of the printer's drawing area to match that of the form, you must do a little extra work to make the printer's scale properties match those of the form. You need to find values for ScaleLeft, ScaleTop, ScaleWidth, and ScaleHeight that make the image of the form appear at its correct size, centered in the printable area.

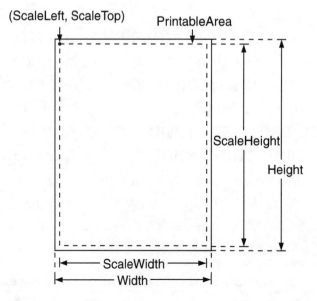

Figure 5.5 How paper size is related to printer properties.

First, use the printer's ScaleX and ScaleY methods to get the printer's dimensions in twips. Then use the form's ScaleX and ScaleY methods to translate these dimensions into the form's coordinate system. This gives the size of the printer's printable area in the form's coordinate system. You will use these dimensions for the printer's new ScaleWidth and ScaleHeight values.

Next, determine where the center of the form is in the form's coordinate system. If you use this point as the center of the printable area, the form's drawing area will be centered.

Now you can compute scaled coordinate values for the printer's upper-left and lower-right corners. Use these in the printer's Scale method to set the scaling properties, and the printer is ready to go.

The SetPrinterScale subroutine shown in the following code uses these steps to make the printer's scale properties match those of a form or picture box.

```
' Set the printer's scale properties so it will
' print the object at the correct size, centered
' in the printable area.
Private Sub SetPrinterScale(obj As Object)
Dim pwid As Single
Dim phgt As Single
Dim xmid As Single
Dim ymid As Single

    ' Get the printer's dimensions in twips.
    pwid = Printer.ScaleX(Printer.ScaleWidth, _
        Printer.ScaleMode, vbTwips)
    phgt = Printer.ScaleY(Printer.ScaleHeight, _
        Printer.ScaleMode, vbTwips)

    ' Convert the printer's dimensions into the
    ' object's coordinates.
    pwid = obj.ScaleX(pwid, vbTwips, obj.ScaleMode)
    phgt = obj.ScaleY(phgt, vbTwips, obj.ScaleMode)

    ' Compute the center of the object.
    xmid = obj.ScaleLeft + obj.ScaleWidth / 2
    ymid = obj.ScaleTop + obj.ScaleHeight / 2

    ' Pass the coordinates of the upper left and
    ' lower right corners into the Scale method.
    Printer.Scale _
        (xmid - pwid / 2, ymid - phgt / 2)- _
        (xmid + pwid / 2, ymid + phgt / 2)
End Sub
```

Example program FrmPrint uses the SetPrinterScale subroutine to display and print a Bowditch curve (also called a curve of Lissajous). When you resize the form, the program resizes the curve to make it as large as possible. When you invoke the File menu's

Print command, the program uses SetPrinterScale and the picture drawing routine DrawPicture to print the curve at its current dimensions.

The left side of Figure 5.6 shows an image of program FrmPrint running on a screen. On the right is a picture showing how the curve fits on a printed page. The two pictures are not drawn at the same scale. The dashed lines indicate where the edges of the form's drawing area are on the printed page.

Scaling Objects to Fit

In some programs, you may want to enlarge or reduce the size of a form when printing it. You might want to make the form as large as possible without changing its shape. You can achieve these goals using techniques similar to those described in the previous section.

First, use the form or picture box object's ScaleX and ScaleY methods to get the object's dimensions in twips. Use the printer's ScaleX and ScaleY methods to convert the printer's size into twips.

Next, compare the aspect ratios (height divided by width) of the object and the printer. If the object is relatively tall and thin, draw the object on the printer as tall as possible, making it as wide as necessary to preserve its aspect ratio.

Similarly, if the object is relatively short and wide, draw it as wide as possible on the printer and make the object's height match.

Once you know how large to make the object on the printer, determine where the center of the form is as before and invoke the printer's Scale method to set the scaling properties.

The following SetLargePrinterScale subroutine performs these steps. It sets the printer's scale properties to make an object as large as possible while preserving the object's shape.

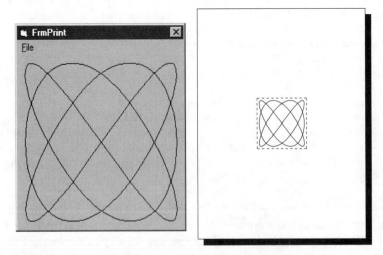

Figure 5.6 Screen and printed output from program FrmPrint.

```
' Set the printer's scale properties so it will
' print the object as large as possible, centered
' in the printable area.
Private Sub SetLargePrinterScale(obj As Object)
Dim owid As Single
Dim ohgt As Single
Dim pwid As Single
Dim phgt As Single
Dim xmid As Single
Dim ymid As Single
Dim s As Single

    ' Get the object's size in twips.
    owid = obj.ScaleX(obj.ScaleWidth, obj.ScaleMode, vbTwips)
    ohgt = obj.ScaleY(obj.ScaleHeight, obj.ScaleMode, vbTwips)

    ' Get the printer's size in twips.
    pwid = Printer.ScaleX(Printer.ScaleWidth, _
        Printer.ScaleMode, vbTwips)
    phgt = Printer.ScaleY(Printer.ScaleHeight, _
        Printer.ScaleMode, vbTwips)

    ' Compare the object and printer aspect ratios.
    If ohgt / owid > phgt / pwid Then
        ' The object is relatively tall and thin.
        ' Use the printer's whole height.
        s = phgt / ohgt ' This is the scale factor.
    Else
        ' The object is relatively short and wide.
        ' Use the printer's whole width.
        s = pwid / owid ' This is the scale factor.
    End If

    ' Convert the printer's dimensions into scaled
    ' object coordinates.
    pwid = obj.ScaleX(pwid, vbTwips, obj.ScaleMode) / s
    phgt = obj.ScaleY(phgt, vbTwips, obj.ScaleMode) / s

    ' See where the center should be.
    xmid = obj.ScaleLeft + obj.ScaleWidth / 2
    ymid = obj.ScaleTop + obj.ScaleHeight / 2

    ' Pass the coordinates of the upper left and
    ' lower right corners into the Scale method.
    Printer.Scale _
        (xmid - pwid / 2, ymid - phgt / 2)- _
        (xmid + pwid / 2, ymid + phgt / 2)
End Sub
```

Example program FrmScale is similar to program FrmPrint except it uses the Set-LargePrinterScale subroutine to make its picture as large as possible before printing it.

The left side of Figure 5.7 shows an image of program FrmScale in action. On the right is a picture showing how the curve fits on a printed page. The dashed lines indicate where the edges of the form's drawing area are on the printed page. These pictures are drawn at the same scales as those in Figure 5.6.

High Resolution PrintForm

The PrintForm method is convenient, but it produces a low-resolution result. By examining the controls contained on a form, you can implement a set of routines that produce a high-resolution approximation of PrintForm.

The idea is simple. Use the form's Controls collection to examine each of the controls on the form. Draw a high-resolution image of each control on the printer. While the basic idea is straightforward, there are many details to consider.

First, different types of controls have different properties and appearances, so you need to draw them differently. Because several graphic properties do not apply to all controls, you need to consider them carefully. For example, picture boxes, labels, and text boxes have a BorderStyle property that you can use to decide whether to draw a box around the control. Option buttons, check boxes, and command buttons do not have this property, so you cannot look at it. If a program tries to look at a command button's BorderStyle property, Visual Basic raises an error.

Second, a wide variety of properties affect the appearance of many controls. Drawing a multiline text box correctly can be difficult for different lengths of text, with and without scroll bars, and with different Alignment property values.

Third, some controls may be contained in other controls. The containers may be contained in still other controls. If some of these controls are picture boxes, they may have their own

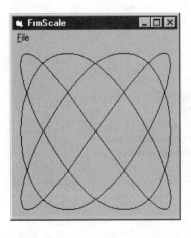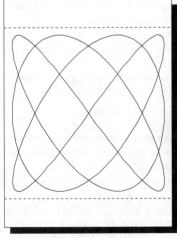

Figure 5.7 Screen and printed output from program FrmScale.

coordinate systems. You must convert the control's coordinate system into that of its parent, then into that of its grandparent, and so forth until you have converted the coordinates into the form's coordinate system. You must also be aware that parts of the control may be hidden because it lies outside the visible area of one of its containers.

Fourth, the fonts available on the printer may not be the same as those on your monitor. In that case, the printed result will not exactly match the print preview.

Finally, even if you get all of these details perfectly correct, the result may still not be exactly what you need. If text is hidden in a scrolled text box, you may want to enlarge the printed output to show all of the text. While there may not be enough room on the screen, there may be plenty of room on the printout.

Example program HiRes, shown in Figure 5.8, use a subroutine named HiResPrint to display a high-resolution version of the form.

Subroutine HiResPrint takes as a parameter a reference to the object on which it should draw the image. The program uses this parameter to provide a print preview. It draws the preview image into a hidden picture box and then uses PaintPicture to display the preview at different scales.

Program HiRes uses techniques described earlier in this chapter to create printouts at either the form's current size or enlarged to fill the printout. When the form's image is enlarged, the program allows text inside controls to expand to fill the available space. For example, suppose a text box contains so much text that it is not all visible at once on the form. When the program prints the form enlarged, it allows the text box to use the extra available space to display more text.

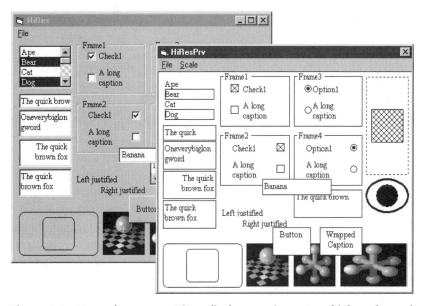

Figure 5.8 Example program HiRes displays previews at multiple scales and produces high-resolution printouts.

Program HiRes is far from perfect, but it demonstrates many useful techniques for providing print previews and multiple scales and for producing high-resolution output. Using the HiResPrint subroutine, you can produce quality output with very little effort.

Summary

Visual Basic's Printer object provides a rich assortment of graphic methods. These methods let a program send lines, curves, text and other graphical objects to the system's printer.

The properties and methods provided by the Printer object are almost exactly the same as those supported by forms and picture boxes. The fact that these properties and methods are the same allows a program to display print previews with relative ease. The program can use a single routine to generate graphics on a form, picture box, or printer. With only a little extra work, you can even display print previews at multiple scales, and fit printed output to the printer. These are powerful features that give any program an appearance of professionalism.

PART TWO

Image Processing

In its most general sense, image processing is the manipulation of visible images. This broad definition includes everything from adding a telephoto lens to a camera or transmitting video signals over microwaves to looking in a mirror or wearing sunglasses. For the purposes of this part, however, image processing means computer manipulation of bitmapped images.

The chapters in this part of the book describe methods you can use to manipulate bitmapped images. The next two chapters cover image processing methods. Chapter 6, Point Processes, explains methods for manipulating images one pixel at a time. Using these techniques, you can adjust an image's color balance, brightness, and contrast.

Chapter 7, Area Processes, demonstrates procedures that modify images using the pixels in an area. It shows how to use filters to soften, sharpen, or emphasize edges in an image. It also describes morphing operations you can use to resize, rotate, warp, and otherwise deform an image.

6

Point Processes

This chapter explains how you can use Visual Basic and a few API functions to perform advanced image processing operations by examining images one pixel at a time. These methods allow you to perform such tasks as adjusting an image's color balance, brightness, and contrast.

Next, the chapter describes *multiple image processing*. Using these techniques, you can combine more than one image to highlight differences between them or to create a composite image containing parts of each.

Obtaining Images

There are many ways you can obtain images that you can use for image processing. First, you can buy a digital camera that stores pictures electronically. With one of these cameras, you do not have to pay for film, developing, or any special processing. Unfortunately, these cameras can be quite expensive, and they provide limited resolution. Once you have taken a picture, you cannot enlarge it much without blurring the image.

Flatbed scanners allow you to digitize photographs, drawings, documents, and almost anything else that you can place on a flat surface. Most scanners come with text recognition software so that you can scan a document and have the software translate it into text that you can then edit in a word processor. Scanners allow you to digitize parts of an image at different scales so that you can enlarge or reduce a picture. Flatbed scanners that provide excellent resolution are now relatively inexpensive. All the photographs in this book were digitized on a flatbed scanner.

Specialized scanners that digitize pictures from film negatives are also available. These scanners may produce images with better resolution, but they are quite expensive and can scan only film negatives. If you occasionally find it useful to scan documents and drawings, a flatbed scanner would be a better choice.

Bulletin boards and online services are excellent sources of inexpensive images. Some of these services make literally millions of images available. Images from online services are often copyrighted by the service or the contributor of the images. This is not a problem if you want the images for your own use. You should not use them in software or anything else that you will distribute to others unless you get permission from the copyright holder first.

The Internet and the World Wide Web are also good sources of inexpensive images. Many companies and government agencies have impressive graphics at their ftp and Web sites. The NASA Web site at www.nasa.gov, for example, contains thousands of pictures of aircraft, spacecraft, planets, stars, comets, and so forth. The White House Web page at www.whitehouse.gov contains images of the White House, president, first lady, and vice president. From these locations, you can follow links to many other interesting government Web sites. Some of the images you find on the Web are copyrighted, though many of the government images are not. If you want to distribute an image, contact the image provider to see if you need permission.

Many copy, graphic arts, and photographic stores can put your own photographs on disk for a reasonable fee. They typically give you software to view and manipulate the images with your first order. This service is ideal if you have one or two old photographs you would like to use on your computer. Because these are your photographs, you do not need someone else's permission to use them.

Finally, some film developers will put images on disk for you when they develop your film. For a reasonable fee, they develop your film and send you prints or slides plus your pictures on disk. If you want electronic copies of all of the pictures in a roll of film, this kind of service is more convenient and probably cheaper than having a copy store scan your photographs one at a time.

Programming Tools

Visual Basic's image processing tools are somewhat limited. Probably the most useful of these are the LoadPicture and SavePicture routines. The Point and PSet routines let you examine the pixels in an image one at a time. These routines are easy to use, but they are relatively slow. A few calls to API routines can make pixel processing much faster. The following sections describe these methods in some detail.

LoadPicture

The LoadPicture function loads a picture from a graphic file. Typically, you use this function to set the Picture property of a form, image control, or picture box control. For example, the following code loads the image stored in the file C:\Images\Planet.bmp into the background of a form named frmPlanet:

```
frmPlanet.Picture = LoadPicture("C:\Images\Planet.bmp")
```

Similarly, you can use LoadPicture to assign images to a form's Icon or to a control's DragIcon property.

```
frmPlanet.Icon = LoadPicture("C:\Images\Planet.ico")
```

To clear the graphic displayed in a form, image, or picture box, use LoadPicture with no parameters.

```
frmPlanet.Picture = LoadPicture()
```

Table 6.1 lists file formats that LoadPicture understands. While these are all standard file formats, you may run into some variations. For example, a wmf file can come with or without a placeable header. LoadPicture can load a wmf file that has a placeable header, but it cannot load one without this header. The easiest way to determine if you can load a particular file is to give it a try. Use the On Error GoTo statement to protect your program when LoadPicture fails.

LoadPicture may also fail to load some kinds of truncated files. If you incompletely download a JPEG file from the Internet, LoadPicture may get stuck reading the file and never stop. If LoadPicture does not finish, your program cannot protect itself using an On Error GoTo statement.

Unfortunately, the LoadPicture function cannot load other graphic file formats, such as tif and pcx files. Several commercially available controls can read files stored in these formats. You may also be able to find some shareware or freeware file conversion utilities on the Web.

LoadImage

After you have loaded a picture using the LoadPicture method, you can use PaintPicture to shrink or stretch the image. PaintPicture enlarges an image by repeating each of the pixels in the input picture several times in the output picture. This can give the result a blocky appearance. When PaintPicture shrinks an image, it removes some of the pixels in the image, which can cause unsightly gaps or artificial jaggedness in the result.

Both of these effects are caused by *aliasing*, a topic covered in more detail in Chapter 7. For now, it is enough to know that resizing an image using PaintPicture can cause these effects.

Table 6.1 Image File Formats That LoadPicture Understands

FILE FORMAT	EXTENSION
Bitmap	bmp
Icon	ico
Cursor	cur
Run-length encoded bitmap	rle
Windows metafile	wmf
Enhanced metafile	emf
GIF (Graphics Interchange Format)	gif
JPEG (Joint Photographic Experts Group)	jpg, jpeg

The LoadImage API function allows you to load a bitmap, cursor, or icon file into a picture of a specified size while reducing aliasing effects. LoadImage cannot load other types of graphic files. This function takes as parameters the name of the file to load and the desired dimensions of the result.

If it succeeds, LoadImage creates a bitmap containing the file's image. The program can then use the SelectObject API function to select the bitmap into a picture box for display. The LoadImageFile subroutine, shown in the following code, uses this technique to load an image file into a picture box, resizing the image to fit.

```
' Load a picture into a PictureBox using LoadImage.
Private Sub LoadImageFile(ByVal pic As PictureBox, _
    ByVal file_name As String)
Dim wid As Long
Dim hgt As Long
Dim hbmp As Long
Dim image_hdc As Long

    ' Get the PictureBox's dimensions in pixels.
    wid = pic.ScaleX(pic.ScaleWidth, pic.ScaleMode, vbPixels)
    hgt = pic.ScaleY(pic.ScaleHeight, pic.ScaleMode, vbPixels)

    ' Load the bitmap.
    hbmp = LoadImage(0, file_name, 0, _
        wid, hgt, LR_LOADFROMFILE)

    ' Make the picture box display the image.
    SelectObject pic.hdc, hbmp

    ' Destroy the bitmap to free its resources.
    DeleteObject hbmp

    ' Refresh the image.
    pic.Refresh
End Sub
```

Example program LoadImg, shown in Figure 6.1, demonstrates the LoadImage function. Enter the name of an image file and a scale factor, and click the Load button. The left image shows the file's original picture. The center image shows the picture resized with PaintPicture. The image on the right is loaded by the LoadImageFile subroutine. In Figure 6.1, you can see that LoadImage produced a much better result.

Example program ThumbImg is very similar to program Thumbs described in Chapter 1, Visual Basics. Both programs display small thumbnail images of the files in a directory. The main difference between the programs is that ThumbImg uses the LoadImage API function to display thumbnails for bitmap files. It uses Visual Basic's PaintPicture function to display thumbnails for other types of files.

Use the program's DriveList, DirectoryList, and FileList controls to search your computer's files. When you select a directory and press F5, the program examines the files

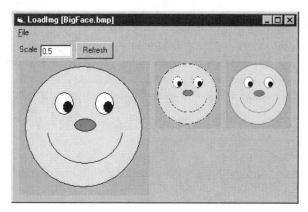

Figure 6.1 Program LoadImg uses the LoadImage API function to resize images while reducing aliasing.

in its FileList control. For each file, the program uses LoadPicture to load the file into a hidden picture box.

The program then checks the file's extension. If the file has a bmp extension, the program uses the LoadImage API function to load the file into a thumbnail picture box. If the file is not a bitmap, the program uses the PaintPicture method to copy the image at a reduced size into the thumbnail picture box.

The Thumbs program is useful for managing directories full of graphic files. One other way the program helps is by allowing you to delete a file. If you click on a thumbnail and press the Delete key, the program moves the file into the system's wastebasket.

SavePicture Routine

Visual Basic's SavePicture routine saves a picture into a bitmap file. For example, the following code saves the picture displayed by the picture box picPerson into the file "Person.bmp."

```
SavePicture picPerson.Picture, "Person.bmp"
```

SavePicture saves images using the same format in which the image was loaded. For example, if you use LoadPicture to load an icon (.ico) file, SavePicture saves the picture as an icon format file. Pictures saved from an Image property are always saved in bitmap (.bmp) format.

While you can make SavePicture use any filename you like, giving image files the appropriate extensions is less confusing. Naming a bitmap format file "Stars.ico" is misleading. While the LoadPicture function will still load this file correctly, other software may not. If you tell CorelDRAW! to import a bitmap but then select a file formatted as an icon file, you will see an error message indicating that the file has an incorrect bitmap format.

Point and PSet Functions

The Point function returns the RGB color specification of a point in a form or picture box. The following code shows a MouseDown event handling procedure for a picture box named picColors. When you click the mouse over the picture box, this routine uses the Point function to display the hexadecimal color value of the pixel pointed to by the mouse.

```
Private Sub picColors_MouseDown(Button As Integer, _
    Shift As Integer, X As Single, Y As Single)

    MsgBox Hex$(Picture1.Point(X, Y))
End Sub
```

The PSet routine sets the color value of a pixel. For example, the following code turns the pixel clicked red in the picture box picColors.

```
Private Sub picColors_MouseDown(Button As Integer, _
    Shift As Integer, X As Single, Y As Single)

    picColors.PSet (X, Y), vbRed
End Sub
```

The Point and PSet routines let you examine and set the colors of every pixel in an image one at a time. They are very simple, but they are also quite slow. The GetBitmapBits and SetBitmapBits functions described in Chapter 3, Advanced Color, are much faster.

Example program SetPix demonstrates three different techniques for setting every pixel in three picture boxes containing 150 * 150 = 22,500 pixels. It sets the pixels in its left picture box using PSet.

SetPix sets its middle picture box's pixels using the SetBitmapPixels subroutine described in Chapter 3. That routine copies color values stored in an RGBTriplet array into the picture box. For more information on this routine, see Chapter 3.

To fill its right picture box, the SetPix program fills an array of bytes with color values. It then calls the SetBitmapBits API function directly. This is the same operation performed by the SetBitmapPixels subroutine. Invoking SetBitmapBits directly is more complex, but it provides somewhat better performance.

Program SetPix assumes it is running on a 24-bit color system. This assumption makes using the SetBitmapPixels and SetBitmapBits functions easier.

In one test, a 133MHz Pentium processor took roughly 8.26 seconds to fill its left picture box using PSet. It took approximately 0.61 seconds to fill the middle picture box using SetBitmapPixels, and it needed only 0.35 seconds to fill its right picture box using SetBitmapBits. These three methods give you a tradeoff between complexity and speed. SetBitmapPixels takes less than 1/10th as long as the PSet method, but it is more complicated. SetBitmapBits takes slightly more than half as long as SetBitmapPixels, but it is even more complicated.

Point Processes

A point process modifies the values of the pixels in an image one pixel at a time. For each pixel in an image, you examine the pixel's value and compute a new value for the corresponding pixel in the output image.

The new value of each pixel does not depend on the values of any other pixels, so you can change the value of the pixel directly in the input image. That means the output image may be in a separate picture box, or it may be in the same picture box as the input image.

While point processes are generally quite simple, some produce dramatic results. Using very simple algorithms, you can complement an image or adjust its brightness, color balance, and contrast.

In most point processes, the output value of a pixel depends only on the input pixel's *value* rather than other factors like its position in the image. In that case, all pixels in the image with a certain input value are mapped to the same output value. If you are using a color model that uses palettes, such as 8-bit color, you can use the palette to make point processes much faster. Instead of examining each pixel in the image, you only need to redefine the nonstatic colors in the picture's palette. Redefining 236 palette entries is much faster than modifying the hundreds of thousands of pixels in even a relatively small image.

Remapping a color palette in this way is called *palette animation*. It is one of the few ways in which 8-bit color is superior to color models with greater depth. Although palette animation is fast, it is much more cumbersome. It requires that you handle all the intricacies of palette management. Because it is much easier to understand, the example in this chapter assumes you are using a 24-bit color system.

Grayscale

One of the simplest image processing tasks is converting an image from color into shades of gray. There are several reasons you might want to do this. First, grayscale images often look better at lower color resolution than color images do. For example, suppose you want to view an image using 8-bit color. A typical 8-bit color system has only 236 colors available for displaying the image. The image may use far more than 236 colors, so it may look strange with only 236 colors. The system may dither the image using small dots of color to approximate colors it cannot display. This may give it a bumpy texture.

On the other hand, grayscale images look fine displayed with 236 shades of gray. If you convert the image into gray scale, the 8-bit color system will produce a smooth result. Of course, at some point you need to load the image in full color so that you can perform an accurate conversion.

Another reason for using grayscale images is that they make many image processing operations easier to understand. For example, you can use image processing techniques to enhance edges in an image. Although you can apply these techniques to color images, the results are easier to understand with a grayscale image.

To convert a pixel's color into a grayscale value, set the pixel's red, green, and blue color components to the average of the three values.

Example program MakeGray uses the TransformImage subroutine shown in the following code to convert the image in picture box picOriginal into a grayscale image displayed in picResult. It uses the GetBitmapPixels subroutine to load the input picture's pixel information. It examines each pixel and sets its color components to the average of the pixel's components. It then uses the SetBitmapPixels subroutine to copy the resulting pixel values into the picResult picture box. Subroutines GetBitmapPixels and SetBitmapPixels are described in Chapter 3.

```
' Transform the image.
Private Sub TransformImage()
Dim pixels() As RGBTriplet
Dim bits_per_pixel As Integer
Dim X As Integer
Dim Y As Integer
Dim shade As Integer

    ' Get the pixels from picOriginal.
    GetBitmapPixels picOriginal, pixels, bits_per_pixel

    ' Set the pixel colors.
    For Y = 0 To picOriginal.ScaleHeight - 1
        For X = 0 To picOriginal.ScaleWidth - 1
            With pixels(X, Y)
                shade = (CInt(.rgbRed) + .rgbGreen + _
                    .rgbBlue) / 3
                .rgbRed = shade
                .rgbGreen = shade
                .rgbBlue = shade
            End With
        Next X
    Next Y

    ' Set picResult's pixels.
    SetBitmapPixels picResult, bits_per_pixel, pixels
    picResult.Picture = picResult.Image
End Sub
```

All the code specific to the grayscale transformation is contained in subroutine Transform-Image. That lets you modify the program to create other point process transformations quickly and easily. In most cases, you will need to change only the four statements that calculate and set the pixels' new values. Several of the other examples in this chapter use this approach and differ from program MakeGray only in these four statements.

When you work with program MakeGray, you will notice that the program quickly loads the image file you select. It then takes a while to create the grayscale version. In one test on a 133MHz Pentium processor, the program loaded a 720 by 486 pixel image almost instantly. It then took about 8 seconds to examine all of the picture's 349,920 pixels and produce the result.

All image processing applications have the same problem. Examining all of the pixels in a large image takes a long time, even if the operation performed on each pixel is fast.

Complement

To complement an image, you simply subtract each pixel's red, green, and blue component values from the largest possible value of 255. For example, the color orange has red, green, and blue components 255, 127, and 0, respectively. The complement of orange has red component 255-255 = 0, green component 255-127 = 128, and blue component 255-0 = 255. This color is sky blue.

Example program Complem, shown in Figure 6.2, uses this technique to display the complement of an image. The figure in this book is grayscale, but the program produces a colored complement image on the computer.

The only significant differences between this program and program MakeGray are in the following statements that set a new pixel's color component values.

```
With pixels(X, Y)
    .rgbRed = 255 - .rgbRed
    .rgbGreen = 255 - .rgbGreen
    .rgbBlue = 255 - .rgbBlue
End With
```

Note that 255 - (255 - value) = 255 - 255 + value = value. That means the complement of a color's complement is the original color. You can verify this result by loading an image in program Complem and saving the complemented image. Then load the complemented image in program Complem. You will see that the new complement is the same as the original image.

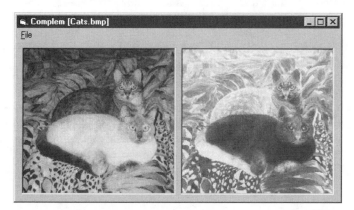

Figure 6.2 Program Complem displays the complement of an image.

Brightness

Adjusting a pixel's brightness is only a little harder than calculating its complement. Suppose your goal is to change a picture's brightness by a percentage value where the value 0 is defined to mean no change, 100 means to increase all colors to the brightest possible value (white), and -100 means to decrease the colors to the darkest possible value (black).

To increase a color's brightness by a certain percentage, the program can add to each pixel's components the percentage times the difference between each component and its largest possible value 255. For example, a program could use the following equations to increase a pixel's components by a 75 percent:

```
red = red + 0.75 * (255 - red)
green = green + 0.75 * (255 - green)
blue = blue + 0.75 * (255 - blue)
```

To decrease a color's brightness by a certain percentage, a program can subtract from each pixel's components the percentage times the component's value. For example, a program could use the following equations to decrease a pixel's components by 75 percent:

```
red = red - 0.75 * red = (1 - 0.75) * red
green = green - 0.75 * green = (1 - 0.75) * green
blue = blue - 0.75 * blue = (1 - 0.75) * blue
```

Example program Bright, shown in Figure 6.3, uses these equations to adjust an image's brightness.

The only significant differences between this program and programs MakeGray and Complem are in the following statements that set a new pixel's color component values.

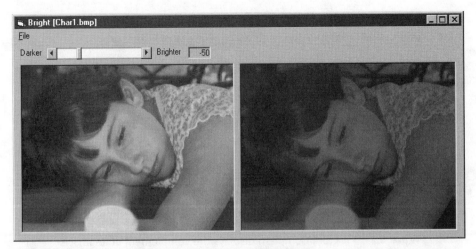

Figure 6.3 Program Bright adjusts an image's brightness.

```
With pixels(X, Y)
    If factor < 0 Then
        ' Make the color darker.
        .rgbRed = (1 + factor) * .rgbRed
        .rgbGreen = (1 + factor) * .rgbGreen
        .rgbBlue = (1 + factor) * .rgbBlue
    Else
        ' Make the color brighter.
        .rgbRed = .rgbRed + factor * (255 - .rgbRed)
        .rgbGreen = .rgbGreen + factor * (255 - .rgbGreen)
        .rgbBlue = .rgbBlue + factor * (255 - .rgbBlue)
    End If
End With
```

Unlike image complements, images with adjusted brightness are not invertible. The reason is some color components may map to fractional values when they are adjusted. Since the color components are converted into byte values, some of the color information is lost. Applying a reverse adjustment cannot reproduce the missing information exactly.

For example, suppose you increase an image's brightness by 99 percent. Many of the pixel values become white. If you now decrease the pixels' component values by 50 percent, trying to recover the original image, the result is mostly gray.

Color Balance

Program Bright adjusts a pixel's brightness by changing its red, green, and blue color components by similar amounts. You can change an image's color balance by adjusting the pixels' components by different amounts. For example, to decrease the amount of blue in an image, you could multiply the blue component of each pixel by 0.5.

Example program ColorBal, shown in Figure 6.4, lets you use scroll bars to specify the amount by which it should adjust each pixel's red, green, and blue components. The result is more striking in color than it is in the grayscale image shown in Figure 6.4.

The only significant differences between this program and the previous programs are in the following statements that set a new pixel's color component values. The values r_factor, g_factor, and b_factor represent the amount by which the red, green, and blue components should be adjusted.

```
With pixels(X, Y)
    If r_factor < 0 Then
        .rgbRed = (1 + r_factor) * .rgbRed
    Else
        .rgbRed = .rgbRed + r_factor * (255 - .rgbRed)
    End If
    If g_factor < 0 Then
        .rgbGreen = (1 + g_factor) * .rgbGreen
    Else
        .rgbGreen = .rgbGreen + g_factor * (255 - .rgbGreen)
    End If
```

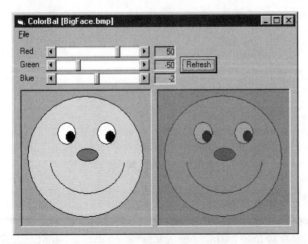

Figure 6.4   Program ColorBal adjusts an image's color balance.

```
    If b_factor < 0 Then
        .rgbBlue = (1 + b_factor) * .rgbBlue
    Else
        .rgbBlue = .rgbBlue + b_factor * (255 - .rgbBlue)
    End If
End With
```

If you set all three scroll bars to the same value, the program acts just as program Bright does, adjusting the image's brightness.

Like brightness adjustments, color balance adjustments are not invertible. If you change an image's color balance, you cannot load the result and adjust its colors to restore the original image exactly.

Contrast

Contrast measures the difference between two colors. There is a lot of contrast between black and white because they are very different. There is less contrast between red and pink because they are fairly similar.

An image's contrast is a measurement of the distribution of the colors it contains. One way to graphically examine an image's contrast is to plot a histogram showing the number of pixels that have each color value.

For grayscale images, this is easy. A program can use an array to hold counts for each of the possible pixel values. It can then examine each pixel in the image and increment the count for that pixel's color value. Because the image is grayscale, each pixel's red, green, and blue color components are the same. If a pixel's color component values are stored in the variable clr, the program would increment the value counts(clr). When it has examined all the pixels, the program can display their values in a histogram.

For color images, the program can make separate counts for the pixels' red, green, and blue color components and draw three histograms.

In Figure 6.5, example program Contrast has loaded a low-contrast picture. The three histograms show the number of pixels with red, green, and blue component values. All the color values that are used are bunched into a small part of the available horizontal space in the histograms. That means all of the pixels have similar color values and the image's contrast is low. If the colors were more evenly distributed, the histograms would have vertical bars across their entire ranges.

The colors are also bunched into the left part of the histograms. That means the color components are relatively small, so the picture is dark.

A program can adjust an image's contrast by changing the distribution of color values in these component histograms. It can use a function to map pixel component values into new values that are more evenly distributed. For example, it could multiply each value by a factor of 2 to spread the pixel values out and make them generally brighter.

Example program Contrast does this. It examines the pixels in an image to build three color component histograms. It then examines each color's counts to find the largest and smallest. For example, the pixels may have red component values only between 50 and 100 instead of the entire possible range of 0 to 255. The program then adjusts the components so that their values are centered on the value 127. It also scales the components so that they occupy more of the space in the histograms.

Figure 6.6 shows program Contrast stretching a low-contrast image's component values so that they span the range 0 to 256. It shows the new image and its component histograms. The new component values fill the histograms.

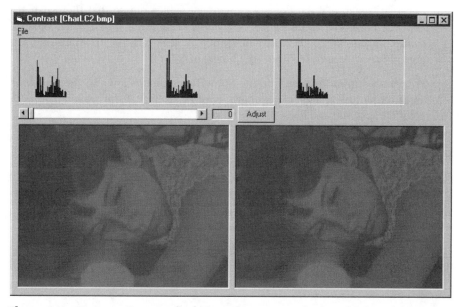

Figure 6.5 Program Contrast displaying a low-contrast image with its color histograms.

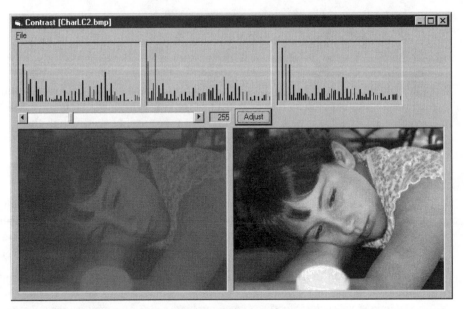

Figure 6.6 Program Contrast increasing an image's contrast.

Note that the stretching operation has introduced gaps in the histograms. If you look closely at the enhanced picture, you may be able to see small jumps in color values where the image should probably be smooth. Increasing the image's contrast sometimes creates this kind of discontinuity.

If you increase the contrast further, this effect becomes stronger. In Figure 6.7, program Contrast has spread the image's component values out so that they span 1000 values. Many of these values lie outside the allowed range of 0 to 255, so those values are changed to 0 or 255. That makes many pixels black or white. The large gaps in the component histograms reflect the large jumps in color in the new image.

Program Contrast uses subroutine ShowHistograms, shown in the following code, to create color histograms for an image. Subroutine TransformImage changes the image's color components to adjust its contrast.

```
' Show the component histograms.
Private Sub ShowHistograms(ByVal picImage As PictureBox, _
    ByVal save_min_max As Boolean)
Dim counts(0 To 2, 0 To 255) As Long
Dim max_count As Long
Dim brightness As Integer
Dim pixels() As RGBTriplet
Dim bits_per_pixel As Integer
Dim X As Integer
Dim Y As Integer
Dim i As Integer
Dim j As Integer
```

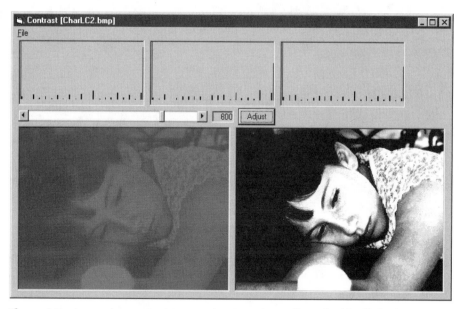

Figure 6.7 Increasing contrast too much creates large discontinuities in the image's colors.

```
' Clear the previous results.
For i = 0 To 2
    picHistogram(i).Cls
    picHistogram(i).Refresh
Next i


' Get the pixels from picImage.
GetBitmapPixels picImage, pixels, bits_per_pixel

' Count the brightness values.
For Y = 0 To picImage.ScaleHeight - 1
    For X = 0 To picImage.ScaleWidth - 1
        With pixels(X, Y)
            counts(0, .rgbRed) = _
                counts(0, .rgbRed) + 1
            counts(1, .rgbGreen) = _
                counts(1, .rgbGreen) + 1
            counts(2, .rgbBlue) = _
                counts(2, .rgbBlue) + 1
        End With
    Next X
Next Y


' Find the largest count value.
For i = 0 To 2
    ' Skip value 0. There tend to be a lot of
    ' them and they dominate things.
```

```
            For j = 1 To 255
                If max_count < counts(i, j) _
                    Then max_count = counts(i, j)
            Next j
        Next i

        ' Display the brightness histograms.
        For i = 0 To 2
            picHistogram(i).ScaleTop = 1.1 * max_count
            picHistogram(i).ScaleHeight = -1.2 * max_count
            picHistogram(i).ScaleLeft = -1
            picHistogram(i).ScaleWidth = 258
            For brightness = 0 To 255
                If counts(i, brightness) > 0 Then _
                    picHistogram(i).Line _
                        (brightness, 0)- _
                        (brightness + 1, _
                            counts(i, brightness)), , BF
            Next brightness
        Next i

        ' Find the largest and smallest non-zero counts.
        If save_min_max Then
            For i = 0 To 2
                MinIndex(i) = 255
                For brightness = 0 To 255
                    If counts(i, brightness) > 0 Then
                        MinIndex(i) = brightness
                        Exit For
                    End If
                Next brightness

                MaxIndex(i) = 0
                For brightness = 255 To 0 Step -1
                    If counts(i, brightness) > 0 Then
                        MaxIndex(i) = brightness
                        Exit For
                    End If
                Next brightness
            Next i
        End If
    End Sub

    ' Transform the image.
    Private Sub TransformImage()
    Dim pixels() As RGBTriplet
    Dim bits_per_pixel As Integer
    Dim r_mid As Integer
    Dim g_mid As Integer
    Dim b_mid As Integer
    Dim r_scale As Single
```

```
Dim g_scale As Single
Dim b_scale As Single
Dim r_diff As Integer
Dim g_diff As Integer
Dim b_diff As Integer
Dim r As Integer
Dim g As Integer
Dim b As Integer
Dim X As Integer
Dim Y As Integer

    ' Get the pixels from picOriginal.
    GetBitmapPixels picOriginal, pixels, bits_per_pixel

    ' Get the middle values for the components.
    r_mid = (MaxIndex(0) + MinIndex(0)) / 2
    g_mid = (MaxIndex(1) + MinIndex(1)) / 2
    b_mid = (MaxIndex(2) + MinIndex(2)) / 2

    ' Calculate the scale factors needed to resize
    ' the color values.
    r_scale = hbarBrightness.value / _
        (MaxIndex(0) - MinIndex(0))
    g_scale = hbarBrightness.value / _
        (MaxIndex(1) - MinIndex(1))
    b_scale = hbarBrightness.value / _
        (MaxIndex(2) - MinIndex(2))

    ' Set the colors for each component separately.
    For Y = 0 To picOriginal.ScaleHeight - 1
        For X = 0 To picOriginal.ScaleWidth - 1
            With pixels(X, Y)
                r_diff = .rgbRed - r_mid
                r_diff = r_diff * r_scale
                r = 127 + r_diff
                If r < 0 Then r = 0
                If r > 255 Then r = 255
                .rgbRed = r

                g_diff = .rgbGreen - g_mid
                g_diff = g_diff * g_scale
                g = 127 + g_diff
                If g < 0 Then g = 0
                If g > 255 Then g = 255
                .rgbGreen = g

                b_diff = .rgbBlue - b_mid
                b_diff = b_diff * b_scale
                b = 127 + b_diff
                If b < 0 Then b = 0
                If b > 255 Then b = 255
```

```
                    .rgbBlue = b
              End With
          Next X
      Next Y


      ' Set picResult's pixels.
      SetBitmapPixels picResult, bits_per_pixel, pixels
      picResult.Picture = picResult.Image

      ' Show the new brightness histogram.
      ShowHistograms picResult, False
  End Sub
```

Unfortunately, the techniques used by program Contrast do not always offer a perfect solution. In some images, the component histograms are not evenly distributed. For example, an image's red component values might be grouped in two clumps, one on the histogram's left and one on the histogram's right. That grouping could produce an image with some parts that are too red and other parts that are not red enough.

In that case, spreading the values out so that they span the range 0 to 255 will not make much difference because the values already span most of that range. Spreading the values out farther will make many fall outside the range 0 to 255, so many will be adjusted to 0 or 255. That will remove the differences between those colors and will reduce contrast for parts of the image.

A better strategy would be to spread the values in the two clumps more smoothly through the existing component range.

Still other images might require other techniques for remapping color component values to achieve the best effect. No single strategy will always produce an ideal result.

Binary Contrast Enhancement

If you use the Contrast program described in the previous section to spread color values too far, many will fall outside the range 0 to 255 and will be adjusted to one of those two values. If you stretch the colors far enough, you may get an image in which every pixel is either black or white.

Binary contrast enhancement performs this operation intentionally. It examines each pixel in an image and compares the pixel's brightness to a cutoff value. It makes pixels that are brighter than the cutoff value white. It makes the other pixels black. The result can often separate two parts of the image that differ in brightness by only a small amount.

Example program BinCont, shown in Figure 6.8, performs binary contrast enhancement. When you click on a position in the image's brightness histogram, BinCont compares the pixels' brightness value to the value you clicked. It makes pixels that are brighter than the value you clicked white and it makes the others black.

Program BinCont is similar to many of the other programs described in this chapter. The main difference is in the TransformImage subroutine shown in the following code. This

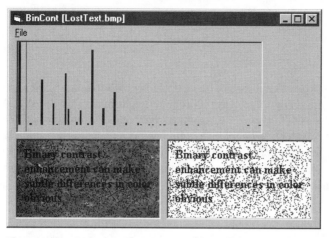

Figure 6.8 Program BinCont uses binary contrast enhancement to make visible subtle differences in color.

routine compares pixel brightness to a cutoff value and determines which should be black and which should be white.

```
' Transform the image.
Private Sub TransformImage(ByVal cutoff As Single)
Dim pixels() As RGBTriplet
Dim bits_per_pixel As Integer
Dim brightness As Integer
Dim X As Integer
Dim Y As Integer

    ' Get the pixels from picOriginal.
    GetBitmapPixels picOriginal, pixels, bits_per_pixel

    ' Set the pixel color values.
    For Y = 0 To picOriginal.ScaleHeight - 1
        For X = 0 To picOriginal.ScaleWidth - 1
            With pixels(X, Y)
                brightness = (CInt(.rgbRed) + _
                    .rgbGreen + .rgbBlue) / 3
                If brightness >= cutoff Then
                    .rgbRed = 255
                    .rgbGreen = 255
                    .rgbBlue = 255
                Else
                    .rgbRed = 0
                    .rgbGreen = 0
                    .rgbBlue = 0
                End If
            End With
        Next X
    Next Y
```

```
    ' Set picResult's pixels.
    SetBitmapPixels picResult, bits_per_pixel, pixels
    picResult.Picture = picResult.Image
End Sub
```

Program BinCont uses pixel brightness to decide which pixels to make black and which to make white. There are many other ways a program might make this decision. Example program BinCont2, shown in Figure 6.9, examines only one of each pixel's color components. When you click on a component histogram, the program uses the value you clicked as the cutoff value for that component. For example, if you click the value 127 in the middle of the green component histogram (in the middle), the program makes pixels with green color components of 127 or more white.

Program BinCont2 uses the following code to set the image's pixel values. The value Index indicates which component to test and is 0 for red, 1 for green, and 2 for blue.

```
With pixels(X, Y)
    Select Case Index
        Case 0
            test_value = .rgbRed
        Case 1
            test_value = .rgbGreen
        Case 2
            test_value = .rgbBlue
    End Select
    If test_value >= cutoff Then
        .rgbRed = 255
        .rgbGreen = 255
```

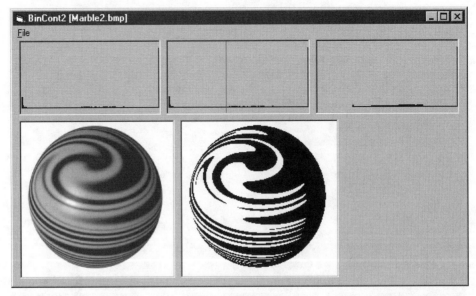

Figure 6.9 Program BinCont2 examines a single color component to decide which pixels to make black and which to make white.

```
            .rgbBlue = 255
        Else
            .rgbRed = 0
            .rgbGreen = 0
            .rgbBlue = 0
        End If
    End With
```

Program BinCont3, shown in Figure 6.10, uses yet another strategy. It uses the following code to make a pixel white if its blue component is more than 5 greater than its green and red components. That makes blue areas on the image white and other areas black.

```
With pixels(X, Y)
    If .rgbBlue > .rgbGreen + 5 And _
        .rgbBlue > .rgbRed + 5 _
    Then
        .rgbRed = 0
        .rgbGreen = 0
        .rgbBlue = 0
    Else
        .rgbRed = 255
        .rgbGreen = 255
        .rgbBlue = 255
    End If
End With
```

Multiple Image Processing

In multiple image processing, a program combines two or more images in some way. One common form of multiple image processing subtracts one image from another. The resulting picture shows where the two images differ.

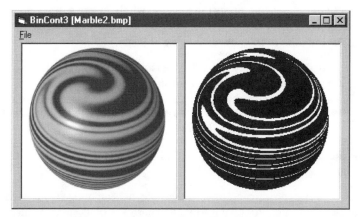

Figure 6.10   Program BinCont3 makes blue pixels white and other pixels black.

You can also use multiple images of the same scene to reduce random noise in the images. If the images are identical except for random noise, the real parts of the images tend to reinforce each other while the random noise tends to cancel itself out.

Finally, you can combine images to create a composite image containing features from each of the original images. Compositing techniques are used extensively in motion pictures and television to create amazing special effects.

The following sections describe these multiple image processing techniques.

Image Subtraction

To subtract two images, a program simply subtracts the color components of the images' corresponding pixels. Where the pixel values are the same, the result of the subtraction is zero, so the output pixel is black. Where the pixel values differ, the result of the subtraction is not zero. The greater the difference between the two values, the farther the result is from zero. When the program subtracts every pixel in the two images, the result highlights the differences between the images.

Because a pixel's value in one image may be darker or lighter than its value in the other, the result of the subtraction might be positive or negative. If you are interested in locating only pixels with brightness greater in the first image than in the second, you can set any negative values to zero. If you want to locate all changes to the pixels' values, you can take the absolute value of any negative results. Then larger changes in pixel values give bright colors in the result no matter which image has the brighter pixels. You can make the differences between the two images even more obvious if you enhance the contrast of the result, possibly using binary contrast enhancement.

Image subtraction has several uses. First, if a scene has changed in a subtle way, subtracting images before and after the change can make the changes obvious.

For example, to locate comets and other rapidly moving objects, astronomers compare two images of the same part of the sky taken at different times. A traditional method for comparing the images is to display them with a slide projector that quickly switches back and forth between them. If an object has moved or disappeared, the astronomer will see the object blinking on and off as the images switch. Image subtraction provides another method for finding these changes. If you subtract the two images, the result is black except in the location of the new or moving object.

You can also use image subtraction to detect edges in a single image. Shift the image by one pixel in the X and Y directions and then subtract it from the original image. The two versions of the image are the same in large regions of constant color. Where the image contains an edge between two colors, the shifted image and the original have different pixel values, so the subtraction gives a bright result.

Example program SubEdge, shown in Figure 6.11, uses this technique to enhance the edges in an image.

The following code shows how program SubEdge subtracts an image from itself. Notice that the For loops do not include the edge pixels where Y = picOriginal.ScaleHeight - 1 and X = picOriginal.ScaleWidth - 1. To calculate values for those pixels, the program

Figure 6.11   Program SubEdge uses image subtraction to detect edges.

would have to examine the color components for the pixel in position (X + 1, Y + 1), and that position lies outside the picture.

It is also important in this code that the each pixel's new value depends only on its current value and the value of another pixel that has not yet been modified. If the code subtracted a pixel's value from a pixel that had already been modified, such as the pixel in position (X - 1, Y - 1), the results would be unpredictable.

```
For Y = 0 To picOriginal.ScaleHeight - 2
    For X = 0 To picOriginal.ScaleWidth - 2
        With pixels(X, Y)
            .rgbRed = Abs(CInt(.rgbRed) - _
                pixels(X + 1, Y + 1).rgbRed)
            .rgbGreen = Abs(CInt(.rgbGreen) - _
                pixels(X + 1, Y + 1).rgbGreen)
            .rgbBlue = Abs(CInt(.rgbBlue) - _
                pixels(X + 1, Y + 1).rgbBlue)
        End With
    Next X
Next Y
```

Example program SubEdge2, shown in Figure 6.12, subtracts each pixel in an image from all of those surrounding it, and it combines the results. The final image shows edges more strongly in all directions.

Image Averaging

As its name suggests, image averaging is the process of averaging the pixel values of several images. The main use for image averaging is noise reduction. If you have several images of the same scene, each containing random noise, you can use the average of the images to reduce the noise.

Figure 6.12 Program SubEdge2 uses multiple image subtraction to detect edges in all directions.

Example program Average, shown in Figure 6.13, demonstrates this technique. The program combines four noisy pictures of the same scene to produce a less noisy result.

Image Compositing

Image compositing is the process of combining parts of one image with parts of another. Compositing is used extensively in the motion picture and television industries to create spectacular visual effects.

Chapter 1 explains how to use the PaintPicture method's opcode parameter to overlay a source image onto a destination image. First, create a mask image that is black over the parts of the source image that you want to copy and white over the rest. Next, copy

Figure 6.13 Program Average combines several noisy images of the same scene to produce a cleaner image.

the mask onto the destination image using the vbMergePaint opcode. This blanks out the portions of the destination that correspond to the black parts of the mask.

Finally, copy the source image onto the destination using the vbSrcAnd opcode. Where the destination image is white, including the areas blanked by the mask, the source image appears. In places where the source image is white, the destination image remains unchanged.

Example program Compose, shown in Figure 6.14, automates part of this process. The program places the foreground image in the upper right on top of the background picture in the upper left. Initially, the foreground picture has a magenta background. The program examines this image's upper-left pixel to find out what color should be transparent in the image.

The program then examines the foreground picture's pixels to make a mask image. When it finds a magenta pixel, it changes the foreground pixel to white and gives the mask picture a white pixel. When it sees any other color pixel, the program leaves the foreground pixel unchanged and gives the mask picture a black pixel. The result for these two pictures is shown in the upper right and lower left in Figure 6.14.

After creating the mask, the program uses the PaintPicture techniques described in Chapter 1 to display the overlaid result.

You can create similar effects directly using image processing techniques. Create foreground and background images as before. The program uses the GetBitmapPixels sub-

Figure 6.14 Program Compose merges two images.

routine to fill two arrays with the pixel values of the foreground and background images. It then examines the foreground pixels. When it finds a magenta pixel, it replaces the foreground pixel value with the background pixel value. When it finds any other pixel value, the program leaves the pixel unchanged. After it has examined all the pixels, the program uses the SetBitmapPixels subroutine to build the result picture directly.

Program Compose2 uses this technique to compose two images much as program Compose does. Program Compose2 is a tiny bit faster and does not require the mask picture for intermediate processing.

There are several techniques you can use to make composite images more realistic. First, place objects in the foreground image both in front of and behind objects in the background image. Doing so increases the appearance of depth and makes the foreground objects seem more integrated into the result.

Another technique uses the fact that the edges of adjacent objects in an image tend to blur together slightly. Blurring the edges of the foreground and background objects slightly makes the foreground objects seem less like you cut them out of a magazine.

Example program Compose3 demonstrates this technique. This program is similar to program Compose2. It examines each pixel to see which are transparent. When it finds a nontransparent pixel, Compose3 examines the adjacent pixels to see which are transparent.

The program then gives the result pixel a color that is a weighted average of the foreground and background pixels' colors. For example, if one-third of the nearby pixels are transparent, the program makes the result pixel one-third of the foreground pixel's value plus two-thirds of the background pixel's value. This program takes longer than the previous programs, but it produces a better result.

A conceptually similar technique produces the composite image at a large scale. It then uses image reduction techniques to shrink the image smoothly. For example, the program could save the results into a file and then use the LoadImage API function described earlier in this chapter to shrink the image. The anti-aliasing effects of LoadImage tend to blur adjacent pixels and remove rough edges from the foreground picture. This technique takes considerably longer than the previous methods because it makes the program work with a much bigger image. For example, if the initial images are twice as tall and wide as the desired final result, the images contain four times as many pixels. Examining all of those pixels may take a while.

Summary

A point process modifies the pixels in an image one at a time. Because only a single pixel is involved in each calculation, most point operations are conceptually very simple. Despite their simplicity, point processes often produce striking results. By adjusting the brightness, color balance, and contrast of an image, you can bring out the best in an otherwise mediocre picture.

CHAPTER 7

Area Processes

I n point processing, the value of an output pixel depends only on its own value. In area processing, the value of an output pixel depends on the values of several different pixels.

Spatial filtering is one kind of area processing. In spatial filtering, a pixel's value depends on the pixels in a square region surrounding it. These other nearby pixels give information about the input pixel's neighborhood. They let the program examine such values as the area's overall brightness, the difference in the pixels' values, and the orientation of features in the area.

Other forms of area processing are based on geometric transformations. Some simple geometric transformations include shrinking, stretching, and rotating an image. More complex transformations let you twist and distort an image in interesting ways.

Spatial Filtering

The most common form of area processing is spatial filtering. In spatial filtering, the program determines a pixel's output value by taking a specially weighted average of the values of the nearby pixels.

The usual way to take this weighted average is to define an array of numbers, called the *kernel*, that defines the coefficients that should be applied to the pixels in the area. Usually, the kernel is square and has an odd number of rows and columns so that the pixel of interest can lie in the exact center. In Visual Basic, you can store the kernel values in an array that is symmetric around zero. For example, a three-by-three kernel might be dimensioned with the following code:

```
Dim kernel(-1 To 1) As Single
```

In any array dimensioned symmetrically around zero, the coefficient corresponding to the center pixel is kernel (0, 0).

The following kernel gives equal weight to all the pixels in a three-by-three area surrounding the center pixel.

1/9	1/9	1/9
1/9	1/9	1/9
1/9	1/9	1/9

To apply this kernel to an area, the program multiplies the surrounding pixel values by their corresponding kernel entries and adds the results. The total gives the output value for the center pixel.

The following example shows the input pixel values for a small part of an image. To compute the output value of the center pixel using the previous kernel, the program would multiply $1/9 * 6 + 1/9 * 2 + 1/9 * 9 + \ldots + 1/9 * 2 = 5$.

6	2	9
4	7	4
3	8	2

More generally, suppose a program contains two picture boxes of the same size named picOriginal and picResult. The following code shows how the program might apply a three-by-three kernel with coefficients stored in the array kernel dimensioned symmetrically around zero.

```
' Apply a filter to an image.
Private Sub ApplyFilter(kernel() As Single)
Dim bound As Integer
Dim input_pixels() As RGBTriplet
Dim result_pixels() As RGBTriplet
Dim bits_per_pixel As Integer
Dim X As Integer
Dim Y As Integer
Dim i As Integer
Dim j As Integer
Dim r As Integer
Dim g As Integer
Dim b As Integer

    ' Get the kernel's bounds.
    bound = UBound(kernel, 1)

    ' Get the pixels from picOriginal.
    GetBitmapPixels picOriginal, input_pixels, bits_per_pixel
```

```
    ' Allocate space for the result pixels.
    ReDim result_pixels( _
        LBound(input_pixels, 1) To UBound(input_pixels, 1), _
        LBound(input_pixels, 2) To UBound(input_pixels, 2))

    ' Set the pixel colors. Note that we
    ' must skip the edges because some of
    ' the kernel values would correspond
    ' to pixels off the image.
    For Y = bound To picOriginal.ScaleHeight - 1 - bound
        For X = bound To picOriginal.ScaleWidth - 1 - bound
            ' Start with no color.
            r = 0
            g = 0
            b = 0
            ' Apply the kernel values to
            ' the nearby pixels.
            For i = -bound To bound
                For j = -bound To bound
                    With input_pixels(X + i, Y + j)
                        r = r + .rgbRed * kernel(i, j)
                        g = g + .rgbGreen * kernel(i, j)
                        b = b + .rgbBlue * kernel(i, j)
                    End With
                Next j
            Next i

            ' Make sure the values are
            ' between 0 and 255.
            If r < 0 Then r = 0
            If r > 255 Then r = 255
            If g < 0 Then g = 0
            If g > 255 Then g = 255
            If b < 0 Then b = 0
            If b > 255 Then b = 255

            ' Set the output pixel value.
            With result_pixels(X, Y)
                .rgbRed = r
                .rgbGreen = g
                .rgbBlue = b
            End With
        Next X
    Next Y

    ' Set picResult's pixels.
    SetBitmapPixels picResult, bits_per_pixel, result_pixels
    picResult.Picture = picResult.Image
End Sub
```

This code has several important points. First, it does not assign values for pixels along the edge of the picture. If it tried, it would need to apply kernel coefficients to pixels that lie beyond the edges of the picture. Since those pixels are not defined, the program would fail.

Second, the subroutine uses separate input_pixels and result_pixels arrays. When it examines a pixel, the code uses pixels with values it has already assigned. For example, to calculate the value of the pixel in position (100, 100), the program examines pixel (99, 99). If it placed new pixel values in the input pixel array, that value would have just been changed. The result for pixel (100, 100) would depend on this new value instead of the original value of pixel (99, 99).

Finally, before it assigns a pixel's color components, the program verifies that they lie between 0 and 255. Depending on the input pixel values and the kernel's coefficients, the new component values could lie outside this range.

Example program Filter, shown in Figure 7.1, uses this code to show all the spatial filters described in this chapter. It also uses code described later in this chapter to implement other area processing techniques.

If you select the Filter menu's Show Filter command, the program displays the current filter's coefficients. The Define Custom Filter command allows you to enter filter coefficients directly.

Spatial filtering can take quite a bit of time. Program Filter took roughly 14 seconds to generate the 5 x 5 low-pass filtered image shown in Figure 7.1 on a 133MHz Pentium processor. The output image contains 205 * 289 = 59,245 pixels that need values. For each of these pixels, the program must perform 9 multiplications and 9 additions for a total of 59,245 * (9 + 9) = just over 1 million mathematical operations. With all these calculations,

Figure 7.1   Program Filter demonstrates many different area processing techniques.

plus the If statements and overhead for the For loops, it should be no big surprise that this may take a while. Bigger images with bigger kernels will take even longer.

Initializing Kernels

Visual Basic does not have a statement that initializes the values in an array of single precision values. That makes initializing large kernels somewhat awkward. The program must include a line to initialize each coefficient in the array as shown in the following code.

```
Dim kernel(-2 To 2) As Single

    kernel(-2, -2) = 1 / 20
    kernel(-2, -1) = 1 / 15
    kernel(-2, 0) = 1 / 10
    :
```

On the other hand, Visual Basic's Array statement creates an array of variants using the values it is passed. The items in the array can be almost anything, including single precision numbers, strings, or other variants that may themselves be arrays.

You can use the Array statement to initialize a variant array containing variant arrays that hold kernel coefficients. You can then use the VariantToArray subroutine shown in the following code to copy the coefficients into a normal, two-dimensional array of singles.

```
' Copy kernel entries from a variant array of
' variant arrays into a normal array.
Private Sub VariantToArray(ByVal var As Variant, _
    ByRef arr() As Single)
Dim bound As Integer
Dim i As Integer
Dim j As Integer

    bound = UBound(var) \ 2
    ReDim arr(-bound To bound, -bound To bound)
    For i = -bound To bound
        For j = -bound To bound
            arr(i, j) = var(i + bound)(j + bound)
        Next j
    Next i
End Sub
```

Program Filter uses this subroutine to initialize many of its kernels. For example, the following code shows how the program initializes the kernel for an embossing filter.

```
VariantToArray Array( _
    Array(1, 0, 0), _
    Array(0, 0, 0), _
    Array(0, 0, -1)), _
    TheKernel
```

Low-Pass Filters

A *low-pass* filter determines a pixel's output value by taking a symmetric average of the nearby pixels. This has a smoothing or blurring effect on the image, so these filters are sometimes called smoothing or blurring filters.

Low-frequency parts of an image are places where the colors change gradually or not at all. In high-frequency portions of an image, the colors change quickly and by large amounts. This kind of averaging filter passes low-frequency portions of the image through with little change while smoothing out higher-frequency portions.

Figure 7.2 shows program Filter applying a low-pass filter to an image. The high-frequency areas at the right and bottom of the image are blurred to an almost uniform gray. The lower-frequency areas in the upper right are still recognizable, though their edges have been softened.

The filter described earlier in this chapter, with every coefficient equal to 1/9, is one kind of low-pass filter. More generally, an N-by-N filter for which each kernel coefficient has value $1/N^2$ is a low-pass filter. Larger kernels soften the image more.

Other low-pass filters give extra weight to the center pixel. These "peaked" kernels make new pixel values more closely resemble their original values while still providing some blurring. The following diagrams show two different kernels for three-by-three peaked low-pass filters.

The first kernel weighs the center pixel slightly more than its neighbors. The second kernel weighs the center pixel quite heavily, so output pixels have values very similar to their input values. The sum of the coefficients in this kernel is 1, so the center coefficient contributes (12/20)/1 = 0.6 or 60 percent of the output pixel's value.

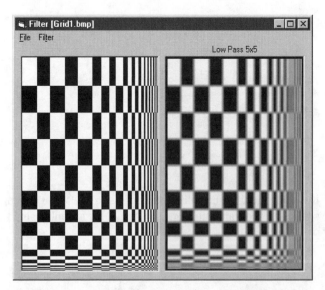

Figure 7.2   Low-pass filters smooth out areas of rapid change.

1/15	2/15	1/15
2/15	3/15	2/15
1/15	2/15	1/15

1/20	1/20	1/20
1/20	12/20	1/20
1/20	1/20	1/20

All low-pass filters have two things in common: They are symmetric around their centers, and the sum of their coefficients equals 1. If a kernel is not symmetric, the filter produces an uneven smoothing. For instance, suppose the coefficients on the right side of the kernel were larger than those on the left. Then the output value for a pixel with bright neighbors to its right would be brighter than one with dark neighbors to its right. Many of the sections that follow use asymmetric kernels to enhance edges with different orientations.

If the weight of the kernel does not equal 1, the resulting image is either lighter or darker than the original. For example, suppose a kernel's coefficients add up to 2 instead of 1. If you apply that kernel to a region where every pixel had a color value of 100, the resulting value would be $2 * 100 = 200$, a much brighter color value than 100. Doubling the total of the coefficients roughly doubles the brightness of the resulting image.

Unsharp Masking

Interestingly, you can sharpen an image by subtracting a scaled version of the result of low-pass filtering from the original image. This process is called *unsharp masking*. Unsharp masking enhances the changes in high-frequency areas, making those areas more noticeable and making the image appear sharper.

Example program Unsharp, shown in Figure 7.3, subtracts a low-pass filtered version of an image from twice the original value. For example, if a pixel's value is P_0 in the original image and P_1 after low-pass filtering, the program makes the pixel's final value $2 * P_0 - P_1$.

High-Pass Filters

Low-pass filters allow low-frequency components of an image to pass through while blurring high-frequency components. High-pass filters do the opposite: They accentuate the high-frequency parts of an image while leaving low-frequency components mostly unchanged.

The following kernels produce high-pass filters. Like the kernels of low-pass filters, they are symmetric around their centers, and the sum of the coefficients in each is 1. These conditions ensure that the kernel produces an even enhancement and does not change the overall brightness of the image.

Figure 7.3 Program Unsharp uses unsharp masking to make images appear sharper.

-1/4	-1/4	-1/4
-1/4	12/4	-1/4
-1/4	-1/4	-1/4

-1	-1	-1
-1	9	-1
-1	-1	-1

0	-1	0
-1	5	-1
0	-1	0

High-pass kernels have a relatively large center coefficient surrounded by negative coefficients. This gives the filter its detail-enhancing effect.

To see why these kernels leave low-frequency details relatively unchanged, suppose a kernel lies over a large area where every pixel has the same value P. Then the output value will be $(P * c_1 + P * c_2 + ... + P * c_n) = P * (c_1 + c_2 + ... + c_n)$. Because the sum of the coefficients is 1, the output value is P, so the pixel's output value is the same as its input value. This fact is what makes high-pass filters leave low-frequency components mostly unchanged. If the colors in an area do not change much, the new pixel values in that area do not change much.

When the kernel passes over an area where the colors change, the negative coefficients tend to push the output value away from the center pixel's value. If the pixels corresponding to the negative coefficients are dark, they tend to make the result brighter. If these coefficients correspond to bright pixels, they tend to make the result darker. Bright pixels that have dark neighbors tend to brighten even more. Dark pixels that have bright neighbors tend to darken further. That tendency makes areas with high-frequency color changes appear sharper.

Figure 7.4 shows program Filter using a strong high-pass filter. The filter's kernel is the third one shown earlier with central coefficient 5.

Some images contain so much detail that high-pass filtering causes strange effects. Recall that a *dithered* image is one in which small dots of one color have been placed in another color to simulate yet a third color. For example, you can simulate pink by placing white dots in a region of red.

If you use a high-pass filter on a dithered image, the filter emphasizes the little dots of color and can produce very strange results. Figure 7.5 shows program Filter applying a relatively weak high-pass filter to an image displayed with 16 dithered colors. While the result is interesting, the transformed dithering effects dominate the image. With stronger high-pass filters, the dithering effects make the image almost unrecognizable.

One way to reduce the effects of a high-pass filter is to make the central coefficient relatively large. Then pixel values corresponding to negative coefficients will still tend to push the result toward darker or lighter values, but they will not be able to influence the result as much as the center pixel does.

Figure 7.4 Program Filter demonstrating a strong high-pass filter.

Figure 7.5   High pass filters can greatly emphasize dithering effects.

Edge Detection

Edge detection operations are useful for identifying objects within an image. Once you have located the edges of the objects, you can use binary contrast enhancement to make the edges even more clearly defined. You can then use the edges in machine vision and other object identification systems.

The SubEdge and SubEdge2 programs described in Chapter 6, Point Processes, enhance edges by shifting an image and subtracting the result from the original image. The two sections that follow describe ways you can use filters to enhance edges.

Prewitt Gradient Edge Detection

The Prewitt gradient edge detection technique uses a simple filter to enhance the edges of an image in a particular direction. For example, one Prewitt filter detects areas in which colors grow darker as you move through the image from the northwest corner toward the southeast corner. Figure 7.6 shows the Filter program using this kind of filter.

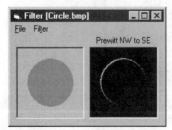

Figure 7.6   Prewitt gradient edge detection filters enhance edges in a particular direction.

The filter used in Figure 7.6 has the following coefficients.

1	1	1
1	2	-1
1	-1	-1

The positive coefficients indicate the direction in which edges are detected. In this kernel, the positive entries are in the upper left corner of the kernel. The resulting image highlights edges where colors change from light to dark while moving from the upper left to the lower right. Program Filter defines similar kernels for Prewitt edge detection in other directions.

Note that the coefficients in this kernel add to zero. In areas with little color variation, applying the coefficients to the pixels gives a value near zero, so output pixels are black. The output image has bright pixels only in areas where pixel colors change quickly and in the appropriate direction.

Laplacian Edge Detection

The Laplacian edge detection method uses a symmetric kernel to detect edges in all directions at the same time. Laplacian edge detection kernels are similar to those of high-pass filters, except the sum of the coefficients is zero rather than 1. This makes the values of most output pixels black, and places where the filter detects a high-frequency feature are brighter. Figure 7.7 shows program Filter using a Laplacian edge detection filter.

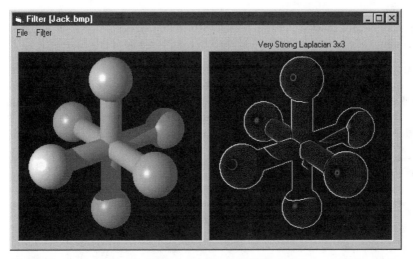

Figure 7.7 Laplacian filters detect edges in all directions.

Embossing

An embossing filter is similar to an edge detection filter. Most of the embossing filter's kernel coefficients are zero. One coefficient on the edge of the kernel has value 1, and the opposite coefficient has value -1. The resulting image has bright highlights where the image grows darker as you move from the direction of the 1 coefficient toward the -1 coefficient. In places where the image grows lighter, the kernel produces a negative value. The results at these positions are rounded up to zero and are black like much of the rest of the image.

You can enhance the three-dimensional appearance of the result by adding 127 to each pixel's color components. Background areas that the kernel would turn black now have a medium gray value of 127. Light areas are brighter, and very dark areas stay dark.

If the image shows a dark object on a lighter background, the embossing process produces an image that looks as if a light is shining on the object from the direction of the 1 coefficient. In Figure 7.8, program Filter is applying a filter with upper left coefficient 1 and lower right coefficient -1.

Restricting an Operation Using a Mask

The Compose2 program described in Chapter 6 uses a mask image to determine which pixels it should copy from a background image and which it should copy from a foreground image. A program can use a similar technique to restrict the effects of a filter to certain parts of an image.

The mask is a grayscale image with each pixel's brightness indicating the amount by which the result pixel's value should depend on the result of the filter. Where the mask is black, the output pixel equals the result of the filter. Where the mask is white, the output pixel equals the input pixel. Where the mask is gray, the result is a weighted average of those values.

For example, if a mask pixel's value is 100, the resulting pixel's value is 100/255 times the original pixel's value plus (255 - 100)/255 times the result of the filter.

Example program MFilter, shown in Figure 7.9, uses this kind of mask to restrict a filter. The mask was initially produced through use of a drawing program to block out the black and white areas. It was then modified with a three-by-three low-pass filter to blur the edges between the black and white areas. This method prevents the filtered areas from having sharp edges.

Figure 7.8   Program Filter applying an embossing filter.

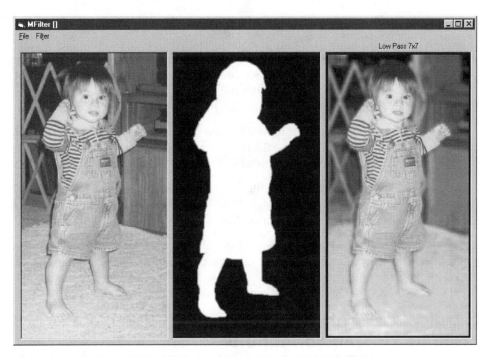

Figure 7.9 Program MFilter uses a mask to restrict a filter to certain areas.

Summary of Spatial Filters

The spatial filters described here use only a tiny fraction of the possible combinations of kernel coefficients. You can use the Filter program's define Custom Filter command to experiment with kernels of your own. Below are a few hints to help you on your way:

- Positive numbers in the center of the kernel reinforce the pixel's current value.
- Negative numbers outside the center emphasize changing pixel values.
- Asymmetric kernels produce asymmetric results.
- If the sum of the kernel's coefficients is 1, the resulting image has roughly the same brightness as the original. If the sum is greater than 1, the result is brighter. If the sum is less than 1, the result is darker.
- If the sum of the kernel coefficients is zero, the resulting image is very dark, possibly with bright highlights.

Rank Filters

The filters discussed so far multiply pixel values and kernel coefficients to obtain new pixel values. Because these calculations use only linear (constant) multiples of the pixel values, this sort of operation is called a *linear* operation.

A *nonlinear* operation computes new pixel values using some method other than multiplication by constants. One type of nonlinear filter is the *rank filter*.

To compute an output value, a rank filter sorts the pixel values in part of the image by their brightness. It then selects one value based on its position in the sorted list and uses that pixel's value for the output value. Filters that select the brightest, darkest, or median value are called maximum, minimum, and median filters, respectively.

You can use a median filter to reduce the noise in an image. If the noise is randomly distributed, it will usually not be the median value when the filter examines an area of the picture. The median filter selects few of the noisy values so the noise is reduced.

On the other hand, the median filter changes the values of many correct pixels, so you lose some resolution in the image. Figure 7.10 shows a noisy image before and after it has been processed using a median filter.

Minimum and maximum ranking filters also produce interesting results. These filters change many of an image's pixel values significantly, but you can still get a sense of the image's overall composition. Both of these filters give an impressionistic quality. Figure 7.11 shows the Filter program using a minimum ranking filter.

Geometric Transformations

Geometric transformations change the physical positioning of the pixels in an image. The most straightforward geometric transformation is *translation*, or moving an image from one location to another. More complicated transformations include scaling, stretching, reflection, and rotation. The sections that follow discuss these and other geometric transformations.

Figure 7.10   Applying a median filter to an image can reduce its noise.

Figure 7.11   A minimum rank filter gives an impressionistic quality.

Bilinear Interpolation

When you want to rotate, stretch, or otherwise transform an image, you often face the problem that you do not have enough data to give values to all the pixels in the resulting image. For example, if you increase an image's height and width by a factor of two, you increase the number of pixels in the image by a factor of four. You have only a quarter of the data you need to assign values to all the pixels.

The PaintPicture method solves this problem by repeating the values of the pixels it has. If you double the width and height of an image, it uses each pixel value four times to fill in the values it needs. If you enlarge the image enough, the image appears blocky.

Example program Stretch, shown in Figure 7.12, uses PaintPicture to display an image at 1, 4, 8, and 16 times its original size. At 8 and 16 times its original size, the image is quite blocky.

Instead of repeating pixel values, you can use the values you know to guess the values in between. The basic idea is that an unknown pixel's color value should be spaced proportionally between the values of the pixels around it. If an unknown pixel is halfway between two known pixels, its value should be halfway between their values. If the unknown pixel is closer to one than the other, its value should be nearer to the value of the closer pixel.

More precisely, if the known pixels have values V_1 and V_2, and the distances from the unknown pixel to the known pixels are D_1 and D_2, the unknown pixel should have the value:

```
V = (V₁ * D₂ + V₂ * D₁) / (D₁ + D₂)
```

This equation has several important properties. If the unknown pixel is very close to the first known pixel, D_1 is close to zero. Then the $V_2 * D_1$ term is close to zero, and the $(D_1 + D_2)$ term is close to D_2. The result becomes $V = V_1 * D_2 / D_2 = V_1$. This makes sense:

Figure 7.12 Using PaintPicture to enlarge an image can make it appear blocky.

If the unknown pixel is close to the first known pixel, it should have a value similar to that of the first pixel.

Similarly, if you assume D_2 is very small, you will find that V is close to V_2. This also makes sense: If the unknown pixel is close to the second known pixel, it should have a value similar to that of the second pixel.

Finally, if $D_1 = D_2$, the equation turns into the ordinary average of the values V_1 and V_2. If the unknown pixel lies exactly between the other two, its value should be the average of the values of the other two.

Assigning an intermediate value proportionally to its distance from known values is called *linear interpolation*. The situation is slightly more complicated with images because images are two dimensional. Some of the unknown pixel values in the enlarged image do not lie exactly between two known pixels.

Suppose you need to assign the value of a pixel at position (x_0, y_0) and you know the values of the four nearest pixels at positions (x_1, y_1), (x_1, y_2), (x_2, y_1), and (x_2, y_2) as shown in Figure 7.13. Then you can estimate the unknown pixel's value by using linear interpolation twice, once horizontally and once vertically. This is called *bilinear interpolation*.

(x_1, y_1) (x_2, y_1)

(x_0, y_0)

(x_1, y_2) (x_2, y_2)

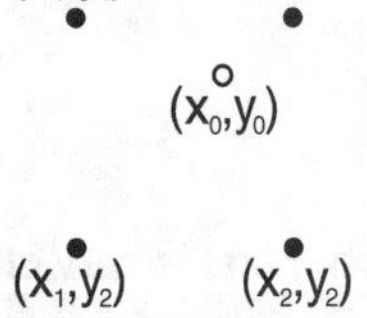

Figure 7.13 Finding a pixel's color using bilinear interpolation.

If the known pixels have values V_{11}, V_{12}, V_{21}, and V_{22}, interpolating horizontally between pixels (x_1, y_1) and (x_2, y_1), and pixels (x_1, y_2) and (x_2, y_2) gives the two values:

```
V₁ = (V₁₁ * dx₂ + V₂₁ * dx₁) / (dx₁ + dx₂)
V₂ = (V₁₂ * dx₂ + V₂₂ * dx₁) / (dx₁ + dx₂)
```

Interpolating these values vertically gives:

```
V = [(V₁₁ * dx₂ + V₂₁ * dx₁) / (dx₁ + dx₂) * dy₂ +
     (V₁₂ * dx₂ + V₂₂ * dx₁) / (dx₁ + dx₂) * dy₁)] / (dy₁ + dy₂)
  = [V₁₁ * dx₂ * dy₂ + V₂₁ * dx₁ * dy₂ +
     V₁₂ * dx₂ * dy₁ + V₂₂ * dx₁ * dy₁]
     / (dx₁ + dx₂) / (dy₁ + dy₂)
```

Because (x_1, y_1), (x_1, y_2), (x_2, y_1), and (x_2, y_2) are adjacent pixels, $dx_1 + dx_2 = 1$ and $dy_1 + dy_2 = 1$. Making these substitutions gives:

```
V = V₁₁ * dx₂ * dy₂ + V₂₁ * dx₁ * dy₂ +
    V₁₂ * dx₂ * dy₁ + V₂₂ * dx₁ * dy₁
```

A Transformation Framework

Using bilinear interpolation, you can build a program that implements a general transformation framework. For each pixel in the output image, the program maps that pixel back to an input pixel location. If that location lies within the input image, the program then uses interpolation to calculate the pixel's value.

Example program Trans demonstrates this technique. Its TransformImage subroutine provides the general framework. For each output pixel, it invokes subroutine MapPixel to map the pixel back to an input location. It then uses bilinear interpolation to calculate the value for the output pixel.

The following code shows the most interesting parts of the TransformImage subroutine. The longest and least interesting parts have been omitted. You can find the complete source code on the CD-ROM.

```
' Transform the image.
Private Sub TransformImage(ByVal pic_from As PictureBox, _
    ByVal pic_to As PictureBox)
Dim input_pixels() As RGBTriplet
Dim result_pixels() As RGBTriplet
Dim bits_per_pixel As Integer
Dim ix_max As Single
Dim iy_max As Single
Dim x_in As Single
Dim y_in As Single
```

```
            :
    ' Get the pixels from pic_from.
    GetBitmapPixels pic_from, input_pixels, bits_per_pixel

    ' Get the pixels from pic_to.
    GetBitmapPixels pic_to, result_pixels, bits_per_pixel

    ' Calculate the output pixel values.
    For iy_out = 0 To pic_to.ScaleHeight - 1
        For ix_out = 0 To pic_to.ScaleWidth - 1
            ' Map the pixel value from
            ' (ix_out, iy_out) to (x_in, y_in).
            MapPixel ix_out, iy_out, x_in, y_in

            ' Interpolate to find the pixel's value.
                :
        Next ix_out
    Next iy_out

    ' Set pic_to's pixels.
    SetBitmapPixels pic_to, bits_per_pixel, result_pixels
    pic_to.Picture = pic_to.Image
End Sub
```

All the information about the particular transformation (rotation, scaling, stretching, etc.) is contained in the MapPixel subroutine. That makes TransformImage very general. You can modify MapPixel to implement a different mapping function without changing the rest of the program.

Although program Trans uses an approach that is very easy to modify, in practice, it imposes some overhead. The program calls subroutine MapPixel for every pixel in the image. With a 100-by-100 pixel output image, for instance, the program calls MapPixel 10,000 times. All those function calls slow the program slightly. You can make the program less general but faster if you move the pixel mapping function directly into subroutine TransformImage.

Program Trans lets you compare these approaches. Use the Transform button to make the program rotate an image using subroutine TransformImage. Use the Rotate button to make the program rotate the image with the pixel mapping directly inside the transformation routine. In one set of tests on a 133MHz Pentium processor, rotating the image took roughly 10 percent longer when the more general TransformImage subroutine was used.

Most of the example programs described in this chapter use the more general technique because it is easier to understand and modify. You can make the programs slightly faster if you bring the pixel mapping functions inside the TransformImage subroutine.

Enlargement

When you enlarge an image, you face the problem described earlier in which you do not have enough data to give values to all the pixels in the result. You can solve this problem using bilinear interpolation, also described earlier.

Example program Stretch2, shown in Figure 7.14, uses bilinear interpolation to enlarge an image. Compare the results to those of program Stretch shown in Figure 7.12. Program Stretch uses PaintPicture to enlarge the image. The images produced by program Stretch2 are less blocky, though they appear fuzzier and they take much longer to create. Because of its greater speed, PaintPicture is still useful when speed is more important than image quality.

Program Stretch2 uses the EnlargePicture subroutine shown in the following code to enlarge its image. EnlargePicture takes as parameters the minimum X and Y coordinates for the input and output areas and saves them in global variables that the MapPixel routine can access later. It also takes parameters giving the widths and heights of the input and output areas. It uses those values to calculate the scale by which the image will be stretched in the X and Y directions.

EnlargePicture subtracts 1 from the input area's width and height so that pixels will map inside the original image. If it used the entire input area, pixels along the right and bottom edges of the result would not map inside the original image, so their values would not be defined.

After setting these global values, EnlargePicture calls the TransformImage routine described in the previous section. TransformImage calls the MapPixel subroutine, which uses the values saved by EnlargePicture.

Figure 7.14   Program Stretch2 uses bilinear interpolation to enlarge an image.

MapPixel must map the output pixel location (ix_out, iy_out) back to the input location (x_in, y_in). Pixels are mapped from input locations to output locations using these formulas:

```
x_out = (x_in - FromXmin) * XScale + ToXmin
y_out = (y_in - FromYmin) * YScale + ToYmin
```

Solving these equations for x_in and y_in gives the reverse mapping from output pixels back to input pixel locations.

```
x_in = FromXmin + (ix_out - ToXmin) / XScale
y_in = FromYmin + (iy_out - ToYmin) / YScale
```

Subroutine MapPixel uses these inverse equations to find input pixel locations.

```
' Copy the picture.
Private Sub EnlargePicture( _
    ByVal pic_from As PictureBox, _
    ByVal pic_to As PictureBox, _
    ByVal from_xmin As Single, ByVal from_ymin As Single, _
    ByVal from_wid As Single, ByVal from_hgt As Single, _
    ByVal to_xmin As Single, ByVal to_ymin As Single, _
    ByVal to_wid As Single, ByVal to_hgt As Single)

    ' Save mapping values.
    FromXmin = from_xmin
    FromYmin = from_ymin
    ToXmin = to_xmin
    ToYmin = to_ymin
    XScale = to_wid / (from_wid - 1)
    YScale = to_hgt / (from_hgt - 1)

    ' Transform the image.
    TransformImage pic_from, pic_to
End Sub

' Map the output pixel (ix_out, iy_out) to the input
' pixel (x_in, y_in).
Private Sub MapPixel( _
    ByVal ix_out As Single, ByVal iy_out As Single, _
    ByRef x_in As Single, ByRef y_in As Single)

    x_in = FromXmin + (ix_out - ToXmin) / XScale
    y_in = FromYmin + (iy_out - ToYmin) / YScale
End Sub
```

Taken together, subroutines EnlargePicture and MapPixel perform a task similar to the one performed by Visual Basic's PaintPicture method. They take the same parameters and produce a stretched image. EnlargePicture and MapPixel produce a smoother result.

Example program Enlarge uses the same technique to enlarge an image. Load a picture file and enter a scale factor that is at least 1.0. Click the Enlarge button to make the program enlarge the image.

Reduction

Enlarging an image with PaintPicture can make the result appear blocky. PaintPicture can also cause problems when it reduces the size of an image. To make an image smaller, PaintPicture omits some of the pixels from the image. Unfortunately, it does not always pick the best pixels to omit. Sometimes it removes pixels that are important to the picture and the results look strange. This problem is called *aliasing*.

In dithered images, where one color is placed on top of another to simulate a third, the reduction may remove most of the top color and leave the background color in ugly splotches. This sort of reduction also often removes pixels that shade a region to make colors blend smoothly. In that case, the edges of the region may become abrupt or jagged.

Even worse, PaintPicture may remove large pieces of thin lines, thus making gaps appear. Example program Shrink, shown in Figure 7.15, draws a series of lines and then uses PaintPicture to copy the lines at half their original size. Almost all the lines in the copy show gaps. The horizontal and vertical lines happen to fall along the rows and columns of pixels that were completely removed by PaintPicture, so they are missing entirely.

When you enlarge an image, you do not have enough input data to fill in all the output pixels. When you reduce an image, you face the opposite problem: You have too much input data. If you just ignore data as PaintPicture does, you may create aliasing effects.

You can prevent these problems by making each output pixel represent the average of its corresponding input pixel values. If you reduce an image to half its original size, for instance, each output pixel corresponds to four input pixels. The value you give the output pixel should be the average of the values of the four input pixels.

Every input pixel's value takes part in determining the value of some output pixel, so you do not actually discard any data. Because every input pixel value is represented, you do not lose the larger structure of the image. In particular, you do not get ugly aliasing effects, and you do not create gaps in thin lines.

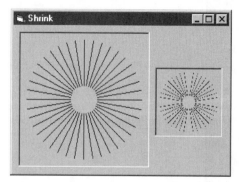

Figure 7.15   PaintPicture can cause gaps in thin lines and other small features.

As is the case when you are enlarging an image, you should consider the output pixels and determine which input pixels contribute to each output pixel. You can use the same equations described in the previous section for enlarging an image. An output pixel at location (x_out, y_out) maps back to an input position (x_in, y_in) where:

```
x_in = FromXmin + (ix_out - ToXmin) / XScale
y_in = FromYmin + (iy_out - ToYmin) / YScale
```

With these equations, the input pixels that map into the output pixel (x_out, y_out) are those with x1 <= x <= x2 and y1 <= y <= y2 where:

```
x1 = Int(FromXmin + (ix_out - ToXmin) / XScale)
x2 = Int(FromXmin + (ix_out + 1 - ToXmin) / XScale) - 1
y1 = Int(FromYmin + (iy_out - ToYmin) / YScale)
y2 = Int(FromYmin + (iy_out + 1 - ToYmin) / YScale) - 1
```

You can now take the average over the values of the input pixels in this area to find the correct value for the output pixel (x_out, y_out).

Example program Reduce, shown in Figure 7.16, uses this technique to shrink images without severe aliasing. The most interesting part of the program's TransformImage subroutine is shown in the following code. The rest of the program is very similar to the other image transformation programs described in this chapter so it is not shown here. You can find the complete source code on the CD-ROM.

```
' Calculate the output pixel values.
For iy_out = 0 To pic_to.ScaleHeight - 1
    For ix_out = 0 To pic_to.ScaleWidth - 1
        ' Map the pixel value from
        ' (ix_out, iy_out) to (x_in, y_in).
        x1 = Int(FromXmin + (ix_out - ToXmin) / XScale)
        x2 = Int(FromXmin + _
            (ix_out + 1 - ToXmin) / XScale) - 1
        y1 = Int(FromYmin + (iy_out - ToYmin) / YScale)
```

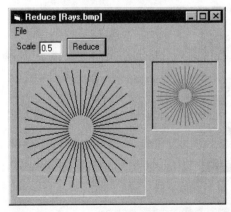

Figure 7.16 Program Reduce reduces an image without severe aliasing.

```
        y2 = Int(FromYmin + _
            (iy_out + 1 - ToYmin) / YScale) - 1

        ' Average the pixels in this area.
        r = 0
        g = 0
        b = 0
        For X = x1 To x2
            For Y = y1 To y2
                With input_pixels(X, Y)
                    r = r + .rgbRed
                    g = g + .rgbGreen
                    b = b + .rgbBlue
                End With
            Next Y
        Next X

        ' Save the result.
        num_pixels = (x2 - x1 + 1) * (y2 - y1 + 1)
        With result_pixels(ix_out, iy_out)
            .rgbRed = r / num_pixels
            .rgbGreen = g / num_pixels
            .rgbBlue = b / num_pixels
        End With
    Next ix_out
  Next iy_out
```

Compare program Reduce's output with the output of program Shrink shown in Figure 7.15. Program Reduce gives a much smoother result, though it takes longer. Program Reduce also gives equal weight to all of the input pixel values. Your image might contain small areas that are important to the structure of the picture. In Figure 7.16, for example, the thin, dark lines are important to the image while the gray background is not. By averaging all of the pixel values, the program dilutes the important data with the background data. This makes the dark, thin lines lighter, and the image appears more blurred.

If you know you are working with this sort of image, you can reduce this effect by unsharp masking or high-pass filtering to sharpen the result.

Example program Resize uses the techniques describe in this and the previous section to enlarge or reduce an image. The ResizePicture subroutine examines its parameters to determine whether it is enlarging or shrinking an image. It then calls the appropriate routine to transform the image.

Cheating with LoadImage

The LoadImage API function loads icons, cursors, and bitmaps. You can use it to load an image from a file with anti-aliasing. This routine does not produce quite as nice a result as the routines described in the previous sections, particularly when you are shrinking an image, but it is much faster. In one test on a 133MHz Pentium, program Resize took 4.28 seconds to enlarge an image while the LoadImage function took only 0.37 seconds.

LoadImage returns a handle to the newly loaded image when it succeeds. To display the image, you must create a device context and use the image's handle to copy it into the device context. Then you can use the BitBlt API function to copy the result into a picture box. Finally, you should destroy the device context and image to free their graphic resources.

The following code shows how a program can use LoadImage to load a picture at a desired size.

```
Private Declare Function LoadImage Lib "user32" Alias _
    "LoadImageA" (ByVal hInst As Long, ByVal lpsz As String, _
    ByVal un1 As Long, ByVal n1 As Long, ByVal n2 As Long, _
    ByVal un2 As Long) As Long
Private Const LR_LOADFROMFILE = &H10
Private Declare Function CreateCompatibleDC Lib "gdi32" ( _
    ByVal hdc As Long) As Long
Private Declare Function DeleteDC Lib "gdi32" ( _
    ByVal hdc As Long) As Long
Private Declare Function DeleteObject Lib "gdi32" ( _
    ByVal hObject As Long) As Long
Private Declare Function SelectObject Lib "gdi32" ( _
    ByVal hdc As Long, ByVal hObject As Long) As Long
Private Declare Function BitBlt Lib "gdi32" ( _
    ByVal hDestDC As Long, ByVal x As Long, ByVal y As Long, _
    ByVal nWidth As Long, ByVal nHeight As Long, _
    ByVal hSrcDC As Long, ByVal xSrc As Long, _
    ByVal ySrc As Long, ByVal dwRop As Long) As Long
Private Const SRCCOPY = &HCC0020

' Use the LoadImage API function to load a picture
' from a file into a PictureBox, filling the PictureBox.
Private Sub LoadImageFromFile(ByVal file_name As String, _
    ByVal pic As PictureBox)
Dim wid As Long
Dim hgt As Long
Dim mem_dc As Long
Dim hbmp As Long

    ' Get the desired size in pixels.
    wid = pic.ScaleX(pic.ScaleWidth, pic.ScaleMode, vbPixels)
    hgt = pic.ScaleY(pic.ScaleHeight, pic.ScaleMode, vbPixels)

    ' Get the bitmap handle from the file.
    hbmp = LoadImage(ByVal 0&, file_name, 0, _
        wid, hgt, LR_LOADFROMFILE)

    ' Create a device context to hold the image.
    mem_dc = CreateCompatibleDC(0)

    ' Select the bitmap into the device context.
    SelectObject mem_dc, hbmp
```

```
    ' Copy the bitmap into picResult.
    BitBlt pic.hdc, 0, 0, wid, hgt, _
        mem_dc, 0, 0, SRCCOPY
    pic.Refresh

    ' Delete the device context and bitmap.
    DeleteDC mem_dc
    DeleteObject hbmp
End Sub
```

Example program Resize2 uses this code to resize images. Compare the program's speed and quality of the results with those of program Resize.

Rotation

At first, rotating an image may seem like a daunting task. If you look closely at the problem, however, you will find that it is very similar to the problem of image enlargement. In both cases, you have a function that maps pixels from a source image to a destination image. The rotation function is a bit more complex than the enlargement function, but the idea is similar.

If you simply copy the source pixels to their corresponding rotated positions in the output image, some pixels will map to the same integral locations. That will leave gaps in the result. This is similar to the problem with enlarging an image, and you can solve it in a similar way. Map the pixels in the output image back to locations in the original image. Then use bilinear interpolation to calculate the output pixel's value.

Example program Trans, shown in Figure 7.17, uses the image transformation framework described earlier in this chapter to rotate images.

The only new part of the transformation process used by program Trans is the MapPixel subroutine that maps output pixels to input pixel positions. The first step in finding this mapping is understanding how the program rotates images.

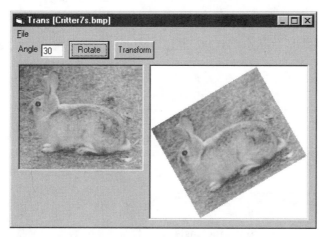

Figure 7.17   Rotating an image.

The program rotates points in the input image around the image's center. It translates the result so that it is centered in the output image.

Figure 7.18 shows how to rotate the point (x, y) around the origin through the angle ϕ. The distance R from (cx, cy) to (x, y) is:

```
R = Sqr(dx * dx + dy * dy)
```

Using the arctangent function, the program can calculate the angle $\theta = \arctan(y/x)$. Unfortunately, Visual Basic's arctangent function Atn returns only values between $-\pi/2$ and $\pi/2$. The ATan2 function shown in the following code uses Atn to return values for angles that fall outside this range.

```
' Return the arctan of dy/dx.
Public Function ATan2( _
    ByVal dy As Single, ByVal dx As Single) As Single
Const PI = 3.14159265

Dim theta As Single

    If Abs(dx) < 0.01 Then
        If dy < 0 Then
            theta = -PI / 2
        Else
            theta = PI / 2
        End If
    Else
        theta = Atn(dy / dx)
        If dx < 0 Then theta = PI + theta
    End If

    ATan2 = theta
End Function
```

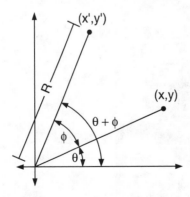

Figure 7.18 Rotating a point through the angle ϕ.

Once the program knows the angle q and the distance R, it can find the new point's position (x', y') using these equations:

```
x' = R * Cos(θ + φ)
y' = R * Sin(θ + φ)
```

Now suppose the original image has center (CxIn, CyIn) and the result picture has center (CxOut, CyOut). The program can rotate the point around (CxIn, CyIn) by first subtracting CxIn and CyIn from the point's coordinates. It can then center the pixel in the output picture by adding CxOut and CyOut to the results.

Inverting these steps to find the inverse mapping would be difficult. Fortunately, the inverse of a rotation through the angle θ is simply a rotation through the angle -θ. To find the inverse operation, you use the same steps with the roles of the input and output pixels switched.

Program Trans uses the MapPixel subroutine shown in the following code to map output pixels back to input positions. First it subtracts CxOut and CyOut from the output pixel's coordinates. This transforms the rotation into a rotation around the origin.

The routine calculates the distance R from the translated point to the origin. It then uses the ATan2 function to find the angle theta to the output point. MapPixel adds the angle of rotation phi to theta and uses the value R to find the input pixel's coordinates with respect to the origin. Finally, it adds the values CxIn and CyIn to center the result in the input image.

```
' Map the output pixel (ix_out, iy_out) to the input
' pixel (x_in, y_in).
Private Sub MapPixel( _
    ByVal ix_out As Single, _
    ByVal iy_out As Single, _
    ByRef x_in As Single, ByRef y_in As Single)
Dim dx As Single
Dim dy As Single
Dim R As Single
Dim theta As Single

    dx = ix_out - CxOut
    dy = iy_out - CyOut
    R = Sqr(dx * dx + dy * dy)
    theta = ATan2(dy, dx)
    x_in = CxIn + R * Cos(theta + Phi)
    y_in = CyIn + R * Sin(theta + Phi)
End Sub
```

There is one other detail you need to consider when rotating an image: The size of the output image is not necessarily the same as the size of the input image. Usually the result is taller and wider than the original. To determine how big the output image should be, you need to compute the dimensions of the rotated input area.

Figure 7.19 shows a rotated rectangle. If the rectangle's original width and height are W and H, then the figure shows that the rotated area's width and height are given by:

```
width  = H * Sin(φ) + W * Cos(φ)
height = H * Cos(φ) + W * Sin(φ)
```

Example program Rotate is similar to program Trans except it does not use the transformation framework. Its RotateImage subroutine contains the inverse pixel mapping code, so it provides slightly better performance.

Reflection

Reflecting an image across the X or Y axis is easy. To reflect an area with bounds x1 <= x <= x2, y1 <= y <= y2 across the X axis, you could use code like this:

```
For Y = y1 To y2
    For X = x1 To x2
        to_pixels(X, -Y) = from_pixels(X, Y)
    Next X
Next Y
```

Of course, the array bounds of the to_bytes and from_bytes arrays are probably positive. In that case, the -Y coordinate value used in the to_bytes entries is outside the array bounds. Your code can check for this condition and ignore any values that do not fit within the output array. In this example, every output pixel lies outside the destination array, so this kind of reflection is not particularly useful.

Reflecting an image across a line other than the X or Y axis is more interesting. You can easily do this by translating the image so that the line of reflection falls along one of the

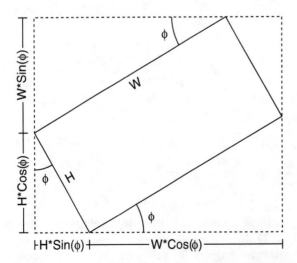

Figure 7.19   Computing the dimensions of a rotated rectangle.

axes, performing the reflection and then translating the image back. For example, to reflect a pixel across the line $y = y0$, you would subtract $y0$ from the pixel's Y coordinate, multiply by -1 to reflect the point, and then add $y0$ to the result. Putting these steps together, you can write an equation for the new location y_out in terms of the old location y_in.

```
y_out = (y_in - y0) * (-1) + y0
```

This simplifies to:

```
y_out = 2 * y0 - y_in
```

Solving this equation for y_in gives:

```
y_in = 2 * y0 - y_out
```

You can use this equation to build a MapPixel subroutine for use with the transformation framework used by other programs in this chapter.

While you could reflect an image vertically or horizontally in this way, PaintPicture is much simpler and faster. The following code shows how you can use PaintPicture to reflect an image vertically. The negative value for the source image's height makes PaintPicture flip the image vertically.

```
Dim wid As Single
Dim hgt As Single

    wid = picOriginal.ScaleWidth
    hgt = picOriginal.ScaleHeight
    picResult.PaintPicture _
        picOriginal.Picture, _
        0, 0, wid, hgt, _
        0, hgt, wid, -hgt
```

Complex Reflection

A more interesting example reflects an image across a line that is not parallel to the X or Y axis. You can accomplish this transformation using simple translation, rotation, and reflection by following these steps:

1. Translate so that the line of reflection intersects the origin.
2. Rotate so that the line of reflection lies along the X axis.
3. Reflect across the X axis by multiplying the pixels' Y values by -1.
4. Reverse the previous rotation.
5. Reverse the previous translation.

The results of these calculations give you the new X and Y coordinates of a point. Following the methods of previous sections, you can build a MapPixel subroutine that performs the inverse of these operations. This routine takes an output pixel and maps it back to an input pixel location. Usually this location will not lie at an integral location, so the program should use bilinear interpolation to calculate the output pixel's value.

Inverting the transformation steps is not difficult. The inverse of translation is a translation in the opposite direction. For example, to invert a translation by distances dx and dy in the X and Y directions, the program can translate by the distances -dx and -dy.

The inverse of rotation by an angle theta is simply a rotation by the angle -theta. Reflection is its own inverse since -(-Y) = Y.

The MapPixel subroutine shown in the following code performs this reverse transformation. The point (0, B) lies on the line of reflection, so MapPixel translates the line to the origin by subtracting B from the pixel's Y coordinate. The sine and cosine of the angle of rotation are calculated before MapPixel executes.

```
' Map the output pixel (ix_out, iy_out) to the input
' pixel (x_in, y_in).
Private Sub MapPixel( _
    ByVal ix_out As Single, ByVal iy_out As Single, _
    ByRef x_in As Single, ByRef y_in As Single)
Dim x1 As Single
Dim y1 As Single
Dim x2 As Single
Dim y2 As Single
Dim x3 As Single
Dim y3 As Single
Dim x4 As Single
Dim y4 As Single

    ' Translate by (0, -B).
    x1 = ix_out
    y1 = iy_out - B

    ' Rotate by angle -theta around the origin.
    x2 = x1 * cos_theta - y1 * sin_theta
    y2 = x1 * sin_theta + y1 * cos_theta

    ' Reflect.
    x3 = x2
    y3 = -y2

    ' Rotate by angle theta around the origin.
    x4 = x3 * cos_theta + y3 * sin_theta
    y4 = -x3 * sin_theta + y3 * cos_theta

    ' Translate by (0, +B).
    x_in = x4
    y_in = y4 + B
End Sub
```

Example program Reflect, shown in Figure 7.20, uses this code to reflect an image across a line with equation Y = M * X + B. Enter the values for M and B on the form and click the Reflect button. Keep in mind that the picture's coordinate system starts with (0, 0) in the upper left corner so the line may seem upside down. Setting B = 0 makes the line pass through the origin.

Shape-Distorting Transformation

So far, the geometric transformations described in this chapter have left the image's shape more or less unchanged. If you enlarge or shrink an image more in one direction than another, you can stretch or flatten an image, but straight lines are still straight lines in the result.

There is no reason you cannot implement transformations that warp an image in stranger ways. The method is the same as before: Map the output pixels to the input pixel locations and use bilinear interpolation to fill in any gaps.

For example, consider the transformation functions below.

```
x_out = x_in
y_out = y_in + 20 * (Sin(x_in / 30) + 1)
```

It is easy to solve these equations for x_in and y_in to find the inverse transformation.

```
x_in = x_out
y_in = y_out - 20 * (Sin(x_in / 30) + 1)
     = y_out - 20 * (Sin(x_out / 30) + 1)
```

Using these equations, you can build a MapPixel subroutine to map output pixels to input pixel locations. Example program Warp, shown in Figure 7.21, uses this technique to demonstrate several different shape-distorting transformations.

Example programs Fish and Pinch use the same technique with different user interfaces. Load a picture and click on it. Program Fish enlarges the position you click. Program Pinch shrinks the position you click.

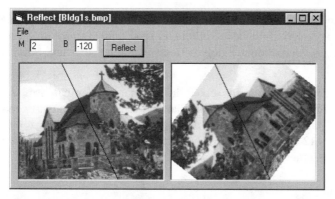

Figure 7.20   Program Reflect reflects an image across an arbitrary line.

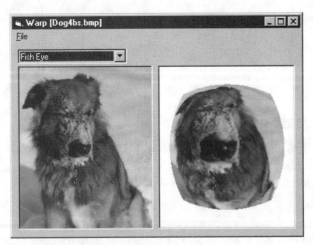

Figure 7.21 Program Warp demonstrates several shape-distorting transformations.

Example program Grid uses a different method to specify its transformation. When you load an image, the program displays the picture overlaid with a grid of control points. Click and drag the control points to new positions. When you click the Transform button, the program maps rectangular areas in the result picture back to the corresponding quadrilateral areas in the control points on the original image. For example, if you make a control area small, the small quadrilateral is stretched to fit the larger corresponding rectangle in the output image.

Program Grid uses bilinear interpolation to map pixels in an output rectangle back to points in the input quadrilateral. If the output pixel is near the upper-left corner of the rectangle, the input pixel is near the upper-left corner of the input quadrilateral. The code for this mapping is fairly long, and it is similar to the bilinear interpolation code shown earlier in this chapter, so it is not shown here. You can see the code in the Grid program on the CD-ROM.

Summary

Area processes modify regions in an image. Spatial filters use the values of pixels in an area to determine a pixel's output value. Although a filter may examine only a small area at one time, it can produce dramatic global effects including softening, sharpening, or embossing an image.

Geometric transformations move the pixels in an image. They can stretch, shrink, rotate, or warp an image. Chapter 9 uses similar methods to implement tweening and morphing, two techniques that allow a program to generate images for animated sequences. Chapters 12 and 13 formalize certain kinds of transformations that are useful in two- and three-dimensional graphics.

PART THREE

Animation

Until recently, few programs used animation. Documents on the World Wide Web, however, use animation extensively. Some are so covered in blinking, flashing, scrolling advertisements that visitors risk severe headaches.

While many Web pages abuse animation, the Web has raised user expectations. Applications that contain animation are becoming more common. Even programs that do not need animation for their core tasks include small animations to break otherwise monotonous chores and hold the user's attention.

The chapters in this part of the book explain how you can add animation to your Visual Basic programs. Chapter 8, Bitmap Animation, explains animation basics. It shows how to use a series of bitmaps to provide the illusion of motion. It explains several different methods for timing images to provide the smoothest animation possible.

Chapter 9, Advanced Animation, describes several different ways a program can control an animation. It tells how to use techniques such as simulation, scripting, and sprites to determine how animation should proceed. It also explains methods for generating animation sequences, including tweening and morphing.

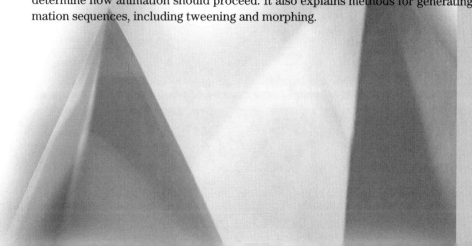

CHAPTER 8

Bitmap Animation

T his chapter describes ways you can add animation to your Visual Basic programs. It begins with a brief explanation of what animation is and how it works. It then describes some of the Visual Basic and API tools you can use to add animation to programs.

As is often the case in programming, some techniques are relatively slow and simple while others are faster and more complex. Using the examples in this chapter and the summary at the end, you can select the right animation method for your application.

Animation Basics

Animation is a process in which you rapidly present a series of images, called *frames*, to create the illusion of motion. If you present the images quickly enough, and if the changes from one image to the next are not too large, an observer perceives the series as a single image that is changing over time.

To give the appearance of smooth motion, you need to display around 16 to 20 frames per second. If you display the images more slowly, the movement appears jerky. Standard motion pictures present 24 frames per second, though that speed is not always possible on a computer.

In the United States, television signals present 30 images per second. These television images are displayed in two parts. First the odd-numbered rows of pixels in the image are displayed, and then even-numbered rows are displayed. This *interlaced scan* makes the changes between frames occur in two smaller stages, so it seems to a television viewer that twice as many images are being presented. That makes motion in the image appear even smoother.

Many computer monitors use *progressive scan* rather than interlaced scan. Here the rows of pixels on the screen are updated in order rather than in alternating odd- and even-numbered rows. To make the image look smooth, progressive scan monitors usually refresh the screen more frequently than those that use an interlaced scan do. A typical progressive scan monitor might refresh its screen 60 or more times per second.

Timing Is Everything

If you present an animation's images too slowly, the motion appears jerky. Presenting images too quickly can also cause problems. If you display images faster than the computer's monitor can update, some of the images may never be visible. This can make the animation appear jerky or produce even stranger effects.

Suppose you have a series of images showing a person running. The person starts with right foot extended, draws the right leg back while putting the left foot forward, and then draws the left leg back while moving the right foot forward again. This cycle of right foot forward to right foot forward requires 10 images.

Now suppose that you present the images 10 times as fast as your monitor can display them. As a result, only every 10th image is visible. All the images presented show your runner with the right foot extended in front. To an observer, the sequence appears to show the runner sliding along the ground with right foot forward.

If you present the images nine times as fast as your monitor can display them, each image will come from a little earlier in the right foot forward to right foot forward cycle. When you run the images together, the person will seem to run backwards, even though the ground underneath indicates that the person is moving forward.

These effects are forms of *temporal aliasing*. By not displaying every image in the appropriate sequence, you have removed important visual information from the animation and created the illusion of motion that does not really exist.

A final problem with displaying images too quickly occurs if you update the image being displayed while your monitor is in the middle of a refresh cycle. In that case, the top half of the screen may show part of one image while the bottom half shows part of another. If the timing is right and this sort of thing occurs frequently, you can see a horizontal line where the two images meet. You may even be able to see the two halves of the images moving independently. The top half of a person running might seem to be slightly in front of the bottom half. Because the image appears torn in the middle, this problem is called *image tearing*.

To prevent all of these problems, you should not display images faster than your monitor can update them. Doing things too quickly is usually not a problem in Visual Basic, but it may be an issue on some of the most modern computers. In one test of the Bmp-Play program described later in this chapter, a 133MHz Pentium processor was able to display a 250 by 250 pixel image roughly 55 times per second. The progressive scan monitor used refreshed itself 60 times per second. This is just fast enough to avoid temporal aliasing problems.

If you run a simple animation on a 400MHz Pentium III with a fast graphics accelerator, you may encounter these problems. In that case, you will need to take special care in timing your animations' frames.

Timing in Visual Basic

To provide smooth motion while preventing temporal aliasing and tearing, you should:

- Display at least 12 images per second—more if possible
- Display images no faster than your monitor can handle them

Whether or not you can achieve these goals, particularly the first one, depends on how you approach the problem. If you store your images as bitmaps in memory, you may be able to display them quickly enough. In fact, you may want to slow things down a bit to prevent temporal aliasing or to allow you to store fewer images for the same duration. For example, if you display 12 images per second even though your computer is fast enough to display 24, you would need to store only half as many images per second of animation.

There are several approaches you can take to timing images in Visual Basic. The simplest is to present the images as quickly as possible. This approach works well in many situations, but it has its drawbacks. You may need to store more images than are really necessary. If each image takes a different amount of time to prepare and display, motion may appear irregular. This method also puts you at the mercy of the hardware running your application. The animation will look very different depending on the type of machine that is running it. This problem grows larger with each new generation of faster computers.

Two more sophisticated methods for timing image display are using a timer control and clock watching.

Fast Display

The easiest way to animate a series of bitmaps is to display them one after another in a loop. The following code shows one method for doing this. The program stores the frames in a hidden array of picture boxes named picFrame. It simply copies the images for each frame into the visible picCanvas control. The routine continues displaying images until it has shown them all or until the Boolean variable Playing is False. The DoEvents statement allows the operating system to perform other actions. In particular, it allows this program's Stop button to set Playing to False.

```
' Run the animation once or until Playing is False.
Private Sub PlayImagesOnce()
Dim i As Integer

    ' Start the animation.
    For i = 0 To NumImages - 1
        ' Display the next frame.
        picCanvas.Picture = picFrame(i).Picture
        DoEvents
        NumPlayed = NumPlayed + 1
```

```
        If Not Playing Then Exit For
    Next i
End Sub
```

Example program PlayFast, shown in Figure 8.1, uses this code to display a series of images as quickly as possible. Select the File menu's Open command to select a series of bitmaps. On the CD-ROM, a file with a name that ends in "_0.bmp" represents a series of bitmaps. For example, select the file morph_0.bmp to load the series morph_0.bmp, morph_1.bmp, morph_3.bmp, and so forth. The program loads the series of pictures and stores them in the picFrame control array.

The code used by program PlayFast is more complicated than the previous code because it provides extra control options. It allows you to start and stop the animation, run through the frames repeatedly, or play them forward and backward.

This display technique is quite fast. In one test on a 133MHz Pentium processor, program PlayFast displayed 395 frames per second. While this is certainly fast enough to provide smooth animation, it also means the program must display more frames than necessary. The program will run at different speeds on different computers, so the animation may not look right on every computer.

Timer Controls

A timer control lets a program execute code at regular intervals. Because you want to display animation frames at regular intervals, using a timer control is a natural choice.

Set the timer's Interval property to indicate how many milliseconds you want to pass between frames. Whenever the control's Timer event is triggered, display the next frame in the animation. You can use a global variable NextFrame to keep track of the next frame to display.

The following code shows how a program's Timer event handler can present the next frame in the series.

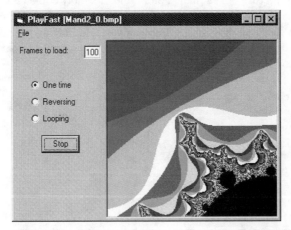

Figure 8.1 Program PlayFast displays images as quickly as it can.

```
Private NextFrame As Integer
Private NumImages As Integer

' Display the next frame.
Private Sub tmrFrame_Timer()
    ' Display the next frame.
    picCanvas.Picture = picFrame(NextImage).Image

    ' Display the next frame next.
    NextImage = NextImage + 1

    ' If that was the last frame, stop.
    If NextImage >= NumImages Then tmrFrame.Enabled = False
End Sub
```

Example program PlayTmr uses this technique to display a series of bitmaps. Load the bitmaps as you would for program PlayFast. Enter the number of frames per second you want displayed and click the Start button.

This technique gives you greater control over the animation speed than the previous technique does. If you set the timer control's Interval property to 50, the program displays roughly 20 frames per second if it can run fast enough. If the computer is too slow to display the images that quickly, it displays them as fast as it can.

Unfortunately, using a timer control has a few drawbacks. First, the timer control imposes some overhead and slows the program down. The same 133MHz Pentium processor that displayed 395 frames per second using program PlayFast could display only 96 frames per second using program PlayTmr. That is still more than fast enough for smooth animation, but on a slower computer, it might make a difference.

A second problem with timers is that they do not count the time spent during the Timer event. Suppose you have a timer set to display an image every 200 milliseconds, and the Timer event takes 50 milliseconds to display a picture. Each Timer event does not occur until at least 200 milliseconds after the previous one finishes. An event may take even longer if other programs are using the system heavily. That means more than 250 milliseconds will pass between the start of one Timer event and the start of the next, rather than the 200 milliseconds you expect.

This unwanted timing adjustment is merely inconvenient if you can display each image in roughly the same amount of time. The images will be displayed at a slightly slower rate than you would like, but after some testing, you could adjust the timer's interval to 150 milliseconds and get reasonably close to the timing you want.

The problem is greater if different frames take different lengths of time to display. Suppose your program generates each image before displaying it. For instance, the images might show a cube being rotated in three dimensions with the program calculating a new position for the cube for each frame. In that case, it might take a different amount of time to generate each frame. To make the timer control present images at a constant rate, you would need to recalculate the timer's Interval property every time you displayed an image. In the Timer event, you would need to follow these steps.

1. Display the current image.

2. Generate the next image.

3. See how much time remains before you need to present the next image, and set the interval property accordingly.

All this makes an otherwise simple process annoyingly complex.

Clock Watching

Another approach to timing frames is to keep checking the clock until it is time to display the next image. The steps you follow are very similar to those for resetting a timer control's Interval property:

1. Display the current image.

2. Generate the next image.

3. See how much time remains before you need to present the next image. Use a Do While loop to wait until that time arrives.

You can use Visual Basic's Timer function to determine the current time, but the API function GetTickCount is faster and more accurate. GetTickCount returns the number of milliseconds that have elapsed since you started Windows. The WaitTill subroutine shown in the following code waits until a specified time arrives.

```
Declare Function GetTickCount Lib "kernel32" () As Long

' Pause until GetTickCount shows the indicated time.
Public Sub WaitTill(next_time As Long)
    Do
        DoEvents
    Loop While GetTickCount() < next_time
End Sub
```

Subroutine WaitTill uses a Do While loop to wait until the indicated time. Each time through the loop, the routine executes the Visual Basic DoEvents statement so that Windows can process events for this program and others. Note that the test to end this loop occurs at the end, so DoEvents is executed at least once.

Because WaitTill uses DoEvents, the program is at the mercy of the operating system to a certain extent. There is no easy way to tell ahead of time how long a call to DoEvents will take. If other programs are using the CPU heavily, DoEvents may take a while, making WaitTill less accurate.

The following code shows one way a program could use WaitTill to animate a series of frames.

```
' Run the animation once or until Playing is False.
Private Sub PlayImagesOnce(ByVal ms_per_frame As Integer)
```

```
Dim i As Integer
Dim next_time As Long

    ' Get the current time.
    next_time = GetTickCount

    ' Start the animation.
    For i = 0 To NumImages - 1
        ' Display the next frame.
        picCanvas.Picture = picFrame(i).Picture
        NumPlayed = NumPlayed + 1

        ' Wait till we should display the next frame.
        next_time = next_time + ms_per_frame
        WaitTill next_time

        If Not Playing Then Exit For
    Next i
End Sub
```

Example program PlayWait uses this code to display a series of images. In one test on a 133MHz Pentium processor, the program displayed 385 frames per second—almost as many frames as program PlayFast described earlier. This technique allows a program close to the best speed possible while giving precise control of the animation speed.

Displaying Files Directly

Programs PlayFast, PlayTmr, and PlayWait all load their frame bitmaps into hidden picture box controls. That lets them display the frame quickly because they are already loaded into memory.

Unfortunately, this also means they must have all the images loaded into memory at the same time. A simple animation might contain 100 frames, each holding a 250 by 250 pixel bitmap. If the bitmaps use 8-bit color, the images take 100 * 250 * 250 * 1, or more than 6MB of memory. If the bitmaps use 24-bit color, the images require more than 18MB of memory. Larger images would require even more memory.

This memory requirement can be a problem. If the program uses too much memory, the system may run out of physical memory. In that case, it must page files to disk, and that slows the entire system dramatically.

An alternative to all this memory use is to display the files as they are loaded using LoadPicture. Only one frame is loaded at a time, so the program uses much less memory. On the other hand, this method relies on the speed of the LoadPicture function reading files from the hard disk. Hard disks are much slower than memory, so this method reduces the maximum number of frames the program can display per second.

Example program PlayFile demonstrates this approach. While programs PlayFast and PlayWait displayed more than 380 frames per second on a 133MHz Pentium processor, program PlayFile can display only around 52. When the frames were stored on a relatively slow CD-ROM, PlayFile could display only 13 frames per second.

The following code shows how program PlayFile displays an animation sequence. The form-level variable FileName contains the base name for the files. For example, if the files are named Map_0.bmp, Map_1.bmp, and so on, then FileName is Map_.

```
' Run the animation once or until Playing is False.
Private Sub PlayImagesOnce(ByVal ms_per_frame As Integer)
Dim i As Integer
Dim next_time As Long

    ' Get the current time.
    next_time = GetTickCount

    ' Start the animation.
    For i = 0 To NumImages - 1
        ' Display the next frame.
        picCanvas.Picture = _
            LoadPicture(FileName & Format$(i) & ".bmp")
        NumPlayed = NumPlayed + 1

        ' Wait till we should display the next frame.
        next_time = next_time + ms_per_frame
        WaitTill next_time

        If Not Playing Then Exit For
    Next i
End Sub
```

Storing Image Bits

Instead of storing bitmap images in controls or loading them from disk, you can load the images one at a time and use the GetBitmapBits API function to save the bitmaps' pixel values in an array. Then you can use the SetBitmapBits API function to display the images when you need them. GetBitmapBits and SetBitmapBits are described in Chapter 3, Advanced Color.

The following code shows how a program might use this technique. The LoadImages routine saves the bits for a series of images in the Bytes array. Subroutine PlayImages uses SetBitmapBits to display the images.

```
Private NumImages As Integer
Private MaxImage As Integer

Private Bytes() As Byte
Private BytesPerImage As Long

' Load the images.
```

```
Private Sub LoadImages(file_name As String)
Dim base As String
Dim i As Integer
Dim bm As BITMAP

    ' Get the base file name.
    base = Left$(file_name, Len(file_name) - 5)

    ' Get the first image.
    picCanvas.AutoSize = True
    picCanvas.Picture = LoadPicture(base & "0.bmp")

    ' See how big it is.
    GetObject picCanvas.Image, Len(bm), bm
    BytesPerImage = bm.bmWidthBytes * bm.bmHeight

    ' Make room for the bitmap bits.
    MaxImage = NumImages - 1
    ReDim Bytes(1 To BytesPerImage, 0 To MaxImage)

    ' Load the images.
    On Error GoTo LoadPictureError
    For i = 0 To MaxImage
        ' Load the picture.
        picFrame.Picture = _
            LoadPicture(base & Format$(i) & ".bmp")

        ' Grab the image's bits.
        GetBitmapBits picFrame.Image, BytesPerImage, _
            Bytes(1, i)
    Next i
End Sub

' Run the animation once or until Playing is False.
Private Sub PlayImagesOnce(ByVal ms_per_frame As Integer)
Dim i As Integer
Dim next_time As Long

    ' Get the current time.
    next_time = GetTickCount

    ' Start the animation.
    For i = 0 To NumImages - 1
        ' Display the next frame.
        SetBitmapBits picCanvas.Image, _
            BytesPerImage, Bytes(1, i)
        picCanvas.Refresh
        NumPlayed = NumPlayed + 1

        ' Wait till we should display the next frame.
```

```
            next_time = next_time + ms_per_frame
            WaitTill next_time

            If Not Playing Then Exit For
        Next i
    End Sub
```

Note that this code does not save palette information, so it works only in color modes that use more than 8 bits per pixel.

This technique saves some overhead because you store only pixel values rather than a whole picture box control for each bitmap, which means you can store more images in memory without paging. GetBitmapBits and SetBitmapBits do not free you completely from paging problems, however. If you load too much data, your program will page, and the program will slow dramatically.

Another advantage to storing picture data in an array is that you can store the array in single file. Then your program needs to load only this file instead of a series of files. The single file takes roughly as much disk space as the series of files, so you will not save much disk space, but you can reduce the clutter on your disk.

Example program PlayBits uses this technique to display images. In one test on a 133MHz Pentium, PlayBits displayed 266 frames per second. This makes it slower than programs PlayFast and PlayWait. Its advantage over those programs is that it can save and load a series of images in a sequence file with a .seq extension.

The following code shows how PlayBits saves and loads sequence files. The SaveSequence subroutine stores the number of images, size of the display picture box, and number of bytes per image in the file. It then writes the entire array of image information in a single Put statement. This is much faster than writing the images into the file one at a time.

Subroutine LoadSequence reloads the number of images, size of the picture box, and number of bytes per image. It sizes the image byte array and then reads the image data in a single Get statement.

```
' Save all the images in a single file.
Private Sub SaveSequence(file_name As String)
Dim fnum As Integer

    ' Open the file.
    fnum = FreeFile
    Open file_name For Binary Access Write As #fnum

    ' Save the number of frames and the frame size.
    Put #fnum, , NumImages
    Put #fnum, , CSng(picCanvas.Width)
    Put #fnum, , CSng(picCanvas.Height)
    Put #fnum, , BytesPerImage
```

```
        ' Save the frames' bytes.
        Put #fnum, , Bytes

        ' Close the file.
        Close #fnum
End Sub

' Load a sequence of images from a single file.
Private Sub LoadSequence(file_name As String)
Dim fnum As Integer
Dim wid As Single
Dim hgt As Single

        ' Open the file.
        fnum = FreeFile
        Open file_name For Binary Access Read As #fnum

        ' Get the number of frames and the frame size.
        Get #fnum, , NumImages
        Get #fnum, , wid
        Get #fnum, , hgt
        Get #fnum, , BytesPerImage

        ' Resize the display picture box.
        picCanvas.AutoRedraw = False
        picCanvas.Width = wid
        picCanvas.Height = hgt
        picCanvas.Picture = picCanvas.Image

        ' Get the frames' bytes.
        MaxImage = NumImages - 1
        ReDim Bytes(1 To BytesPerImage, 0 To MaxImage)
        Get #fnum, , Bytes

        ' Close the file.
        Close #fnum

        ' Display the first image.
        SetBitmapBits picCanvas.Image, BytesPerImage, Bytes(1, 0)
        picCanvas.Refresh
        lblResults.Caption = ""
        txtNumFrames.Text = Format$(NumImages)
End Sub
```

The Need for Speed

The programs described so far may seem to take the pursuit for speed to extremes. Program PlayWait can display far more than the 20 or so frames per second needed for smooth animation. So why bother with such elaborate methods to achieve this overkill?

The answer is that animation performance sometimes varies greatly. The tests described in this chapter were run on a relatively fast computer that was not doing much else at the time. On a slower computer or one that was heavily loaded, the programs would not run as quickly.

Even more important, the performance of these programs depends on the size of the images they are displaying. If the images are large, the programs take more memory and must move more memory in and out of the display picture box. Program PlayFile must move more data from the hard disk. All this slows down the programs.

In one test, program PlayWait was able to display more than 285 frames per second when the images were 130 by 130 pixels in size. With 250 by 250 images, the program could display only 140 frames per second. With 800 by 600 pixel images, the program could display only 29 frames per second. Add some other programs running on a slower computer, and the program could have trouble displaying even 12 frames per second. Of course, even at this slow speed, 5 seconds of animation using 24-bit color would take up to more than 84MB of memory, so this program may be impractical in any case.

Table 8.1 shows the number of frames per second displayed by the programs discussed so far. The tests were run on a 133MHz Pentium and used the same 130 by 130 pixel 24-bit color images.

Drawing Animation

Bitmap animation gives you excellent control over the images that are displayed. When you create the frames, you can spend as much time as you like making sure they show exactly what you want. On the other hand, bitmap animation takes a huge amount of memory. Animating even a few seconds for a small image can take several megabytes.

In some applications, you can save a lot of memory by generating the frames as you need them rather than storing them as images ahead of time. This gives a space-versus-time tradeoff that is common in computer programming. Generating images as you need them saves memory, but it may take more time.

Table 8.1 Frames per Second

PROGRAM	FRAMES PER SECOND	ADVANTAGES	DISADVANTAGES
PlayFast	395	Very fast. Simple.	No speed control.
PlayTmr	96	Adequate speed control.	Slower.
PlayWait	385	Fast. Excellent speed control.	Somewhat complex.
PlayFile	52	Less memory required.	Slow.
PlayBits	266	Very fast. Images in one file.	Very complex.

For example, the files Mand1_0.bmp, Mand1_1.bmp, and so forth on the CD-ROM form an animation that zooms in on part of the Mandelbrot set. Some of those images took several minutes to generate. A typical personal computer cannot generate those images quickly enough to display them in an animation program.

If your program can generate images quickly enough, you can take a couple of different approaches to displaying them. The clear-and-redraw method is simple and uses only Visual Basic graphic methods. It is fairly slow, however, and limited to a few dozen frames per second for a simple animation.

The save-and-restore method achieves better speed by updating only the parts of the image that change between frames. This technique also uses only Visual Basic graphic methods.

By using the GetBitmapBits and SetBitmapBits API functions, you can improve the speed of these methods to make them useful in a wider variety of circumstances.

Clear and Redraw

In the simplest form of drawing animation, you clear the entire picture and redraw it for each frame. Example program Stocks1, shown in Figure 8.2, uses this method to animate a random stock portfolio.

The following code shows how program Stocks1 works. The stock price data is stored in the array Data where Data(F, S) is the price for stock number S in frame number F.

Before starting the animation, the program draws the animation's background on the pic-Graph picture box. It then sets the control's Picture property equal to its Image property. That makes the image a permanent part of the control's background. Before it draws each frame, the program uses the Cls method to clear the picture box and restore this background quickly and easily. It then draws rectangles to represent the stock values.

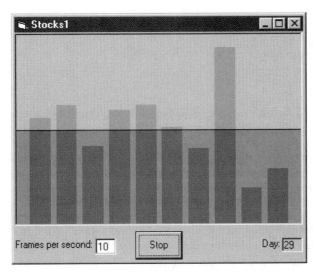

Figure 8.2   Program Stocks1 animates a random stock portfolio.

```
' Play the animation.
Private Sub PlayImages(ByVal ms_per_frame As Long)
Dim frame As Integer
Dim stock As Integer
Dim next_time As Long

    ' Start the animation.
    next_time = GetTickCount()
    For frame = 1 To NUM_FRAMES
        ' Restore the background.
        picGraph.Cls

        ' Draw the stock data.
        For stock = 1 To NUM_STOCKS
            If Data(frame, stock) > 50 Then
                picGraph.Line (stock, 0)- _
                    (stock + 0.75, 50), _
                    vbRed, BF
                picGraph.Line (stock, 50)- _
                    (stock + 0.75, Data(frame, stock)), _
                    vbGreen, BF
            Else
                picGraph.Line (stock, 0)- _
                    (stock + 0.75, Data(frame, stock)), _
                vbRed, BF
            End If
        Next stock
        picGraph.Line (0, 50)- _
            (NUM_STOCKS + 1.25, 50), vbBlack, BF
        lblDay.Caption = Format$(frame)

        ' Wait until it's time for the next frame.
        next_time = next_time + ms_per_frame
        WaitTill next_time

        If Not Playing Then Exit For
    Next frame
End Sub
```

Program Stocks1 animates a series of precomputed values. That makes sense for a stock application that displays historical data.

Example program Bounce1, shown in Figure 8.3, takes a different approach. This program displays a collection of balls bouncing in front of a background of rectangles. Instead of using precomputed data, program Bounce1 generates the data it needs as it displays the frames.

The following code shows how program Bounce1 displays its collection of bouncing balls. The BallX and BallY arrays store the balls' coordinates. BallDx and BallDy store the distances in pixels that each ball moves between frames. The BallRadius and BallColor

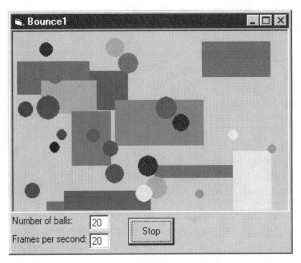

Figure 8.3 Program Bounce1 generates data when it is needed.

arrays tell the program how to draw each ball. The variables xmax and ymax store the largest coordinates inside the picCourt control where the program draws the balls.

For each frame, the program adds each ball's BallDx and BallDy values to its current position. It then checks that the ball lies completely within the picture box. If the ball does falls outside, the program moves it back into the picture box and reverses the sign of the corresponding BallDx or BallDy value. For example, if a ball crosses the left edge of the drawing area, the program sets BallDx(ball) = -BallDx(ball). That reverses the ball's direction of movement and makes it appear to bounce off the left wall.

```
Private xmax As Integer
Private ymax As Integer

Private NumBalls As Integer
Private BallX() As Integer
Private BallY() As Integer
Private BallDx() As Integer
Private BallDy() As Integer
Private BallRadius() As Integer
Private BallColor() As Long

' Play the animation.
Private Sub PlayImages(ByVal ms_per_frame As Long)
Dim ball As Integer
Dim next_time As Long

    ' Get the current time.
    next_time = GetTickCount()

    ' Start the animation.
```

```
Do While Playing
    NumPlayed = NumPlayed + 1

    ' Restore the background.
    picCourt.Cls

    ' Draw the balls.
    For ball = 1 To NumBalls
        picCourt.FillColor = BallColor(ball)
        picCourt.Circle _
            (BallX(ball), BallY(ball)), _
            BallRadius(ball), BallColor(ball)
    Next ball

    ' Move the balls for the next frame,
    ' keeping them within picCourt.
    For ball = 1 To NumBalls
        BallX(ball) = BallX(ball) + BallDx(ball)
        If BallX(ball) < BallRadius(ball) Then
            BallX(ball) = 2 * BallRadius(ball) - _
                BallX(ball)
            BallDx(ball) = -BallDx(ball)
        ElseIf BallX(ball) > xmax - BallRadius(ball) Then
            BallX(ball) = 2 * (xmax - _
                BallRadius(ball)) - BallX(ball)
            BallDx(ball) = -BallDx(ball)
        End If

        BallY(ball) = BallY(ball) + BallDy(ball)
        If BallY(ball) < BallRadius(ball) Then
            BallY(ball) = 2 * BallRadius(ball) - _
                BallY(ball)
            BallDy(ball) = -BallDy(ball)
        ElseIf BallY(ball) > ymax - BallRadius(ball) Then
            BallY(ball) = 2 * (ymax - _
                BallRadius(ball)) - BallY(ball)
            BallDy(ball) = -BallDy(ball)
        End If
    Next ball

    ' Wait until it's time for the next frame.
    next_time = next_time + ms_per_frame
    WaitTill next_time

    If Not Playing Then Exit Do
Loop
End Sub
```

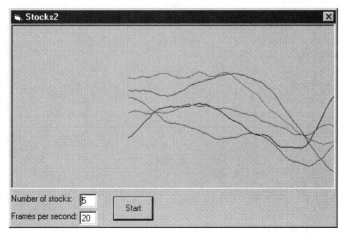

Figure 8.4 Program Stocks2 uses PaintPicture to make curves scroll across the drawing area.

Program Stocks2, shown in Figure 8.4, uses a slightly different approach. Instead of clearing the entire drawing area, this program uses the PaintPicture method to copy the current image shifted slightly to the left. It then draws its newest data on the right. This makes the stock value curves scroll across the form from right to left.

Save and Restore

Another strategy for animating moving objects is to save an image of the part of the background beneath each object. To draw the next frame, use the saved images to redraw the background. Under some circumstances, saving and restoring the parts of the image that change is faster than using Cls to erase the whole image. After restoring the original background, move the images and draw them in their new locations.

Example program Bounce2 uses the following code to animate bouncing balls. Before it draws the balls for a frame, it uses PaintPicture to save an image of the area under each ball in the picHidden picture box array. It then draws the balls and waits until it should display the next frame. At that time, the program restores the saved areas before continuing with the next frame.

```
' Play the animation.
Private Sub PlayImages(ByVal ms_per_frame As Long)
Dim ball As Integer
Dim next_time As Long

    ' Get the current time.
    next_time = GetTickCount()

    ' Start the animation.
    Do While Playing
        NumPlayed = NumPlayed + 1
```

```vbnet
' Save the background where the balls
' will be placed.
For ball = 1 To NumBalls
    picHidden(ball).PaintPicture _
        picCourt.Picture, _
        0, 0, _
        2 * BallRadius(ball) + 4, _
        2 * BallRadius(ball) + 4, _
        BallX(ball) - BallRadius(ball) - 2, _
        BallY(ball) - BallRadius(ball) - 2, _
        2 * BallRadius(ball) + 4, _
        2 * BallRadius(ball) + 4
    picHidden(ball).Picture = picHidden(ball).Image
Next ball


' Draw the balls.
For ball = 1 To NumBalls
    picCourt.FillColor = BallColor(ball)
    picCourt.Circle _
        (BallX(ball), BallY(ball)), _
        BallRadius(ball), BallColor(ball)
Next ball


' Wait until it's time for the next frame.
next_time = next_time + ms_per_frame
WaitTill next_time


' Restore the background information.
For ball = 1 To NumBalls
    picCourt.PaintPicture _
        picHidden(ball).Picture, _
        BallX(ball) - BallRadius(ball) - 2, _
        BallY(ball) - BallRadius(ball) - 2, _
        2 * BallRadius(ball) + 4, _
        2 * BallRadius(ball) + 4, _
        0, 0, _
        2 * BallRadius(ball) + 4, _
        2 * BallRadius(ball) + 4
Next ball


' Move the balls for the next frame,
' keeping them within picCourt.
For ball = 1 To NumBalls
    BallX(ball) = BallX(ball) + BallDx(ball)
    If BallX(ball) < BallRadius(ball) Then
        BallX(ball) = 2 * BallRadius(ball) - _
            BallX(ball)
        BallDx(ball) = -BallDx(ball)
    ElseIf BallX(ball) > xmax - BallRadius(ball) Then
        BallX(ball) = 2 * (xmax - _
```

```
                    BallRadius(ball)) - BallX(ball)
              BallDx(ball) = -BallDx(ball)
          End If

          BallY(ball) = BallY(ball) + BallDy(ball)
          If BallY(ball) < BallRadius(ball) Then
              BallY(ball) = 2 * BallRadius(ball) - _
                  BallY(ball)
              BallDy(ball) = -BallDy(ball)
          ElseIf BallY(ball) > ymax - BallRadius(ball) Then
              BallY(ball) = 2 * (ymax - _
                  BallRadius(ball)) - BallY(ball)
              BallDy(ball) = -BallDy(ball)
          End If
      Next ball

      If Not Playing Then Exit Do
    Loop
End Sub
```

This technique works well when the animation is moving a few small objects across a large background. In that case, the program needs to save and restore just a few small areas. The clear and redraw technique, on the other hand, would need to clear a large background area.

Using the API

Programs Stocks2, Bounce1, and Bounce2 all have marginal performance. For a reasonably small drawing area on a 133MHz Pentium, program Bounce2 can display around 12 frames per second. Program Stocks2 can display only around 8 frames per second. This is just barely fast enough to create meaningful animation.

You can improve the speed of these programs significantly using API functions. Programs Stocks2 and Bounce2 use PaintPicture to copy parts of pictures. You can make them faster if you use the BitBlt API function instead.

Program Bounce1 uses the Cls method to restore its background before drawing a new frame in the animation. To make this program faster, save the background's bitmap information in a byte array using the GetBitmapBits API function. Then instead of using Cls to restore the background, use SetBitmapBits. Programs Stocks2b, Bounce1b, and Bounce2b use these methods to improve performance.

Table 8.2 summarizes the speeds of these techniques. Programs Bounce1b and Bounce2b that use the API functions are always faster than programs Bounce1 and Bounce2, but neither is always fastest. Bounce1b is faster when the program is moving many objects. Bounce2b is faster when the program is moving only a few objects.

Table 8.2 Speeds of Different Animation Techniques

METHOD	PROGRAM	FRAMES/SECOND (2 BALLS)	FRAMES/SECOND (20 BALLS)
Cls clear and redraw	Bounce1	15	13
PaintPicture save and restore	Bounce2	12	2
SetBitmapBits clear and redraw	Bounce1b	36	27
BitBlt save and restore	Bounce2b	47	12

Summary

Producing animation that works well on all sorts of computers can be tricky. Depending on the size of the images, the speed of the computer, and the other programs running on the system, it may be difficult to present the images quickly enough to provide smooth animation.

Try the different techniques described in this chapter and select the one best suited for your application. Use the simplest technique that gives good enough performance on your system.

9

Advanced Animation

The previous chapter describes methods for adding animation to your programs. It explains how to present images at regular intervals to produce the illusion of smooth motion.

This chapter describes ways a program can determine what is displayed by the animation. It uses the concepts of simulation, scripting, and sprites to determine how animation should work. It explains methods for generating animation sequences, including tweening and morphing, a technique that uses image processing methods to produce fascinating animated sequences.

This chapter also explains a variety of scene transition effects. Using these techniques, you can add extra interest to even the simplest graphical programs.

Controlling Animation

When you create the frames for a bitmap animation, you determine the exact color of each pixel in every frame. When your program creates frames as it runs, you need some method to control the way in which the program generates the frames. The sections that follow describe two important methods for controlling animation: simulation and scripting.

Simulation

In a simulation, a program uses a set of rules to determine how objects in the animation behave over time. In many programs, the rules are based on the physical laws of the universe. These laws include those that describe falling objects, elastic collisions, the force of gravity between objects, and the way water flows through pipes. Often these laws are greatly simplified to make calculations faster. If the calculations between frames take too long, the program cannot display the frames quickly enough to produce the illusion of smooth motion.

The bouncing object programs presented in Chapter 8 all perform a simulation of moving objects. They use a simple set of physical laws to determine how each object moves over time. In these programs the laws of movement are:

- Objects have constant velocities with X and Y components Vx and Vy.
- If an object is at position (Cx, Cy) at a given time, in the next frame, it has position (Cx + Vx, Cy + Vy).
- If an object touches the left or right edge of the drawing area, it bounces back, reversing the direction of its X velocity component.
- If an object touches the top or bottom edge of the drawing area, it bounces back, reversing the direction of its Y velocity component.

Program Stocks2 also generates its data using rules. Its rules make it select random stock values with some bounding operations to ensure that the values do not vary too quickly.

Simple planetary motion is governed by the physical laws:

```
F = m₁ * m₂ / d²
```

```
F = m * a
```

The first equation gives the gravitational force that two objects exert on each other. In this equation, m_1 and m_2 are the masses of two objects, and d is the distance between them.

You can rewrite the second equation as a = F/m. In other words, if you apply a force F to an object of mass m, it accelerates by amount a.

Using these two equations, you can build a simulation of planetary motion. The program must keep track of each object's mass, position, and velocity.

The main difference between this simulation and the previous bouncing ball programs is that this program calculates acceleration. For each frame, the program computes the force each object exerts on the others. It does this using the equation $F = m_1 * m_2/d^2$ for each pair of objects.

Once it has a force acting on an object, the program uses the second equation to compute the acceleration of the object due to that force. If the force F is acting on an object with mass m, its acceleration is a = F/m.

Acceleration is the rate of change in the velocity of an object. The acceleration due to another object is in the direction of the other object. To find the X and Y components of the acceleration, the program multiplies the acceleration by the X and Y components of the vector from one object to the other. In other words, if dx and dy are the distances between the two objects in the X and Y directions, and d = Sqr(dx * dx + dy * dy) is the distance between the objects, the components of the acceleration are:

```
X component = dx / d * acceleration
Y component = dy / d * acceleration
```

Once the program has calculated the acceleration components for an object, it adds the components to the object's velocity. It can then use the object's velocity to compute its new position.

Example program Planets uses these equations to simulate planetary motion. Select the File menu's Open command to load a file containing object data. The file should begin with the number of planets defined by the file. Then for each planet, the file should contain the planet's initial position, velocity, mass, and the color the program should use when drawing it.

For example, the following sample values describe two planets. The first begins centered at position (100, 175) with velocity components 0 in the X direction and –8 in the Y direction. It has mass 20 and color &H880000&, which is dark blue. The Ch9 directory on the CD-ROM contains several planet data files with .pla extensions.

```
2
100 175 0 -8 20 &H880000&
300 175 0  8 20 &H008800&
```

The following Visual Basic code shows the main animation subroutine used by program Planets.

```
' Make the planets move until Playing is false.
Private Sub PlayImages(ByVal ms_per_frame As Long)
Const F_SCALE = 1000

Dim next_time As Long
Dim i As Integer
Dim j As Integer
Dim dx As Double
Dim dy As Double
Dim d2 As Double
Dim d As Double
Dim f As Double
Dim a_d As Double

    ' Start the animation.
    next_time = GetTickCount()
    Do While Playing
        ' Calculate the forces on the planets.
        For i = 1 To NumPlanets - 1
            For j = i + 1 To NumPlanets
                ' Calculate the force between planets
                ' i and j. Translate the force into a
                ' change in velocity.
                dx = Cx(i) - Cx(j)
                dy = Cy(i) - Cy(j)
                d2 = dx * dx + dy * dy
                f = F_SCALE * M(i) * M(j) / d2
                d = Sqr(d2)
```

```
            a_d = f / M(i) / d
            Vx(i) = Vx(i) - a_d * dx
            Vy(i) = Vy(i) - a_d * dy

            a_d = f / M(j) / d
            Vx(j) = Vx(j) + a_d * dx
            Vy(j) = Vy(j) + a_d * dy
        Next j
    Next i

    ' Move all the planets.
    For i = 1 To NumPlanets
        Cx(i) = Cx(i) + Vx(i)
        Cy(i) = Cy(i) + Vy(i)
    Next i

    ' Restore the background.
    SetBitmapBits picCanvas.Image, _
        BitmapNumBytes, Bytes(1, 1)

    ' Redraw the planets.
    For i = 1 To NumPlanets
        picCanvas.FillColor = Clr(i)
        picCanvas.Circle (Cx(i), Cy(i)), R(i), Clr(i)
    Next i

    ' Wait until it's time for the next frame.
    next_time = next_time + ms_per_frame
    WaitTill next_time
  Loop
End Sub
```

Example program Cannon uses gravitational rules to simulate cannon fire. Enter the cannon's angle and the projectile's initial speed. At each step in the animation, the program subtracts a downward acceleration due to gravity from the projectile's vertical velocity component.

Using other physical laws, you can build other animation programs that simulate colliding balls, springs, objects in magnetic fields, objects in flight, and so forth.

Scripts

Simulation programs such as the Bounce programs, Planets, and Cannon use physical laws to determine where objects should be drawn. Given information about the simulation, the program uses the laws to decide how the objects move.

A script explicitly lists the locations of the objects for different frames in the animation. A script must describe everything the program needs to know to display objects properly. That might include the position, orientation, shape, and color of the objects being displayed.

The Stocks1 program described earlier in this chapter uses a simple kind of script. When it starts, the program fills its Data array with random stock values. The value of stock number S during frame F is given by Data(F, S). The Data array indicates exactly what values the animation should display during each frame, so it forms a script for the program's animation.

Example program Robot, shown in Figure 9.1, is a robot script editor. The program's drawing area shows a stick figure robot. Using the commands in the Frames menu, you can add or delete frames from the script. Use the scrollbar to select a frame to edit. Then use the mouse to click and drag the robot's control points. The program saves the robot's position and the angles at which its arms and legs are bent in an array entry corresponding to the frame you have selected. This array forms the script for the animation.

When you are satisfied with the script, select the type of animation you want to see, and click the Play button. If you select the Once option, the program runs the animation once and then stops. If you select Looping, the program plays the script repeatedly until you click the Stop button. If you click the Reversing button, the program runs the script forward and backward until you stop it.

To make working with scripts easier, the program's File menu contains commands for loading and saving scripts. The file Jacks.rob in the Ch9 directory on the CD-ROM contains a script that makes the robot do jumping jacks. Try running this script in a reversing animation at 20 frames per second. The script file Run.rob makes the robot run. Play this file in a looping animation.

This simple scripted animation is quite fast. With a 133MHz Pentium, it can display more than 400 frames per second. The program achieves its remarkable performance by using a blank background. Because the background is blank, the program can set the drawing area's AutoRedraw property to False and quickly clear it using SetBitmapBits. If the

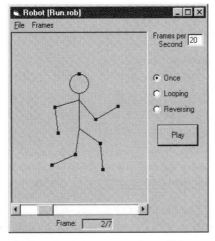

Figure 9.1   Program Robot editing a robot script.

background was not blank, the program would need to use the techniques described earlier in this chapter to redraw it.

This program can display images much faster than a typical monitor can display them. When it displays more than 30 or so frames per second, the program can cause strange temporal aliasing effects.

Because the program is so fast, you can extend it to animate much more complicated scenes involving many objects while still displaying the 20 or so frames per second you need to produce smooth animation.

Sprites

A *sprite* is a programming abstraction that represents some object in an animation. A sprite should contain all the information needed to describe, update, and draw the object it represents. To make a program showing an animation of bouncing balls, you could make a sprite to represent each ball. The sprites would need to keep track of the position and velocity of the balls they represent. They would also need to be able to move their balls and to draw them when necessary.

In Visual Basic, you can build a sprite using a class. You can create a different class for each different kind of sprite your program needs. You might have classes for sprites representing bouncing balls, spinning rectangles, growing and shrinking triangles, and so forth.

All sprite classes should provide two key methods: MoveSprite and DrawSprite. The main program can use these methods to make the sprites move and display themselves. The sprite classes should also define whatever data they need to draw their particular objects.

To give the main program a consistent way to manage the sprites, create a generic Sprite class. Make this class declare public MoveSprite and DrawSprite methods. This class does not need to implement these routines; it merely defines them as shown in the following code.

```
' Move the sprite keeping it in bounds.
Public Sub MoveSprite( _
    ByVal xmin As Integer, ByVal xmax As Integer, _
    ByVal ymin As Integer, ByVal ymax As Integer)

End Sub


' Draw the sprite on the PictureBox.
Public Sub DrawSprite(pic As PictureBox)

End Sub
```

Now add the statement Implements Sprite to the other sprite classes. That tells Visual Basic that the class implements the MoveSprite and DrawSprite methods defined by the Sprite class.

At this point, Visual Basic adds a Sprite section to the class's code. If you click on the left ComboBox in the class's code window, you will see the Sprite section. Select that section, and you will find that Visual Basic has defined stub routines named Sprite_MoveSprite and Sprite_DrawSprite. Enter the code needed by the particular sprite class in those routines.

The following code shows a complete BallSprite class. The private variables and the InitializeBall method are specific to this class and are not defined by the generic Sprite class. Other sprite classes will have their own variables and initialization methods.

```
' Bouncing ball sprite.
Option Explicit

Implements Sprite

Private Radius As Integer
Private Cx As Integer        ' Position of center.
Private Cy As Integer
Private Vx As Integer        ' Velocity.
Private Vy As Integer
Private Color As Long

' Initialize the ball.
Public Sub InitializeBall(ByVal new_radius As Integer, _
    ByVal new_cx As Integer, ByVal new_cy As Integer, _
    ByVal new_vx As Integer, ByVal new_vy As Integer, _
    ByVal new_color As Long)

    Radius = new_radius
    Cx = new_cx
    Cy = new_cy
    Vx = new_vx
    Vy = new_vy
    Color = new_color
End Sub

' Add the velocity components to the sprite's
' position components.
Public Sub Sprite_MoveSprite( _
    ByVal xmin As Integer, ByVal xmax As Integer, _
    ByVal ymin As Integer, ByVal ymax As Integer)

    Cx = Cx + Vx
    Cy = Cy + Vy

    ' Keep the object within the drawing area.
    If (Cx < xmin) Then
        Cx = 2 * xmin - Cx
        Vx = -Vx
    ElseIf (Cx > xmax) Then
        Cx = 2 * xmax - Cx
```

```
            Vx = -Vx
        End If
        If (Cy < ymin) Then
            Cy = 2 * ymin - Cy
            Vy = -Vy
        ElseIf (Cy > ymax) Then
            Cy = 2 * ymax - Cy
            Vy = -Vy
        End If
    End Sub

    ' Draw the circle on the indicated picture box.
    Public Sub Sprite_DrawSprite(ByVal pic As PictureBox)
        pic.FillColor = Color
        pic.Circle (Cx, Cy), Radius, Color
    End Sub
```

Because each sprite class implements the generic Sprite methods, the program can treat the different kinds of sprites uniformly. The program can create a sprite of any sprite class and assign it to a variable of type Sprite. The program can then invoke the object's MoveSprite and DrawSprite methods without worrying about which kind of object it really is.

Example program Sprites, shown in Figure 9.2, uses this method to animate balls, triangles, and rectangles that bounce and spin.

The following code shows how program Sprites animates its sprite objects. References to the sprites are stored in the Sprites array. For each frame, the program loops through the Sprites array telling each sprite to draw itself and then move itself to a new position for the next frame.

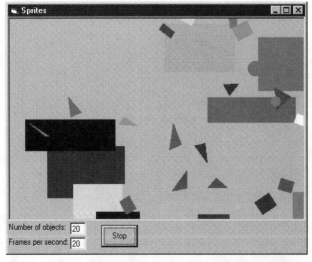

Figure 9.2   Program Sprites draws balls, triangles, and rectangles that bounce and spin.

Note that this code does not need to know what kind of sprite object it is using. The entries in the Sprites array can be from the BallSprite, TriangleSprite, or Rectangle-Sprite class. As long as the entries are all from classes that implement the generic Sprite class, the program can use their MoveSprite and DrawSprite methods.

```
Private NumSprites As Integer
Private Sprites() As Sprite

' Play the animation.
Private Sub PlayImages(ByVal ms_per_frame As Long)
Dim sprite_number As Integer
Dim next_time As Long

    ' Get the current time.
    next_time = GetTickCount()

    ' Start the animation.
    Do While Playing
        NumPlayed = NumPlayed + 1

        ' Restore the background.
        SetBitmapBits picCanvas.Image, _
            BitmapNumBytes, Bytes(1, 1)

        ' Draw and move the sprites.
        For sprite_number = 1 To NumSprites
            Sprites(sprite_number).DrawSprite picCanvas
            Sprites(sprite_number).MoveSprite _
                xmin, xmax, ymin, ymax
        Next sprite_number

        ' Wait until it's time for the next frame.
        next_time = next_time + ms_per_frame
        WaitTill next_time
    Loop
End Sub
```

Sprites make it easier to manage many different kinds of graphic objects, but they do come at a price. Calling the sprite methods slows the animation. In some cases, the extra overhead required to use sprites may make the program too slow to be usable. If your program can display only five frames per second, you should probably consider rewriting it. You might need to move sprite data into global variables and execute the moving and drawing code in the PlayImages subroutine rather than in sprite subroutines.

Tweening and Morphing

In traditional cartoon animation, all the frames are sketched, cleaned up, inked, and colored by hand. A feature-length animation might run 70 or 80 minutes. At one to two dozen frames per second, that can add up to more than 100,000 frames, all drawn by hand. To make such an enormous undertaking possible, animators work in large teams.

The 100,000 frames must be drawn consistently. No one wants the main characters to become taller or thinner during the film. One way to make the frames consistent is to have a single animator draw every frame. This would be a long process, with no guarantee that the animator's style will remain unchanged over the several years that would probably be needed to finish.

A more common strategy is to have senior animators draw frames that show key action in the script. Then less senior animators draw the frames in between the key frames. These animators are called *inbetweeners* or just *tweeners*, and the frames they draw are called *tweens*. By frequently comparing the tweens with the key frames, the animators can keep all the drawings consistent.

The sections that follow explain how you can add tweening to your Visual Basic programs. Tweening lets you quickly generate extra animation frames that can make motion appear smoother.

Tweening

The general problem in tweening is to smoothly transform the objects in one key frame into the objects in the next. To keep things simple for the time being, consider only frames that are composed of line segments. Then you can break this problem down into one of transforming the line segments that make up the objects.

Figure 9.3 shows a line segment in two key frames. The goal is to create tweens that smoothly transform the line segment on the left into the segment on the right. The following sections describe three approaches you can take.

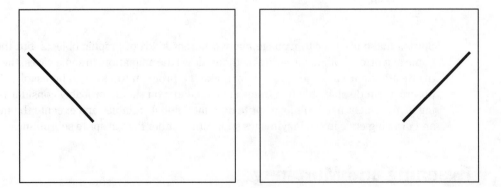

Figure 9.3 The goal of tweening is to smoothly transform one key frame into another.

Endpoint Interpolation

In endpoint interpolation, you use linear interpolation to compute the endpoints of the line segment in the tweens. Suppose you want to create seven tweens between two key frames. Starting from the first key frame, you move the segment's endpoints one-eighth of the distance closer to their final positions during each tween. This produces seven sets of endpoints evenly spaced between the key frames. Another one-eighth of the distance gives the final segment's position.

The following code fragment shows how you could compute the endpoint positions. The values (x11, y11) and (x12, y12) are the endpoint coordinates in the first key frame, and (x21, y21) and (x22, y22) are the coordinates in the second.

```
Dim i As Integer
Dim x1 As Single
Dim y1 As Single
Dim x2 As Single
Dim y2 As Single
Dim dx1 As Single
Dim dy1 As Single
Dim dx2 As Single
Dim dy2 As Single

    ' Compute the differences between the tweens.
    dx1 = (x21 - x11) / (num_tweens + 1)
    dy1 = (y21 - y11) / (num_tweens + 1)
    dx2 = (x22 - x12) / (num_tweens + 1)
    dy2 = (y22 - y12) / (num_tweens + 1)

    ' Compute the tweens' end points.
    x1 = x11
    y1 = y11
    x2 = x12
    y2 = y12
    For i = 1 To num_tweens
        ' Compute the new endpoint coordinates.
        x1 = x1 + dx1
        y1 = y1 + dy1
        x2 = x2 + dx2
        y2 = y2 + dy2

        ' Save the tween end points (x1, y1) and (x2, y2).
            :
    Next i
```

Figure 9.4 shows the resulting frames for the segments in Figure 9.3. The segments are drawn on the same picture so you can see how they change from frame to frame.

Example program TweenEnd creates tweens using endpoint interpolation. Select Load from the File menu to load a data file describing an animation. This file should begin

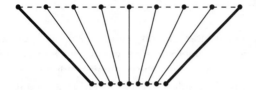

Figure 9.4 Tweening with endpoint interpolation.

with the number of frames in the animation. Then for each frame, it should contain the number of polylines making up the frame.

Each polyline consists of a number of points that should be connected to form a continuous series of line segments. For each polyline in each frame, the file must contain the number of points in the polyline followed by the coordinates of the points themselves.

For example, the file Square.twe, which is located in the Ch9 directory on the CD-ROM, defines two frames. Each frame shows a square consisting of a single polyline made up of five points. The comments to the right have been added to make the following listing easier to understand and are not part of the file.

```
2               ' 2 frames in the animation.
1               ' 1 polyline in the first frame.
5               ' 5 points in the polyline.
50, 50          ' Point data.
50, 150
150, 150
150, 50
50, 50
1               ' 1 polyline in the second frame.
5               ' 5 points in the polyline.
50, 150         ' Point data.
150, 150
150, 50
50, 50
50, 150
```

Endpoint interpolation is relatively simple and fast. It also ensures that segments that share an endpoint in the key frames share an endpoint in the tweens, too. Unfortunately, it can also distort the image. As you can see in Figure 9.4, the segment in the middle tween is significantly shorter than those in the key frames.

In some animations, this distortion may not be noticeable. The file Smile.twe defines three frames showing a sad face turning happy. Run the TweenEnd program and load this file. Create five tweens between the key frames and run the animation once at 20 frames per second. The endpoint interpolation introduces some distortion in the tweens. The curves in the key frames do not have the same shape, however, so the changes between key frames are distortions as well. Any distortion introduced by the tweens is lost in the larger distortion between the key frames, and the animation appears smooth.

In other animations, the distortion caused by endpoint interpolation can be very noticeable. The file Square.twe describes two frames showing the same square rotated by 90 degrees. Run TweenEnd and load this file. Create 10 tweens between the key frames, and run the animation reversing at 20 frames per second. As you watch the animation, you can see the distorting effects of endpoint interpolation. As the square rotates back and forth, it shrinks and grows noticeably.

One way to reduce these distortions is to create more key frames. By increasing the number of key frames, you reduce the amount of change between them so the tweens cannot distort the image as much. Of course, this requires that you create more key frames, the very thing that tweening was invented to prevent.

The file Square2.twe shows the same animation as Square.twe, with one extra key frame in the middle. Load this file, and create five tweens between key frames. When you run the animation, you will still see some distortion but not as much as before.

Script Interpolation

If your animation is controlled by a script, you can create tweens by interpolating the script parameters. For example, the Robot program described earlier in this chapter uses several control variables to determine the robot's position. To create tweens, you can interpolate the values of these variables between key frames.

Because the animation is controlled by script variables, tweening does not introduce distortions. No matter what parameters the interpolations create, the program can create the corresponding scene without distortion.

Example program TweenRob creates tweens for simple robot scripts by interpolating script variables. Select the File menu's Load command to load the file Jacks.rob. This file defines seven frames that make the robot do jumping jacks. Run the file as a reversing animation at 20 frames per second, and you will see relatively smooth motion.

Now load the file Jackstw.rob. This file defines only three jumping jacks frames. Enter 10 for the number of tweens to create and press the Tween button. Then run the file as a reversing animation at 60 frames per second. You should run this animation at about three times the speed of the other because it uses about three times as many frames to define the same amount of action. This gives you roughly the same number of jumps per second. The file Jackstw.rob takes less room to store than Jacks.rob because it defines only three frames instead of seven. You can still use it to produce smooth animation by creating tweens.

It is interesting to see what happens if you remove the middle frame from the file Jackstw.rob. Load the file, select the second frame, and invoke the Frames menu's Delete command. Then create 10 tweens between the two remaining frames and run the animation. You will see a very different result than you saw before.

During the parameter interpolations, the program "takes the shortest path" from one parameter value to the next. After you delete the middle key frame, the shortest path between the remaining frames looks more like a toe touch than a jumping jack. When you tween, you must provide enough key frames to determine the route the program takes between them.

Tween Smoothing

When you use linear interpolation to compute tween values, values vary smoothly between key frames. When you reach a key frame, however, there is a sudden change in the direction the key values are moving. In the previous tweens, the key values have been moving toward this key frame's value. Now they start moving toward those of the next key frame. Figure 9.5 shows a graph of one of an animation's parameters. For instance, this might be the value of the X coordinate of one of a segment's endpoints during endpoint interpolation. Notice the sharp changes in direction at the key frames.

Sudden changes in the movement of the parameters can make the animation appear jerky. The file Square3.twe describes four frames that animate a moving square. The square begins in the upper left of the screen, moves down to the lower left, across to the lower right, and then up to the upper right. The square makes large changes in direction when it reaches the key frames. If you load the file in program TweenEnd, create 10 tweens between the key frames, and run the animation, the motion changes abruptly when it reaches the key frames.

One way to reduce the jerkiness is to create more key frames. By making the differences between the key frames smaller, you reduce the size of the jerks. Of course, this approach requires that you create and store more key frames.

Another way to prevent this jerkiness is to smooth the values used by the tweens as shown in Figure 9.6. Instead of using linear interpolation, you can compute values using some sort of smoothing function. One such function is a *Hermite curve*.

Suppose you want to create a smoothly varying set of values connecting the two end-points (x1, y1) and (x2, y2). Suppose you also want the tangents at the two endpoints to

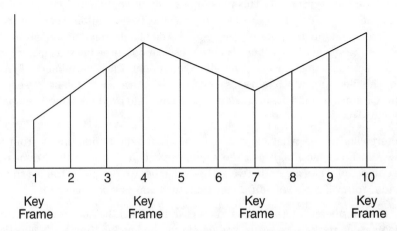

Figure 9.5 Linear interpolation causes sudden changes in a variable's direction of change at key frames.

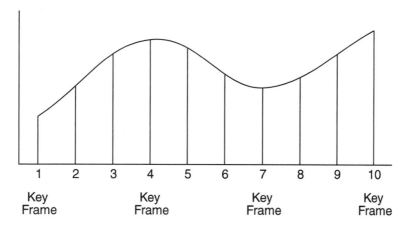

1	2	3	4	5	6	7	8	9	10
Key Frame			Key Frame			Key Frame			Key Frame

Figure 9.6 Smoothing the values used by tweens can reduce jerkiness.

be the vectors <dx1, dy1> and <dx2, dy2>. Then the coordinates of the points in the Hermite curve between the two endpoints are given by the equations:

```
x(t) = x1 * (2 * t³ - 3 * t² + 1) + x2 * (-2 * t³ + 3 * t²) +
       dx1 * (t³ - 2 * t² + t) + dx2 * (t³ - t²)
y(t) = y1 * (2 * t³ - 3 * t² + 1) + y2 * (-2 * t³ + 3 * t²) +
       dy1 * (t³ - 2 * t² + t) + dy2 * (t³ - t²)
```

Here the value t varies from 0 to 1. Figure 9.7 shows two points connected by a Hermite curve. The dashed lines show the tangent vectors at the endpoints.

To create smoothly varying tweens, use these equations with values of t that are multiples of 1/(number of tweens + 1). For example, to create nine tweens, use the values t = 1/10, 2/10, 3/10, ..., 9/10.

To use the Hermite equations for smooth tweening, you need to pick tangent vectors at the endpoints. Suppose you are connecting the key frame points p1, p2, p3, and p4. To make the curve smooth at the point p2, you need the tangent vector at p2 in the p1-p2 curve to be parallel to the tangent vector at p2 in the p2–p3 curve. Figure 9.8 shows this situation.

One way to ensure that the tangents are parallel is to make them parallel to the line connecting the points on either side of the one you are examining. In Figure 9.8, the tangents at point p2 are parallel to the line connecting points p1 and p3.

Example program TweenSmo uses Hermite curves to create smooth tweens. Load the file Square3.twe and create 10 tweens between the key frames. When you run this animation, the motion appears much smoother than it is in program TweenEnd.

Morphing

Tweening is useful for creating frames that fit between key frames. There is no reason you can use tweening only on similar frames. You can also use tweening on two images

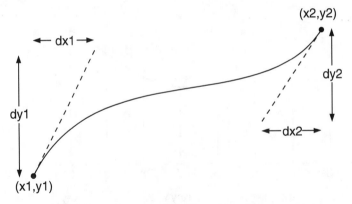

Figure 9.7 Two points connected by a Hermite curve.

that have very little in common. This creates a sequence of images that transforms one image into another that may be very little like the first. Creating such a sequence is called *morphing*.

The data file Morph.twe contains two key frames. One shows a truck, and the other shows a plane. Corresponding shapes in the drawings contain the same number of points. For example, the main body of both the truck and plane contain 32 points.

The points are arranged in the two frames in generally the same order. The first point in both the truck and plane bodies is at the lower left. The other points proceed counterclockwise around the two figures. Keeping the points approximately lined up allows tweening to transform the first shape into the second without major twisting and tearing.

Load the file Morph.twe in either tweening program: TweenEnd or TweenSmo. Create tweens, and run the animation to morph the truck into the plane. Because the two key frames have little in common, this animation looks best if you create a lot of tweens. If you have a fast computer, create 50 tweens and run the animation at 50 frames per second. If this animation is too slow on your computer, try again with fewer tweens until your computer can display them all in about one second.

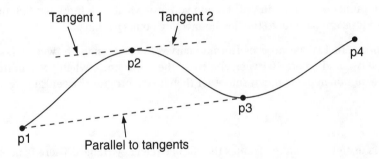

Figure 9.8 Connecting two Hermite curves smoothly.

Morphing full-color images has recently become popular in television and motion pictures. The basic idea is the same as for morphing line drawings. The differences lie in matching points in the key images and in handling color.

In the truck-to-plane animation, corresponding parts of the truck and plane are defined by the same number of points. The points are even arranged so that they line up somewhat. For example, points at the top of the truck correspond to points at the top of the plane. When you work with photographic images, making the points that define areas line up nicely is a little more difficult.

One method for mapping points between two images involves dividing the images into quadrilaterals. You can map the points in one quadrilateral to those in another using some rather messy mapping calculations. The process is similar to the way some of the programs described at the end of Chapter 7, Area Processes, map pixels from an output image back to an input image. The details of the calculation, however, are rather long, so they are not described here. You can see them in all their glory in the source code on the CD-ROM.

Program QuadMap, shown in Figure 9.9, uses these calculations to map points among three quadrilaterals. Click a point in one of the areas, and the program displays the corresponding points in the other two.

The values S and T tell how far through the quadrilaterals the points are positioned horizontally and vertically, though the quadrilaterals may be bent so far that these directions have little meaning. For example, in Figure 9.9, T is 0.90, so the points are 90 percent of the way from the left edge of the quadrilaterals to the right edge. S is 0.14, so the points are 14 percent of the way from the top of the quadrilaterals to the bottom.

Once you have code that maps points from one quadrilateral to another, you can specify these quadrilaterals on the images you want to morph. Superimpose a grid on both images. Adjust the points in the grids until corresponding points lie over corresponding points of the images. The grids define quadrilaterals that you can use to map points in one image to points in the other.

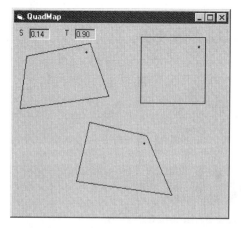

Figure 9.9 Program QuadMap maps points in one quadrilateral to points in two others.

At this point, you have a way to determine which points in the first image correspond to which points in the second image. It is still not completely obvious how to use that mapping to morph the images.

Use tweening techniques to smoothly convert the points in the first grid into the points in the second. For each of these tweens, consider the pixels in the intermediate image. Use the quadrilateral mapping techniques to find the corresponding points in the two key images. Finally, use linear interpolation to pick the intermediate pixel's color. For example, if the tween is one-quarter of the distance between the first and second key frame, make the intermediate pixel one-quarter of the color of the first image's pixel plus three-quarters of the second image's pixel.

Notice that this process contains two interpolation steps: transforming the starting grid into the ending grid and blending the colors of the starting and ending images.

Example program Morph, shown in Figures 9.10 and 9.11, uses this technique to create morphing animation sequences. Figure 9.10 shows the program's transformation grids. Click and drag on the grid points to make corresponding features in the two images line up. For example, in Figure 9.10, corresponding grid points mark the images' eyes, noses, cheeks, ears, and so forth.

Figure 9.11 shows program Morph after it has created 20 out of 30 tweens. The calculations required to create each tween are fairly complex, so the whole process can take a while. The program took 11 minutes to generate 30 tweens for the images shown in Figures 9.10 and 9.11.

Specialized Animation

The previous sections of this chapter explain some of the ways you can create and display images to produce the illusion of motion. You can use these techniques to add animation to almost any kind of Visual Basic program. The following sections take a look at some more specialized animation techniques.

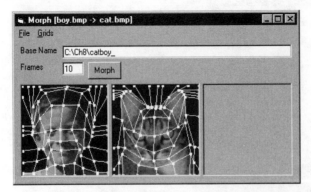

Figure 9.10 Program Morph displaying transformation grids.

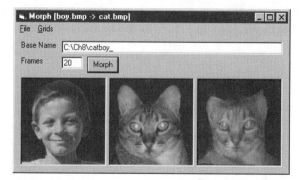

Figure 9.11 Program Morph displaying the 20th of 30 tweens.

The next several sections describe ways you can create animated scene transitions. With only a little work, you can replace one image with another using wipes, tiles, and spirals. These methods are simple but produce impressive results that can make an otherwise dull operation interesting.

The final sections of the chapter explain how you can build screen savers and animated icons. These sections discuss mostly Visual Basic programming details. By applying these details to the techniques presented in previous sections, you can create interesting and useful animated utilities.

Scene Transitions

When a program switches from one image to another, it can add extra interest using animation techniques. By copying parts of the new image over the old one, you can create wipes, tiles, and other motion picture style transition effects.

Example program Scenes demonstrates several different transitions. Click the button for the technique you want to see, and the program will switch between two images using that technique. The routines that implement the different effects are stored in module Wipes.bas to make it easier for you to include them in your applications.

You can use either Visual Basic's PaintPicture method or the BitBlt API function to copy parts of one image onto another. PaintPicture is a little easier to use, but BitBlt is faster. Program Scenes uses BitBlt so that it can produce useful effects on slower computers.

Wipes

A *wipe* is one image drawn across another. A horizontal wipe, for example, might begin drawing the new image over the left edge of the old image. Over time, more and more of the new image is drawn on top of the old one, until only the new image remains.

Wipes are relatively straightforward with Visual Basic. The program uses PaintPicture or BitBlt to copy more and more of the new image over the old one. The following code shows how program Scenes wipes a picture over another one from left to right. The code starts by copying a thin slice of the new image over the left side of the old image. Each time the program should display some more of the new image, it increases the width of the area it copies.

```
Private Wiping As Boolean

' Wipe pic_new onto pic_old from left to right.
Public Sub WipeLeftToRight( _
    ByVal pic_new As PictureBox, _
    ByVal pic_old As PictureBox, _
    ByVal ms_per_frame As Long, _
    ByVal pixels_per_frame As Integer)
Dim next_time As Long
Dim wid As Single
Dim hgt As Single
Dim X As Single

    ' Prevent more than one wipe at a time.
    If Wiping Then Exit Sub
    Wiping = True

    wid = pic_old.ScaleWidth
    hgt = pic_old.ScaleHeight

    ' Start moving the image.
    X = 0
    next_time = GetTickCount()
    Do While X <= wid
        ' Copy the area.
        BitBlt pic_old.hDC, 0, 0, X, hgt, _
            pic_new.hDC, 0, 0, vbSrcCopy
        pic_old.Refresh

        ' Wait for the next frame's time.
        next_time = next_time + ms_per_frame
        WaitTill next_time

        X = X + pixels_per_frame
    Loop

    ' Finish up.
    pic_old.Picture = pic_new.Picture
    Wiping = False
End Sub
```

Other wipes are almost as simple as this one. The only difference between the routines is in they way they decide which part of the new image to copy over the old one next. For example, a right-to-left wipe copies parts of the new picture over the right side of the old one.

Module Wipes.bas includes eight wipe routines that move the new image over the old one from left to right, upper left to lower right, top to bottom, and so forth. A ninth subroutine makes the new image start in the center of the old image and grow outward. You can see the complete source code for each of these subroutines on the CD-ROM.

Push

In a *push*, a new picture pushes the old one out of the way as it slides into view. The code to perform a push is similar to the code for a wipe. The difference is in the calls to BitBlt. Before displaying a new piece of the new image, the program moves the old picture over to make room. Instead of sliding over the old picture, this makes the new image appear to push the old one out of its way.

```
' Push pic_new onto pic_old from left to right.
Public Sub PushLeftToRight( _
    ByVal pic_new As PictureBox, _
    ByVal pic_old As PictureBox, _
    ByVal ms_per_frame As Long, _
    ByVal pixels_per_frame As Integer)
Dim next_time As Long
Dim wid As Single
Dim hgt As Single
Dim X As Single

    ' Prevent more than one wipe at a time.
    If Wiping Then Exit Sub
    Wiping = True

    wid = pic_old.ScaleWidth
    hgt = pic_old.ScaleHeight

    ' Start moving the image.
    X = 0
    next_time = GetTickCount()
    Do While X <= wid
        ' Move the existing area.
        BitBlt pic_old.hDC, X, 0, wid - X, hgt, _
            pic_old.hDC, X - pixels_per_frame, 0, vbSrcCopy

        ' Copy the area.
        BitBlt pic_old.hDC, 0, 0, X, hgt, _
            pic_new.hDC, wid - X, 0, vbSrcCopy
        pic_old.Refresh

        ' Wait for the next frame's time.
        next_time = next_time + ms_per_frame
        WaitTill next_time

        X = X + pixels_per_frame
```

```
    Loop

        ' Finish up.
        pic_old.Picture = pic_new.Picture
        Wiping = False
End Sub
```

The Wipes.bas module contains routines to push images from left to right, right to left, top to bottom, and bottom to top.

One interesting combination pushes a blank image over the current one from left to right and then pushes a new image over the blank one from right to left. This gives an effect similar to that of a slide projector. The old slide disappears moving to the right, and the new slide appears moving to the left. The following code shows how a program can use the routines in Wipes.bas to make this kind of transition. Here picCanvas is the visible display area, picNew contains the new image, and picBlank contains a blank picture.

```
    PushLeftToRight picBlank, picCanvas, _
        ms_per_frame, pixels_per_frame
    PushRightToLeft picNew, picCanvas, _
        ms_per_frame, pixels_per_frame
```

Tile Overs

In a *tile over*, the program replaces the old image gradually, using rectangular blocks of the new image. Figure 9.12 shows program Scenes after it has partially replaced an image with randomly selected tiles from the new image.

Different tile overs display the tiles in the new image in different orders. Program Scenes demonstrates three tile overs. A random tile over selects the next tile to display randomly.

The following code shows how program Scenes displays random tile overs. Subroutine TileRandom begins by creating chunk_row and chunk_col arrays to hold the rows and columns of the tiles it will present. It initializes the entries in these arrays in their most natural order: (0, 0), (0, 1), ..., (1, 0), (1, 1), and so forth.

Next TileRandom randomizes the entries in these arrays. For each entry in the array, the program selects another entry that has not yet been positioned. It then swaps the two entries. This produces a random arrangement of the tile rows and columns.

TileRandom then calls subroutine DisplayTiles to display the tiles in their randomized order, waiting the right amount of time between them.

```
    ' Tile the pic_old with pic_new randomly.
    Public Sub TileRandom( _
        ByVal pic_new As PictureBox, _
        ByVal pic_old As PictureBox, _
        ByVal ms_per_frame As Long, _
        ByVal divisions_per_side As Integer)
```

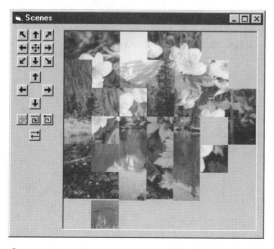

Figure 9.12 Program Scenes showing a partially completed random tile over.

```
Dim chunk_row() As Integer
Dim chunk_col() As Integer
Dim num_chunks As Integer
Dim chunk As Integer
Dim i As Integer
Dim j As Integer
Dim tmp As Integer

    ' Prevent more than one wipe at a time.
    If Wiping Then Exit Sub
    Wiping = True

    ' Allocate the chunk_row and chunk_col arrays.
    num_chunks = divisions_per_side * divisions_per_side
    ReDim chunk_row(1 To num_chunks)
    ReDim chunk_col(1 To num_chunks)

    ' Put the row and column numbers in the
    ' chunk_row and chunk_col arrays.
    chunk = 1
    For i = 1 To divisions_per_side
        For j = 1 To divisions_per_side
            chunk_row(chunk) = i - 1
            chunk_col(chunk) = j - 1
            chunk = chunk + 1
        Next j
    Next i

    ' Randomize the chunks.
    For i = 1 To num_chunks - 1
        ' Pick a random entry between i
        ' and divisions_per_side.
```

```
        j = Int((num_chunks - i + 1) * Rnd + i)

        ' Swap that entry with the one in position i.
        If i <> j Then
            tmp = chunk_row(i)
            chunk_row(i) = chunk_row(j)
            chunk_row(j) = tmp
            tmp = chunk_col(i)
            chunk_col(i) = chunk_col(j)
            chunk_col(j) = tmp
        End If
    Next i

    ' Display the tiles.
    DisplayTiles pic_new, pic_old, ms_per_frame, _
        divisions_per_side, chunk_row, chunk_col

    Wiping = False
End Sub

' Display the tiles in the indicated order.
Private Sub DisplayTiles( _
    ByVal pic_new As PictureBox, _
    ByVal pic_old As PictureBox, _
    ByVal ms_per_frame As Long, _
    ByVal divisions_per_side As Integer, _
    chunk_row() As Integer, _
    chunk_col() As Integer)
Dim num_chunks As Integer
Dim chunk As Integer
Dim next_time As Long
Dim wid As Single
Dim hgt As Single

    wid = pic_old.ScaleWidth / divisions_per_side
    hgt = pic_old.ScaleHeight / divisions_per_side
    num_chunks = divisions_per_side * divisions_per_side

    ' Start displaying the tiles.
    next_time = GetTickCount()
    For chunk = 1 To num_chunks
        ' Copy the tile area.
        BitBlt pic_old.hDC, _
            wid * chunk_col(chunk), _
            hgt * chunk_row(chunk), _
            wid, hgt, _
            pic_new.hDC, _
            wid * chunk_col(chunk), _
            hgt * chunk_row(chunk), _
            vbSrcCopy
        pic_old.Refresh
```

```
        ' Wait for the next frame's time.
        next_time = next_time + ms_per_frame
        WaitTill next_time
    Next chunk

    ' Finish up.
    pic_old.Picture = pic_new.Picture
End Sub
```

Program Scenes also displays tiles spiraling inward or spiraling outward. The differences between these routines are in how they order the tiles' row and column values in the chunk_row and chunk_col arrays. After they have ordered the tiles, they all use the DisplayTiles subroutine to display the results.

Dissolves and Fades

In a *dissolve*, the old image gradually blends into the new one. The old image gradually grows darker while the new image gradually grows lighter. Eventually, the new image is completely displayed, and the old image is gone.

Example program Dissolve demonstrates this technique. The following code shows how the program works. For each frame in the dissolve sequence, the program combines appropriate fractions of the pixel values in the two images. For example, one-quarter of the way through the animation sequence, the program uses three-quarters of the first image's pixel values plus one-quarter of the second image's values.

```
' Make the fade frames.
Private Sub cmdDissolve_Click()
Dim num_frames As Integer
Dim base_name As String
Dim pic0_pixels() As RGBTriplet
Dim pic1_pixels() As RGBTriplet
Dim new_pixels() As RGBTriplet
Dim bits_per_pixel As Integer
Dim X As Integer
Dim Y As Integer
Dim i As Integer
Dim f0 As Single
Dim f1 As Single

    If Not IsNumeric(txtNumFrames.Text) Then -
        txtNumFrames.Text = "10"
    num_frames = CInt(txtNumFrames.Text)
    base_name = txtBaseName.Text

    ' Get the input pixels.
    GetBitmapPixels picCanvas(0), pic0_pixels, bits_per_pixel
    GetBitmapPixels picCanvas(1), pic1_pixels, bits_per_pixel
```

```
' Make room for the output pixels.
ReDim new_pixels(0 To UBound(pic0_pixels, 1), _
                 0 To UBound(pic0_pixels, 2))

' Build the frames.
For i = 1 To num_frames
    lblFrameNumber.Caption = Format$(i)
    DoEvents

    f1 = i / num_frames
    f0 = 1 - f1
    For X = 0 To picCanvas(0).ScaleWidth - 1
        For Y = 0 To picCanvas(0).ScaleHeight - 1
            With new_pixels(X, Y)
                .rgbRed = _
                    f0 * pic0_pixels(X, Y).rgbRed + _
                    f1 * pic1_pixels(X, Y).rgbRed
                .rgbGreen = _
                    f0 * pic0_pixels(X, Y).rgbGreen + _
                    f1 * pic1_pixels(X, Y).rgbGreen
                .rgbBlue = _
                    f0 * pic0_pixels(X, Y).rgbBlue + _
                    f1 * pic1_pixels(X, Y).rgbBlue
            End With
        Next Y
    Next X

    ' Update the image.
    SetBitmapPixels picCanvas(0), bits_per_pixel, _
        new_pixels
    picCanvas(0).Picture = picCanvas(0).Image

    ' Save the results.
    SavePicture picCanvas(0).Picture, _
        base_name & Format$(i) & ".bmp"
Next i

' Restore the original image.
SetBitmapPixels picCanvas(0), bits_per_pixel, pic0_pixels
picCanvas(0).Picture = picCanvas(0).Image
lblFrameNumber.Caption = ""
End Sub
```

The program uses the GetBitmapPixels and SetBitmapPixels functions described in Chapter 3, Advanced Color, to get reasonable performance. Unfortunately, the program is still not fast enough to build the images in real time. You will need to generate the frames ahead of time and store them for later use.

In a *fade*, the old image grows gradually darker until it is black. This is just a special case of a dissolve in which the old image dissolves into a black one. Often a fade (fade out) is followed by a reversed fade (fade in) to present a new image.

If your computer uses color palettes, you can use *palette animation* to make fades extremely fast. Use the SetPaletteEntries API function to make the image's palette colors darker and darker until they are all black. An 8-bit color image has only 256 colors in its color palette. For a large image, updating the 256 values is much faster than updating the colors of each pixel individually. For example, a 200 by 200 pixel image contains 40,000 pixels. Setting the values of 40,000 pixels takes much longer than updating 256 palette entries.

Unfortunately, palette animation does not work if you are not using color palettes. If you are using 16- or 24-bit color, you must update each of the pixels individually. Example program Fade does this to produce fading animation sequences.

Screen Savers

Screen savers were originally created to protect computer monitors. If the contents of a screen did not change for a very long time, the images being displayed might burn the phosphors on the screen, leaving a ghostly picture as a permanent addition to the monitor. A screen saver either blanks the screen so that there is no image to burn in or displays a series of moving images. By keeping the images moving, the program ensures that nothing stays in one place long enough to burn the phosphors. Today, screen savers are used more for entertainment than to protect monitors.

Screen savers are executable programs much like any other. One thing that makes them seem different is that they have a .scr extension instead of ending in .exe. This is just a naming convention, and you can simply rename your executable screen saver so that it has a .scr extension.

The program must also handle a few screen saver details. When Windows starts a screen saver, it passes it command line arguments telling it how to run. These arguments include:

/c   The program should display its configuration screen.

/s   The program should run as a normal screen saver.

/p   The program should display a preview.

To capture those arguments, you should start your program with a subroutine named Main in a .bas module instead of with a startup form. Use the Command$ function to see what arguments were passed to the program.

If the program sees the /c flag, it should display a configuration form to allow the user to tell it how to run. For example, a bouncing ball program might let the user decide the number of balls to display. If the user accepts the new values, the form should save the values to the registry so that it can read the values later when it must run as a screen saver.

If the program receives the /s flag, it should run as a normal screen saver.

The strangest case occurs when the program receives the /p flag. In that case, the program should display a preview of the screen saver as shown in Figure 9.13.

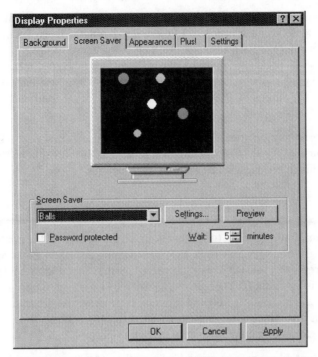

Figure 9.13 A screen saver should display a preview when it receives the /p flag.

When Windows passes the program the /p flag, it also passes the preview window's window handle. The screen saver should draw its preview on that window. For example, if the program receives the command string "/p 787482," it should display its preview on the window with window handle 787482.

This is not hard if the program normally draws using the API. The program can use the GetDC API function to get the window's device context handle and then use API functions to draw on that device context.

In Visual Basic, drawing using the API functions is inconvenient. It is much easier to use Visual Basic's Line, Circle, and other drawing methods. With a little creative API use, you can display the preview using normal Visual Basic methods.

First, load the drawing form on which the program draws its animation. Use GetWindowLong to get the form's window style. Add the WS_CHILD style to this value and set the form's new style using SetWindowLong. This converts the form so that you can display it inside another window.

Next, break the preview window handle out of the command string. Use SetParent to make the drawing form have as its parent the preview window. Use SetWindowLong to save the preview window's handle in the drawing window's GWL_HWNDPARENT entry. At this point, the drawing window is an official child of the preview area.

Use the GetClientRect API function to get the preview window's dimensions. Finally, use SetWindowPos to make the drawing window fill the preview window.

These may seem to be obscure steps, but once you are done, you can draw on the form you normally would if the program were running as a normal screen saver instead of in preview mode.

Example program SSaver uses these steps to display a bouncing ball screen saver. The following code shows the Main subroutine that starts the program.

```
' Start the program.
Public Sub Main()
Dim args As String
Dim preview_hwnd As Long
Dim preview_rect As RECT
Dim window_style As Long

    ' Get the command line arguments.
    args = LCase$(Trim$(Command$))

    ' Examine the first 2 characters.
    Select Case Left$(args, 2)
        Case "/c"       ' Display configuration dialog.
            RunMode = rmConfigure
        Case "", "/s"   ' Run as a screen saver.
            RunMode = rmScreenSaver
        Case "/p"       ' Run in preview mode.
            RunMode = rmPreview
        Case Else       ' This shouldn't happen.
            RunMode = rmScreenSaver
    End Select

    Select Case RunMode
        Case rmConfigure    ' Display configuration dialog.
            frmConfig.Show

        Case rmScreenSaver  ' Run as a screen saver.
            ' Make sure there isn't another one running.
            CheckShouldRun

            ' Display the cover form.
            frmCover.Show
            ShowCursor False

        Case rmPreview      ' Run in preview mode.
            ' Set the caption for Windows 95.
            Load frmCover
            frmCover.Caption = "Preview"

            ' Get the current window style.
            window_style = GetWindowLong(frmCover.hwnd, _
                GWL_STYLE)

            ' Add WS_CHILD to make this a child window.
```

```
        window_style = (window_style Or WS_CHILD)

        ' Set the window's new style.
        SetWindowLong frmCover.hwnd, _
            GWL_STYLE, window_style

        ' Get the preview area hWnd.
        preview_hwnd = GetHwndFromCommand(args)

        ' Set the window's parent so it appears
        ' inside the preview area.
        SetParent frmCover.hwnd, preview_hwnd

        ' Save the preview area's hWnd in
        ' the form's window structure.
        SetWindowLong frmCover.hwnd, _
            GWL_HWNDPARENT, preview_hwnd

        ' Get the dimensions of the preview area.
        GetClientRect preview_hwnd, preview_rect

        ' Show the preview.
        SetWindowPos frmCover.hwnd, _
            HWND_TOP, 0&, 0&, _
            preview_rect.Right, _
            preview_rect.Bottom, _
            SWP_NOZORDER Or SWP_NOACTIVATE Or _
                SWP_SHOWWINDOW
    End Select
End Sub
```

Screen savers must handle a few other details that are much less confusing. To protect the screen as completely as possible, make the program run maximized with no title bar. Set the form's background color to black to reduce the chances of burning the screen phosphors. You can complete these steps by setting the main form's property values as shown in Table 9.1.

Table 9.1 Main Form Property Values for Screen Savers

PROPERTY	VALUE
BackColor	&H00000000
Caption	" "
ControlBox	False
MaxButton	False
MinButton	False
WindowState	2 - maximized

To ensure that the mouse pointer does not burn the phosphors, hide the pointer. You can do this with the ShowCursor API function.

Next, create whatever animation you want to run during the screen saver. You can use bouncing balls, revolving planets, sliding bitmaps, or whatever you like. The only requirement is that you do not allow an image to remain in one place for very long.

To allow the user to stop the screen saver, add code that exits your program in all MouseMove, MouseDown, and KeyDown event handlers. Unfortunately, Visual Basic sometimes generates a few spurious MouseMove events as soon as a screen saver starts. It also generates a MouseMove event once in a while when the mouse has not actually moved.

To prevent the screen saver from exiting when it receives these "false" events, see if the mouse has moved more than a few pixels. If the mouse has not moved much, ignore the event.

```
Private Sub Form_MouseMove(Button As Integer, _
    Shift As Integer, X As Single, Y As Single)
Static x0 As Integer
Static y0 As Integer

    ' Do nothing except in screen saver mode.
    If RunMode <> rmScreenSaver Then Exit Sub

    ' Unload on large mouse movements.
    If ((x0 = 0) And (y0 = 0)) Or _
        ((Abs(x0 - X) < 5) And (Abs(y0 - Y) < 5)) _
        Then
            ' It's a small movement.
            x0 = X
            y0 = Y
            Exit Sub
    End If

    ' This is a big movement. Stop the screen saver.
    Unload Me
End Sub
```

Windows may start a screen saver when another copy of it is already running. The program should check App.PrevInstance and exit if another instance is running.

Once you have tested and debugged your program, you are ready to turn it into an executable screen saver. In the Visual Basic development environment, select the File menu's Make EXE File command. In the File name box, specify a .scr extension instead of the usual .exe. Then click on the Options button and add the string "SCRNSAVE:" at the front of the application's title. For example, to create a screen saver named Bounce, set the title to "SCRNSAVE:Bounce." Create the executable and then move it into your Windows directory. You now have a working screen saver.

Animating Program Icons

A form may not always be visible, but its icon is always present in the task bar. Because a form's icon is always visible yet never gets in the way of other programs, it makes sense to put information there.

As you start more and more tasks, the task bar becomes crowded. Each time you start a new application, Windows adds the application's icon and caption text to the task bar. If there is not enough room in the task bar for the new application, Windows shrinks all of the other items to make room. That reduces the amount of text each item can display.

Because the shrinking occurs on the right side and the icons are displayed on the left, the icons usually remain visible. Eventually, if you start enough applications, the text will be completely hidden, but the icons will still be there.

This arrangement makes task bar icons an ideal place to put information that you want to be able to find easily and quickly. Of course, the icons in Windows 95 are very small, so you cannot put much information there. Still, there are times when changing or animating a task bar icon can be useful.

To change the picture displayed in a task bar icon, set the form's Icon property to an object containing an icon property. For example, if you have an image control named imgWaiting that contains an icon, you can display that icon in the task bar with the following code.

```
frmSearch.Icon = imgWaiting.Picture
```

You can also set the icon using the LoadPicture function, as in:

```
frmSearch.Icon = LoadPicture("C:\Search\Waiting.ico")
```

Once you know how to change a program's icon, you can animate it by rapidly cycling through a series of icons. You can use all the techniques described earlier for bitmap animation. You can regulate the speed of display using a timer control, or you can write your own routines to keep time using the Timer function or the GetTickCount API function.

Example program IconAnim displays an animated icon. Click the option buttons to see different animations.

There are a few very important considerations you should keep in mind when you animate an application's icon. First, the icons in the task bar are very small. If you assign a larger icon to a form's Icon property, Windows shrinks the icon to fit in the task bar. When it is shrunk, the icon loses some of its resolution and may become meaningless. To ensure that your icons are meaningful, always test them and see what they look like in the task bar.

Second, if you change the icon displayed by an application, finding the application in the task bar may be difficult. If the icon could hold any of a dozen different shapes, the user will need to look carefully to find the application's icon. To make finding an application's icons easier, make sure they have something in common. For example, you might make them the same shape with different colors.

One last thing you should consider is that motion grabs attention. This can be useful if your program has some urgent information to convey. If a printer monitor notices a printer is stuck, it might flash its icon rapidly to get attention.

On the other hand, excessive motion can be annoying. Use animation sparingly. It is fine to change a program's icon to indicate what it is doing. It can be irritating if an icon is rapidly blinking in a rainbow of bright colors for no particular reason.

Summary

The Internet's recent popularity has raised users' graphical expectations. Using the techniques described in this chapter, you can meet those expectations. Simulation and scripting allow you to add simple animations to your programs. Tweening lets you display longer animated sequences with less effort and using less memory. Morphing and scene transitions can lend interest to otherwise monotonous operations and satisfy even the most jaded Web surfers.

PART FOUR

Two-Dimensional Graphics

Three-dimensional graphics can make some concepts easier to understand. Nothing shows the changes in altitude of a geographic area as intuitively as a three-dimensional map. Despite the power and visual appeal of three-dimensional images, the vast majority of graphics are still two-dimensional. You can see this at any business office or on a random stroll through the Web. Unless you stumble into a site dedicated to three-dimensional graphics, you see mostly flat images and text.

The chapters in this part cover an assortment of topics in two-dimensional graphics. Chapter 10 describes fractals and tilings. The techniques explained in this chapter allow you to generate fascinating images of infinite complexity with remarkably simple code.

Chapter 11 explains how to draw several important types of curves. It describes parametric curves and shows how you can use them to draw a variety of interesting shapes. It shows how to draw data smoothly using such methods as polynomial least squares, Hermite curves, and splines.

Chapter 12 extends some of the ideas presented in Chapter 11 to explain general two-dimensional transformations. It tells how you can transform two-dimensional objects and manipulate two-dimensional transformations in a uniform way. These techniques provide a useful foreshadowing of the three-dimensional techniques described later. Working through these transformations in two dimensions makes generalizing them to three dimensions easier.

CHAPTER 10

Fractals and Tilings

This chapter shows several techniques for producing amazing fractal and tiled images. While the sections that follow mention some of the mathematics behind fractals, chaos, and tilings, they concentrate more on drawing interesting graphics rather than on explaining mathematical theory. For the hardcore mathematics, you should read a book about fractals or chaos theory.

Fractals

Simply defined, without a morass of mathematical definitions, a fractal is a curve with *fractional dimension*. Simple curves, like a line segment or the edge of an ellipse, are one-dimensional objects. Filled shapes, like rectangles and circles, have two dimensions. In some strange way, many fractals seem to have more than one dimension but fewer than two. The tree in Figure 10.1, for example, does not cover a two-dimensional area as completely as a square does. Yet as the tree grows more and more complicated, it seems to cover more area than a simple one-dimensional line segment.

Fractals have several interesting properties. Many are *self-similar*. That means parts of the curve resemble the whole curve. The tree in Figure 10.1, for instance, is made up of a trunk attached to two branches. Each of those branches is a smaller tree that looks just like a copy of the larger tree that has been rotated and shrunk. At every part of the tree, you will find branches that resemble the tree as a whole.

Many other fractals, while self-similar, do not repeat themselves exactly. If you explore the Mandelbrot set, you will find parts of it that closely resemble the set as a whole. When you look closer, you will find slight differences in these areas. While every position in the tree in Figure 10.1 looks exactly like the tree as a whole, parts of the Mandelbrot set are similar but not identical to the whole.

Many fractals are produced by remarkably simple methods. The Mandelbrot set is generated by repeated evaluation of the equation $Z_{n+1} = Z_n^2 + C$, where the Z_n and C are complex

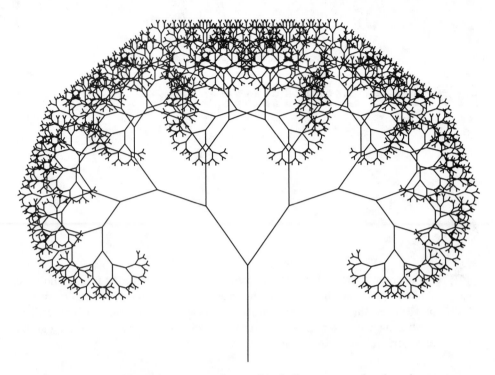

Figure 10.1 A tree covers more area than a simple line segment but less than two-dimensional objects like rectangles.

numbers. By evaluating this simple equation many times, you can create a picture of amazing intricacy.

The sections that follow describe several different kinds of fractals. Some, like trees, are simple and regular. Others, such as the Mandelbrot set, seem almost alien in their twisted complexity.

Trees

You can define a tree recursively as a trunk attached to zero or more smaller trees. More intuitively, the trunk is attached to branches. The branches are attached to smaller branches that are attached to still smaller branches and so forth until you reach some point in the tree where there are no more branches. For example, you could write a program that continued drawing smaller and smaller branches until the new branches were less than one pixel long. At that point, the program would stop.

You can define the *level* or *depth* of a tree to be the number of branches between the bottom and the top of the tree. The tree in Figure 10.2, for instance, has five levels.

Drawing a tree like the one shown in Figure 10.2 is easy using a tree drawing subroutine that closely follows the recursive definition of a tree. This routine draws a branch of a given length in a given direction. It then calls itself recursively to draw smaller branches

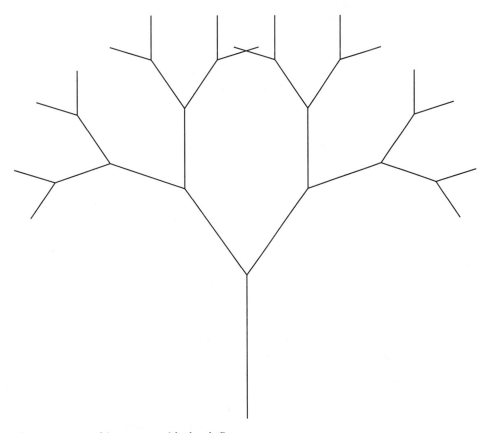

Figure 10.2 A binary tree with depth five.

suitably rotated. The routine takes as a parameter its level in the tree so that it knows when to stop drawing.

The DrawBranch routine shown in the following code does this. First it calculates where its main branch should end, and it draws the branch. Its length parameter gives the branch's length. Parameter theta gives the branch's direction in radians.

If the current depth is greater than one, the routine recursively calls itself to draw two new branches. Those branches are shorter than the main branch by a factor of LENGTH_SCALE and are drawn in the directions theta + DTHETA and theta - DTHETA.

```
Private Const PI = 3.14159

Private Const LENGTH_SCALE = 0.75
Private Const DTHETA = PI / 5

' Recursively draw a binary tree branch.
Private Sub DrawBranch(ByVal depth As Integer, _
    ByVal X As Single, ByVal Y As Single, _
```

```
        ByVal length As Single, ByVal theta As Single)
Dim x1 As Integer
Dim y1 As Integer

    ' See where this branch should end.
    x1 = X + length * Cos(theta)
    y1 = Y + length * Sin(theta)
    picCanvas.Line (X, Y)-(x1, y1)

    ' If depth > 1, draw the attached branches.
    If depth > 1 Then
        DrawBranch depth - 1, x1, y1, _
            length * LENGTH_SCALE, theta + DTHETA
        DrawBranch depth - 1, x1, y1, _
            length * LENGTH_SCALE, theta - DTHETA
    End If
End Sub
```

Example program BinTree uses this routine to draw binary trees. Enter the depth of the tree and click the Go button to make the program draw the tree.

There are several modifications you can make to program BinTree to make it more interesting. First, you can adjust the scale factor LENGTH_SCALE by which the branches at each level are shortened. If you increase LENGTH_SCALE, you get a bushier tree like the one on the left in Figure 10.3. You can also change the value of DTHETA that determines the angle new branches make with the branches below.

Figure 10.4 shows a tree in which DTHETA is set to 90 degrees. You can also vary the thickness of branches, making each smaller than its parent.

Example program BinTree2 is similar to program BinTree except it allows you to change the values of LENGTH_SCALE and DTHETA. If you check the Taper Branches box, the program makes each branch a little thinner than the previous one.

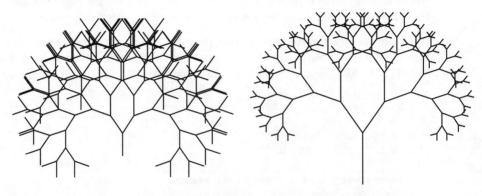

Figure 10.3   Depth eight trees with LENGTH_SCALE = 0.95 (left) and 0.75 (right).

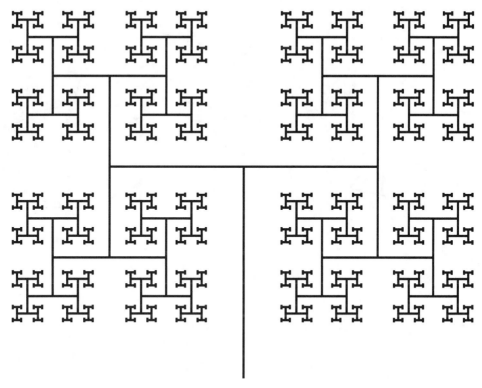

Figure 10.4   A depth 11 tree with DTHETA = 90 degrees.

By adjusting the parameters in program BinTree2, you can create trees that look very different, but they are all symmetrical. You need to look at only a few real trees to realize they are not symmetrical. Branches are rarely straight for more than a few feet; they are bent by wind and gravity, and they do not always divide into two smaller branches. By adding a little randomness to your programs, you can make trees that look much more natural. These trees still look like computer-generated drawings, but a little randomness gives them a pleasing asymmetry.

There are several tree parameters you can adjust randomly. You can vary the lengths and angles of the branches slightly to produce a much less symmetric tree that looks more natural. You can also vary the number of branches that appear when a branch splits.

With a little extra work, you can make the branches bend slightly. Instead of drawing to the end of each branch in a single step, add to the branch a little bit at a time. Each time you add a piece to the branch, add a small random amount to the angle in which the branch is growing. Figure 10.5 shows a depth seven tree with a variable number of bending branches of different lengths.

The following code recursively draws a tree with randomized branch length, angle, and number of branches at each split. If the thickness parameter is greater than zero, the routine uses that value as the line's thickness. It then passes a smaller value into the recursive subroutine calls, making branches grow thinner as the tree progresses.

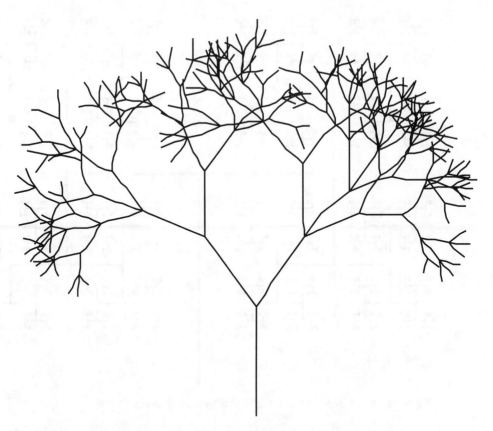

Figure 10.5 A depth seven tree with a variable number of bending branches.

The bend parameter indicates by how much the branch should bend as it grows. If bend is zero, the branch is straight. Otherwise, the direction of each segment in a branch is modified by a random amount between -bend/2 and bend/2 radians. When the subroutine recursively calls itself, it increases the bend parameter so that smaller branches are likely to bend more than larger branches.

```
' Recursively draw a tree branch.
Private Sub DrawBranch(ByVal bend As Single, _
    ByVal thickness As Single, ByVal Depth As Integer, _
    ByVal X As Single, ByVal Y As Single, _
    ByVal length As Single, ByVal length_scale As Single, _
    ByVal rnd_scale As Single, ByVal theta As Single, _
    ByVal dtheta As Single, ByVal rnd_dtheta As Single, _
    ByVal max_branches As Integer)
Const DIST_PER_BEND = 5#
Const BEND_FACTOR = 2#
Const MAX_BEND = PI / 6

Dim x1 As Integer
```

```
Dim y1 As Integer
Dim x2 As Integer
Dim y2 As Integer
Dim status As Integer
Dim num_bends As Integer
Dim num_branches As Integer
Dim i As Integer
Dim new_length As Integer
Dim new_theta As Single
Dim new_bend As Single
Dim dt As Single
Dim t As Single

    If thickness > 0 Then picCanvas.DrawWidth = thickness

    ' Draw the branch.
    If bend > 0 Then
        ' This is a bending branch.
        num_bends = length / DIST_PER_BEND
        t = theta
        x1 = X
        y1 = Y
        For i = 1 To num_bends
            x2 = x1 + DIST_PER_BEND * Cos(t)
            y2 = y1 + DIST_PER_BEND * Sin(t)
            picCanvas.Line (x1, y1)-(x2, y2)

            t = t + bend * (Rnd - 0.5)
            x1 = x2
            y1 = y2
        Next i
    Else
        ' This is a straight branch.
        x1 = X + length * Cos(theta)
        y1 = Y + length * Sin(theta)
        picCanvas.Line (X, Y)-(x1, y1)
    End If

    ' If depth > 1, draw the attached branches.
    If Depth > 1 Then
        num_branches = Int((max_branches - 1) * Rnd + 2)
        dt = 2 * dtheta / (num_branches - 1)
        t = theta - dtheta
        For i = 1 To num_branches
            new_length = length * _
                (length_scale + rnd_scale * (Rnd - 0.5))
            new_theta = t + rnd_dtheta * (Rnd - 0.5)
            t = t + dt
            If bend > 0 Then
                new_bend = bend * BEND_FACTOR
                If new_bend > MAX_BEND Then _
```

```
                    new_bend = MAX_BEND
            Else
                new_bend = bend
            End If
            DrawBranch new_bend, thickness - 1, _
                Depth - 1, x1, y1, new_length, _
                length_scale, rnd_scale, new_theta, _
                dtheta, rnd_dtheta, max_branches
        Next i
    End If
End Sub
```

Example program RndTree uses this subroutine to draw randomized trees. This program is similar to program BinTree2, but it also allows you to specify additional parameters for randomizing the tree.

These programs only scratch the surface of approaches you can take to create more "natural" trees. Real trees show endless variety. Some have long straight branches from which many side branches spring, and others have thick twisted branches. Some branches grow horizontally while others grow at an upward angle or are bent downward by their own weight. Using RndTree as a starting point, you can experiment with these and other variations to create different kinds of trees.

Snowflakes

The basic snowflake begins with an equilateral triangle like the one shown on the left in Figure 10.6. This triangle is called the curve's *initiator*. The program replaces each of the initiator's edges with a properly scaled and rotated version of the curve on the right in Figure 10.6. This curve is called the *generator*.

The program then replaces each of the straight segments in the new figure with a smaller version of the generator. The program replaces the newer straight segments with smaller and smaller versions of the generator until it reaches the curve's desired depth. Figure 10.7 shows the snowflakes that result when the depth of recursion is 1, 2, and 3.

To make creating new snowflakes easier, a program can store the coordinates of the points that make up the initiator in two arrays, InitiatorX and InitiatorY. It can store the amount by which it needs to turn to draw the segments that make up the generator in the array GeneratorDTheta.

Figure 10.6   The initiator and generator for a snowflake.

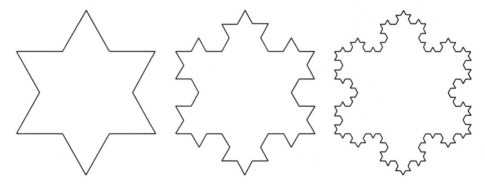

Figure 10.7   Snowflakes of depth 1, 2, and 3.

Whenever the program must recursively draw a line segment, it draws segments that are scaled down by some factor. The program can store this factor in the variable ScaleFactor.

For example, consider the generator and initiator in Figure 10.6. When the program recursively draws a line segment, it begins by drawing a third of the length of the segment in its current direction. It then turns 60 degrees and draws another third of the length of the segment. Next, it turns –120 degrees and draws another third. Finally, it turns 60 degrees again and draws yet another third of the length of the original segment. In this case, you could use the following code to initialize the generator data.

```
ScaleFactor = 1/3                 ' Make subsegments 1/3 size.
GeneratorDTheta(1) = 0            ' Draw in original direction.
GeneratorDTheta(2) = PI / 3       ' Turn 60 degrees.
GeneratorDTheta(3) = -2 * PI / 3  ' Turn -120 degrees.
GeneratorDTheta(4) = PI / 3       ' Turn 60 degrees.
```

Using the generator array GeneratorDTheta and the value ScaleFactor, you can write a subroutine to draw a segment in the snowflake. The DrawFlakeEdge routine shown in the following code recursively draws a segment that starts at position (x1, y1) and moves in the direction theta by distance dist. When it is finished, it leaves the values x1 and y1 so they indicate the endpoint of the segment. That makes it easier to perform all of the necessary recursive calls one after another.

```
' Recursively draw a snowflake edge starting at
' (x1, y1) in direction theta and distance dist.
' Leave the coordinates of the endpoint in
' (x1, y1).
Private Sub DrawFlakeEdge(ByVal depth As Integer, _
    ByRef x1 As Single, ByRef y1 As Single, _
    ByVal theta As Single, ByVal dist As Single)
Dim status As Integer
Dim i As Integer
Dim x2 As Single
Dim y2 As Single
```

```
    If depth <= 0 Then
        x2 = x1 + dist * Cos(theta)
        y2 = y1 + dist * Sin(theta)
        picCanvas.Line (x1, y1)-(x2, y2)
        x1 = x2
        y1 = y2
        Exit Sub
    End If

    ' Recursively draw the edge.
    dist = dist * ScaleFactor
    For i = 1 To NUM_GENERATOR_ANGLES
        theta = theta + GeneratorDTheta(i)
        DrawFlakeEdge depth - 1, x1, y1, theta, dist
    Next i
End Sub
```

You can use the DrawFlakeEdge subroutine to draw each of the edges in the curve's initiator. The following Visual Basic code loops through the initiator's coordinates stored in the InitiatorX() and InitiatorY() arrays and draws the edges of the snowflake. The ATan2 function takes as parameters dy and dx, the changes in a line segment's Y and X coordinates. It returns the angle with tangent dy / dx.

```
' Draw the snowflake.
For i = 1 To NUM_INITIATOR_POINTS
    x1 = InitiatorX(i - 1)
    y1 = InitiatorY(i - 1)
    x2 = InitiatorX(i)
    y2 = InitiatorY(i)
    dx = x2 - x1
    dy = y2 - y1
    theta = ATan2(dy, dx)
    DrawFlakeEdge depth, x1, y1, _
        theta, length
Next i
```

With only a little more work, you can make the generator more general. When the program recursively breaks up a line segment, you can allow the program to turn by angles

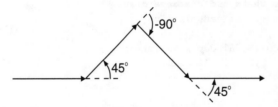

Figure 10.8   A snowflake generator beginning with a 45-degree turn.

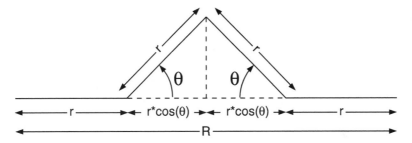

Figure 10.9   Calculating the dimensions of a snowflake generator.

other than 60 degrees. Figure 10.8 shows a generator that turns 45 degrees, -90 degrees, and then 45 degrees again.

More generally, if you want the first turn to be θ degrees, the second should be $-2 * \theta$, and the third should be θ again. Suppose the total length of the segment should be R, and the length of the shorter pieces is r. Then Figure 10.9 shows that $R = 2 * r + 2 * r * Cos(\theta)$. Solving this equation for r, you get $r = R / (2 * (1 + Cos(\theta)))$. Using these facts, you can write a routine to initialize the generator for any angle θ.

Example program Flake lets you build snowflakes. Enter the level of recursion you want and the first angle the generator should use. Then click the Go button to have the program draw the appropriate snowflake. Figure 10.10 shows snowflakes created with generators that start with different angles.

Animated Snowflakes

Example program FlakeAn1 displays animated snowflakes. The program starts by displaying a depth zero snowflake. It then gradually pulls the midpoints of each edge out until they reach their correct positions for a level-one snowflake. Figure 10.11 shows three frames in the sequence between a level-zero snowflake and a level-one snowflake.

Figure 10.10   Depth four snowflakes with generators beginning with 45, 80, and 90 degree turns.

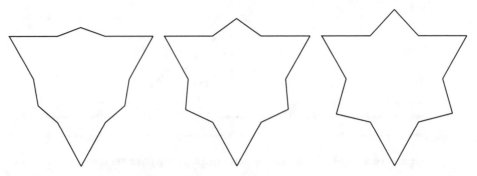

Figure 10.11 Frames produced by program FlakeAn1.

Next, the program pulls the midpoints of the level-one snowflake edges outward until they lie in their proper positions for a level-two snowflake. The program continues this process until it has created the complete snowflake.

When you specify higher levels for the snowflakes, the program takes longer to draw each frame. For that reason, the animation starts to slow down when the maximum level drawn is around three or four. The snowflake does not show much detail beyond level four anyway, so you really do not need to animate higher levels.

Example program FlakeAn2 animates snowflakes in a different way. For each frame, the program displays a snowflake of the level specified in the Level text box. It starts by making the initial angle in the generator zero. This makes the snowflake look like a triangle no matter what level you specify. The program then gradually increases the angles in the generator, displaying a new frame for each angle.

As is the case with program FlakeAn1, higher-level snowflakes take longer to display, so the animation starts to slow down when you specify a level above three or four. The reduced detail at these higher levels makes them uninteresting anyway.

Other Snowflakes

Using program Flake as a starting point, you can make other snowflake programs that use different initiators and generators. The initiators are usually regular polygons like triangles, squares, or hexagons. The points in the generators are usually selected to fall on the points of a lattice made up of regular polygons.

For example, Figure 10.12 shows the generator and initiator for a Gosper curve. The initiator is a hexagon. The points in the generator fall on the points of a triangular lattice. Figure 10.13 shows some of the snowflakes produced by this initiator and generator.

Example program Flake2 lets you load a file with a .sno extension that describes a snowflake's initiator and generator. These files have a format similar to the following file, which describes a von Koch snowflake. The comments to the right make the listing easier to follow and are not part of the file.

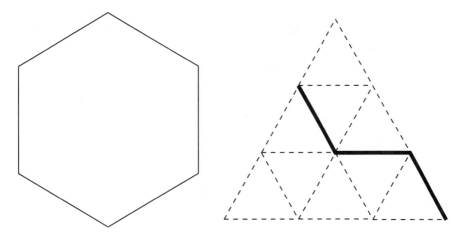

Figure 10.12   The initiator and generator for a Gosper snowflake.

```
4                ' Number of points in the initiator.
230, 54          ' Initiator point 1.
54, 54           ' Initiator point 2.
54, 230          ' Initiator point 3.
230, 230         ' Initiator point 4.
0.4472136        ' ScaleFactor.
3                ' Number of turns in the generator.
26.565051        ' Generator turn 1.
-90              ' Generator turn 2.
90               ' Generator turn 3.
```

The Ch10 directory on the CD-ROM contains several snowflake definition files that you can load using program Flake2. When you load a new .sno file, be sure you run the program with a small level of recursion until you know how complex the snowflake will be. In one test on a 133MHz Pentium, a level-four von Koch snowflake with the 18-segment generator described in file Koch18.sno took more 52 seconds to draw.

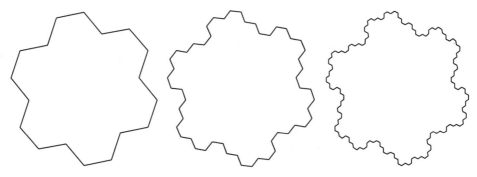

Figure 10.13   Depth one, two, and three Gosper snowflakes.

You can easily create your own snowflake definition files. Start by defining the initiator. Any shape will work, though regular polygons tend to produce some of the best pictures because they are symmetrical.

Give each segment in your generator the same length. This is easiest if you make the edges in the generator fall along the edges of triangles or squares in a regular lattice. Then the value of DistFactor is the ratio of the length of these segments to the distance from the first to the last point in the generator. Usually, a little geometry and trigonometry will help you calculate this ratio.

The generator shown in Figure 10.12, for example, lies in a lattice of equilateral triangles. If the side length of an equilateral triangle is S, its height is $(S/2) * Sqr(3)$. Then this generator is $2 * S$ wide and $2 * (S/2) * Sqr(3) = S * Sqr(3)$ tall. That means the distance between the first and last points in the generator is $Sqr((2 * S)^2 + (S * Sqr(3))^2) = Sqr(4 * S^2 + S^2 * 3) = S * Sqr(4 + 3) = S * Sqr(7)$. The ratio of the side length S to this distance is $S/(S * Sqr(7)) = 1/Sqr(7)$, or roughly 0.3779645. That is the value DistFactor should have for this generator.

The last thing you need to do is to compute the generator's turn angles. If you lay your generator out on a triangular or square grid, most of the angles will be multiples of 60 or 90 degrees, respectively. You can make use of geometry and trigonometry again to determine the first angle.

In Figure 10.12, the angle between the first generator segment and the X axis is 60 degrees. The generator is $2 * S$ units wide and $2 * (S/2) * Sqr(3) = S * Sqr(3)$ units tall. Then the angle between the line connecting the first and last points and the X axis has tangent $(S * Sqr(3))/(2 * S) = Sqr(3)/2$. The first angle in the generator tells how much you need to turn to move from the path between the first and last generator points to the path toward the second generator point. In this case, that angle is the difference between the angles 60 degrees and arctangent($Sqr(3)/2$). That difference $60 -$ arctangent($Sqr(3)/2$) is about 19.1 degrees.

The top pictures in Figure 10.14 show the initiator and a three-segment generator for a von Koch snowflake. The initiator is a square, and the points in the generator fall on the points of a square lattice. The bottom three pictures show the depth one, two, and three von Koch snowflakes produced by this initiator and generator.

If you create a snowflake using certain generators, pieces of the snowflake will overlap with others. This can produce a whole new kind of snowflake. The top of Figure 10.15 shows a hexagonal initiator and a seven-segment generator on a triangular lattice. The bottom pictures show the corresponding level one, two, and three overlapping snowflakes.

Once you have built up a collection of initiators and generators, you can mix and match them to produce new snowflakes. For example, you can use a hexagon instead of a square as an initiator with a three-segment rectangular generator. Figure 10.16 shows this initiator and generator, together with level one, two, and three snowflakes.

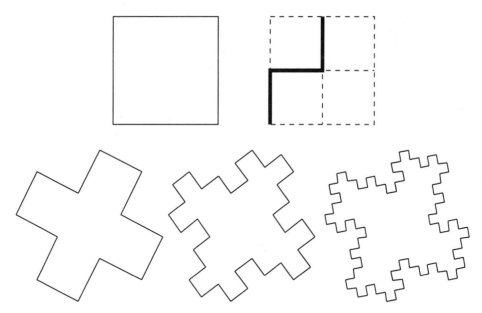

Figure 10.14   A von Koch initiator and generator with depth one, two, and three snowflakes.

Figure 10.15   An initiator and generator with depth one, two, and three overlapping snowflakes.

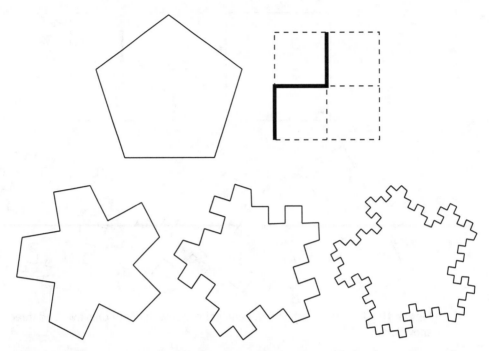

Figure 10.16   A pentagonal initiator and square generator with depth one, two, and three snowflakes.

Space-Filling Curves

Space-filling curves, like snowflakes, are defined recursively. As the level of recursion increases, the curve becomes more and more complex. Eventually a space-filling curve covers the area it occupies in a very special way. For any point (x, y) within the area and for any distance D, no matter how small, the curve will eventually pass within distance D of the point (x, y).

To think of this in another way, suppose a space-filling curve occupies the area 0 <= x <= 1, 0 <= y <= 1. Now suppose the value for D is 1 millionth of a unit. For a large enough level of recursion, the space-filling curve will pass within 1 millionth of a unit of every point in the area.

As with snowflakes, you create a space-filling curve by breaking a large curve into smaller pieces. You then use the curve itself, properly scaled and rotated, to build the pieces. You can continue to break the pieces into smaller and smaller pieces until you have reached some desired level of recursion.

The sections that follow describe three different space-filling curves: Hilbert, Sierpinski, and Peano.

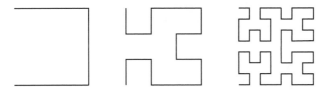

Figure 10.17   Depth one, two, and three Hilbert curves.

Hilbert Curves

Figure 10.17 shows Hilbert curves of level one, two, and three. To create a Hilbert curve of a given level, you draw four Hilbert curves of one less level and connect them with line segments. The picture on the left in Figure 10.18 shows how four level-one curves make up a level-two curve. The picture on the right shows how four level-two curves make up a level-three curve. The smaller curves in each picture are shown in bold lines so that you can see them easily.

Because the smaller curves that make up a Hilbert curve are rotated, the drawing routine must be able to draw curves with different orientations. The easiest way to accomplish this is to pass the routine two parameters, dx and dy, that indicate the direction in which the first line in the curve should be drawn. Then if the curve is a level-one curve, the first drawing command is Line -Step(dx, dy), assuming the drawing position is already at the correct location.

If the curve is not a level-one curve, the drawing routine begins by recursively calling itself to draw a smaller curve with the parameters dx and dy switched. This gives the smaller curve the proper orientation.

For example, consider the curve on the left in Figure 10.18. This level-two curve begins with parameters dx = S and dy = 0 where S is the length of one of the curve's segments. The drawing routine begins by calling itself recursively with dx = 0 and dy = S to draw a level-one curve. Because the new curve has level one, the drawing routine draws the level-one curve beginning with the statement Line -Step(dx, dy), which, in this case, is equivalent to Line -Step(0, S). Keeping in mind that the positive Y direction is down, you can see that this agrees with the first segment in the curve in Figure 10.18.

The Hilbert curve-drawing routine is surprisingly concise in Visual Basic, but it is a little hard to understand. You may need to step through the code several times in the debugger to understand how dx and dy switch to produce the different pieces of the curves.

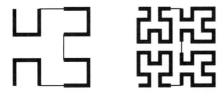

Figure 10.18   Hilbert curves made up of smaller Hilbert curves.

```
Private Sub Hilbert(ByVal depth As Integer, _
    ByVal dx As Single, ByVal dy As Single)

    If depth > 1 Then Hilbert depth - 1, dy, dx
    Canvas.Line -Step(dx, dy)
    If depth > 1 Then Hilbert depth - 1, dx, dy
    Canvas.Line -Step(dy, dx)
    If depth > 1 Then Hilbert depth - 1, dx, dy
    Canvas.Line -Step(-dx, -dy)
    If depth > 1 Then Hilbert depth - 1, -dy, -dx
End Sub
```

Example program Hilbert uses this routine to draw Hilbert curves. Enter the depth of the curve you want to draw and click the Go button. Because some Hilbert curves take a long time to draw, you should run the program for relatively small levels (four or five) until you know how long the program takes on your computer.

Hilbert curves have some properties that make them particularly useful as decorations. First, all the lines in a Hilbert curve are vertical or horizontal. That means all the lines have the same brightness and none suffers from the aliasing problems that sometimes affect diagonal line segments as described in Chapters 6 and 7.

Second, computing the size of a Hilbert curve is relatively easy. If a depth N curve has line segments of length S, the total width and height of the curve is $S * (2^N - 1)$. To think

Figure 10.19 A box made from Hilbert curves.

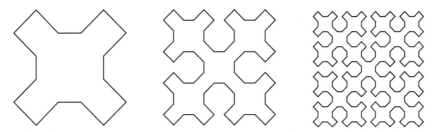

Figure 10.20   Level one, two, and three Sierpinski curves.

of this in another way, if you want a depth N Hilbert curve to have width and height W, make the line segments $W / (2^N - 1)$ long.

Finally, Hilbert curves are square with their starting and ending positions located in two adjacent corners. Together, these features make it easy to design borders, dividers, and other decorations using Hilbert curves. Figure 10.19 shows a box made from 12 level-three Hilbert curves connected by short line segments.

Sierpinski Curves

Sierpinski curves are also self-similar curves that are naturally defined recursively. Figure 10.20 shows Sierpinski curves of levels one, two, and three.

The Hilbert curve subroutine in the previous section calls itself recursively to draw Hilbert curves. Sierpinski curves are easier to draw with four routines working together than with a single routine. These four routines are named SierpA, SierpB, SierpC, and SierpD. The routines are indirectly recursive. Each routine calls the others, which may later call the first. The different routines draw the top, left, bottom, and right parts of a Sierpinski curve. In Figure 10.21, these parts of the curve are labeled A, B, C, and D so that you can see which routine draws the different parts of the curve.

Each of the four curve types is composed of a diagonal line segment, a vertical or horizontal line segment, and another diagonal line segment. When the depth of recursion is greater than 1, the program breaks each curve's two diagonal line segments into two smaller curves. For example, to break up a type A curve, the program breaks the first diagonal segment into a type A curve followed by a type B curve. Next, the program draws a horizontal line segment. It then breaks the second diagonal segment into a type D curve followed by a type A curve.

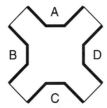

Figure 10.21   The four basic types of Sierpinski subcurves.

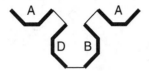

Figure 10.22 A depth two type A curve made up of four level-one curves.

Figure 10.22 shows how level-one curves make up a level-two type A curve. Figure 10.23 shows how 16 level-one curves make up a complete level-two Sierpinski curve. Each of the level-two subcurves is circled with dashed lines so that it is easy to see.

If you use arrows to indicate the types of lines that connect the subcurves (the thin lines in Figures 10.22 and 10.23), you can list the recursive relationships among the four types of curves, as shown in Figure 10.24.

The routines that draw the Sierpinski subcurves are all very similar, so only one is shown here. Figure 10.24 shows how to combine smaller curves to form larger ones. You can follow the steps in Figure 10.24 for drawing a type A curve in the following code. You can use the other relationships to reproduce the other curve-drawing routines.

```
' Draw a type A sierpinski sub-curve.
Private Sub SierpA(ByVal depth As Integer, _
    ByVal dist As Single)

    If depth = 1 Then
        picCanvas.Line -Step(-dist, dist)
        picCanvas.Line -Step(-dist, 0)
        picCanvas.Line -Step(-dist, -dist)
    Else
        SierpA depth - 1, dist
        picCanvas.Line -Step(-dist, dist)
        SierpB depth - 1, dist
```

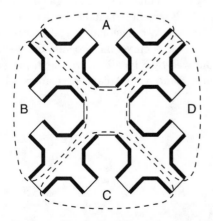

Figure 10.23 A complete depth two Sierpinski curve made up of depth one curves.

A: A ↗ B ← D ↘ A
B: B ↘ C ↓ A ↗ B
C: C ↗ D → B ↘ C
D: D ↘ A ↑ C ↗ D

Figure 10.24   Recursive relationships among Sierpinski subcurves.

```
        picCanvas.Line -Step(-dist, 0)
        SierpD depth - 1, dist
        picCanvas.Line -Step(-dist, -dist)
        SierpA depth - 1, dist
    End If
End Sub
```

In addition to the routines that draw each of the four basic curve types, the program needs a routine that uses the four to create the completed Sierpinski curve.

```
' Draw the complete Sierpinski curve.
Private Sub Sierpinski(depth As Integer, dist As Single)
    SierpB depth, dist
    picCanvas.Line -Step(dist, dist)
    SierpC depth, dist
    picCanvas.Line -Step(dist, -dist)
    SierpD depth, dist
    picCanvas.Line -Step(-dist, -dist)
    SierpA depth, dist
    picCanvas.Line -Step(-dist, dist)
End Sub
```

Example program Sierp uses these recursive routines to draw Sierpinski curves. Be sure to test the program with relatively small levels of recursion (three or four) until you know how long the program takes on your computer.

Peano Curves

Figure 10.25 shows Peano curves of depths one, two, and three. Arrows on the level-one curve show the order in which the segments were drawn.

High-level Peano curves are made up of smaller curves appropriately scaled and rotated. Like the Hilbert curve code presented earlier, the Peano curve routine uses two variables, dx and dy, to indicate the direction in which it is drawing. When the routine recurses, it calls itself nine times with the dx and dy parameters scaled by a factor of one-third and switched around to produce an appropriately rotated curve.

Example program Peano uses the following code to draw Peano curves. You may want to step through the routine in the debugger a few times to see how dx and dy are switched to draw the correct curves.

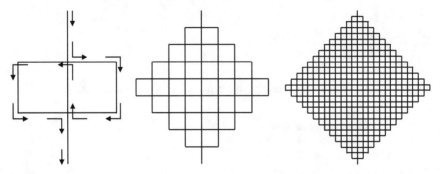

Figure 10.25   Depth one, two, and three Peano curves.

```
' Draw a Peano curve.
Private Sub Peano(ByVal depth As Integer, _
    ByVal dx As Single, ByVal dy As Single)
Dim dx3 As Single
Dim dy3 As Single

    If depth > 0 Then
        dx3 = dx / 3
        dy3 = dy / 3
        Peano depth - 1, dx3, dy3
        Peano depth - 1, dy3, dx3
        Peano depth - 1, dx3, dy3
        Peano depth - 1, -dy3, -dx3
        Peano depth - 1, -dx3, -dy3
        Peano depth - 1, -dy3, -dx3
        Peano depth - 1, dx3, dy3
        Peano depth - 1, dy3, dx3
        Peano depth - 1, dx3, dy3
    Else
        picCanvas.Line -Step(dx, dy)
    End If
End Sub
```

Gaskets

You can think of a fractal gasket as a geometric shape with some holes cut in it. The gasket shown in Figure 10.26 is called the Sierpinski gasket. The simplest way to create a Sierpinski gasket is to draw a large filled triangle. Break the triangle into four smaller triangles and erase the middle one. Then recursively call a subroutine to erase the middle triangles from the three remaining triangles.

The following source code uses this method to draw Sierpinski gaskets.

```
Private Type POINTAPI
    X As Long
```

Figure 10.26   A Sierpinski gasket.

```
    Y As Long
End Type
Private Declare Function Polygon Lib "gdi32" ( _
    ByVal hdc As Long, lpPoint As POINTAPI, _
    ByVal nCount As Long) As Long

' Draw a complete Sierpinski gasket.
Private Sub SierpinskiGasket(ByVal depth As Integer, _
    ByVal x1 As Single, ByVal y1 As Single, _
    ByVal x2 As Single, ByVal y2 As Single, _
    ByVal x3 As Single, ByVal y3 As Single)
Dim points(1 To 3) As POINTAPI

    ' Erase the picture.
    picCanvas.Line (0, 0)- _
        (picCanvas.ScaleWidth, picCanvas.ScaleHeight), _
        picCanvas.BackColor, BF

    ' Draw the main filled triangle.
    picCanvas.AutoRedraw = True
    picCanvas.FillStyle = vbFSSolid
    picCanvas.FillColor = vbBlack
    points(1).X = x1
    points(1).Y = y1
    points(2).X = x2
    points(2).Y = y2
    points(3).X = x3
    points(3).Y = y3
    Polygon picCanvas.hdc, points(1), 3

    ' If depth > 0, call SierpinskiErase to
    ' erase the center of this triangle.
    If depth >= 0 Then
        picCanvas.FillColor = picCanvas.BackColor
        SierpinskiErase depth, x1, y1, x2, y2, x3, y3
    End If
```

```
        ' Make the results visible.
        picCanvas.Refresh
        picCanvas.Picture = picCanvas.Image
End Sub

' Erase the center triangle from this one.
Private Sub SierpinskiErase(ByVal depth As Integer, _
    ByVal x1 As Single, ByVal y1 As Single, _
    ByVal x2 As Single, ByVal y2 As Single, _
    ByVal x3 As Single, ByVal y3 As Single)
Dim newy As Single
Dim newx1 As Single
Dim newx2 As Single
Dim newx3 As Single
Dim points(1 To 3) As POINTAPI

        ' Find the corners of the middle triangle.
        newy = (y1 + y2) / 2
        newx1 = (3 * x1 + x3) / 4
        newx2 = (x1 + x3) / 2
        newx3 = (x1 + 3 * x3) / 4

        ' Erase the middle triangle.
        points(1).X = newx1
        points(1).Y = newy
        points(2).X = newx3
        points(2).Y = newy
        points(3).X = newx2
        points(3).Y = y1
        Polygon picCanvas.hdc, points(1), 3

        ' Recursively erase other subtriangles.
        If depth > 0 Then
            SierpinskiErase depth - 1, _
                x1, y1, newx1, newy, newx2, y1
            SierpinskiErase depth - 1, _
                newx1, newy, newx2, y2, newx3, newy
            SierpinskiErase depth - 1, _
                newx2, y1, newx3, newy, x3, y1
        End If
End Sub
```

Example program SierpG uses this code to create Sierpinski gaskets. Start by drawing curves of small depth (four or five) until you know how long the program takes on your computer. Your monitor probably does not have enough resolution to show the difference between gaskets of higher depths, anyway.

Sierpinski Gasket Curves

An interesting thing about the Sierpinski gasket is that there are several other very different ways you can create figures that look almost the same. Figure 10.27 shows the first six levels of a curve that looks like the Sierpinski gasket.

The remarkably simple curve-drawing subroutine that follows takes as parameters the angle at which it should draw, the distance it must cover, and the amount it should initially turn if it needs to call itself recursively.

```
' Draw a gasket-like Sierpinski curve.
Private Sub SierpinskiGasketCurve(ByVal depth As Integer, _
    ByVal theta As Single, ByVal dist As Single, _
    ByVal turn As Single)

    If depth > 0 Then
        SierpinskiGasketCurve depth - 1, _
            theta + turn, dist / 2, -turn
        SierpinskiGasketCurve depth - 1, _
            theta, dist / 2, turn
        SierpinskiGasketCurve depth - 1, _
            theta - turn, dist / 2, -turn
    Else
        picCanvas.Line - _
            Step(dist * Cos(theta), dist * Sin(theta))
    End If
End Sub
```

Figure 10.27 Six levels of a curve that approximates a Sierpinski gasket.

Example program SierpG2 uses this code to draw a Sierpinski gasket-like curve. The program initially invokes the SierpinskiGasketCurve routine with a direction of 0 (horizontally moving to the right), a distance large enough to cross most of the picture box, and a turn angle of 60 degrees. This produces images like those shown in Figure 10.27.

Sierpinski Chaos

Another way you can create Sierpinski gaskets is using a program called the *chaos game*. Before playing the game, you select several anchor points within a picture box. The program starts by picking a random point anywhere within the box. Then it repeatedly selects one of the anchor points randomly and moves halfway from its currently selected point to the anchor point. It plots that position and makes that the next selected point. As the game progresses, the program sometimes creates ghostly images one pixel at a time.

The following code shows the heart of the chaos game. The arrays AnchorX and AnchorY store the coordinates of the anchor points as fractions of the size of the picCanvas picture box. For example, if AnchorX(i) = 0.1, the ith anchor point is 10 percent of the way through the picture box from left to right.

```
' Play the chaos game.
Private Sub PlayGame()
Dim wid As Single
Dim hgt As Single
Dim X As Single
Dim Y As Single
Dim anchor As Integer
Dim i As Integer

    ' See how much room we have.
    wid = picCanvas.ScaleWidth
    hgt = picCanvas.ScaleHeight

    ' Pick a random starting point.
    X = wid * Rnd
    Y = hgt * Rnd

    ' Start the game.
    i = 0
    Do While Running
        ' Pick a random anchor point.
        anchor = Int(NumAnchors * Rnd + 1)

        ' Move halfway there.
        X = (X + wid * AnchorX(anchor)) / 2
        Y = (Y + hgt * AnchorY(anchor)) / 2
        picCanvas.PSet (X, Y)
```

```
        ' To make things faster, only DoEvents
        ' every 100 times.
        i = i + 1
        If i > 100 Then
            i = 0
            DoEvents
        End If
    Loop
End Sub
```

Example program Chaos uses this code to play the chaos game. Select the File menu's Open command and pick a file with a .cha extension. These files contain a number of anchor points and then list the points.

The following text shows the contents of the file Sierp.cha. The comments to the right make the listing easier to follow and are not part of the file.

```
3               ' Number of anchor points.
0.1, 0.9        ' Anchor point 1.
0.5, 0.1        ' Anchor point 2.
0.9, 0.9        ' Anchor point 3.
```

Using the anchor points defined by file Sierp.cha, program Chaos generates the shape shown in Figure 10.28. The boxes at the corners of the gasket are the anchor points.

Other Gaskets

Program SierpG breaks a triangle into four smaller triangles and removes the middle one. It then recursively calls itself to turn the remaining three triangles into gaskets. You can use a similar technique to create other gaskets.

The following code divides a square into nine smaller squares. It erases the middle square and recursively calls itself to turn the remaining eight squares into gaskets.

```
 ' Erase the center rectangle from this one.
Private Sub SierpinskiErase(ByVal depth As Integer, _
```

Figure 10.28 Program Chaos generating a Sierpinski gasket.

```
        ByVal x1 As Single, ByVal y1 As Single, _
        ByVal x4 As Single, ByVal y4 As Single)
Dim x2 As Single
Dim y2 As Single
Dim x3 As Single
Dim y3 As Single

    ' Find the corners of the middle square.
    x2 = (2 * x1 + x4) * 0.3333
    x3 = (x1 + 2 * x4) * 0.3333
    y2 = (2 * y1 + y4) * 0.3333
    y3 = (y1 + 2 * y4) * 0.3333

    ' Erase the middle rectangle.
    picCanvas.Line (x2, y2)-(x3, y3), picCanvas.BackColor, BF

    ' Recursively erase other rectangles.
    If depth > 0 Then
        SierpinskiErase depth - 1, x1, y1, x2, y2
        SierpinskiErase depth - 1, x2, y1, x3, y2
        SierpinskiErase depth - 1, x3, y1, x4, y2
        SierpinskiErase depth - 1, x1, y2, x2, y3
        SierpinskiErase depth - 1, x3, y2, x4, y3
        SierpinskiErase depth - 1, x1, y3, x2, y4
        SierpinskiErase depth - 1, x2, y3, x3, y4
        SierpinskiErase depth - 1, x3, y3, x4, y4
    End If
End Sub
```

Example program SierpBox uses this routine to create gaskets like the one shown in Figure 10.29. This object is known as the *Sierpinski carpet* or the *Sierpinski box*.

The Mandelbrot Set

The Mandelbrot set is probably the most widely recognized fractal. Its ever-changing whorls, twists, spikes, and ridges give it an alien beauty that makes it a popular subject

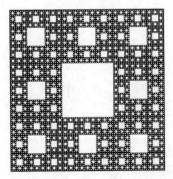

Figure 10.29 A Sierpinski carpet.

for graphic programs, screen savers, calendars, T-shirts, and all sorts of other colorful products. Figure 10.30 shows four different views of the Mandelbrot set.

While infinitely complex in appearance, the Mandelbrot set is based on a very simple equation:

$$Z_n = Z_{n-1}^2 + C$$

where the Z_n and C are complex numbers.

As a quick review, recall that complex numbers have a real part and an imaginary part. A complex number with real part R and imaginary part I is written as R + I * i, where i is a special number representing the square root of –1. Now if $Z_{n-1} = R_{n-1} + I_{n-1} * i$ and C = $R_C + I_C * i$, you can rewrite the equation above as:

$$
\begin{aligned}
Z_n &= Z_{n-1}^2 + C \\
&= (R_{n-1} + I_{n-1} * i)^2 + (R_C + I_C * i) \\
&= (R_{n-1}^2 + 2 * R_{n-1} * I_{n-1} * i + I_{n-1}^2 * i^2) + (R_C + I_C * i)
\end{aligned}
$$

Because i is the square root of –1, $i^2 = -1$ by definition. Then you can regroup the real and imaginary parts of the equation to get:

$$Z_n = (R_{n-1}^2 - I_{n-1}^2 + R_C) + (2 * R_{n-1} * I_{n-1} + I_C) * i$$

You can rewrite this equation as two separate equations for the real and imaginary parts.

$$
\begin{aligned}
R_n &= R_{n-1}^2 - I_{n-1}^2 + R_C \\
I_n &= 2 * R_{n-1} * I_{n-1} + I_C
\end{aligned}
$$

Figure 10.30 Different views of the Mandelbrot set.

Using these equations, you can compute the real and imaginary parts of Z_n in Visual Basic for different values of n. For instance, suppose you start with $Z_0 = 0 + 0 * i$ and $C = 1 + 1 * i$. Then the values for Z_n would be:

```
Z₀ = 0 + 0 * i
Z₁ = (0² - 0² + 1) + (2 * 0 * 0 + 1) * i = 1 + 1 * i
Z₂ = (1² - 1² + 1) + (2 * 1 * 1 + 1) * i = 1 + 3 * i
Z₃ = (1² - 3² + 1) + (2 * 1 * 3 + 1) * i = -7 + 7 * i
Z₄ = (7² - 7² + 1) + (2 * (-7) * 7 + 1) * i = 1 - 97 * i
Z₅ = (1² - (-97)² + 1) + (2 * 1 * (-97) + 1) * i = -9407 - 193 * i
```

After this, the values for R_n and I_n become huge. In fact, it can be shown that, if the magnitude of Z_n given by $Sqr(R_n^2 + I_n^2)$ ever exceeds 2, the magnitude of the Zn values will eventually head toward infinity.

The Mandelbrot set is a map showing how quickly the magnitude of Z_n goes toward infinity for different values of C. Let the X and Y coordinates of a point correspond to the real and imaginary parts of the number C. Starting with $Z_0 = 0$, compute the series of values Z_n for that value of C. If you find a value for Z_n that has magnitude greater than 2, you know the magnitudes will eventually head toward infinity. Use the number of iterations it took to find a magnitude greater than 2 to compute a color for that pixel. If you want to use NumColors colors and Z_n is the first value that has a magnitude greater than 2, you would give the pixel color number n Mod NumColors.

For some values of C, the magnitude of the Z_n will not grow toward infinity. After you have examined some predefined number of values, stop. All the values of C that make you stop in this way end up with the same color. If the maximum number of Z_n you compute is a multiple of the number of colors you use, these pixels will all be colored with color number 0. For example, if you are using 16 colors and you compute up to 64 values for Z_n, all these pixels will have color number 64 Mod 16 = 0.

The following code shows a Mandelbrot set drawing routine. This routine uses the Get-BitmapPixels and SetBitmapPixels subroutines described in Chapter 3, Advanced Color, to update the image quickly.

```
' Draw the Mandelbrot set.
Private Sub DrawMandelbrot()
' Work until the magnitude squared > 4.
Const MAX_MAG_SQUARED = 4

Dim pixels() As RGBTriplet
Dim bits_per_pixel As Integer
Dim wid As Long
Dim hgt As Long
Dim clr As Long
Dim i As Integer
Dim j As Integer
Dim ReaC As Double
Dim ImaC As Double
```

```
Dim dReaC As Double
Dim dImaC As Double
Dim ReaZ As Double
Dim ImaZ As Double
Dim ReaZ2 As Double
Dim ImaZ2 As Double
Dim r As Integer
Dim b As Integer
Dim g As Integer

    picCanvas.Line (0, 0)-(picCanvas.ScaleWidth, _
        picCanvas.ScaleHeight), vbBlack, BF
    DoEvents

    ' Get the image's pixels.
    GetBitmapPixels picCanvas, pixels, bits_per_pixel

    ' Adjust the coordinate bounds to fit picCanvas.
    AdjustAspect

    ' dReaC is the change in the real part
    ' (X value) for C. dImaC is the change in the
    ' imaginary part (Y value).
    wid = picCanvas.ScaleWidth
    hgt = picCanvas.ScaleHeight
    dReaC = (m_Xmax - m_Xmin) / (wid - 1)
    dImaC = (m_Ymax - m_Ymin) / (hgt - 1)

    ' Calculate the values.
    ReaC = m_Xmin
    For i = 0 To wid - 1
        ImaC = m_Ymin
        For j = 0 To hgt - 1
            ReaZ = 0
            ImaZ = 0
            ReaZ2 = 0
            ImaZ2 = 0
            clr = 1
            Do While clr < MaxMandelbrotIterations And _
                    ReaZ2 + ImaZ2 < MAX_MAG_SQUARED
                ' Calculate Z(clr).
                ReaZ2 = ReaZ * ReaZ
                ImaZ2 = ImaZ * ImaZ
                ImaZ = 2 * ImaZ * ReaZ + ImaC
                ReaZ = ReaZ2 - ImaZ2 + ReaC
                clr = clr + 1
            Loop

            clr = m_Colors(1 + clr Mod NumColors)
            With pixels(i, j)
                .rgbRed = clr And &HFF&
```

```
                    .rgbGreen = (clr And &HFF00&) \ &H100&
                    .rgbBlue = (clr And &HFF0000) \ &H10000
                End With

                ImaC = ImaC + dImaC
            Next j
            ReaC = ReaC + dReaC

            ' Let the user know we're not dead.
            If i Mod 10 = 0 Then
                picCanvas.Line (0, 0)-(wid, i), vbWhite, BF
                picCanvas.Refresh
            End If
        Next i

        ' Update the image.
        SetBitmapPixels picCanvas, bits_per_pixel, pixels
        picCanvas.Refresh
        picCanvas.Picture = picCanvas.Image

        Caption = "Mand (" & Format$(m_Xmin) & ", " & _
            Format$(m_Ymin) & ")-(" & _
            Format$(m_Xmax) & ", " & _
            Format$(m_Ymax) & ")"
    End Sub
```

Example program Mand uses this subroutine to draw the Mandelbrot set. If you click and drag to select part of the image, the program zooms in on that area. You can later use the Scale menu's x2, x4, x8, and Full Scale commands to zoom out so that you can see more of the Mandelbrot set. You can save the image displayed by selecting Save As from the File menu.

The program can also save a series of images for animation. First, zoom in on an area of the Mandelbrot set that you find interesting. Then select the Movie menu's Create Movie command. The program then asks you to select a filename to use as the base name for the images. For instance, if you specify the file C:\Temp\Mand1, the program saves the movie frames in the files C:\Temp\Mand1_0.bmp, C:\Temp\Mand1_1.bmp, and so forth.

Next the program asks you how many images you want to create. After you have entered a value, the program creates the series of images. The first image is at full scale centered on the area you are currently displaying. Subsequent images zoom in on your selected area.

The Options menu's Set Options command lets you select colors and specify the maximum number of iterations the program performs when computing pixel values. This number determines how many values of Z_n the program calculates before it decides that the magnitude of Z_n is probably not heading toward infinity. Smaller values make the program run more quickly. You might want to set this value to something small, like 64 or even 16, while you are exploring the Mandelbrot set. Once you have found an interesting area, you can increase this value to 128 or 512 to see more detail.

Julia Sets

To draw a Mandelbrot set, you evaluate the sequence of values:

```
Zₙ = Zₙ₋₁² + C
```

where Z_n and C are complex numbers. For the Mandelbrot set, you start with $Z_n = 0$ and use the coordinates of the pixels in the image to give you the value of C. For each value of C, you calculate the series of Z_n values to see if the magnitude of the values tends toward infinity.

You use the same equation to create Julia sets. There are only two differences between drawing the Mandelbrot set and drawing Julia sets. The first difference is in how you select Z_0 and C. To draw a Julia set, you pick some constant value for C. You then use the coordinates of the pixels in the image to get the value Z_0.

The second difference is in selecting colors for the pixels. The Mandelbrot program sets a pixel's color based on how quickly the magnitude of Z_n exceeds 2. A Julia set program sets a pixel's color based on how large its magnitude is if it does *not* exceed 2 after a certain number of iterations. If the magnitude does exceed 2, the pixel is given a default background color.

The following code shows a Julia set drawing routine.

```
' Draw the Mandelbrot set.
Private Sub DrawJulia()
' Work until the magnitude squared > 4.
Const MAX_MAG_SQUARED = 4

Dim pixels() As RGBTriplet
Dim bits_per_pixel As Integer
Dim wid As Long
Dim hgt As Long
Dim clr As Long
Dim color As Long
Dim i As Integer
Dim j As Integer
Dim dReaZ0 As Double
Dim dImaZ0 As Double
Dim ReaZ0 As Double
Dim ImaZ0 As Double
Dim ReaZ As Double
Dim ImaZ As Double
Dim ReaZ2 As Double
Dim ImaZ2 As Double
Dim r As Integer
Dim b As Integer
Dim g As Integer

    picCanvas.Line (0, 0)-(picCanvas.ScaleWidth, _
```

```vb
            picCanvas.ScaleHeight), vbBlack, BF
DoEvents

' Get the image's pixels.
GetBitmapPixels picCanvas, pixels, bits_per_pixel

' Adjust the coordinate bounds to fit picCanvas.
AdjustAspect

' dReaZ0 is the change in the real part
' (X value) for Z0. dImaZ0 is the change in the
' imaginary part (Y value).
wid = picCanvas.ScaleWidth
hgt = picCanvas.ScaleHeight
dReaZ0 = (m_Xmax - m_Xmin) / (wid - 1)
dImaZ0 = (m_Ymax - m_Ymin) / (hgt - 1)


' Calculate the values.
ReaZ0 = m_Xmin
For i = 0 To wid - 1
    ImaZ0 = m_Ymin
    For j = 0 To hgt - 1
        ReaZ = ReaZ0
        ImaZ = ImaZ0
        ReaZ2 = ReaZ * ReaZ
        ImaZ2 = ImaZ * ImaZ
        clr = 1
        Do While clr < MaxJuliaIterations And _
                ReaZ2 + ImaZ2 < MAX_MAG_SQUARED
            ' Calculate Z(clr).
            ReaZ2 = ReaZ * ReaZ
            ImaZ2 = ImaZ * ImaZ
            ImaZ = 2 * ImaZ * ReaZ + m_Julia_ImaC
            ReaZ = ReaZ2 - ImaZ2 + m_Julia_ReaC
            clr = clr + 1
        Loop

        If clr >= MaxJuliaIterations Then
            ' Use a non-background color.
            color = m_Colors(((ReaZ2 + ImaZ2) * _
                (numcolors - 1)) Mod _
                (numcolors - 1) + 1)
        Else
            ' Use the background color.
            color = m_Colors(1)
        End If
        With pixels(i, j)
            .rgbRed = color And &HFF&
            .rgbGreen = (color And &HFF00&) \ &H100&
            .rgbBlue = (color And &HFF0000) \ &H10000
        End With
```

```
            ImaZ0 = ImaZ0 + dImaZ0
        Next j
        ReaZ0 = ReaZ0 + dReaZ0

        ' Let the user know we're not dead.
        If i Mod 10 = 0 Then
            picCanvas.Line (0, 0)-(wid, i), vbWhite, BF
            picCanvas.Refresh
        End If
    Next i

    ' Update the image.
    SetBitmapPixels picCanvas, bits_per_pixel, pixels
    picCanvas.Refresh
    picCanvas.Picture = picCanvas.Image

    Caption = "Julia (" & Format$(m_Xmin) & ", " & _
        Format$(m_Ymin) & ")-(" & _
        Format$(m_Xmax) & ", " & _
        Format$(m_Ymax) & ")"
End Sub
```

Interestingly, the Mandelbrot set forms a strange kind of map for Julia sets. You can use the coordinates of any point in a Mandelbrot set as the real and imaginary parts of the value C for drawing a Julia set. Some of the most interesting Julia sets are created when C corresponds to a point close to one of the fuzzy edges of the Mandelbrot set.

Example program Julia is similar to program Mand. You can use it to display a Mandelbrot set and zoom in on areas of interest. If you select the Options menu's Julia command, the program displays the Julia set with the value of C corresponding to the point in the center of the currently displayed area in the Mandelbrot set. In other words, to select a value of C that corresponds to a point near the edge of the Mandelbrot set, zoom in on that point in the Mandelbrot display and then invoke the Julia command.

While you are displaying a Julia set, you can zoom in on areas much as you can for the Mandelbrot set. You can also alter the appearance of the picture by changing the maximum number of iterations the program computes for each pixel. If you increase the number of iterations, the magnitude of Z_n exceeds 2 for more of the pixels. The program gives those pixels the default background color, so the resulting image contains fewer non-background pixels.

Often, you need to adjust the number of iterations for a particular Julia set to produce the best result. If the number is too small, the program makes many pixels colorful, but the picture may not have much detail. If the number is too large, the program will set most or all of the pixels to the background color, and there may be very little to see.

After you have finished looking at the current Julia set, select the Options menu's Mandelbrot command. The program once again displays the Mandelbrot set, so you can zoom in on a new value for C and create a different Julia set.

Figure 10.31 shows views of four different Julia sets.

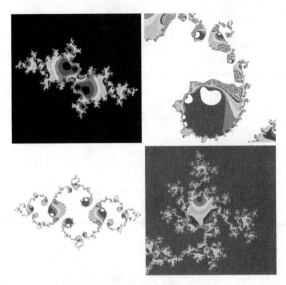

Figure 10.31   Four different Julia sets.

Strange Attractors

Suppose you have a system of equations that produce a series of values. For example, the equation $Z_n = Z_{n-1}^2 + C$ produces a series of values Z_0, Z_1, Z_2 and so forth used to draw the Mandelbrot and Julia sets. This equation is equivalent to two equations that give the real and imaginary parts R_n and I_n of the number Z_n.

You can examine the values produced by such an equation in the system's *phase space*. This is a coordinate space with enough dimensions to plot each value produced by the system of equations. In this example, there are two equations R_n and I_n, so the phase space is two-dimensional.

In this case, you can use the values of R_n and I_n to give the X and Y coordinates of points to plot. If you plot the values produced for many of different initial conditions, you may get one of several possible results. First, the plot may approach a single value. For example, consider the following equations.

```
Xₙ = Xₙ₋₁ / 2
Yₙ = Yₙ₋₁ / 4
```

As the value n grows large, the values for X_n and Y_n approach zero, no matter what the initial values of X_0 and Y_0 are. If you plot the values of X_n and Y_n, you will find that the curves for different initial conditions are all drawn toward the point (0, 0). The collection of points toward which the plotted curves are drawn is called an *attractor*. When all the curves are drawn toward a single point, as in this example, that point is called a *fixed-point attractor*.

For other systems of equations, the plotted points may eventually settle into a steady state in which they follow a repeating cycle. This sort of attractor is called a *limit cycle*.

Still other systems produce points that seem to jump randomly around in phase space. When you plot enough values, however, a pattern emerges. While individually the points seem randomly placed and they do not really follow a curve, they are still constrained in some bizarre way. The unusual shapes these plots are drawn toward are called *strange attractors*.

The following equations discovered by Clifford Pickover generate points that are drawn toward a strange attractor.

```
X_n = Sin(A * Y_{n-1}) - Z_{n-1} * Cos(B * X_{n-1})
Y_n = Z_n * Sin(C * X_{n-1}) - Cos(D * Y_{n-1})
Z_n = Sin(X_{n-1})
```

where A, B, C, D, and E are constants.

Because there are three equations in this system, the phase space is three dimensional and the generated points have X, Y, and Z components. To visualize what this shape looks like, you can plot its projections onto the XY, XZ, and YZ planes. To project points onto the XZ plane, for example, simply ignore the points' Y coordinates.

Figure 10.32 shows three images of the Pickover attractor. Each image contains 30,000 points. You can see from the figure that the points are not arranged completely randomly. Although they do not follow a simple curve, they are arranged in some sort of strange pattern.

Example program Pickover lets you experiment with the Pickover equations. Enter values for the parameters A, B, C, D, and E. Use the option buttons to tell the program whether to project the points onto the XY, XZ, or YZ plane. Then click the Go button to make the program begin plotting points.

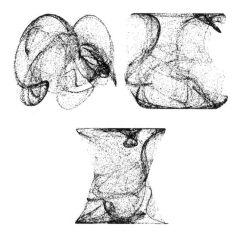

Figure 10.32   The Pickover attractor.

Let the program run for several seconds and click the Stop button. Then click the Go button again. Several seconds pass before the program begins plotting new points. The program spends the first several seconds replotting the exact same points it plotted before.

Stop the program again and change the value of X0 slightly. If the initial value of X0 was 0, change it to 0.0001. Then click the Go button again. This time, the program begins to generate new points immediately. This demonstrates an important feature of many chaotic systems: Initial conditions that differ by only a tiny amount often produce very different results. Even though the two initial conditions differed by only 0.0001, the equations produced different points right away. If you experiment with other initial values, you will see the same effect. Different values produce different points, but they all follow the same strange attractor.

Tilings

Mathematically speaking, a *tiling* is a collection of sets that covers the plane without gaps or overlaps. By that definition, the squares in a checkerboard and the pieces in a jigsaw puzzle form tilings.

The study of tilings in mathematics is a huge and complex field. The following sections examine only a few of the simplest kinds of tiles that are possible. These tiles produce patterns that are interesting and easy to use in Visual Basic.

The easiest type of tiling to implement in Visual Basic is one that is defined by a rectangular tile. You can cover a form, picture box, or printer object with the tile by repeatedly copying it using the PaintPicture method.

The most straightforward way to cover a destination area is to copy the tile in rows and columns. The TilePicture subroutine shown in the following code tiles a picture box with a tile stored in an image control.

```
' Tile a PictureBox with the picture in an Image control.
Private Sub TilePicture(ByVal pic As PictureBox, _
    ByVal tile_image As Image)
Dim wid As Integer
Dim hgt As Integer
Dim rows As Integer
Dim cols As Integer
Dim r As Integer
Dim c As Integer
Dim x As Integer
Dim y As Integer

    pic.Cls     ' Clear the picture box.
    wid = ScaleX(tile_image.Width, _
        tile_image.Parent.ScaleMode, pic.ScaleMode)
    hgt = ScaleY(tile_image.Height, _
        tile_image.Parent.ScaleMode, pic.ScaleMode)
```

```
    ' See how many rows and columns we will need.
    cols = Int(pic.ScaleWidth / wid + 1)
    rows = Int(pic.ScaleHeight / hgt + 1)

    ' Copy the tile.
    y = 0
    For r = 1 To rows
        x = 0
        For c = 1 To cols
            pic.PaintPicture tile_image.Picture, x, y
            x = x + wid
        Next c
        y = y + hgt
    Next r
End Sub
```

Example program Tile, shown in Figure 10.33, uses the subroutine TilePicture a variety of tiles. Click on a pattern to make the tile its drawing area with it.

Some tilings are easiest to define when you use nonrectangular tiles. For example, you can define the tile shown in Figure 10.34 using the hexagonal tile surrounded by bold lines. Covering an area using this tile is a bit more complicated than it is to use a rectangular tile for a couple reasons.

Rows and columns are harder to locate in this tiling than they are in a rectangular tiling. A copy of the tile in a row does not lie immediately next to the tiles on its left and right. A row does not lie directly below the row above.

To correctly place the tiles, you can pass parameters into the tiling routine indicating the X offset it should use between tiles on the same row and the X and Y offsets it should use between rows.

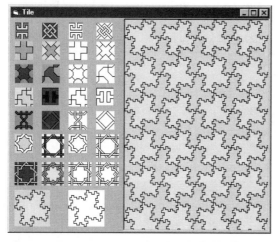

Figure 10.33 Program Tile tiling a picture box.

Figure 10.34 Tiling with a hexagonal tile.

Another complication arises because the PaintPicture method copies only rectangular regions. Because these tiles are not rectangular, you cannot just use PaintPicture to copy them. If you did, PaintPicture would copy a rectangular area surrounding the tile, including some of the background area. The background would then obscure parts of the other nearby tiles.

To avoid obscuring other tiles, you can create a mask for the tile. The mask should be the same size as the tile's bitmap. It should be black where its pixels correspond to pixels you want to draw in the tile bitmap and white where its pixels correspond to background pixels in the tile bitmap. Then instead of copying the tile in a single call to PaintPicture, you first copy the mask using the vbMergePaint raster operation. You then copy the tile bitmap using the vbSrcAnd raster operation. These two operations together copy the tile's bitmap to the destination area only in the places that correspond to black pixels in the mask.

The TilePicture subroutine shown in the following code tiles a picture box using a tile and mask stored in image controls. The parameter cdx gives the X offset between adjacent tiles in a row. The rdx and rdy parameters give the X and Y offsets between tiles in different rows.

```
' Tile the PictureBox with the image in the image control.
Private Sub TilePicture(ByVal pic As PictureBox, _
    ByVal tile_image As Image, ByVal mask_image As Image, _
    ByVal cdx As Integer, _
    ByVal rdx As Integer, ByVal rdy As Integer)
Dim wid As Single
Dim hgt As Single
Dim x As Integer
Dim y As Integer
Dim x1 As Integer
Dim x2 As Integer
Dim startx As Integer

    pic.Cls      ' Clear the picture box.
```

```
' Start above and to the left of the drawing area.
wid = tile_image.Parent.ScaleX(tile_image.Width, _
    tile_image.Parent.ScaleMode, pic.ScaleMode)
hgt = tile_image.Parent.ScaleY(tile_image.Height, _
    tile_image.Parent.ScaleMode, pic.ScaleMode)
y = -hgt
x1 = -wid
x2 = x1 + rdx
startx = x1

' Copy the tile until we're to the right and
' below the drawing area.
Do While y <= pic.ScaleHeight
    x = startx
    Do While x <= pic.ScaleWidth
        ' Copy the mask with vbMergePaint.
        pic.PaintPicture mask_image.Picture, _
            x, y, , , , , , vbMergePaint

        ' Copy the mask with vbSrcAnd.
        pic.PaintPicture tile_image.Picture, _
            x, y, , , , , , vbSrcAnd
        x = x + cdx
    Loop

    If startx = x1 Then
        startx = x2
    Else
        startx = x1
    End If
    y = y + rdy
Loop
End Sub
```

Example program TileHex uses this routine to display several different tiles. Click a tile image to make the program tile its drawing area with that tile. The offsets for the bottom two tiles are set so that the tiles do not cover the whole draw area. They incorporate the background color into the pattern displayed.

Summary

The programs described in this chapter are mostly decorative. They produce interesting images you can use to make a program unique. The self-similar fractal programs also provide interesting examples of recursive programming. By calling themselves to produce different parts of a curve, routines such as the Hilbert and Sierpinski subroutines generate images of remarkable complexity with surprisingly little code.

CHAPTER 11

Drawing Curves

V isual Basic comes with a reasonable assortment of drawing routines. Forms, picture boxes, and printer objects provide methods for drawing lines, circles, arcs, pie slices, boxes, and text. You can use these methods, particularly the Line method, to draw more complex shapes than those provided by Visual Basic directly.

For example, you can use the Circle method to draw a circle. You can also use Circle to draw an ellipse with axes parallel to the X and Y axes. However, you cannot use this method to draw an ellipse that has been rotated by 30 degrees. Even the Windows API, which contains routines for drawing ellipses, arcs, chords, and pie slices, does not contain routines for drawing these objects rotated. If you want to display these shapes, you must draw them yourself.

This chapter describes some of the issues you face when you want to display one of these shapes in Visual Basic. It shows how you can draw circles and rotated ellipses quickly and easily.

It also describes several different types of curves you can use to represent data. Curves such as least square fits, splines, and Bezier curves follow a set of data points while providing a balance between close fit and smoothness. By following the general pattern of the points instead of following the points exactly, they show the overall shape of the data and can make patterns clear.

Lines and Circles

Over the years programmers have developed extremely efficient algorithms for scan converting fundamental shapes like lines and circles. Bresenham's circle algorithm, for example, uses clever techniques to decide which pixels belong to a circle while minimizing the number of complex mathematical operations that would make the algorithm slow.

These algorithms are quite interesting, but they are not very useful to a typical Visual Basic programmer. Visual Basic and the Windows operating systems use these techniques to draw lines and circles much more quickly than you could on your own. Rather than implementing your own circle- and line-drawing routines, use those provided by Visual Basic whenever possible.

The sections that follow describe some curves that Visual Basic methods cannot easily draw. You can draw these curves yourself using the Line method.

Parametric Curves

A *parametric curve* is a curve with X and Y coordinates defined in terms of a third parameter. Usually the parameter is called "t," and the equations for the coordinates of the points on the curve are written as X(t) and Y(t).

For example, you can write the parametric equations for a circle with radius R centered at the origin as X(t) = R * Cos(t), Y(t) = R * Sin(t). As the parameter t varies between the values 0 and 2 * π, the functions X(t) and Y(t) give the coordinates of the points on the circle.

In Visual Basic, drawing a curve written with parametric equations is easy. Create a variable t and use a While loop to run the variable over the range of parameter values needed to draw the curve. Connect the points on the curve using the Visual Basic Line command.

The DrawCurve subroutine shown in the following code does this. The values cx and cy are chosen to center the drawing in the picture box.

```
' Draw the curve on the indicated picture box.
Private Sub DrawCurve(ByVal pic As PictureBox, _
    ByVal start_t As Single, ByVal stop_t As Single, _
    ByVal dt As Single)
Dim cx As Single
Dim cy As Single
Dim t As Single

    cx = pic.ScaleLeft + pic.ScaleWidth / 2
    cy = pic.ScaleTop + pic.ScaleHeight / 2

    pic.Cls
    pic.CurrentX = cx + X(start_t)
    pic.CurrentY = cy + Y(start_t)

    t = start_t + dt
    Do While t < stop_t
        pic.Line -(cx + X(t), cy + Y(t))
        t = t + dt
    Loop

    pic.Line -(cx + X(stop_t), cy + Y(stop_t))
End Sub
```

If you make dt too large in this routine, the points you connect on the curve are far apart and the curve does not appear smooth. If you make dt smaller, the curve appears smoother. If you make dt too small, you waste a lot of time finding points on the curve that you do not need. When the points you calculate are drawn at the nearest pixels, many of the points will end up at the same position. You could have used fewer points to get the same result.

Figure 11.1 shows a circle drawn three times with this method. To create the picture on the left, dt was set to $\pi/4$. This value is not small enough, so the circle does not appear smooth. In the middle picture, dt is $\pi/8$. This makes the circle smoother, but straight edges are still visible. The value of dt in the right picture is $\pi/16$. This circle appears reasonably smooth. Making dt smaller than $\pi/16$ makes the routine take longer without producing great improvements in the result.

Example program Circle1 uses this method to draw circles like those shown in Figure 11.1. Enter minimum and maximum values for t and the value of dt. Then when you click on the Go button, the program draws the corresponding circle.

The following code shows the parametric functions X(t) and Y(t) that program Circle1 uses to draw circles. The value Radius was chosen to make the circle fill the picture box.

```
' The parametric function X(t).
Private Function X(ByVal t As Single) As Single
    X = Radius * Cos(t)
End Function

' The parametric function Y(t).
Private Function Y(ByVal t As Single) As Single
    Y = Radius * Sin(t)
End Function
```

DrawCurve

Program Circle1 uses the DrawCurve subroutine shown earlier to draw circles. The functions X(t) and Y(t) return the points on the circle for different values of t.

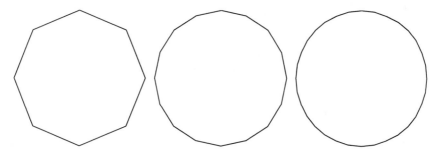

Figure 11.1　Circles drawn with dt $= \pi/4$, $\pi/8$, and $\pi/16$.

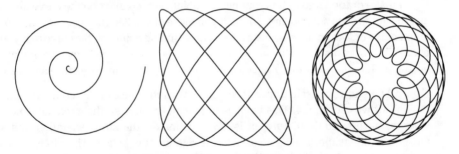

Figure 11.2 Parametric spiral, Bowditch curve, and cycloid.

If the DrawCurve routine were good for drawing nothing but circles, it would not be very useful. Visual Basic's Circle routine draws smooth circles more quickly and easily. There are two reasons the DrawCurve subroutine is important. First, it works for many other kinds of parametric curves.

Figure 11.2 shows three other parametric curves. A program can draw all three of these curves using the same DrawCurve subroutine. Only the parametric functions X and Y need to change. Table 11.1 lists the parametric equations and the values covered by t for these curves, as well as the name of the example program that displays them.

The second reason the DrawCurve subroutine is important is that it turns a set of parametric equations into a series of points along a curve. Before you connect the points with lines, you can perform actions on the points to transform the curve.

For example, if you multiply the values returned for X(t) by 2 before you draw the points, the curve is stretched by a factor of two in the X direction. The following code draws a circle scaled in both the X and Y directions.

```
' Draw the curve on the indicated picture box
' scaled.
Private Sub DrawCurve(ByVal pic As PictureBox, _
    ByVal start_t As Single, ByVal stop_t As Single, _
    ByVal dt As Single, _
    ByVal x_scale As Single, ByVal y_scale As Single)
Dim cx As Single
Dim cy As Single
Dim t As Single

    cx = pic.ScaleLeft + pic.ScaleWidth / 2
    cy = pic.ScaleTop + pic.ScaleHeight / 2

    pic.Cls
    pic.CurrentX = cx + x_scale * X(start_t)
    pic.CurrentY = cy + y_scale * Y(start_t)

    t = start_t + dt
    Do While t < stop_t
```

Table 11.1 Equations for the Curves in Figure 11.2

PROGRAM	X(T)	Y(T)	VALUES OF T
Spiral	7 * t² / 350 * Cos(t)	-7 * t² / 350 * Sin(t)	0 <= t <= 6 * π
Bditch	2000 * Sin(4 * t)	2000 * Sin(5 * t)	0 <= t <= 2 * π
Cycloid	2000 * (27 * Cos(t) + 15 * Cos(t * 20 / 7)) / 42	2000 * (27 * Sin(t) + 15 * Sin(t * 20 / 7)) / 42	0 <= t <= 14 * π

```
        pic.Line -(cx + x_scale * X(t), cy + y_scale * Y(t))
        t = t + dt
    Loop

    pic.Line -(cx + x_scale * X(stop_t), _
        cy + y_scale * Y(stop_t))
End Sub
```

Example program Circle2 uses this code to display stretched circles. Enter the scale factors and click the Go button. The program adjusts the circle's radius and center to keep the ellipse in the middle of the picture box.

Figure 11.3 shows a circle drawn by the Circle2 program. In this picture, the points have been scaled by a factor of 0.5 in the Y direction, making the circle appear squashed.

Rotating Points

Another way you can transform a curve is to rotate each of its points. If you want to rotate the points by an angle of θ radians, transform the X and Y coordinates of each point like this:

```
new X(t) = X(t) * Cos(θ) - Y(t) * Sin(θ)
new Y(t) = X(t) * Sin(θ) + Y(t) * Cos(θ)
```

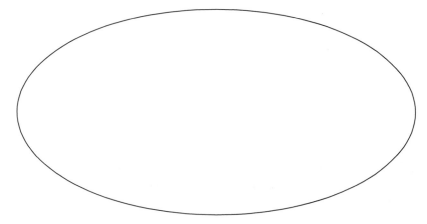

Figure 11.3 A circle scaled by a factor of 0.5 in the Y direction.

The following source code displays a circle that is first scaled in the X and Y directions and then rotated.

```vb
' Draw the curve on the indicated picture box,
' scaled and rotated.
Private Sub DrawCurve(ByVal pic As PictureBox, _
    ByVal start_t As Single, ByVal stop_t As Single, _
    ByVal dt As Single, _
    ByVal x_scale As Single, ByVal y_scale As Single, _
    ByVal theta As Single)
Dim cx As Single
Dim cy As Single
Dim sin_theta As Single
Dim cos_theta As Single
Dim old_x As Single
Dim old_y As Single
Dim new_x As Single
Dim new_y As Single
Dim t As Single

    cx = pic.ScaleLeft + pic.ScaleWidth / 2
    cy = pic.ScaleTop + pic.ScaleHeight / 2

    ' Get Cos(theta) and Sin(theta)
    sin_theta = Sin(theta)
    cos_theta = Cos(theta)

    pic.Cls
    old_x = x_scale * X(start_t)
    old_y = y_scale * Y(start_t)
    pic.CurrentX = cx + old_x * cos_theta - old_y * sin_theta
    pic.CurrentY = cy + old_x * sin_theta + old_y * cos_theta

    t = start_t + dt
    Do While t < stop_t
        old_x = x_scale * X(t)
        old_y = y_scale * Y(t)
        pic.Line -( _
            cx + old_x * cos_theta - old_y * sin_theta, _
            cy + old_x * sin_theta + old_y * cos_theta)
        t = t + dt
    Loop

    old_x = x_scale * X(stop_t)
    old_y = y_scale * Y(stop_t)
    pic.Line -( _
        cx + old_x * cos_theta - old_y * sin_theta, _
        cy + old_x * sin_theta + old_y * cos_theta)
End Sub
```

Example program Circle3 uses this code to display circles that have been scaled and rotated. Enter the scaling factors in the X and Y directions and the angle through which the circle should be rotated in degrees. Then click the Go button to make the program display the resulting rotated ellipse. You will not see the rotation if the scaling factors are the same because then the ellipse is a circle. Figure 11.4 shows a circle that has been scaled by a factor of 0.5 in the Y direction and then rotated 30 degrees.

Example programs Spiral2, BDitch2, and Cycloid2 use the same DrawCurve code to draw scaled and rotated spirals, Bowditch curves, and cycloids like the ones shown in Figure 11.5. The only differences between these programs are in their definitions of the parametric functions X(t) and Y(t). These functions define the basic curve shape for each program. The DrawCurve subroutine stretches and rotates these figures in exactly the same way for all three programs.

You can use similar techniques to scale and rotate any parametric curve. Chapter 12, Two-Dimensional Transformations, describes scaling and rotation transformations more generally, along with some other transformations such as reflecting a figure across a line and shape-distorting transformations. Chapter 12 also explains how you can combine transformations to perform complex actions like rotating a figure around an arbitrary point quickly and easily.

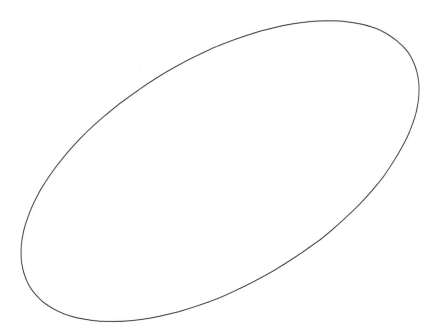

Figure 11.4 A circle scaled by a factor of 0.5 in the Y direction and then rotated 30 degrees.

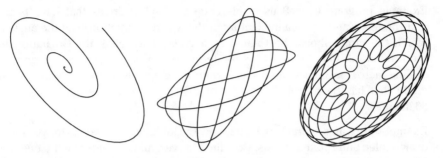

Figure 11.5 A scaled and rotated spiral, Bowditch curve, and cycloid.

Curve Fitting

Many applications must represent a series of data points as a curve. The following sections discuss several different ways you can fit curves to data points. These methods provide different tradeoffs between a close fit to the data and a smooth curve.

On one extreme, you can connect each point to the next with a straight line, as shown in Figure 11.6. This makes the curve fit the data exactly. The curve is not very smooth, however, and it bends sharply at each of the data points. It does a poor job of showing the overall trends in the data.

At the other extreme, you can fit the data points with a single straight line, as shown in Figure 11.7. This makes the curve very smooth. The curve never bends or changes direction at all, so in some sense, it is perfectly smooth. It does a good job of showing the data's overall trend, but it may not fit the data very closely.

Other methods for fitting curves to data provide solutions that lie somewhere between these two extremes. They tend to follow the data, but not too exactly. As a result, they provide a reasonably smooth curve such as the one in Figure 11.8.

Figure 11.6 Fitting data points with line segments matches the data closely but is not smooth.

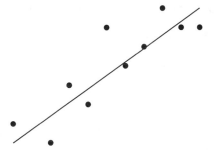

Figure 11.7 A straight line fits points smoothly but may not match the data closely.

Polynomial Curve Fitting

A polynomial is a function of the form $F(x) = a0 + a_1 * x^1 + a_2 * x^2 + ... + a_N * x^N$ where the values a_i are constants. The *degree* of a polynomial is the greatest power to which x is raised. The degree in this example is N.

By selecting suitable values for the parameters $a_0, a_1, ..., a_N$, you can make a polynomial that fits a collection of points. Using polynomials of different degrees, you can make curves that trade off between a close fit to the data and a smooth curve that does not wiggle around too much. The following sections explain how you can find a linear or quadratic function to fit your data. By generalizing these techniques, you can create data-fitting curves of even higher degree.

Linear Least Squares

The *method of least squares* fits a curve to a set of data points so that the sum of the squares of the differences between the curve and the data points is as small as possible. If the Y coordinates for the points along the curve are given by the equation $y = F(x)$, and the data values are at position (x_i, y_i) for $1 <= i <= N$, the least squares method tries to minimize the sum:

```
E(F(x))  =  Σ  (F(x_i)  -  y_i)²
```

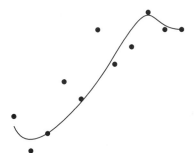

Figure 11.8 Fitting points with a curve provides a tradeoff between smoothness and accuracy.

Here the symbol Σ means to add the values for all of the data points (x_i, y_i).

If you think your data points lie more or less along a straight line, you can write the equation of a line to fit the points as $y = m * x + b$. Then the sum of the squares of the distances from the line to the data points becomes:

```
E(m, b) = Σ (m * xᵢ + b - yᵢ)²
```

You can find the minimum of this equation using a little calculus. If your calculus is rusty, you can either take this on faith or skip down to the results.

Take the partial derivatives of $E(m, b)$ with respect to m and b, set the derivatives equal to zero, and solve for the values of m and b. Those values give the equation for the line that minimizes the error equation $E(F(x))$. The partial derivatives are given by:

```
δE/δm = Σ 2 * (m * xᵢ + b - yᵢ) * xᵢ
      = m * Σ 2 * xᵢ² + b * Σ 2 * xᵢ - Σ 2 * xᵢ * yᵢ
δE/δb = Σ 2 * (m * xᵢ + b - yᵢ)
      = m * Σ 2 * xᵢ + b * Σ 2 - Σ 2 * yᵢ
```

By setting these equations equal to zero and rearranging a bit, you get:

```
m * Σ xᵢ² + b * Σ xᵢ = Σ xᵢ * yᵢ
m * Σ xᵢ + b * Σ 1 = Σ yᵢ
```

Keep in mind that the x_i and y_i are just numbers that define the positions of your data points. That means the values of Σx_i^2, Σx_i, $\Sigma x_i * y_i$, and Σy_i are only numbers that you can easily compute. For convenience, calculate these values and let:

```
A = Σ xᵢ²
B = Σ xᵢ
C = Σ xᵢ * yᵢ
D = Σ yᵢ
```

If you have N data points numbered from 1 to N, the value of $\Sigma 1$ is simply N. Substituting all of these values into the previous equations, you get:

```
m * A + b * B = C
m * B + b * N = D
```

This gives you two equations with two unknowns. Solving them for m and b gives:

```
m = (B * D - C * N) / (B² - A * N)
b = (B * C - A * D) / (B² - A * N)
```

Notice that these values are undefined if $B^2 - A * N = 0$. That happens when all of the data points have the same X coordinate x_1. In that case:

$$(B^2 - A * N) = (\Sigma\ x_i)^2 - \Sigma\ x_i^2 * N$$
$$= (N * x_i)^2 - (N * x_i^2) * N$$
$$= (N^2 * x_i^2) - (N^2 * x_i^2)$$
$$= 0$$

The equations for m and b give you the values you need to find the straight line that best fits the data points. As a quick check, consider what happens if all the data points have the same Y value y_1. In that case, the values of the constants C and D become:

```
C = S xᵢ * yᵢ = y₁ * S xᵢ = y₁ * B
D = S yᵢ = y₁ * S 1 = y₁ * N
```

Substituting these values in the equations for m and b, you get:

```
m   = (B * D - C * N) / (B² - A * N)
    = (B * (y₁ * N) - (y₁ * B) * N) / (B² - A * N)
    = 0
b   = (B * C - A * D) / (B² - A * N)
    = (B * (y₁ * B) - A * (y₁ * N)) / (B² - A * N)
    = y₁ * (B² - A * N) / (B² - A * N)
    = y₁
```

In this case, the least squares line is the horizontal line $y = y_1$, as it should be.

The GetLeastSquaresValues subroutine shown in the following code calculates the values of m and b. GetLeastSquaresValues takes as parameters two arrays containing the X and Y coordinates of the points it should fit. Subroutine DrawCurve uses GetLeastSquaresValues to find the endpoints of the least squares line.

```
' Compute the m and b values for the least squares line.
Private Sub GetLeastSquaresValues( _
    X() As Single, Y() As Single, _
    ByRef m_value As Single, ByRef b_value As Single)
Dim num_points As Integer
Dim A As Single
Dim B As Single
Dim C As Single
Dim D As Single
Dim i As Integer

    ' Compute the sums.
    num_points = UBound(X)
    For i = 1 To num_points
        A = A + PtX(i) * PtX(i)
        B = B + PtX(i)
        C = C + PtX(i) * PtY(i)
        D = D + PtY(i)
    Next i
    m_value = (B * D - C * num_points) / _
```

```
            (B * B - A * num_points)
    b_value = (B * C - A * D) / _
            (B * B - A * num_points)
End Sub


' Draw the least squares line.
Private Sub DrawCurve()
Dim m_value As Single
Dim b_value As Single
Dim x1 As Single
Dim x2 As Single
Dim y1 As Single
Dim y2 As Single
Dim i As Integer

    ' Get the m and b values for the line.
    GetLeastSquaresValues PtX, PtY, m_value, b_value

    ' Find the minimum and maximum X values.
    x1 = PtX(1)      ' This will be the minimum X value.
    x2 = x1          ' This will be the maximum X value.
    For i = 2 To numpts
        If x1 > PtX(i) Then x1 = PtX(i)
        If x2 < PtX(i) Then x2 = PtX(i)
    Next i

    ' Draw the line.
    y1 = m_value * x1 + b_value
    y2 = m_value * x2 + b_value
    picCanvas.Line (x1, y1)-(x2, y2)
End Sub
```

Example program LeastSq uses this code to display a linear least squares fit to a set of points. Click several times in the drawing area to select some points. When you click the Go button, the program displays the least squares line. It then resets itself so that you can start clicking to create a new set of points. Figure 11.9 shows program LeastSq fitting a least squares line to a set of data points.

Quadratic Least Squares

You can use techniques similar to those described in the previous section to fit a higher-order polynomial to fit a set of data points. For instance, you might believe your data has a shape that fits an equation like $a * x^2 + b * x + c$ rather than a line. In that case, you can write the sum of the squares of the differences between the curve and the data points as:

$$E(a, b, c) = \Sigma (a * x_i^2 + b * x_i + c - y_i)^2$$

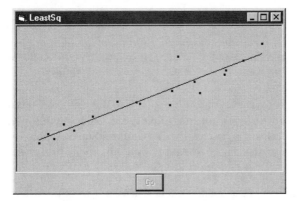

Figure 11.9 Program LeastSq fitting a line to a set of points.

You can then take the partial derivatives of this equation with respect to a, b, and c.

```
δE/δa = Σ 2 * (a * xᵢ² + b * xᵢ + c - yᵢ) * xᵢ²
      = 2 * (a * Σ xᵢ⁴ + b * Σ xᵢ³ + c * Σ xᵢ² - Σ yᵢ * xᵢ²)
δE/δb = Σ 2 * (a * xᵢ² + b * xᵢ + c - yᵢ) * xᵢ
      = 2 * (a * Σ xᵢ³ + b * Σ xᵢ² + c * Σ xᵢ - Σ yᵢ * xᵢ)
δE/δc = Σ 2 * (a * xᵢ² + b * xᵢ + c - yᵢ)
      = 2 * (a * Σ xᵢ² + b * Σ xᵢ + c * Σ 1 - Σ yᵢ)
```

Once again, the values x_i and y_i values are just numbers, so you can compute the values of the summations. For convenience, let:

```
A = Σ xᵢ⁴
B = Σ xᵢ³
C = Σ xᵢ²
D = Σ yᵢ * xᵢ²
E = Σ xᵢ
F = Σ yᵢ * xᵢ
G = Σ yᵢ
```

Substituting these values into the partial derivatives, setting them equal to zero, and rearranging a bit gives you the three equations:

```
a * A + b * B + c * C = D
a * B + b * C + c * E = F
a * C + b * E + c * N = G
```

You can now solve these three equations for the three unknowns a, b, and c to get:

```
a = [(C * D - B * F) * (E² - C * N) - (E * F - C * G) * (C² - B * E)] /
    [(A * C - B²) * (E² - C * N) + (C² - B * E)²]
```

```
b = [(C * F - B * G) * (B * C - A * E) - (B * D - A * F) * (C * E - B *
N)] / [(B * C - A * E) * (C² - B * E) - (C * E - B * N) * (B² - A * C)]

c = [(B * D - A * F) * (C² - B * E) - (C * F - B * G) * (B² - A * C)] /
[(B * C - A * E) * (C² - B * E) - (C * E - B * N) * (B² - A * C)]
```

You can use these equations to write a subroutine similar to the GetLeastSquaresValues routine described in the previous section for finding the least squares parameters. Example program LeastSq2 uses the new version of GetLeastSquaresValues to display quadratic least squares curves to fit sets of data points. Figure 11.10 shows program LeastSq2 in action.

Note that a straight line is a form of the quadratic function $a * x^2 + b * x + c$, where the constant $a = 0$. If you compute the parameters for a quadratic least squares curve and the data points fall mostly along a straight line, the value you calculate for parameter a will be close to zero. This gives you a quadratic that is almost identical to the line you would have obtained had you used the linear least squares methods. In this sense, you have not lost anything by using the quadratic method. You will still find a more or less straight line if one fits the data well. Of course, you need to do a lot more work to find this curve using the quadratic method.

Higher-Order Least Squares

Using these same methods, you can fit polynomials of even higher degree to your collection of data points. Higher-degree polynomials can contain more bends, so they will tend to match your data values more closely.

You can write the equation for the polynomial function as:

```
y = A₀ + A₁ * x + A₂ * x² + ... + Aₙ * xᴺ
```

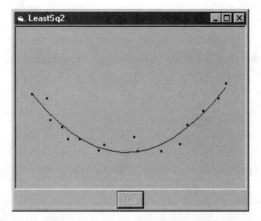

Figure 11.10 Program LeastSq2 fitting a quadratic to a set of points.

Then the error equation is:

```
E = Σ (y_i - (A_0 + A_1 * x_i + A_2 * x_i² + ... + A_N * x_i^N))²
```

Following the methods of the previous sections, you take the partial derivatives of this equation with respect to the constants $A_1, A_2, ... , A_N$. For example, the partial derivative with respect to A_j is:

```
δE/δA_j = Σ -2 * (y_i - (A_0 + A_1 * x_i + ... + A_N * x_i^N)) * (x_i^j)
        = -2 * Σ (x_i^j * y_i - A_0 * x_i^j - A_1 * x_i^{j+1} - ... - A_N * x_i^{j+N})
```

If you set this equation equal to zero, divide both sides of the equation by -2, and rearrange a little, you get:

```
A_0 * Σ x_i^j + A_1 * Σ x_i^{j+1} + ... + A_N * Σ x_i^{j+N} = Σ (x_i^j * y_i)
```

This mess seems more complicated than the equations in the previous sections, but it is not really too different. Remember that the x_i and y_i are the data values you are trying to fit. The only unknowns in these equations are the A_i values. That means all the summations are simple numeric values you can calculate using the data points. Then the ith equation simplifies to:

```
A_0 * C_{i0} + A_1 * C_{i1} + ... + A_N * C_{iN} = C_{N+1}
```

If you calculate all the partial derivatives and set them all equal to zero, you have N + 1 equations and N + 1 unknowns. You can solve the equations to find the A_i values.

The previous sections solved systems of two and three equations directly. To solve a system of an unknown number of equations, you need a more systematic approach. You can do this using *Gaussian elimination*.

First, place the equations' coefficients in a two-dimensional array. Each row in the array corresponds to an equation. Each column corresponds to the coefficients of an A_i value. The entries in the array look like this:

C_{00}	C_{00}	C_{02}	...	C_{0N+1}
C_{10}	C_{11}	C_{12}	...	C_{1N+1}
⋮				⋮
C_{N0}	C_{N1}	C_{N2}	...	C_{NN+1}

The first step in Gaussian elimination is to divide each value in the first row by the value in the upper left corner C_{00}. Dividing every entry by the same value keeps the meaning of the system of equations unchanged. The solution to the new equations is the same as the solution to the original equations. Dividing by the first entry in the first row by itself makes that entry 1.

Next, for each row i, except the first, subtract C_{i0} times the first row's values. At this point, the first entry in the first row is 1, so subtracting C_{i0} times 1 from C_{i0} makes the first entry in the ith row 0. The other entries have other values depending on the values in the other columns. For example, the entry in the jth column of the ith row will have value $C_{ij} - C_{i0} * C_{10}$.

After you have finished this step, the first row has a 1 in its first column and all the other rows have 0s in their first columns.

Now repeat these steps for the second column using the second row. Divide each value in the second row by C_{11} to make the second entry in the second row 1. Then subtract multiples of the second row from every other row to make all the other entries in the second column 0.

There is one other strange case that may arise. When the program should convert the entry C_{ii} to 1 and use it to eliminate the ith entries in the other rows, the value C_{ii} may be 0. In that case, it cannot be used to eliminate the other entries in its columns.

When this happens, the program should search the remaining rows and find one with a nonzero entry in this column. It should swap the two rows and continue. This corresponds to switching the order of two of the original equations and does not change the eventual solution.

Continue this process for each column until the array looks like this:

1	0	...	0	D_0
0	1	...	0	D_1
:				:
0	0	...	1	D_N

The ith row in this array corresponds to the equation:

$$A_0 * 0 + A_1 * 0 + \ldots + A_i * 1 + \ldots + A_N * 0 = D_i$$

From this equation, it is easy to see that $A_i = D_i$.

Example program LeastSq3, shown in Figure 11.11, uses this method for finding higher-order polynomial least square curves. Click several times to select points and enter the degree you want for the polynomial. When you click the Go button, the program finds a polynomial to approximate the points you selected.

The following code shows how program LeastSq3 works. Subroutine DrawCurve orchestrates the process and draws the final curve. It calls GetLeastSquareValues to calculate the polynomial's coefficients. It then uses the PolynomialValue function to compute the coordinates of the points on the curve.

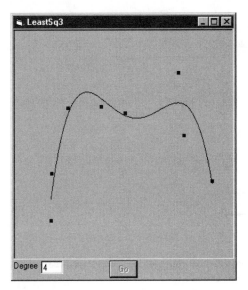

Figure 11.11 Program LeastSq3 fitting points with a degree 4 polynomial.

Subroutine GetLeastSquareValues creates the coefficient arrays representing the partial derivatives. It calls subroutine GaussianEliminate to perform the Gaussian elimination. It copies the polynomial's coefficients into the a_values array for use by the PolynomialValue function.

```
' Draw the least squares line.
Private Sub DrawCurve(ByVal degree As Integer)
Dim a_values() As Single
Dim x1 As Single
Dim x2 As Single
Dim i As Integer
Dim X As Single
Dim dx As Single

    ' Get the parameters for the quadratic.
    If GetLeastSquaresValues(degree, PtX, PtY, a_values) Then
        ' There is a solution.
        ' Find the minimum and maximum X values.
        x1 = PtX(1) ' This will be the minimum X value.
        x2 = x1     ' This will be the maximum X value.
        For i = 2 To NumPts
            If x1 > PtX(i) Then x1 = PtX(i)
            If x2 < PtX(i) Then x2 = PtX(i)
        Next i

        ' Draw the curve.
        picCanvas.CurrentX = x1
        picCanvas.CurrentY = PolynomialValue(a_values, x1)
```

```
        ' Make dx = 1 pixel.
        dx = picCanvas.ScaleX(1, vbPixels, _
            picCanvas.ScaleMode)

        X = x1 + dx
        Do While X < x2
            picCanvas.Line -(X, PolynomialValue(a_values, X))
            X = X + dx
        Loop

        picCanvas.Line -(x2, PolynomialValue(a_values, x2))
    Else
        ' There is no solution.
        MsgBox "There is no solution."
    End If
End Sub


' Compute the a, b, and c values for quadratic least squares.
' Return True if there is a solution.
Private Function GetLeastSquaresValues( _
    ByVal degree As Integer, X() As Single, Y() As Single, _
    a_values() As Single) As Boolean
Dim max_point As Integer
Dim coeff() As Single
Dim row As Integer
Dim col As Integer
Dim i As Integer
Dim total As Single

    max_point = UBound(X) - 1

    ' Find the coefficients for the equations.
    ReDim coeff(0 To degree, 0 To degree + 1)
    For row = 0 To degree
        ' Find the coefficients for the columns.
        For col = 0 To degree
            ' Find Sum(Xi^(row + col)) over all i.
            total = 0
            For i = 0 To max_point
                total = total + X(i + 1) ^ (row + col)
            Next i
            coeff(row, col) = total
        Next col

        ' Find the constant term.
        total = 0
        For i = 0 To max_point
            total = total + Y(i + 1) * X(i + 1) ^ row
        Next i
        coeff(row, degree + 1) = total
    Next row
```

```
        ' Perform the Gaussian elimination.
        If GaussianEliminate(coeff) Then
            ' There is a solution.
            ' Save the results.
            ReDim a_values(0 To degree)
            For row = 0 To degree
                a_values(row) = coeff(row, degree + 1)
            Next row
            GetLeastSquaresValues = True
        Else
            ' There is no solution.
            GetLeastSquaresValues = False
        End If
End Function

' Perform Gaussian elimination on this array.
' Return True if there is a solution.
Private Function GaussianEliminate(coeff() As Single) _
    As Boolean
Dim max_row As Integer
Dim max_col As Integer
Dim row As Integer
Dim col As Integer
Dim i As Integer
Dim j As Integer
Dim factor As Single
Dim tmp As Single

    max_row = UBound(coeff, 1)
    max_col = UBound(coeff, 2)
    For row = 0 To max_row
        ' Make sure coeff(row, row) <> 0.
        factor = coeff(row, row)
        If Abs(factor) < 0.001 Then
            ' Switch this row with one that is not
            ' zero in position. Find this row.
            For i = row + 1 To max_row
                If Abs(coeff(i, row) > 0.001) Then
                    ' Switch rows i and row.
                    For j = 0 To max_col
                        tmp = coeff(row, j)
                        coeff(row, j) = coeff(i, j)
                        coeff(i, j) = tmp
                    Next j
                    factor = coeff(row, row)
                End If
            Next i

            ' See if we found a good row.
            If Abs(factor) < 0.001 Then
                ' We found no good row.
```

```
                    ' There is no solution.
                    GaussianEliminate = False
                    Exit Function
                End If
            End If


            ' Divide each entry in this row by
            ' coeff(row, row).
            For i = 0 To max_col
                coeff(row, i) = coeff(row, i) / factor
            Next i


            ' Subtract this row from the others.
            For i = 0 To max_row
                If i <> row Then
                    ' See what factor we will multiply
                    ' by before subtracting for this row.
                    factor = coeff(i, row)
                    For j = 0 To max_col
                        coeff(i, j) = coeff(i, j) - _
                            factor * coeff(row, j)
                    Next j
                End If
            Next i
        Next row


        ' There is a solution.
        GaussianEliminate = True
End Function


' Find the value of the polynomial with the given
' coefficients.
Private Function PolynomialValue(a_values() As Single, _
    ByVal X As Single) As Single
Dim max_coeff As Integer
Dim total As Single
Dim i As Integer
Dim x_power As Single

    max_coeff = UBound(a_values)
    x_power = 1#
    For i = 0 To max_coeff
        total = total + x_power * a_values(i)
        x_power = x_power * X
    Next i

    PolynomialValue = total
End Function
```

Note that there is no reason to use a polynomial with a degree greater than or equal to the number of points. For example, if you select three points, they can be connected exactly with a degree two polynomial so there is no reason to use a degree four polynomial. In fact, if you use a polynomial of degree greater than two, the curve may wiggle around in an arbitrary manner and still pass exactly through all the points.

To prevent this kind of strangeness, program LeastSq3 allows the degree to be no more than one less than the number of points. If you enter a greater value, the program reduces it.

If you use a polynomial of high enough degree, you may eventually find a curve that passes through each of your data points exactly. This is not necessarily a good thing, however. Figure 11.12 shows a curve that passes exactly through each of the data points. While this curve matches the data closely, it does not correctly convey the fact that these points lie very close to a straight line. A linear least squares fit would make this more obvious and emphasize an important trend in the data values.

For these reasons, you should start by trying to fit your data to a polynomial that agrees with your knowledge of the data. If you think the points were produced by a linear process, use a linear least squares fit. If you think the data values start small, rise as X increases, and then drop off again, try using a quadratic fit. Only if you have some reason to believe that the processes that generated the data included higher-degree effects should you attempt to fit the data with polynomials of high degree.

Many programs need only to present a smoothed version of the data; the exact shape of the function is unimportant. In that case, one of the techniques described in the following sections is probably more appropriate than a polynomial least squares curve.

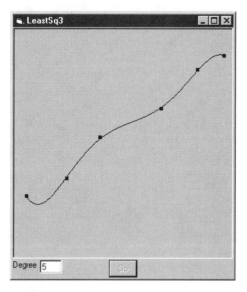

Figure 11.12 A high-degree polynomial may fit the data too closely, hiding the data's underlying structure.

Parametric Curve Fitting

Instead of using a single polynomial to fit a set of data points, you can use two polynomials to define parametric equations X(t) and Y(t) to fit the points. Parametric equations allow a curve far more flexibility than a simple polynomial does. A parametric curve can move straight up or even turn back and cross itself like the curve shown in Figure 11.13. The following sections describe different ways you can create parametric curves that fit a set of data points.

Hermite Curves

Hermite curves use cubic (degree-three polynomial) parametric equations of the form:

```
X(t) = aₓ * t³ + bₓ * t² + cₓ * t + dₓ
Y(t) = a_y * t³ + b_y * t² + c_y * t + d_y
```

for appropriate constants a_x, b_x, c_x, d_x, a_y, b_y, c_y, and d_y. Using these equations, you can connect two points with a curve that has a specified slope at each end. You can use several Hermite curves with matching slopes to connect more than two points.

In the Hermite form, you specify two endpoints for the curve and the tangent vectors at the two endpoints. The curve should pass through the two endpoints heading in the directions of the tangent vectors.

Suppose the endpoints are at coordinates (E_{x1}, E_{y1}) and (E_{x2}, E_{y2}), and that the tangent vectors are $<V_{x1}, V_{y1}>$ and $<V_{x2}, V_{y2}>$. Now suppose you want to create a parametric equation X(t) for the X coordinate of the points on the curve with $0 <= t <= 1$. If the

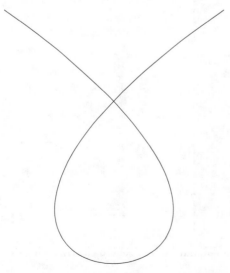

Figure 11.13   The parametric curve $X(t) = t^3 - t$, $Y(t) = t^2$.

equation for the X coordinate of the curve is given by $X(t) = a_x * t^3 + b_x * t^2 + c_x * t + d_x$, the endpoint conditions require that:

```
X(0) = Ex1 = ax * 0³ + bx * 0²+ cx * 0 + dx = dx
X(1) = Ex2 = ax * 1³ + bx * 1²+ cx * 1 + dx = ax + bx + cx + dx
```

At the endpoints, the X component of the tangent vectors should match the derivative of X(t). The derivative of X(t) is $X'(t) = 3 * a_x * t^2 + 2 * b_x * t + c_x$ so the tangent conditions require:

```
X'(0) = Vx1 = 3 * ax * 0² + 2 * bx * 0 + cx = cx
X'(1) = Vx2 = 3 * ax * 1² + 2 * bx * 1 + cx = 3 * ax + 2 * bx + cx
```

Using these four equations defined by the endpoint and tangent conditions, you can solve for the constants a_x, b_x, c_x, and d_x to get:

```
ax = Vx2 + Vx1 - 2 * Ex2 + 2 * Ex1
bx = 3 * Ex2 - 2 * Vx1 - 3 * Ex1 - Vx2
cx = Vx1
dx = Ex1
```

Similar equations hold for the Y components of the endpoints and tangent vectors.

With these equations, you can write a GetHermiteValues subroutine in Visual Basic to compute the parameters you need to draw the Hermite curve. The parameter declarations are longer than the calculations themselves.

```
' Compute the Hermite curve parameters.
Private Sub GetHermiteValues( _
    ByVal ex1 As Single, ByVal ey1 As Single, _
    ByVal ex2 As Single, ByVal ey2 As Single, _
    ByVal vx1 As Single, ByVal vy1 As Single, _
    ByVal vx2 As Single, ByVal vy2 As Single, _
    ByRef Ax As Single, ByRef Bx As Single, _
    ByRef Cx As Single, ByRef Dx As Single, _
    ByRef Ay As Single, ByRef By As Single, _
    ByRef Cy As Single, ByRef Dy As Single)

    Ax = vx2 + vx1 - 2 * ex2 + 2 * ex1
    Bx = 3 * ex2 - 2 * vx1 - 3 * ex1 - vx2
    Cx = vx1
    Dx = ex1

    Ay = vy2 + vy1 - 2 * ey2 + 2 * ey1
    By = 3 * ey2 - 2 * vy1 - 3 * ey1 - vy2
    Cy = vy1
    Dy = ey1
End Sub
```

You can then use the subroutines presented earlier that display parametric curves to display Hermite curves. Example program Hermite, shown in Figure 11.14, does just that. Enter the values of V_{x1}, V_{y1}, V_{x2}, and V_{y2} in text boxes. Use the mouse to drag the curve's endpoints to new positions. When you have made the changes you want, click the Go button to have the program display the curve.

If you check the Show Control Points check box, the program also draws the endpoints and the tangent vectors. The vectors are scaled by a factor of 1/5 because interesting values for the vectors tend to be fairly large.

Hermite Blending Functions

If you take the equations for a_x, b_x, and so forth, and plug them into the equation for the finished curve $X(t) = a_x * t^3 + b_x * t^2 + c_x * t + d_x$, you get:

$$
\begin{aligned}
X(t) &= \quad (V_{x2} + V_{x1} - 2 * E_{x2} + 2 * E_{x1}) * t^3 + \\
&\quad (3 * E_{x2} - 2 * V_{x1} - 3 * E_{x1} - V_{x2}) * t^2 + \\
&\quad V_{x1} * t + E_{x1} \\
&= \quad E_{x1} * (2 * t^3 - 3 * t^2 + 1) + \\
&\quad E_{x2} * (-2 * t^3 + 3 * t^2) + \\
&\quad V_{x1} * (t^3 - 2 * t^2 + t) + \\
&\quad V_{x2} * (t^3 - t^2)
\end{aligned}
$$

The functions multiplying the E_{x1}, E_{x2}, V_{x1}, and V_{x2} terms are called *blending functions*. They produce values for the points on the curve by blending together different amounts of E_{x1}, E_{x2}, V_{x1}, and V_{x2} as t varies from 0 to 1.

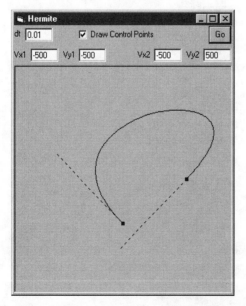

Figure 11.14 Program Hermite displaying a Hermite curve.

For example, when t = 0, the second, third, and fourth blending functions all have value zero, and the first blending function has value 1. This makes $X(0) = E_{x1}$, which agrees with the way the curve was constructed.

Figure 11.15 shows a graph of the four blending functions. Notice that all but one of the functions have value zero when t = 0 and when t = 1. Notice also that the first two functions are generally larger than the others. This indicates that the coordinates of the endpoints contribute more to the curve's value than the tangent vectors do. That is why the tangent vector components tend to be quite large for interesting curves.

Connecting Hermite Curves

To make two Hermite curves meet, you need the curves to share an endpoint. If you want the curves to meet smoothly, you must also make the tangent vectors at that position point in the same direction.

Suppose you have a curve with endpoints (E_{x1}, E_{y1}) and (E_{x2}, E_{y2}) and tangent vectors $<V_{x1}, V_{y1}>$ and $<V_{x2}, V_{y2}>$. Suppose you have a second curve with endpoints (F_{x1}, F_{y1}) and (F_{x2}, F_{y2}) and tangent vectors $<W_{x1}, W_{y1}>$ and $<W_{x2}, W_{y2}>$. If you want to connect the second endpoint from the first curve to the first endpoint of the second curve, you need:

```
E_x2  =  F_x1
E_y2  =  F_y1
```

If you want the curves to meet smoothly, you must also ensure that:

```
V_x2  *  W_y1  =  V_y2  *  W_x1  *  k
```

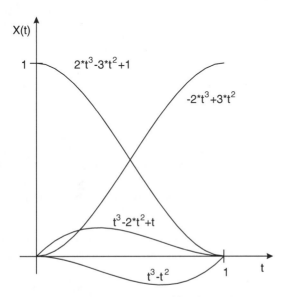

Figure 11.15 Hermite curve blending functions.

for some constant k. This makes both tangent vectors $<V_{x2}, V_{y2}>$ and $<W_{x1}, W_{y1}>$ point in the same direction. The value of the constant k depends on the relative lengths of the tangent vectors.

Bezier Curves

Hermite curves have a couple of drawbacks. First, specifying tangent vectors is not a very intuitive process. Second, the tangent vectors must be fairly large for most interesting curves. That means you need to make large changes to the vectors to make a noticeable effect on the shape of the curve. Bezier curves address both of these problems.

Bezier curves are very similar to Hermite curves. Instead of specifying the tangent vectors for the curve explicitly, however, in a Bezier curve you specify two new control points that determine the tangent vectors indirectly. The tangent vector at the first endpoint is three times the vector connecting the first endpoint to the first new control point. The tangent vector at the second endpoint is three times the vector connecting the second new control point and the second endpoint. In other words, if the two new control points have coordinates (x_1, y_1) and (x_2, y_2), then:

```
Vx1 = 3 * (x1 - Ex1)
Vy1 = 3 * (y1 - Ey1)
Vx2 = 3 * (Ex2 - x2)
Vy2 = 3 * (Ey2 - y2)
```

The factors of three in these equations give the new control points more influence over the shape of the curve.

If you substitute these values into the equations for the Hermite parameters a_x, b_x, c_x, d_x, a_y, b_y, c_y, and d_y, you get:

```
ax   = 3 * (Ex2 - x2) + 3 * (x1 - Ex1) - 2 * Ex2 + 2 * Ex1
     = Ex2 - Ex1 - 3 * x2 + 3 * x1
bx   = 3 * Ex2 - 2 * 3 * (x1 - Ex1) - 3 * Ex1 - 3 * (Ex2 - x2)
     = 3 * Ex1 - 6 * x1 + 3 * x2
cx   = -3 * Ex1 + 3 * x1
dx   = Ex1
```

Using these equations, you can write a program similar to program Hermite to draw Bezier curves. Example program Bezier, shown in Figure 11.16, is such a program. Use the mouse to drag the curve's endpoints and control points to new positions, and the program displays the appropriate curve.

If you check the Show Control Points check box, the program also draws the endpoints and the control points. You can use the Go button to redraw the curve if you change the value of dt.

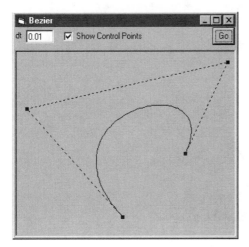

Figure 11.16 Program Bezier drawing a Bezier curve.

Bezier Blending Functions

You can enter the equations representing a_x, b_x, and so forth into the equations for the finished Bezier curve $X(t) = a_x * t^3 + b_x * t^2 + c_x * t + d_x$ and $Y(t) = a_y * t^3 + b_y * t^2 + c_y * t + d_y$. You can rearrange these equations to group together terms that involve the endpoints and control points.

```
X(t) =        (E_x2 - E_x1 - 3 * x_2 + 3 * x_1) * t^3 +
       (3 * E_x1 - 6 * x_1 + 3 * x_2) * t^2 +
       (-3 * E_x1 + 3 * x_1) * t +
       E_x1
    =  E_x1 * (-t^3 + 3 * t^2 - 3 * t + 1) +
       E_x2 * t^3 +
       x_1 * (3 * t^3 - 6 * t^2 + 3 * t) +
       x_2 * (-3 * t^3 + 3 * t^2)
```

In this equation, the functions multiplying the values E_{x1}, E_{x2}, x_1, and x_2 terms are the blending functions for the Bezier curve. Like the blending functions for Hermite curves, they produce values for the points on the curve by blending different amounts of the control parameters as the value of t varies from 0 to 1.

Figure 11.17 shows the Bezier curve blending functions. Like the Hermite blending functions, all but one have value zero when t = 0 and when t = 1. The sum of these functions is 1 for any value of t. You many be able to see this from the picture, but it is easier to understand if you add the blending function equations together algebraically.

```
(-t^3 + 3 * t^2 - 3 * t + 1) +
(t^3) +
(3 * t^3 - 6 * t^2 + 3 * t) +
```

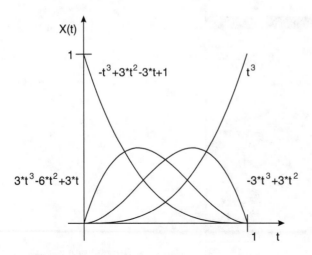

Figure 11.17 Bezier curve blending functions.

```
      (-3 * t³ + 3 * t²)
   =  t³ * (-1 + 1 + 3 - 3) + t² * (3 - 6 + 3) + t * (-3 + 3) + 1
   =  1
```

Because the sum of the Bezier blending functions is 1 for all t, the curve essentially takes a weighted average of the endpoints and control points.

Connecting Bezier Curves

Making two Bezier curves connect is similar to making two Hermite curves connect. If two Bezier curves should meet, they must share an end point. If the curves should meet smoothly, you must also arrange their interior control points so that the tangents at the endpoints point in the same direction.

Suppose you have a curve with endpoints (x_{11}, y_{11}) and (x_{14}, y_{14}) and interior control points (x_{12}, y_{12}) and (x_{13}, y_{13}). Suppose your second curve has endpoints (x_{21}, y_{21}) and (x_{24}, y_{24}), and interior control points (x_{22}, y_{22}) and (x_{23}, y_{23}). To make the second endpoint of the first curve meet the first endpoint of the second curve, you need:

```
   x₁₄ = x₂₁
   y₁₄ = y₂₁
```

To make the curves meet smoothly, you must also ensure that:

```
   (x₁₄ - x₁₃) * (y₂₂ - y₂₁) = (y₁₄ - y₁₃) * (x₂₂ - x₂₁) * k
```

for some constant k. This makes the tangent vectors $<x_{14} - x_{13}, y_{14} - y_{13}>$ and $<x_{22} - x_{21}, y_{22} - x_{21}>$ point in the same direction. As before, the value of the constant k depends on the relative lengths of the tangent vectors.

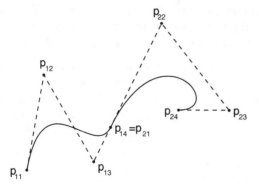

Figure 11.18 Two Bezier curves meeting smoothly at a common point.

Figure 11.18 shows two Bezier curves meeting smoothly at a common point. The curves' control points are labeled p_{11}, p_{12}, and so forth. The curves are connected because $p_{14} = p_{21}$. They meet smoothly because the tangent vectors $(p_{14} - p_{13}) = (p_{22} - p_{21}) * 1/3$.

Higher-Order Bezier Curves

By properly arranging the control points that define a sequence of Bezier curves, you can create a series of curves that connect many different points smoothly. Instead of using a sequence of curves to fit a series of points, you can use more general blending functions to create a single higher-order Bezier curve that connects many data points.

Suppose you have $N + 1$ control points with coordinates (x_0, y_0), (x_1, y_1), ..., (x_N, y_N). Then you can write the equation for the X coordinate of a Bezier curve as:

```
X(t) = S x_i * B_i,N(t)
```

Here $B_{i,N}(t)$ is the blending function:

```
B_i,N(t) = t^i * (1 - t)^N-i * N! / i! / (N - i)!
```

The Bezier curves in the previous section used four data points: two endpoints and two additional control points. In that case $N = 3$, so the blending functions are:

```
B_0,3(t)        = t^0 * (1 - t)^3-0 * 3! / 0! / (3 - 0)!
       = (1 - t)^3
       = -t^3 + 3 * t^2 - 3 * t + 1
B_1,3(t)        = t^1 * (1 - t)^3-1 * 3! / 1! / (3 - 1)!
       = t * (1 - t)^2 * 6 / 2
       = 3 * t^3 - 6 * t^2 + 3 * t
B_2,3(t)        = t^2 * (1 - t)^3-2 * 3! / 2! / (3 - 2)!
       = t^2 * (1 - t) * 6 / 2
       = -3 * t^3 + 3 * t^2
B_3,3(t)        = t^3 * (1 - t)^3-3 * 3! / 3! / (3 - 3)!
       = t^3
```

These agree with the blending functions presented in the previous section. To make these equations match up properly with the previous versions, the endpoints must be the data points numbered 0 and 3. The additional control points must be data points 1 and 2.

Using the generalized equation for the Bezier blending functions, you can write a Visual Basic program to create a Bezier curve that uses many control points. To make the code a bit easier to understand, create separate functions to compute factorials and the blending function values for inputs i, N, and t. Then use these functions to compute X(t) and Y(t). The drawing routine DrawCurve can use these functions as before.

```
' Return the factorial of a number.
Private Function Factorial(ByVal N As Integer) As Long
Dim value As Long
Dim i As Integer

    value = 1
    For i = 2 To N
        value = value * i
    Next i
    Factorial = value
End Function

' The blending function for i, N, and t.
Private Function Blend(ByVal i As Integer, _
    ByVal N As Integer, ByVal t As Single) As Single

    Blend = Factorial(N) / Factorial(i) / _
        Factorial(N - i) * t ^ i * (1 - t) ^ (N - i)
End Function

' The parametric function X(t).
Private Function X(ByVal t As Single) As Single
Dim i As Integer
Dim value As Single

    For i = 0 To MaxPt
        value = value + PtX(i) * Blend(i, MaxPt, t)
    Next i
    X = value
End Function

' The parametric function Y(t).
Private Function Y(ByVal t As Single) As Single
Dim i As Integer
Dim value As Single

    For i = 0 To MaxPt
        value = value + PtY(i) * Blend(i, MaxPt, t)
    Next i
    Y = value
End Function
```

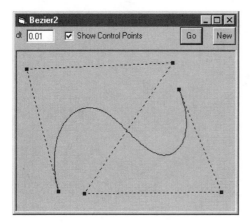

Figure 11.19 Program Bezier2 displaying a high-order Bezier curve.

Example program Bezier2, shown in Figure 11.19, demonstrates this code. Click with the mouse to create a series of control points. When you click the Go button, the program displays the corresponding Bezier curve. While the curve is displayed, you can use the mouse to drag the control points to see the effect on the curve. If you click the New button, the program clears the screen and lets you select a new set of control points.

Notice that the curve in Figure 11.19 does not touch any control points except the two endpoints. The other control points determine only the general shape of the curve.

B-Splines

By correctly placing control points, you can give a higher-order Bezier curve the general shape you want it to have. One inconvenient feature of Bezier curves is that the value of every point on the curve, except the endpoints, depends on the location of every control point. If you move one control point in the middle of the curve, the entire curve changes slightly. As a result, you cannot adjust the shape of the curve locally without affecting its shape globally.

One way to make a curve with local control is to build it using several different Bezier curves connected at their endpoints. You can then modify the control points of one curve to change its shape without changing the shapes of the other curves. If you want the curves to meet smoothly, you may also need to adjust one of the neighboring curve's control points so that the tangents of the two curves remain pointed in the same direction.

B-splines give you a simpler way to create a complicated curve with local control. The basic construction of a B-spline is similar to that of a Bezier curve defined using blending functions. Suppose you have $N + 1$ control points with coordinates (x_0, y_0), (x_1, y_1), ..., (x_N, y_N). You can write the equation for the X coordinate of a B-spline as:

```
X(t) = Σ xᵢ * Bᵢ,ₖ(t)
```

where the $B_{i,k}(t)$ are the curve's blending functions. The parameter k determines the smoothness of the curve. If k is small, the curve matches the data points relatively closely.

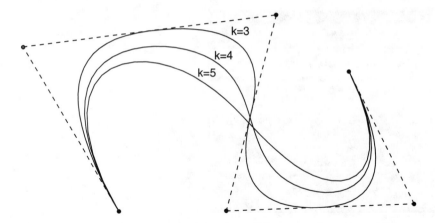

Figure 11.20 B-splines defined by the same control points but with different levels of smoothness.

If k is large, the curve is smoother but may not fit the data as well. Figure 11.20 shows three B-splines defined by the same control points but with different values for k. The curve with k = 3 matches the points most closely; the curve with k = 5 is the smoothest.

For Bezier curves, the parameter t varies between 0 and 1. For a B-spline, t varies between 0 and N - k + 2 where k is the smoothness parameter and the control points are numbered from 0 to N.

Figure 11.21 shows the blending functions for a B-spline curve with seven control points and k = 3. Notice that the sum of the values of the functions for any given value of t is 1. That means the B-spline is essentially taking a weighted average of the control points at each t value.

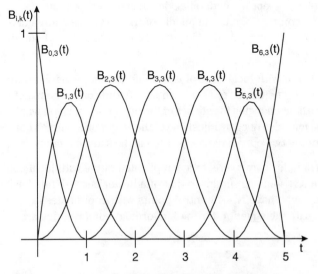

Figure 11.21 B-spline blending functions for k = 3.

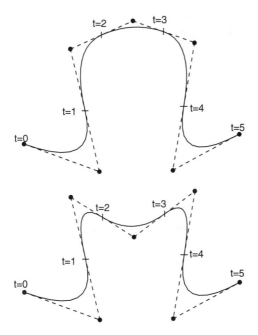

Figure 11.22 B-spline blending functions give the curve local control.

You can see from Figure 11.21 that at most, three of the functions are nonzero for any given value of t. Only the three control points corresponding to those three functions contribute to the value of the curve's coordinates.

Also notice that each blending function is nonzero for only some t values. The blending function $B_{3,3}(t)$, for example, is nonzero only for $1 <= t <= 4$. This is what gives the B-spline local control of its shape. If you move one control point, the B-spline changes only for values of t where that point's blending function is nonzero. Other parts of the curve remain unchanged.

Figure 11.22 shows two B-splines with positions marked on the curve where t is 0, 1, 2, 3, 4, and 5. Only control point number 3 differs in the two curves. Figure 11.21 shows that the corresponding blending function $B_{3,3}(t)$ is nonzero only when $1 < t < 4$, so this control point affects only the middle part of the curve. You can see from Figure 11.22 that the two curves are identical where $t <= 1$ and where $t >= 4$.

The blending functions $B_{i,k}(t)$ are defined recursively in terms of a set of *knot values* that make up a *knot vector*. The knot values relate the values of t to the control points and they help determine the shape of the curve. The most common knot values are used to build *uniform nonperiodic B-splines*. The knot values are defined by:

```
Knot(i) =      0       if i < k
        i - k+ 1       if k <= i <= N
        N - k + 2      if N < i
```

These knot values are used to create open-ended curves like the ones shown in Figure 11.22. In Visual Basic, you can easily write a function to compute these knot values.

```
' Return the ith knot value.
Private Function Knot(ByVal i As Integer) As Integer
    If i < Kvalue Then
        Knot = 0
    ElseIf i <= MaxPt Then
        Knot = i - Kvalue + 1
    Else
        Knot = MaxPt - Kvalue + 2
    End If
End Function
```

Using the knot values, you can define the B-spline blending functions recursively.

```
B_{i,1}(t) =
```

$$
B_{i,1}(t) =
\begin{cases}
1 & \text{if Knot(i)} <= t < \text{Knot(i + 1)} \\
1 & \text{if Knot(i)} <= t <= \text{Knot(i + 1) and } t = N - K + 2 \\
0 & \text{otherwise}
\end{cases}
$$

```
B_{i,k}(t) =    (t - Knot(i)) * B_{i,k-1}(t) / (Knot(i + k - 1) - Knot(i)) +
        (Knot(i + k) - t) * B_{i+1,k-1}(t) / (Knot(i + k) - Knot(i + 1))
```

If the denominator of either of the fractions is zero, that fraction is defined to have value zero.

While these equations are fairly confusing, writing a Visual Basic function to compute the blending function values is not hard.

```
' Recursively compute the blending function.
Private Function Blend(ByVal i As Integer, _
    ByVal k As Integer, ByVal t As Single) As Single
Dim numer As Single
Dim denom As Single
Dim value1 As Single
Dim value2 As Single

    ' Base case for the recursion.
    If k = 1 Then
        If (Knot(i) <= t) And (t < Knot(i + 1)) Then
            Blend = 1
        ElseIf (t = MaxT) And (Knot(i) <= t) And _
            (t <= Knot(i + 1)) _
        Then
            Blend = 1
        Else
            Blend = 0
        End If
```

```
        Exit Function
    End If

    denom = Knot(i + k - 1) - Knot(i)
    If denom = 0 Then
        value1 = 0
    Else
        numer = (t - Knot(i)) * Blend(i, k - 1, t)
        value1 = numer / denom
    End If

    denom = Knot(i + k) - Knot(i + 1)
    If denom = 0 Then
        value2 = 0
    Else
        numer = (Knot(i + k) - t) * Blend(i + 1, k - 1, t)
        value2 = numer / denom
    End If

    Blend = value1 + value2
End Function
```

Using function Blend, you can now write functions to compute the X and Y values for the curve. When you write a program that uses these functions to draw the curve, remember that t varies from 0 to $N - k + 2$ rather than from 0 to 1.

```
' The parametric function X(t).
Private Function X(ByVal t As Single) As Single
Dim i As Integer
Dim value As Single

    For i = 0 To MaxPt
        value = value + PtX(i) * Blend(i, Kvalue, t)
    Next i
    X = value
End Function
```

```
' The parametric function Y(t).
Private Function Y(ByVal t As Single) As Single
Dim i As Integer
Dim value As Single

    For i = 0 To MaxPt
        value = value + PtY(i) * Blend(i, Kvalue, t)
    Next i
    Y = value
End Function
```

Example program BSpline uses these functions to draw B-splines. Click with the mouse to create the set of control points. When you click the Go button, the program displays the appropriate curve. While the curve is displayed, you can use the mouse to drag the control points and change the curve. If you click the New button, the program clears the screen and lets you select a new set of control points.

You can check the Show Control Points check box to make the program display the control points. Check the Show t Values check box to make the program mark the positions on the curve where t has an integer value. Use the K text box to change the smoothness of the curve.

Closed B-Splines

To create a closed B-spline like the one shown in Figure 11.23, you can use a set of knot values and blending functions that produce a *uniform periodic B-spline*. Unlike the blending functions for an open B-spline, these blending functions all look the same and are all symmetrical. They have the general form of function $B_{2,3}(t)$ shown in Figure 11.21. You can generate functions of this shape by setting the knot values to:

```
Knot(i) = i
```

You can then make the function $B_{0,k}(t)$ similar to its previous definition.

```
B₀,₁(t) =
        1        if Knot(0) <= t < Knot(1)
        1        if Knot(0) <= t <= Knot(1) and t = N - k + 2
        0        otherwise

B₀,ₖ(t) =     (t - Knot(0)) * B₀,ₖ₋₁(t) / (Knot(k - 1) - Knot(0)) +
        (Knot(k) - t) * B₁,ₖ₋₁(t) / (Knot(k) - Knot(1))
```

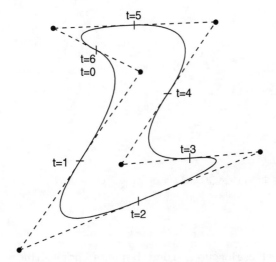

Figure 11.23 A closed B-spline.

Next you can define the other blending functions in terms of $B_{0,k}(t)$.

```
B_i,k(t) =      B_0,k((t - i + N + 1) Mod (N + 1))
```

This makes each blending function look like a copy of $B_{0,k}(t)$ that has been shifted in the X direction. Figure 11.24 shows the blending functions for the curve drawn in Figure 11.23. To draw the entire curve using these functions, t must vary from 0 to N + 1.

In Visual Basic the Knot and Blend functions for the closed curve are:

```
' Return the ith knot value.
Private Function Knot(ByVal i As Integer) As Integer
    Knot = i
End Function


' Recursively compute the blending function.
Private Function Blend(ByVal i As Integer, _
    ByVal k As Integer, ByVal t As Single) As Single
Dim numer As Single
Dim denom As Single
Dim value1 As Single
Dim value2 As Single
Dim newt As Single

    If i > 0 Then
        newt = t - i + MaxPt + 1
        Do While newt >= MaxPt + 1
            newt = newt - (MaxPt + 1)
        Loop
        Do While newt < 0
```

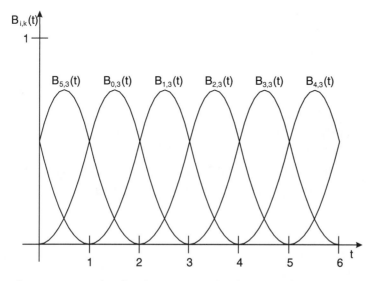

Figure 11.24 Blending functions for the closed B-spline shown in Figure 11.23.

25

```
            newt = newt + (MaxPt + 1)
        Loop
        Blend = Blend(0, k, newt)
        Exit Function
    End If

    ' Base case for the recursion.
    If k = 1 Then
        If (Knot(i) <= t) And (t < Knot(i + 1)) Then
            Blend = 1
        ElseIf (t = MaxT) And (Knot(i) <= t) And _
            (t <= Knot(i + 1)) _
        Then
            Blend = 1
        Else
            Blend = 0
        End If
        Exit Function
    End If

    denom = Knot(i + k - 1) - Knot(i)
    If denom = 0 Then
        value1 = 0
    Else
        numer = (t - Knot(i)) * Blend(i, k - 1, t)
        value1 = numer / denom
    End If

    denom = Knot(i + k) - Knot(i + 1)
    If denom = 0 Then
        value2 = 0
    Else
        numer = (Knot(i + k) - t) * Blend(i + 1, k - 1, t)
        value2 = numer / denom
    End If

    Blend = value1 + value2
End Function
```

The only other difference in drawing open and closed B-splines is that t must vary from 0 to N + 1 to draw the entire closed curve.

Example program BSpline2 uses these functions to draw closed B-splines in a manner very similar to the way program BSpline draws open B-splines.

Summary

The programs in this chapter demonstrate several methods for drawing useful curves. Using parametric curves, you can convert the problem of drawing a complex shape into one of connecting a series of points with line segments. By transforming the points before you connect them, you can draw complex stretched and rotated curves in a simple manner.

Other types of curves show the general shape of a sequence of data values. Polynomial least squares curves minimize the distance between a polynomial function and a set of data points. Using a polynomial of an appropriate degree, you can emphasize polynomial trends in a confusing data set. Hermite curves and B-splines follow a set of points even more approximately. You can use these curves to show the overall shape of a series of points smoothly.

CHAPTER 12

Two-Dimensional Transformations

This chapter explains the basics of two-dimensional transformations. It begins by discussing object-oriented techniques you can use to manage the objects in your pictures. Besides drawing graphical objects, these techniques let you quickly load or save pictures to a file.

Next, the chapter describes windowing, viewports, scrolling, panning, and zooming. Using the mapping between a world window and a viewport, you can display different parts of a picture at different levels of magnification and with different scales along the X and Y axes.

The chapter then explains the matrix representations of translation, scaling, and rotation transformations. Once you can represent these operations using matrices, you can compose them to build complex transformations represented by a single matrix.

The chapter finishes by describing quadtrees. A quadtree is a spatial data structure for locating and displaying items quickly in even the largest pictures.

Modeling Two-Dimensional Objects

Before you can draw an object on your computer's screen, you must have some way to describe that object in memory. You can use a Type statement to create a user-defined data type for storing object information. For example, you might use the following data type to store information about line segments.

```
Private Type MyLine
    x1 As Single
    y1 As Single
    x2 As Single
    y2 As Single
End Type
```

This method works for simple objects, but it is limited. You can make much more powerful representations using classes rather than user-defined data types. You can add methods to object classes that allow an object to read itself from a file, write itself into a file, draw itself on a picture box, and perform other tasks that make sense for that kind of object.

For example, the following code describes a simple TwoDLine class (TwoD stands for two-dimensional). The class defines public variables to hold the line segment's end points. The Draw method makes the object draw itself on a form, printer, or picture box.

```
Option Explicit

' A two-dimensional line.

Public X1 As Single
Public Y1 As Single
Public X2 As Single
Public Y2 As Single

' Draw the line on a Form, Printer, or PictureBox.
Public Sub Draw(Canvas As Object)
    Canvas.Line (X1, Y1)-(X2, Y2)
End Sub
```

You can define other classes to represent other graphical objects such as arcs, circles, ellipses, and rectangles.

All these objects have some things in common. They must all be able to draw themselves. Many programs need to know how big an object is. To make this easier, these objects can provide a Bound method that returns the object's minimum and maximum X and Y coordinate values.

It would also be convenient if the objects could read and create standard text representations of themselves. This kind of representation is called a *serialization*. Using serializations, a program can save and restore representations of its objects in a text file or database.

To ensure that the objects handle these common tasks consistently, you can make a TwoDObject class that defines these common methods. The other classes can then use the Implements keyword to indicate that they provide the features defined by the TwoDObject class.

This not only guarantees that the objects provide these methods in the same way, it also gives a slight performance advantage. A program can refer to any of these objects using the generic TwoDObject data type. It can invoke the methods defined by TwoDObject without knowing the particular type of object it is using. You can achieve the same effect using the Object data type, but using the more specific TwoDObject type is faster.

The following code shows how the TwoDObject class defines the common methods provided by the specific object classes.

```
Option Explicit
' Two-dimensional object parent class.



' The object's textual serialization.
Public Serialization As String

' Draw the object on the canvas.
Public Sub Draw(ByVal canvas As Object)

End Sub

' Return this object's bounds.
Public Sub Bound( _
    ByRef xmin As Single, ByRef xmax As Single, _
    ByRef ymin As Single, ByRef ymax As Single)

End Sub
```

The following code shows a more complete implementation of the TwoDLine class. The Serialization property defined by the TwoDObject class is implemented with property procedures. Notice the strange syntax for declaring the methods defined by the TwoDObject class.

```
Option Explicit
' Two-dimensional line object.

Implements TwoDObject

Public X1 As Single
Public Y1 As Single
Public X2 As Single
Public Y2 As Single

' Return this object's bounds.
Public Sub TwoDObject_Bound( _
    ByRef xmin As Single, ByRef xmax As Single, _
    ByRef ymin As Single, ByRef ymax As Single)

    If X1 < X2 Then
        xmin = X1
        xmax = X2
    Else
        xmin = X2
        xmax = X1
    End If
    If Y1 < Y2 Then
        ymin = Y1
        ymax = Y2
```

```
        Else
            ymin = Y2
            ymax = Y1
        End If
End Sub


' Return a serialization string for the object.
Public Property Get TwoDObject_Serialization() As String
Dim txt As String

    txt = txt & "X1(" & Format$(X1) & ")"
    txt = txt & "Y1(" & Format$(Y1) & ")"
    txt = txt & "X2(" & Format$(X2) & ")"
    txt = txt & "Y2(" & Format$(Y2) & ")"
    TwoDObject_Serialization = "TwoDLine(" & txt & ")"
End Property


' Initialize the object using a serialization string.
' The serialization does not include the
' "TwoDLine(...)" part.
Private Property Let TwoDObject_Serialization( _
    ByVal RHS As String)
Dim token_name As String
Dim token_value As String

    ' Read tokens until there are no more.
    Do While Len(RHS) > 0
        ' Read a token.
        GetNamedToken RHS, token_name, token_value
        Select Case token_name
            Case "X1"
                X1 = CSng(token_value)
            Case "Y1"
                Y1 = CSng(token_value)
            Case "X2"
                X2 = CSng(token_value)
            Case "Y2"
                Y2 = CSng(token_value)
        End Select
    Loop
End Property
```

The TwoDObject_Serialization property let procedure uses the GetNamedToken subroutine to break a serialization string into pieces. Each token is of the form Token-Name(TokenValue). Subroutine GetNamedToken searches the string for the first opening parenthesis to tell where the token name ends. It then searches for the next unmatched closing parenthesis to see where the token value ends.

```
    ' Return a named token from the string txt.
    ' Tokens have the form TokenName(TokenValue).
    Public Sub GetNamedToken(ByRef txt As String, _
```

```
                   ByRef token_name As String, ByRef token_value As String)
Dim pos1 As Integer
Dim pos2 As Integer
Dim open_parens As Integer
Dim ch As String

    ' Find the "(".
    pos1 = InStr(txt, "(")
    If pos1 = 0 Then
        ' No "(" found. Return the rest as the token name.
        token_name = Trim$(txt)
        token_value = ""
        txt = ""
        Exit Sub
    End If

    ' Find the corresponding ")". Note that
    ' parentheses may be nested.
    open_parens = 1
    pos2 = pos1 + 1
    Do While pos2 <= Len(txt)
        ch = Mid$(txt, pos2, 1)
        If ch = "(" Then
            open_parens = open_parens + 1
        ElseIf ch = ")" Then
            open_parens = open_parens - 1
            If open_parens = 0 Then
                ' This is the corresponding ")".
                Exit Do
            End If
        End If
        pos2 = pos2 + 1
    Loop

    ' At this point, pos1 points to the ( and
    ' pos2 points to the ).
    token_name = Trim$(Left$(txt, pos1 - 1))
    token_value = Trim$(Mid$(txt, pos1 + 1, pos2 - pos1 - 1))
    txt = Trim$(Mid$(txt, pos2 + 1))
End Sub
```

This method of using object serializations to save and restore object properties has a couple of benefits. First, the serializations are simple strings. You can save them in files, database fields, or any other medium that works with text. You could pass a serialization to an ActiveX control on a Web page and make the control display the drawing objects in the browser. You could e-mail a serialization to someone who has a program that can read serializations.

This system promotes backward compatibility. If a later version of your program creates a new object property type, your program will still be able to read older serializations. For example, suppose you add a ForeColor property to the TwoDLine class. When a TwoDLine object reads an older serialization, it will not find a ForeColor value. That will not make the program fail, though. It just means the object's ForeColor property is not initialized.

The serializations also provide forward compatibility. Suppose you send a new serialization with the ForeColor property to someone whose program does not support that property. When it reads the serialization, the TwoDLine object simply ignores the property it does not understand. It does not crash.

The convenience of forward and backward compatibility does come at the price of reduced error checking. If a serialization contains the property ForeColor misspelled as FireColor, the program will quietly ignore this value without telling you there is a potential problem.

Using techniques similar to those demonstrated by the TwoDLine class, you can create other objects with other properties. Example program Show2D supports a variety of object types including lines, circles, ellipses, rectangles, squares, and polygons.

Program Show2D also includes a TwoDScene class that contains references to other objects in its SceneObjects collection. This class allows the program to group objects and perform operations on all of them together. For example, the following code shows how the TwoDScene object's Draw method allows the program to draw all of the objects in the scene.

```
' Draw the object on the canvas.
Private Sub TwoDObject_Draw(ByVal canvas As Object)
Dim obj As TwoDObject

    For Each obj In SceneObjects
        obj.Draw canvas
    Next obj
End Sub
```

The classes used by program Show2D implement the drawing properties DrawWidth, DrawStyle, ForeColor, FillStyle, and FillColor. These allow a program to create objects with different colors and drawing styles.

The objects used by program Show2D can also draw themselves into Windows metafiles. Many applications can load metafiles, so this gives you a way to export drawings into other programs. For example, you can create a scene using a Visual Basic program, save the results into a metafile, and then load the metafile into CorelDRAW! or some other drawing program.

Example program Show2D, shown in Figure 12.1, is based on the Styles program described in Chapter 1, Visual Basics. You can use the option buttons to select drawing attributes and objects. Then click and drag to draw the objects. When you have finished, use the File menu's Save 2D File command to save the picture's object serialization in a file. Use the Save Metafile command to make the objects draw themselves into a metafile.

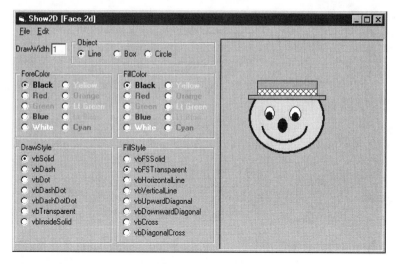

Figure 12.1   Program Show2D.

Windows and Viewports

You can think of a picture as existing in its own coordinate space. This is some abstract place that has boundaries that make sense for the particular picture. For example, suppose you want to graph stock prices over a 12-month period when the stock had values ranging from $10 to $30 per share. You can work in a coordinate space with $1 <= x <= 12$ and $10 <= y <= 30$. This space is called *world coordinate space* or *global coordinate space*. You specify points in this space using *world* or *global coordinates*.

Often, you will not want to display the entire picture drawn in the world coordinate space. You may want to zoom in and display only a small part of the picture, or you may want to zoom out to display the picture at a smaller scale. In traditional graphics programming terms, the region of world coordinate space that you want to display is called a *window*. Unfortunately, the word "window" has been overused in recent years, so this can be confusing. This book uses the term *world window* to mean the area in world coordinate space that you want to display.

Once you know what you want to display, you need to decide where on the computer's screen to display it. This screen area is traditionally called a *viewport*. The relationship between a world window and viewport is shown in Figure 12.2.

Panning and Zooming

The size and position of the world window determine which part of the picture is drawn. The relative sizes of the world window and the viewport determine the scale at which the picture is displayed on the screen. For a given viewport, a relatively large world window produces a small picture because you are drawing a large piece of world coordinate space into a small viewport. A relatively small world window produces a

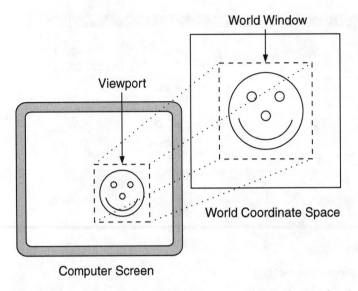

Figure 12.2 The relationship between a world window and a viewport.

large, zoomed-in picture. Figure 12.3 shows the effects of different world windows for the same viewport. Using different world windows, you can *pan* (show different parts of the picture) and *zoom* (show parts of the picture at different scales).

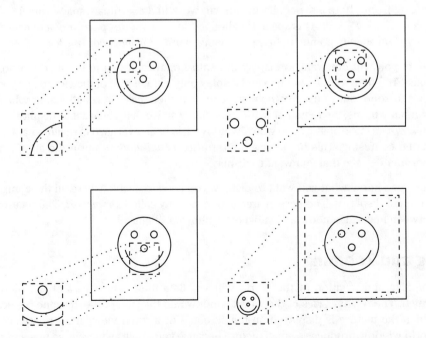

Figure 12.3 Different world windows can produce panning and zooming.

Aspect Ratios

For a region like a viewport or world window, the region's *aspect ratio* is defined as the ratio of the region's height to its width. A square always has an aspect ratio of 1 because its height and width are the same. A viewport with a height of 1 inch and a width of 2 inches has an aspect ratio of 1/2.

If a world window and a viewport have the same aspect ratio, the image displayed on the screen appears normally. If the world window and viewport have different aspect ratios, the image appears stretched or squashed. Figure 12.4 shows several world windows and viewports that have different aspect ratios.

In many programs, you do not want a picture to appear stretched or squashed. A mapping program, for example, would look quite strange if the user could stretch the map out of proportion. Judging distances in a stretched map would be difficult, especially if the map is stretched by different amounts at different times.

To prevent this sort of confusion, you must ensure that the viewport and world windows always have the same aspect ratio. When the user of your program wants to zoom in on part of the picture, you must be certain that the aspect ratios remain the same. Several different approaches you can take to achieve this goal are discussed in the following sections.

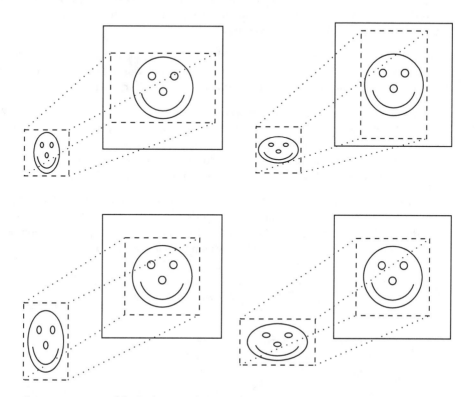

Figure 12.4 World windows and viewports with different aspect ratios.

Fixed Levels of Magnification

First, you can allow the user to specify only certain fixed levels of magnification. To zoom in on an area, the user might select the Scale x2 command from a menu. The program then reduces the height and width of the world window by a factor of two, giving two times magnification. Because the program decreases the world window's width and height by the same amount, it has not changed the aspect ratio, so it still matches the aspect ratio of the viewport.

Similarly, if the user selects the Scale 1/2 option, the program multiplies the world window's width and height by 2. This step reduces the magnification factor by 1/2 and keeps the aspect ratio unchanged.

After the program has resized the world window, it must decide where to place it in the world coordinate space. Probably the most sensible choice is to center it over its old position. If the world window is enlarged, the program can also check to see if the new world window extends far beyond the edge of the picture. If it does, the program can reposition the window so that it displays more of the picture and less empty space.

Adjusting a Selected World Window

A second method for keeping the world window and viewport aspect ratios synchronized is to allow the user to specify an area within the viewport to examine. Let the user pick a rectangle using a rubber band box.

Once the user has chosen a rectangle, resize it so that it has the same aspect ratio as the viewport. To allow the user to see the entire area that was selected, only increase the size of the rectangle in one dimension; do not decrease it in the other.

For example, suppose you are using a square viewport with an aspect ratio of 1. With a rubber band box, the user selects a region with upper-left corner at (1000, 1000) and lower-right corner (2000, 3000). This region has an aspect ratio of 2000/1000 = 2. Because the aspect ratio of the world window (2) is greater than the aspect ratio of the viewport (1), the world window is too tall and thin compared with the viewport.

To make the aspect ratios match without reducing the size of the world window, you must make it wider. To give the world window an aspect ratio of 1 while keeping its height at 2000, you need to set the width to 2000. More generally, you can compute the proper coordinates for the world window using the following code.

```
Private Sub AdjustAspect(ByVal view_aspect As Single, _
    ByRef ww_wid As Single, ByRef ww_hgt As Single)
Dim ww_aspect As Single

    ' Don't divide by zero.
    If ww_wid = 0 Or ww_hgt = 0 Or view_aspect = 0 _
        Then Exit Sub

    ww_aspect = ww_hgt / ww_wid
```

```
      If ww_aspect > view_aspect Then
          ' The world window is too tall and thin.
          ' Make it wider.
          ww_wid = ww_hgt / view_aspect
      Else
          ' The world window is too short and wide.
          ' Make it taller.
          ww_hgt = view_aspect * ww_wid
      End If
  End Sub
```

As is the case with fixed levels of magnification, once you have adjusted the world window, you must decide where to place it. As before, the most sensible choice is to center it over its old position. If you are enlarging the world window, you can also check to see if the new world window extends far beyond the edge of the picture. If it does, you can move the window so that it displays more of the picture and less empty space.

Selecting a Constrained Region

A third method that ensures the world window and viewport have the same aspect ratios is to allow the user to select only regions of the proper shape. You can use a rubber band technique to allow the user to select a region as before. As the user stretches the region, however, you adjust the aspect ratio of the region so that it always matches the aspect ratio of the viewport.

When you use the previous methods, you sometimes need to enlarge the world window so that its aspect ratio matches that of the viewport. This means parts of the picture that were not explicitly selected by the user are included in the new world window. The new, constrained method has the advantage that the user sees exactly what region will be displayed.

On the other hand, with the previous methods, the region the user selects is centered in the viewport. If the user selects a single object of interest, that object is placed in the viewport's center. The constrained method makes it a bit harder for the user to center the viewport over a specific region. To make the constrained rubber band box include an area of interest, the user may need to include other parts of the picture that are less interesting. When the user finishes the selection, the most important part of the picture may not be centered in the viewport.

The Visual Basic code to manage this sort of constrained rubber band box is similar to the code for normal rubber band boxes used by program RubrBox described in Chapter 1, Visual Basics. The major difference is in the MouseMove and MouseUp events. Before these routines use the new coordinates for the rectangle's corner, they call subroutine AdjustAspect to figure out what dimensions the newly selected region should have. They then use these dimensions to adjust the corners of the selected region before drawing the rubber band box.

The AdjustAspect routine used by these event handlers is also a little different from the one presented earlier. To allow the user to create a rubber band box to the left or above the initial mouse position, this version of AdjustAspect must handle the case where the aspect ratio of the selected region is negative. The subroutine first computes the region's new width and height based on the absolute value of the region's aspect ratio. It then uses the sign of the original aspect ratio to make the width or height of the selected area negative if necessary.

Example program Aspect demonstrates this type of constrained region selection. Enter an aspect ratio in the text box. Then use the mouse to select a region. Notice what happens if you drag the mouse to the left or above the point you originally select.

If you select an aspect ratio that is very large or very close to zero, the region you select will grow very quickly as you move the mouse. In fact, it may grow so quickly that the rubber band box coordinates become too large to fit within an integer variable, and the program will crash. The following code shows the key parts of sample program Aspect.

```
Option Explicit

Private SelectInProgress As Boolean
Private StartX As Single
Private StartY As Single
Private LastX As Single
Private LastY As Single
Private OldMode As Integer
Private ViewAspect As Single

' Begin selecting the region.
Private Sub Form_MouseDown(Button As Integer, _
    Shift As Integer, X As Single, Y As Single)

    SelectInProgress = True

        ' For demonstration purposes, get the desired

        ' aspect ratio from a TextBox.

    ViewAspect = CSng(txtAspect.Text)


        ' Save the current drawing mode.
    OldMode = DrawMode

        ' Use invert mode for the rubberband box.
    DrawMode = vbInvert

    StartX = X
    StartY = Y
    LastX = X
    LastY = Y
    Line (StartX, StartY)-(LastX, LastY), , B
End Sub

' Update the region selected.
Private Sub Form_MouseMove(Button As Integer, _
```

```
        Shift As Integer, X As Single, Y As Single)
Dim wid As Single
Dim hgt As Single

    If Not SelectInProgress Then Exit Sub

    ' Erase the old box.
    Line (StartX, StartY)-(LastX, LastY), , B

    wid = X - StartX
    hgt = Y - StartY
    AdjustAspect ViewAspect, wid, hgt
    LastX = StartX + wid
    LastY = StartY + hgt

    ' Draw the new box.
    Line (StartX, StartY)-(LastX, LastY), , B
End Sub

' Finish selecting the region.
Private Sub Form_MouseUp(Button As Integer, _
    Shift As Integer, X As Single, Y As Single)
Dim wid As Single
Dim hgt As Single

    If Not SelectInProgress Then Exit Sub
    SelectInProgress = False

    ' Erase the old box.
    Line (StartX, StartY)-(LastX, LastY), , B

    ' Restore the original drawing mode.
    DrawMode = OldMode

    wid = X - StartX
    hgt = Y - StartY
    AdjustAspect ViewAspect, wid, hgt
    LastX = StartX + wid
    LastY = StartY + hgt

    ' Do something with the region
    ' (StartX, StartY) - (LastX, LastY).
    Line (StartX, StartY)-(LastX, LastY), vbRed, B
End Sub
```

Windows and Viewports in Visual Basic

World windows and viewports are interesting, but how do you use them in Visual Basic? The Visual Basic picture box control is ideal for use as a viewport.

Place the picture box on your form as you would any other control. When you select a size for your viewport, keep in mind that picture box controls may have borders. To take the border into account, you need to examine the control's ScaleWidth and ScaleHeight properties to determine how large your viewport will be.

The following code sizes a picture box so that its interior is two inches square. This code uses the picture box's current Width, Height, ScaleWidth, and ScaleHeight properties to determine how much extra space it needs to allow for the control's borders. It assumes the control and its parent use the same ScaleMode.

```
Dim X As Single
Dim Y As Single
Dim border_wid As Single
Dim border_hgt As Single
Dim wid As Single
Dim hgt As Single

    ' Find the PictureBox's border sizes.
    border_wid = picViewport.Width - picViewport.ScaleWidth
    border_hgt = picViewport.Height - picViewport.ScaleHeight
    wid = 2 * 1440 + border_wid
    hgt = 2 * 1440 + border_hgt

    ' Make the viewport 2 inches square.
    X = picViewport.Left
    Y = picViewport.Top
    picViewport.Move X, Y, wid, hgt
```

At this point you have a viewport mapped onto your computer's screen. You still need to create a world window to define the mapping from world coordinates into the viewport. You can accomplish this using the picture box's scale properties as described in Chapter 1, Visual Basics.

The ScaleLeft, ScaleTop, ScaleWidth, and ScaleHeight values are the same as the coordinates that define the world window. For instance, to map a world window with an upper-left corner (0, 10) and lower-right corner (10, 0) into the viewport as shown in Figure 12.5, you could use the following code.

```
picViewport.ScaleLeft = 0
picViewport.ScaleTop = 10
picViewport.ScaleWidth = (10 - 0)
picViewport.ScaleHeight = (0 - 10)
```

Now you are ready to draw in world coordinate space. When you use the picture box's line, circle, and point drawing routines, the control's scale properties automatically transform your commands into the viewport's coordinate system.

Example program Viewport demonstrates this code. It creates a picture box with an interior viewport area two inches square. It then uses the picture box's scale properties

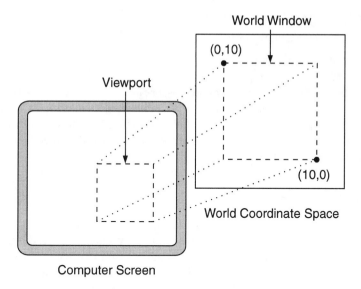

Figure 12.5 Defining a world window using a picture box's scale properties.

to map the viewport to a world window with corners at (0, 10) and (10, 0). Finally, the viewport's Paint event handler calls subroutine DrawSmiley to draw a smiley face centered on the point (5, 5) in world coordinates.

You can modify this program to experiment with different viewport and world window parameters. For example, try changing the world window corners to (-10, 20) and (20, -10) using the following statements.

```
picViewport.ScaleLeft = -10
picViewport.ScaleTop = 20
picViewport.ScaleWidth = (20 - -10)
picViewport.ScaleHeight = (-10 - 20)
```

Practice changing the viewport and world window parameters until you get a feel for how you can use them to pan, zoom, and stretch the image.

Zooming and Panning in Visual Basic

Using picture boxes together with world windows and viewports, you can easily write programs that magnify and pan across a picture. If you attach these techniques to menus and scrollbars, you can build a sophisticated drawing system with surprisingly little effort.

Zooming In

To zoom in on a picture, let the user select a new magnification level using one of the three methods described earlier:

- Selecting a fixed level of magnification
- Adjusting a selected world window
- Selecting a constrained region

Once you know the new world window boundaries, create a new mapping from the world window into the viewport using the viewport's scale properties. Then erase the old picture and redraw it. If your picture drawing commands are invoked in the viewport control's Paint event handler, you can do this by calling the viewport's Refresh method. This method forces an immediate repaint of the entire control.

Zooming Out

To zoom out, let the user select a new level of magnification from a menu. Create a Magnify 1/2 command to decrease the level of magnification by a factor of 1/2. Similarly, the commands Magnify 1/4, Magnify 1/8, and so forth allow faster decreases in the level of magnification. You can also implement a Full Scale command that immediately brings the program back to a default scale that shows the entire picture.

At this point, you might want to restrict the possible level of magnification. If you allow the user to decrease the level of magnification indefinitely, the picture will eventually become a dot in the middle of the screen. To prevent this, you can calculate a minimum allowed level of magnification. This should also be the magnification level given by the Full Scale command.

Make this minimum level of magnification small enough that the user can display a margin of empty space around the picture. Not only is this aesthetically pleasing, but it gives the user some confidence that the entire picture is visible. If your picture is not too complicated, allow a 10 percent margin around each edge. If your picture is very densely packed with lines, a 5 percent margin will do. When an empty margin is visible around a complex picture, it is easy to understand that the whole picture is visible.

Once you have computed the world window's new size, you can center it over its previous position. At this point, the world window may be so far to one side that it displays a lot of space beyond the edge of the picture. Figure 12.6 shows a world window before and after the level of magnification was decreased by a factor of 1/4. Because the old world window was close to the left edge of the picture, the new one extends far beyond the edge of the drawing.

In this case you can move the world window so that it no longer extends beyond the margins you have set for your picture. In Figure 12.6 you would move the world window to the right so that it contains less empty space.

If the aspect ratio of the area containing your complete picture in world coordinates does not match the aspect ratio of your viewport, the user must be able to display some empty space. If the picture is tall and thin and the viewport is relatively short and wide, the program must display a lot of empty space if it is to show the user all of the data at once. Figure 12.7 shows this situation.

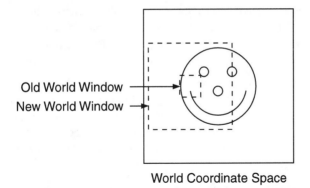

World Coordinate Space

Figure 12.6   Resizing a world window may make it extend off the edge of the picture.

Panning

To implement a complete windowing system, you also need to allow the user to scroll or pan through a picture. Vertical and horizontal scrollbars provide an easy way to do this. Place a horizontal scrollbar at the bottom of your picture and a vertical scrollbar to the right.

A scrollbar's Min and Max properties determine the values that the user can select. If you set Min = 1 and Max = 100, the user will be able to use the scrollbar to select values between 1 and 100.

When you attach a scrollbar to a picture, keep in mind that the world window takes up space in world coordinates. If your picture occupies the range $1 <= y <= 100$ in world coordinates, and your world window is 10 units tall, set the vertical scrollbar's properties to Min = 10 and Max = 100. You can use the value selected by the user to position

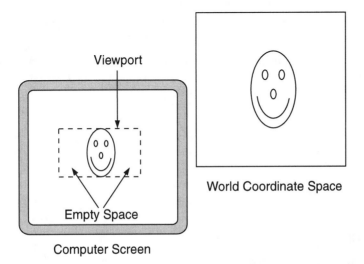

Figure 12.7   Sometimes a viewport must contain empty space to show the whole picture.

the top of the world window. When the scrollbar value is 100, set the world window so that its top is at position 100, the picture's largest world coordinate. When the scrollbar's value is 10, set the world window so that its top is at position 10. This puts its bottom at position 1, so the world window displays the bottommost part of the picture.

In addition to Min and Max, you must set the scrollbars' SmallChange and LargeChange properties. SmallChange determines the amount by which a scrollbar's value changes when the user clicks on its arrow buttons. LargeChange determines the amount by which the value changes when the user clicks on the space between an arrow button and the thumb. Figure 12.8 shows the parts of a scrollbar where the user can click to cause a small or large change.

Set the SmallChange values so that the world window moves only a fraction of its own size across the picture when the user clicks on the arrows. Setting SmallChange to 10 or 20 percent of the size of the world window usually produces good results.

Set LargeChange to move the world window its current size across the picture when the user clicks between the arrows and the thumb. If the world window is 10 units tall, set LargeChange = 10. This not only lets the user move the picture a reasonable amount, but it also allows the scrollbar thumb to size itself proportionally. If the viewport displays half of the world window space, the scrollbar thumb occupies half of the scrollbar's area.

Scrollbars have two events that the program must handle. The Change event occurs when the value of the scrollbar has changed. This happens when the user clicks on the scrollbar to change its value or when the program explicitly sets the value of the scrollbar. Whenever the program receives a Change event, it should reposition the world window using the scrollbar's new value.

The second scrollbar event is the Scroll event. This occurs when the user has grabbed a scrollbar's thumb and is dragging it to a new position. As the user drags the thumb, Visual Basic may generate many Scroll events.

When the program receives Scroll events, it can reposition the world window using the scrollbar's new value. This makes the picture appear to move as the user is dragging the scrollbar's thumb. This produces a nice, smooth, interactive result.

If the picture is particularly time consuming to draw, however, the picture may seem to flicker. If the picture is extremely complicated, the picture may even repeatedly disappear and then slowly redraw as the user drags the thumb.

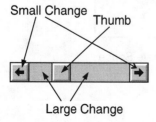

Figure 12.8 The parts of a scrollbar.

To prevent these problems, you can simply ignore Scroll events. If you do not redraw the picture during scroll events, Visual Basic generates a final Change event when the user finishes moving the thumb. The program can reposition the world window when it receives this Change event. While the picture does not scroll interactively as the thumb moves, the user can still use the thumb to quickly display other parts of the picture.

Using the SetWorldWindow Subroutine

Individually, the adjustments needed to reposition a world window are simple. Together they add up to a fair amount of code. The SetWorldWindow subroutine shown in the following code adjusts the world window coordinates given by Wxmin, Wxmax, Wymin, and Wymax. The values DataXmin, DataXmax, DataYmin, and DataYmax are the bounds of the picture in world coordinates. The values DataMinWid, DataMaxWid, DataMinHgt, and DataMaxWid are the maximum and minimum dimensions you want to allow for the world window. For instance, you could set DataMaxWid = DataXmax - DataXmin plus a 10 percent margin.

This subroutine makes sure that the world window is not ridiculously large or small. It then adjusts the world window's aspect ratio so the data is not distorted. It places the world window in the correct location, maps the world window, and forces it to redraw. Finally, the subroutine sets values for the scrollbar properties Min, Max, SmallChange, and LargeChange.

```
' Adjust the world window so it is not too big,
' too small, off to one side, or of the wrong
' aspect ratio. Then map the world window to the
' viewport and force the viewport to repaint.
Private Sub SetWorldWindow()
Dim wid As Single
Dim hgt As Single
Dim xmid As Single
Dim ymid As Single
Dim aspect As Single

    ' Find the size and center of the world window.
    wid = Wxmax - Wxmin
    hgt = Wymax - Wymin
    xmid = (Wxmax + Wxmin) / 2
    ymid = (Wymax + Wymin) / 2

    ' Make sure we're not too big or too small.
    If wid > DataMaxWid Then
        wid = DataMaxWid
    ElseIf wid < DataMinWid Then
        wid = DataMinWid
    End If
    If hgt > DataMaxHgt Then
        hgt = DataMaxHgt
    ElseIf hgt < DataMinHgt Then
```

```
        hgt = DataMinHgt
    End If


    ' Make the aspect ratio match the viewport
    ' aspect ratio, VAspect (set in Form_Resize).
    aspect = hgt / wid
    If aspect > VAspect Then
            ' Too tall and thin. Make it wider.
        wid = hgt / VAspect
    Else
            ' Too short and wide. Make it taller.
        hgt = wid * VAspect
    End If


    ' Compute the new coordinates
    Wxmin = xmid - wid / 2
    Wxmax = xmid + wid / 2
    Wymin = ymid - hgt / 2
    Wymax = ymid + hgt / 2


    ' See if we're off to one side.
    If wid > DataMaxWid Then
            ' We're wider than the picture. Center.
        xmid = (DataXmax + DataXmin) / 2
        Wxmin = xmid - wid / 2
        Wxmax = xmid + wid / 2
    Else
            ' Else see if we're too far to one side.
        If Wxmin < DataXmin And Wxmax < DataXmax Then
                ' Adjust to the right.
            Wxmax = Wxmax + DataXmin - Wxmin
            Wxmin = DataXmin
        End If
        If Wxmax > DataXmax And Wxmin > DataXmin Then
                ' Adjust to the left.
            Wxmin = Wxmin + DataXmax - Wxmax
            Wxmax = DataXmax
        End If
    End If
    If hgt > DataMaxHgt Then
            ' We're taller than the picture. Shrink.
        ymid = (DataYmax + DataYmin) / 2
        Wymin = ymid - hgt / 2
        Wymax = ymid + hgt / 2
    Else
            ' See if we're too far to top or bottom.
        If Wymin < DataYmin And Wymax < DataYmax Then
                ' Adjust downward.
            Wymax = Wymax + DataYmin - Wymin
            Wymin = DataYmin
```

```
            End If
        If Wymax > DataYmax And Wymin > DataYmin Then
            ' Adjust upward.
            Wymin = Wymin + DataYmax - Wymax
            Wymax = DataYmax
        End If
    End If
End If


' Map the world window to the viewport.
picViewport.ScaleLeft = Wxmin
picViewport.ScaleTop = Wymax
picViewport.ScaleWidth = Wxmax - Wxmin
picViewport.ScaleHeight = Wymin - Wymax


' Force the viewport to repaint.
picViewport.Refresh


' Reset the scroll bars.
IgnoreSbarChange = True
HScrollBar.Visible = (wid < DataXmax - DataXmin)
VScrollBar.Visible = (hgt < DataYmax - DataYmin)


' The values of the scroll bars will be where
' the top/left of the world window should be.
VScrollBar.Min = 100 * (DataYmax)
VScrollBar.Max = 100 * (DataYmin + hgt)
HScrollBar.Min = 100 * (DataXmin)
HScrollBar.Max = 100 * (DataXmax - wid)


' SmallChange moves the world window 1/10
' of its width/height.
VScrollBar.SmallChange = 100 * (hgt / 10)
VScrollBar.LargeChange = 100 * hgt
HScrollBar.SmallChange = 100 * (wid / 10)
HScrollBar.LargeChange = 100 * wid


' Set the current scroll bar values.
VScrollBar.Value = 100 * Wymax
HScrollBar.Value = 100 * Wxmin


    IgnoreSbarChange = False
End Sub
```

Example program Panview1 lets you zoom and pan to examine a picture of a smiley face. You can change the magnification by a factor of 2, 4, 1/2, or 1/4 in addition to returning to full scale. Zoom in and experiment with the scrollbars. Click on the arrow buttons and between the buttons and the thumb to see how the SmallChange and LargeChange properties affect the scrollbars. Drag the thumb to watch the picture scroll as you change the scrollbars' values.

On my 133MHz Pentium, program Panview1 draws its smiley face just a little too slowly to pan without flickering. If you click and drag the scrollbar thumbs, you will see a slight but noticeable flicker.

Example program Panview2 is similar to program Panview1 but uses different zooming and scrolling styles. Rather than providing certain fixed-scale factors, this program lets you zoom in on an arbitrary region. To do this, select the Zoom command from the Scale menu. Then click and drag to select the area in the picture that you would like to examine more closely. The program adjusts the world window so that it has the correct aspect ratio before it updates the picture.

Panview2 does not scroll its picture as you drag a scrollbar's thumb. If you grab a thumb and drag it, the program waits until you release the thumb before it updates the world window's boundaries. This method is particularly useful if the picture you are drawing is extremely complicated and redrawing whenever the thumb moves causes the image to flicker annoyingly.

Two-Dimensional Transformations

By changing the world window mapping, you can easily move a picture to another part of a viewport. If the picture contains more than one object, you might like to move one of the objects without moving the others. In that case, you cannot use the world window mapping to move the object because that would move the other objects as well.

Instead you can apply a *transformation* to the object you want to move. A transformation changes the position of the points and lines that make up the object. The following sections describe transformations that translate, scale, and rotate an object.

Some Visual Basic drawing methods do not transform easily. The Circle method, for instance, can draw arcs of ellipses. While the Circle method can draw arcs that have been scaled or translated, it cannot draw an arc that has been rotated. Similarly, you can use the Line method to draw a rectangle as shown in the following code:

```
Line (x1, y1) - (x2, y2), , B
```

You can modify this statement to draw a rectangle that has been scaled or translated but not one that has been rotated. To draw a rotated rectangle, you must use the Line command four times, once for each side of the rectangle. Figure 12.9 shows some arcs and rectangles that Visual Basic's Circle and Line commands cannot draw directly.

You can draw these sorts of shapes using the Line command. If you draw an arc as a sequence of short line segments, you can transform the arc by transforming the points that make up the segments. If the segments are small enough, the arc appears smooth to the user. Chapter 11, Drawing Curves, discusses this sort of curve drawing in detail.

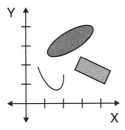

Figure 12.9   Arcs and rectangles that Visual Basic's Circle and Line methods cannot draw directly.

Simple Transformations

While the most general transformations possible are quite complicated, you can build many useful transformations by combining simple translation, scaling, and rotation. The next several sections describe these simpler transformations. The sections following those explain how you can compose these simple transformations to create more general ones.

Translation

To translate an object, you add an appropriate offset to the X and Y coordinates of the points that make up the object. For example, to move an object 10 units in the positive X direction and 3 units in the negative Y direction in world coordinates, add 10 to the X coordinate and subtract 3 from the Y coordinate of each point in the object. You can write the new coordinates of a point as:

```
new_x = old_x + x_offset
new_y = old_y + y_offset
```

Scaling

It is just as easy to scale an object. To scale or stretch an object in the X direction, multiply the X coordinate of each of the object's points by some number. For example, to make an object twice as wide, multiply the X coordinates of its points by a factor of two. You can scale an object in the Y direction similarly. You can write the new coordinates of a point as:

```
new_x = old_x * x_scale
new_y = old_y * y_scale
```

Figure 12.10 shows a picture before and after it has been scaled by a factor of 2 in the X direction. Notice that multiplying each point's X coordinate has moved the object twice as far from the Y axis as it was before.

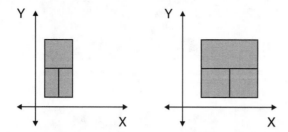

Figure 12.10 A figure scaled by a factor of two in the X direction.

Reflection

By reflecting an object across the X or Y axis, you can create a mirror image of the object. Figure 12.11 shows an object and its reflection across the Y axis.

Reflecting an object across an axis is equivalent to scaling it with a negative scale factor. For instance, to reflect an object across the Y axis as shown in Figure 12.11, you can scale the object by a factor of -1 in the X direction. You can write the new coordinates of a point as:

```
new_x = old_x * (-1)
new_y = old_y
```

You can reflect an object across the X axis similarly by scaling it by a factor of -1 in the Y direction.

```
new_x = old_x
new_y = old_y * (-1)
```

Rotation

Rotating an object is a little trickier than translating or scaling one. The equations for rotating a point around the origin by an angle θ are:

```
new_x = old_x * Cos(θ) - old_y * Sin(θ)
new_y = old_x * Sin(θ) + old_y * Cos(θ)
```

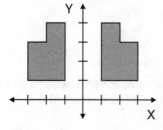

Figure 12.11 An object and its reflection across the Y axis.

Because both of the old values of the point's X and Y coordinates are used in both of these equations, you must be careful when using the equations in Visual Basic. You might try to execute the statements in order like this:

```
X = X * Cos(theta) - Y * Sin(theta)
Y = X * Sin(theta) + Y * Cos(theta)
```

Unfortunately the first statement changes the value of the variable X. The original value of X is not available for use in the second statement, so the new value for Y is wrong. The following three lines show one way you can rotate a point correctly in Visual Basic.

```
new_x = X * Cos(theta) - Y * Sin(theta)
Y = X * Sin(theta) + Y * Cos(theta)
X = new_x
```

Figure 12.12 shows a small picture before and after rotation through an angle of 30 degrees.

The Mathematics of Rotation

This section explains why the rotation equations described in the previous section work. If your trigonometry is a little rusty, feel free to skip this section and take the equations on faith.

To see why the rotation equations work, look at Figure 12.13. The point (x_1, y_1) is distance R from the origin. Using simple trigonometry, you know that:

```
x₁ = R * Cos(φ)
y₁ = R * Sin(φ)
```

The point (x_2, y_2) is the same point rotated by an angle of θ. Because it is also distance R from the origin, its coordinates are given by:

```
x₂ = R * Cos(φ + θ)
y₂ = R * Sin(φ + θ)
```

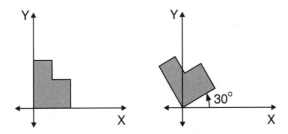

Figure 12.12 An object rotated by 30 degrees.

You can rewrite these two equations using the following trigonometric identities.

```
Cos(φ + θ) = Cos(φ) * Cos(θ) - Sin(φ) * Sin(θ)
Sin(φ + θ) = Cos(φ) * Sin(θ) + Sin(φ) * Cos(θ)
```

Making these substitutions you get:

```
x₂ = R * Cos(φ) * Cos(θ) - R * Sin(φ) * Sin(θ)
y₂ = R * Cos(φ) * Sin(θ) + R * Sin(φ) * Cos(θ)
```

Now substituting the values $x_1 = R * Cos(\phi)$ and $y_1 = R * Sin(\phi)$ into these equations gives the equations for rotation.

```
x₂ = x₁ * Cos(θ) - y₁ * Sin(θ)
y₂ = x₁ * Sin(θ) + y₁ * Cos(θ)
```

Combining Transformations

The equations for translation, scaling, and rotation use very different operations. To translate a point, you add values to the point's coordinates. To scale a point, you multiply its coordinates by scale factors. To rotate a point, you must use more complicated equations involving both of the point's coordinates in addition to sines and cosines.

Before you can easily combine these simple operations to form more complex transformations, you must be able to treat the different simple transformations in a uniform or homogeneous way.

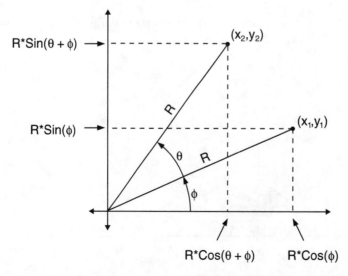

Figure 12.13 The mathematics of rotation.

The following section introduces *homogeneous coordinates* that allow you to manipulate all of these transformations with matrices. The sections after that explain how you can combine simple transformation matrices to create more complicated transformations.

Homogeneous Coordinates

To represent a two-dimensional point in homogeneous coordinates, you store the point as a vector [S * x, S * y, S]. Here x and y are the point's normal X and Y coordinates, and S is a scale factor. For example, the point (10, 4) might be stored as [20, 8, 2] or as [5, 2, 0.5]. Both of these vectors represent the same point (10, 4). In the first case, the value of S is 2. In the second, S is 0.5.

Usually, for convenience, the components in a vector are *normalized* by dividing them by the scale factor S. This makes the new scale factor 1 and the other components the same as their normal X and Y coordinates. The normalized representation of the point (10, 4) is [10, 4, 1].

When you represent points as vectors, you can represent translation, scaling, and rotation as matrices. To apply a transformation matrix to a point, you multiply the point's vector by the transformation matrix. The result is a new vector that gives the point's transformed coordinates.

Before specific transformation matrices are described, the following two sections review matrix/vector and matrix/matrix multiplication. If you are comfortable with these operations, you can safely skip these sections.

Vector/Matrix Multiplication

When you multiply a vector by a matrix, the result is a new vector. To find the value of the ith component in the result, multiply the components in the vector by the corresponding entries in the ith column of the matrix and add them together. This makes more sense after you have worked through a few examples.

Suppose you want to multiply the vector [a, b, c] with the matrix:

```
m11 m12 m13
m21 m22 m23
m31 m32 m33
```

The first component of the result is given by the sum of the products of [a, b, c] with the entries in the first column of the matrix. This value is a * m11 + b * m21 + c * m31. In a similar way, you can compute the values for the second and third components in the new vector.

You can use the following Visual Basic code to multiply a vector and a matrix. Here V is an array holding the vector, M is a two-dimensional array holding the matrix, and Result is the array that should hold the resulting vector.

```
For i = 1 To 3
```

```
         ' Compute the ith component.
        Result(i) = 0
        For j = 1 To 3
            ' Multiply vector components with the corresponding
            ' matrix entries in the ith column.
            Result(i) = Result(i) + V(j) * M(i, j)
        Next j
    Next i
```

Matrix/Matrix Multiplication

When you multiply two matrices, the result is a new matrix. To multiply two matrices, you can think of each row in the first matrix as a vector. You can then use vector/matrix multiplication to find the corresponding row in the result.

The following Visual Basic code multiplies two matrices. Here L and R are two-dimensional arrays that represent the left and right matrices respectively. Result is a two-dimensional array that will hold the result. In other words, Result = L * R.

```
For i = 1 To 3
    ' Compute result row i.
    For j = 1 To 3
        ' Compute the result in row i, column j.
        Result(i, j) = 0
        For k = 1 to 3
            Result(i, j) = Result(i, j) + L(i, k) * R(k, j)
        Next k
    Next j
Next i
```

Translation

Now that you know how to multiply vectors and matrices, you can use them to represent transformations. You can represent translation by distance Tx in the X direction and Ty in the Y direction with the matrix:

$$\begin{vmatrix} 1 & 0 & 0 \\ 0 & 1 & 0 \\ Tx & Ty & 1 \end{vmatrix}$$

To apply the transformation to the point [x, y, 1], you multiply the vector by the matrix.

$$[x, y, 1] \begin{vmatrix} 1 & 0 & 0 \\ 0 & 1 & 0 \\ Tx & Ty & 1 \end{vmatrix} = [x + Tx, y + Ty, 1]$$

The new vector [x + Tx, y + Ty, 1] correctly represents the point (x, y) after it has been translated to the point (x + Tx, y + Ty).

If this seems like a lot of work for little benefit, you are right. Performing a matrix/vector multiplication takes six additions, nine multiplications, and some overhead for running two For loops. This is a good deal more work than the two additions it would take to directly add Tx and Ty to the point's coordinates.

The real advantage of this method comes when you combine transformations. You will see the power of homogeneous coordinates a little later in the section "Composing Transformations."

Scaling

Just as you can represent translation using a matrix, you can represent scaling by a factor of Sx in the X direction and Sy in the Y direction with the matrix:

$$\begin{vmatrix} Sx & 0 & 0 \\ 0 & Sy & 0 \\ 0 & 0 & 1 \end{vmatrix}$$

When you multiply the point [x, y, 1] with this matrix you get:

$$[x, \ y, \ 1] \ \begin{vmatrix} Sx & 0 & 0 \\ 0 & Sy & 0 \\ 0 & 0 & 1 \end{vmatrix} \ = \ [x \ * \ Sx, \ y \ * \ Sy, \ 1]$$

The resulting vector [x * Sx, y * Sy, 1] correctly represents the point (x, y) after it has been scaled to (x * Sx, y * Sy).

Rotation

You can represent rotation by an angle θ with the transformation matrix:

$$\begin{vmatrix} Cos(\theta) & Sin(\theta) & 0 \\ -Sin(\theta) & Cos(\theta) & 0 \\ 0 & 0 & 1 \end{vmatrix}$$

Multiplying the vector [x, y, 1] by this matrix, you get [x * Cos(θ) - y * Sin(θ), x * Sin(θ) + y * Cos(θ), 1]. This agrees with the previous result for rotating a point (x, y) by the angle θ to the point (x * Cos(θ) - y * Sin(θ), x * Sin(θ) + y * Cos(θ)).

Inverse Transformations

Each of these basic transformations has a simple inverse that undoes whatever operation was performed by the transformation. If you apply a transformation to an object and then apply the transformation's inverse, the object ends up in its original position.

The inverse of a translation by distance Tx in the X direction and Ty in the Y direction is simply a translation by distances -Tx and -Ty. The transformation matrix for this operation is:

$$\begin{vmatrix} 1 & 0 & 0 \\ 0 & 1 & 0 \\ -Tx & -Ty & 1 \end{vmatrix}$$

The inverse of a transformation that scales by factors Sx and Sy is one that scales by factors 1/Sx and 1/Sy.

$$\begin{vmatrix} 1/Sx & 0 & 0 \\ 0 & 1/Sy & 0 \\ 0 & 0 & 1 \end{vmatrix}$$

Finally, the inverse of a rotation through the angle θ is a rotation through the angle $-\theta$.

$$\begin{vmatrix} Cos(-\theta) & Sin(-\theta) & 0 \\ -Sin(-\theta) & Cos(-\theta) & 0 \\ 0 & 0 & 1 \end{vmatrix}$$

Because $Cos(-\theta) = Cos(\theta)$ and $Sin(-\theta) = -Sin(\theta)$, you can simplify this to:

$$\begin{vmatrix} Cos(\theta) & -Sin(\theta) & 0 \\ Sin(\theta) & Cos(\theta) & 0 \\ 0 & 0 & 1 \end{vmatrix}$$

Composing Transformations

Representing translation, scaling, and rotation as the same sort of matrices is convenient, but the real value of homogeneous coordinates comes when you compose transformations.

Suppose you want to rotate a point P by applying a rotation matrix R and then translate the point by applying translation matrix T. You can write the transformation equation for this operation as (P * R) * T.

Multiplication of vectors and matrices is associative. That means it does not matter whether you multiply P and R first or R and T first. This lets you rewrite the operation as P * (R * T). That means you can compute the matrix R * T first and then multiply this new matrix by the point P. Instead of multiplying the point P by two matrices, you only need to multiply it by one matrix that combines both transformations.

This is not much of an improvement if you are only transforming a single point. Multiplying a vector by a matrix requires 9 multiplications and 6 additions. Multiplying two matrices takes 27 multiplications and 18 additions. By combining the two matrices, you save one vector/matrix multiplication. You perform an extra 27 multiplications and 18 additions to save only 9 multiplications and 6 additions.

Most of the time, however, a program must apply a transformation to all of the points that make up some sort of object in a picture. If there are many points in the object, saving one matrix multiplication per point can add up quickly. If the object contains only three points, you will save as many multiplications and additions as you gain. For more complicated objects that contain hundreds of data points, the savings can be quite large.

Even more important, many graphic operations require a complex series of transformations. One operation may require a translation, rotation, scaling, inverse rotation, and inverse scaling. Combining all these operations into one matrix can save a lot of time when the program applies it to every point in a complex scene.

To examine a concrete example of composing transformation matrices, look at Figure 12.14. Here the object on the left has been rotated 30 degrees and then translated three units in the X direction and two units in the Y direction to produce the object on the right. The transformation matrix representing the rotation is:

$$\begin{vmatrix} \text{Cos}(30) & \text{Sin}(30) & 0 \\ -\text{Sin}(30) & \text{Cos}(30) & 0 \\ 0 & 0 & 1 \end{vmatrix}$$

The matrix representing the translation is:

$$\begin{vmatrix} 1 & 0 & 0 \\ 0 & 1 & 0 \\ 3 & 2 & 1 \end{vmatrix}$$

Multiplying these two matrices gives the combined transformation matrix:

$$\begin{vmatrix} \text{Cos}(30) & \text{Sin}(30) & 0 \\ -\text{Sin}(30) & \text{Cos}(30) & 0 \\ 0 & 0 & 1 \end{vmatrix} * \begin{vmatrix} 1 & 0 & 0 \\ 0 & 1 & 0 \\ 3 & 2 & 1 \end{vmatrix} = \begin{vmatrix} \text{Cos}(30) & \text{Sin}(30) & 0 \\ -\text{Sin}(30) & \text{Cos}(30) & 0 \\ 3 & 2 & 1 \end{vmatrix}$$

Instead of multiplying the object's six points by two separate matrices, you can multiply them by the single combined transformation matrix.

Note that the order in which you multiply transformation matrices is very important. Figure 12.15 shows the same object as Figure 12.14. In this case, the translation matrix was placed on the left side of the multiplication, and the rotation matrix was placed on

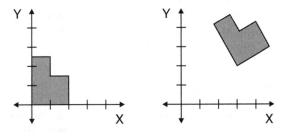

Figure 12.14   Rotation followed by translation.

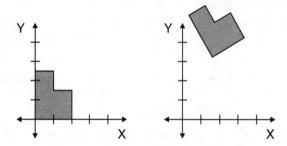

Figure 12.15 Translation followed by rotation.

the right. Geometrically, this corresponds to a translation followed by a rotation rather than a rotation followed by a translation, as is shown in Figure 12.14.

Scaling Without Translation

The scaling transformation described earlier moves points further away from the origin. Figure 12.10, for example, shows an object scaled by a factor of two in the X direction. This operation moves each point twice as far from the Y axis as it was originally.

The one point that is immune to this movement is the origin itself. Because the X and Y coordinates of the origin are both zero, they remain zero if you multiply them by any scale factors. You can use this fact to scale an object without moving it.

Begin by translating the object so that it is located at the origin. Then scale the object and use the inverse of the original translation to move the object back to where it started. By composing the three transformation matrices, you can represent the combined operation with a single matrix. Figure 12.16 shows an object translated to the origin, scaled, and translated back to its original position in this way.

Because the size of a scaled object has changed, you cannot put it back exactly where it was when you started. Only one of the object's points can return to its original position. In Figure 12.16, the object is placed centered over the position from which it came. The center point in the object was returned to its original position. Translating the center point to the origin made it easy to translate that point back to its original position after the scaling.

To return the object so that a different point remains unmoved, translate that point to the origin. After you scale the object, that point is still at the origin, so it is easy to translate it back to its original location. Figure 12.17 shows an object similar to the one shown in Figure 12.16. In this case, the object is translated, scaled, and translated again so its lower-left corner is returned to its original position.

Reflection across an Arbitrary Line

Simple scaling transformation matrices scale an object with respect to the origin. Similarly, the reflections described earlier allow you to reflect an object only across the X or Y axis. By translating an object to the origin before scaling it, you can change the way

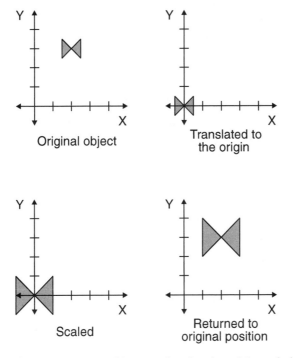

Figure 12.16 An object translated to the origin, scaled, and translated back to its original position.

the object is scaled. You can use a similar technique to reflect an object across an arbitrary line.

Begin by translating the object and the line across which you want to reflect it so that the line passes through the origin. Next, rotate the object and line until the line corresponds to the X axis. Then reflect the object across the X axis. Finally, use the inverses of the original rotation and translation to put the line back in its original position. Figure 12.18 shows an object being reflected across a line.

Rotation around an Arbitrary Point

You can use a similar technique to rotate an object around a point other than the origin. First, translate the point of rotation to the origin. Then rotate the object and use the inverse translation to move the point of rotation back to its original position.

Figure 12.19 shows how to rotate a square around its center. First, translate the square so that its center is at the origin. Then rotate the square using a simple rotation transformation. Finally, translate the square so that its center is back in its original position.

Transformation Matrices in Visual Basic

You can easily write Visual Basic subroutines to make the creation of the simpler transformation matrices easier. The most fundamental of these subroutines initializes an

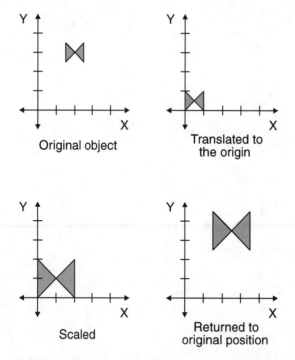

Figure 12.17 Scaling an object at its lower left corner.

identity transformation. The identity transformation matrix leaves any point's coordinates unchanged.

$$\begin{vmatrix} 1 & 0 & 0 \\ 0 & 1 & 0 \\ 0 & 0 & 1 \end{vmatrix}$$

You can use the identity matrix to initialize the parts of a transformation that you will not be modifying. To build a scaling matrix, for example, you can start with the identity matrix and then modify the X and Y scaling terms.

The first of the subroutines that follow sets a transformation equal to the identity matrix. The next three routines use the identity matrix as the basis for creating simple translation, scaling, and rotation transformations.

```
' Create a 2-dimensional identity matrix.
Public Sub m2Identity(M() As Single)
Dim i As Integer
Dim j As Integer

    For i = 1 To 3
        For j = 1 To 3
            If i = j Then
                M(i, j) = 1
```

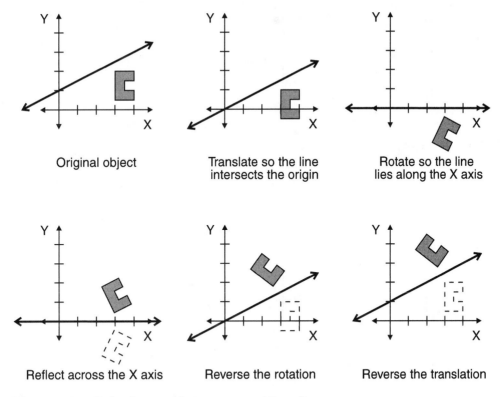

Figure 12.18 Reflecting an object across an arbitrary line.

```
            Else
                M(i, j) = 0
            End If
        Next j
    Next i
End Sub


' Create a translation matrix for translation by
' distances tx and ty.
Public Sub m2Translate(Result() As Single, _
    ByVal tx As Single, ByVal ty As Single)

    m2Identity Result
    Result(3, 1) = tx
    Result(3, 2) = ty
End Sub


' Create a scaling matrix for scaling by factors
' of sx and sy.
Public Sub m2Scale(Result() As Single, _
    ByVal sx As Single, ByVal sy As Single)

    m2Identity Result
```

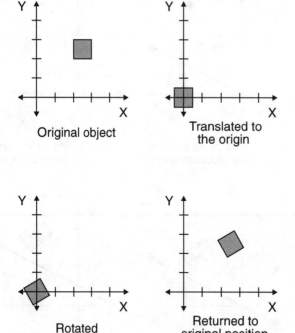

Figure 12.19 Rotating an object around its center.

```
        Result(1, 1) = sx
        Result(2, 2) = sy
End Sub


    ' Create a rotation matrix for rotating by the
    ' given angle (in radians).
    Public Sub m2Rotate(Result() As Single, ByVal theta As Single)
        m2Identity Result
        Result(1, 1) = Cos(theta)
        Result(1, 2) = Sin(theta)
        Result(2, 1) = -Result(1, 2)
        Result(2, 2) = Result(1, 1)
    End Sub
```

Sometimes you will find it easier to specify a rotation with a point that should be rotated until it lies along the X or Y axis rather than specifying an angle of rotation. When you want to reflect across an arbitrary line, for instance, you need to rotate the line until it lies in the X axis. Specifying a point on the line is easier than calculating the angle through which the line must be rotated.

Figure 12.20 shows a point that should be rotated into the X axis. The distance d is the distance from the point to the origin and equals $Sqr(x * x + y * y)$. Because θ is measured in the negative direction, $Cos(\theta) = x / d$ and $Sin(\theta) = -y / d$. In that case, the rotation transformation matrix becomes:

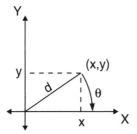

Figure 12.20 Rotating the point (x, y) until it lies on the X axis.

$$\begin{vmatrix} x/d & -y/d & 0 \\ y/d & x/d & 0 \\ 0 & 0 & 1 \end{vmatrix}$$

Using this fact, you can write a Visual Basic routine that initializes a transformation matrix to rotate a point until it lies in the X axis without calling the relatively slow Sin and Cos functions.

```
' Create a rotation matrix that rotates the point
' (x, y) onto the X axis.
Public Sub m2RotateIntoX(Result() As Single, _
    ByVal x As Single, ByVal y As Single)
Dim d As Single

    m2Identity Result
    d = Sqr(x * x + y * y)
    Result(1, 1) = x / d
    Result(1, 2) = -y / d
    Result(2, 1) = -Result(1, 2)
    Result(2, 2) = Result(1, 1)
End Sub
```

With these routines as tools, you can build more complicated combinations of transformations. The following routines use these tools to create transformation matrices for scaling around a point other than the origin, reflection around an arbitrary line, and rotation around a specified point.

```
' Create a scaling matrix for scaling by factors
' of sx and sy at the point (x, y).
Public Sub m2ScaleAt(Result() As Single, _
    ByVal sx As Single, ByVal sy As Single, _
    ByVal x As Single, ByVal y As Single)
Dim T(1 To 3, 1 To 3) As Single
Dim S(1 To 3, 1 To 3) As Single
Dim T_Inv(1 To 3, 1 To 3) As Single
Dim M(1 To 3, 1 To 3) As Single
```

```vb
    ' Translate the point to the origin.
    m2Translate T, -x, -y

    ' Compute the inverse translation.
    m2Translate T_Inv, x, y

    ' Scale.
    m2Scale S, sx, sy

    ' Combine the transformations.
    m2MatMultiply M, T, S          ' T * S
    m2MatMultiply Result, M, T_Inv ' T * S * T_Inv
End Sub

' Create a matrix for reflecting across the line
' passing through (x, y) in direction <dx, dy>.
Public Sub m2ReflectAcross(Result() As Single, _
    ByVal x As Single, ByVal y As Single, _
    ByVal dx As Single, ByVal dy As Single)
Dim T(1 To 3, 1 To 3) As Single
Dim R(1 To 3, 1 To 3) As Single
Dim S(1 To 3, 1 To 3) As Single
Dim R_Inv(1 To 3, 1 To 3) As Single
Dim T_Inv(1 To 3, 1 To 3) As Single
Dim M1(1 To 3, 1 To 3) As Single
Dim M2(1 To 3, 1 To 3) As Single
Dim M3(1 To 3, 1 To 3) As Single

    ' Translate the point to the origin.
    m2Translate T, -x, -y

    ' Compute the inverse translation.
    m2Translate T_Inv, x, y

    ' Rotate so the direction vector lies in the Y axis.
    m2RotateIntoX R, dx, dy

    ' Compute the inverse translation.
    m2RotateIntoX R_Inv, dx, -dy

    ' Reflect across the X axis.
    m2Scale S, 1, -1

    ' Combine the transformations.
    m2MatMultiply M1, T, R      ' T * R
    m2MatMultiply M2, S, R_Inv  ' S * R_Inv
    m2MatMultiply M3, M1, M2    ' T * R * S * R_Inv

    ' T * R * S * R_Inv * T_Inv
    m2MatMultiply Result, M3, T_Inv
End Sub
```

```
' Create a rotation matrix for rotating through
' angle theta around the point (x, y).
Public Sub m2RotateAround(Result() As Single, _
    ByVal theta As Single, _
    ByVal x As Single, ByVal y As Single)
Dim T(1 To 3, 1 To 3) As Single
Dim R(1 To 3, 1 To 3) As Single
Dim T_Inv(1 To 3, 1 To 3) As Single
Dim M(1 To 3, 1 To 3) As Single

    ' Translate the point to the origin.
    m2Translate T, -x, -y

    ' Compute the inverse translation.
    m2Translate T_Inv, x, y

    ' Rotate.
    m2Rotate R, Theta

    ' Combine the transformations.
    m2MatMultiply M, T, R
    m2MatMultiply Result, M, T_Inv
End Sub
```

You can find the routines described in this section, along with other routines that manipulate two-dimensional transformation matrices, in the file M2Ops.bas. Example programs ScaleAt, ReflAt, and RotAt demonstrate the m2ScaleAt, m2ReflectAcross, and m2RotateAround subroutines respectively.

Program ScaleAt draws a square. When you click on the Big, Normal, and Little option buttons, the program uses subroutine m2ScaleAt to scale the square around its center by a factor of 2, 1, or 1/2 respectively.

Program ReflAt draws a square and a line. When you check the Reflect box, the program uses subroutine m2ReflectAcross to reflect the square across the line. When you uncheck this box, the program places the square back in its original position.

Program RotAt also draws a square. When you press the right arrow key, the program uses subroutine m3RotateAround to rotate the square clockwise around its center. When you press the left arrow key, the program uses m3RotateAround to rotate the square counterclockwise.

Vector and Matrix Operations in Visual Basic

Whenever you multiply two matrices that both have 0, 0, 1 in the final column, you get another matrix with 0, 0, 1 in the final column. No matter how you compose translation, scaling, and rotation matrices, the resulting matrix will always have the form:

$$
\begin{vmatrix}
m11 & m12 & 0 \\
m21 & m22 & 0 \\
m31 & m32 & 1
\end{vmatrix}
$$

You can use this fact to speed up vector/matrix multiplication. When you multiply a normalized vector (with 1 as the scale factor in the final component) by this sort of matrix, you can skip calculating the resulting vector's last entry because it is always 1.

The following subroutine uses this fact to multiply a vector by a matrix. It also saves a little time by not using For loops. Writing the calculations out makes the code a little more cluttered, but it also makes it a bit faster. In one series of tests, a similar subroutine that did not use these tricks took about 2.5 times as long to perform the same calculations.

```
' Apply a transformation matrix to a point.
Public Sub m2Apply(V() As Single, A() As Single, _
    Result() As Single)

    Result(1) = V(1) * A(1, 1) + V(2) * A(2, 1) + A(3, 1)
    Result(2) = V(1) * A(1, 2) + V(2) * A(2, 2) + A(3, 2)
    Result(3) = 1#
End Sub
```

If you need to apply a matrix to many points at the same time, you can also speed things up by moving these calculations into the routine transforming the points instead of calling a subroutine. Avoiding all the subroutine calls will make the code a little faster. It is rarely worth complicating code to avoid a subroutine call, but if an application must transform thousands of points, this may be worthwhile.

In the following example, the global variable V is a three-dimensional array that contains the vectors representing the points that make up an object. This routine transforms each of the points in array V and draws lines connecting them. The routine performs all of its calculations directly rather than by calling a subroutine. Because the final components in the transformed points are always 1 and because they are not needed to draw the lines, this routine further increases its speed by ignoring them completely.

```
Private Sub DrawPoints()
Dim i As Integer
Dim x As Single
Dim y As Single

    CurrentX = V(1, 1) * A(1, 1) + V(1, 2) * A(2, 1) + A(3, 1)
    CurrentY = V(1, 1) * A(1, 2) + V(1, 2) * A(2, 2) + A(3, 2)
    For i = 2 To NumPoints
        x = V(i, 1) * A(1, 1) + V(i, 2) * A(2, 1) + A(3, 1)
        y = V(i, 1) * A(1, 2) + V(i, 2) * A(2, 2) + A(3, 2)
        Line -(x, y)
    Next i
End Sub
```

Similarly, you can avoid some calculations when you multiply two matrices. Because you know the last column in the result always contains 0, 0, 1, you do not need to compute the values for the last column. Once again, you can save a little extra time by computing each entry in the resulting matrix without using nested For loops.

The following Visual Basic subroutine uses these facts to multiply two matrices. In some tests, a similar subroutine that did not take advantage of the special structure of the matrices took more than three times as long to perform the same calculations.

```
' Multiply two transformation matrices.
Public Sub m2MatMultiply(Result() As Single, A() As Single, _
    B() As Single)

    Result(1, 1) = A(1, 1) * B(1, 1) + A(1, 2) * B(2, 1)
    Result(1, 2) = A(1, 1) * B(1, 2) + A(1, 2) * B(2, 2)
    Result(1, 3) = 0#
    Result(2, 1) = A(2, 1) * B(1, 1) + A(2, 2) * B(2, 1)
    Result(2, 2) = A(2, 1) * B(1, 2) + A(2, 2) * B(2, 2)
    Result(2, 3) = 0#
    Result(3, 1) = A(3, 1) * B(1, 1) + A(3, 2) * B(2, 1) + _
        B(3, 1)
    Result(3, 2) = A(3, 1) * B(1, 2) + A(3, 2) * B(2, 2) + _
        B(3, 2)
    Result(3, 3) = 1#
End Sub
```

You can find these and other routines for manipulating two-dimensional matrices and vectors in the file M2Ops.bas on the CD-ROM.

Transforming Objects

Once you have created a transformation, you might like to apply it to the drawing objects described earlier in this chapter. For each object class, create a Transform subroutine that applies a transformation matrix to the object. For instance, the following Visual Basic code applies a transformation matrix to a TwoDPolygon object with points stored in the m_Points array.

```
' Transform the object using a two-dimensional
' transformation matrix.
Public Sub Transform(M() As Single)
Dim i As Integer
Dim new_x As Single
Dim new_y As Single

    For i = 1 To m_NumPoints
        With m_Points(i)
            new_x = .X * M(1, 1) + .Y * M(2, 1) + M(3, 1)
            new_y = .X * M(1, 2) + .Y * M(2, 2) + M(3, 2)
            .X = new_x
            .Y = new_y
        End With
```

```
    Next i
End Sub
```

As was mentioned earlier, this sort of transformation will not work for all Visual Basic drawing commands. The Circle method, for instance, cannot draw an arc that has been arbitrarily scaled and rotated. Similarly, you can use the Line statement to draw a rectangle but not a rotated rectangle.

If you want to be able to apply general transformations to all your graphical objects, you cannot use Visual Basic commands that are hard to transform. Instead, use the Line command to draw arcs and other more complicated shapes using short line segments. Then you can transform the object by applying a transformation matrix to the points that make up the line segments.

Because the TwoDPolygon object can hold any number of points, it makes a convenient tool for drawing other kinds of objects. For example, to draw a transformed rectangle, you can create a TwoDPolygon object that draws lines connecting the rectangle's four corners. To draw a circle, you can use a TwoDPolygon object holding a large number of points along the circle's edge.

Example program RotRect, shown in Figure 12.21, demonstrates a greatly simplified TwoDPolygon class. This class provides none of the drawing attribute functions implemented by the previous version, but it does have a Transform routine.

Enter an angle of rotation in program RotRect's text box. Then click and drag to define a rectangle. The program creates a TwoDPolygon object and initializes it using the points you selected. It then uses the m2RotateAround subroutine to create a transformation matrix that rotates around the rectangle's center. It applies the transformation using the Transform routine and displays the result.

Shape-Distorting Transformations

The transformations described so far have all been shape preserving. You can use scaling to stretch an object, but scaling stretches all the points in an object by an equal amount. While you can change the aspect ratio of an object, a straight line remains a straight line no matter what combination of translation, scaling, and rotation you apply to it.

It is convenient to represent transformations as matrices, but there are other types of transformations that you cannot represent in this way. For example, you could transform the points in an object using the following equations:

```
new_x = old_x + Amplitude * Sin(old_y * 6.28 / Period)
new_y = old_y + Amplitude * Sin(old_x * 6.28 / Period)
```

In this transformation, the new X coordinate depends on the sine of the Y coordinate, and the new Y coordinate depends on the sine of the X coordinate. Because multiplying a vector and a matrix cannot produce the sine of a number, you cannot use matrices to represent this transformation. Figure 12.22 shows a grid and three shape-distorting transformations of the grid. The image in the upper right was produced with this transformation.

When you have a transformation stored in a matrix, you can pass the matrix into a graphical object's Transform subroutine. The Transform subroutine can then apply the matrix to the points that make up the object.

Because you cannot store shape-distorting transformations in matrices, this strategy does not work for them. What you really need to do is pass a shape-distorting *function* into one of the graphical object's routines. Then that routine can use the function to transform the points making up the object. While you cannot pass a function into a Visual Basic subroutine, you can do something almost as good: You can pass an object.

Create a class to represent the shape-distorting transformation. If you like, you can give the class variables to make the transformation more general. The previous example uses the values Amplitude and Period to modify the basic transformation.

Next, give the class a Transform subroutine. This routine takes as parameters the coordinates of a point and applies a shape-distorting transformation to them. The following code shows the complete definition of the TransWave transformation class. The interface class Transformation defines the single method Transform, so this routine is called Transformation_Transform in the TransWave class that implements it. A program can treat this class and others that implement the Transformation class as Transformation objects.

```
Option Explicit
' A wavy transformation.

Implements Transformation

' Transformation parameters.
Public Amplitude As Single
Public Period As Single

' Transform the point (X, Y).
Private Sub Transformation_Transform(X As Single, Y As Single)
```

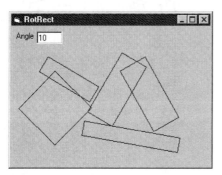

Figure 12.21   Program RotRect uses the Transform subroutine to rotate rectangles.

```
Dim new_x As Single

    new_x = X + Amplitude * Sin(Y * 6.28 / Period)
    Y = Y + Amplitude * Sin(X * 6.28 / Period)
    X = new_x
End Sub
```

Example program Distort uses this kind of class to transform a two-dimensional array of points. It then connects the points to draw a transformed grid similar to those shown in Figure 12.22.

Once you have created a transformation class, you can use it to transform graphical objects much as previous examples transform them using matrices. Write an Apply-TransformationObject subroutine that takes as a parameter a Transformation object. That routine can then invoke the transformation object's Transform method for each of the points in the object. The following code shows how a TwoDPolygon object would perform this transformation.

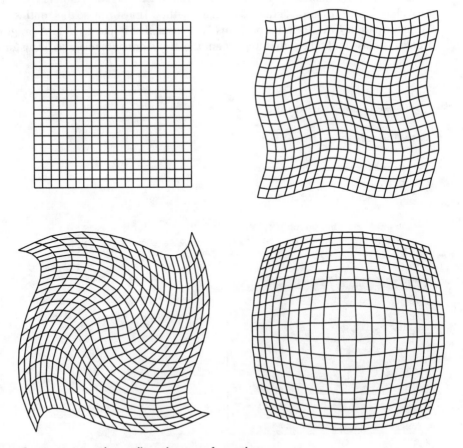

Figure 12.22 Shape-distorting transformations.

```
' Apply a transformation object's Transform
' method to the points.
Public Sub TwoDObject_ApplyTransformationObject( _
    ByRef obj As Transformation)
Dim i As Integer

    For i = 1 To m_NumPoints
        obj.Transform m_Points(i).X, m_Points(i).Y
    Next i
End Sub
```

Using transformation objects, you can create a transformation that is the composition of two other transformations. If TransWave and TransTwist are two transformation classes, you could use the following Visual Basic code to create a class representing a TransWave transformation followed by a TransTwist transformation.

```
Option Explicit
' A TransWave followed by a TransTwist.

Implements Transformation

' The sub-transformations.
Public wave As New TransWave
Public twist As New TransTwist

' Transform the point (X, Y).
Private Sub Transformation_Transform(X As Single, Y As Single)
Dim obj As Transformation

    ' Apply the wave transformation.
    Set obj = wave
    obj.Transform X, Y

    ' Apply the twist transformation.
    Set obj = twist
    obj.Transform X, Y
End Sub
```

Treating Types of Transformation Differently

Using transformation objects, you can easily manipulate shape-distorting transformations. You could even use these techniques to store the matrix transformations described earlier as transformation objects. You could place a transformation matrix inside one of these objects and make the object's Transform subroutine transform points by applying the matrix. There are a couple of reasons you should treat these two kinds of transformations differently.

First, invoking the Transform subroutine of a transformation object adds an extra subroutine call to the transformation process. To make matters worse, that subroutine call is particularly slow. If the program uses a generic Transformation class object, the subroutine call is a bit slower than it would be if the program used a more specific class such as TransWave. It is certainly slower than calling a matrix/vector multiplication subroutine or performing the multiplication directly.

Transformation objects also do not combine as well as matrices do. While building a combined transformation object is easy, that object executes the transformations it represents one at a time. On the other hand, you can combine as many transformation matrices as you like and still end up with a single matrix to represent the combined transformations. This capability is particularly important for complex operations that require many intermediate transformations.

To reflect an object across an arbitrary line, for example, you must translate the line of reflection to the origin, rotate the line until it lies along the X axis, reflect the object, reverse the rotation, and finally translate the line back to where it started—a total of five transformations. Using matrices, you can accomplish all these steps with a single transformation. Using a transformation class, the program would need to perform each operation separately.

Finally, although shape-distorting transformations are interesting, the standard matrix transformations described earlier are much more common. It would be nice to be able to treat all transformations in the same way, but making the most important transformations as efficient as possible is worth the extra effort.

Display Data Structure

For small pictures, it is easy enough to redraw every part of the picture whenever you need to draw a piece of it. When you zoom in on one corner of the picture, redrawing everything is the easiest approach. Visual Basic takes care of cropping the picture at the viewport's boundaries.

For complex pictures, however, this approach can be wasteful. If you have zoomed in on a small part of the picture, you might spend a lot of time drawing objects that are cropped off by Visual Basic.

Example program Hexes1 lets you pan and zoom on a picture containing a 50-by-50 grid of small hexagons. On a 133MHz Pentium processor, the program takes more than two seconds to draw the picture at full scale. On slower computers, it may take much longer.

If you zoom in on a tiny portion of the picture, it still takes more than two seconds to draw the picture, even though only a fraction of a second is needed to draw the visible part of the picture. Drawing a smaller portion of the picture is a little faster than drawing the whole thing because Visual Basic needs a little less time to clip part of the picture off than to draw it. Still, the program is wasting a lot of time drawing hexagons that are never displayed.

This program also lets you select one of the hexagons by clicking it. When you click one, the program searches through its list of objects until it finds the hexagon that contains the point where you clicked. It then highlights that hexagon. The hexagons are ordered from bottom to top, so it takes the program longer to find hexagons near the top. The program can find hexagons near the bottom almost instantly, but it takes more than a second to find those at the top.

Quadtrees

You can make both the display and location of objects faster using a *quadtree*. A quadtree is a tree that recursively divides parts of world coordinate space into four segments. The four segments represent the upper-left, upper-right, lower-left, and lower-right quadrants of the drawing area. The four segments are also referred to as the northwest, northeast, southwest, and southeast quadrants.

Each node in a quadtree contains a list of the objects that are within its part of the display area. If a node contains too many objects, it is further divided into four subnodes, and the items are assigned to the proper quadrants. This process is repeated until each node contains at most some predetermined maximum number of objects.

Figure 12.23 shows how a small quadtree represents a picture containing six objects. Nodes in this quadtree have been divided until no node contains more than two items.

Once you have created a quadtree, you can use it to help you decide which objects to draw. Figure 12.24 shows a world window drawn on top of the quadtree from Figure 12.23. The first quadtree node contains four subnodes. Because the world window overlaps only the northwest subnode, you need to examine only that subnode when you are drawing the objects in the world window. By not considering the other three nodes in the quadtree, you remove three of the picture's objects (D, E, and F) from consideration. You do not need to draw these objects or examine them further.

The northwest subnode contains four subnodes of its own. The world window intersects all four of these nodes, so you must draw all of the objects within them. Those nodes contain the picture objects A, B, and C, so you would draw those three objects. Only two, A and B, actually lie within the world window, so Visual Basic must clip object C out of the picture.

Locating Objects

Quadtrees are also helpful in locating objects. Suppose a user clicks on object C in Figure 12.24. When you examine the first quadtree node, you find that the point the user

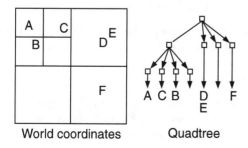

World coordinates   Quadtree

Figure 12.23   Dividing a display area with a quadtree.

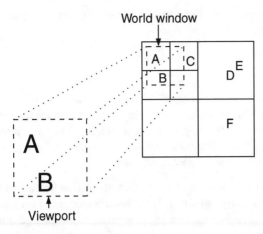

Figure 12.24 Using a quadtree to decide which objects to draw.

clicked is in the northwest quadrant, so you examine the node's northwest child. When you examine that node, you find that the selected point is in its the northeast quadrant. That node is not subdivided further. The object clicked by the user must be in that node, so you need to search only the objects in that node.

In this example, you would find that object C contained the point the user selected. Instead of examining every object in the picture, you are able to use the quadtree to narrow the search down to the objects contained in a single quadtree node. In this case, that node contained only the single object C, and that was the one you wanted to find.

Quadtrees in Visual Basic

You must handle a couple of details when implementing quadtrees in Visual Basic. First, there is a tradeoff between the number of quadtree nodes you use and the number of objects you can eliminate when displaying or searching the picture. If you use many quadtree nodes, each will contain only a few objects, so searches will be relatively fast. On the other hand, you will have used a lot of memory to create the nodes. If you use too many nodes, the extra memory you use will slow the drawing noticeably.

On the other hand, if you use too few quadtree nodes, you will not eliminate many of the nodes when you are drawing or searching, and the quadtree will be of little help. In that case, you will have made your job more complicated for little gain.

You must find a balance when deciding how many objects to allow in each quadtree node. As a rule, allowing 100 or so objects per node usually provides reasonable performance without too much memory overhead. You will need to experiment a little with your application to see what numbers are best.

A second detail to consider is that most graphical objects have a nonzero width and height. This means a single object can intersect more than one quadtree node. Figure 12.25 shows several objects that intersect more than one quadtree node.

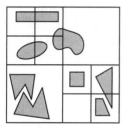

Figure 12.25 Objects may intersect more than one quadtree node.

You must be careful to avoid drawing objects that lie in more than one quadtree node multiple times. Modify the drawing object classes so that they contain a Boolean variable Drawn to indicate whether the object has already been drawn. In the objects' Draw subroutines, check this value. If the object has already been drawn, do not draw it again.

A Quadtree Implementation

The code that follows shows a Visual Basic implementation of the QtreeNode class representing quadtree nodes. Its xmin, xmax, ymin, and ymax variables store the bounds of the drawing area represented by the node. The NWchild, NEchild, SWchild, and SEchild variables are references to the node's children. The Objects collection holds the drawing objects contained in the node if the node is a leaf node.

The Add subroutine adds a new object to the node. First it determines whether the node has been divided into subnodes. If so, it calls subroutine PlaceObject to place the new object in the correct subnodes. Otherwise, the Add routine inserts the new object in the node's Objects collection. Then, if the collection contains too many objects, the routine calls subroutine Divide to split the node into subnodes and divide the objects among the children.

Subroutine PlaceObject compares the object's bounds with the bounds of the quadtree node's children. It then invokes the Add subroutine for any children that intersect the new object's bounds.

Subroutine Divide first creates four new QtreeNode objects, one for each quadtree child node. It then examines the objects in the Objects collection and uses PlaceObject to put each in the correct child nodes. Finally, it sets the Objects collection to Nothing because this node is no longer a child node.

The SetDrawn method sets the Drawn flag for all the objects contained in a node. The main program uses this routine to reset the objects' Drawn flags after drawing them.

The Draw subroutine takes as parameters the coordinate bounds of the area to draw. If that area does not intersect the area represented by the node, the routine does nothing. Otherwise, if the node is a leaf node, it makes each of the objects it contains draw itself. Finally, if the node is not a leaf node, it calls its children's Draw methods so they can draw the objects they contain.

Finally, the ObjectAt function returns the object at a given point. If the point does not lie within the area represented by the quadtree node, the routine returns Nothing. Otherwise, if the node is a leaf node, it uses its objects' IsAt function to find the object at the indicated point. Finally, if the node is not a leaf node, the routine finds the child node that contains the point and invokes its ObjectAt function.

```
Option Explicit
' A quadtree node.

' If this is a leaf node, its Objects
' collection contains the objects to draw.
'
' Otherwise the object's children contain other
' QtreeNode objects.

' The maximum number of objects the node can hold.
Private Const MAX_OBJECTS = 100

' The bounds this quadtree node represents.
Public xmin As Single
Public ymin As Single
Public xmid As Single
Public ymid As Single
Public xmax As Single
Public ymax As Single

' The objects, if this is a leaf node.
Private Objects As Collection

' The quadtree children otherwise.
Public NWchild As QtreeNode
Public NEchild As QtreeNode
Public SWchild As QtreeNode
Public SEchild As QtreeNode

' Add an object to the Objects collection.
'
' If this gives us too many objects, create
' child nodes and subdivide.
Public Sub Add(obj As Object)
    If Objects Is Nothing Then
        ' We are not a leaf node. Put the
        ' object in the appropriate child.
        PlaceObject obj
    Else
        ' We are a leaf node. Add the object
        ' to the Objects collection.
        Objects.Add obj

        ' See if need to subdivide.
```

```
            If Objects.Count > MAX_OBJECTS Then Divide
        End If
End Sub


' Place this object in the proper child(ren).
Private Sub PlaceObject(ByVal obj As Object)
Dim x1 As Single
Dim x2 As Single
Dim y1 As Single
Dim y2 As Single

    obj.Bound x1, y1, x2, y2
    If y2 > ymid And x1 < xmid Then NWchild.Add obj
    If y2 > ymid And x2 > xmid Then NEchild.Add obj
    If y1 < ymid And x1 < xmid Then SWchild.Add obj
    If y1 < ymid And x2 > xmid Then SEchild.Add obj
End Sub


' Create the children and divide the object.
Private Sub Divide()
Dim obj As Object

    ' Create the children.
    Set NWchild = New QtreeNode
    NWchild.SetBounds xmin, xmid, ymid, ymax

    Set NEchild = New QtreeNode
    NEchild.SetBounds xmid, xmax, ymid, ymax

    Set SWchild = New QtreeNode
    SWchild.SetBounds xmin, xmid, ymin, ymid

    Set SEchild = New QtreeNode
    SEchild.SetBounds xmid, xmax, ymin, ymid

    ' Move the objects into the proper children.
    For Each obj In Objects
        PlaceObject obj
    Next obj

    ' Remove the Objects collection.
    Set Objects = Nothing
End Sub


' Set the bounds for this quadtree node.
Public Sub SetBounds(ByVal x1 As Single, ByVal x2 As Single, _
    ByVal y1 As Single, ByVal y2 As Single)

    xmin = x1
    ymin = y1
    xmax = x2
```

```
        ymax = y2
        xmid = (xmin + xmax) / 2
        ymid = (ymin + ymax) / 2
End Sub

' Set the Drawn properties of the objects.
Public Sub SetDrawn(ByVal new_value As Boolean)
Dim obj As Object

    If Objects Is Nothing Then
            ' We are not a leaf. Make our children
            ' set Drawn for their objects.
        NWchild.SetDrawn new_value
        NEchild.SetDrawn new_value
        SWchild.SetDrawn new_value
        SEchild.SetDrawn new_value
    Else
            ' We are a leaf. Set Drawn for our objects.
        For Each obj In Objects
            obj.Drawn = new_value
        Next obj
    End If
End Sub

' Draw the objects in this node on a PictureBox.
Public Sub Draw(ByVal pic As PictureBox, _
    ByVal x1 As Single, ByVal y1 As Single, _
    ByVal x2 As Single, ByVal y2 As Single)
Dim obj As Object

    ' Stop if we don't intersect the region
    ' we're trying to draw.
    If x2 < xmin Or x1 > xmax Or _
        y2 < ymin Or y1 > ymax _
        Then Exit Sub

    ' Draw a red box around our display region.
    pic.Line (xmin, ymin)-(xmax, ymax), vbRed, B

    ' Draw the objects.
    If Objects Is Nothing Then
            ' We are not a leaf. Make our children
            ' draw themselves.
        NWchild.Draw pic, x1, y1, x2, y2
        NEchild.Draw pic, x1, y1, x2, y2
        SWchild.Draw pic, x1, y1, x2, y2
        SEchild.Draw pic, x1, y1, x2, y2
    Else
            ' We are a leaf. Make the objects
            ' draw themselves.
        For Each obj In Objects
```

```
            obj.Draw pic
        Next obj
    End If
End Sub

' Find an object that contains this point.
Public Function ObjectAt( _
    ByVal X As Single, ByVal Y As Single) As Object
Dim obj As Object

    Set ObjectAt = Nothing

    ' Stop if we don't contain the point.
    If X < xmin Or X > xmax Or _
        Y < ymin Or Y > ymax _
        Then Exit Function

    ' Find the object.
    If Objects Is Nothing Then
        ' This is not a leaf node.
        ' Search our children.
        If Y > ymid Then
            If X < xmid Then
                ' Search the northwest child.
                Set ObjectAt = NWchild.ObjectAt(X, Y)
            Else
                ' Search the northeast child.
                Set ObjectAt = NEchild.ObjectAt(X, Y)
            End If
        Else
            If X < xmid Then
                ' Search the southwest child.
                Set ObjectAt = SWchild.ObjectAt(X, Y)
            Else
                ' Search the southeast child.
                Set ObjectAt = SEchild.ObjectAt(X, Y)
            End If
        End If
    Else
        ' This is a leaf node.
        ' Search the objects it contains.
        For Each obj In Objects
            If obj.IsAt(X, Y) Then
                Set ObjectAt = obj
                Exit Function
            End If
        Next obj
    End If
End Function
```

The pictures shown in Figures 12.23 through 12.25 contain only a few objects, so using quadtrees is overkill. Drawing and searching through all the objects one at a time is fast enough for most purposes. On the other hand, a more complex picture might contain hundreds or thousands of objects. In that case, the savings you get by using a quadtree can be tremendous.

Example program Hexes2 is similar to program Hexes1 except it uses a quadtree to display and locate hexagons more quickly. In addition to displaying the hexagons, this program draws red lines around each of the quadtree nodes so that you can see them.

Although this program takes about as long as program Hexes1 to display the complete picture, it is much faster when you zoom in closely. If you zoom in as far as possible on a 133MHz Pentium, Hexes1 needs more than two seconds to display the part of the picture that is visible. Hexes2 takes about half the time.

The quadtree gives an even more dramatic improvement when the program must locate an object. The time needed by program Hexes1 to locate a hexagon depends on where the hexagon is located in the program's list of objects. If the hexagon is near the end of the list, this program takes more than a second to locate it on a 133MHz Pentium. Program Hexes2 can locate any hexagon almost instantly.

Programs Hexes1 and Hexes2 have one other feature worth noting. If you zoom in on an area that is too small, Visual Basic is unable to draw all of the picture. When it tries to scale the world coordinates to fit in the viewport, some of the points that fall far outside the world window fall *very* far outside the viewport. In fact, these points fall so far outside that their coordinates overflow the values allowed for the viewport PictureBox, and Visual Basic generates an overflow error. To prevent this, these programs do not allow the user to zoom in too far.

Summary

The most important concept described in this chapter is the use of homogeneous coordinates. Using homogeneous coordinates, you can represent translation, scaling, reflection, and rotation uniformly with matrices. You can combine a complex series of transformations into a single matrix which you can then apply quickly and easily to the points in your objects.

Understanding homogeneous coordinates in two dimensions is particularly important since later chapters build on these concepts. Chapter 13, Three-Dimensional Transformations, extends the ideas presented here to manipulate three-dimensional objects. If you have a good understanding of the two-dimensional concepts, you will be able to build programs that draw three-dimensional scenes with little trouble.

PART FIVE

Three-Dimensional Graphics

Throughout its existence, the field of three-dimensional computer graphics has been a never-ending pursuit of visual realism. Early graphics programs could display recognizable shapes and structures. They were useful for visualizing engineering concepts, but there was little danger of anyone mistaking them for real objects. Today, computers can generate images so realistic that they are virtually indistinguishable from photographs.

The next several chapters parallel some of the most important developments along the path to visual realism. Chapter 13, Three-Dimensional Transformations, explains the mathematics used to display three-dimensional objects on two-dimensional surfaces.

Chapter 14, Surfaces, shows how to display three-dimensional surface data. It explains how to estimate missing values when the data is incomplete, and it describes two specialized algorithms that let you display surfaces with hidden surfaces removed.

Chapter 15, Hidden Surface Removal, tells how to remove hidden surfaces in more general three-dimensional scenes. It covers the relatively simple backface removal algorithm that works for convex solids and the more involved depth-sort algorithm that works in more general circumstances.

Chapter 16, Shading Models, explains how to shade the surfaces that make up an object. Using a simplified model of the physics of light, a program can greatly increase the realism of the objects it displays.

Chapter 17, Ray Tracing, shows how to create ray traced images that display reflective, shadowed, transparent, and textured objects.

CHAPTER 13

Three-Dimensional Transformations

This chapter explains the basics of three-dimensional transformations. Most three-dimensional transformations are analogous to the two-dimensional transformations described in Chapter 12, Two-Dimensional Transformations. In fact, many three-dimensional transformations are simply special uses of two-dimensional transformations that ignore the third dimension.

Using homogeneous coordinates and a matrix representation similar to the one used in two-dimensions, this chapter explains how to perform translation, scaling, reflection, and rotation in three dimensions. It also describes matrices that represent *projections*, transformations that let you view three-dimensional objects on a two-dimensional computer screen. As is the case in two dimensions, you can combine three-dimensional transformation matrices to represent complex transformations with a single matrix.

The chapter finishes by explaining how you can use Visual Basic classes to model three-dimensional objects. These classes let you create and manipulate objects with relative ease.

Simple Transformations

The most general transformations possible in three dimensions are quite complicated. As is the case in two dimensions, however, you can build the most useful of these with combinations of simple translation, scaling, rotation, and projection. The following sections describe these fundamental transformations. Once you understand how to use the simpler transformations in three dimensions, you can compose them to create more general ones.

Homogeneous Coordinates

As is the case in two dimensions, you can easily represent points and transformations in three dimensions using homogeneous coordinates. In two dimensions, you represent a point in as a vector [S * x, S * y, S], where x and y are the point's normal X and Y coordinates and S is a scale factor.

In three dimensions, you simply add another coordinate before the scaling factor. A typical point is represented as [S * x, S * y, S * z, S]. Here, x, y, and z are the point's coordinates in three-dimensional space, and S is a scale factor. For example, you could represent the point (1, 4, 2) as [10, 40, 20, 10] or as [0.5, 2, 1, 0.5]. As is the case in two-dimensional homogeneous coordinates, vectors are often *normalized* so that their scale factor is one. The normalized representation of the point (1, 4, 2) is [1, 4, 2, 1].

You can represent three-dimensional translation, scaling, and rotation as matrices. To apply one of these transformations to a point, you multiply the point's homogeneous vector representation by the corresponding transformation matrix. Just as you can in two dimensions, you can combine transformation matrices by multiplying them to represent complex combinations of translation, scaling, and rotation in a single matrix.

Vector and Matrix Operations in Visual Basic

As was the case in two dimensions, you can use the special structure of homogeneous coordinates and transformation matrices to speed up matrix operations. Most three-dimensional transformation matrices contain 0, 0, 0, 1 in their last columns. The following routine uses this fact to apply a transformation matrix to a point quickly. This routine also gains a slight speed benefit by performing its multiplications and additions directly without For loops.

```
' Apply a transformation matrix to a point.
Public Sub m3Apply(V() As Single, M() As Single, _
    Result() As Single)

    Result(1) = V(1) * M(1, 1) + _
                V(2) * M(2, 1) + _
                V(3) * M(3, 1) + M(4, 1)
    Result(2) = V(1) * M(1, 2) + _
                V(2) * M(2, 2) + _
                V(3) * M(3, 2) + M(4, 2)
    Result(3) = V(1) * M(1, 3) + _
                V(2) * M(2, 3) + _
                V(3) * M(3, 3) + M(4, 3)
    Result(4) = 1#
End Sub
```

Whenever you multiply two matrices containing 0, 0, 0, 1 in their final columns, you get another matrix with 0, 0, 0, 1 in the final column. The following subroutine uses this fact to make multiplying two matrices faster.

```
' Multiply two matrices together.
Public Sub m3MatMultiply(Result() As Single, _
    A() As Single, B() As Single)

    Result(1, 1) = A(1, 1) * B(1, 1) + A(1, 2) * B(2, 1) + _
        A(1, 3) * B(3, 1)
    Result(1, 2) = A(1, 1) * B(1, 2) + A(1, 2) * B(2, 2) + _
        A(1, 3) * B(3, 2)
    Result(1, 3) = A(1, 1) * B(1, 3) + A(1, 2) * B(2, 3) + _
        A(1, 3) * B(3, 3)
    Result(1, 4) = 0#

    Result(2, 1) = A(2, 1) * B(1, 1) + A(2, 2) * B(2, 1) + _
        A(2, 3) * B(3, 1)
    Result(2, 2) = A(2, 1) * B(1, 2) + A(2, 2) * B(2, 2) + _
        A(2, 3) * B(3, 2)
    Result(2, 3) = A(2, 1) * B(1, 3) + A(2, 2) * B(2, 3) + _
        A(2, 3) * B(3, 3)
    Result(2, 4) = 0#

    Result(3, 1) = A(3, 1) * B(1, 1) + A(3, 2) * B(2, 1) + _
        A(3, 3) * B(3, 1)
    Result(3, 2) = A(3, 1) * B(1, 2) + A(3, 2) * B(2, 2) + _
        A(3, 3) * B(3, 2)
    Result(3, 3) = A(3, 1) * B(1, 3) + A(3, 2) * B(2, 3) + _
        A(3, 3) * B(3, 3)
    Result(3, 4) = 0#

    Result(4, 1) = A(4, 1) * B(1, 1) + A(4, 2) * B(2, 1) + _
        A(4, 3) * B(3, 1) + B(4, 1)
    Result(4, 2) = A(4, 1) * B(1, 2) + A(4, 2) * B(2, 2) + _
        A(4, 3) * B(3, 2) + B(4, 2)
    Result(4, 3) = A(4, 1) * B(1, 3) + A(4, 2) * B(2, 3) + _
        A(4, 3) * B(3, 3) + B(4, 3)
    Result(4, 4) = 1#
End Sub
```

These routines work for most transformation matrices, but the perspective transformation matrix described later in this chapter does not contain 0, 0, 0, 1 in its final column. That means you cannot use these Visual Basic subroutines when you are using a perspective transformation. Instead, you should use the following versions that do not assume the transformation matrices contain 0, 0, 0, 1 in their final columns.

```
' Apply a transformation matrix to a point where
' the transformation may not have 0, 0, 0, 1 in
' its final column.
Public Sub m3ApplyFull(V() As Single, M() As Single, _
    Result() As Single)
Dim i As Integer
Dim j As Integer
Dim value As Single
```

```
      For i = 1 To 4
          value = 0#
          For j = 1 To 4
              value = value + V(j) * M(j, i)
          Next j
          Result(i) = value
      Next i

      ' Renormalize the point.
      ' Note that value still holds Result(4).
      Result(1) = Result(1) / value
      Result(2) = Result(2) / value
      Result(3) = Result(3) / value
      Result(4) = 1#
  End Sub

  ' Multiply two matrices together. The matrices
  ' may not contain 0, 0, 0, 1 in their last columns.
  Public Sub m3MatMultiplyFull(Result() As Single, _
      A() As Single, B() As Single)
  Dim i As Integer
  Dim j As Integer
  Dim k As Integer
  Dim value As Single

      For i = 1 To 4
          For j = 1 To 4
              value = 0#
              For k = 1 To 4
                  value = value + A(i, k) * B(k, j)
              Next k
              Result(i, j) = value
          Next j
      Next i
  End Sub
```

These subroutines and others that manipulate three-dimensional points and matrices are contained in module M3Ops.bas.

Translation

Generalizing a two-dimensional translation matrix for the three-dimensional case is easy. To translate a point by distance Tx in the direction of the X axis, Ty along the Y axis, and Tz along the Z axis, you can multiply the point by the transformation matrix:

$$
\begin{vmatrix}
1 & 0 & 0 & 0 \\
0 & 1 & 0 & 0 \\
0 & 0 & 1 & 0 \\
Tx & Ty & Tz & 1
\end{vmatrix}
$$

To see that this transformation matrix works, multiply a generic point (x, y, z) by the generic translation matrix.

$$[x, y, z, 1] \begin{vmatrix} 1 & 0 & 0 & 0 \\ 0 & 1 & 0 & 0 \\ 0 & 0 & 1 & 0 \\ Tx & Ty & Tz & 1 \end{vmatrix} = [x + Tx, y + Ty, z + Tz, 1]$$

The result, (x + Tx, y + Ty, z + Tz), is the correct translation of the point (x, y, z).

To make translation easy in Visual Basic, you can write a routine that initializes the entries in a transformation matrix to represent translation. This routine calls subroutine m3Identity to initialize the matrix to the identity matrix. It then sets the three entries needed for translation.

```
' Create a 3-D transformation matrix for
' translation by Tx, Ty, and Tz.
Public Sub m3Translate(M() As Single, _
    Tx As Single, Ty As Single, Tz As Single)
Dim i As Integer

    m3Identity M()
    M(4, 1) = Tx
    M(4, 2) = Ty
    M(4, 3) = Tz
End Sub
```

Scaling

Three-dimensional scaling also generalizes easily from two dimensions. To scale a point by a factor of Sx in the X direction, Sy in the Y direction, and Sz in the Z direction, multiply the point by the matrix:

$$\begin{vmatrix} Sy & 0 & 0 & 0 \\ 0 & Sx & 0 & 0 \\ 0 & 0 & Sz & 0 \\ 0 & 0 & 0 & 1 \end{vmatrix}$$

You can verify that this matrix properly represents scaling by multiplying it by the point (x, y, z).

$$[x, y, z, 1] \begin{vmatrix} Sx & 0 & 0 & 0 \\ 0 & Sy & 0 & 0 \\ 0 & 0 & Sz & 0 \\ 0 & 0 & 0 & 1 \end{vmatrix} = [x * Sx, y * Sy, z * Sz, 1]$$

The following code shows a routine that initializes scaling transformation matrices.

```
' Create a 3-D transformation matrix for scaling
' by scale factors Sx, Sy, and Sz.
Public Sub m3Scale(M() As Single, _
    Sx As Single, Sy As Single, Sz As Single)
Dim i As Integer

    m3Identity M()
    M(1, 1) = Sx
    M(2, 2) = Sy
    M(3, 3) = Sz
End Sub
```

Reflection

In two dimensions, reflection across the X or Y axis is simple. To reflect an object across an axis, you scale it using a negative scale factor. For instance, to reflect an object across the Y axis, you scale it by a factor of -1 in the X direction using a transformation matrix like this one:

$$\begin{vmatrix} -1 & 0 & 0 \\ 0 & 1 & 1 \\ 0 & 0 & 1 \end{vmatrix}$$

When you apply this matrix to the point (x, y), you get:

$$[x, y, 1] \begin{vmatrix} -1 & 0 & 0 \\ 0 & 1 & 1 \\ 0 & 0 & 1 \end{vmatrix} = [-x, y, 1]$$

In three dimensions, you must reflect an object across a plane instead of a line. Reflecting an object across the X-Y, X-Z, or Y-Z planes is easy. Simply scale the point using -1 as one of the scale factors. For example, to reflect an object across the X-Y plane, use a scaling transformation matrix where Sx = 1, Sy = 1, and Sz = -1. To perform one of these simple reflections, use the appropriate transformation matrix shown in Table 13.1.

Because these reflection matrices are the same as simple scaling matrices, you do not need to write separate Visual Basic routines to initialize reflection transformations.

Table 13.1 Reflection Transformation Matrices

ACROSS THE X-Y PLANE	ACROSS THE X-Z PLANE	ACROSS THE Y-Z PLANE
$\begin{vmatrix} 1 & 0 & 0 & 0 \\ 0 & 1 & 0 & 0 \\ 0 & 0 & -1 & 0 \\ 0 & 0 & 0 & 1 \end{vmatrix}$	$\begin{vmatrix} 1 & 0 & 0 & 0 \\ 0 & -1 & 0 & 0 \\ 0 & 0 & 1 & 0 \\ 0 & 0 & 0 & 1 \end{vmatrix}$	$\begin{vmatrix} -1 & 0 & 0 & 0 \\ 0 & 1 & 0 & 0 \\ 0 & 0 & 1 & 0 \\ 0 & 0 & 0 & 1 \end{vmatrix}$

Instead you can use the corresponding scaling matrix. For example, to create a matrix representing a reflection across the X-Y plane, you can write:

```
Dim M(1 To 4, 1 To 4) As Single

    m3Scale M, 1, 1, -1
```

Right-Handed Coordinates

If you keep the standard arrangement of the X and Y axes in two dimensions, you can add the Z axis in two possible ways. If you think of the X-Y plane as lying parallel to the surface of this page, the Z axis could point into or out of the page. These different choices are called *right-handed* and *left-handed* coordinate systems, respectively, because you can use your hands to remember how the axes are related.

If you point your right thumb along the Z axis in the positive direction in a right-handed coordinate system, your fingers curl in the direction leading from the X axis toward the Y axis. If you point your left thumb along the Z axis in the positive direction in a left-handed coordinate system, your fingers also curl in the direction leading from the X axis toward the Y axis. Figure 13.1 shows right- and left-handed coordinate systems.

When you translate or scale an object, you do not need to think too much about the exact arrangement of the coordinate axes. When you rotate an object, however, you need to decide whether you are working in a right- or left-handed coordinate system. Some authors use left-handed systems and some use right-handed systems. The right-handed system seems to be more common, so it is the one used here.

Different authors also measure angles of rotation in different directions. Some measure angles clockwise as you look down an axis toward the origin, and others measure them counterclockwise. Counterclockwise angles seem to be more common, so they are used in this book.

Counterclockwise angles have the additional advantage that rotating around the Z axis agrees with rotation in two dimensions. If you look down the positive Z-axis toward the origin, angles increase as you rotate from the positive X axis toward the positive Y axis.

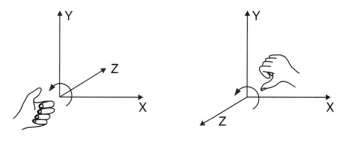

Left-handed coordinates   Right-handed coordinates

Figure 13.1   Right- and left-handed coordinate systems.

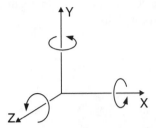

Figure 13.2 Measuring angles of rotation.

Finally, if you point your right thumb in the positive direction along an axis as in Figure 13.1, your fingers curl in the counterclockwise direction—the direction in which you measure angles of rotation. Figure 13.2 shows how you should measure angles of rotation around each of the three axes.

Rotation

Rotating an object around an arbitrary line in three dimensions is complicated. Rotating an object around the X, Y, or Z axis, on the other hand, is simple. To rotate a point around the Z axis, for example, simply ignore the Z coordinate of the point and handle the rotation as if it were taking place in two dimensions. Because you are rotating the point around the Z axis, its Z coordinate does not change. The new coordinates for the point are given by the equations:

```
new_x = old_x * Cos(θ) - old y * Sin(θ)
new_y = old_x * Sin(θ) + old y * Cos(θ)
new_z = old_z
```

Table 13.2 shows matrices that rotate a point through an angle θ around the three coordinate axes.

Using this information, you can write Visual Basic routines that initialize rotation matrices.

```
' Create a 3-D transformation matrix for rotation
' around the X axis (angle measured in radians).
Public Sub m3XRotate(M() As Single, ByVal theta As Single)
Dim i As Integer
```

Table 13.2 Rotation Transformation Matrices

AROUND THE X AXIS	AROUND THE Y AXIS	AROUND THE Z AXIS
$\begin{vmatrix} 1 & 0 & 0 & 0 \\ 0 & Cos(θ) & Sin(θ) & 0 \\ 0 & -Sin(θ) & Cos(θ) & 0 \\ 0 & 0 & 0 & 1 \end{vmatrix}$	$\begin{vmatrix} Cos(θ) & 0 & -Sin(θ) & 0 \\ 0 & 1 & 0 & 0 \\ Sin(θ) & 0 & Cos(θ) & 0 \\ 0 & 0 & 0 & 1 \end{vmatrix}$	$\begin{vmatrix} Cos(θ) & Sin(θ) & 0 & 0 \\ -Sin(θ) & Cos(θ) & 0 & 0 \\ 0 & 0 & 1 & 0 \\ 0 & 0 & 0 & 1 \end{vmatrix}$

```
    m3Identity M()
    M(2, 2) = Cos(theta)
    M(3, 3) = M(2, 2)
    M(2, 3) = Sin(theta)
    M(3, 2) = -M(2, 3)
End Sub


' Create a 3-D transformation matrix for rotation
' around the Y axis (angle measured in radians).
Public Sub m3YRotate(M() As Single, ByVal theta As Single)
Dim i As Integer

    m3Identity M()
    M(1, 1) = Cos(theta)
    M(3, 3) = M(1, 1)
    M(3, 1) = Sin(theta)
    M(1, 3) = -M(3, 1)
End Sub


' Create a 3-D transformation matrix for rotation
' around the Z axis (angle measured in radians).
Public Sub m3ZRotate(M() As Single, ByVal theta As Single)
Dim i As Integer

    m3Identity M()
    M(1, 1) = Cos(theta)
    M(2, 2) = M(1, 1)
    M(1, 2) = Sin(theta)
    M(2, 1) = -M(1, 2)
End Sub
```

Sometimes it is more convenient to specify a rotation with a point that should be rotated until it lies in the X-Y, Y-Z, or X-Z plane. This is no different from the two-dimensional case in which it was convenient to specify a rotation with a point that should be rotated into the X or Y axis. For example, rotating a point into the X-Z plane in three dimensions is equivalent to ignoring the point's Z coordinate and rotating the point into the X axis in two dimensions.

Figure 13.3 shows a point that should be rotated around the Z axis until it lies in the X-Z plane. The distance d is the distance from the projection of the point into the X-Y plane, to the origin. This distance equals $Sqr(x * x + y * y)$. Because θ is measured in the negative direction, $Cos(\theta) = x/d$ and $Sin(\theta) = -y/d$. Leaving the Z coordinate of the point unchanged, the rotation transformation matrix is:

$$
\begin{vmatrix}
Cos(\theta) & Sin(\theta) & 0 & 0 \\
-Sin(\theta) & Cos(\theta) & 0 & 0 \\
0 & 0 & 1 & 0 \\
0 & 0 & 0 & 1
\end{vmatrix}
=
\begin{vmatrix}
x/d & -y/d & 0 & 0 \\
y/d & x/d & 0 & 0 \\
0 & 0 & 1 & 0 \\
0 & 0 & 0 & 1
\end{vmatrix}
$$

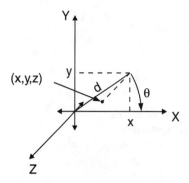

Figure 13.3 Rotating a point around the Z axis until it lies in the X-Z plane.

You can write a Visual Basic subroutine to initialize a transformation matrix that rotates around the Z axis until a point lies in the X-Z plane like this:

```
' Create a matrix that rotates around the Y axis
' so the point (x, y, z) lies in the X-Z plane.
Public Sub m3YRotateIntoXZ(Result() As Single, _
    ByVal x As Single, ByVal y As Single, ByVal z As Single)
Dim d As Single

    m2Identity Result
    d = Sqr(x * x + y * y)
    Result(1, 1) = x / d
    Result(1, 2) = -y / d
    Result(2, 1) = -Result(1, 2)
    Result(2, 2) = Result(1, 1)
End Sub
```

Notice that you could also have rotated around the X axis to move the point into the X-Z plane, as shown in Figure 13.4. While both of these rotations move the point into the X-Z plane, they place the point in different positions.

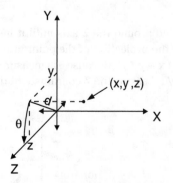

Figure 13.4 Rotating a point around the X axis until it lies in the X-Z plane.

You can use similar methods to rotate around other axes to move a point into the Y-Z or X-Z planes.

Inverse Transformations

As is the case in two dimensions, each of the simple three-dimensional transformations examined so far has a simple inverse. The inverse of a translation by distances Tx, Ty, and Tz is a translation by distances -Tx, -Ty, and -Tz.

$$
\begin{vmatrix}
1 & 0 & 0 & 0 \\
0 & 1 & 0 & 0 \\
0 & 0 & 1 & 0 \\
-Tx & -Ty & -Tz & 1
\end{vmatrix}
$$

The inverse of a scaling by factors Sx, Sy, and Sz is a scaling by factors 1/Sx, 1/Sy, and 1/Sz.

$$
\begin{vmatrix}
1/Sy & 0 & 0 & 0 \\
0 & 1/Sx & 0 & 0 \\
0 & 0 & 1/Sz & 0 \\
0 & 0 & 0 & 1
\end{vmatrix}
$$

Finally, the inverse of a rotation through angle θ around an axis is a rotation through angle $-\theta$ around the same axis. An inverse rotation around the Z axis is given by the matrix:

$$
\begin{vmatrix}
Cos(-\theta) & Sin(-\theta) & 0 & 0 \\
-Sin(-\theta) & Cos(-\theta) & 0 & 0 \\
0 & 0 & 1 & 0 \\
0 & 0 & 0 & 1
\end{vmatrix}
$$

Because $Cos(-\theta) = Cos(\theta)$ and $Sin(-\theta) = -Sin(\theta)$, you can simplify this to:

$$
\begin{vmatrix}
Cos(\theta) & -Sin(\theta) & 0 & 0 \\
Sin(\theta) & Cos(\theta) & 0 & 0 \\
0 & 0 & 1 & 0 \\
0 & 0 & 0 & 1
\end{vmatrix}
$$

Projections

Because your computer's screen is two dimensional, it cannot directly display three-dimensional objects. If you want to display three-dimensional objects on your two-dimensional screen, you must *project* the objects from three dimensions to two.

More generally, a projection translates an object's representation from one set of dimensions to another. The most common projections are from three to two dimensions, though Chapter 18, Higher-Dimensional Transformations, shows how to project from higher dimensional spaces into two dimensions.

The most common types of projections are called *planar geometric projections*. They are defined by the passing of a ray called a *projector* from a *center of projection* through the points being projected onto a *plane of projection*. Figure 13.5 shows the projection of a triangle.

This sort of projection is called "planar geometric" because objects are projected onto a plane with straight projectors. Though less common, there are other kinds of projections that are not described here. For example, because the earth is not flat, cartographers often use nonplanar or nongeometric projections when mapping it. That allows them to map the curved surface of the earth onto a flat map.

Planar geometric projections can be grouped into two classes: *parallel* and *perspective*. These are described in the following sections.

Parallel Projection

In a parallel projection, the projectors are parallel to each other. If you move the center of projection farther and farther away from the plane of projection, the projectors become closer and closer to parallel. If you take this to its limit, you can think of the projectors as originating at a point infinitely far away so they are parallel. Instead of specifying a center of projection, for a parallel projection, you need to specify a direction of projection. Figure 13.6 shows the parallel projection of a triangle.

There are several useful kinds of parallel projections. These fall into two subcategories: *orthographic* and *oblique*. In an orthographic projection, the projectors are perpendicular to the plane of projection; in an oblique projection, they are not.

Orthographic Projections

Orthographic projections are often used in architectural and mechanical drawings. The most common orthographic projections show the front, side, and top views of an object. Figure 13.7 shows an object and its front, side, and top views.

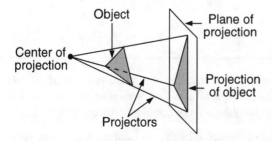

Figure 13.5 Projecting a triangle from three dimensions to two.

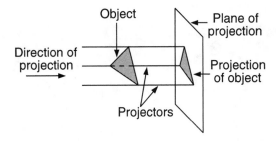

Figure 13.6 The parallel projection of a triangle.

These projections are quite simple. To project a point, simply ignore the point's unneeded third coordinate. To create a front view, ignore the point's Z coordinate. The point's new coordinates are given by the equations:

```
new_x = old_x
new_y = old_y
```

To create a side view, ignore the point's X coordinate. You may also want to map the point's Y and Z coordinates into X and Y coordinates to make it easier to display on a computer screen. In that case, the point's new coordinates are given by the equations:

```
new_x = -old_z
new_y = old_y
```

Similarly, to create a top view you should ignore the point's Y coordinates. To map the point into the X-Y plane, you should use:

```
new_x = old_x
new_y = -old_z
```

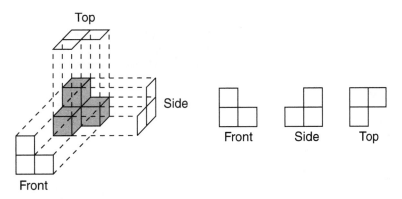

Figure 13.7 Front, side, and top orthographic projections.

Table 13.3 Transformation Matrices for Orthographic Projections

FRONT VIEW (PROJECTING ALONG THE Z AXIS)	SIDE VIEW (PROJECTING ALONG THE X AXIS)	TOP VIEW (PROJECTING ALONG THE Y AXIS)
1 0 0 0 0 1 0 0 0 0 0 0 0 0 0 1	0 0 0 0 0 1 0 0 -1 0 0 0 0 0 0 1	1 0 0 0 0 0 0 0 0 -1 0 0 0 0 0 1

The transformation matrices for these projections are shown in Table 13.3.

Example program Orth demonstrates these transformations. The program draws a shape like the one shown in Figure 13.7 together with its front, side, and top orthographic projections.

Axonometric Orthographic Projections

The front, side, and top orthographic projections preserve distances and angles. In other words you can measure distances and angles directly from the projection of an object. In a front view, for example, the X and Y coordinates of the object are unchanged. That means the distances between points in the X and Y directions are the same as in the original object.

Because the front, side, and top views preserve distances and angles, labeling distances and angles on architectural and mechanical drawings that use these projections is easy. It is also sometimes useful to be able to measure directly from these drawings.

On the other hand, it is often difficult to understand the three-dimensional structure of an object by examining only its front, side, and top views. Reproducing an object like the one in Figure 13.7 from these views takes experience and good spatial intuition. In any case, the front, side, and top views are not completely unambiguous. Both of the objects shown in Figure 13.8 have the same front, side, and top views as the object shown in Figure 13.7.

To make the three-dimensional nature of an object easier to understand, you can use projections that are not parallel to the X, Y, or Z axis. This type of projection is called an *axonometric orthographic projection*. Figure 13.9 shows an axonometric orthographic projection of the object in Figure 13.7.

Figure 13.8 Two objects with the same front, top, and side views.

Figure 13.9 An axonometric orthographic projection.

While this type of projection may seem more complicated than the front, side, and top views, it is easy to build using translations, rotations, and the simpler orthographic projections.

Suppose you want to project an object as shown in Figure 13.10. The focus point (Fx, Fy, Fz) will be projected to the origin. The direction of projection is given by the vector $<Px, Py, Pz>$. To build the transformation for this projection, follow these steps:

1. Translate the focus (Fx, Fy, Fz) to the origin.
2. Rotate to place the direction of projection in the Y-Z plane.
3. Rotate to place the direction of projection in the Y axis.
4. Project along the Y axis (top view).

Once you have calculated the matrices necessary for each of these steps, you can combine them to make one matrix representing the complete transformation.

Figure 13.11 shows the individual steps for projecting a cube with the focus at the cube's center. The direction of projection is drawn with a bold line so that it is easy to see.

Example program Axon follows the steps one at a time to produce a display similar to Figure 13.11. You can use the left, right, up, and down arrow keys to make the program display different views of the intermediate steps in the projection.

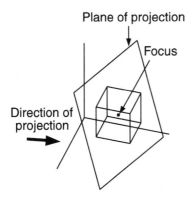

Figure 13.10 An axonometric orthographic projection of a cube.

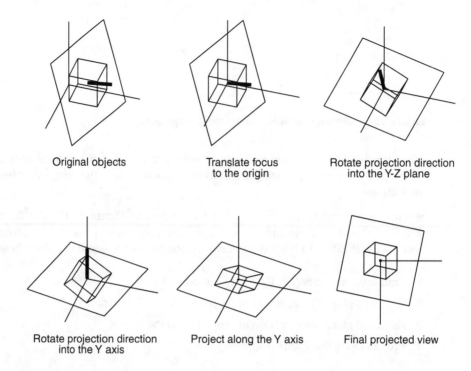

Original objects	Translate focus to the origin	Rotate projection direction into the Y-Z plane
Rotate projection direction into the Y axis	Project along the Y axis	Final projected view

Figure 13.11 The steps in an axonometric orthographic projection.

Isometric Projections

An *isometric projection* is a common type of axonometric orthographic projection in which the direction of projection makes equal angles with all three coordinate axes. Figure 13.12 shows an axonometric projection and an isometric projection of an object.

Because the direction of projection makes the same angle with all three axes, you can measure distances along all three axes using the same scale. For example, in the projection on the right in Figure 13.12, all line segments have the same length. In the projection on the left, however, line segments parallel to the Y axis are the longest, those parallel to the X axis are slightly shorter, and those parallel to the Z axis are quite a bit shorter.

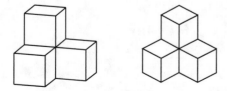

Figure 13.12 Axonometric (left) and isometric (right) projections.

Oblique Projections

Like front, top, and side view orthographic projections, oblique projections are made with the plane of projection perpendicular to one of the coordinate axes. Because the projectors are not perpendicular to the plane of projection, however, more than one face of an object is visible. Figure 13.13 shows front view and oblique projections for a cube.

Because one face of the object is parallel to the plane of projection, you can measure distances and angles on that face. The front of the cube in Figure 13.13 is parallel to the plane of projection, so you can measure distances and angles in the X and Y directions. Distances and angles that involve points with different Z coordinates are not preserved, so you cannot meaningfully measure them.

Cavalier Projections

One useful type of oblique projection is the *cavalier projection*. Here the projectors meet the plane of projection at a 45-degree angle. With this sort of projection, a line perpendicular to the plane of projection is transformed into a line that has the same length as the original line. This means you can measure lengths using the same scale along all three axes.

Figure 13.14 shows three different cavalier projections of a cube. The lengths of all lines in this figure are unchanged by the projection. Lines parallel to the Z axis are tilted by an angle θ. This angle is often chosen to be 30 or 45 degrees. In Figure 13.14, the angles θ are 45, 30, and 15 degrees.

Cabinet Projections

In a cavalier projection, the projectors meet the plane of projection at a 45-degree angle. In a *cabinet projection*, the projectors meet the plane of projection at an angle of Atn(2). In other words, the tangent of the angle between the direction of projection and the plane of projection is 2.

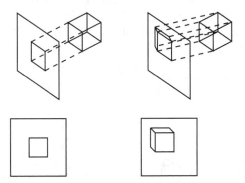

Figure 13.13   Front view (left) and oblique (right) projections.

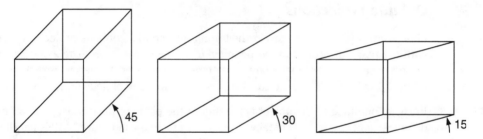

Figure 13.14 Cavalier projections.

While distances are preserved along all three axes by a cavalier projection, distances in one direction are scaled by a factor of 1/2 in a cabinet projection. This makes cabinet projections a bit more aesthetically appealing than cavalier projections. Making the receding axis shorter than the others agrees more closely with orthographic projections and your visual experience, so the picture looks more realistic. Because you know the shortened lines are scaled by a factor of 1/2, you can still measure them meaningfully. Figure 13.15 shows three cabinet projections in which the Z axis is tilted by 45, 30, and 15 degrees.

Oblique Projections in Visual Basic

Figure 13.16 shows an oblique projection of the point (Px, Py, Pz) onto the X-Y plane. This is not a picture of some operation occurring in three dimensions—it is the actual projection onto a page in this book. In this projection, the Z axis makes angle θ with the X axis. Distances parallel to the Z axis are scaled by a factor of S. The factor S is 1 for a cavalier projection and 1/2 for a cabinet projection.

Before projection, the point has X coordinate Px. Because distances parallel to the Z axis are scaled by a factor of S, the point's projection is distance S * Abs(Pz) from the point's original position. In this case, the Z coordinate of the point Pz is negative, so this distance is S * -Pz.

Because lines parallel to the Z axis are tilted by angle θ, the distance between the point's X coordinate and the projection's X coordinate is S * -Pz * Cos(θ). Because the point starts with X coordinate Px, the projection's X coordinate is Px + S * -Pz * Cos(θ).

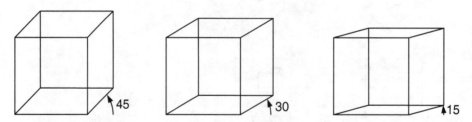

Figure 13.15 Cabinet projections.

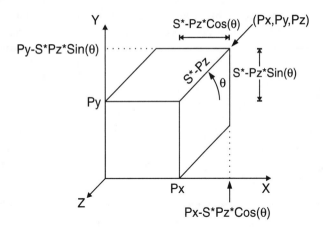

Figure 13.16   The oblique projection of the point (Px, Py, Pz).

Similarly, the distance between the point's Y coordinate and the projection's Y coordinate is S * -Pz * Sin(θ). Because the point starts with Y coordinate Py, the projection's Y coordinate is Py + S * -Pz * Sin(θ). Putting these facts together, the equations for the projection's coordinates are:

```
new_x = old_x + S * -(old_z) * Cos(θ)
new_y = old_y + S * -(old_z) * Sin(θ)
new_z = 0
```

You can represent these equations with the transformation matrix:

$$\begin{vmatrix} 1 & 0 & 0 & 0 \\ 0 & 1 & 0 & 0 \\ -S*\text{Cos}(\theta) & -S*\text{Sin}(\theta) & 0 & 0 \\ 0 & 0 & 0 & 1 \end{vmatrix}$$

Using this information, you can write a Visual Basic routine to initialize a transformation matrix to represent oblique projection onto the X-Y plane.

```
' Create a transformation matrix for an oblique
' projection onto the X-Y plane.
Public Sub m3ObliqueXY(M() As Single, ByVal S As Single, _
    ByVal theta As Single)

    m3Identity M()
    M(3, 1) = -S * Cos(theta)
    M(3, 2) = -S * Sin(theta)
    M(3, 3) = 0
End Sub
```

Example program Oblique uses this subroutine to display cavalier and cabinet projections of a cube. It also displays an orthographic projection of the cube for reference. You can use the left, right, up, and down arrow keys to change the viewing direction in the orthographic projection.

Perspective Projection

In a perspective projection, the projectors pass from a *center of projection* through each point in the object to the plane of projection. Because the projectors pass through a single point, the projection of an object far from the center of projection is smaller than the projection of an object that is closer.

Figure 13.17 shows the perspective projection of two squares. The square that is further from the center of projection is projected into a smaller image on the plane of projection. This effect is called *foreshortening*.

One of the consequences of foreshortening is that the projections of parallel lines that are not parallel to the plane of projection appear to converge. Because the lines are not parallel to the plane of projection, one end of the lines is further from the center of projection than the other. Foreshortening makes the distance between the projections of the lines at that end smaller, so the lines appear to move closer together. Figure 13.18 shows two parallel lines and their perspective projections converging.

The point at which the projection of two parallel lines would meet if they were extended is called a *vanishing point*. A vanishing point where lines parallel to a coordinate axis would meet is called a *principal vanishing point*.

Perspective projections are classified by the number of principal vanishing points they contain. This is determined by the relationship between the plane of projection and the coordinate axes. If the plane of projection is parallel to two coordinate axes, the projection has one principal vanishing point. All lines that are parallel to the third coordinate axis have projections that lead toward this vanishing point.

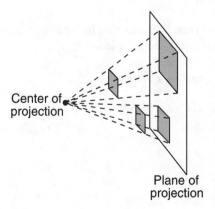

Figure 13.17   Objects farther from the center of projection appear smaller than closer objects.

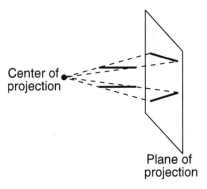

Center of
projection

Plane of
projection

Figure 13.18 The perspective projections of parallel lines converge.

If the plane of projection is parallel to one axis, the projection contains two principal vanishing points. Lines that are parallel to either of the other two coordinate axes have projections that lead toward one of the principal vanishing points.

Finally, if the plane of projection is not parallel to any of the axes, the projection has three principal vanishing points. Lines that are parallel to any of the coordinate axes have projections that lead toward a principal vanishing point.

These types of projections are called *one-point, two-point,* and *three-point perspective projections.* Figure 13.19 shows examples of each for different views of a cube.

The perspective projection of an object may also have other, nonprincipal vanishing points. Any parallel lines that are not also parallel to the plane of projection must converge toward a vanishing point. If the lines are not parallel to a coordinate axis, the

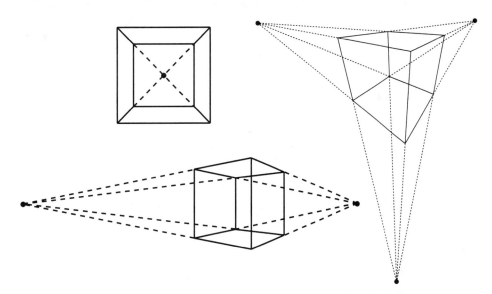

Figure 13.19 Perspective projections with one, two, and three principal vanishing points.

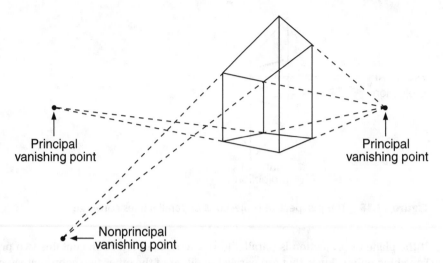

Principal vanishing point

Principal vanishing point

Nonprincipal vanishing point

Figure 13.20 Parallel lines that are not parallel to the plane of projection converge toward a vanishing point.

vanishing point will be nonprincipal. The object shown in Figure 13.20 has two parallel lines that are not parallel to any of the coordinate axes.

As is the case with other transformations, a general perspective projection can be quite complicated. There are special cases, however, that are simple. Projecting onto the X-Y plane when the center of projection lies on the Z axis, for example, is relatively easy.

Figure 13.21 shows a point P = (Px, Py, Pz) being projected into the point P' = (P'x, P'y, P'z) in the X-Y plane. The center of projection is at (0, 0, d), distance d along the Z axis. On the right in Figure 13.21 is a side view of the projection showing the Y and Z axes. The point A is the center of projection, and the point B is the point on the Z axis with the same Z coordinate as the point being projected.

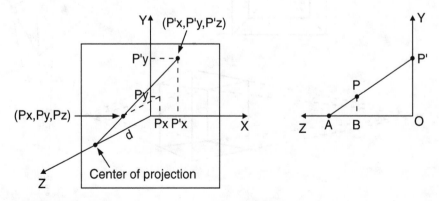

Figure 13.21 The perspective transformation of a point.

In this picture, the triangles ΔABP and ΔAOP' have the same angles, so they are similar triangles. The ratio of corresponding side lengths in similar triangles must be the same, so |OP'| / |AO| = |BP| / |AB|. At the left part of Figure 13.21, you can see that |OP'| = P'y, |AO| = d, |BP| = Py, and |AB| = (d - Pz), so P'y/d = Py/(d - Pz). Solving for P'y, you get P'y = d * Py/(d - Pz). This gives the projected point's Y coordinate.

By examining a similar picture showing the X and Z axes, you can find that P'x = d * Px/(d - Pz). Using these facts, you can conclude that the equations for perspective projection onto the X-Y plane where the center of projection lies at position (0, 0, d) are:

```
new_x = d * (old_y) / (d - (old_z))
new_y = d * (old_x) / (d - (old_z))
new_z = 0
```

You can represent these equations with the transformation matrix:

$$
\begin{vmatrix}
1 & 0 & 0 & 0 \\
0 & 1 & 0 & 0 \\
0 & 0 & 0 & -1/d \\
0 & 0 & 0 & 1
\end{vmatrix}
$$

When you multiply a point (x, y, z, 1) by this matrix you get:

$$
[x, y, z, 1]
\begin{vmatrix}
1 & 0 & 0 & 0 \\
0 & 1 & 0 & 0 \\
0 & 0 & 0 & -1/d \\
0 & 0 & 0 & 1
\end{vmatrix}
= [x, y, 0, 1 - z/d]
$$

Remember that the fourth component in a homogeneous representation of a point is a scale factor. If you normalize the point [x, y, 0, 1 - z/d] by dividing by the fourth component 1 - z/d, the point becomes:

```
[x / (1 - z / d), y / (1 - z / d), 0, 1] =
[d * x / (d - z), d * y / (d - y), 0, 1]
```

This agrees with the previous equations for the new values of x, y, and z.

Using the perspective projection matrix shown here, you can easily write a Visual Basic routine that initializes a transformation matrix that projects onto the X-Z plane.

```
' Create a 3-D transformation matrix for a
' perspective projection into the X-Z plane with
' center of projection at the origin and the plane
' of projection at distance D.
Public Sub m3PerspectiveXZ(M() As Single, ByVal D As Single)
    m3Identity M
    If D <> 0 Then
        M(3, 4) = -1 / D
        M(3, 3) = 0
```

```
        End If
    End Sub
```

Note that transformation matrices representing perspective transformations do not contain 0, 0, 0, 1 in their final columns. To work with these matrices, you must use routines that take this into account. To apply such a transformation to a point, use subroutine m3ApplyFull rather than m3Apply. To multiply such a matrix by another matrix, use subroutine m3MatMultiplyFull rather than subroutine m3MatMultiply.

Summary of Projections

Remembering the definitions for all of the kinds of projection can be quite difficult. Table 13.4 summarizes the projections described in the previous sections. The names of the projections are indented to show how the classifications relate. For example, the entry for parallel projection is indented to show that it is one kind of planar geometric projection.

Perspective Viewing

The equations for perspective projection work equally well for points that lie between the plane of projection and the center of projection and for points that lie behind the plane of projection. This makes it a little easier to specify the plane of projection. You can place it anywhere in front of, behind, or even inside the object you are viewing, and the projection will produce reasonable results.

Table 13.4 Summary of Projection Types

TYPE OF PROJECTION	DESCRIPTION
Planar Geometric	Projectors start at a center of projection and pass through the object to a plane of projection.
Parallel	Projectors are parallel. You can think of the center of projection as being infinitely far away.
Orthographic	Projectors are perpendicular to the plane of projection.
Axonometric	Projectors are not parallel to the X, Y, or Z axis.
Isometric	Direction of projection makes equal angles with all three coordinate axes.
Oblique	Plane of projection is perpendicular to a coordinate axis. Projectors are not perpendicular to the plane of projection.
Cavalier	Projectors meet plane of projection at a 45-degree angle.
Cabinet	Projectors meet plane of projection at an angle of Atn(2).
Perspective	Projectors pass through a center of projection.

The equations also work when the center of projection lies between a point and the plane of projection. This can produce weird results. Generally, you can think of yourself as standing at the center of projection looking toward a screen that lies in the plane of projection. Unfortunately, objects that are behind you will also appear on the screen. If those objects are close behind you, their perspective projections may also appear quite large and distorted.

Even worse, if a point lies directly to the side, at the same distance from the screen as your eye, the equations for the point's new coordinates cause a divide-by-zero error. When you project along the Z axis onto the X-Y plane, for example, the point's new coordinates are given by the equations:

```
new_x = d * (old_y) / (d - (old_z))
new_y = d * (old_x) / (d - (old_z))
new_z = 0
```

If the point is right beside you, d = old_z, so (d - (old_z)) = 0, and you cannot compute the new X and Y coordinates.

Figure 13.22 shows several different triangles and their projections. The top and bottom projections—those of the triangle beyond the plane of projection and of the triangle between the center and plane of projection—are meaningful. The projection of the triangle behind the center of projection is upside down and is probably not meaningful. The projection of the point that lies beside the center of projection does not exist.

Figure 13.23 shows a perspective transformation of a cube in which the center of projection was within the cube. The three lines drawn in bold meet at the corner of the cube that is furthest from the center of projection. The point behind the center of projection is projected fairly close to that corner. The other points are almost the same distance from the origin as the center of projection is, so their projections are quite strange. This results in a somewhat bizarre picture having little resemblance to a cube.

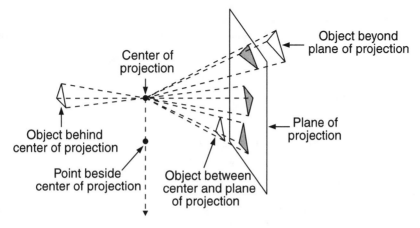

Figure 13.22 Perspective projections.

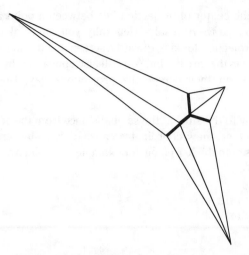

Figure 13.23 Perspective projection of a cube containing the center of projection.

One easy way to prevent all these odd effects is to check whether either of a line segment's endpoints lies beside or behind the center of projection. If so, clip that segment out of the picture and do not draw it.

The ideal time to decide whether a point is behind the center of projection is after translating and rotating the center of projection into the Z axis but before performing the perspective transformation. At that point, you can check to see if the Z coordinate of the point is smaller than the Z coordinate of the center of projection. If so, the point lies in front of the center of projection, so you can draw it.

Unfortunately, when you apply a perspective transformation to a point, you destroy the point's Z coordinate information. That means you can no longer compare the points' Z coordinates to see if they lie behind the center of projection. However, if you modify the perspective transformation matrix and the way transformations are applied to points, you can preserve the Z coordinate information.

First, change the perspective transformation matrix so that the Z coordinate is not lost.

$$\begin{vmatrix} 1 & 0 & 0 & 0 \\ 0 & 1 & 0 & 0 \\ 0 & 0 & 1 & -1/d \\ 0 & 0 & 0 & 1 \end{vmatrix}$$

Now when you multiply a point [x, y, z, 1] with this new matrix you get:

$$[x, y, z, 1] \begin{vmatrix} 1 & 0 & 0 & 0 \\ 0 & 1 & 0 & 0 \\ 0 & 0 & 1 & -1/d \\ 0 & 0 & 0 & 1 \end{vmatrix} = [x, y, z, 1 - z/d]$$

Next, you would usually normalize the vector by dividing each component by (1 - z/d). This step would confuse the Z coordinate information. To preserve the information, normalize only the X and Y components of the point. Then the result becomes:

```
[x / (1 - z / d), y / (1 - z / d), z, 1]
```

The subroutine m3ApplyFull included in module M3Ops.bas applies a perspective transformation matrix to a point. It then normalizes the X and Y coordinates of the result, leaving the Z coordinate unchanged.

```
' Apply a transformation matrix to a point where
' the transformation may not have 0, 0, 0, 1 in
' its final column. Normalize only the X and Y
' components of the result to preserve the Z
' information.
Public Sub m3ApplyFull(V() As Single, M() As Single, _
    Result() As Single)
Dim i As Integer
Dim j As Integer
Dim value As Single

    For i = 1 To 4
        value = 0#
        For j = 1 To 4
            value = value + V(j) * M(j, i)
        Next j
        Result(i) = value
    Next i

    ' Renormalize the point.
    ' Note that value still holds Result(4).
    If value <> 0 Then
        Result(1) = Result(1) / value
        Result(2) = Result(2) / value
        ' Do not transform the Z component.
    Else
        ' Make the Z value greater than that of
        ' the center of projection so the point
        ' will be clipped.
        Result(3) = INFINITY
    End If
    Result(4) = 1#
End Sub
```

Example program Clip, shown in Figure 13.24, demonstrates these techniques. Use the left, right, up, and down arrow keys to change the program's viewing direction. Enter the distance you want between the center of projection and the origin. Click the Clip check box to make the program clip lines behind the center of projection. If you make the distance small (1 or 2), clipping makes a huge difference.

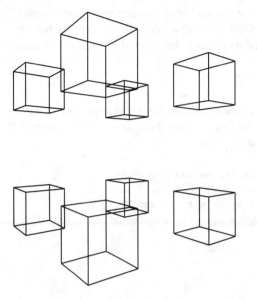

Figure 13.24   Program Clip displaying eight cubes.

If you move the center of projection until it lies at the origin, the projection fails. You cannot perform a perspective projection when the center of projection lies within the plane of projection.

Composing Transformations

One of the main reasons for writing transformations as matrices is so that you can compose them to store complicated combinations of transformations in a single matrix. This allows you to build complex transformations as combinations of simpler ones. Many of these complex operations are similar to their two-dimensional equivalents.

Scaling without Translation

When you scale an object in three dimensions, its X, Y, and Z coordinates are all scaled so that the object tends to move further from, or closer to, the origin. To scale an object without moving it, you can follow a procedure similar to the one described in Chapter 12, Two-Dimensional Transformations, for scaling an object in two dimensions.

First, translate the object to the origin. Next, scale the object. Then use the inverse of the initial translation to move the object back to its original position. Figure 13.25 shows a cube being translated to the origin, scaled, and translated back to its original position.

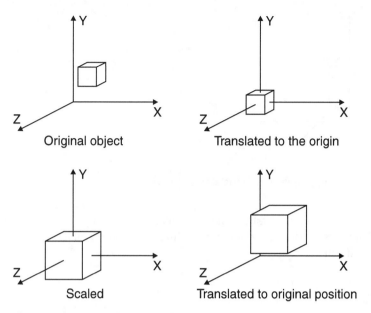

Figure 13.25 An object translated to the origin, scaled, and then translated back to its original position.

Reflection across an Arbitrary Plane

Reflecting an object across the X-Y, Y-Z, or X-Z planes is easy. To reflect an object across an arbitrary plane, first translate and rotate the object until the plane of reflection coincides with the X-Y, Y-Z, or X-Z plane. Then you can perform the simpler reflection and use the inverses of the initial rotations and translation to move the object back to its original position. While this operation is easy to describe, it is fairly complicated to perform.

To reflect objects across a plane, you first need to be able to describe the plane of reflection. One simple way to describe a plane is by giving a point on the plane and a vector that is perpendicular to the plane. This kind of vector is called a *normal vector* for the plane. Figure 13.26 shows a plane that passes through the point (p1, p2, p3) and has normal vector <n1, n2, n3>.

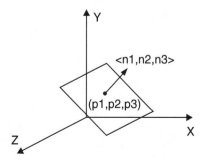

Figure 13.26 A plane passing through (p1, p2, p3) with normal vector <n1, n2, n3>.

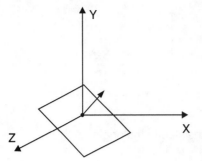

Figure 13.27 Plane of reflection translated to the origin.

To reflect across this plane, first translate the plane so that it intersects the origin as shown in Figure 13.27. Because the point (p1, p2, p3) is on the plane, you can do this using the transformation:

$$
T = \begin{vmatrix} 1 & 0 & 0 & 0 \\ 0 & 1 & 0 & 0 \\ 0 & 0 & 1 & 0 \\ -p1 & -p2 & -p3 & 1 \end{vmatrix}
$$

Next, you must perform rotations until the plane coincides with the X-Y, Y-Z, or X-Z plane. You can do this by rotating until the plane's normal vector lies along one of the coordinate axes. If you rotate the vector so that it lies along the Y axis, for example, the plane of reflection will lie in the X-Z plane.

You can begin by rotating around the Z axis until the normal vector lies in the Y-Z plane. Figure 13.28 shows the projection of the normal vector onto the X-Y plane. To place the vector in the Y-Z plane, you must rotate by angle θ around the Z axis as shown in Figure 13.28. The transformation matrix corresponding to this rotation is:

$$
R_1 = \begin{vmatrix} \text{Cos}(\theta) & \text{Sin}(\theta) & 0 & 0 \\ -\text{Sin}(\theta) & \text{Cos}(\theta) & 0 & 0 \\ 0 & 0 & 1 & 0 \\ 0 & 0 & 0 & 1 \end{vmatrix}
$$

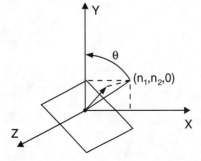

Figure 13.28 Rotating the normal vector into the Y-Z plane.

The X and Y coordinates of the projection of the vector are n1 and n2, so the length of the projection is $D = Sqr(n1 * n1 + n2 * n2)$. Then $Sin(\theta) = n1/D$ and $Cos(\theta) = n2/D$. This makes the first rotation's transformation matrix:

$$
R1 = \begin{vmatrix}
n2 / D & n1 / D & 0 & 0 \\
-n1 / D & n2 / D & 0 & 0 \\
0 & 0 & 1 & 0 \\
0 & 0 & 0 & 1
\end{vmatrix}
$$

Figure 13.29 shows the plane translated and rotated so that the normal vector lies in the Y-Z plane.

Now you must rotate by angle $-\phi$ around the X axis to make the normal vector lie along the Y axis. The angle of rotation is $-\phi$, not ϕ, because you must measure angles in the counterclockwise direction as you look down the axis toward the origin. The angle ϕ is measured in the clockwise direction, so you must rotate by the angle $-\phi$. The transformation matrix for this rotation is:

$$
R2 = \begin{vmatrix}
1 & 0 & 0 & 0 \\
0 & Cos(-\phi) & Sin(-\phi) & 0 \\
0 & -Sin(-\phi) & Cos(-\phi) & 0 \\
0 & 0 & 0 & 1
\end{vmatrix}
$$

The Y coordinate of the tip of the translated and rotated vector is now $D = Sqr(n1 * n1 + n2 * n2)$. The total length of the vector is $L = Sqr(n1 * n1 + n2 * n2 + n3 * n3)$. This means $Sin(-\phi) = -Sin(\phi) = -n3/L$ and $Cos(-\phi) = Cos(\phi) = D/L$. With these values, the second rotation matrix becomes:

$$
R2 = \begin{vmatrix}
1 & 0 & 0 & 0 \\
0 & D / L & -n3 / L & 0 \\
0 & n3 / L & D / L & 0 \\
0 & 0 & 0 & 1
\end{vmatrix}
$$

Figure 13.30 shows the plane of reflection and its normal vector after you have applied the translation and two rotations. At this point, reflecting objects across the X-Z plane is easy. Simply use a scaling transformation where the X and Z coordinates are unchanged and the Y coordinate is scaled by a factor of -1. The matrix for this operation is:

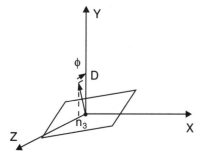

Figure 13.29 The normal vector in the Y-Z plane.

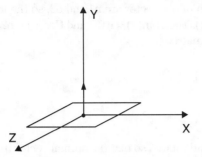

Figure 13.30 The normal vector lies along the Y axis.

$$S = \begin{vmatrix} 1 & 0 & 0 & 0 \\ 0 & -1 & 0 & 0 \\ 0 & 0 & 1 & 0 \\ 0 & 0 & 0 & 1 \end{vmatrix}$$

Once you have finished the reflection, apply the inverses of the rotations and translation you performed earlier to move the plane of reflection back to its original position. Suppose $T1^{-1}$, $R1^{-1}$, and $R2^{-1}$ are the inverses of the translation and the first and second rotations respectively. Then the complete transformation for reflecting an object across the plane is given by the matrix equation:

$$T \ R1 \ R2 \ S \ R2^{-1} \ R1^{-1} \ T1^{-1}$$

Now you can combine these seven matrices by multiplying them to obtain a single transformation matrix to represent the reflection operation. Module M3Ops.bas contains the subroutine m3Reflect, which uses these methods to initialize a transformation matrix that performs reflection across an arbitrary plane.

```
' Create a transformation matrix for reflecting
' across the plane passing through (p1, p2, p3)
' with normal vector <n1, n2, n3>.
Public Sub m3Reflect(M() As Single, ByVal p1 As Single, _
    ByVal p2 As Single, ByVal p3 As Single, _
    ByVal n1 As Single, ByVal n2 As Single, _
    ByVal n3 As Single)
Dim T(1 To 4, 1 To 4) As Single       ' Translate.
Dim R1(1 To 4, 1 To 4) As Single      ' Rotate 1.
Dim R2(1 To 4, 1 To 4) As Single      ' Rotate 2.
Dim S(1 To 4, 1 To 4) As Single       ' Reflect.
Dim R2i(1 To 4, 1 To 4) As Single     ' Unrotate 2.
Dim R1i(1 To 4, 1 To 4) As Single     ' Unrotate 1.
Dim Ti(1 To 4, 1 To 4) As Single      ' Untranslate.
Dim D As Single
Dim L As Single
Dim M12(1 To 4, 1 To 4) As Single
```

```
Dim M34(1 To 4, 1 To 4) As Single
Dim M1234(1 To 4, 1 To 4) As Single
Dim M56(1 To 4, 1 To 4) As Single
Dim M567(1 To 4, 1 To 4) As Single

    ' Translate the plane to the origin.
    m3Translate T, -p1, -p2, -p3
    m3Translate Ti, p1, p2, p3

    ' Rotate around Z-axis until the normal is in
    ' the Y-Z plane.
    m3Identity R1
    D = Sqr(n1 * n1 + n2 * n2)
    R1(1, 1) = n2 / D
    R1(1, 2) = n1 / D
    R1(2, 1) = -R1(1, 2)
    R1(2, 2) = R1(1, 1)

    m3Identity R1i
    R1i(1, 1) = R1(1, 1)
    R1i(1, 2) = -R1(1, 2)
    R1i(2, 1) = -R1(2, 1)
    R1i(2, 2) = R1(2, 2)

    ' Rotate around the X-axis until the normal
    ' lies along the Y axis.
    m3Identity R2
    L = Sqr(n1 * n1 + n2 * n2 + n3 * n3)
    R2(2, 2) = D / L
    R2(2, 3) = -n3 / L
    R2(3, 2) = -R2(2, 3)
    R2(3, 3) = R2(2, 2)

    m3Identity R2i
    R2i(2, 2) = R2(2, 2)
    R2i(2, 3) = -R2(2, 3)
    R2i(3, 2) = -R2(3, 2)
    R2i(3, 3) = R2(3, 3)

    ' Reflect across the X-Z plane.
    m3Identity S
    S(2, 2) = -1

    ' Combine the matrices.
    m3MatMultiply M12, T, R1
    m3MatMultiply M34, R2, S
    m3MatMultiply M1234, M12, M34
    m3MatMultiply M56, R2i, R1i
    m3MatMultiply M567, M56, Ti
    m3MatMultiply M, M1234, M567
End Sub
```

Example program Reflect demonstrates the steps in performing a reflection across an arbitrary plane. It applies the transformation matrices used to reflect an object one at a time and shows the object after each step. When you run the program, you can use the left, right, up, and down arrow keys to change the program's viewing direction.

Rotation around an Arbitrary Line

You can follow similar steps to rotate an object around an arbitrary line.

1. Translate the line to the origin.
2. Rotate around the Z axis until the line lies in the Y-Z plane.
3. Rotate around the X axis until the line lies along the Y axis.
4. Rotate around the Y axis.
5. Reverse the second rotation.
6. Reverse the first rotation.
7. Reverse the translation.

Example program Rotate demonstrates the steps used to rotate an object around an arbitrary line. It applies the required transformations one at a time and shows the object after each step. When you run the program, you can use the left, right, up, and down arrow keys to change the program's viewing direction.

Subroutine m3LineRotate, included in module M3Ops.bas, initializes a single, combined transformation matrix for rotating around an arbitrary line.

```
' Create a transformation atrix for rotating

' through angle theta around a line passing
' through (p1, p2, p3) in direction <d1, d2, d3>.
' Theta is measured counterclockwise as you look
' down the line opposite the line's direction.
Private Sub m3LineRotate(M() As Single, ByVal p1 As Single, _
    ByVal p2 As Single, ByVal p3 As Single, _
    ByVal d1 As Single, ByVal d2 As Single, _
    ByVal d3 As Single, ByVal theta As Single)
Dim T(1 To 4, 1 To 4) As Single        ' Translate.
Dim R1(1 To 4, 1 To 4) As Single       ' Rotate 1.
Dim R2(1 To 4, 1 To 4) As Single       ' Rotate 2.
Dim Rot3(1 To 4, 1 To 4) As Single     ' Rotate.
Dim R2i(1 To 4, 1 To 4) As Single      ' Unrotate 2.
Dim R1i(1 To 4, 1 To 4) As Single      ' Unrotate 1.
Dim Ti(1 To 4, 1 To 4) As Single       ' Untranslate.
Dim D As Single
Dim L As Single
Dim M12(1 To 4, 1 To 4) As Single
Dim M34(1 To 4, 1 To 4) As Single
Dim M1234(1 To 4, 1 To 4) As Single
```

```
Dim M56(1 To 4, 1 To 4) As Single
Dim M567(1 To 4, 1 To 4) As Single

    ' Translate the plane to the origin.
    m3Translate T, -p1, -p2, -p3
    m3Translate Ti, p1, p2, p3

    ' Rotate around Z-axis until the line is in
    ' the Y-Z plane.
    m3Identity R1
    D = Sqr(d1 * d1 + d2 * d2)
    R1(1, 1) = d2 / D
    R1(1, 2) = d1 / D
    R1(2, 1) = -R1(1, 2)
    R1(2, 2) = R1(1, 1)

    m3Identity R1i
    R1i(1, 1) = R1(1, 1)
    R1i(1, 2) = -R1(1, 2)
    R1i(2, 1) = -R1(2, 1)
    R1i(2, 2) = R1(2, 2)

    ' Rotate around the X-axis until the line
    ' lies along the Y axis.
    m3Identity R2
    L = Sqr(d1 * d1 + d2 * d2 + d3 * d3)
    R2(2, 2) = D / L
    R2(2, 3) = -d3 / L
    R2(3, 2) = -R2(2, 3)
    R2(3, 3) = R2(2, 2)

    m3Identity R2i
    R2i(2, 2) = R2(2, 2)
    R2i(2, 3) = -R2(2, 3)
    R2i(3, 2) = -R2(3, 2)
    R2i(3, 3) = R2(3, 3)

    ' Rotate around the line (Y axis).
    m3YRotate Rot3, theta

    ' Combine the matrices.
    m3MatMultiply M12, T, R1
    m3MatMultiply M34, R2, Rot3
    m3MatMultiply M1234, M12, M34
    m3MatMultiply M56, R2i, R1i
    m3MatMultiply M567, M56, Ti
    m3MatMultiply M, M1234, M567
End Sub
```

Projection onto an Arbitrary Plane

Using similar steps, you can create a transformation matrix that represents parallel or perspective projection onto an arbitrary plane. One simple way to specify a projection system is to give a focus point and the center of projection or eye. The focus point is some point of interest that you want to view. The plane of projection passes through the focus point. The normal to the plane of projection is given by the vector from the focus point to the center of projection. Figure 13.31 shows a viewing system specified in this way.

Using this specification, you can follow these steps to perform the projection:

1. Translate the focus to the origin.
2. Rotate around the Y axis to place the center of projection in the Y-Z plane.
3. Rotate around the X axis until the center of projection lies on the Z axis.
4. Project (parallel or perspective) along the Z axis onto the X-Y plane.

The goal of steps 2 and 3 is to rotate the center of projection into the Z axis. These instructions rotate around the center of projection into the Y-Z plane and then rotate it into the Z axis, but there are other ways you can achieve the same result. For example, you could rotate the center of projection into the X-Z plane and then rotate it into the Z axis. Or you could rotate around a line that moved the center of projection directly into the Z axis.

Figure 13.32 shows these three possibilities. The top pictures show a point on a triangle being rotated into the Z axis. The bottom pictures show the corresponding projections onto the X-Y plane. Each of the three methods moves the selected point to the same position on the Z axis. Other points, however, are not necessarily moved to the same locations by each transformation. This means the three orders of rotation give three different projections.

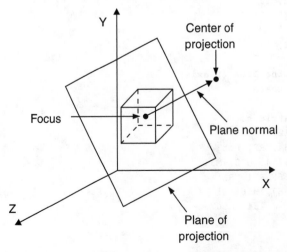

Figure 13.31   Specifying a viewing system with a focus point and a center of projection.

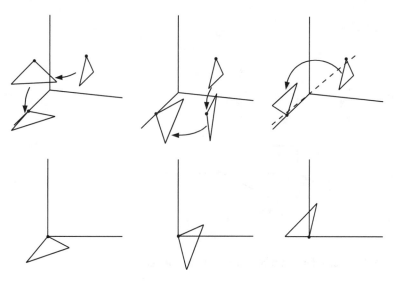

Figure 13.32 Different ways to rotate a point into the Z axis.

Example program RotOrder performs these three sets of rotations and displays the results in pictures much like those in Figure 13.32. You can use the left, right, up, and down arrow keys to change the viewing directions in the three upper pictures.

The UP Vector

The three projections at the bottom of Figure 13.32 are identical except they have been rotated by different amounts around the Z axis. In addition to a center of projection and a focus point, you must decide at what angle to rotate objects around the Z axis to completely specify the projection. One way to do that is to indicate an UP vector as shown in Figure 13.33. After rotating the center of projection into the Z axis, you can rotate around the Z axis until the UP vector lies in the Y-Z plane. Then the steps for projection become:

1. Translate the focus to the origin.
2. Rotate around the Y axis to place the center of projection in the Y-Z plane.
3. Rotate around the X axis until the center of projection lies on the Z axis.
4. Rotate around the Z axis until the UP vector lies in the Y-Z plane.
5. Project (parallel or perspective) along the Z axis onto the X-Y plane.

These steps are illustrated in Figure 13.34. Here the viewing direction is drawn as a bold line between the focus point and the center of projection. The UP vector is drawn as an arrow starting at the focus point.

Example program Up follows these steps one at a time to produce pictures like those in Figure 13.34. This program draws the viewing direction in green and the UP vector in red.

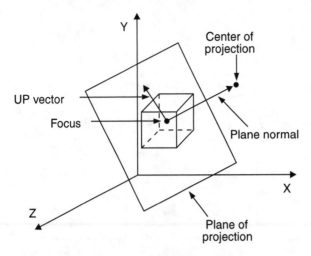

Figure 13.33 Specifying a projection with an UP vector.

You can use the arrow keys to make the program display the steps in the projection from different angles.

Using Subroutine m3Project

Subroutine m3Project in module M3Ops.bas uses these steps to initialize a transformation matrix representing a projection. This routine takes as parameters the matrix to be initialized, a flag indicating whether this should be a perspective or parallel projection, the center of projection, the focus point, and the UP direction vector.

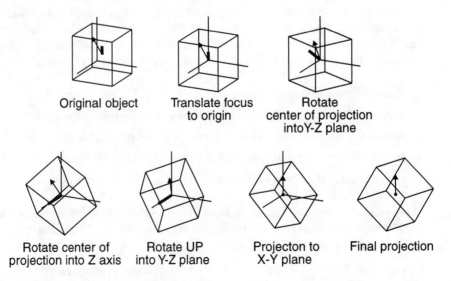

Figure 13.34 Projecting an object with an UP vector.

```
' Create a 3-D transformation matrix for a
' projection with:
'       center of projection    (cx, cy, cz)
'       focus                   (fx, fy, fx)
'       UP vector               <ux, yx, uz>
' ptype should be m3Perspective or m3Parallel.
Public Sub m3Project(M() As Single, ByVal ptype As Integer, _
    ByVal cx As Single, ByVal cy As Single, _
    ByVal cz As Single, ByVal Fx As Single, _
    ByVal Fy As Single, ByVal Fz As Single, _
    ByVal ux As Single, ByVal uy As Single, _
    ByVal uz As Single)
Static M1(1 To 4, 1 To 4) As Single
Static M2(1 To 4, 1 To 4) As Single
Static M3(1 To 4, 1 To 4) As Single
Static M4(1 To 4, 1 To 4) As Single
Static M5(1 To 4, 1 To 4) As Single
Static M12(1 To 4, 1 To 4) As Single
Static M34(1 To 4, 1 To 4) As Single
Static M1234(1 To 4, 1 To 4) As Single
Dim sin1 As Single
Dim cos1 As Single
Dim sin2 As Single
Dim cos2 As Single
Dim sin3 As Single
Dim cos3 As Single
Dim A As Single
Dim B As Single
Dim C As Single
Dim d1 As Single
Dim d2 As Single
Dim d3 As Single
Dim up1(1 To 4) As Single
Dim up2(1 To 4) As Single

    ' Translate the focus to the origin.
    m3Translate M1, -Fx, -Fy, -Fz

    A = cx - Fx
    B = cy - Fy
    C = cz - Fz
    d1 = Sqr(A * A + C * C)
    If d1 <> 0 Then
        sin1 = -A / d1
        cos1 = C / d1
    End If
    d2 = Sqr(A * A + B * B + C * C)
    If d2 <> 0 Then
        sin2 = B / d2
        cos2 = d1 / d2
    End If
```

```
' Rotate around the Y axis to place the
' center of projection in the Y-Z plane.
m3Identity M2

' If d1 = 0 then the center of projection
' already lies in the Y axis and thus the Y-Z plane.
If d1 <> 0 Then
    M2(1, 1) = cos1
    M2(1, 3) = -sin1
    M2(3, 1) = sin1
    M2(3, 3) = cos1
End If

' Rotate around the X axis to place the
' center of projection in the Z axis.
m3Identity M3

' If d2 = 0 then the center of projection
' lies at the origin. This makes projection
' impossible.
If d2 <> 0 Then
    M3(2, 2) = cos2
    M3(2, 3) = sin2
    M3(3, 2) = -sin2
    M3(3, 3) = cos2
End If

' Apply the rotations to the UP vector.
up1(1) = ux
up1(2) = uy
up1(3) = uz
up1(4) = 1
m3Apply up1, M2, up2
m3Apply up2, M3, up1

' Rotate around the Z axis to put the UP
' vector in the Y-Z plane.
d3 = Sqr(up1(1) * up1(1) + up1(2) * up1(2))
m3Identity M4

' If d3 = 0 then the UP vector is a zero
' vector so do nothing.
If d3 <> 0 Then
    sin3 = up1(1) / d3
    cos3 = up1(2) / d3
    M4(1, 1) = cos3
    M4(1, 2) = sin3
    M4(2, 1) = -sin3
    M4(2, 2) = cos3
End If
```

```
' Project.
If ptype = m3Perspective And d2 <> 0 Then
    m3PerspectiveXZ M5, d2
Else
    m3Identity M5
End If

' Combine the transformations.
m3MatMultiply M12, M1, M2
m3MatMultiply M34, M3, M4
m3MatMultiply M1234, M12, M34
If ptype = m3Perspective Then
    m3MatMultiplyFull M, M1234, M5
Else
    m3MatMultiply M, M1234, M5
End If
End Sub
```

Spherical Coordinates

In normal, Cartesian coordinates, you specify a point using X, Y, and Z coordinates. Other coordinate systems are also possible, and sometimes they are more convenient.

In spherical coordinates, a point is specified by three parameters: R, ϕ, and θ. R is the distance from the point to the origin. ϕ is the angle between the line from the origin to the point and the X-Z plane. θ is the angle the vertical plane containing the point and the Y axis makes with the X axis. Figure 13.35 shows the spherical representation of a point. Using Figure 13.35 and a little trigonometry, you can see that:

```
y = R * Sin(φ)
x = R * Cos(φ) * Cos(θ)
z = R * Cos(φ) * Sin(θ)
```

Sometimes it is more convenient to specify a center of projection in spherical coordinates instead of the usual Cartesian coordinates. If the focus point is at the origin, you

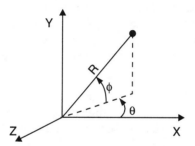

Figure 13.35   Spherical coordinates.

can use spherical coordinates to easily change the angle of projection without changing the distance from the center of projection to the focus point.

Many of the example programs in this chapter use this method for specifying the center of projection. The distance R is fixed by the program. As the program runs, you can use the right and left arrow keys to increase and decrease the value of θ. Similarly, you can use the up and down arrow keys to increase and decrease the value of ϕ.

The m3PProject routine in module M3Ops.bas is similar to subroutine m3Project, except it specifies the center of projection in spherical coordinates. All this routine does is convert the spherical coordinates into Cartesian coordinates and then call m3Project to initialize the transformation matrix.

```
' Create a 3-D transformation matrix for a
' perspective projection with:
'       center of projection     (r, phi, theta)
'       focus                    (fx, fy, fx)
'       up vector                <ux, uy, uz>
' ptype should be m3Perspective or m3Parallel.
Public Sub m3PProject(M() As Single, ByVal ptype As Integer, _
    ByVal r As Single, ByVal phi As Single, _
    ByVal theta As Single, ByVal Fx As Single, _
    ByVal Fy As Single, ByVal Fz As Single, _
    ByVal ux As Single, ByVal uy As Single,
    ByVal uz As Single)
Dim cx As Single
Dim cy As Single
Dim cz As Single
Dim r2 As Single

    ' Convert to Cartesian coordinates.
    cy = r * Sin(phi)
    r2 = r * Cos(phi)
    cx = r2 * Cos(theta)
    cz = r2 * Sin(theta)
    m3Project M, ptype, cx, cy, cz, Fx, Fy, Fz, ux, uy, uz
End Sub
```

Example program Platonic uses subroutine m3PProject to display the five Platonic solids. These solids, the tetrahedron, cube (or hexahedron), octahedron, dodecahedron, and icosahedron, were classified by the Greek philosopher Plato (B.C. 427-347). They are the only three-dimensional solids you can make using regular polygons for sides.

Using check boxes, you can indicate which solids the program should display and whether it should draw the coordinate axes. Click on the drawing area to give it the keyboard focus. Then you can use the arrows to change the values of the center of projection's spherical coordinates ϕ and θ.

Three-Dimensional Objects

As is the case in two dimensions, you can use Visual Basic's classes to manage three-dimensional objects more easily. At a minimum, such an object should be able to store points for drawing, apply a transformation to those points, and draw the transformed points on a picture box, form, or printer.

The Polyline3d class in module Pline3d.cls represents a collection of three-dimensional line segments. It contains an array of points and an array that indicates which points should be connected.

Polyline3d objects use the private function AddPoint to add new points to its point array. This function first checks to see if the point is already in the array. If so, the function reuses that point rather than creating a duplicate entry. This saves time later when you want to transform the Polyline3d object. You need to transform each point only once rather than once for each of the segments that contains it.

```
Option Explicit

' Point3D and Segment3D are defined in module M3OPS.BAS as:
'    Type Point3D
'        coord(1 To 4) As Single
'        trans(1 To 4) As Single
'    End Type
'
'    Type Segment3D
'        pt1 As Integer
'        pt2 As Integer
'    End Type

Private NumPoints As Integer ' Number of points.
Private Points() As Point3D  ' Data points.

Private NumSegs As Integer   ' Number of segments.
Private Segs() As Segment3D  ' The segments.

' Add a point to the polyline or reuse a point.
' Return the point's index.
Private Function AddPoint(ByVal x As Single, _
    ByVal y As Single, ByVal z As Single) As Integer
Dim i As Integer

    ' See if the point is already here.
    For i = 1 To NumPoints
        If x = Points(i).coord(1) And _
           y = Points(i).coord(2) And _
           z = Points(i).coord(3) Then _
                Exit For
```

```
        Next i
        AddPoint = i

        ' If so, we're done.
        If i <= NumPoints Then Exit Function

        ' Otherwise create the new point.
        NumPoints = NumPoints + 1
        ReDim Preserve Points(1 To NumPoints)
        Points(i).coord(1) = x
        Points(i).coord(2) = y
        Points(i).coord(3) = z
        Points(i).coord(4) = 1#
    End Function
```

The AddSegment routine adds one or more segments to a Polyline3d object. This routine uses the ParamArray keyword to take a variable number of point coordinates as parameters. AddSegment creates new segments in the object to connect each point to the one after it in the parameter list.

```
    ' Add one or more line segments to the polyline.
    Public Sub AddSegment(ParamArray coord() As Variant)
    Dim num_segs As Integer
    Dim i As Integer
    Dim last As Integer
    Dim pt As Integer

        num_segs = (UBound(coord) + 1) \ 3 - 1
        ReDim Preserve Segs(1 To NumSegs + num_segs)

        last = AddPoint((coord(0)), (coord(1)), (coord(2)))
        pt = 0
        For i = 1 To num_segs
            Segs(NumSegs + i).pt1 = last
            pt = pt + 3
            last = AddPoint((coord(pt)), _
                (coord(pt + 1)), (coord(pt + 2)))
            Segs(NumSegs + i).pt2 = last
        Next i

        NumSegs = NumSegs + num_segs
    End Sub
```

The Polyline3d class also includes subroutine Transform, which applies a distorting transformation to the points that make up the object. This routine takes as a parameter an object representing a distorting transformation, and that has a transform subroutine. The Polyline3d object invokes that object's Transform routine for each of the points that make up the object.

```
    ' Apply a nonlinear transformation.
    Public Sub Transform(ByVal T As Object)
```

```
Dim i As Integer

    For i = 1 To NumPoints
        T.Transform Points(i).coord(1), _
            Points(i).coord(2), Points(i).coord(3)
    Next i
End Sub
```

You can see the complete source code for the Polyline3d class in Pline3d.cls.

Example program Distort uses the Polyline3d class to demonstrate several shape-distorting transformations. When you run the program, it creates grids on the top and two sides of a cube, as shown in the upper left in Figure 13.36. Click on the option buttons to make the program apply one of the transformations shown in Figure 13.36.

Example program Shapes uses the Polyline3d class to display several three-dimensional scenes. Use the option buttons to select the scene you want to see.

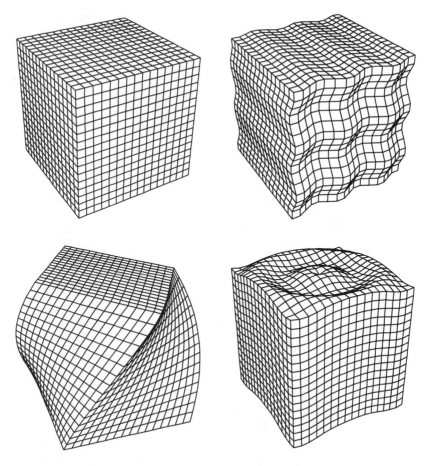

Figure 13.36   Shape-distorting transformations.

Summary

The techniques described in this chapter begin the search for visual realism. Using homogeneous coordinates and the transformation matrices described here, you can write programs that display three-dimensional objects.

These methods only let you display wireframe objects, however. A program can draw lines in three dimensions, but it cannot draw solid surfaces that obscure the things behind them. The following chapters continue the quest for visual realism by showing how to remove hidden lines and shade the surfaces that are visible.

CHAPTER 14

Surfaces

This chapter covers the broad topic of surfaces in three dimensions. The chapter begins by describing data structures you can use to store, manipulate, and display simple surfaces. Using these structures, you can manage many kinds of simple surfaces, including surfaces that contain incomplete data.

The chapter then covers a few specialized techniques you can use to manipulate simple surfaces. Fractal techniques allow you to turn simple surfaces into interesting, irregular terrains. The Hi-Lo and Z-Order algorithms use the special characteristics of simple surfaces to remove hidden areas from the display.

Some programs make use of a list of control points that determine only the overall shape of the surface. The exact nature of the surface is not critical as long as the surface generally follows the control points. In cases like this, you need to use other methods for managing your data. The next few sections explain ways you can create smooth parametric surfaces using Bezier curves and B-splines in three dimensions.

The final sections in the chapter describe surfaces of transformation. By applying the three-dimensional transformations described in Chapter 13, Three-Dimensional Transformations, to a curve, you can create all sorts of strange and interesting surfaces.

Simple Surfaces

Often in mathematics, you think of a surface as a function that returns a Z value for each X and Y coordinate in a region of interest. Many of the viewing routines described in previous chapters are oriented so that the Y axis gives the viewing "up" direction. To be consistent, this chapter considers surfaces defined by functions that return a Y value for each X and Z coordinate in a region. To translate a function from a system that gives Z as a function of X and Y, simply reverse the roles of Y and Z.

For each X and Z value, a simple surface can have at most one Y value. Figure 14.1 shows a simple surface drawn with the coordinate axes. Simple surfaces include objects such as

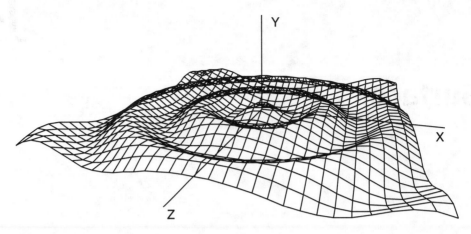

Figure 14.1 A simple surface.

planes, pyramids, and bowls. They do not include objects like spheres, cubes, and tetrahedrons that have more than one Y value corresponding to the same X and Z coordinates.

The grid data structures described in the next few sections let you manage many kinds of simple surfaces, including those for which you are working with incomplete data.

Grids

The simplest way to store surface data is in a two-dimensional array. For each point (X, Z) in the area defined for the surface, the (X, Z) entry in the array gives the Y coordinate of the corresponding point on the surface.

Drawing this kind of surface is easy. Simply draw the three-dimensional line segments connecting points on the surface that have adjacent X or Z values. The following Visual Basic code fragment shows how you could draw the line segments, assuming the data values are stored in the two-dimensional array Data.

```
Dim x As Integer
Dim z As Integer

    ' Draw the segments parallel to the X axis.
    For z = zmin To zmax
        For x = xmin + 1 To xmax
            ' Draw the 3-D line connecting the points
            ' (x - 1, Data(x - 1, z), z) and
            ' (x, Data(x, z), z).
                :
        Next x
    Next z

    ' Draw the segments parallel to the Z axis.
    For x = xmin To xmax
        For z = zmin + 1 To zmax
```

```
            ' Draw the 3-D line connecting the points
            ' (x, Data(x, z - 1), z - 1) and
            ' (x, Data(x, z), z).
                :
        Next z
    Next x
```

Figure 14.2 shows a surface drawn in this way. For smoothly varying surfaces like this one, the line segments appear to cover the surface with rectangles. Nearby lines on the surface do not necessarily lie within the same plane, however, so they actually form "bent rectangles" like the one shown in Figure 14.3.

A Grid Class

To make managing surfaces easier, you can create a Grid3d class. The class should contain variables to describe the data it contains. The class described in this section stores its minimum X and Z values, the spacing between the rows of data in the X and Z directions, and the number of data points in the X and Z directions.

The actual data values are stored in the Points array, a two-dimensional array of Point3D data structures. Point3D structures contain room for a point's original coordinates as well as the coordinates after they have been transformed and projected. This makes Point3D structures useful for storing, projecting, and displaying the data.

```
Option Explicit

Private Xmin As Single       ' Min X and Y values.
Private Zmin As Single
Private Dx As Single         ' Spacing between rows of data.
Private Dz As Single
Private NumX As Integer      ' Number of X and Y entries.
Private NumZ As Integer
Private Points() As Point3D  ' Data values.
```

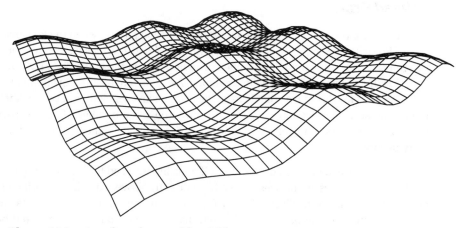

Figure 14.2 A surface drawn with a grid.

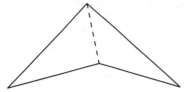

Figure 14.3   Close-up of a "bent rectangle" on a surface.

Using an array of Point3D structures duplicates some of the surface's data. Because you know the X and Z coordinates of each point by its location in the array, you really do not need to store those coordinates in the Point3D structure. In other words, for the point corresponding to array entry Points(A, B), you know the point's untransformed X and Z coordinates are A and B.

```
Points(A, B).coord(1) = A
Points(A, B).coord(3) = B
```

If you were to omit this data from the Point3D structure, however, you would need to rewrite the routines that apply a transformation matrix to the points. For a program with lots of surface data, this additional effort might be worth the space saved. In most cases, however, it is better to reuse the existing subroutines rather than creating a whole new set of routines to debug and maintain.

The Grid3d class contains methods that make transforming and drawing the grid easy. The Apply method applies a transformation matrix to the surface. ApplyFull applies a matrix, such as a parallel projection matrix, that may not contain 0, 0, 0, 1 in its final column. The Draw method displays the transformed grid coordinates on a PictureBox.

Example program Surface1 uses the Grid3d class to display several different kinds of surfaces. Use the option buttons to select the surface you want to display. Use the arrow keys to display the surface from different angles.

Refined Grids

In some cases, you can increase the number points you plot between the key locations in a grid. For instance, suppose you have a grid with X and Z values spaced one unit apart. In a normal grid, you would draw a line segment between the point (x1, y1, z1) and (x1 + 1, y2, z1). If you can calculate the extra data value, you can insert a new point at position (x1 + 0.5, y3, z1). This extra point breaks the original line segment into two segments that follow the surface more closely. You still draw the same number of curves parallel to the X and Z axes, but the curves contain more data points, so they represent the surface more accurately.

Figure 14.4 shows a diagram of the X and Z coordinates used to draw a surface. You can think of these images as surfaces shown from directly above. The black dots indicate data points that are drawn to display the surface. The picture on the left connects each grid location as before. The picture on the right has one extra data point inserted between

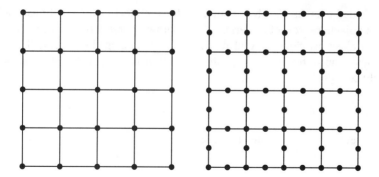

Figure 14.4 Data points used to display a grid (left) and a refined grid (right).

each pair of adjacent grid locations. This makes the drawing on the right follow the surface more precisely.

Figure 14.5 shows three pictures of the same surface. The picture on the left does not use enough data points to follow the surface closely, particularly at the base of the hemisphere.

The middle picture uses twice as many data points, so it follows the surface more closely. This picture does a better job of accurately portraying the surface, but it is cluttered with lines. If there were other objects in the picture, it would be hard to see any that were behind this object.

The picture on the right uses the same number of curves as the one on the left, but it places five intermediate data points between each pair of grid locations. This makes the drawing follow the surface very closely without becoming cluttered.

The easiest way to create this kind of refined grid in Visual Basic is to create a Polyline3d object for each of the curves parallel to the X and Z axes. The Polyline3d class represents a series of points that should be connected and is described in Chapter 13, Three-Dimensional Transformations.

Where a refined grid's curves intersect, the polylines store duplicate information, so this method wastes a little space. If the number of points between grid locations is relatively large, however, the amount of space wasted is only a small percentage of the total space needed. Using polylines in this way also allows you to build refined grids using existing tools rather than by creating a whole new class with new subroutines to debug and maintain.

Figure 14.5 A grid (left), grid with more points (middle), and a refined grid (right).

The RefinedGrid3d class is simply a container for a collection of Polyline3d objects. Each of these objects represents a series of lines drawn parallel to the X or Z axis. The RefinedGrid3d class provides several methods for managing the Polyline3d objects. These methods simply iterate through the collection of Polyline3d objects, passing requests to those objects.

```
Option Explicit

' The collection of Polyline3d objects.
Public Polylines As Collection

' Create the empty Polylines collection.
Private Sub Class_Initialize()
    Set Polylines = New Collection
End Sub

' Apply a transformation matrix which may not
' contain 0, 0, 0, 1 in the last column to the
' object.
Public Sub ApplyFull(M() As Single)
Dim pline As Polyline3d

    For Each pline In Polylines
        pline.ApplyFull M
    Next pline
End Sub

' Apply a transformation matrix to the object.
Public Sub Apply(M() As Single)
Dim pline As Polyline3d

    For Each pline In Polylines
        pline.Apply M
    Next pline
End Sub

' Draw the transformed points on a PictureBox.
Public Sub Draw(ByVal pic As Object)
Dim pline As Polyline3d

    For Each pline In Polylines
        pline.Draw pic
    Next pline
End Sub
```

Example program Surface2 uses the following code to initialize its surface data. The YValue function returns the Y coordinate for a surface for given X and Z coordinates. Program Surface2 displays the same surfaces shown by program Surface1. Surface2's grid uses fewer curves that contain more data points.

```
' Create the surface.
Private Sub CreateData()
Const Subdivisions = 3
Const MajorDx = 0.6
Const MajorDz = 0.6
Const MinorDx = MajorDx / Subdivisions
Const MinorDz = MajorDz / Subdivisions
Const NumX = -2 * Xmin / MajorDx
Const NumZ = -2 * Zmin / MajorDz

Dim i As Integer
Dim j As Integer
Dim k As Integer
Dim X As Single
Dim Y As Single
Dim Z As Single
Dim x1 As Single
Dim y1 As Single
Dim z1 As Single
Dim x2 As Single
Dim y2 As Single
Dim z2 As Single
Dim pline As Polyline3d

    Set TheGrid = New RefinedGrid3d

    SphereRadius = (Xmin + 3 * MajorDx) * (Xmin + 3 * MajorDx)

    ' Make polylines parallel to the X axis.
    X = Xmin
    For i = 1 To NumX
        Set pline = New Polyline3d
        z1 = Zmin
        ' Get the starting point.
        y1 = YValue(X, z1)
        For j = 1 To NumZ - 1
            For k = 1 To Subdivisions
                z2 = z1 + MinorDz
                y2 = YValue(X, z2)
                pline.AddSegment X, y1, z1, X, y2, z2
                y1 = y2
                z1 = z2
            Next k
        Next j
        TheGrid.Polylines.Add pline

        X = X + MajorDx
    Next i

    ' Make polylines parallel to the Z axis.
    Z = Zmin
```

```
    For i = 1 To NumZ
        Set pline = New Polyline3d
        x1 = Xmin
        ' Get the starting point.
        y1 = YValue(x1, Z)
        For j = 1 To NumX - 1
            For k = 1 To Subdivisions
                x2 = x1 + MinorDx
                y2 = YValue(x2, Z)
                pline.AddSegment x1, y1, Z, x2, y2, Z
                y1 = y2
                x1 = x2
            Next k
        Next j
        TheGrid.Polylines.Add pline

        Z = Z + MajorDz
    Next i
End Sub
```

There is one main drawback to the refined grid method. If you look too closely at part of the surface that is changing rapidly, the segments connecting two grid locations may appear to stick up beyond the surface. Figure 14.6 shows this sort of area highlighted.

Irregular Grids

If the surface you want to display is generated from experimental or observed data, you may not have all the values you would like. You may be missing some values in the middle of a region, or you may have data for only a few positions scattered throughout a large area.

One way you can display this sort of surface is to estimate the missing values in the grid. To make managing this kind of sparse grid easier, you can create a SparseGrid3d class. This class contains the actual data values, plus a grid object to display a surface approximating those values. You can store the data values in an array of Point3D structures.

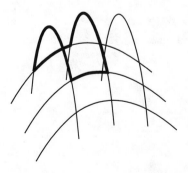

Figure 14.6   In a refined grid, curves may appear to stick up above the surface.

```
Private TheGrid As Grid3d    ' The display grid.

Private NumPts As Integer    ' # actual data values.
Private Data() As Point3D     ' Actual data values.
```

You can use a couple of methods to generate grid data using the incomplete data values you have available. The first method is to simply use the data value that is closest to the position you need. For each location (a, b) where you want a data value in the grid, find the data point (x, y, z) where $(a - x)^2 + (b - z)^2$ is smallest. Use that data point's Y value for the grid value at (a, b).

The NearestPoint subroutine shown in the following code simply looks through the array of data values to find the one that is closest to a given point. For very large data sets, you could make this search faster using the quadtree techniques described in Chapter 12, Two-Dimensional Transformations.

```
' Return the index of the closest data point.
Private Function NearestPoint(ByVal X As Single, _
    ByVal Z As Single) As Integer
Dim i As Integer
Dim best_i As Integer
Dim best_dist2 As Single
Dim diffx As Single
Dim diffz As Single
Dim dist2 As Single

    ' Start with no data point.
    best_i = 0
    best_dist2 = 1E+30

    ' See which points are closer.
    For i = 1 To NumPts
        ' See if this point is closer than the ones
        ' already chosen.
        diffx = X - Data(i).coord(1)
        diffz = Z - Data(i).coord(3)
        dist2 = diffx * diffx + diffz * diffz
        If dist2 < best_dist2 Then
            best_i = i
            best_dist2 = dist2
        End If
    Next i

    NearestPoint = best_i
End Function
```

The InitializeGrid subroutine provided by the SparseGrid3d class uses NearestPoint to set points in the display grid. First, it examines the data to find the largest and smallest X and Z values. It creates the display grid object and gives it appropriate data bounds.

The routine then uses NearestPoint to locate the data value nearest to each of the points in the grid. It sets the grid value equal to that data point's Y value.

```vb
' Create the grid values for display.
'
' Dx and Dz tell how far apart to make the grid
' lines.
Public Sub InitializeGrid(ByVal Dx As Single, _
    ByVal Dz As Single)
Dim Xmin As Single
Dim Xmax As Single
Dim Zmin As Single
Dim Zmax As Single
Dim NumX As Integer
Dim NumZ As Integer
Dim wid As Single
Dim hgt As Single
Dim i As Integer
Dim j As Integer
Dim X As Single
Dim Y As Single
Dim Z As Single
Dim best_i As Integer

    ' Find the X and Z data bounds.
    Xmin = Data(1).coord(1)
    Xmax = Xmin
    Zmin = Data(1).coord(3)
    Zmax = Zmin
    For i = 2 To NumPts
        If Xmin > Data(i).coord(1) Then _
            Xmin = Data(i).coord(1)
        If Xmax < Data(i).coord(1) Then _
            Xmax = Data(i).coord(1)
        If Zmin > Data(i).coord(3) Then _
            Zmin = Data(i).coord(3)
        If Zmax < Data(i).coord(3) Then _
            Zmax = Data(i).coord(3)
    Next i

    ' Set the data boundaries.
    wid = Xmax - Xmin
    hgt = Zmax - Zmin
    NumX = wid / Dx + 1
    NumZ = hgt / Dz + 1
    X = (wid - NumX * Dx) / 2
    Z = (hgt - NumZ * Dz) / 2
    Xmin = Xmin - X
    Xmax = Xmax + X
    Zmin = Zmin - Z
    Zmax = Zmax + Z
```

```
' Create the new grid object.
Set TheGrid = New Grid3d
TheGrid.SetBounds Xmin, Dx, NumX, Zmin, Dz, NumZ

' Fill in data values.
X = Xmin
For i = 1 To NumX
    Z = Zmin
    For j = 1 To NumZ
        ' Find the closest data value.
        best_i = NearestPoint(X, Z)

        ' Add the value to the grid.
        TheGrid.SetValue X, Data(best_i).coord(2), Z
        Z = Z + Dz
    Next j
    X = X + Dx
Next i
End Sub
```

Example program Surface3 uses the SparseGrid3d class to display a surface that approximates incomplete data. Use the option buttons to select a surface type. The program randomly picks several hundred X and Z values on the surface within the region -5 <= X <= 5, -5 <= Z <= 5. It stores those data values in a SparseGrid3d object.

Next, the program invokes the object's InitializeGrid routine to create and initialize the display grid. The program then uses the object's Draw method to make the SparseGrid3d display the data.

Figure 14.7 shows a grid approximating a set of data randomly chosen from the values displayed in Figure 14.2. The surface shown in Figure 14.7 follows the general shape of the data, but it is quite blocky. As you move through the display grid's X and Z coordinates, the nearest data value suddenly jumps from one value to another. Because you use only the nearest data value to set the grid values, the grid values also jump suddenly, creating steep slopes and artificial flat surfaces that are probably not part of the true data. You can reduce the effects of these sudden jumps by initializing the grid data in a different way.

Instead of considering only the data value nearest to each grid position, consider several values and take a weighted average. The version of the subroutine InitializeGrid that follows begins as before, finding bounds for the data, creating the display grid object, and setting its data bounds.

Then, for each grid location, the routine locates the four closest data points to the upper left, upper right, lower left, and lower right of the grid location. This gives the routine data values that surround the grid location's value.

Sometimes one or two of these surrounding values will be missing. If the grid location is at the left edge of the data, there will be no data values to the upper left or lower left of the grid location. Still, for most grid locations, this method gives several points surrounding the target location.

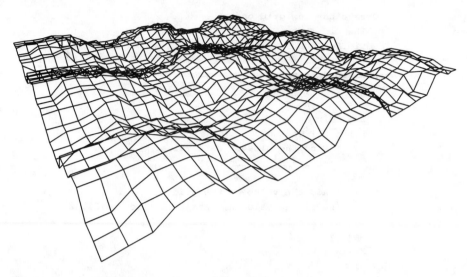

Figure 14.7 A grid approximating an incomplete data set.

Next, InitializeGrid calls the routine WeightedAverage to compute a weighted average of the values found in the previous step. Suppose the four nearest data points have coordinates (x1, y1, z1), ..., (x4, y4, z4). Let d1, d2, d3, and d4 be the squares of the distances from those points to the grid location of interest in the X-Z plane. For instance, if the grid point is at (x, z), then $d1 = (x - x1)^2 + (z - z1)^2$. Routine WeightedAverage sets the Y value at the grid location to be:

```
(y1 * d2 * d3 * d4 +
 y2 * d1 * d3 * d4 +
 y3 * d1 * d2 * d4 +
 y4 * d1 * d2 * d3) /
(d2 * d3 * d4 +
 d1 * d3 * d4 +
 d1 * d2 * d4 +
 d1 * d2 * d3)
```

This weighted average has two important properties. First, as one of the distances di approaches zero, the value of y approaches the corresponding data value yi. For example, if d1 is close to zero, then the equation above is close to:

```
(y1 * d2 * d3 * d4)/(d2 * d3 * d4) = y1
```

This property is important because it means a grid point close to an actual data point gets a Y value close to the actual data point's Y value.

The second property of this weighted average is that it emphasizes closer points heavily. By using the squares of the distances in its calculations, the routine gives nearby data points much greater weight than points farther away. This is particularly important when one of the data points is very far from the grid location. In that case, the value at that location is deemphasized so that it cannot influence the result too greatly.

```
' Create the grid values for display.
'
' Dx and Dz tell how far apart to make the grid
' lines.
Public Sub InitializeGrid(ByVal Dx As Single, _
    ByVal Dz As Single)
Dim Xmin As Single
Dim Xmax As Single
Dim Zmin As Single
Dim Zmax As Single
Dim NumX As Integer
Dim NumZ As Integer
Dim wid As Single
Dim hgt As Single
Dim i As Integer
Dim j As Integer
Dim X As Single
Dim Y As Single
Dim Z As Single
Dim best_i(1 To 4) As Integer
Dim num_close As Integer

    ' Find the X and Z data bounds.
    Xmin = Data(1).coord(1)
    Xmax = Xmin
    Zmin = Data(1).coord(3)
    Zmax = Zmin
    For i = 2 To NumPts
        If Xmin > Data(i).coord(1) Then _
            Xmin = Data(i).coord(1)
        If Xmax < Data(i).coord(1) Then _
            Xmax = Data(i).coord(1)
        If Zmin > Data(i).coord(3) Then _
            Zmin = Data(i).coord(3)
        If Zmax < Data(i).coord(3) Then _
            Zmax = Data(i).coord(3)
    Next i

    ' Set the data boundaries.
    wid = Xmax - Xmin
    hgt = Zmax - Zmin
    NumX = wid / Dx + 1
    NumZ = hgt / Dz + 1
    X = (wid - NumX * Dx) / 2
    Z = (hgt - NumZ * Dz) / 2
    Xmin = Xmin - X
    Xmax = Xmax + X
```

```vb
        Zmin = Zmin - Z
        Zmax = Zmax + Z

        ' Create the new grid object.
        Set TheGrid = New Grid3d
        TheGrid.SetBounds Xmin, Dx, NumX, Zmin, Dz, NumZ

        ' Fill in data values.
        X = Xmin
        For i = 1 To NumX
            Z = Zmin
            For j = 1 To NumZ
                    ' Find close points to the upper left,
                    ' upper right, lower left, and lower
                    ' right. Average them.
                    num_close = 1
                    best_i(num_close) = NearestPoint( _
                        X, Z, True, True)
                    If best_i(num_close) > 0 Then _
                        num_close = num_close + 1

                    best_i(num_close) = NearestPoint( _
                        X, Z, True, False)
                    If best_i(num_close) > 0 Then _
                        num_close = num_close + 1

                    best_i(num_close) = NearestPoint( _
                        X, Z, False, True)
                    If best_i(num_close) > 0 Then _
                        num_close = num_close + 1

                    best_i(num_close) = NearestPoint( _
                        X, Z, False, False)
                    If best_i(num_close) > 0 Then _
                        num_close = num_close + 1

                    Y = WeightedAverage(X, Z, best_i, num_close - 1)

                    ' Add the value to the grid.
                    TheGrid.SetValue X, Y, Z
                    Z = Z + Dz
            Next j
            X = X + Dx
        Next i
End Sub


' Return a weighted average for this point's value.
Private Function WeightedAverage(ByVal X As Single, _
    ByVal Z As Single, best_i() As Integer, _
    ByVal num As Integer) As Single
Dim i As Integer
```

```
Dim j As Integer
Dim diffx As Single
Dim diffz As Single
Dim dist2(1 To 4) As Single
Dim wgt As Single
Dim tot As Single
Dim Y As Single

    ' Compute the distance squared to each point.
    For i = 1 To num
        diffx = X - Data(best_i(i)).coord(1)
        diffz = Z - Data(best_i(i)).coord(3)
        dist2(i) = diffx * diffx + diffz * diffz
        If dist2(i) = 0 Then
            Y = Data(best_i(i)).coord(2)
            Exit Function
        End If
    Next i

    ' Compute the contribution due to each point.
    Y = 0
    For i = 1 To num
        ' Compute the weight for point i.
        wgt = 1
        For j = 1 To num
            If j <> i Then
                wgt = wgt * dist2(j)
            End If
        Next j
        Y = Y + wgt * Data(best_i(i)).coord(2)
        tot = tot + wgt
    Next i

    WeightedAverage = Y / tot
End Function


' Return the index of the nearest point in the
' indicated direction.
Private Function NearestPoint(ByVal X As Single, _
    ByVal Z As Single, ByVal on_left As Boolean, _
    ByVal on_top As Boolean) As Integer
Dim i As Integer
Dim best_i As Integer
Dim best_dist2 As Single
Dim diffx As Single
Dim diffz As Single
Dim dist2 As Single

    ' Start with the first data point.
    best_i = 0
    best_dist2 = 1E+30
```

```
    ' See which points are closer.
    For i = 1 To NumPts
        ' See if the point satisfies on_left/on_top.
        If CBool(X < Data(i).coord(1)) = on_left And _
            CBool(Z > Data(i).coord(3)) = on_top Then

            ' See if this point is closer than the
            ' best one so far.
            diffx = X - Data(i).coord(1)
            diffz = Z - Data(i).coord(3)
            dist2 = diffx * diffx + diffz * diffz
            If dist2 < best_dist2 Then
                best_i = i
                best_dist2 = dist2
            End If
        End If
    Next i

    NearestPoint = best_i
End Function
```

Example program Surface4 uses the WeightedGrid3d class to approximate a surface with missing data values. The results are much smoother than those generated by program Surface3. Figure 14.8 shows a grid approximating a set of data randomly chosen from the values displayed in Figure 14.2. This is a much better approximation than the one shown in Figure 14.7.

Figure 14.9 shows approximations for two other surfaces. The pictures on the left show the true surfaces from which sample data was randomly selected. The middle pictures show an approximation to the sample data using the data point nearest to each grid location. The pictures on the right show approximations using weighted averages.

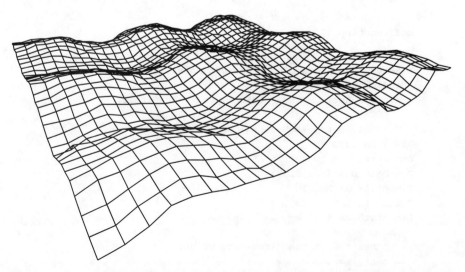

Figure 14.8   A grid approximating an incomplete data set using weighted averages.

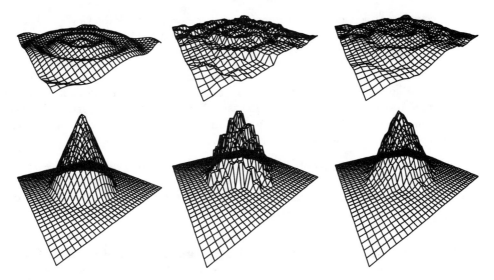

Figure 14.9   Comparing approximations for two data sets.

The Hi-Lo Algorithm

The Hi-Lo algorithm is a specialized technique for performing hidden surface removal for simple surfaces. By removing hidden surfaces from a picture, you can make it more realistic and easier to understand.

The basic idea behind the Hi-Lo algorithm is to draw the bent rectangles that make up the surface in order, starting with the areas closest to the center of projection, and working back toward the furthest.

Suppose you want to draw a surface like the one shown in Figure 14.10. In this picture, the center of projection lies between the positive X and Z axes. The direction of projection points back toward the origin. With the center of projection in this position, the edges of the surface with the largest X and Z values contain points that are relatively close to the

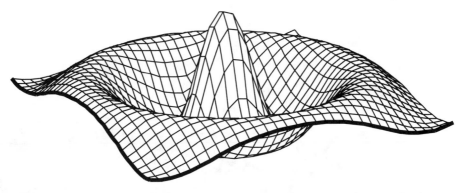

Figure 14.10   The front edges of a surface (heavy lines) are not obscured by the rest of the surface.

center of projection. Other parts of the surface cannot block the view of these edges, so you know that these edges should be drawn. In Figure 14.10 these two edges are drawn with heavy lines.

Once you have drawn the front edges, you can begin drawing the bent rectangles that make up the rest of the surface. You can draw them ordered by their X and Z values, with rows of "rectangles" having the same X values drawn first. Figure 14.11 shows the same surface as Figure 14.10, with the first row and part of the second outlined with heavy lines to show you the order in which they should be drawn.

Because each area you draw has larger X or Z values than all of the areas you have not yet drawn, you know that the undrawn areas cannot obscure the one you are drawing. If you follow the pattern of drawing areas in Figure 14.11, you will find that some areas are obscured by areas you have already drawn. None is covered by an area that you will draw later, however.

To make this drawing method into a hidden surface removal algorithm, you still need to take into account the cases in which an area you draw later is covered by one you have already drawn. This is where the "Hi-Lo" comes in. To keep track of the parts of the screen that are already covered by an area, you create two arrays: hi and lo. For each X value in your projected surface, the lo entry records the smallest Y coordinate value used so far on the screen. The corresponding hi entry records the greatest Y value used so far on the screen.

As you prepare to display a new area, you check to see if the points you need to draw fall between the array values lo and hi. If you need to plot the point (a, b) on the screen, for example, you check to see if lo(a) <= b <= hi(a). If so, the point (a, b) is obscured by a previously drawn area, so you do not draw the point.

In practice, it is faster to examine the line segments that define a region than to examine all the points it contains. To draw a line segment, start at one of the segment's endpoints. Move along the segment, one X coordinate value at a time, checking to see if the segment has moved into or out of the range spanned by the hi and lo values. Draw the portions of the segment that are visible. Whenever you find a point that lies above the corresponding hi value, update hi to have the new value. Similarly, when you find a point that lies below the corresponding lo value, update lo to have the new value.

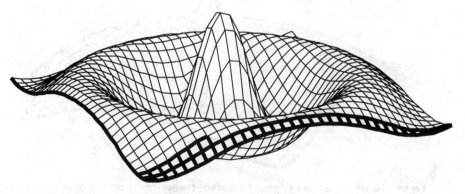

Figure 14.11 In the Hi-Lo algorithm, areas are drawn from front to back.

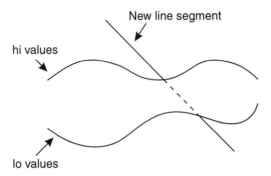

hi values

New line segment

lo values

Figure 14.12 Line segments are hidden where they lie between the hi and lo values.

Figure 14.12 shows a line segment and the lo and hi values already displayed. In this case, you would draw the two end portions of the segment, where the segment does not lie between the hi and lo values. The part of the segment that you should not draw is shown with a dashed line in Figure 14.12. Note that the segment could be completely visible or completely obscured, or it could have several visible and hidden regions, depending on the particular segment and the values in the hi and lo arrays.

Implementing the Hi-Lo Algorithm

The following code implements the Hi-Lo algorithm. Subroutine DrawWithoutHidden controls the operation. It begins by calling subroutine DrawAndSetLine to draw the front edges of the surface.

Subroutine DrawAndSetLine draws the edges of the surface without checking the hi and lo arrays. It also initializes those arrays so that the hi and lo values equal the values displayed by the routine.

After drawing the front edges, DrawWithoutHidden uses subroutine DrawLine to draw the rest of the segments that make up the surface. DrawLine uses the hi and lo arrays to draw the visible portions of line segments. When it draws parts of a line, it updates the hi and lo arrays.

```
' Draw the grid without hidden surfaces using the
' Hi-Lo algorithm.
Public Sub DrawWithoutHidden(ByVal pic As Object, _
    Optional R As Variant)
Dim Xmin As Integer
Dim Xmax As Integer
Dim lo() As Integer
Dim hi() As Integer
Dim ix As Integer
Dim i As Integer
Dim j As Integer
```

```
' Bound the X values.
Xmin = Points(1, 1).trans(1)
Xmax = Xmin
For i = 1 To NumX
    For j = 1 To NumZ
        ix = CInt(Points(i, j).trans(1))
        If Xmin > ix Then Xmin = ix
        If Xmax < ix Then Xmax = ix
    Next j
Next i

' Create the hi and lo arrays.
ReDim lo(Xmin To Xmax)
ReDim hi(Xmin To Xmax)

' Draw the X and Z front edges.
For i = 2 To NumX
    ' Draw the edge between
    ' Points(i - 1, NumZ) and Points(i, NumZ)
    ' and set hi and lo for its values.
    DrawAndSetLine pic, _
        Points(i - 1, NumZ).trans(1), _
        Points(i - 1, NumZ).trans(2), _
        Points(i, NumZ).trans(1), _
        Points(i, NumZ).trans(2), _
        hi, lo
Next i
For i = 2 To NumZ
    ' Draw the edge between
    ' Points(NumX, i - 1) and Points(NumX, i)
    ' and set hi and lo for its values.
    DrawAndSetLine pic, _
        Points(NumX, i - 1).trans(1), _
        Points(NumX, i - 1).trans(2), _
        Points(NumX, i).trans(1), _
        Points(NumX, i).trans(2), _
        hi, lo
Next i

' Draw the "rectangles."
For i = NumX - 1 To 1 Step -1
    For j = NumZ - 1 To 1 Step -1
        ' Draw the edges between:
        '    Points(i, j) and Points(i + 1, j)
        '    Points(i, j) and Points(i, j + 1)

        ' If the right side of the "rectangle"
        ' leans over the top like this:
        '    +_
        '    | \_
        '    |   \_
```

```
'     +        \_
'       \        \
'        +------+
' draw the top first so the right side
' doesn't make hi() too bit and stop
' the top from being drawn.
'
' This only happens with perspective
' projection.
If Points(i + 1, j).trans(1) >= _
    Points(i, j).trans(1) _
Then
    DrawLine pic, _
        Points(i, j).trans(1), _
        Points(i, j).trans(2), _
        Points(i, j + 1).trans(1), _
        Points(i, j + 1).trans(2), _
        hi, lo
    DrawLine pic, _
        Points(i, j).trans(1), _
        Points(i, j).trans(2), _
        Points(i + 1, j).trans(1), _
        Points(i + 1, j).trans(2), _
        hi, lo
Else
    DrawLine pic, _
        Points(i, j).trans(1), _
        Points(i, j).trans(2), _
        Points(i + 1, j).trans(1), _
        Points(i + 1, j).trans(2), _
        hi, lo
    DrawLine pic, _
        Points(i, j).trans(1), _
        Points(i, j).trans(2), _
        Points(i, j + 1).trans(1), _
        Points(i, j + 1).trans(2), _
        hi, lo
End If
            Next j
        Next i
End Sub


' Draw a line between the points. Set the hi and
' lo values for the line.
Private Sub DrawAndSetLine(ByVal pic As PictureBox, _
    ByVal x1 As Single, ByVal y1 As Single, _
    ByVal x2 As Single, ByVal y2 As Single, _
    hi() As Integer, lo() As Integer)
Dim tmp As Single
Dim ix As Integer
Dim iy As Integer
```

```vb
Dim Y As Single
Dim dy As Single

    ' Deal only with integers.
    x1 = CInt(x1)
    y1 = CInt(y1)
    x2 = CInt(x2)
    y2 = CInt(y2)

    ' Make x1 < x2.
    If x2 < x1 Then
        tmp = x1
        x1 = x2
        x2 = tmp
        tmp = y1
        y1 = y2
        y2 = tmp
    End If

    ' Draw the line.
    pic.Line (x1, y1)-(x2, y2)

    ' Deal with vertical lines separately.
    If x1 = x2 Then
        If y1 < y2 Then
            lo(x1) = y1
            hi(x1) = y2
        Else
            lo(x1) = y2
            hi(x1) = y1
        End If
        Exit Sub
    End If

    ' Deal with non-vertical lines.
    dy = (y2 - y1) / CInt(x2 - x1)
    Y = y1
    For ix = x1 To x2
        iy = CInt(Y)

        lo(ix) = iy
        hi(ix) = iy

        Y = Y + dy
    Next ix
End Sub

' Draw a line between the points using and
' updating the hi and lo arrays.
Private Sub DrawLine(ByVal pic As PictureBox, _
    ByVal x1 As Single, ByVal y1 As Single, _
```

```
        ByVal x2 As Single, ByVal y2 As Single, _
        hi() As Integer, lo() As Integer)
Dim tmp As Single
Dim ix As Integer
Dim iy As Integer
Dim Y As Single
Dim dy As Single
Dim firstx As Integer
Dim firsty As Integer
Dim skipping As Boolean
Dim above As Boolean

    ' Deal only with integers.
    x1 = CInt(x1)
    y1 = CInt(y1)
    x2 = CInt(x2)
    y2 = CInt(y2)

    ' Make x1 < x2.
    If x2 < x1 Then
        tmp = x1
        x1 = x2
        x2 = tmp
        tmp = y1
        y1 = y2
        y2 = tmp
    End If

    ' Deal with vertical lines separately.
    If x1 = x2 Then
        ' Make y1 < y2.
        If y2 < y1 Then
            tmp = y1
            y1 = y2
            y2 = tmp
        End If
        If y1 <= lo(x1) Then
            If y2 <= lo(x1) Then
                pic.Line (x1, y1)-(x2, y2)
            Else
                pic.Line (x1, y1)-(x2, lo(x2))
            End If
            lo(x1) = y1
        End If
        If y2 >= hi(x2) Then
            If y1 >= hi(x2) Then
                pic.Line (x1, y1)-(x2, y2)
            Else
                pic.Line (x1, hi(x1))-(x2, y2)
            End If
            hi(x2) = y2
```

```
        End If
        Exit Sub
End If


' Deal with non-vertical lines.
dy = (y2 - y1) / CInt(x2 - x1)
Y = y1


' Find the first visible point.
skipping = True
For ix = x1 To x2
    iy = CInt(Y)
    ' See if this point is visible.
    If iy <= lo(ix) Then
        If skipping Then
            ' Start a new line below.
            skipping = False
            above = False
            firstx = ix
            firsty = lo(ix)
        End If
    ElseIf iy >= hi(ix) Then
        If skipping Then
            ' Start a new line above.
            skipping = False
            above = True
            firstx = ix
            firsty = hi(ix)
        End If
    Else
        ' This point is not visible.
        If Not skipping Then
            ' Draw the previous visible line.
            If above Then
                ' The line is coming from
                ' above. Connect it to hi(ix).
                pic.Line (firstx, firsty)-(ix, hi(ix))
            Else
                ' The line is coming from
                ' below. Connect it to lo(ix).
                pic.Line (firstx, firsty)-(ix, lo(ix))
            End If

            skipping = True
        End If
    End If

    If iy < lo(ix) Then lo(ix) = iy
    If iy > hi(ix) Then hi(ix) = iy

    Y = Y + dy
Next ix
```

```
' Draw to the last point if necessary.
If Not skipping Then _
    pic.Line (firstx, firsty)-(x2, y2)
End Sub
```

Example program HiLo uses the HiLoGrid3d class to display surfaces with hidden lines removed. Use the option buttons to select the surface you want to display. Use the Remove Hidden check box to tell the program whether it should display the hidden portions of the surface.

Restrictions

In order for the Hi-Lo algorithm to work correctly, your program must meet a couple of constraints. First, the object you display must be a surface defined by a grid. The Hi-Lo algorithm uses the ordering imposed on the data by the grid to display the areas in the correct order. The algorithm will not work as it is described here for displaying other objects such as cubes and spheres. More general algorithms that handle these cases are described in later chapters.

Second, the algorithm is not guaranteed to work with perspective projections. In a perspective projection, the area you are drawing can sometimes be obscured by an area that you draw later. The front edges of the surface are not always visible. The picture on the left in Figure 14.13 shows a parallel projection of a surface with hidden surfaces removed. The edges with the largest X and Z coordinates are drawn in heavy lines. The picture on the right shows a perspective projection of the same surface with the same direction of projection. Because the center of projection is quite close to the surface, foreshortening makes closer regions much larger than those further from the center of projection. Some of the closer regions obscure parts of the front edge that have the largest Z values.

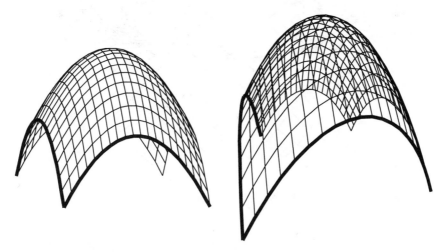

Figure 14.13 The Hi-Lo algorithm works for parallel projections (left) but not all perspective projections.

On the other hand, the Hi-Lo algorithm often produces fine results, even for perspective projections. As long as the center of projection is not too close to the surface and does not lie too close to either the X-Y or Y-Z plane, the Hi-Lo algorithm may produce correct results. Figure 14.14 shows a perspective projection of a surface in which the Hi-Lo algorithm works correctly.

Finally, the code presented earlier works only when the corner of the surface with the largest X and Z values is closest to the center of projection. You can write similar code to handle viewing from other directions. It may be easier, however, to apply a transformation to your data to rotate the surface rather than move the center of projection.

The Z-Order Algorithm

The Hi-Lo algorithm uses two arrays to ensure that it never draws a line that will later be obscured by another part of the surface. This is very important when you are drawing on a plotter or other device that cannot erase. It is also important if you want to save a drawing in a metafile. Using the Hi-Lo algorithm ensures that any application that imports the metafile will display it correctly. For some complex surfaces, the algorithm may also remove a lot of data, substantially reducing the size of the metafile.

While plotters cannot erase, computer monitors can. The Z-Order algorithm uses that fact to draw surfaces with hidden lines removed in a remarkably simple way.

The Hi-Lo algorithm draws a surface's "rectangles" in order from front to back. Since one of these areas cannot be obscured by one that will be drawn later, the program can tell which parts of each area are visible.

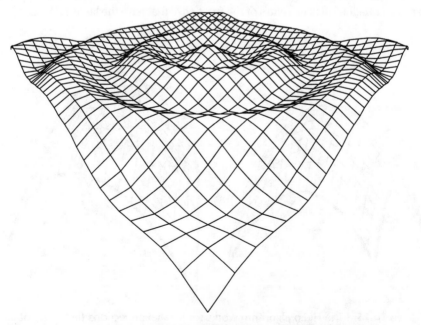

Figure 14.14 The Hi-Lo algorithm works for some perspective projections.

The Z-Order algorithm takes the opposite approach. It draws the areas in order from back to front. When drawn in this order, an area can obscure only an area that has been drawn before it. When it draws an area, the program fills it so that it covers up any lines that it should obscure.

The following code shows how a program can draw the areas that make up a surface in the correct order if the center of projection lies between the positive X and Z axes.

```vb
Private Type POINTAPI
    X As Long
    Y As Long
End Type
Private Declare Function Polygon Lib "gdi32" ( _
    ByVal hdc As Long, lpPoint As POINTAPI, _
    ByVal nCount As Long) As Long


' Draw the transformed points on a PictureBox.
Public Sub Draw(ByVal pic As Object)
Dim i As Integer
Dim j As Integer
Dim api_points(1 To 4) As POINTAPI

    On Error Resume Next

    ' See if we should fill the "rectangles."
    If RemoveHidden Then
        pic.FillStyle = vbFSSolid
        pic.FillColor = vbWhite
    Else
        pic.FillStyle = vbFSTransparent
    End If

    ' Draw the "rectangles."
    For i = 1 To NumX - 1
        For j = 1 To NumZ - 1
            ' Load the POINTAPI array.
            With api_points(1)
                .X = points(i, j).trans(1)
                .Y = points(i, j).trans(2)
            End With
            With api_points(2)
                .X = points(i + 1, j).trans(1)
                .Y = points(i + 1, j).trans(2)
            End With
            With api_points(3)
                .X = points(i + 1, j + 1).trans(1)
                .Y = points(i + 1, j + 1).trans(2)
            End With
            With api_points(4)
                .X = points(i, j + 1).trans(1)
                .Y = points(i, j + 1).trans(2)
```

```
            End With

            Polygon pic.hdc, api_points(1), 4
        Next j
    Next i
End Sub
```

Example program ZOrder uses the ZOrderGrid3d class to display surfaces. Use the option buttons to select the surface you want to see. Use the check box to determine whether the program removes the hidden surfaces.

Fractal Surfaces

Using a straightforward fractal technique, you can turn a simple surface into an interesting, irregular terrain. Start with any simple surface modeled as a grid. Break each bent rectangle that makes up the surface into four smaller rectangles as shown on the left in Figure 14.15. Initially, set the Y coordinates of each of the five newly created points to be the averages of the surrounding points. For example, if y1 and y2 are the Y coordinates of two adjacent corners in the original rectangle, set the Y coordinate of the point between them to (y1 + y2)/2.

Next, modify each of the new Y coordinates by a small random amount. This gives you a set of four new bent rectangles like the ones shown on the right in Figure 14.15.

By breaking up all the regions representing the original surface, you create a new, slightly randomized surface containing four times as many regions. You can then recursively break up the new regions into smaller and smaller regions until you have reduced them to some acceptable size.

Figures 14.16 and 14.17 show surfaces that were created pseudo-randomly and drawn through use of the Hi-Lo algorithm. The data for Figure 14.16, for example, was created with code similar to the code that follows. The first Cos term gives the surface a ridge down the middle, parallel to the X axis. The next two Sin terms give the ridge some bumps of different sizes. The final Rnd term gives the basic surface a bit of randomness.

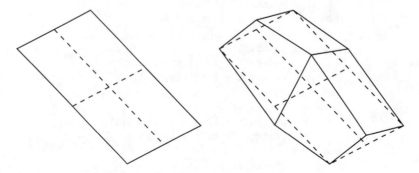

Figure 14.15   Subdividing a region on a surface.

```
X = Xmin
For i = 1 To NumX
    Z = Zmin
    For j = 1 To NumZ
        Y = 2 * Cos(2 * PI / 10 * z) * (5 - Abs(z)) / 5 + _
            0.25 * Sin(2 * x + x1) + _
            0.25 * Sin(1# * x + x1) + 0.5 * Rnd
        TheGrid.SetValue X, Y, Z
        Z = Z + Dz
    Next j
    X = X + Dx
Next i
```

Figures 14.18 and 14.19 show the resulting pictures after the grids have been subdivided three times. Because each subdivision increases the number of areas in the grid by a factor of four, these pictures contain $4^3 = 64$ times as many regions as the original grids. The underlying shape of the surfaces is determined by the original data shown in Figures 14.16 and 14.17. The subdivision of the grids adds further randomness to the surfaces and makes them look like surprisingly realistic mountain ranges.

Fractal Surfaces in Visual Basic

The FractalGrid3d class manages this kind of fractal surface. In most respects it behaves like the ZOrderGrid3d class. The major difference is that the FractalGrid3d class also includes routines to subdivide the grid randomly.

The GenerateSurface subroutine shown in the following code starts by resizing the Points array to make room for all the new data points it is about to generate. Next, it

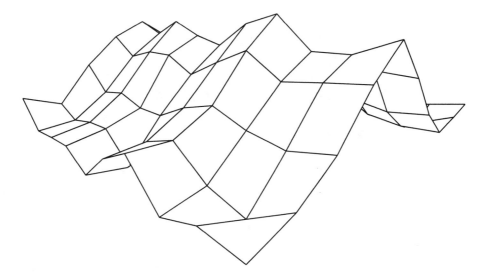

Figure 14.16   A simple, pseudo-random surface.

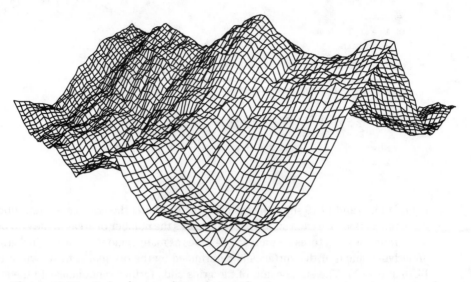

Figure 14.17 A simple, pseudo-random surface.

copies the original data points into their correct locations in the resized array. It then invokes subroutine Subdivide for each of the regions representing the original surface.

Subdivide breaks one of the surface's defining regions into four smaller regions, randomly adjusting each of the five new data points. It then recursively calls itself to divide the smaller regions if necessary.

The parameter Dy tells subroutine Subdivide the maximum amount by which it can adjust each of the new points. When the routine calls itself, it decreases Dy by a factor

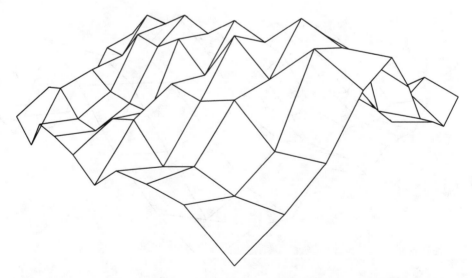

Figure 14.18 A fractal surface produced by subdividing the surface in Figure 14.16 three times.

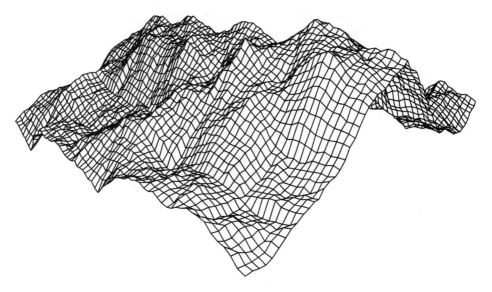

Figure 14.19   A fractal surface produced by subdividing the surface in Figure 14.17 three times.

of two. This allows random changes to be relatively large during the highest-level calls to Subdivide. As the regions are broken into smaller and smaller pieces, the amount of random change allowed is smaller. Changes during the higher-level calls set the general shape of the surface. Changes during the lower-level calls refine it.

```
' Generate the fractal surface.
Public Sub GenerateSurface(ByVal divisions As Integer, _
    ByVal Dy As Single)
Dim oldpoints() As Point3D
Dim oldx As Integer
Dim oldz As Integer
Dim factor As Integer
Dim newx As Integer
Dim newz As Integer
Dim i As Integer
Dim j As Integer
Dim newi As Integer
Dim newj As Integer

    ' Make room for the new data.
    factor = 2 ^ divisions
    newx = (NumX - 1) * factor + 1
    newz = (NumZ - 1) * factor + 1

    ' Copy the original data.
    ReDim oldpoints(1 To NumX, 1 To NumZ)
    For i = 1 To NumX
        For j = 1 To NumZ
```

```
                    oldpoints(i, j) = points(i, j)
            Next j
        Next i

        ' Resize and initialize the Points array.
        oldx = NumX
        oldz = NumZ
        SetBounds Xmin, Dx / factor, newx, _
                Zmin, Dz / factor, newz

        ' Move the old data to the new positions.
        newi = 1
        For i = 1 To oldx
            newj = 1
            For j = 1 To oldz
                points(newi, newj) = oldpoints(i, j)
                newj = newj + factor
            Next j
            newi = newi + factor
        Next i

        ' Subdivide each area in the data.
        newi = 1
        For i = 2 To oldx
            newj = 1
            For j = 2 To oldz
                Subdivide newi, newi + factor, _
                        newj, newj + factor, Dy
                newj = newj + factor
            Next j
            newi = newi + factor
        Next i
End Sub

' Recursively subdivide the indicated area.
Private Sub Subdivide(ByVal i1 As Integer, _
    ByVal i2 As Integer, ByVal j1 As Integer, _
    ByVal j2 As Integer, ByVal Dy As Single)
Dim y11 As Single
Dim y12 As Single
Dim y21 As Single
Dim y22 As Single
Dim imid As Integer
Dim jmid As Integer

        If (i2 - i1 <= 1) Or (j2 - j1 <= 1) Then Exit Sub

        ' Compute the midpoint locations.
        y11 = points(i1, j1).coord(2)
        y12 = points(i1, j2).coord(2)
        y21 = points(i2, j1).coord(2)
        y22 = points(i2, j2).coord(2)
```

```
        imid = (i1 + i2) \ 2
        jmid = (j1 + j2) \ 2
        points(i1, jmid).coord(2) = _
            (y11 + y12) / 2 + 2 * Dy * Rnd - Dy
        points(i2, jmid).coord(2) = _
            (y21 + y22) / 2 + 2 * Dy * Rnd - Dy
        points(imid, j1).coord(2) = _
            (y11 + y21) / 2 + 2 * Dy * Rnd - Dy
        points(imid, j2).coord(2) = _
            (y12 + y22) / 2 + 2 * Dy * Rnd - Dy
        points(imid, jmid).coord(2) = _
            (y11 + y12 + y21 + y22) / 4 + 2 * Dy * Rnd - Dy

    ' Recursively subdivide the four new areas.
        Subdivide i1, imid, j1, jmid, Dy / 2
        Subdivide imid, i2, j1, jmid, Dy / 2
        Subdivide i1, imid, jmid, j2, Dy / 2
        Subdivide imid, i2, jmid, j2, Dy / 2
    End Sub
```

Example program Fractal demonstrates the FractalGrid3d class. Use the option buttons to select a basic surface type. The program generates a rough grid to guide the development of the surface pseudo-randomly. It then uses the GenerateSurface subroutine to refine the grid. Click on the picture box and use the arrow keys to change the viewing direction.

Enter the level of recursion and the maximum amount of random change allowed in the text boxes. If you set the level of recursion to 0, the program displays a basic pseudo-random grid surface that has not been modified by the GenerateSurface routine. As you set the level of recursion to higher values, the program creates more refined surfaces. Be careful not to set the level of recursion too high until you know how long the program takes on your computer.

Example program Altitude uses similar techniques to display a colored surface. It creates a pseudo-random surface and displays it using the Z-Order algorithm much as program Fractal does. Before it fills each area, however, this program sets its fill color to a value that depends on the area's Y value. The colors are chosen from a smooth gradient with green for the smallest Y values and red for the largest. This display makes it easier to see the highest and lowest points on the surface.

Example program Valley, shown in Figure 14.20, uses similar code to create a moderately realistic valley scene. It begins with a pseudo-random valley shape and then makes some specialized adjustments. First it flattens the valley floor and carves a riverbed in it. It then displays the surface using the ZOrder algorithm but it colors the areas specially. It makes the low areas in the riverbed blue and it makes the highest areas white to simulate snow. The program colors steep areas gray to represent rock cliffs. It colors the remaining areas green, using different shades of green for different altitudes.

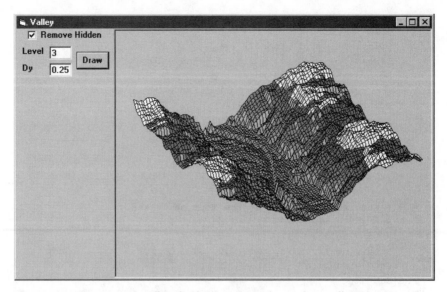

Figure 14.20   Program Valley displaying a pseudo-random valley scene.

Few people would be fooled into thinking the image produced by program Valley is a photograph of a real valley. At the same time, few people would have trouble understanding what the image represents, particularly in color.

Program Valley uses different color shades to make its image easier to understand. Chapter 16, Shading Models, extends these methods to produce more realistic images for objects other than surfaces.

Parametric Surfaces

Sometimes you might like to create a surface of a certain shape, but you do not know exactly what data points should make up the surface. For instance, you might like to create a shape like the one shown in Figure 14.21. Calculating where every point on this surface belonged would be quite tedious. Furthermore, this surface does not represent a simple function. For certain values of X and Z, this surface has more than one Y value. That means you cannot use the methods of the previous sections to store and display the data.

One way to represent this sort of surface is using a system of parametric equations. For variables u and v, these equations give the X, Y, and Z coordinates of points on the surface. Usually the equations are chosen so that the surface is traced out when the variables u and v run between 0.0 and 1.0. The two particular kinds of parametric curves described in the following sections are Bezier surfaces and B-splines. These surfaces are the three-dimensional counterparts of the Bezier curves and B-splines described in Chapter 11, Drawing Curves.

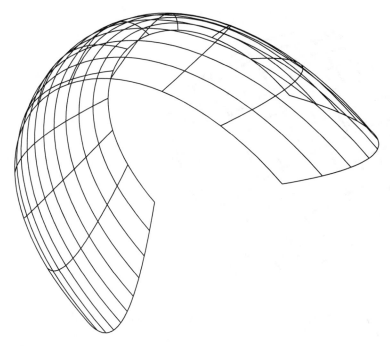

Figure 14.21   A complex surface.

Bezier Surfaces

Like their two-dimensional counterparts, Bezier surfaces are defined by a set of control points. The control points are arranged in a two-dimensional mesh that determines the approximate shape of the surface. Figure 14.22 shows a Bezier surface and its control points. The surface is shown in bold lines. The control points are drawn as large dots connected by fine lines showing which control points are adjacent in the mesh.

Notice that the control points touch the surface only at the surface's corners. The control points determine the overall shape of the surface, but the surface generally meets the control points only at the corners.

Suppose you have an M+1 by N+1 two-dimensional mesh of control points with coordinates stored in the arrays ControlX(0 To M, 0 To N), ControlY(0 To M, 0 To N), and ControlZ(0 To M, 0 To N). Then the X coordinates of the points on the Bezier surface are given by the equation:

```
          M   N
X(u, v) =  Σ   Σ   ControlX(i, j) * B_{i,M}(u) * B_{j,N}(v)
          i=0 j=0
```

where:

```
B_{i,M}(u) = M! / i! / (M - i)! * u^i * (1 - u)^{M-i}
```

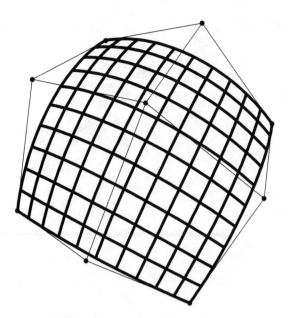

Figure 14.22 A Bezier surface (bold lines) with its control points (dots) and control grid (thin lines).

The $B_{i,M}$ equations are called the curve's *blending functions* because they blend different amounts of the coordinates of the control points as u and v take values between 0.0 and 1.0. The blending functions work much as they do for the two-dimensional Bezier curves described in Chapter 11, Drawing Curves.

Corner Points

Figure 14.22 shows a three-by-three control grid, so for that surface, M = 2 and N = 2. Consider what happens when u = 0 and v = 0. In that case the value of $B_{i,M}(u)$ when u = 0 is:

```
B_i,2(0) = 2! / i! / (2 - i)! * 0^i * (1 - 0)^2-i
         = 2! / i! / (2 - i)! * 0^i
```

Because the value of 0^0 is defined as 1, but $0^i = 0$ for i > 0, all of the $B_{i,M}$ terms have value zero except when i = 0. When i = 0, this equation becomes

```
B_0,2(0) = 2! / 0! / (2 - 0)! * 0^0 = 2! / 1 / 2! * 1 = 1
```

Similarly, when v = 0, the value of $B_{j,N}(v)$ is zero, unless j = 0, in which case $B_{j,N}(v) = 1$. That means every term in the summation has value zero except the first term where i = j = 0. Then the value for the X coordinate of the surface when u = v = 0 is:

```
X(0, 0) = ControlX(0, 0) * 1 * 1 = ControlX(0, 0)
```

If you compute the Y and Z coordinates of the surface in the same way, you will find that they are ControlY(0, 0) and ControlZ(0, 0). In other words, when u = v = 0, the surface coincides with the first point in the control grid. If you perform similar calculations for u = 0 and v = 1, u = 1 and v = 0, and u = 1 and v = 1, you will see that the equation includes only a single nonzero term in those cases as well. Those conditions make the surface match the control grid at all of its corners.

Interior Points

Now suppose u = 0 and v = 0.5. The values for $B_{i,M}$ are still 1 when i = 0 and 0 otherwise, so the equation for the surface's X coordinate becomes:

```
          M   N
 X(u, v) = Σ   Σ  ControlX(i, j) * B_i,M(u) * B_j,N(v)
          i=0 j=0

   = ControlX(0, 0) * 1 * (2! / 0! / (2 - 0)! * 0.5^0 * (1 - 0.5)^(2-0)) +
     ControlX(0, 1) * 1 * (2! / 1! / (2 - 1)! * 0.5^1 * (1 - 0.5)^(2-1)) +
     ControlX(0, 2) * 1 * (2! / 2! / (2 - 2)! * 0.5^2 * (1 - 0.5)^(2-2))

   = ControlX(0, 0) * 0.5^2 +
     ControlX(0, 1) * 2 * 0.5 * 0.5 +
     ControlX(0, 2) * 0.5^2 *

   = ControlX(0, 0) * 0.25 +
     ControlX(0, 1) * 0.5 +
     ControlX(0, 2) * 0.25
```

The coordinates of this point are given by a weighted average of the coordinates of the control points. Note that the middle control point is given a greater weight than the other two. This pulls the curve toward the middle control point, though the curve will generally not reach that point.

Similarly, other values of u and v give weighted averages of the control points. The result is a surface that follows the general shape of the control points, though it matches those points exactly only at the corners.

Displaying Bezier Curves

The classes described earlier in this chapter display a surface by drawing curves in the surface that have constant X or Z coordinates. Finding such curves in a Bezier surface is quite difficult. A Bezier surface may twist and turn in all sorts of strange directions that do not line up nicely with the coordinate axes.

A much easier method for displaying these surfaces is to draw curves in the surface with constant u and v parameter values. This method works well with a refined grid technique. For example, you could draw the curves where u = 0.0, 0.2, 0.4, ..., 1.0. For each of those curves, you could let v range from 0.0 to 1.0 in steps of 0.05.

The Bezier3d class stores and displays Bezier surfaces. This class holds the control point data in an array of the Point3D data type. Variables MaxU and MaxV hold the maximum values for u and v needed to draw the surface. The class provides a SetControlPoint method to initialize the control point coordinates.

After the control points are initialized, the InitializeGrid subroutine creates points on the surface and stores them in Polyline3d objects. To manipulate the data, the Bezier3dclass passes subroutine calls to these objects. For example, to apply a transformation matrix to the surface, the object calls the Apply method for each of its Polyline3d objects.

InitializeGrid calls the SurfaceValue subroutine to calculate the coordinates of points on the surface. Subroutine SurfaceValue uses the Bezier surface equations to calculate the X, Y, and Z coordinates of a point with particular u and v parameter values. The most interesting parts of the Bezier3d object are shown in the following code. You can see the rest of the code in the module Bezier.cls on the CD-ROM.

```
Private MaxU As Integer        ' Dimensions of control grid.
Private MaxV As Integer
Private Points() As Point3D ' Control points.

' Holds polylines containing the refined
' grid to display the surface.
Private Polylines As Collection

' u and v increment parameters.
Private GapU As Single
Private GapV As Single
Private Du As Single
Private Dv As Single

' Set MaxU and MaxV and allocate room for the
' control points.
Public Sub SetBounds(_
    ByVal NumX As Integer, ByVal NumZ As Integer)

    MaxU = NumX - 1
    MaxV = NumZ - 1
    ReDim Points(0 To NumX, 0 To NumZ)
End Sub

' Set the value for a control point.
Public Sub SetControlPoint( _
    ByVal i As Integer, ByVal j As Integer, _
    ByVal X As Single, ByVal Y As Single, ByVal Z As Single)

    Points(i - 1, j - 1).coord(1) = X
    Points(i - 1, j - 1).coord(2) = Y
    Points(i - 1, j - 1).coord(3) = Z
    Points(i - 1, j - 1).coord(4) = 1
End Sub
```

```
' Create polylines to represent the surface.
Public Sub InitializeGrid( _
    ByVal gap_x As Single, ByVal gap_z As Single, _
    ByVal d_x As Single, ByVal d_z As Single)
Dim u As Single
Dim v As Single
Dim X As Single
Dim Y As Single
Dim Z As Single
Dim x1 As Single
Dim y1 As Single
Dim z1 As Single
Dim pline As Polyline3d

    GapU = gap_x
    GapV = gap_z
    Du = d_x
    Dv = d_z

    Set Polylines = New Collection

    ' Create curves with constant u.
    For u = 0 To 1 + GapU / 10 Step GapU
        Set pline = New Polyline3d
        Polylines.Add pline

        SurfaceValue u, 0, x1, y1, z1

        For v = Dv To 1 + Dv / 10 Step Dv
            SurfaceValue u, v, X, Y, Z
            pline.AddSegment x1, y1, z1, X, Y, Z
            x1 = X
            y1 = Y
            z1 = Z
        Next v
    Next u

    ' Create curves with constant v.
    For v = 0 To 1 + GapV / 10 Step GapV
        Set pline = New Polyline3d
        Polylines.Add pline

        SurfaceValue 0, v, x1, y1, z1
        For u = Du To 1 + Du / 10 Step Du
            SurfaceValue u, v, X, Y, Z
            pline.AddSegment x1, y1, z1, X, Y, Z
            x1 = X
            y1 = Y
            z1 = Z
        Next u
    Next v
End Sub
```

```vb
' Return the (X, Y, Z) coordinates of the
' Bezier surface for these u and v values.
Private Sub SurfaceValue( _
    ByVal u As Single, ByVal v As Single, _
    ByRef X As Single, ByRef Y As Single, ByRef Z As Single)
Dim P As Integer
Dim i As Integer
Dim j As Integer
Dim pt As Point3D
Dim Bix As Single
Dim Bjz As Single

    For i = 0 To MaxU
        ' Compute Bix.
        Bix = Factorial(MaxU) / Factorial(i) / _
            Factorial(MaxU - i) * _
            u ^ i * (1 - u) ^ (MaxU - i)

        For j = 0 To MaxV
            ' Compute Bjz.
            Bjz = Factorial(MaxV) / Factorial(j) / _
                Factorial(MaxV - j) * _
                v ^ j * (1 - v) ^ (MaxV - j)

            ' Add to the coordinates.
            For P = 1 To 3
                pt.coord(P) = pt.coord(P) + _
                    Points(i, j).coord(P) * _
                    Bix * Bjz
            Next P
        Next j
    Next i

    ' Prepare the output.
    X = pt.coord(1)
    Y = pt.coord(2)
    Z = pt.coord(3)
End Sub

' Return the factorial of a number (n!).
Function Factorial(ByVal n As Single) As Single
Dim i As Integer
Dim tot As Single

    tot = 1
    For i = 2 To n
        tot = tot * i
    Next i
    Factorial = tot
End Function
```

```
' Draw the transformed object on a PictureBox.
Public Sub Draw(ByVal pic As PictureBox, _
    Optional R As Variant)
Dim pline As Polyline3d

    ' Draw the grid if it exists.
    If Not Polylines Is Nothing Then
        For Each pline In Polylines
            pline.Draw pic, R
        Next pline
    End If

    ' Uninteresting code that draws the
    ' control points and grid omitted.
        :
End Sub
```

Example program Bezier, shown in Figure 14.23, demonstrates the Bezier3d class. Use the option buttons to select the surface you want to see. Use the arrow keys to change the viewing direction. Click the check boxes to make the program display the control points or the control grid.

Joining Bezier Surfaces

By adding enough control points, you can create a Bezier surface that approximates almost any shape you want. However, each control point contributes to the value of every point on the surface. This arrangement has two consequences. First, as you add more control

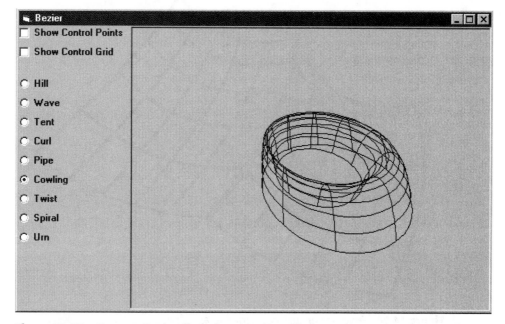

Figure 14.23   Program Bezier displaying a Bezier surface.

points, calculating the values of each point on the surface takes longer. Second, when you change the location of a control point, you change the location of every point on the surface except at the corners. This makes it difficult to modify part of the surface while leaving the rest unchanged. Like the two-dimensional Bezier curves described in Chapter 11, Drawing Curves, three-dimensional Bezier surfaces do not give you local control.

One way around these drawbacks is to build your surface out of several different Bezier surfaces joined at the edges. You can make the edges of two Bezier surfaces match by giving the surfaces the same control points along that edge. Figure 14.24 shows two Bezier surfaces. Thin lines show the control point grid and dots mark the three control points that are shared by the two surfaces. Because they share control points along one edge, the surfaces also share a corresponding edge, drawn with an extra thick line in the figure.

If you want two Bezier surfaces to share an edge and also meet smoothly, the control points on the common edge must match, and the control points adjacent to them must lie along straight lines. Figure 14.25 shows two Bezier surfaces meeting smoothly at a common edge. Dots indicate the shared control points. Extra thick lines connect the shared control points with the others that must lie along a straight line.

B-Splines

Using Bezier surfaces joined at the edges, you can gain local control over your surface's shape. If you change the position of an interior control point for one of the surfaces, the shape of that surface changes, but the shapes of the others do not.

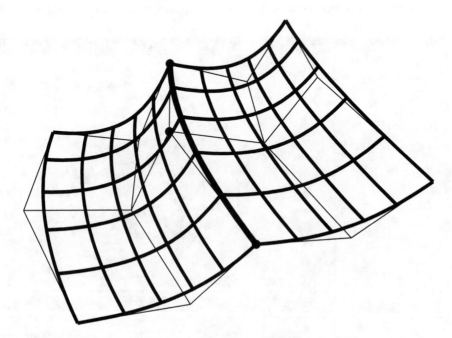

Figure 14.24   Two Bezier surfaces joined at an edge.

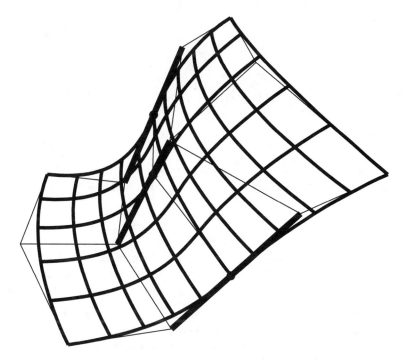

Figure 14.25   Two Bezier surfaces joined smoothly at an edge.

While this gives you a good deal of flexibility, it also places you under quite a few constraints. If you move a control point on the edge of a surface, you must also move the corresponding control points on any surfaces that share the point. If you want the surfaces to meet smoothly, you also need to move the neighboring control points so that they still lie along a straight line. When you move one of those neighboring control points, you also need to make adjustments to keep the points properly aligned.

Like two-dimensional B-spline curves, three-dimensional B-spline surfaces give you local control over your surface without all of these constraints. As is the case with two-dimensional B-splines, B-spline surfaces are defined in terms of blending functions that generate the points on the surface as weighted averages of the control points' coordinate values.

Suppose you have a two-dimensional grid of control points as before with coordinates stored in the arrays ControlX(0 To M, 0 To N), ControlY(0 To M, 0 To N), and ControlZ(0 To M, 0 To N). Then the X coordinates of the points on the B-spline surface are given by the equation:

```
            m    n
X(u, v) = Σ    Σ   ControlX(i, j) * N_{i,k}(u) * N_{j,1}(v)
           i=0  j=0
```

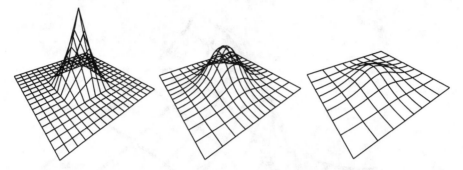

Figure 14.26 B-spline surfaces of degree two, three, and four.

Before learning the definition of the blending functions $N_{i,k}(u)$, you can explore their behavior. $N_{i,k}(u)$ is a blending function of degree k. As is the case for two-dimensional B-splines, the degree of the blending functions determines how smoothly the surface fits the control points. If the degree is small, the surface fits the data closely. If the degree is larger, the surface is smoother and does not match the data as closely.

Figure 14.26 shows three B-spline surfaces of degree two, three, and four defined by a control grid arranged in a cone shape. The picture on the left fits the data fairly closely. The middle picture is smoother and does not fit the data as well. The picture on the right is very smooth and bears only the slightest resemblance to the original data.

To define the blending functions, you need to define a set of *knot values* that relate the parameters u and v to the control points. Suppose the coordinates of your control points are contained in arrays dimensioned (0 To M, 0 To N). The most commonly used knot values t_0 through t_{M+k} for the parameter u are defined for a surface of degree k by the equations:

```
t_i = 0          if i < k
      i - k + 1        if k <= i <= M
      M - k + 2        if i > M
```

For example, Table 14.1 shows the knot values for a degree three surface where the control points are contained in arrays dimensioned as (0 To 4, 0 To 4).

Once you can compute knot values, you can use them to define the blending functions recursively using the following equations:

```
N_i,1(u) =     0       if t_i <= u < t_i+1
           1       otherwise

N_i,k(u) =     (u - t_i) * N_i,k-1(u) / (t_i+k-1 - t_i) +
           (t_i+k - u) * N_i+1,k-1(u) / (t_i+k - t_i+1)
```

Table 14.1 Knot Values for a Degree Three Surface

i	0	1	2	3	4	5	6	7
t_i	0	0	0	1	2	3	3	3

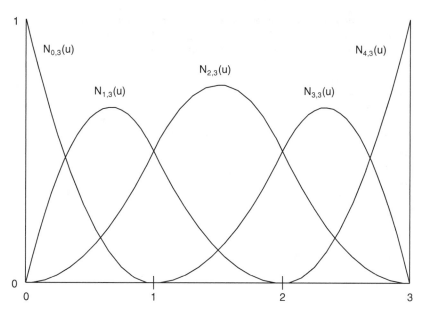

Figure 14.27 B-spline blending functions for the knot values 0, 0, 0, 1, 2, 3, 3, 3.

Figure 14.27 shows the blending functions for parameter u of a degree three surface where the control point arrays are dimensioned as (0 To 4, 0 To 4). From this picture, you can see several important properties of the blending functions. These properties are similar to those of the blending functions for two-dimensional B-spline curves.

First, for any value of u, the sum of the values of all of the functions on input u equals one. This makes the coordinates of the points on the surface a weighted average of the coordinates of some of the control points.

Second, each blending function is nonzero over only part of the domain of u values. The function $N_{1,3}(u)$, for instance, is nonzero where $0 < u < 2$. Because the nonzero domain for each function is limited, the coordinates of the points on the surface that are affected by each function are also limited. If you change the position of a control point, the surface is affected only for values of u and v for which that control point's blending function is nonzero. This gives you local control over the shape of the surface.

The code for displaying B-spline surfaces is very similar to that for displaying Bezier surfaces. The largest difference is in the way you vary the parameters u and v. To draw a Bezier surface, you vary u and v between 0.0 and 1.0. To draw a degree k B-spline surface with control points stored in arrays dimensioned (0 To M, 0 To N), you need to vary u and v over the ranges $0 <= u <= M - k + 2$ and $0 <= v <= N - k + 2$.

To convert the Bezier3d class into a BSpline3d class, you need to change the Initialize-Grid subroutine so it uses these ranges for u and v.

```
' Create polylines to represent the surface.
Public Sub InitializeGrid( _
```

```
            ByVal degree_u As Integer, ByVal degree_v As Integer, _
            ByVal gap_u As Single, ByVal gap_v As Single, _
            ByVal d_u As Single, ByVal d_v As Single)
Dim u As Single
Dim v As Single
Dim stopu As Single
Dim stopv As Single
Dim X As Single
Dim Y As Single
Dim Z As Single
Dim x1 As Single
Dim y1 As Single
Dim z1 As Single
Dim pline As Polyline3d

    DegreeU = degree_u
    DegreeV = degree_v
    GapU = gap_u
    GapV = gap_v
    Du = d_u
    Dv = d_v

    Set Polylines = New Collection

    ' Create curves with constant u.
    stopu = MaxU - DegreeU + 2 + GapU / 10
    stopv = MaxV - DegreeV + 2 + Dv / 10
    For u = 0 To stopu Step GapU
        Set pline = New Polyline3d
        Polylines.Add pline

        SurfaceValue u, 0, x1, y1, z1

        For v = Dv To stopv Step Dv
            SurfaceValue u, v, X, Y, Z
            pline.AddSegment x1, y1, z1, X, Y, Z
            x1 = X
            y1 = Y
            z1 = Z
        Next v
    Next u

    ' Create curves with constant v.
    stopv = MaxV - DegreeV + 2 + GapV / 10
    stopu = MaxU - DegreeU + 2 + Du / 10
    For v = 0 To stopv Step GapV
        Set pline = New Polyline3d
        Polylines.Add pline

        SurfaceValue 0, v, x1, y1, z1
        For u = Du To stopu Step Du
```

```
            SurfaceValue u, v, X, Y, Z
            pline.AddSegment x1, y1, z1, X, Y, Z
            x1 = X
            y1 = Y
            z1 = Z
        Next u
    Next v
End Sub
```

The Bspline3d class computes surface values much as the Bezier3d class does. The SurfaceValue routine uses the blending functions to create a weighted average of the control points. Although the details of the blending functions themselves are quite different from their Bezier surface counterparts, the way they are used by the Surface-Value function to calculate points on the surface is the same.

```
' Return the (X, Y, Z) coordinates of the
' B-spline surface for these u and v values.
Private Sub SurfaceValue( _
    ByVal u As Single, ByVal v As Single, _
    ByRef X As Single, ByRef Y As Single, ByRef Z As Single)
Dim P As Integer
Dim i As Integer
Dim j As Integer
Dim pt As Point3D
Dim Ni As Single
Dim Nj As Single

    For i = 0 To MaxU
        ' Compute Ni.
        Ni = NValue(i, MaxU, DegreeU, DegreeU, u)

        For j = 0 To MaxV
            ' Compute Nj.
            Nj = NValue(j, MaxV, DegreeV, DegreeV, v)

            ' Add to the coordinates.
            For P = 1 To 3
                pt.coord(P) = pt.coord(P) + _
                    Points(i, j).coord(P) * _
                    Ni * Nj
            Next P
        Next j
    Next i

    ' Prepare the output.
    X = pt.coord(1)
    Y = pt.coord(2)
    Z = pt.coord(3)
End Sub
```

```
' Return the value of N.
Private Function NValue(ByVal i As Integer, _
    ByVal max As Integer, ByVal degree As Integer, _
    ByVal max_degree As Integer, ByVal u As Single) As Single
Dim denom As Single
Dim v1 As Single
Dim v2 As Single

    If degree = 1 Then
        If Knot(i, max, max_degree) <= u And _
         u < Knot(i + 1, max, max_degree) Then
            NValue = 1
        Else
            NValue = 0
        End If

        ' Recall that:
        '   Ni,1(u) = 0      if ti <= u < ti+1
        '             1      otherwise
        ' The following test handles u = tmax.
        If i = max And _
            Knot(i, max, max_degree) <= u And _
            u <= Knot(i + 1, max, max_degree) + 0.001 Then
                NValue = 1
        End If
        Exit Function
    End If

    denom = Knot(i + degree - 1, max, max_degree) - _
        Knot(i, max, max_degree)
    If denom = 0 Then
        v1 = 0
    Else
        v1 = (u - Knot(i, max, max_degree)) * _
            NValue(i, max, degree - 1, max_degree, u) / _
            denom
    End If

    denom = Knot(i + degree, max, max_degree) - _
        Knot(i + 1, max, max_degree)
    If denom = 0 Then
        v2 = 0
    Else
        v2 = (Knot(i + degree, max, max_degree) - u) * _
            NValue(i + 1, max, degree - 1, max_degree, u) / _
            denom
    End If

    NValue = v1 + v2
End Function
```

```
' Return a B-spline knot value.
Private Function Knot(ByVal i As Integer, _
    ByVal max As Integer, ByVal degree As Integer) As Integer

    If i < degree Then
        Knot = 0
    ElseIf i <= max Then
        Knot = i - degree + 1
    Else
        Knot = max - degree + 2
    End If
End Function
```

Example program Bspline uses these routines to draw B-splines much as the program Bezier draws Bezier surfaces. Use the option buttons to select the surface you want to see. Use the arrow keys to change the viewing direction. Click the check boxes to make the program display the control points or the control grid.

Example program Bspline2, shown in Figure 14.28, is a simple B-spline editor. Enter the number of control points you want in the X and Z directions, and click the Initialize

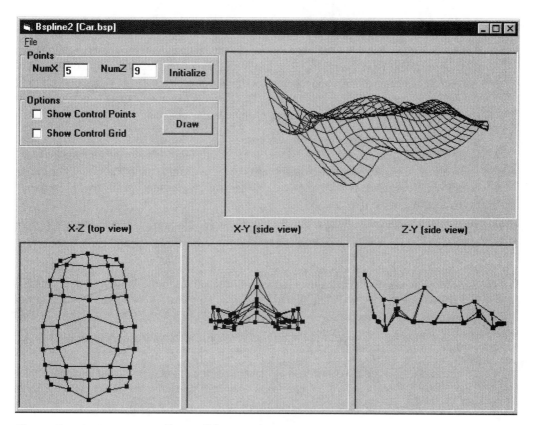

Figure 14.28   Program Bspline2 editing a surface.

button to create a set of control points. Click and drag the points in the top and side views, and then click the Draw button to make the program display the corresponding B-spline surface.

Surfaces of Transformation

Suppose you have a curve. You can transform the curve by translating, rotating, reflecting, scaling, and applying a shape-distorting transformation to it. If you then connect the corresponding points in the original and transformed curves, you will have created a *transformation surface*.

The following two sections describe the most common forms of transformation surfaces: extruded surfaces and surfaces of revolution. These use only a subset of the possible transformations you might apply to a curve.

The section after that describes more general surfaces of transformation. Using less restricted forms of transformation, you can create all sorts of surfaces that are interesting and sometimes truly bizarre.

Extruded Surfaces

Extrusion is the process of forcing a substance through some sort of restricted opening to produce a kind of ribbon. The cross-section of the ribbon has the shape of the opening. Examples of extrusion are forcing toothpaste out of a tube or squeezing frosting through a pastry cone to decorate a cake. By changing the opening in the cone, you can change the cross-section of the frosting ribbons you produce.

In three-dimensional graphics, you can perform a similar operation by moving a *base curve* through space along a *generating path*. As you move the curve, it sweeps out a three-dimensional surface. This kind of surface is called an *extruded* surface. The cross-sections of the surface look like the base curve you are moving. This curve corresponds to the opening in the pastry cone.

As a simple example, if you move a line segment in a direction perpendicular to it, you will sweep out a rectangle. In this case the cross-sections of the surface are line segments.

The simplest extrusions move the base curve along a straight line. Figure 14.29 shows a horizontal rectangle that has been extruded a small distance vertically. The original rectangle is drawn in bold. The line segments connecting corresponding points in the original and transformed curve are drawn in dashed lines.

There is no reason the base curve cannot be moved along a longer path or a curved path. After all, as you squeeze a pastry cone, you can move the cone around on the cake. You can also change the base curve much as you can change the opening in the pastry cone. Figure 14.30 shows a semicircle that has been extruded along a curved generating path. Figure 14.31 shows a rectangle that has been extruded along a similar path.

If you look carefully at Figures 14.29 through 14.31, you will notice a couple of interesting features of extruded surfaces. First, each of the areas that make up the surface is a

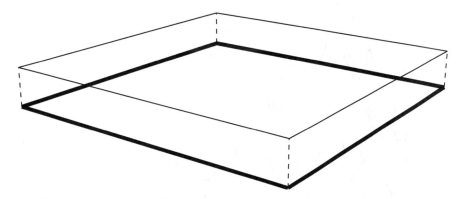

Figure 14.29   A square extruded a small distance vertically.

parallelogram. Each time the base curve is moved along the generating path, the points along the curve are moved a fixed distance and direction determined by the generating path. Because the distance and direction are the same for any two adjacent points along the curve, the line segments connecting the points' new and old positions are parallel. Because these segments are also all the same length, connecting any two of these segments gives a parallelogram.

A second interesting fact about extruded surfaces is that you can create the same surface by moving the base curve along the generating path or by moving the generating path along the base curve. Figure 14.31, for example, was produced when a rectangle was moved more or less horizontally along an S-shaped path. You could have created the same surface by moving an S-shaped curve along a rectangular path. Figure 14.32

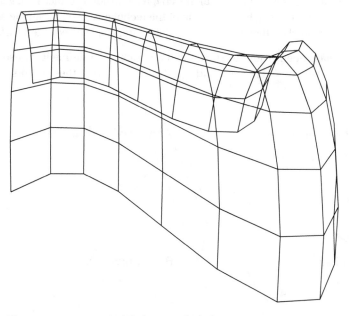

Figure 14.30   A semicircle extruded along a curved path.

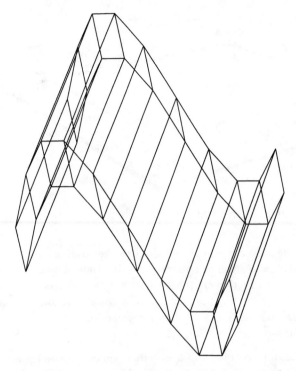

Figure 14.31   A rectangle extruded along a curved path.

shows the base curves and generating paths used by these two methods.

Like the simple surfaces described earlier in this chapter, extruded surfaces are generated from a set of data points. You can borrow some of the techniques used by simple surfaces to create an Extrusion3d class that stores, manipulates, and displays extruded surfaces.

The Extrusion3d class needs room to store the data points that define it. These are the points along the base curve and the generating path. You can store these points in arrays

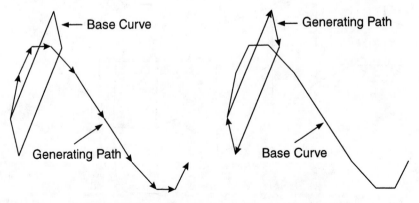

Figure 14.32   Two ways to generate the surface shown in Figure 14.31.

and create subroutines AddCurvePoint and AddPathPoint to allow your program to define the curve and path.

The Extrusion3d class can use Polyline3d objects to display the surface. The public Extrude method uses the base curve and generator to create these Polyline3d objects.

```
Option Explicit

Private NumCurvePts As Integer
Private NumPathPts As Integer

Private CurvePoints() As Point3D
Private PathPoints() As Point3D

Private ThePolyline As Polyline3d

' Add a point to the base curve.
Public Sub AddCurvePoint(ByVal X As Single, _
    ByVal Y As Single, ByVal Z As Single)

    NumCurvePts = NumCurvePts + 1
    ReDim Preserve CurvePoints(1 To NumCurvePts)

    With CurvePoints(NumCurvePts)
        .coord(1) = X
        .coord(2) = Y
        .coord(3) = Z
        .coord(4) = 1
    End With
End Sub

' Add a point to the generating path.
Public Sub AddPathPoint(ByVal X As Single, _
    ByVal Y As Single, ByVal Z As Single)

    NumPathPts = NumPathPts + 1
    ReDim Preserve PathPoints(1 To NumPathPts)

    With PathPoints(NumPathPts)
        .coord(1) = X
        .coord(2) = Y
        .coord(3) = Z
        .coord(4) = 1
    End With
End Sub

' Create the display polylines.
Public Sub Extrude()
Dim i As Integer
Dim j As Integer
```

```
Dim xoff1 As Single
Dim yoff1 As Single
Dim zoff1 As Single
Dim xoff2 As Single
Dim yoff2 As Single
Dim zoff2 As Single
Dim x1 As Single
Dim y1 As Single
Dim z1 As Single
Dim x2 As Single
Dim y2 As Single
Dim z2 As Single

    Set ThePolyline = New Polyline3d

    ' Create the translated images of the curve.
    For i = 1 To NumPathPts
        ' Calculate offsets for this path point.
        xoff1 = PathPoints(i).coord(1) - _
            PathPoints(1).coord(1)
        yoff1 = PathPoints(i).coord(2) - _
            PathPoints(1).coord(2)
        zoff1 = PathPoints(i).coord(3) - _
            PathPoints(1).coord(3)

        x1 = CurvePoints(1).coord(1) + xoff1
        y1 = CurvePoints(1).coord(2) + yoff1
        z1 = CurvePoints(1).coord(3) + zoff1
        For j = 2 To NumCurvePts
            x2 = CurvePoints(j).coord(1) + xoff1
            y2 = CurvePoints(j).coord(2) + yoff1
            z2 = CurvePoints(j).coord(3) + zoff1
            ThePolyline.AddSegment x1, y1, z1, x2, y2, z2
            x1 = x2
            y1 = y2
            z1 = z2
        Next j
    Next i

    ' Create the translated images of the path.
    xoff1 = PathPoints(1).coord(1) - PathPoints(1).coord(1)
    yoff1 = PathPoints(1).coord(2) - PathPoints(1).coord(2)
    zoff1 = PathPoints(1).coord(3) - PathPoints(1).coord(3)
    For i = 2 To NumPathPts
        ' Calculate offsets for this path point.
        xoff2 = PathPoints(i).coord(1) - _
            PathPoints(1).coord(1)
        yoff2 = PathPoints(i).coord(2) - _
            PathPoints(1).coord(2)
```

```
        zoff2 = PathPoints(i).coord(3) - _
            PathPoints(1).coord(3)

        For j = 1 To NumCurvePts
            ThePolyline.AddSegment _
                CurvePoints(j).coord(1) + xoff1, _
                CurvePoints(j).coord(2) + yoff1, _
                CurvePoints(j).coord(3) + zoff1, _
                CurvePoints(j).coord(1) + xoff2, _
                CurvePoints(j).coord(2) + yoff2, _
                CurvePoints(j).coord(3) + zoff2
        Next j
        xoff1 = xoff2
        yoff1 = yoff2
        zoff1 = zoff2
    Next i
End Sub
```

Most of the rest of the Extrusion3d routines pass requests to the points that make up the curve and path or to the display polyline if it exists. For instance, the following code shows the ApplyFull routine, which applies a transformation matrix to the object.

```
' Apply a transformation matrix which may not
' contain 0, 0, 0, 1 in the last column to the object.
Public Sub ApplyFull(M() As Single)
Dim i As Integer

    ' Transform the base curve.
    For i = 1 To NumCurvePts
        m3ApplyFull CurvePoints(i).coord, M, _
                    CurvePoints(i).trans
    Next i

    ' Transform the generating path.
    For i = 1 To NumPathPts
        m3ApplyFull PathPoints(i).coord, M, _
                    PathPoints(i).trans
    Next i

    ' Transform the display polyline if it exists.
    If Not (ThePolyline Is Nothing) Then _
        ThePolyline.ApplyFull M
End Sub
```

Example program Extrude, shown in Figure 14.33, demonstrates the Extrusion3d class. Use the option buttons to pick a base curve and a generating path. Then click the Extrude button to see the resulting surface. Use the arrow keys to change the viewing direction.

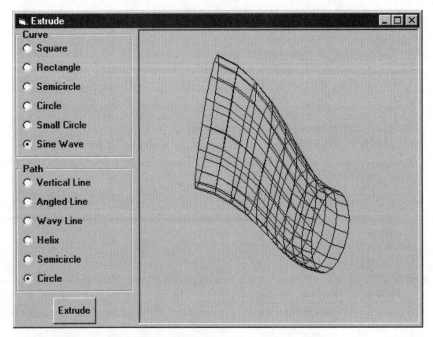

Figure 14.33   Program Extrude creating an extruded surface.

Surfaces of Revolution

To create an extruded surface, you move a base curve along a generating path. To make a surface of revolution, rotate a base curve around an axis of rotation. Figure 14.34 shows a surface of revolution with the base curve drawn in heavy lines. To produce this surface, the base curve was rotated around the Y axis.

Creating a surface of revolution is very similar to creating an extruded surface. In both cases you take a base curve and repeatedly transform it. At each step, you draw the transformed curve and connect the points on the transformed curve to the corresponding points on the previously transformed version.

You can produce a surface of revolution by rotating the base curve around any line in three-dimensional space. In practice, it is much easier to rotate around the X, Y, or Z coordinate axis. If you want to rotate a curve around some other line, you can first apply translations and rotations until the line coincides with a coordinate axis. Then perform the rotation and translate and rotate the line back to its original position. These operations are described in detail in Chapter 13, Three-Dimensional Transformations.

The surface in Figure 14.34 appears to be made up of trapezoids. It can be shown that the areas that make up a surface of revolution are trapezoids as long as the surface's base curve lies in a plane that passes through the axis of rotation. On the other hand, if the curve does not lie in such a plane, the areas that make up the surface are "bent trapezoids" similar to the bent rectangles that make up many other types of surfaces.

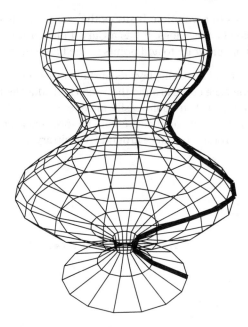

Figure 14.34   A surface of revolution created by the rotation of a curve (heavy lines) around an axis of rotation.

Figure 14.35 shows a surface of revolution created with a curve that does not lie in a plane containing the axis of rotation. The base curve is drawn with bold lines. On the right, the figure shows an enlarged view of one of the regions that make up the surface. From this picture, you can see that the region does not lie flat.

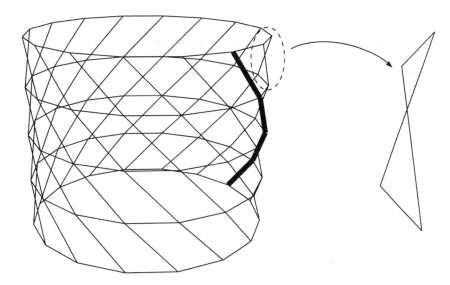

Figure 14.35   When the base curve and axis of rotation do not lie in the same plane, a surface of revolution is made of "bent trapezoids."

The Rotated3d class manages surfaces of revolution. It stores the points that make up the base curve much as the Extrusion3d class does. It has a CurvePoints array and an AddCurvePoint method that allows the program to add points to the base curve.

Like the Extrusion3d class, the Rotated3d class displays its surface using a Polyline3d object. The Rotate method rotates the base curve around the Y axis and adds the resulting line segments to the Polyline3d object. You could easily make similar routines for rotating the curve around the X or Z axis. You could also create a more general routine that uses translations and rotations to rotate the curve around an arbitrary line.

```vb
Option Explicit

Private NumCurvePts As Integer
Private CurvePoints() As Point3D

Private ThePolyline As Polyline3d     ' The display polyline.

' Add a point to the curve.
Public Sub AddCurvePoint(ByVal X As Single, _
    ByVal Y As Single, ByVal Z As Single)

    NumCurvePts = NumCurvePts + 1
    ReDim Preserve CurvePoints(1 To NumCurvePts)

    With CurvePoints(NumCurvePts)
        .coord(1) = X
        .coord(2) = Y
        .coord(3) = Z
        .coord(4) = 1
    End With
End Sub

' Create the display polyline by rotating around
' the Y axis.
Public Sub Rotate()
Dim i As Integer
Dim R As Single
Dim theta As Single
Dim dtheta As Single
Dim T As Single
Dim X As Single
Dim Z As Single
Dim x1 As Single
Dim y1 As Single
Dim z1 As Single
Dim x2 As Single
Dim y2 As Single
Dim z2 As Single

    Set ThePolyline = New Polyline3d
```

```
' Create the translated images of the curve.
dtheta = PI / 8
For theta = 0 To 2 * PI - dtheta + 0.01 Step dtheta
    X = CurvePoints(1).coord(1)
    Z = CurvePoints(1).coord(3)
    R = Sqr(X * X + Z * Z)
    T = ATan2(Z, X)
    x1 = R * Cos(T + theta)
    y1 = CurvePoints(1).coord(2)
    z1 = R * Sin(T + theta)
    For i = 2 To NumCurvePts
        X = CurvePoints(i).coord(1)
        Z = CurvePoints(i).coord(3)
        R = Sqr(X * X + Z * Z)
        T = ATan2(Z, X)
        x2 = R * Cos(T + theta)
        y2 = CurvePoints(i).coord(2)
        z2 = R * Sin(T + theta)

        ThePolyline.AddSegment x1, y1, z1, x2, y2, z2
        x1 = x2
        y1 = y2
        z1 = z2
    Next i
Next theta

' Create the circles of rotation.
For i = 1 To NumCurvePts
    X = CurvePoints(i).coord(1)
    Z = CurvePoints(i).coord(3)
    R = Sqr(X * X + Z * Z)
    T = ATan2(Z, X)
    x1 = R * Cos(T)
    y1 = CurvePoints(i).coord(2)
    z1 = R * Sin(T)
    For theta = dtheta To 2 * PI - dtheta + 0.01 _
            Step dtheta

        x2 = R * Cos(T + theta)
        z2 = R * Sin(T + theta)
        ThePolyline.AddSegment x1, y1, z1, x2, y1, z2
        x1 = x2
        z1 = z2
    Next theta
    x2 = R * Cos(T)
    z2 = R * Sin(T)
    ThePolyline.AddSegment x1, y1, z1, x2, y1, z2
Next i
End Sub
```

The other routines needed by the Rotated3d class are very similar to those used by the Extrusion3d class.

Example program Rotate, shown in Figure 14.36, demonstrates the Extrusion3d class. Use the option buttons to pick the surface you want to see. Use the arrow keys to change the program's viewing direction.

Figure 14.37 shows several surfaces of rotation produced by the program with their base curves drawn in heavy lines. All the surfaces' base curves lie in the X-Y plane, so each of the surfaces is made up of trapezoids.

Other Surfaces of Transformation

You create extruded surfaces by translating a curve along a path. You create a surface of revolution by rotating a curve around an axis of rotation. In both cases, you create a series of copies of the original base curve, properly transformed.

You can generalize this method to allow other types of transformations. To create the series of curves, you can use translation, rotation, reflection, stretching, and even shape-distorting transformations. This usually produces a surface made up of bent trapezoids like the ones that make up the surface in Figure 14.35. Only when the base curve and the transformations have the proper relationships will the areas that define the surface be flat trapezoids.

The generating path used to construct extruded surfaces and the axis of rotation used to construct surfaces of revolution provide easy, intuitive ways to specify the transformations that should be applied to the base curve. Specifying a series of more general transformations is not as intuitive. One way to manage these transformations is to explicitly create them and store them in a transformation array. You can then apply the transformations to the base curve to create the surface.

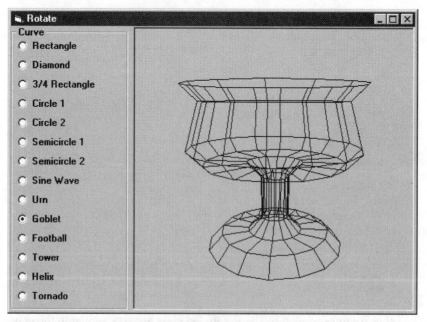

Figure 14.36 Program Rotate creating a surface of revolution.

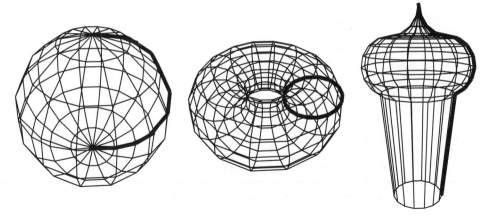

Figure 14.37 Surfaces of revolution with base curves drawn in heavy lines.

The Transformed3d class manages these kinds of surfaces of transformation. Like the Extrusion3d and Rotated3d classes, Transformed3d stores the points that define its base curve using an array of points and an AddCurvePoint method.

The class stores transformation matrices in its Transformations array. Its SetTransformation method allows a program to define these matrices.

Finally, the Transform subroutine applies the transformations to the object's base curve to produce the line segments representing the surface. For each transformation in the Trans array, the object transforms the curve and adds the transformed version to its display polyline object. It also connects the points in the transformed version to the corresponding points in the previous version.

```
Option Explicit

Private NumCurvePts As Integer
Private CurvePoints() As Point3D

Private NumTransformations As Integer
Private Transformations() As Transformation

Private ThePolyline As Polyline3d    ' The display polyline.

' Set a transformation.
Public Sub SetTransformation(M() As Single)
    NumTransformations = NumTransformations + 1
    ReDim Preserve Transformations(1 To NumTransformations)
    m3MatCopy Transformations(NumTransformations).M, M
End Sub

' Create the display polyline by applying the
' series of transformations in array M().
Public Sub Transform()
Dim i As Integer
```

```
Dim j As Integer
Dim x0 As Single
Dim y0 As Single
Dim z0 As Single
Dim x1 As Single
Dim y1 As Single
Dim z1 As Single
Dim x2 As Single
Dim y2 As Single
Dim z2 As Single

    Set ThePolyline = New Polyline3d

    ' Add the original curve to ThePolyline.
    x1 = CurvePoints(1).coord(1)
    y1 = CurvePoints(1).coord(2)
    z1 = CurvePoints(1).coord(3)
    For j = 2 To NumCurvePts
        x2 = CurvePoints(j).coord(1)
        y2 = CurvePoints(j).coord(2)
        z2 = CurvePoints(j).coord(3)
        ThePolyline.AddSegment x1, y1, z1, x2, y2, z2
        x1 = x2
        y1 = y2
        z1 = z2
    Next j

    ' Start with the transformed coordinates
    ' the same as the original coordinates.
    For j = 1 To NumCurvePts
        CurvePoints(j).trans(1) = CurvePoints(j).coord(1)
        CurvePoints(j).trans(2) = CurvePoints(j).coord(2)
        CurvePoints(j).trans(3) = CurvePoints(j).coord(3)
    Next j

    ' Create the transformed copies of the curve.
    For i = 1 To NumTransformations
        ' Place the first point.
        x1 = CurvePoints(1).trans(1)
        y1 = CurvePoints(1).trans(2)
        z1 = CurvePoints(1).trans(3)
        m3ApplyFull _
            CurvePoints(1).coord, _
            Transformations(i).M, _
            CurvePoints(1).trans
        x0 = CurvePoints(1).trans(1)
        y0 = CurvePoints(1).trans(2)
        z0 = CurvePoints(1).trans(3)
        ThePolyline.AddSegment x1, y1, z1, x0, y0, z0

        ' Add the rest of the points.
        For j = 2 To NumCurvePts
```

```
                x1 = CurvePoints(j).trans(1)
                y1 = CurvePoints(j).trans(2)
                z1 = CurvePoints(j).trans(3)
                m3ApplyFull _
                    CurvePoints(j).coord, _
                    Transformations(i).M, _
                    CurvePoints(j).trans
                x2 = CurvePoints(j).trans(1)
                y2 = CurvePoints(j).trans(2)
                z2 = CurvePoints(j).trans(3)
                ' (x0, y0, z0) = previous point, new.
                ' (x1, y1, z1) = current point, old.
                ' (x2, y2, z2) = current point, new.
                ThePolyline.AddSegment x0, y0, z0, x2, y2, z2
                ThePolyline.AddSegment x1, y1, z1, x2, y2, z2
                x0 = x2
                y0 = y2
                z0 = z2
            Next j
        Next i
    End Sub
```

Example program Trans, shown in Figure 14.38, demonstrates the Transformed3d class. Use the option buttons to pick a base curve and a set of transformations for the program to apply. Then click the Transform button to make the program display the corresponding surface. Use the arrow keys to change the viewing direction.

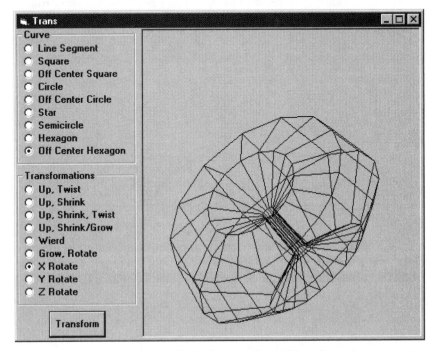

Figure 14.38   Program Trans displaying a surface of transformation.

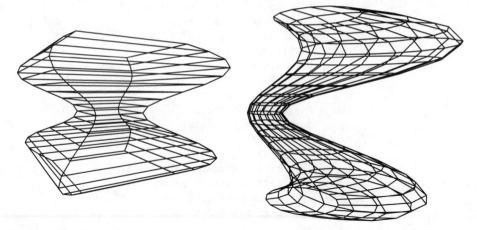

Figure 14.39 Surfaces created with transformations that scale horizontally and translate vertically.

Figure 14.39 shows two transformation surfaces. The base curve for the surface on the left is a square in the X-Z plane centered on the origin. The base curve for the surface on the right is a circle in the X-Z plane with center at (2, 0, 2). Both surfaces use the same set of transformations that scale horizontally and translate vertically.

The transformations used to produce Figure 14.39 were created and stored in the Transformations array by the following code. Later, when the program was ready to display the surfaces, it used the Transformed3d object's SetTransformation routine to copy the transformations into the Transformed3d object.

```
NumTrans = 18
ReDim Trans(1 To NumTrans)
dtheta = PI / 12
For i = 1 To NumTrans
    y = i / 4
    theta = i * dtheta
    R = 1 + Sin(2 * theta) / 2
    m3Scale A, R, 1, R        ' Scale.
    m3Translate B, 0, y, 0    ' Translate.
    m3MatMultiply Trans(i).M, A, B  ' Combine.
Next i
```

Figure 14.40 shows two transformation surfaces created with a set of transformations that rotate around the Y axis and translate vertically. The base curve for the surface on the left was a semicircle in the X-Z plane centered at the origin. The base curve for the surface on the right was a circle in the X-Z plane with center at (2, 0, 2).

Many transformation surfaces are self-intersecting and quite bizarre. Figure 14.41 shows two surfaces generated by transformations that rotate around the Z axis and

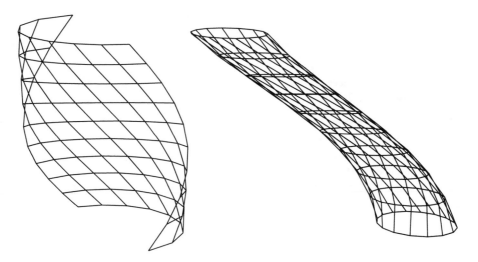

Figure 14.40   Surfaces created with transformations that rotate around the Y axis and translate vertically.

translate vertically. The base curves of both surfaces were circles in the X-Z plane. The base curve for the surface on the left was centered on the origin. The base curve for the surface on the right was centered on the point at (2, 0, 2).

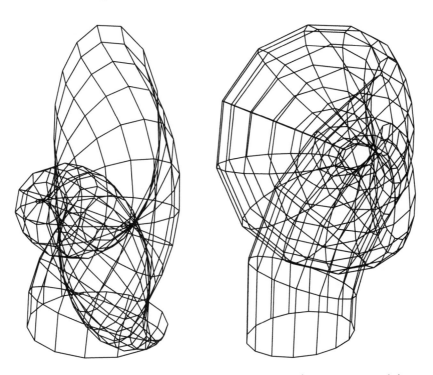

Figure 14.41   Surfaces created with transformations that rotate around the Z axis and translate vertically.

Summary

This chapter shows how to build several kinds of surfaces. It shows how to display three-dimensional surfaces defined by functions, data points, randomized data, and surfaces of transformation. These kinds of surfaces allow you to visualize complex data sets.

Using the Hi-Lo and Z-Order algorithms, you can remove the parts of a surface that should be hidden. Example programs Altitude and Valley shade different parts of a surface specially to make the surface even easier to understand. The following chapters extend these techniques to provide hidden surface removal for objects other than surfaces, and they show how to use more general shading models to create more realistic images.

CHAPTER 15

Hidden Surface Removal

The hi-lo and Z-order algorithms described in Chapter 14, Surfaces, let you perform hidden surface removal for simple surfaces. They work only for simple surfaces, however, and are not guaranteed to work for perspective projections.

This chapter describes more general hidden surface removal techniques that do not have these limitations. The chapter starts by describing a relatively simple backface removal algorithm. You can use backface removal to perform hidden surface removal for convex solids. Backface removal is also useful as a preprocessing step for hidden surface removal in other solids.

The sections that follow describe the Depth-Sort algorithm. Using Depth-Sort, you can perform hidden surface removal for almost any set of three-dimensional objects.

Backface Removal

Figure 15.1 shows the geometry of a perspective projection of a cube. The side of the cube farthest from the center of projection is hidden by the rest of the cube. Because this face is on the back side as seen from the center of projection, it is called a *backface*. Because you cannot see a backface from the center of projection, you do not need to draw it. The process of identifying backfaces is called *backface removal* or *culling*.

Figure 15.1 shows something very important about backfaces. The line from the center of projection to a backface points in more or less the same direction as a perpendicular vector pointing outward from the face. This vector is called the *surface normal*.

More precisely, if the viewing direction makes an angle less than 90 degrees with a surface normal, the surface is a backface, so you do not need to draw it. If the line and normal meet at an angle of greater than 90 degrees, the surface is not a backface. If the two meet at exactly 90 degrees, the surface is seen edge on from the center of projection. In that case, the surface appears as a line segment in the projected image. Unless your solid is infinitely thin, the edges of the surface will meet those of other surfaces, some

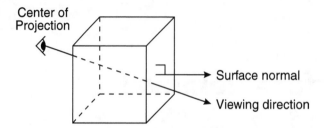

Figure 15.1 A backface is hidden from the center of projection by the solid's body.

of which will not be backfaces. In that case, you do not need to draw this surface because its visible edges will be drawn by other surfaces.

To use this information to perform backface removal, you need to do two things. First, you must be able to compute surface normals. Second, you must be able to determine what angle the viewing direction makes with the surface normals.

Finding Surface Normals

You can easily find a surface normal by taking the vector cross-product between two of the surface's adjacent edges. The cross-product of two vectors with components A = <x1, y1, z1> and B = <x2, y2, z2> is written "A x B" and is defined as:

```
<y1 * z2 - y2 * z1, x2 * z1 - x1 * z2, x1 * y2 - x2 * y1>
```

You can use the m3Cross subroutine defined in module M3Ops.bas to compute vector cross-products. This routine takes as parameters the X, Y, and Z components of the vectors A and B. It returns through parameters the components of the vector cross-product.

```
' Compute the cross product of two vectors.
' Set <X, Y, Z> = <x1, y1, z1> X <x2, y2, z2>.
Public Sub m3Cross(ByRef X As Single, ByRef Y As Single, _
    ByRef Z As Single, ByVal x1 As Single, _
    ByVal y1 As Single, ByVal z1 As Single, _
    ByVal x2 As Single, ByVal y2 As Single, _
    ByVal z2 As Single)

    X = y1 * z2 - z1 * y2
    Y = z1 * x2 - x1 * z2
    Z = x1 * y2 - y1 * x2
End Sub
```

If |A| and |B| are the lengths of the vectors A and B, respectively, and θ is the angle between them, the cross-product vector has length $|A| * |B| * Sin(\theta)$.

The cross-product is a vector that is perpendicular to both vectors A and B, but there are two directions perpendicular to vectors A and B. For example, if A and B lie in a horizontal plane, a perpendicular vector could point upward or downward. The direction of the vector created by the cross-product is given by the right-hand rule. If you hold the fingers of your right hand pointed in the direction of vector A and then curl them toward the direction of vector B, your thumb points in the direction of the new vector. Figure 15.2 shows how the right-hand rule gives the direction of the new vector.

For a solid like the cube shown in Figure 15.1, you can use two adjacent edges of a face for the vectors A and B. In that case, the cross-product A × B is a surface normal. Because you are going to use the normal for backface removal, you must be sure that the normal you pick is the outward-pointing normal. Otherwise, you will not know whether the viewing direction would make an angle greater or less than 90 degrees with the normal to a backface.

To ensure that the cross-product always gives you an outward-pointing normal, you can arrange the points that make up each face so that they are listed in a counterclockwise direction, as seen from outside the solid. Then you can use the first three points in the surface to compute the vectors A and B, and the cross-product will give you an outward-pointing normal. This orientation of a surface's data points is called the surface's *outward orientation*. Figure 15.3 shows how you can use the cross-product of two adjacent edges to find a surface normal for a face on a cube.

Testing Angles with Normals

Now that you know how to find a surface normal vector, you need to use it to determine whether the viewing direction makes an angle greater than, less than, or equal to 90 degrees with the surface normal. Vector dot products make this test easy.

Suppose two vectors A and B have components <x1, y1, z1> and <x2, y2, z2>. The *dot product* of the two vectors, written "A · B," is given by the equation:

```
A · B = x1 * x2 + y1 * y2 + z1 * z2
```

Let |A| and |B| represent the lengths of the vectors A and B. Let θ be the angle between them, as shown in Figure 15.2. Then the dot product of the vectors equals |A| * |B| * Cos(θ). You can use this fact to easily determine whether the viewing direction and the surface normal make an angle less than, greater than, or equal to 90 degrees.

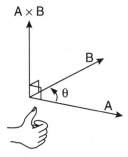

Figure 15.2 The right-hand rule gives the direction of a cross-product vector.

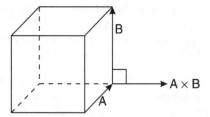

Figure 15.3 The cross-product of two adjacent vectors on a face gives an outward-pointing surface normal.

The value of $\cos(\theta)$ is greater than zero if θ is less than 90 degrees. It is less than zero if θ is greater than 90 degrees. Finally, $\cos(\theta)$ equals zero if θ equals 90 degrees. Because the lengths |A| and |B| are always positive, the dot product $A \cdot B$ is greater than zero if and only if $\cos(\theta) > 0$ and therefore $\theta < 90$ degrees.

Putting It All Together

Using cross-products and dot products, you can implement the backface removal algorithm in Visual Basic. For each surface in the solid:

1. Take the cross-product of the first two edges of the surface to get an outward-pointing normal vector.

2. Take the dot product of the normal vector and the viewing direction. If the result is less than or equal to zero, the surface is a backface (or seen edge on), so you do not need to draw it.

Backface removal eliminates roughly half of the surfaces you need to consider when drawing three-dimensional solids. If necessary, you can then use one of the more complicated algorithms described later in this chapter to determine which parts of the remaining surfaces you should draw.

Convex Solids

A solid is *convex* if the angles between each of its adjacent surfaces are all greater than zero degrees. This means there are no nooks, crannies, or holes in the solid. Another way to think of this is to imagine extending each of the solid's surfaces infinitely in all directions. If none of the extended surfaces cuts through the body of the solid, the solid is convex. The solid on the left in Figure 15.4 is convex; the solid on the right is not.

If you are drawing a single convex solid, backface removal identifies all the surfaces that you should draw. All the backfaces are completely hidden, and all other surfaces are completely visible. The solid on the left in Figure 15.4 has four backfaces drawn with dashed lines. The other four surfaces are not backfaces and they are completely visible.

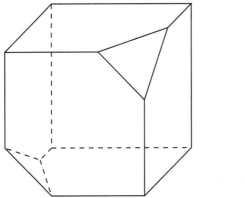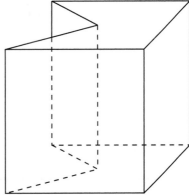

Figure 15.4 A convex solid (left) and a nonconvex solid (right).

The solid on the right is not convex. It has three backfaces. Because they are backfaces, they are completely hidden by the body of the solid, so you definitely should not draw them. This solid also has three surfaces that are completely visible. It has one surface, however, that is not a backface and is still not completely visible. It is this sort of surface that makes backface removal insufficient for drawing nonconvex solids.

You can still perform backface removal for nonconvex objects. All the backfaces are completely hidden, so you do not need to draw them. However, just because a surface is not a backface does not mean it is completely visible in a nonconvex solid.

Backface Removal in Visual Basic

The previous chapters treated most three-dimensional objects as collections of three-dimensional line segments. This approach lets you display objects, but it does not give you enough information about how the segments make up the surfaces to use backface removal.

To provide the information you need, you can use Face3d and Solid3d classes. A Face3d object represents an outwardly oriented face on a solid. A Solid3d object contains a collection of Face3d objects that represent its faces.

The data needs for the Face3d class are simple. The class contains an array that holds the points that make up the surface. For convenience, it also contains a Boolean flag IsCulled that is set to true if the surface is a backface. The object skips most other tasks if IsCulled is true. For example, the object does not bother to apply transformations to its points or draw itself if it has been culled.

Most of the Face3d methods are straightforward. The AddPoints routine adds one or more new points to the polygon. The Apply routine applies a transformation to each of the points in the polygon.

The ClipEye routine checks to see if any of the polygon's transformed points lie behind the center of projection. This prevents strange effects when the viewing direction points away from the polygon. If any point lies behind the center of projection, this routine sets the IsCulled flag to true, indicating the polygon should not be drawn.

Subroutine NormalVector takes the vector cross-product of the polygon's first two edges to find an outward pointing normal vector. Subroutine Cull uses this subroutine to determine whether the polygon is a backface.

```vb
Private NumPts As Long       ' Number of points.
Private Points() As Point3D  ' Data points.


Public IsCulled As Boolean


' Add one or more points to the polygon.
Public Sub AddPoints(ParamArray coord() As Variant)
Dim num_pts As Integer
Dim i As Integer
Dim pt As Integer

    num_pts = (UBound(coord) + 1) \ 3
    ReDim Preserve Points(1 To NumPts + num_pts)

    pt = 0
    For i = 1 To num_pts
        Points(NumPts + i).coord(1) = coord(pt)
        Points(NumPts + i).coord(2) = coord(pt + 1)
        Points(NumPts + i).coord(3) = coord(pt + 2)
        Points(NumPts + i).coord(4) = 1#
        pt = pt + 3
    Next i

    NumPts = NumPts + num_pts
End Sub


' Apply a transformation matrix to the object.
Public Sub Apply(M() As Single)
Dim i As Integer

    ' Do nothing if we are culled.
    If IsCulled Then Exit Sub

    For i = 1 To NumPts
        m3Apply Points(i).coord, M, Points(i).trans
    Next i
End Sub


' Cull if any points are behind the center of projection.
Public Sub ClipEye(ByVal R As Single)
Dim pt As Integer

    ' Do nothing if we are already culled.
```

```
        If IsCulled Then Exit Sub

        For pt = 1 To NumPts
            If Points(pt).trans(3) >= R Then Exit For
        Next pt

        If pt <= NumPts Then IsCulled = True
End Sub

' Perform backface removal for the center
' of projection (X, Y, Z).
Public Sub Cull(ByVal X As Single, ByVal Y As Single, _
    ByVal Z As Single)
Dim Ax As Single
Dim Ay As Single
Dim Az As Single
Dim Nx As Single
Dim Ny As Single
Dim Nz As Single

    ' Compute a normal to the face.
    NormalVector Nx, Ny, Nz

    ' Compute a vector from the center of
    ' projection to the face.
    Ax = Points(1).coord(1) - X
    Ay = Points(1).coord(2) - Y
    Az = Points(1).coord(3) - Z

    ' See if the vectors meet at an angle < 90.
    IsCulled = (Ax * Nx + Ay * Ny + Az * Nz > -0.0001)
End Sub

' Compute a normal vector for this polygon.
Public Sub NormalVector(ByRef Nx As Single, _
    ByRef Ny As Single, ByRef Nz As Single)
Dim Ax As Single
Dim Ay As Single
Dim Az As Single
Dim Bx As Single
Dim By As Single
Dim Bz As Single

    Ax = Points(2).coord(1) - Points(1).coord(1)
    Ay = Points(2).coord(2) - Points(1).coord(2)
    Az = Points(2).coord(3) - Points(1).coord(3)
    Bx = Points(3).coord(1) - Points(2).coord(1)
    By = Points(3).coord(2) - Points(2).coord(2)
    Bz = Points(3).coord(3) - Points(2).coord(3)
    m3Cross Nx, Ny, Nz, Ax, Ay, Az, Bx, By, Bz
End Sub
```

The Solid3d class represents a solid made up of Face3d objects. It stores the Face3d objects in a collection. Most of the Solid3d's routines simply pass requests on to the solid's polygons. For example, the solid's Cull subroutine invokes each polygon's Cull routine.

```
Public Faces As Collection

' Perform backface removal on the faces for
' center of projection at (X, Y, Z).
Public Sub Cull(ByVal X As Single, ByVal Y As Single, _
    ByVal Z As Single)
Dim obj As Face3d

    For Each obj In Faces
        obj.Cull X, Y, Z
    Next obj
End Sub
```

Example program Backface, shown in Figure 15.5, uses the Solid3d and Face3d classes to demonstrate backface removal. Use the option buttons to display different solids. Use the check box to indicate whether the program should perform backface removal.

The first six solids are convex, so hidden surface removal displays them with all hidden surfaces correctly removed. The last three scenes are not convex solids, so hidden surface removal is not enough. If you view these scenes at certain angles, you can still see some lines that should be hidden.

Figure 15.6 shows two situations in which backface removal does not remove all the hidden surfaces. The pictures on the top show the results of backface removal. The pictures on the bottom show the correct images with all hidden surfaces removed. The stellate octahedron on the left is not convex, so some faces partially obscure others. The picture on the right contains several different convex solids. Some of the solids obscure

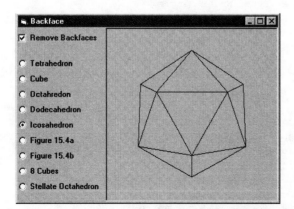

Figure 15.5 Program Backface displays solids with backface removal.

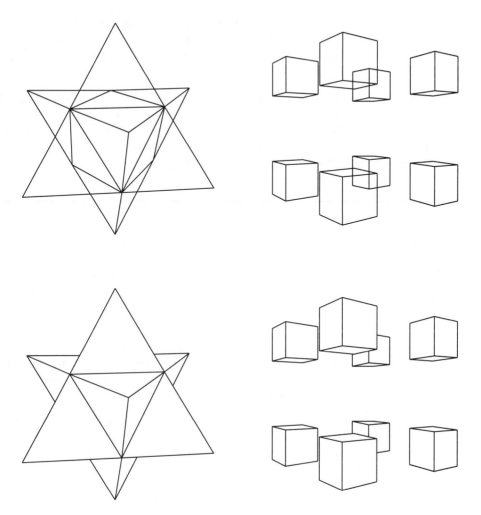

Figure 15.6   Two situations in which backface removal does not remove all the hidden surfaces.

parts of others. Use the option buttons in program Backface to display these solids and the one on the right in Figure 15.4.

Depth-Sort

One way to handle some of the problems left unresolved by backface removal is the *Depth-Sort algorithm*. The basic idea is simple. First, sort the objects in the picture according to their distances from the center of projection. Then draw them, starting with the objects furthest away and moving to those that are closer. As you draw each object, fill each visible face with some color. If you do not want the object to have a color of its own, fill it with the form or picture box's background color. This makes the object cover any objects that were drawn previously and that should be behind the new object.

Because you are drawing the objects in order, with the closest objects drawn last, closer objects obscure objects that are further away. When you are finished, the objects appear on the screen with the hidden lines buried under objects that are closer to the center of projection.

This process is similar to the way you could create a painting. You could begin by painting the background areas. You could then add the objects in the middle distance, painting them over the background. Eventually you would add the foreground objects on top of the background and objects in the middle distance. Because the Depth-Sort algorithm is similar to painting in this way, it is sometimes called the *painter's algorithm*.

Determining the distance from an object to the center of projection can be quite time consuming. For each point in each object, you need to perform several multiplications, additions, and even a square root.

You can make the calculations simpler if you apply the projection transformation to the objects before you order them. Recall that the perspective transformation described in Chapter 13, Three-Dimensional Transformations, preserves each point's Z coordinate. After the objects have been translated, rotated, and projected, you can use the points' Z coordinates to decide which is farthest from the center of projection.

If the objects are convex solids and they are not too close together, the Depth-Sort algorithm combined with backface removal hides all the hidden surfaces correctly. First, perform backface removal so that you can skip examining backfaces in the later steps. Then arrange the convex solids in order from back to front as seen from the center of projection. Finally, draw the solids in their proper order.

The following code shows how a program can sort the objects it contains. The Solid3d class has a SetZmax routine that finds and records the largest transformed Z coordinate value of any of the points it contains. The SortSolids subroutine examines the ZMax values to reorder the Solids collection so that those farthest from the center of projection come first. The program then draws them in this order.

```
' Sort the solids in depth-sort order.
Private Sub SortSolids()
Dim solid As Solid3d
Dim ordered_solids As Collection
Dim besti As Integer
Dim bestz As Single
Dim newz As Single
Dim i As Integer

    ' Compute each solid's Zmax value.
    For Each solid In Solids
        solid.SetZmax
    Next solid

    ' Sort the objects by their Zmax values.
    Set ordered_solids = New Collection
```

```
Do While Solids.Count > 0
    ' Find the face with the smallest Zmax
    ' left in the Faces collection.
    besti = 1
    bestz = Solids(1).ZMax
    For i = 2 To Solids.Count
        newz = Solids(i).ZMax
        If bestz > newz Then
            besti = i
            bestz = newz
        End If
    Next i

    ' Add the best object to the sorted list.
    ordered_solids.Add Solids(besti)
    Solids.Remove besti
Loop

' Replace the Solids collection with the
' ordered_solids collection.
Set Solids = ordered_solids
End Sub
```

Example program Depth1, shown in Figure 15.7, uses this method to draw scenes that contain convex solids. Use the option buttons to pick a scene to display. Use the Remove Backfaces check box to tell the program whether to hide the hidden surfaces.

Nonconvex Solids

Program Depth1 uses the Depth-Sort algorithm to draw convex solids in their proper order. To draw a nonconvex solid, you can use the same technique to draw the faces that make up the solid in their correct order.

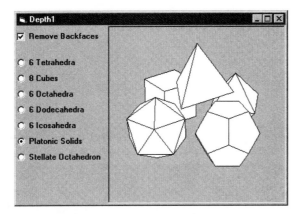

Figure 15.7 Program Depth1 uses backface removal and the Depth-Sort algorithm to draw groups of convex solids.

The Solid3d's SortFaces subroutine rearranges the solid's faces so that those furthest from the center of projection come first. The solid can then draw its faces in farthest-to-nearest order to cover any surfaces that should be hidden.

Program Depth1 uses a very simple method for determining the order in which the solids should be drawn. It assumes that the object with the smallest Z coordinate after transformation is the one furthest from the center of projection.

This works well for convex solids that are relatively far apart. When the objects are close together, however, this method sometimes fails. Unfortunately, the surfaces that make up a nonconvex solid are guaranteed to be close together. In that case, this simple method does not always work.

Figure 15.8 shows a solid after its points have been transformed for projection. Surface A has a smaller Z coordinate than surface B, even though it obscures surface B. The Depth-Sort algorithm as written above would draw surface A first, even though it belonged in front of surface B and therefore should have been drawn second. If you use program Depth1 to view the stellate octahedron, you can find some viewing directions from which this happens, and surfaces that should be hidden are visible.

To make the algorithm handle this common situation, the SortFaces routine used by the Solid3d class must be a bit more sophisticated. This routine begins by moving any backfaces into the collection that will hold the sorted faces. Because the backfaces are never drawn, it does not matter where they are in the rearranged list. By removing them right away, SortFaces reduces the number of objects it must consider so that it can run more quickly.

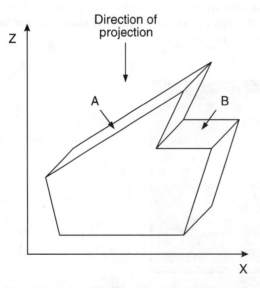

Figure 15.8 A simple Depth-Sort algorithm does not work for this solid.

Next, the routine checks to see if any face is further from the center of projection than the first face in the Faces collection. If so, that face is moved to the front of the list. The routine repeats this process until no face is further than the face at the front.

At that point, SortFaces moves the first face to the sorted output collection, and it starts all over again. When all the faces have been moved to the output collection, SortFaces sets the Faces collection to point to the rearranged objects, and the routine is finished.

There are two major complications to this method. First, it may not be possible to find a face that is further than any other from the center of projection. Figure 15.9 shows two overlapping surfaces. Because they overlap each other, neither one is further from the center of projection. The simplest way to take care of this situation is to break the mutually overlapping surfaces into smaller pieces that do not overlap in this way. Then this problem does not arise.

To be certain it does not become stuck in an infinite loop if this situation does occur, SortFaces keeps track of the number of times it has moved a face to the front of the list. If there are N items remaining to be ordered and the routine has moved N items to the front of the list, the subroutine is stuck in an infinite loop. In that case, the routine breaks out of the loop by moving the first item on the list to the output collection. While this does not guarantee a proper ordering of the faces, it allows the program to continue and produce some sort of output.

Comparing Faces

The second complication to the ordering process is that it is not always easy to determine whether one of a solid's faces obscures another. The SortFaces routine performs a series of tests to determine if two faces overlap. First, it checks the maximum and minimum X and Y coordinates of the two faces. If the X and Y coordinate ranges of the two faces do not overlap, the faces themselves cannot overlap. In this case, one face lies to the side of the other, so neither can block the view of the other from the center of projection.

The routine also checks whether the largest Z coordinate of the first face is smaller than the smallest Z coordinate of the second. If it is, the first face must be further from the center of projection than the second face so that the program does not need to move the second face to the front of the list.

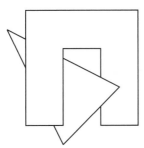

Figure 15.9 Mutually overlapping faces.

Next, the routine uses the IsAbove function to see if the second face is completely above the plane containing the first face. If it is, the first face cannot block the view of the second from the center of projection. Once again the subroutine does not need to move the second face to the front of the list.

Similarly, the routine uses the IsBelow function to see if the first face is completely below the plane that contains the second. If so, the first face cannot block the view of the second from the center of projection, so the subroutine does not need to rearrange the faces.

Any of these tests might determine that the faces do not overlap, but none can conclude that they do. In the final test, SortFaces uses the function Obscures to attempt to determine whether the first face really does block the view of the second from the center of projection.

The following code shows the SortFaces subroutine. The IsAbove and Obscures functions are listed and described in more detail in the following sections.

```
' Sort the faces so those with the largest
' transformed Z coordinates come first.
'
' As we switch faces around, we keep track of the
' number of switches we have made. If it's clear we
' are stuck in an infinite loop, just move the
' first face to the ordered_faces collection so we
' can continue.
Public Sub SortFaces()
Dim ordered_faces As Collection
Dim face_1 As Face3d
Dim face_i As Face3d
Dim i As Integer
Dim Xmin As Single
Dim xmax As Single
Dim ymin As Single
Dim ymax As Single
Dim zmin As Single
Dim zmax As Single
Dim xmini As Single
Dim xmaxi As Single
Dim ymini As Single
Dim ymaxi As Single
Dim zmini As Single
Dim zmaxi As Single
Dim overlap As Boolean
Dim switches As Integer
Dim max_switches As Integer

    Set ordered_faces = New Collection

    ' Pull out any that are culled. These are not
    ' drawn so we can put them at the front of
```

```
' the ordered_faces collection.
For i = Faces.Count To 1 Step -1
    If Faces(i).IsCulled Then
        ordered_faces.Add Faces(i)
        Faces.Remove i
    End If
Next i

' Order the remaining faces.
max_switches = Faces.Count
Do While Faces.Count > 0
    ' Get the first item's extent.
    Set face_1 = Faces(1)
    face_1.GetExtent Xmin, xmax, ymin, ymax, zmin, zmax

    ' Compare this face to the others.
    overlap = False      ' In case Face.Count = 0.
    For i = 2 To Faces.Count
        Set face_i = Faces(i)

        ' Get item i's extent.
        face_i.GetExtent xmini, xmaxi, _
            ymini, ymaxi, zmini, zmaxi
        overlap = True
        If xmaxi <= Xmin Or xmini >= xmax Or _
            ymaxi <= ymin Or ymini >= ymax Or _
            zmini >= zmax _
        Then
            ' The extents do not overlap.
            overlap = False
        ElseIf face_i.IsAbove(face_1) Then
            ' Face i is all above the plane
            ' of face 1.
            overlap = False
        ElseIf face_1.IsBelow(face_i) Then
            ' Face 1 is all beneath the plane
            ' of face i.
            overlap = False
        ElseIf Not face_1.Obscures(face_i) Then
            ' If face_1 does not lie partly above
            ' face_i, then there is no problem.
            overlap = False
        End If

        If overlap Then Exit For
    Next i

    If overlap And switches < max_switches Then
        ' There's overlap, move face i to the
        ' top of the list.
        Faces.Remove i
        Faces.Add face_i, , 1 ' Before position 1.
```

```
                    switches = switches + 1
            Else
                ' There's no overlap. Move face 1 to
                ' the ordered_faces collection.
                ordered_faces.Add face_1
                Faces.Remove 1
                max_switches = Faces.Count
                switches = 0
            End If
        Loop ' Loop until we've ordered all the faces.

        ' Replace the Faces collection with the
        ' ordered_faces collection.
        Set Faces = ordered_faces
    End Sub
```

The IsAbove Function

The IsAbove function checks to see if a polygon lies completely above the plane containing another polygon. Figure 15.10 shows this situation. The routine uses cross-products and dot products to decide if all the points in the first polygon lie above the plane in a manner similar to that for the backface removal test.

First, IsAbove uses the cross-product to find a normal vector for the plane. Because the function needs to decide whether the first polygon lies above the plane, it reverses

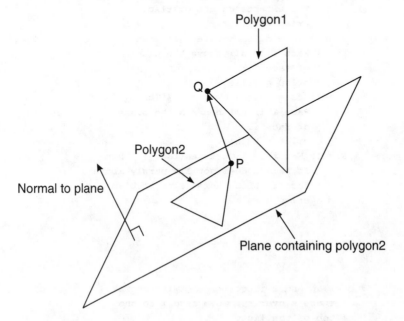

Figure 15.10 Testing whether a face lies completely above the plane containing another face.

the normal if necessary to ensure it is an upward-pointing normal. That makes the normal point more or less toward the transformed center of projection.

For each point Q in the first polygon, IsAbove then computes the vector from a fixed point P on the plane to the point Q as shown in Figure 15.10. It evaluates the dot product of this vector and the normal vector. If the result is greater than zero, the vector points in roughly the same direction as the normal vector, so the point lies above the plane. Otherwise, the point lies below the plane.

In Visual Basic, the routine actually checks whether the dot product is less than –0.01. This prevents the program from incorrectly classifying points because of round-off errors. Because you use this routine to compare the faces of a solid, two polygons will often share a common point or edge. The dot product for points in the first polygon that lie within the plane of the second should be zero. After the points have been translated, rotated, scaled, and projected, however, rounding errors sometimes make the value a small negative number. By comparing the value to -0.01 instead of zero, the routine avoids incorrect results that would be caused by rounding errors.

The following code shows the IsAbove function. The IsBelow function, which determines whether a polygon is entirely below another, is very similar. The only difference is that IsBelow uses a downward-pointing normal rather than one that points upward.

```
' Return True if this polygon is completely above
' the plane containing target.
Public Function IsAbove(ByVal target As Face3d) As Boolean
Dim nx As Single
Dim ny As Single
Dim nz As Single
Dim px As Single
Dim py As Single
Dim pz As Single
Dim dx As Single
Dim dy As Single
Dim dz As Single
Dim Cx As Single
Dim Cy As Single
Dim Cz As Single
Dim i As Integer

    ' Compute an upward pointing normal to the plane.
    target.TransformedNormalVector nx, ny, nz
    If nz < 0 Then
        nx = -nx
        ny = -ny
        nz = -nz
    End If

    ' Get a point on the plane.
    target.GetTransformedPoint 1, px, py, pz

    ' See if the points in this polygon all lie
```

```
    ' above the plane containing target.
    For i = 1 To NumPts
        ' Get the vector from plane to point.
        dx = Points(i).trans(1) - px
        dy = Points(i).trans(2) - py
        dz = Points(i).trans(3) - pz

        ' If the dot product < 0, the point is
        ' below the plane.
        If dx * nx + dy * ny + dz * nz < -0.01 Then
            IsAbove = False
            Exit Function
        End If
    Next i
    IsAbove = True
End Function
```

The Obscures Function

The Obscures function makes one final attempt to determine whether one polygon actually obscures another. First it compares each line segment in the first polygon with each segment in the second. If a segment in one polygon passes above a segment in the other, the function then compares the Z coordinate values of the two segments where they cross. If the first Z value is greater than the second, the function knows with certainty that the first polygon lies above the other. Similarly, if the second Z value is greater than the first, the second polygon must lie above the first.

If the two values are equal, the function continues to check other edges. If the routine later finds two edges that cross each other and have different Z values, it can determine which polygon is on top. If it finds no such edges, then the polygons probably do not overlap, but there are still two cases that the function needs to consider.

First, one polygon might completely surround the other. To check for this situation, function Obscures tests whether the projection of a point on the first polygon lies within the projection of the second. Because the edges of the polygons do not cross, if one point lies within the second polygon, they all do.

Remember that the IsAbove and IsBelow tests have already ruled out the possibility that the second polygon lies entirely above the plane of the first or that the first polygon lies entirely below the plane of the second. In that case, if the points in the first polygon lie within the projection of the second, parts of the second polygon must lie further from the center of projection than the first. In this case, the program needs to move the second polygon to the front of the list.

If there is still no overlap after this test, function Obscures determines whether a point in the second polygon lies within the projection of the first. If so, there is an overlap once again, and the program must move the second polygon to the front of the list.

The final odd situation that function Obscures does not handle is when one polygon has an edge that lies within the other polygon. If one polygon's edges enter and leave the other polygon only at vertices, the Z values where the edges cross are the same. In that

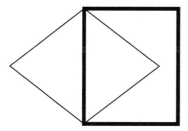 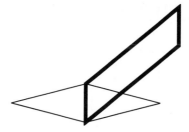

Figure 15.11 Function Obscures does not notice when one polygon enters and exits another only at vertices.

case, the function is not able to tell which polygon is on top. The points in one polygon also do not all lie within the other so the polygon containment test does not work either.

Figure 15.11 shows a square with one edge that lies within a diamond. The picture on the left shows the polygons from the top while the picture on the right shows an oblique view. The square is shown in bold lines, so it is easy to tell which lines belong to each polygon.

The easiest way to handle this problem is to not allow faces that touch in this way. If one polygon has an edge that lies within another, break the second polygon into two pieces along that edge. Then the program does not need to handle this unusual case.

```
' Return True if this polygon partially obscures
' (has greater Z value than) polygon target.
'
' We assume one polygon may obscure the other, but
' they cannot obscure each other.
'
' This check is executed by seeing where the
' projections of the edges of the polygons cross.
' Where they cross, see if one Z value is greater
' than the other.
'
' If no edges cross, see if one polygon contains
' the other. If so, there is an overlap.
Public Function Obscures(ByVal target As Face3d) As Boolean
Dim num As Integer
Dim i As Integer
Dim j As Integer
Dim xi1 As Single
Dim yi1 As Single
Dim zi1 As Single
Dim xi2 As Single
Dim yi2 As Single
Dim zi2 As Single
Dim xj1 As Single
Dim yj1 As Single
Dim zj1 As Single
Dim xj2 As Single
```

```
    Dim yj2 As Single
    Dim zj2 As Single
    Dim X As Single
    Dim Y As Single
    Dim z1 As Single
    Dim z2 As Single

        num = target.NumPts

        ' Check each edge in this polygon.
        GetTransformedPoint NumPts, xi1, yi1, zi1
        For i = 1 To NumPts
            GetTransformedPoint i, xi2, yi2, zi2

            ' Compare with each edge in the other.
            target.GetTransformedPoint num, xj1, yj1, zj1
            For j = 1 To num
                target.GetTransformedPoint j, xj2, yj2, zj2
                ' See if the segments cross.
                If FindCrossing( _
                    xi1, yi1, zi1, _
                    xi2, yi2, zi2, _
                    xj1, yj1, zj1, _
                    xj2, yj2, zj2, _
                    X, Y, z1, z2) _
                Then
                    If z1 - z2 > 0.01 Then
                        ' z1 > z2. We obscure it.
                        Obscures = True
                        Exit Function
                    End If
                    If z2 - z1 > 0.01 Then
                        ' z2 > z1. It obscures us.
                        Obscures = False
                        Exit Function
                    End If
                End If

                xj1 = xj2
                yj1 = yj2
                zj1 = zj2
            Next j

            xi1 = xi2
            yi1 = yi2
            zi1 = zi2
        Next i

        ' No edges cross. See if one polygon contains
        ' the other.

        ' If any points of one polygon are inside the
        ' other, then they must all be. Since the
```

```
    ' IsAbove tests were inconclusive, some points
    ' in one polygon are on the "bad" side of the
    ' other. In that case there is an overlap.

    ' See if this polygon is inside the other.
    GetTransformedPoint 1, xi1, yi1, zi1
    If target.PointInside(xi1, yi1) Then
        Obscures = True
        Exit Function
    End If

    ' See if the other polygon is inside this one.
    target.GetTransformedPoint 1, xi1, yi1, zi1
    If PointInside(xi1, yi1) Then
        Obscures = True
        Exit Function
    End If

    Obscures = False
End Function
```

The FindCrossing Function

Function Obscures uses the FindCrossing function to see where two polygon edges cross each other. This routine takes as parameters the endpoints of two line segments. It determines if the segments cross over each other, and if they do, it determines the Z coordinate values of the segments where they cross.

The function uses parametric representations for the line segments. If a line segment connects the points (ax1, ay1) and (ax2, ay2), you can represent the X and Y coordinates of the points along the segment using a variable t1, like this:

```
X(t1) = ax1 + t1 * (ax2 - ax1)
Y(t1) = ay1 + t1 * (ay2 - ay1)
```

To generate the points on the segment, you vary the value of t1 between 0.0 and 1.0. You can create similar equations using a variable t2 to represent the second line segment connecting the points (bx1, by1) and (bx2, by2).

Where the segments intersect, the values of the X and Y coordinates of both segments are the same. The equations give:

```
ax1 + t1 * (ax2 - ax1) = bx1 + t2 * (bx2 - bx1)
ay1 + t1 * (ay2 - ay1) = by1 + t2 * (by2 - by1)
```

These two equations contain two unknown values, t1 and t2. The FindCrossing function solves the equations to find these values. If both values are between 0.0 and 1.0, the segments cross each other. FindCrossing then uses the values of t1 and t2 to calculate the Z coordinates of each segment where they cross.

```vb
' See where the projections of two segments cross.
' Return true if the segments cross, false
' otherwise.
Private Function FindCrossing(ByVal ax1 As Single, _
    ByVal ay1 As Single, ByVal az1 As Single, _
    ByVal ax2 As Single, ByVal ay2 As Single, _
    ByVal az2 As Single, ByVal bx1 As Single, _
    ByVal by1 As Single, ByVal bz1 As Single, _
    ByVal bx2 As Single, ByVal by2 As Single, _
    ByVal bz2 As Single, _
    ByRef X As Single, ByRef Y As Single, _
    ByRef z1 As Single, ByRef z2 As Single) _
        As Boolean
Dim dxa As Single
Dim dya As Single
Dim dza As Single
Dim dxb As Single
Dim dyb As Single
Dim dzb As Single
Dim t1 As Single
Dim t2 As Single
Dim denom As Single

    dxa = ax2 - ax1
    dya = ay2 - ay1
    dxb = bx2 - bx1
    dyb = by2 - by1

    FindCrossing = False

    denom = dxb * dya - dyb * dxa
    ' If the segments are parallel, stop.
    If denom < 0.01 And denom > -0.01 Then Exit Function

    t2 = (ax1 * dya - ay1 * dxa - bx1 * dya + by1 * dxa) / _
        denom
    If t2 < 0 Or t2 > 1 Then Exit Function

    t1 = (ax1 * dyb - ay1 * dxb - bx1 * dyb + by1 * dxb) / _
        denom
    If t1 < 0 Or t1 > 1 Then Exit Function

    ' Compute the points of overlap.
    X = ax1 + t1 * dxa
    Y = ay1 + t1 * dya
    dza = az2 - az1
    dzb = bz2 - bz1
    z1 = az1 + t1 * dza
    z2 = bz1 + t2 * dzb
    FindCrossing = True
End Function
```

The PointInside Function

The final important function used in this process is the PointInside function. This function determines whether a point lies within the projection of a polygon. It does this by adding up the angles between the lines drawn from the point to each vertex of the polygon. If the point lies outside the polygon, the sum is zero. If the point lies inside the polygon, the sum will be $2 * \pi$ or $-2 * \pi$, depending on the direction in which you examine the vertices.

To see why this works, imagine running a line segment from the point to one of the vertices in the polygon. Then rotate the line segment to the next vertex. Continue rotating the segment to visit the vertices in order around the polygon's edges.

Suppose the point lies far to the left of the polygon. Then the segment will move up and down, making various angles with the vertices. The positive angles are canceled by the negative angles, so you finish where you started and the total sum of the angles is zero.

Now suppose the point is in the middle of the polygon. Then as you rotate the segment through the vertices, the segment rotates 360 degrees around the point. It finishes where it started, but it has made a loop around the point. That makes the sum of the angles between the segment's positions add up to 360 or –360 degrees.

```
' Return True if the point projection lies within
' this polygon's projection.
Public Function PointInside( _
    ByVal X As Single, ByVal Y As Single) As Boolean
Dim i As Integer
Dim theta1 As Double
Dim theta2 As Double
Dim dtheta As Double
Dim dx As Double
Dim dy As Double
Dim angles As Double

    dx = Points(NumPts).trans(1) - X
    dy = Points(NumPts).trans(2) - Y
    theta1 = ATan2(CSng(dy), CSng(dx))
    If theta1 < 0 Then theta1 = theta1 + 2 * PI
    For i = 1 To NumPts
        dx = Points(i).trans(1) - X
        dy = Points(i).trans(2) - Y
        theta2 = ATan2(CSng(dy), CSng(dx))
        If theta2 < 0 Then theta2 = theta2 + 2 * PI
        dtheta = theta2 - theta1
        If dtheta > PI Then dtheta = dtheta - 2 * PI
        If dtheta < -PI Then dtheta = dtheta + 2 * PI
        angles = angles + dtheta
        theta1 = theta2
    Next i

    PointInside = (Abs(angles) > 0.001)
End Function
```

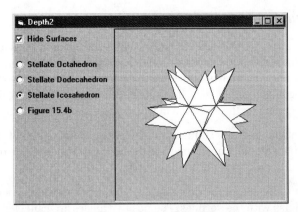

Figure 15.12 Program Depth2 displaying a seriously nonconvex stellate icosahedron.

You can see that ordering polygons is a complicated process full of special cases. The tests that handle these cases are arranged so that the tests that are fastest and most likely to give conclusive results are performed first. More time-consuming tests, like those used by function Obscures, are performed only if absolutely necessary.

Example program Depth2, shown in Figure 15.12, uses these routines to display nonconvex solids. Use the option buttons to select a solid to view. Use the Hide Surface check box to tell the program to use the Depth-Sort algorithm to remove the hidden surfaces.

Surfaces Revisited

Chapter 14, Surfaces, describes ways you can create and display different kinds of three-dimensional surfaces. It also explains the hi-lo and Z-order algorithms for performing hidden surface removal for many kinds of simple surfaces. Unfortunately, this algorithm is not guaranteed to work for all perspective transformations. It also does not handle more complex surfaces like Bezier surfaces, B-splines, and surfaces of transformation. You can use the Depth-Sort algorithm to perform hidden surface removal in these other situations.

Before you can use Depth-Sort, you must make a few changes to the way you store surfaces. The programs described in Chapter 14 create and store surfaces as collections of polyline objects. This is fine for displaying a skeleton view of a surface, but the Depth-Sort algorithm works only with polygons. To display these surfaces using Depth-Sort, you must first modify the programs to generate surface polygons.

Many of the surfaces described in Chapter 14 are made up of areas that are not flat polygons. Bezier surfaces, B-splines, and surfaces of transformation all consist of some sort of bent rectangle or quadrilateral. The easiest way to convert a bent quadrilateral into a group of polygons is to break it into two triangles, as shown in Figure 15.13. With this strategy in mind, you can modify the programs that generate these surfaces so that they produce triangles rather than bent quadrilaterals.

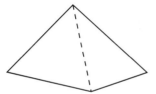

Figure 15.13 Breaking a "bent quadrilateral" into two triangles.

For instance, a program that creates a surface of transformation would build triangles between the vertices of adjacent copies of the transformed base curve. Figure 15.14 shows two transformed versions of a base curve and the triangles between them.

The program can also create a polygon to represent the untransformed base curve and one to represent the final transformation of the curve. This would seal the ends of the surface to create a solid. If the program uses backface removal, it must ensure that all the triangles as well as the two closing polygons are oriented so that their normals point outward.

The following code generates these polygons. The routine assumes that the base curve is closed, so the first and last points are the same. To make the triangles and polygons outwardly oriented, the routine also assumes that the base curve is inwardly oriented with respect to the transformations. In other words, the normal to the base curve should point in the general direction of the transformations. If the base curve lies in the X–Z plane and the transformations move the curve in the positive Y direction (upward), the base curve should be oriented counterclockwise. Then its normal also points in the positive Y direction.

```
' Create the display solid by applying the
' series of transformations in array M().
Public Sub Transform(Optional cap_ends As Variant)
Dim face As Face3d
Dim i As Integer
Dim j As Integer
Dim x0 As Single
Dim y0 As Single
```

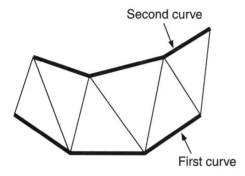

Second curve

First curve

Figure 15.14 Creating triangles for a surface of transformation.

```
Dim z0 As Single
Dim x1 As Single
Dim y1 As Single
Dim z1 As Single
Dim x2 As Single
Dim y2 As Single
Dim z2 As Single
Dim x3 As Single
Dim y3 As Single
Dim z3 As Single

    If IsMissing(cap_ends) Then cap_ends = True

    Set solid = New Solid3d

    ' Add the base curve to solid assuming the
    ' curve is stored oriented towards the
    ' transformations.
    If cap_ends Then
        Set face = New Face3d
        solid.Faces.Add face
        For i = NumCurvePts - 1 To 1 Step -1
            face.AddPoints _
                CurvePoints(i).coord(1), _
                CurvePoints(i).coord(2), _
                CurvePoints(i).coord(3)
        Next i
    End If

    ' Start with the transformed coordinates
    ' the same as the original coordinates.
    For i = 1 To NumCurvePts
        CurvePoints(i).trans(1) = CurvePoints(i).coord(1)
        CurvePoints(i).trans(2) = CurvePoints(i).coord(2)
        CurvePoints(i).trans(3) = CurvePoints(i).coord(3)
    Next i

    ' Create the transformed copies of the curve.
    For i = 1 To NumTrans
        x0 = CurvePoints(1).trans(1)
        y0 = CurvePoints(1).trans(2)
        z0 = CurvePoints(1).trans(3)
        m3ApplyFull _
            CurvePoints(1).coord, trans(i).M, _
            CurvePoints(1).trans
        x1 = CurvePoints(1).trans(1)
        y1 = CurvePoints(1).trans(2)
        z1 = CurvePoints(1).trans(3)

        For j = 2 To NumCurvePts
            x2 = CurvePoints(j).trans(1)
```

```
            y2 = CurvePoints(j).trans(2)
            z2 = CurvePoints(j).trans(3)
            m3ApplyFull _
                CurvePoints(j).coord, trans(i).M, _
                CurvePoints(j).trans
            x3 = CurvePoints(j).trans(1)
            y3 = CurvePoints(j).trans(2)
            z3 = CurvePoints(j).trans(3)

            solid.AddFace _
                x0, y0, z0, _
                x2, y2, z2, _
                x1, y1, z1

            solid.AddFace _
                x2, y2, z2, _
                x3, y3, z3, _
                x1, y1, z1
            x0 = x2
            y0 = y2
            z0 = z2
            x1 = x3
            y1 = y3
            z1 = z3
        Next j
    Next i

    ' Add the final curve to solid assuming
    ' the curve is stored oriented towards the
    ' transformations.
    If cap_ends Then
        Set face = New Face3d
        solid.Faces.Add face
        For i = 2 To NumCurvePts
            face.AddPoints _
                CurvePoints(i).trans(1), _
                CurvePoints(i).trans(2), _
                CurvePoints(i).trans(3)
        Next i
    End If
End Sub
```

This code uses two polygons to close the surface to form a solid. Other surfaces, like fractal terrains and Bezier surfaces, are generally not closed solids. The Depth-Sort algorithm works with these open surfaces, but backface removal does not. No matter how you orient the triangles, there will be places you can put the center of projection so that backface removal eliminates triangles that should be displayed. This produces holes in the surface.

For some well-behaved surfaces, you can restrict the allowed positions of the center of projection and still use hidden surface removal. If the surface is mostly flat, like a fractal terrain surface, backface removal works as long as the center of projection is relatively high above the surface. For more general surfaces that twist and turn, like Bezier surfaces and B-splines, it is unlikely that you will be able to properly restrict the placement of the center of projection. In that case, you can add sides and a bottom to the surface to make it a closed solid.

Example program Trans uses the previous code to display surfaces of transformation. The program is similar to the Trans program presented in Chapter 14, Surfaces, except it has a Hide Surfaces check box. When you check this box, the program uses backface removal and the Depth-Sort algorithm to display the solid with hidden surfaces removed. Figure 15.15 shows several complex solids created by the program.

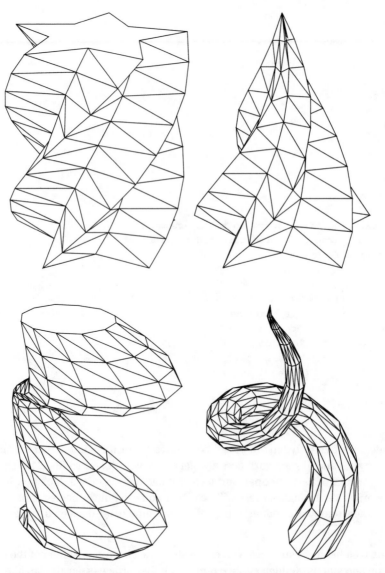

Figure 15.15 Surfaces of transformation with hidden surfaces removed.

Example program Rotate uses these techniques to display surfaces of revolution. This program is similar to the Rotate program presented in Chapter 14. Like program Trans, it has a Hide Surfaces check box that lets you tell the program to remove hidden surfaces.

Summary

Hidden surface removal is an important step on the path to visual realism. Removing lines that should be hidden makes complicated three-dimensional scenes much easier to understand. Left in the picture, these lines clutter the image, usually without adding useful information.

While these images are easier to understand, they are still not very aesthetically appealing. No one is likely to mistake them for photographs of actual objects. Chapter 16, Shading Models, shows how a program can use shading to make three-dimensional objects appear much more realistic. Chapter 17, Ray Tracing, extends these shading techniques to produce even more realistic images.

CHAPTER 16

Shading Models

Chapter 15, Hidden Surface Removal, describes several different kinds of hidden surface removal algorithms. By removing hidden surfaces, you can make the display of three-dimensional objects easier to understand.

The Valley example program described in Chapter 14, Surfaces, uses color to produce a fractal valley landscape. It uses blue for a river, white for snow, gray for steep cliffs, and different shades of green for vegetation. This technique makes the result much more realistic than a simple wire frame or even an image with hidden surfaces removed.

You can make images even more realistic by using a *shading model* (sometimes called a *lighting model*). A shading model embodies some of the physics that determine how light falls on an object. By considering diffuse and specular reflection, ambient light, and the distance from the light source, you can shade objects realistically, making three-dimensional scenes more believable and easier to understand.

The Physics of Lighting

The physical laws that describe how light interacts with an object are extremely complex. They involve such factors as the brightness of the light, whether the light comes from a point source or a bright surface, the wavelengths present in the light, the angle of incidence of the light on an object's surface, the roughness of the surface with respect to the wavelengths present in the light, and the amount of light reflected off other objects onto this one.

Fortunately, to display an object on a computer you do not need to understand every last detail of the physics involved. Instead you can use a mathematical model that takes into account the most important aspects of the physical situation. The level of detail your model should have depends on your needs and your available processing power. To display a spinning cube in real time, you need a fairly simple model. Without an extremely powerful computer, your program cannot compute values for a complex shading model fast enough to display the results in real time.

If you want to create a series of bitmaps for later animation, you can use a much more sophisticated model. You could let your computer spend a few hours computing each frame in the animation. Later, you can play the frames back at the much faster rate of 10 or 20 frames per second, which is fast enough to produce smooth motion.

Diffuse Reflection

Most objects do not emit light of their own. Instead, light from some other source falls on them. The object absorbs some of the light and reflects some of it. For instance, when you shine white light on a blue object, the object absorbs many of the green and red frequencies in the light and reflects most of the blue frequencies. Your eye detects the reflected blue frequencies, so you see the object as blue.

A perfectly dull, matte surface reflects light equally in all directions. This sort of reflection is called *diffuse reflection*. A normal piece of paper is a reasonably matte surface. When you shine white light on a white piece of paper, the paper appears white no matter what your viewing angle.

In reality, few surfaces are perfectly dull, so from some viewing angles you see highlights and other effects. If you place a piece of paper on a desk and move your eyes to different positions around the paper, you will see that the paper grows brighter and darker depending on the angle from which you are viewing it. Still, diffuse reflection plays a large role in determining the appearance of reasonably dull surfaces.

For a perfect matte surface, the intensity of the diffuse reflected light from a point-sized light source is given by Lambert's law:

```
I_d = I_i * k_d * Cos(θ) for 0 <= θ <= π/2
```

In this equation:

I_d is the resulting intensity of the diffuse reflected light. Since this value will be used with the RGB function to calculate a color, it must eventually lie between 0 and 255.

I_I is the intensity of the incident light hitting the surface. Usually this is between 0 and 255, so I_d is between 0 and 255.

kd is a constant between 0.0 and 1.0 that represents the way the surface reacts to these wavelengths of light. The larger the value, the more light is reflected.

θ is the angle between the vector L pointing from the surface to the light source and the surface normal N.

Figure 16.1 shows a light source shining on a surface with the angle θ labeled.

Suppose A and B are two vectors with components <xa, ya, za> and <xb, yb, zb>. Recall that the dot product of two vectors written A ⟨ B is defined as:

```
A · B = xa * xb + ya * yb + za + zb
```

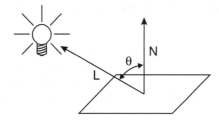

Figure 16.1 Light hitting a matte surface.

If |A| and |B| are the lengths of the vectors, recall also that:

```
A · B = |A| * |B| * Cos(θ)
```

where θ is the angle between the vectors.

You can *normalize* a vector by dividing its X, Y, and Z components by the vector's length. This produces a vector of length 1 pointing in the same direction as the original vector. Because normalized vectors have length one, they are often called *unit* vectors.

If the vectors A and B are unit vectors, the dot product becomes simply:

```
A · B = Cos(θ)
```

Now return to Lambert's law. If you normalize the vector L from the surface to the light source and the surface normal N, you can rewrite Lambert's law using vectors.

```
I_d = I_i * k_d * (L · N)
```

You should calculate the intensities of the surface's red, green, and blue color components separately and then combine them using Visual Basic's RGB function. Break both the incident light and the surface's color coefficients into red, green, and blue values. This gives you three equations:

```
I_d,red   = I_I,red   * k_d,red   * (L · N)
I_d,green = I_I,green * k_d,green * (L · N)
I_d,blue  = I_I,blue  * k_d,blue  * (L · N)
```

Notice that the value L · N is the same in all three equations so you only need to calculate it once.

The components of the incident light and the surface's reflection coefficients determine the general colors of the light and the surface. For example, a blue-green light source might give incident light values of $I_{i,red} = 0$, $I_{i,green} = 255$, and $I_{i,blue} = 255$. If the surface is yellow, its diffuse reflection coefficients might be $k_{d,red} = 1.0$, $k_{d,green} = 1.0$, and $k_{d,blue} = 0.0$.

If you assume that the light source is far away from the polygons you are drawing, the vector L from a polygon to the light source is approximately the same for every point in the polygon. Because the points in the polygon all lie in the same plane, they all have the same surface normal vector N.

In that case, the intensity at all points in the polygon is roughly the same. Using these facts, you can easily add a simple shading model to the hidden surface removal programs described in previous chapters. For each polygon that must be drawn, use the previous formula to compute the intensity of a point on the polygon. Compute the corresponding color and fill the polygon with that color.

Just as you can add a point's red, green, and blue intensities to get its color, you can also add the effects of multiple light sources. Calculate the color component values due to each light source separately, add them, and use the RGB function to calculate the final color value.

After you add the components due to several light sources, the result may be greater than 255. If you pass a value greater than 255 into the RGB function, your program crashes. To avoid crashing, test the color components and make sure none are too big before you call RGB.

To make it easier to manage light sources, you can create a LightSource class. This class holds the light source's location and intensities.

```
Option Explicit

Public X As Single
Public Y As Single
Public Z As Single
Public Ir As Single
Public Ig As Single
Public Ib As Single
```

Now you can pass a collection of LightSource objects to a Face3d object. The face can use the light sources' locations and intensities to calculate its color. The SurfaceColor function shown in the following code performs this calculation.

```
' Return the proper shade for this face
' due to the indicated light source.
Private Function SurfaceColor( _
    ByVal light_sources As Collection) As Long
Dim light As LightSource
Dim Lx As Single
Dim Ly As Single
Dim Lz As Single
Dim L_len As Single
Dim Nx As Single
Dim Ny As Single
Dim Nz As Single
Dim NdotL As Single
Dim R As Integer
```

```
Dim G As Integer
Dim B As Integer

    ' Find the unit surface normal. It is the
    ' same for all the light sources.
    UnitNormalVector Nx, Ny, Nz

    For Each light In light_sources
        ' Find the unit vector pointing towards the light.
        Lx = light.X - Points(1).coord(1)
        Ly = light.Y - Points(1).coord(2)
        Lz = light.Z - Points(1).coord(3)
        L_len = Sqr(Lx * Lx + Ly * Ly + Lz * Lz)
        Lx = Lx / L_len
        Ly = Ly / L_len
        Lz = Lz / L_len

        ' See how intense to make the color.
        NdotL = Nx * Lx + Ny * Ly + Nz * Lz

        ' The light does not hit the top of the
        ' surface if NdotL <= 0.
        If NdotL > 0 Then
            R = R + light.Ir * DiffuseKr * NdotL
            G = G + light.Ig * DiffuseKg * NdotL
            B = B + light.Ib * DiffuseKb * NdotL
        End If
    Next light

    ' Keep the color components <= 255.
    If R > 255 Then R = 255
    If G > 255 Then G = 255
    If B > 255 Then B = 255

    ' Return the color.
    SurfaceColor = RGB(R, G, B)
End Function
```

Example program Light1, shown in Figures 16.2 and 16.3, uses this subroutine to display objects with diffuse reflection. Use the option buttons to select a scene. The objects in the scenes all have their own predefined diffuse reflection coefficients.

Use the check boxes to determine which predefined light sources the program should use. The spheres in the two last scenes are white and can be particularly interesting with the nonwhite color sources.

Note that the program's light sources are stationary. When you press the arrow keys, the viewing position changes, but the objects and light sources do not. That means the angles the light makes with the objects do not change, so each polygon's color remains the same.

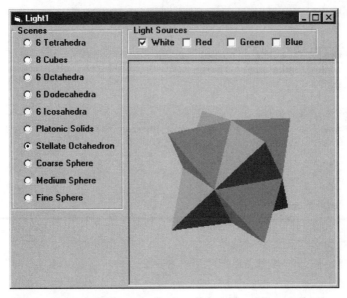

Figure 16.2 A stellate octahedron lighted by diffuse reflection.

Ambient Light

As you work with program Light1, you will notice that the images appear rather stark, particularly with only one light source. Surfaces that are not illuminated by some light source are completely black. In reality, surfaces that are blocked from a light source are

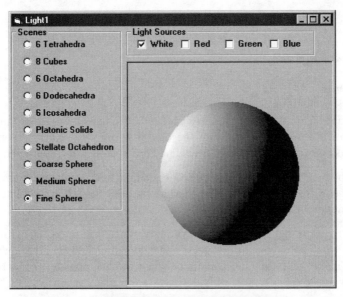

Figure 16.3 A sphere lighted by diffuse reflection.

usually still visible to some extent because of *ambient light*. Ambient light is light that reaches an object after being reflected off other objects.

In a typical room, objects hidden under desks and chairs are visible because ambient light reflected off the floor, walls, and other surfaces in the room illuminate them. Even if you turn off the lights during the day, the room is lit by ambient sunlight reflected by the sky and entering through windows.

A simple way to model ambient light is to add a constant term I_a to indicate the amount of ambient light in the scene. Then give each object in the scene a constant factor k_a that indicates how much of the ambient light is reflected by the object. For color, use three ambient light terms—$I_{a,red}$, $I_{a,green}$, and $I_{a,\ blue}$—and three coefficients for each object—$k_{a,red}$, $k_{a,green}$, and $k_{a,blue}$.

Determining exactly how much ambient light truly reaches a given object is very difficult. For example, when a dark object lies close to another object, the first object blocks some of the ambient light that would otherwise strike the second. Assuming the ambient light intensity I_a is constant throughout the scene is a good first approximation and is much easier.

When the ambient light term is added to the component because of diffuse reflection, the intensity of light a viewer sees from an object is given by the equation:

```
I = Ia * ka + Ii * kd * (L · N)
```

The only change you need to make to the SurfaceColor subroutine is to add the new ambient term. Note that this term does not depend on the light sources, so it is added only once.

```
' Add the ambient term.
R = R + ambient_light * AmbientKr
G = G + ambient_light * AmbientKg
B = B + ambient_light * AmbientKb
```

Example program Light2 is similar to program Light1, except it uses ambient light. Because the ambient term tends to make objects brighter, this program's light sources are slightly darker than those in program Light1.

Distance

If two polygons lie in parallel planes, the angles their normals make with the vectors to a light source that is far away are almost the same. In that case, the two polygons are shaded with the same color. If one polygon overlaps the other, you cannot distinguish the boundary between them.

Figure 16.4 shows this problem. The darkest faces on the four middle cubes have the same color. These faces overlap, so the boundary between them vanishes, making the picture more confusing.

You can prevent this sort of problem by adding a distance term to the shading model. In the real world, light intensity decreases proportionally to the square of the distance to the light source. Adding a term that decreases with the distance squared does not work well in practice, however. If you try to place the light source infinitely far away, you will have trouble dividing by the square of an infinite number. Even if the light source is not infinitely far away, it is often relatively far away compared with the distances between the objects. In that case, the differences in light intensity between different objects are very small.

A solution that works well in practice is to make the light intensity I_d at an object proportional to $1/(r + k_{dist})$ where k_{dist} is a constant and r is the distance from the object to the light source. When this correction is added, the shading model becomes:

```
I = I_a * k_a + I_i * k_d * (L · N) / (r + k_dist)
```

If you add this term and make no other correction, the overall brightness of your image is greatly reduced. Because you are dividing the term representing diffuse reflection by a large number, particularly if the light source is far from the polygons so that r is large, the image is much darker.

To prevent this, you can increase the intensity of the light source I_i. If r_{min} is the smallest distance from any polygon to the light source, you can adjust I_i by a factor of $(r_{min} + k_{dist})$. Then the intensity at polygons closest to the light source is roughly the same as it would be without the distance term. The intensity at polygons farther away is reduced. Adding this scaling term to the lighting equation gives:

```
I = I_a * k_a + I_i * k_d * (L · N) * (r_min + k_dist) / (r + k_dist)
```

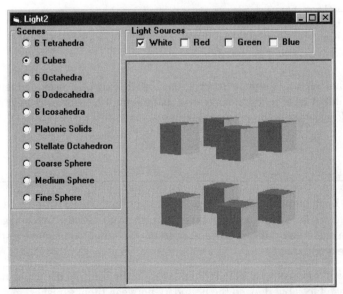

Figure 16.4   Parallel faces are the same color with diffuse and ambient lighting.

To make the differences in intensity between different polygons noticeable, you also need to select k_{dist} carefully. You need to make $(r_{min} + k_{dist})$ reasonably sized compared with the differences in the distances from the polygons to the light source.

If k_{dist} is very small, the difference between $(r_{min} + k_{dist})$ and $(r_{max} + k_{dist})$ is relatively large. In that case, the intensity at polygons further from the light source is very small, and those polygons are too dark.

On the other hand, if k_{dist} is very large, the difference between $(r_{min} + k_{dist})$ and $(r_{max} + k_{dist})$ is relatively small. In that case, the intensity at polygons far from the light source is almost the same as at those that are closer. This makes it difficult to notice the differences in the intensities.

Often you can get good results by making the intensity drop by roughly 50 percent across the scene. To do that, you need to satisfy the equation:

```
(r_min + k_dist) / (r_max + k_dist) = 0.5
```

Solving for k_{dist} gives:

```
k_dist = r_max - 2 * r_min
```

To calculate color values with the distance term, the SurfaceColor function must know the values of k_{dist}, r_{min}, and the distance between a polygon and a light source. Because the distance terms depend on the position of the light source, these values should be properties of the light source objects, not the scene as a whole or of the objects in the scene. With these extra terms, the LightSource class has the following declarations:

```
Option Explicit

Public X As Single
Public Y As Single
Public Z As Single
Public Ir As Single
Public Ig As Single
Public Ib As Single
Public Kdist As Single
Public Rmin As Single
```

The ScaleIntensityForDepth subroutine shown in the following code sets the values of Kdist and Rmin for a light source. The Solids collection contains the Solid3d objects in the scene. The solid class used by this program provides a GetRminRmax routine that sets the minimum and maximum distances from the light source to the solid.

```
' Set this light source's Kdist and Rmin values.
Private Sub ScaleIntensityForDepth(ByVal light As LightSource)
Dim solid As Solid3d
Dim Rmin As Single
Dim Rmax As Single
```

```
Dim new_rmin As Single
Dim new_rmax As Single

    Rmin = 1E+30
    Rmax = -1E+30

    For Each solid In Solids
        solid.GetRminRmax new_rmin, new_rmax, _
            light.X, light.Y, light.Z
        If Rmin > new_rmin Then Rmin = new_rmin
        If Rmax < new_rmax Then Rmax = new_rmax
    Next solid

    light.Rmin = Rmin
    light.Kdist = Rmax - 2 * Rmin
End Sub
```

Example program Light3, shown in Figure 16.5, is similar to program Light2 except it adds the distance term to the shading model. Use the option buttons to select a scene. Use the check boxes to determine which light sources are used. Compare Figures 16.4 and 16.5 to see how the distance term works.

You may want to experiment with different formulas for setting k_{dist}. For example, setting k_{dist} to the following value makes the darkest polygons much darker.

$$k_{dist} = (r_{max} - 5 * r_{min}) \ / \ 4$$

Because only the few polygons closest to the light source keep their original intensities, the scene as a whole is darker.

Specular Reflection

Most objects do not have perfectly dull, matte surfaces. Most surfaces have some degree of reflectiveness. When you view a surface at a certain angle, much of the incident light that strikes the surface is reflected toward your eyes. This is called *specular reflection*.

For example, when you look at a red billiard ball under a bright white light, you see a bright highlight on the ball. The highlight is due to specular reflection. The light that reaches your eyes after striking other parts of the ball is due to diffuse reflection and ambient light.

If you look closely at the highlight, you will see it is much whiter than the rest of the ball. In the highlight, the ball reflects most of the white light that hits it. Other parts of the ball reflect mostly red light, so they appear redder.

A mirror is an almost perfectly reflective surface. Light that strikes a mirror making angle θ with the surface normal reflects off the mirror, making another angle θ with the normal as shown in Figure 16.6.

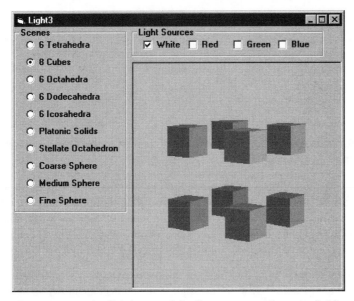

Figure 16.5 The lighting model's distance term gives parallel faces slightly different colors.

While most objects are not perfectly dull, most are not perfectly reflective, either. Light transmitted by specular reflection leaves the surface mostly, but not entirely, in the direction of the mirror angle θ. Figure 16.7 shows light reflecting off an imperfectly reflective surface. The lengths of the arrows in the shaded region indicate the amount of light reflected in directions close to the mirror angle.

The amount of reflected light drops off very quickly as the direction moves away from the mirror angle. Figure 16.8 shows light reflecting off a surface toward a viewpoint. The viewpoint receives less reflected light than it would if it were directly in the mirror direction.

Bui-Tong Phong developed a model that approximates specular reflection using a term that involves $\cos^n(\phi)$. If n is large, $\cos^n(\phi)$ grows small very quickly as ϕ increases. That makes most of the specularly reflected light move in directions close to the angle θ, which agrees with the behavior of a good reflector.

For a perfect reflector, n is infinitely large. In that case $\cos^n(\phi) = 0$, except when $\phi = 0$, in which case $\cos^n(\phi) = 1$. That makes all of the reflected light follow the mirror angle.

When n is small, $\cos^n(\phi)$ does not decrease as quickly when ϕ increases. That allows more reflected light at larger angles ϕ. This produces a larger, less intense highlight on the surface.

Adding the new term for specular reflection to the shading model gives:

```
I = I_a * k_a +
    I_i * (k_d * (L · N) + k_s * Cos^n(φ)) *
        (r_min + k_dist) / (r + k_dist)
```

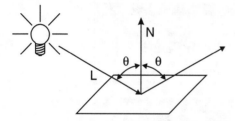

Figure 16.6 For a perfect reflector, light arrives and leaves, making the same angle with the surface normal.

The value k_s is a new specular reflection constant that depends on the particular surface. Unlike with other lighting model constants, there is only one specular constant κ_σ rather than one each for the surface's red, green, and blue components. Specular reflection brightens each color component in equal amounts, so you only need one constant.

Suppose V is the unit vector from the point on the surface to the viewpoint, and R is the unit vector pointing in the direction of the angle of reflection as shown in Figure 16.8. Then you can rewrite $\text{Cos}^n(\phi)$ as:

```
Cosⁿ(φ) = (R · V)ⁿ
```
$$\text{Cos}^n(\phi) = (R \cdot V)^n$$

Substituting this value into the previous equation gives:

$$
\begin{aligned}
I = I_a * k_a + \\
I_i * (k_d * (L \cdot N) + k_s * (R \cdot V)^n) * \\
(r_{min} + k_{dist}) / (r + k_{dist})
\end{aligned}
$$

The vectors L, N, and V are easy to calculate, but R is not. Fortunately, you can find the vector R using a little vector algebra. Figure 16.9 shows the unit vector L pointing from the surface toward the light source, and the surface's unit normal vector N. The vector B is chosen to be perpendicular to N. The vector A is the projection of the vector L along the vector N.

In terms of vector addition, A = L + B. In other words, you can get the components of vector A by adding the corresponding components of vectors L and B. For example,

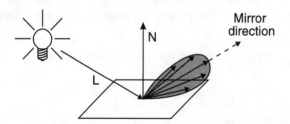

Figure 16.7 For an imperfect reflector, light leaves in directions close to the mirror direction.

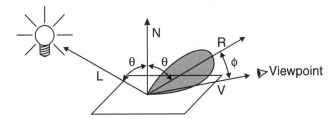

Figure 16.8 Specular reflection decreases quickly as the angle ϕ increases.

the X component of vector A is $A_x = L_x + B_x$. You can turn this around slightly to see that $B = A - L$.

The geometry of the situation implies that the length of A is $|L| * Cos(\theta)$. Because L is a unit vector, $|L| = 1$, so this becomes simply $Cos(\theta)$. The vector A lies along the unit normal N, so the exact value for A is $N * Cos(\theta)$. Because L and N are unit vectors, the dot product $L \langle N = Cos(\theta)$.

Putting these results together, you get $B = A - L = N * (L \langle N) - L$.

Finally, Figure 16.9 shows that $R = L + 2 * B$. Substituting the value for B gives $R = L + 2 * (N * (L \langle N) - L) = 2 * N * (L \langle N) - L$. You can use this equation to compute the vector R in terms of the vectors N and L. For instance, the X component of the vector R is given by the equation:

```
R_x = 2 * N_x * (L_x * N_x + L_y * N_y + L_z * N_z) - L_x
```

Using these results, you can update the SurfaceColor subroutine used by the Face3d class. The following code show the routine in its entirety.

```
' Return the proper shade for this face
' due to the indicated light source.
Private Function SurfaceColor( _
    ByVal light_sources As Collection, _
    ByVal ambient_light As Integer, ByVal eye_x As Single, _
```

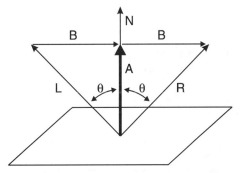

Figure 16.9 Calculating the mirror direction R.

```
        ByVal eye_y As Single, ByVal eye_z As Single) As Long
Dim light As LightSource
Dim Lx As Single
Dim Ly As Single
Dim Lz As Single
Dim L_len As Single
Dim Nx As Single
Dim Ny As Single
Dim Nz As Single
Dim NdotL As Single
Dim R As Integer
Dim G As Integer
Dim B As Integer
Dim distance_factor As Single
Dim diffuse_factor As Single
Dim Vx As Single
Dim Vy As Single
Dim Vz As Single
Dim V_len As Single
Dim Rx As Single
Dim Ry As Single
Dim Rz As Single
Dim RdotV As Single
Dim specular_factor As Single

    ' Find the unit surface normal. It is the
    ' same for all the light sources.
    UnitNormalVector Nx, Ny, Nz

    For Each light In light_sources
        ' ***********************
        ' * Diffuse Reflection *
        ' ***********************
        ' Find the unit vector pointing towards the light.
        Lx = light.X - Points(1).coord(1)
        Ly = light.Y - Points(1).coord(2)
        Lz = light.Z - Points(1).coord(3)
        L_len = Sqr(Lx * Lx + Ly * Ly + Lz * Lz)
        Lx = Lx / L_len
        Ly = Ly / L_len
        Lz = Lz / L_len

        ' See how intense to make the color.
        NdotL = Nx * Lx + Ny * Ly + Nz * Lz

        ' The light does not hit the top of the
        ' surface if NdotL <= 0.
        If NdotL > 0 Then
            distance_factor = (light.Rmin + light.Kdist) / _
                (L_len + light.Kdist)
            diffuse_factor = NdotL * distance_factor
            R = R + light.Ir * DiffuseKr * diffuse_factor
```

```
        G = G + light.Ig * DiffuseKg * diffuse_factor
        B = B + light.Ib * DiffuseKb * diffuse_factor

        ' ***********************
        ' * Specular Reflection *
        ' ***********************
        ' Find the unit vector V from the surface
        ' to the viewing position.
        Vx = eye_x - Points(1).coord(1)
        Vy = eye_y - Points(1).coord(2)
        Vz = eye_z - Points(1).coord(3)
        V_len = Sqr(Vx * Vx + Vy * Vy + Vz * Vz)
        Vx = Vx / V_len
        Vy = Vy / V_len
        Vz = Vz / V_len

        ' Find the mirror vector R.
        Rx = 2 * Nx * NdotL - Lx
        Ry = 2 * Ny * NdotL - Ly
        Rz = 2 * Nz * NdotL - Lz

        ' Calculate the specular component.
        RdotV = Rx * Vx + Ry * Vy + Rz * Vz
        specular_factor = SpecularK * (RdotV ^ SpecularN)
        R = R + light.Ir * specular_factor
        G = G + light.Ig * specular_factor
        B = B + light.Ib * specular_factor
      End If ' End if NdotL > 0 ...
  Next light

    ' Add the ambient term.
    R = R + ambient_light * AmbientKr
    G = G + ambient_light * AmbientKg
    B = B + ambient_light * AmbientKb

    ' Keep the color components <= 255.
    If R > 255 Then R = 255
    If G > 255 Then G = 255
    If B > 255 Then B = 255

    ' Return the color.
    SurfaceColor = RGB(R, G, B)
End Function
```

Example program Light4, shown in Figures 16.10 and 16.11, uses this method to display three-dimensional objects. In both Figures 16.10 and 16.11, the constant k_s in the equation $k_s * (R \cdot V)^n$ was 0.5. The constant n was 10 in Figure 16.10 and 100 in Figure 16.11. Larger values for n give smaller highlights.

You may recall that the lighting model ignores several of the more complicated aspects of the physics of lighting. For instance, the ambient term does not take into account other nearby objects. If a large, dark object lies near a second object, the first may block some of the ambient light that would otherwise reach the second. A large bright object may reflect extra light onto other nearby objects.

In using $Cos^n(\phi)$ to model specular reflection, the lighting model equation makes a similar assumption. The model assumes that light reflected from a shiny surface does not increase the light falling on nearby objects. This means nearby objects are darker than they should be. It also means you are unable to see the reflection of one object in another. Reflection in this model applies only to light coming from the light source directly to an object and then reflecting toward the viewpoint. Chapter 17, Ray Tracing, describes a more general reflection model that allows you to see the reflection of one object in another.

Smooth Shading

Many programs use polygons to simulate a smooth surface. You can use a few techniques to smooth out the edges between the polygons when you shade them. The two most common techniques are *Gouraud shading* and *Phong shading*. Unfortunately, both methods are slow and difficult in Visual Basic, so they are only briefly described here. Smooth shading is accomplished in a different way by the ray tracing algorithm described in Chapter 17.

Gouraud Shading

In *Gouraud shading*, or *intensity interpolation shading*, you begin by creating surface normal vectors at each vertex of each polygon. In some cases, you can compute these

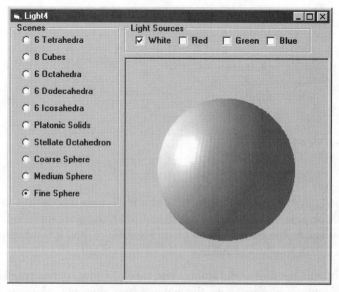

Figure 16.10 Program Light4 displaying a sphere with specular constant n = 10.

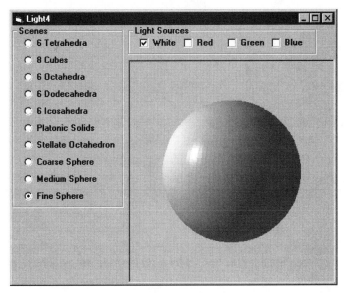

Figure 16.11   Program Light4 displaying a sphere with specular constant n = 100.

normals as you generate the surface. When you create a sphere of radius R, for example, the unit normal vector at the point (x, y, z) on the sphere is <x / R, y / R, z / R>. As you create the polygons that represent the surface, you store these normals for later use.

In other cases, you can approximate the normal vectors by taking the average of the normals of the surrounding polygons. Figure 16.12 shows four polygons meeting at a common vertex. The normal at the vertex is the average of the four polygon normals.

Using the vertex normals and the lighting model equations, you can calculate the color values for each vertex. You can then use interpolation to find the colors for the other points inside the polygon. As the colors vary smoothly across the polygon, they produce a smoother image than you get if you give every point in the polygon the same color. For example, you can use this technique to create a smoother image of a sphere using fewer data points than you would need without Gouraud shading.

Unfortunately, interpolating for each point in the polygon is slow and complicated. In fact, just listing the points is tricky. You cannot use the Polygon API function to draw the polygon because the interior points are not all the same color.

One way to identify the pixels in the polygon is to use the CreatePolygonRgn API function to create a region to represent the polygon. Next, use the GetRgnBox function to get the minimum and maximum X and Y values in the region. Then loop over all these points and use the PtInRegion function to determine whether the point is inside the region.

For each of the points in the region, take a weighted average of the colors of the polygon's vertexes. Even doing that can be difficult. Interpolation is straightforward if the region is a rectangle, but for other shapes, it is not as easy. Depending on the type of data you are drawing, the polygon may be a triangle, quadrilateral, or some other more strangely shaped area.

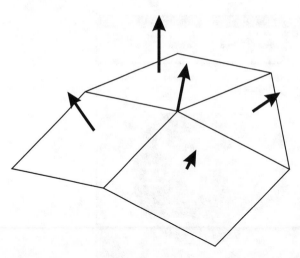

Figure 16.12 Approximating a vertex normal by averaging the adjacent face normals.

Example program Gouraud draws spheres with Gouraud shading. Figure 16.13 shows a sphere made of 100 polygons. The image is much smoother than those produced by the programs described earlier in this chapter. The edges of the polygons are still visible along the outline of the sphere, however. These edges give the sphere a lumpy appearance.

If you look very closely at Figure 16.13, you can also see several faint pale traces running vertically and horizontally across the surface of the sphere. Program Gouraud uses linear interpolation to calculate values for the points within a polygon. That makes the colors of those points blend smoothly.

The speed of change in the interpolation may change at polygon edges, however. In this case, the colors vary linearly, but the surface is actually curved. This difference produces the small light areas. If you add a few more polygons to the sphere, this problem shrinks until it is not noticeable. Figure 16.14 shows program Gouraud displaying a sphere with more data points. The lighter areas are no longer visible.

Many programs, though not program Gouraud, drop the specular reflection terms from the lighting model when they use this shading method. Gouraud shading calculates only colors at polygon vertexes and uses them to calculate the interior points' colors.

Unless a vertex normal just happens to fall near the mirror direction for the viewing position, the specular term does not contribute significantly. If the polygons are relatively large, as they are in Figure 16.13, it is unlikely that a vertex normal will point in the mirror direction. If it does, it greatly brightens the surrounding polygons, producing an abnormally large specular highlight.

You can see this effect in Figure 16.13. The sphere is slightly brighter in the upper left, but there is no specular highlight. In Figure 16.14, the size of the polygons is small enough that some of the vertex normals point in the mirror direction, so they produce a specular highlight. The polygons are small, so the highlight has a reasonably normal appearance.

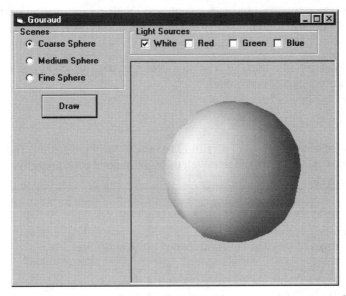

Figure 16.13   Gouraud shading of a sphere containing 100 polygons.

Example program GZOrder, shown in Figure 16.15, uses Gouraud shading to draw several kinds of surfaces. The most interesting difference between this program and program Gouraud is in how it calculates vertex normals.

Program Gouraud uses the fact that the normal of the point (x, y, z) on the surface of a sphere of radius R centered at the origin is <x/R, y /R, z/R>. That does not work for more

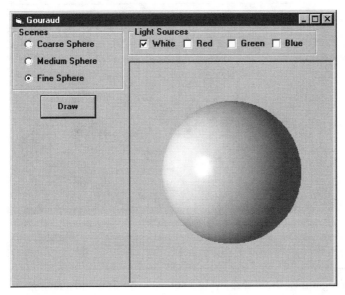

Figure 16.14   Gouraud shading of a sphere containing 10,000 polygons.

general surfaces. Program GZOrder uses calculus to explicitly find vertex normals. If your calculus is a little rusty, do not worry too much about this. Feel free to skip to the next section.

If F(x, y) is the equation of a surface, a normal vector to the surface at point (x, y) is given by the equation's partial derivatives:

```
<∂F/∂x (x, y), ∂F/∂y (x, y), -1>
```

For example, the surface shown in Figure 16.15 has the following equation. The roles of the Y and Z coordinates are reversed to match the right-handed coordinate system used by the projection code.

```
Y = Amplitude1 * (Cos(Period1 * X) + Cos(Period1 * Z))
```

The partial derivatives of this equation with respect to X and Z are:

```
∂F/∂x = Amplitude1 * Period1 * Sin(Period1 * X)
∂F/∂z = Amplitude1 * Period1 * Sin(Period1 * Z)
```

Program GZOrder uses these equations to find the vertex normals for the surface.

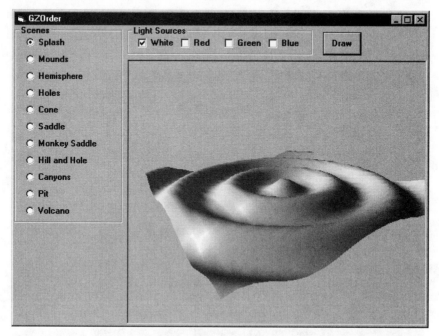

Figure 16.15 Program GZOrder displaying a surface with Gouraud shading.

Phong Shading

Phong shading also uses vertex normals to create smooth shading. Gouraud shading uses the vertex normals to compute vertex colors. It then interpolates using those colors to find the colors of the points inside a polygon. Phong shading interpolates using the vertex normals to find normals for each point in a polygon. It then uses those normals to compute the points' colors individually.

The most time-consuming part of both methods is computing the color of a point given its surface normal. Interpolating colors or normal vectors is relatively fast. Because Gouraud shading computes only the colors of the vertices and Phong shading computes the color of each point individually, Phong shading takes longer.

On the other hand, Phong shading generally produces a better result. Interpolating normals instead of colors means the change in color varies more evenly, so the edges between polygons are less noticeable.

Phong shading calculates colors for every point based on a smoothly varying normal vector. For some points, the vector is likely to point in the mirror direction for the viewing position. Those points have significant specular reflection terms, so the surface has highlights.

Example program Phong, shown in Figures 16.16 and 16.17, draws a sphere with Phong shading. Compare Figure 16.16 with Figures 16.13 and 16.14. Phong shading produces an excellent result for the interior of the sphere, though the edges are still lumpy. It produces a much better result than the sphere with Gouraud shading shown in Figure 16.13.

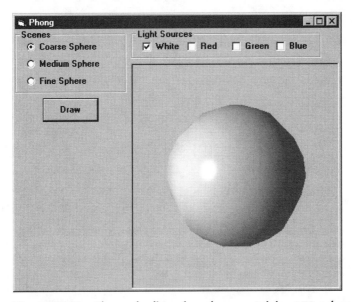

Figure 16.16   Phong shading of a sphere containing 100 polygons.

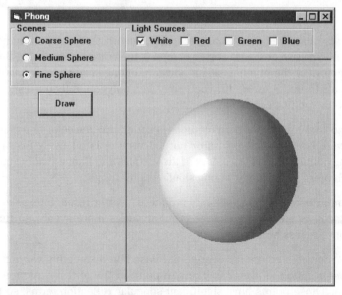

Figure 16.17 Phong shading of a sphere containing 10,000 polygons.

Example program PZOrder, shown in Figure 16.18, displays surfaces with Phong shading. The edges between polygons are much less obvious than they are in the image produced by Gouraud shading shown in Figure 16.15. The specular highlights are also

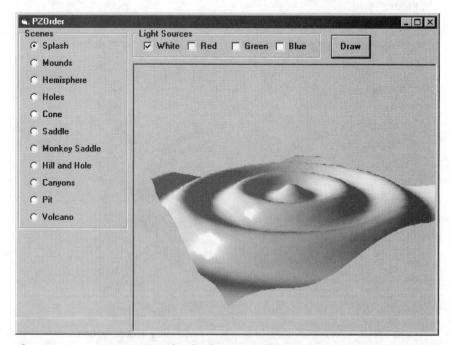

Figure 16.18 Program PZOrder displaying a surface with Phong shading.

brighter. The polygons used to draw the surface are fairly large, so the edges of the surface and the highlights are still somewhat lumpy.

Summary

Shading models are the next step in the quest for visual realism. Simple lines and hidden surface removal algorithms produce images that can be meaningful, but there is little doubt that they are computer generated. No one would mistake the images in Chapter 13, Three-Dimensional Transformations, for a photograph.

Shading models give dramatic improvements over hidden surface algorithms. Gouraud and Phong shading produce images that are almost realistic enough to be believable. The smoothly varying colors make the result appear quite natural, though perhaps a bit rubbery.

This extra realism comes at a price. The Gouraud and Phong shading programs are much more complicated than the simple line drawing and hidden surface programs described earlier. They are also much slower. On a 133MHz Pentium, program Light4 described earlier in this chapter can display a 100-polygon sphere almost instantly. Program Gouraud takes roughly 6 seconds, and program Phong needs more than 13 seconds.

The Gouraud and Phong shading programs presented in this chapter are still missing several important features. They do not allow reflective or transparent surfaces, they do not display shadows, and they do not take into account interactions between objects in a scene.Chapter 17, Ray Tracing, takes the quest for realism one step further. It uses a simple conceptual model to generate images of near photographic realism.

CHAPTER 17

Ray Tracing

The previous chapters describe methods for displaying three-dimensional objects that have grown increasingly realistic. At the same time, they have grown more complex. Chapter 13, Three-Dimensional Transformations, starts the discussion of three-dimensional objects by describing transformations in three-dimensions. Using translation, rotation, and projection transformations, you can write programs to display three-dimensional objects like the sphere shown in Figure 17.1.

Chapter 14, Surfaces, describes different ways to manage and display three-dimensional surfaces. This chapter explained the Hi-Lo and Z-Order algorithms that allow you to remove the hidden parts of a three-dimensional surface.

Chapter 15, Hidden Surface Removal, describes more general hidden surface removal techniques like backface removal and the Depth-Sort algorithm. By removing hidden surfaces, you can reduce the clutter in an image and make it easier to understand. Figure 17.2 shows a sphere similar to the one shown in Figure 17.1 with the hidden surfaces removed. While these algorithms provide a greater degree of realism, they are also fairly complex, requiring code to handle many special cases.

Chapter 16, Shading Models, improves the hidden surface methods by shading the surfaces that make up three-dimensional solids. Shading provides visual clues about the depth and surface features of three-dimensional objects, making·them appear more realistic and easier to understand. Figure 17.3 shows a sphere similar to those in Figures 17.1 and 17.2 with shading added.

The shading model described in Chapter 16 takes into account ambient light, diffuse and specular reflection, and distance effects. Gouraud and Phong shading produce smoothly shaded surfaces, though the code is time consuming and complex. You can also extend the shading models used to handle transparency and shadows, but these extensions are quite complicated.

In some sense, ray tracing is a generalization of the lighting models described in Chapter 16. By following light rays, ray tracing lets you model complex interactions between light and the objects in a scene. Using a single elegant algorithm, ray tracing handles:

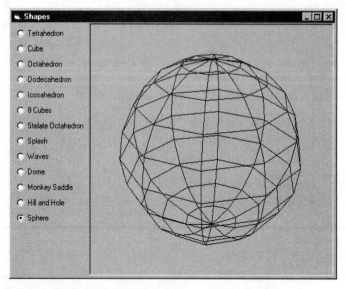

Figure 17.1 A sphere displayed with line segments.

- Ambient light
- Diffuse and specular reflection
- Intensity reduction due to distance
- Hidden surface removal
- Smooth shading of curved surfaces
- Shadows
- Reflective surfaces
- Transparent surfaces
- Mutually overlapping objects
- Objects that pierce other objects

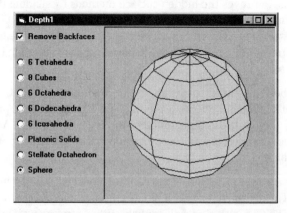

Figure 17.2 A sphere displayed with hidden surfaces removed.

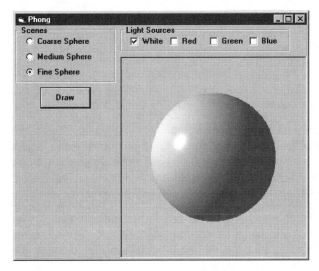

Figure 17.3   A sphere with Phong shading.

Some of these effects are very difficult to implement when one uses the methods described in previous chapters.

A Brief Warning

Before continuing, be aware that ray tracing relies on some fairly involved mathematics. Calculating how light refracts when it passes through a transparent object or finding the intersection between a ray and a cylinder is complicated.

If you find you are overwhelmed by the mass of equations, skip them. The basic ray-tracing concepts are fairly intuitive, and you should be able to understand them even if you skip some of the details. Once you understand the basics, you will be able to modify the example programs to produce new arrangements of objects even if you have not memorized every last equation.

The programs described in this chapter also include a lot of code—too much code to print all of it here. To keep this chapter down to a manageable size, much detail is omitted. Only the code needed to illustrate important concepts is printed here. You can find the complete source code on the CD-ROM.

Ray-Tracing Basics

The Z-Order and Depth-Sort hidden surface removal algorithms draw surfaces in order, drawing those furthest from the center of projection first. Surfaces that are drawn later cover up any previously drawn surfaces if necessary.

For each surface, these algorithms determine which pixels make up that surface. They then color the surface appropriately. Programs that use a shading model or smooth shading use the scene's geometry to determine the colors of the pixels.

Ray tracing approaches the problem from the opposite point of view. Instead of determining which pixels make up each object in the scene, a ray-tracing algorithm determines for each pixel in the screen what that pixel's color should be.

The idea behind ray tracing is simple. For each pixel on the screen, the program passes a *ray* from the center of projection through the pixel. It follows the ray into the scene until it strikes an object. It then uses the geometry of that object, the direction of the ray, and the position of the light sources to determine the pixel's color. This basic process is illustrated in Figure 17.4.

Because the algorithm follows each ray only until it reaches the closest surface, this method provides hidden surface removal. Any surface that lies behind another is ignored because the rays passing from the center of projection to the hidden object are blocked by the closer object, as shown in Figure 17.5.

Ray tracing even handles mutually overlapping objects and situations like the one shown in Figure 17.6 where one object pierces another. These are difficult special cases that are not handled by the Depth-Sort hidden surface removal algorithm.

To calculate a pixel's color, the ray-tracing algorithm can use any of the shading models described in Chapter 16, Shading Models. If you use the most complete model, your picture gets the benefits of ambient light, diffuse and specular reflection, and intensity reduction due to distance.

With only a small change, you can make the algorithm display shadows as well. Before you calculate the diffuse and specular reflection components of a pixel's color, you should check to see if there is any object between the pixel and each light source. You can do this

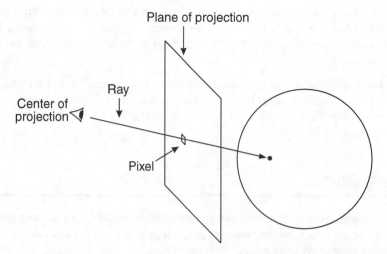

Figure 17.4   Ray tracing follows a ray from the center of projection, through a pixel on the screen, until it reaches an object.

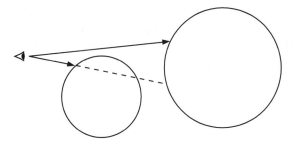

Figure 17.5   Ray tracing provides hidden surface removal.

by tracing a ray from each light source toward the surface or from the surface toward each light source. This ray is called a *shadow feeler*.

If the shadow feeler finds an object between a light source and the surface you are drawing, the light does not shine directly on the surface. In that case, the surface is in shadow and the pixel's color is due entirely to ambient light. This test even detects cases in which one part of an object shadows another part of the same object. For instance, when the light source is on the far side of a sphere, the far surface of the sphere shadows the near side.

Ray Tracing in Visual Basic

In practice, most programs do not really trace a ray until it reaches an object. Instead, they examine each object in the scene and find the point where the ray intersects the object. The program then picks the object for which the point of intersection is closest to the center of projection.

One way to do this is to think of the ray as a line segment starting at a point and extending along a vector. To trace a ray from the center of projection through a pixel on the screen,

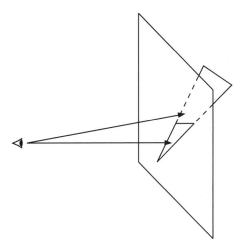

Figure 17.6   Ray tracing handles objects that pierce other objects.

use the center of projection as the starting point. The direction vector leads from the center of projection through the pixel. If the center of projection is at (cx, cy, cz) and the pixel has coordinates (px, py, pz), the vector has components <px - cx, py - cy, pz - cz>.

The points along this ray have coordinates given by (cx, cy, cz) + t * <px - cx, py - cy, pz - cz> for different values of t. For example, the X coordinate of a point on this ray is given by:

```
cx + t * (px - cx)
```

where t >= 0. Values of t less than zero correspond to points behind the center of projection.

To find the point where the ray intersects the nearest object, the program can calculate t for the point of intersection with each object. It then takes the intersection with the smallest positive value for t.

To make it easier to handle different kinds of objects, you can create a RayTraceable class that defines the methods that an object must implement to be ray traced. The FindT function takes as parameters the ray's starting point and its direction vector. It returns the smallest positive values for t in the previous equations.

For example, the equation for a sphere of radius R centered at position (cx, cy, cz) is:

```
(cx - x)² + (cy - y)² + (cz - z)² - R² = 0
```

You can write the equation of a line through point (px, py, pz) along the vector <vx, vy, vz> using parametric equations like this:

```
X(t) = px + t * vx
Y(t) = py + t * vy
Z(t) = pz + t * vz
```

If you substitute these values into the equation for a sphere, you get:

```
(cx - px + t * vx)² + (cy - py + t * vy)² + (cz - pz + t * vz)² - R² = 0
```

After rearranging this a bit, you get:

```
A * t² + B * t + C = 0
```

where:

```
A =  vx² + vz² + vz²
B =  2 * vx * (px - cx) + 2 * vy * (py - cy) + 2 * vz * (pz - cz)
C =  cx² + cy² + cz² + px² + py² + pz²
     - 2 * (cx * px + cy * py + cz * pz) - R²
```

The solutions to this equation are given by the quadratic formula as:

```
t = -B ± Sqr(B² - 4 * A * C) / 2 / A
```

All the values you need to compute A, B, and C are constants determined by the particular sphere and line. When you plug in the values for A, B, and C, you get one of three possible results. First, if $B^2 - 4 * A * C < 0$, the square root has no real solutions. In this case, the ray does not intersect the sphere in real, three-dimensional space.

Second, if $B^2 - 4 * A * C = 0$, the equation has a single solution -B/2/A. In this case, the ray is tangent to the sphere, meeting it at a single point.

Finally, if $B^2 - 4 * A * C > 0$, the equation gives two possible values for t. Values less than zero represent points behind the point at which the ray originates. Larger values for t represent points further from the beginning of the ray than the points represented by smaller values. Thus the position on the sphere closest to the point (px, py, pz) in the direction of the vector <vx, vy, vz> corresponds to the smaller positive value of t.

Once you have found the correct value for t, you can plug it into the parametric equations for the line to determine the exact point of intersection.

The following code shows the FindT function for the RaySphere class. The RaySphere class implements the RayTraceable class and FindT is defined by RayTraceable, so the RaySphere class declares this function as RayTraceable_FindT.

```
' Return the value T for the point of intersection
' between the vector from point (px, py, pz) in
' the direction <vx, vy, vz>.
'
' direct_calculation is true if we are finding the
' intersection from a viewing position ray. It is
' false if we are finding a reflected intersection
' or a shadow feeler.
Public Function RayTraceable_FindT( _
    ByVal direct_calculation As Boolean, _
    ByVal px As Single, ByVal py As Single, _
    ByVal pz As Single, ByVal Vx As Single, -
    ByVal Vy As Single, ByVal Vz As Single) As Single
Dim A As Single
Dim B As Single
Dim C As Single
Dim Cx As Single
Dim Cy As Single
Dim Cz As Single
Dim B24AC As Single
Dim T1 As Single
Dim T2 As Single
Dim dx As Single
Dim dy As Single
Dim dz As Single

    Cx = Center.Trans(1)
    Cy = Center.Trans(2)
    Cz = Center.Trans(3)

    ' Get the coefficients for the quadratic.
```

```
        A = Vx * Vx + Vy * Vy + Vz * Vz
        B = 2 * Vx * (px - Cx) + _
            2 * Vy * (py - Cy) + _
            2 * Vz * (pz - Cz)
        C = Cx * Cx + Cy * Cy + Cz * Cz + _
            px * px + py * py + pz * pz - _
            2 * (Cx * px + Cy * py + Cz * pz) - _
            Radius * Radius

        ' Solve the quadratic A*t^2 + B*t + C = 0.
        B24AC = B * B - 4 * A * C
        If B24AC < 0 Then
            ' There is no real intersection.
            RayTraceable_FindT = -1
        ElseIf B24AC = 0 Then
            ' There is one intersection.
            T1 = -B / 2 / A
        Else
            B24AC = Sqr(B24AC)
            T1 = (-B + B24AC) / 2 / A
            T2 = (-B - B24AC) / 2 / A
            ' Use only positive t values.
            If T1 < 0.01 Then T1 = T2
            If T2 < 0.01 Then T2 = T1
            ' Use the smaller t value.
            If T1 > T2 Then T1 = T2
        End If

        ' If there is no positive t value, there's no
        ' intersection in this direction.
        If T1 < 0.01 Then
            RayTraceable_FindT = -1
        Else
            RayTraceable_FindT = T1
        End If
    End Function
```

Calculating Hit Color

Once the ray-tracing algorithm has determined which object is closest to the center of projection, it must determine the color of the object at that point. You can use the techniques explained in Chapter 16, Shading Models, to calculate the color.

The RayTraceable class defines the FindHitColor subroutine. This routine takes as parameters the coordinates of the point of interest. It returns the point's red, green, and blue color components through parameters passed by reference.

The following code shows how the RaySphere class calculates hit color. It calculates the sphere's unit normal vector at the point and then calls the CalculateHitColor subroutine to actually calculate the color. It passes CalculateHitColor the point of intersection, the surface normal at that point, and the sphere's shading model parameters.

Subroutine CalculateHitColor uses the shading model described in Chapter 16 to calculate the color of a pixel on an arbitrary object. For details on how this calculation works, see the code or look in Chapter 16.

```
' Return the red, green, and blue components of
' the surface at the hit position.
Public Sub RayTraceable_FindHitColor( _
    ByVal depth As Integer, Objects As Collection, _
    ByVal eye_x As Single, ByVal eye_y As Single, _
    ByVal eye_z As Single, ByVal px As Single, _
    ByVal py As Single, ByVal pz As Single, _
    ByRef R As Integer, ByRef G As Integer, _
    ByRef B As Integer)
Dim Nx As Single
Dim Ny As Single
Dim Nz As Single
Dim n_len  As Single

    ' Find the unit normal at this point.
    Nx = px - Center.Trans(1)
    Ny = py - Center.Trans(2)
    Nz = pz - Center.Trans(3)
    n_len = Sqr(Nx * Nx + Ny * Ny + Nz * Nz)
    Nx = Nx / n_len
    Ny = Ny / n_len
    Nz = Nz / n_len

    ' Get the hit color.
    CalculateHitColor depth, Objects, Me, _
        eye_x, eye_y, eye_z, _
        px, py, pz, _
        Nx, Ny, Nz, _
        DiffuseKr, DiffuseKg, DiffuseKb, _
        AmbientKr, AmbientKg, AmbientKb, _
        SpecularK, SpecularN, _
        ReflectedKr, ReflectedKg, ReflectedKb, IsReflective, _
        TransmittedKr, TransmittedKg, TransmittedKb, TransN, _
        n1, n2, IsTransparent, _
        R, G, B
End Sub
```

Tracing Rays

Using the FindT and FindHitColor routines, a program can trace rays through a scene. The TraceRay subroutine shown in the following code traces a ray from the center of projection through a pixel until it hits an object. It examines each object in the scene to find the one with the smallest value t returned by FindT. It then uses that object's FindHitColor routine to decide what color to make the pixel.

```
' Return the pixel color given by tracing from
' point (px, py, pz) in direction <vx, vy, vz>.
Public Sub TraceRay(ByVal direct_calculation As Boolean, _
    ByVal depth As Integer, _
    ByVal skip_object As RayTraceable, ByVal px As Single, _
    ByVal py As Single, ByVal pz As Single, _
    ByVal Vx As Single, ByVal Vy As Single, _
    ByVal Vz As Single, ByRef R As Integer, _
    ByRef G As Integer, ByRef B As Integer)
Dim obj As RayTraceable
Dim best_obj As RayTraceable
Dim best_t As Single
Dim t As Single

    ' Find the object that's closest.
    best_t = INFINITY
    For Each obj In Objects
        ' Skip the object skip_object. We use this
        ' to avoid erroneously hitting the object
        ' casting out a ray.
        If Not (obj Is skip_object) Then
            t = obj.FindT(direct_calculation, px, py, pz, _
                Vx, Vy, Vz)
            If (t > 0) And (best_t > t) Then
                best_t = t
                Set best_obj = obj
            End If
        End If
    Next obj

    ' See if we hit anything.
    If best_obj Is Nothing Then
        ' We hit nothing. Return the background color.
        R = BackR
        G = BackG
        B = BackB
    Else
        ' Compute the color at that point.
        best_obj.FindHitColor depth, Objects, _
            px, py, pz, _
            px + best_t * Vx, _
            py + best_t * Vy, _
            pz + best_t * Vz, _
            R, G, B

        ' This is a problem for some values of Kdist.
        If R < 0 Then R = 0
```

```
            If G < 0 Then G = 0
            If B < 0 Then B = 0
        End If
End Sub
```

Subroutine TraceAllRays traces all the rays passing from the center of projection through the pixels in a picture box. This routine takes a parameter skip that indicates how many pixels it should skip in its calculations. For example, if skip is 2, the routine examines every second pixel. It then uses the result it gets to draw a two-by-two area on the picture box, so you can see a low-resolution preview of the final image. If skip is large, this can be much faster than generating the entire image at full resolution. Figure 17.7 shows an image of three spheres in which skip is 8. Figure 17.8 shows the same image with skip set to 1 so that every pixel's value is calculated separately.

```
' Ray trace on this picture box.
Public Sub TraceAllRays(ByVal pic As PictureBox, _
    ByVal skip As Integer, ByVal depth As Integer)
Dim pixels() As RGBTriplet
Dim bits_per_pixel As Integer
Dim pix_x As Long
Dim pix_y As Long
Dim real_x As Long
Dim real_y As Long
Dim Xmin As Integer
Dim Xmax As Integer
Dim Ymin As Integer
Dim Ymax As Integer
Dim xoff As Integer
Dim yoff As Integer
Dim R As Integer
Dim G As Integer
Dim B As Integer
Dim obj As RayTraceable
```

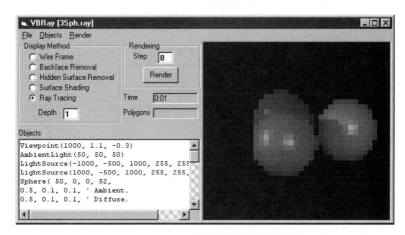

Figure 17.7   A low-resolution preview image.

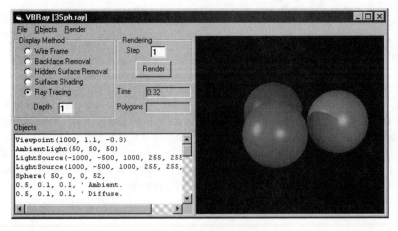

Figure 17.8 A high-resolution ray-traced image.

```
If skip < 2 Then
        ' Get the picture box's pixels.
    GetBitmapPixels pic, pixels, bits_per_pixel
End If

' Get the transformed coordinates of the eye.
xoff = pic.ScaleWidth / 2
yoff = pic.ScaleHeight / 2
Xmin = pic.ScaleLeft
Xmax = Xmin + pic.ScaleWidth - 1
Ymin = pic.ScaleTop
Ymax = Ymin + pic.ScaleHeight - 1
For pix_y = Ymin To Ymax Step skip
    real_y = pix_y - yoff

    For pix_x = Xmin To Xmax Step skip
        real_x = pix_x - xoff
        ' Calculate the value of pixel (x, y).
        ' After transformation the eye is
        ' at (0, 0, EyeR) and the plane of
        ' projection lies in the X-Y plane.
        TraceRay True, depth, Nothing, _
            0, 0, EyeR, _
            CSng(real_x), CSng(real_y), -EyeR, _
            R, G, B

        ' Draw the pixel.
        If skip < 2 Then
            ' Save the pixel value.
            With pixels(pix_x, pix_y)
                .rgbRed = R
                .rgbGreen = G
                .rgbBlue = B
```

```
                             End With
                     Else
                         pic.Line (pix_x, pix_y)- _
                             Step(skip - 1, skip - 1), _
                             RGB(R, G, B), BF
                     End If
                 Next pix_x

                 ' Let the user see what's going on.
                 If skip < 2 Then
                     pic.Line (pic.ScaleLeft, pix_y)-(Xmax, pix_y), _
                         vbWhite
                 Else
                     pic.Refresh
                 End If

                 ' If the Stop button was pressed, stop.
                 DoEvents
                 If Not Running Then Exit Sub
             Next pix_y

             If skip < 2 Then
                 SetBitmapPixels pic, bits_per_pixel, pixels
             End If
         End Sub
```

Performance

As you might imagine, ray tracing can be slow. Ray tracing even a simple scene can require many calculations. For a 300 by 300 pixel image containing four spheres, the program must compute the color for 90,000 pixels.

For each of those pixels, it uses the FindT function to determine the distance between the center of projection and each of the four spheres in the scene. The FindT function involves roughly 34 multiplications and divisions, 29 additions and subtractions, and even two square roots. Assuming the ray through a pixel strikes some object in the scene, you also need to add about 100 more operations to compute the pixel's color using the FindHitColor and CalculateHitColor functions. The total number of operations needed to display the four spheres is roughly:

```
(90,000 pixels) *
[(65 operations per FindT) * (4 spheres) +
 (100 operations per FindHitColor)]
≈ 32 million operations
```

This does not take into account all the overhead of making 4 * 90,000 = 360,000 calls to function FindT and as many as 90,000 calls to function FindHitColor and CalculateHit-Color. All of these calculations add up to make ray tracing quite slow.

This is slow enough that ray tracing a complicated scene can take hours or even days. This glacial speed is the one major drawback to ray tracing. While it provides many powerful features, such as hidden surface removal, shadows, and a complete lighting model, ray tracing takes far longer than the less realistic Depth-Sort algorithm. You can do a few things to make the process faster. Two of the simpler techniques are using bounding volumes and scanline culling. These techniques are described in the following sections.

Bounding Volumes

In a complicated scene, you may be able to use the arrangement of the objects to avoid calculating some ray-object intersections. You may be able to group several nearby objects and surround them with a bounding volume like a sphere. If a ray does not intersect the sphere, you know that it does not intersect any of the objects within the sphere, so you do not need to test for intersections with each of the objects separately.

This method is most useful when the scene contains a large number of small objects. In particular, if the scene contains a solid object made up of many polygonal faces, bounding volumes may greatly reduce the number of intersections you need to compute. If a ray does not intersect the bounding volume, you do not need to intersect it with each of the polygonal faces.

Even for relatively simple objects, you can sometimes improve performance by using bounding volumes. For instance, even though a cube is a fairly simple object, it takes less time to find the intersection between a ray and a sphere bounding the cube than it does to test each of the cube's six faces separately. If the ray does not intersect the bounding sphere, you do not need to test the faces individually.

On the other hand, if a ray does intersect a bounding volume, you still need to test the objects inside. If a bounding volume occupies most of the scene space, most of the rays intersect it. Then you need to test the objects inside almost all the time. In that case, the bounding volume test is extra work that does not save you much time, so you are better off without it.

For many objects, spheres make convenient bounding volumes, but for some objects, other volumes are more appropriate. For example, suppose a scene contains a collection of squares arranged in a rectangle in a plane. It would make sense to use a rectangle that contains the squares as a bounding volume. Before checking the squares to see if a ray intersects them, you could see if it intersects the bounding rectangle.

In this case the bounding rectangle might occupy much of the resulting image, so you will have gained only a small improvement. You can take advantage of the special geometry of the situation to gain a much greater improvement. If the squares do not overlap, a ray can intersect at most one of them at a time. While testing the squares, if you find one that the ray intersects, you do not need to check any of the others. With a little extra work, you can even use the point of intersection between the ray and bounding rectangle to directly compute which of the squares contains the point. The RayCheckerboard class described later in this chapter uses that method to treat a collection of squares as a single object.

Scanline Culling

Many objects do not occupy a large portion of a scene, so many of the object-ray intersection tests yield no intersection. In that case, you can usually speed things up by performing *scanline culling*.

Before starting to work on a scanline or row of pixels, you can calculate the intersection between the plane containing that scanline and the objects in the scene. If the plane does not intersect the object, none of the rays for that scanline intersect the object either, so you can skip all the ray intersection calculations for that scanline.

Figure 17.9 shows the plane through the center of projection and a scanline. The plane does not intersect the top sphere, so none of the rays for this scanline do either.

For convex objects such as spheres, you can make scanline culling even more useful. Suppose a scanline plane intersects an object. As the program traces rays through the pixels on the scanline, it will eventually find a ray that hits the object. It may find other rays that hit the object and then it may find a ray that does not hit the object. After that point, no more rays through this scanline will hit the object. The program can mark the object as culled for this scanline and not consider it again until it checks the next scanline.

Similarly as the program moves down through the scanlines, it may find the first several scanline planes do not intersect an object and then some planes will intersect it. Once the program reaches another scanline plane that does not intersect the object, no other planes will intersect it. After that point, no rays will intersect the object again so it can be permanently culled.

Example program VBRay, shown in Figure 17.10, demonstrates many of the three-dimensional techniques described so far in this book.

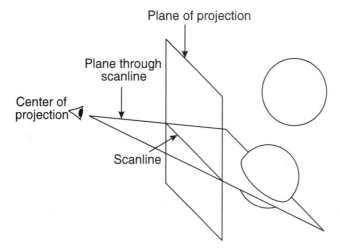

Figure 17.9   Scanline culling.

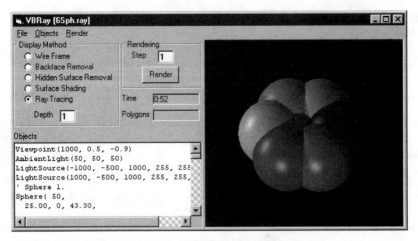

Figure 17.10   Program VBRay ray tracing three spheres.

Enter commands to describe a scene in the Objects text box. The entries in the Objects menu add dummy entries to the end of the object list. You can edit dummy entries and fill in the values you want. For example, the Sphere command adds the following code to the text box.

```
Sphere( Radius, X, Y, Z,
   ka_r, ka_g, ka_b,     ' Ambient
   kd_r, kd_g, kd_b,     ' Diffuse
   spec_n, spec_s,       ' Specular
   kr_r, kr_g, kr_b,     ' Reflected
   kt_n, n1, n2,         ' TransN, n1, n2
   kt_r, kt_g, kt_b      ' Transmitted
)
```

You can modify these values to set the sphere's radius, position, and color parameters.

The File menu's Open Scene and Save Scene commands allow you to load and save object descriptions in files. Using the examples on the CD-ROM and the commands in the Objects menu, you can figure out how to create scenes of your own.

Select the display method you want to use and click the Render button. You can use the simpler display methods to view complex scenes before you use more advanced methods. For example, you can move objects and adjust the viewing position using a wire frame display. When you are satisfied with the results, you can ray trace the final image.

The Polygons box tells how many polygons were used when you click the Hidden Surface Removal or Surface Shading options. Figure 17.11 shows program VBRay displaying eight spheres using hidden surface removal. This example contains 360 polygons.

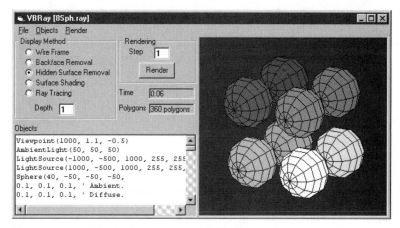

Figure 17.11   Displaying a scene with hidden surface removal.

Other Objects

The geometry of a sphere is relatively simple. It is easy to transform a sphere using translations and rotations by transforming the sphere's center. As long as you know the sphere's radius and the transformed location of its center, you know where the sphere belongs. It is also easy to determine where a ray intersects a sphere, and it is easy to find the surface normal at any point on a sphere. For these reasons, spheres are extremely common in ray traced scenes.

Unfortunately, the whole world does not consist of spheres. If you want to use other kinds of objects in ray traced scenes, you must be able to write appropriate FindT and FindHitColor functions for them. If this proves too difficult for a particular object, you can approximate the object using polygons. While ray tracing will not give you smooth shading for objects approximated by polygons, you get all the other benefits of ray tracing such as hidden surface removal and shadows.

The following sections explain how to find ray-object intersections and surface normals for planes, disks, polygons, checkerboards, and cylinders.

Planes

Suppose you have a plane that passes through the point P = (px, py, pz) and that has normal vector N = <nx, ny, nz>. A point S = (x, y, z) lies on the plane if the vector between S and P is perpendicular to the normal vector N.

Recall that the value of the dot product of two vectors A and B is $A \cdot B = |A| * |B| * \cos(\theta)$, where θ is the angle between the two vectors. If the vector between points S and P is perpendicular to the normal vector N, $\cos(\theta) = 0$ between these two vectors, so the dot product must be zero. This gives one form of the equation of a plane:

```
(x - px) * nx + (y - py) * ny + (z - pz) * nz = 0
```

You can rewrite this equation as:

```
A * x + B * y + C * z + D = 0
```

where

```
A = nx
B = ny
C = nz
D = -(nx * px + ny * py + nz * pz)
```

Now suppose you want to find the intersection between this plane and a ray passing through the point C = (cx, cy, cz) in the direction of the vector V = <vx, vy, vz>. You can represent the ray using parametric equations like this:

```
X(t) = cx + t * vx
Y(t) = cy + t * vy
Z(t) = cz + t * vz
```

Substituting these values into the plane equation you get:

```
A * (cx + t * vx) + B * (cy + t * vy) + C * (cz + t * vz) + D = 0
```

Solving this equation for t gives:

```
t * (A * vx + B * vy + C * vz) + A * cx + B * cy + C * cz + D = 0
t = -(A * cx + B * cy + C * cz + D) / (A * vx + B * vy + C * vz)
```

If the denominator (A * vx + B * vy + C * vz) equals zero, the ray is parallel to the plane and does not intersect it. Otherwise, the equation gives the value for t at the intersection.

If t < 0, the ray intersects the plane behind the point at which the ray originates, so the intersection is not interesting to a ray tracing program. Otherwise you can insert the value of t into the parametric equations for the ray to determine the exact point of intersection.

Because you will need to transform the plane, you should store the information that generates the plane in a way that allows you to transform it. For instance, you could store the coordinates of a point on the plane and the components of the plane's normal vector. You can rotate the plane by applying the rotation to the point and vector. Unfortunately, translations do not work properly for the vector. If you translated the vector's components by 1 unit in the X direction, for example, you would change the vector's direction and length. This would distort the vector and change the orientation of the plane.

A better solution is to store the coordinates of a point on the plane and the coordinates of a point that lies along the normal vector placed at that point. If the point on the plane is (px, py, pz) and the normal vector has components <vx, vy, vz>, the second point you should store is P2 = (px + nx, py + ny, pz + nz). To transform the plane, you can now transform both of these points. As long as you do not use any shape-deforming transformations like perspective projection, the normal vector between these two points is transformed correctly. When you need to use the normal vector, you can compute it by subtracting the two points.

The RayPlane class represents a plane. This class stores the coordinates of a point on the plane in the Point3D variable Point1. It stores the point that defines the normal vector in variable Point2. The following code shows the FindT function for the RayPlane class.

```
' Return the value T for the point of intersection
' between the vector from point (px, py, pz) in
' the direction <vx, vy, vz>.
'
' direct_calculation is true if we are finding the
' intersection from a viewing position ray. It is
' false if we are finding a reflected intersection
' or a shadow feeler.
Public Function RayTraceable_FindT( _
    ByVal direct_calculation As Boolean, ByVal px As Single, _
    ByVal py As Single, ByVal pz As Single, _
    ByVal Vx As Single, ByVal Vy As Single, _
    ByVal Vz As Single) As Single
Dim A As Single
Dim B As Single
Dim C As Single
Dim D As Single
Dim Nx As Single
Dim Ny As Single
Dim Nz As Single
Dim denom As Single
Dim t As Single

    ' Do not cull planes.

    ' Find the unit normal at this point.
    GetUnitNormal Nx, Ny, Nz

    ' Compute the plane's parameters.
    A = Nx
    B = Ny
    C = Nz
    D = -(Nx * Point1.Trans(1) + _
          Ny * Point1.Trans(2) + _
          Nz * Point1.Trans(3))

    ' If the denominator = 0, the ray is parallel
    ' to the plane so there's no intersection.
    denom = A * Vx + B * Vy + C * Vz
    If denom = 0 Then
        RayTraceable_FindT = -1
        Exit Function
```

```
        End If

        ' Solve for t.
        t = -(A * px + B * py + C * pz + D) / denom

        ' If there is no positive t value, there's no
        ' intersection in this direction.
        If t < 0.01 Then
            RayTraceable_FindT = -1
            Exit Function
        End If

        ' We had a hit.
        If direct_calculation Then HadHit = True

        RayTraceable_FindT = t
    End Function
```

There is one significant difference between the FindHitColor functions used by the RayPlane and RaySphere classes. After finding the plane's normal vector, the RayPlane class makes sure that the vector points in the direction of the center of projection. That allows the CalculateHitColor subroutine to color the plane correctly. If the center of projection and a light source lie on opposite sides of the plane, using this normal allows the program to correctly omit the specular and diffuse reflection components in the plane's lighting model. The plane blocks the light source, so it receives only ambient light.

```
    ' Return the red, green, and blue components of
    ' the surface at the hit position.
    Public Sub RayTraceable_FindHitColor(ByVal depth As Integer, _
        Objects As Collection, ByVal eye_x As Single, _
        ByVal eye_y As Single, ByVal eye_z As Single, _
        ByVal px As Single, ByVal py As Single, _
        ByVal pz As Single, ByRef R As Integer, _
        ByRef G As Integer, ByRef B As Integer)
Dim Nx As Single
Dim Ny As Single
Dim Nz As Single
Dim Vx As Single
Dim Vy As Single
Dim Vz As Single
Dim NdotV As Single

        ' Find the unit normal at this point.
        GetUnitNormal Nx, Ny, Nz

        ' Make sure the normal points towards the
        ' center of projection.
        Vx = EyeX - px
        Vy = EyeY - py
        Vz = EyeZ - pz
```

```
    NdotV = Nx * Vx + Ny * Vy + Nz * Vz
    If NdotV < 0 Then
        Nx = -Nx
        Ny = -Ny
        Nz = -Nz
    End If

    ' Get the hit color.
    CalculateHitColor depth, Objects, Me, _
        eye_x, eye_y, eye_z, _
        px, py, pz, _
        Nx, Ny, Nz, _
        DiffuseKr, DiffuseKg, DiffuseKb, _
        AmbientKr, AmbientKg, AmbientKb, _
        SpecularK, SpecularN, _
        ReflectedKr, ReflectedKg, ReflectedKb, IsReflective, _
        TransmittedKr, TransmittedKg, TransmittedKb, TransN, _
        n1, n2, IsTransparent, R, G, B
End Sub
```

Figure 17.12 shows seven spheres and a plane. The smaller spheres sit on top of the plane. The plane cuts the larger sphere slightly above its middle.

Disks

A disk is a circular area on a plane. Once you have mastered the ability to intersect rays with planes, it is only a small step to intersect rays with circular disks. To determine where a ray intersects a disk, first determine where the ray intersects the plane containing the disk. Then simply determine whether the point of intersection lies within the radius of the disk.

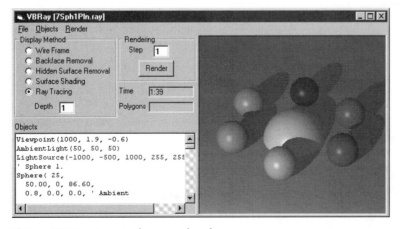

Figure 17.12   Seven spheres and a plane.

The RayDisk class manages disk objects. This class is very similar to the RayPlane class. It uses the first point defining the plane as the center of the disk. It also has a Radius variable that gives the disk's radius.

RayDisk's FindT function first determines whether a ray intersects the plane that contains the disk. It does this exactly as the RayPlane object does. If the ray intersects the plane, FindT determines whether the point of intersection lies within the radius of the disk. If it does not, the point is on the plane but not the disk, so the intersection is not useful.

```
' Return the value T for the point of intersection
' between the vector from point (px, py, pz) in
' the direction <vx, vy, vz>.
'
' direct_calculation is true if we are finding the
' intersection from a viewing position ray. It is
' false if we are finding a reflected intersection
' or a shadow feeler.
Public Function RayTraceable_FindT( _
    ByVal direct_calculation As Boolean, _
    ByVal px As Single, ByVal py As Single, _
    ByVal pz As Single, ByVal Vx As Single, _
    ByVal Vy As Single, ByVal Vz As Single) As Single
Dim A As Single
Dim B As Single
Dim C As Single
Dim D As Single
Dim Nx As Single
Dim Ny As Single
Dim Nz As Single
Dim denom As Single
Dim t As Single
Dim Cx As Single
Dim Cy As Single
Dim Cz As Single
Dim dx As Single
Dim dy As Single
Dim dz As Single
Dim X As Single
Dim Y As Single
Dim Z As Single

    ' See if we have been culled.
    If direct_calculation And DoneOnThisScanline Then
        RayTraceable_FindT = -1
        Exit Function
    End If

    ' Find the unit normal at this point.
    GetUnitNormal Nx, Ny, Nz

    ' Compute the plane's parameters.
```

```
A = Nx
B = Ny
C = Nz
D = -(Nx * Point1.Trans(1) + _
       Ny * Point1.Trans(2) + _
       Nz * Point1.Trans(3))

' If the denominator = 0, the ray is parallel
' to the plane so there's no intersection.
denom = A * Vx + B * Vy + C * Vz
If denom = 0 Then
    RayTraceable_FindT = -1
    Exit Function
End If

' Solve for t.
t = -(A * px + B * py + C * pz + D) / denom

' If there is no positive t value, there's no
' intersection in this direction.
If t < 0.01 Then
    RayTraceable_FindT = -1
    Exit Function
End If

' Get the coordinates of the disk's center.
Cx = Point1.Trans(1)
Cy = Point1.Trans(2)
Cz = Point1.Trans(3)

' Get the point of intersection with the plane.
X = px + t * Vx
Y = py + t * Vy
Z = pz + t * Vz

' See if the point is within distance
' Radius of the center.
dx = Cx - X
dy = Cy - Y
dz = Cz - Z
If dx * dx + dy * dy + dz * dz > Radius * Radius Then
    ' We are not within distance Radius.
    RayTraceable_FindT = -1
    Exit Function
End If

' We had a hit.
If direct_calculation Then HadHit = True

RayTraceable_FindT = t
End Function
```

RayDisk has more useful scanline clipping capabilities than the RayPlane class because it is much more tightly bounded. In most other respects, the two classes are similar. Figure 17.13 shows program VBRay displaying three spheres and a disk.

Polygons

Like disks, polygons lie in a plane. The RayPolygon class is very similar to the RayDisk class. The only difference between the two classes lies in the way they find their intersections with rays in the FindT function.

Both classes begin by determining whether the ray intersects the plane containing the polygon. The RayDisk class then uses the distance from the disk's center to the point of intersection to determine whether the point lies within the disk.

The RayPolygon class must determine whether the point of intersection lies within the polygon. At first, this task might seem difficult. Actually, it is fairly easy if you use a modified version of the PointInside function described in Chapter 15, Hidden Surface Removal. This function determines whether a point lies within a two-dimensional polygon. In the present case, however, the polygon is three-dimensional—it does not lie in the X-Y plane.

Fortunately, a point lies within a polygon if the projection of the point lies within the projection of the polygon for any reasonable projection, as shown in Figure 17.14. This means you can project the polygon onto the X-Y plane before you test to see if a point lies inside it. Then you can use the PointInside function from Chapter 15.

This test can fail if the plane containing the polygon is perpendicular to the X-Y plane. In that case, the projections of all the points in the polygon lie along a line, so you cannot tell if the point lies in the projected polygon.

If the plane is perpendicular to the X-Y plane, it must not be perpendicular to the X-Z plane, the Y-Z plane, or both. In that case, you can project the polygon onto one of those other planes before testing to see if the point lies within the polygon.

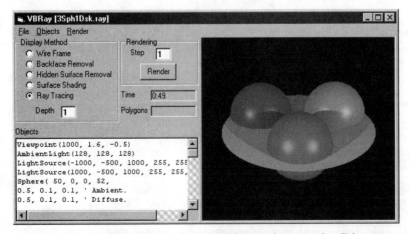

Figure 17.13   Program VBRay displaying three spheres and a disk.

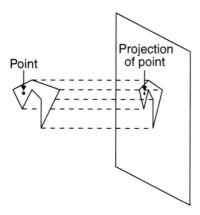

Figure 17.14 A point lies within a polygon if its projection lies within the projection of the polygon.

The new PointInside routine shown in the following code first decides onto which plane it can project the polygon. It then calls function PointInsideXY, PointInsideYZ, or PointInsideXZ as necessary. The code that follows shows the PointInsideXY function. The other functions are very similar.

```
' Return true if the point is in the polygon.
Private Function PointInside(ByVal X As Single, _
    ByVal Y As Single, ByVal Z As Single) As Boolean
Dim i As Integer
Dim xok As Boolean
Dim yok As Boolean
Dim zok As Boolean

    ' See in which coordinates the points differ.
    ' X coordinates.
    xok = False
    For i = 2 To NumPoints
        If Points(i - 1).Trans(1) <> Points(i).Trans(1) _
        Then
            xok = True
            Exit For
        End If
    Next i

    ' Y coordinates.
    yok = False
    For i = 2 To NumPoints
        If Points(i - 1).Trans(2) <> Points(i).Trans(2) _
        Then
            yok = True
            Exit For
        End If
    Next i
```

```vb
    ' Z coordinates.
    zok = False
    For i = 2 To NumPoints
        If Points(i - 1).Trans(3) <> Points(i).Trans(3) _
        Then
            yok = True
            Exit For
        End If
    Next i

    ' Test the appropriate projection.
    If xok And yok Then
        PointInside = PointInsideXY(X, Y)
    ElseIf yok And zok Then
        PointInside = PointInsideYZ(Y, Z)
    ElseIf xok And zok Then
        PointInside = PointInsideXZ(X, Z)
    Else
        PointInside = False
    End If
End Function

' Return true if the point's projection lies within
' this polygon's projection onto the X-Y plane.
Private Function PointInsideXY( _
    ByVal X As Single, ByVal Y As Single) As Boolean
Dim i As Integer
Dim theta1 As Double
Dim theta2 As Double
Dim dtheta As Double
Dim dx As Double
Dim dy As Double
Dim angles As Double

    dx = Points(NumPoints).Trans(1) - X
    dy = Points(NumPoints).Trans(2) - Y
    theta1 = ATan2(CSng(dy), CSng(dx))
    If theta1 < 0 Then theta1 = theta1 + 2 * PI
    For i = 1 To NumPoints
        dx = Points(i).Trans(1) - X
        dy = Points(i).Trans(2) - Y
        theta2 = ATan2(CSng(dy), CSng(dx))
        If theta2 < 0 Then theta2 = theta2 + 2 * PI
        dtheta = theta2 - theta1
        If dtheta > PI Then dtheta = dtheta - 2 * PI
        If dtheta < -PI Then dtheta = dtheta + 2 * PI
        angles = angles + dtheta
        theta1 = theta2
    Next i

    PointInsideXY = (Abs(angles) > 0.001)
End Function
```

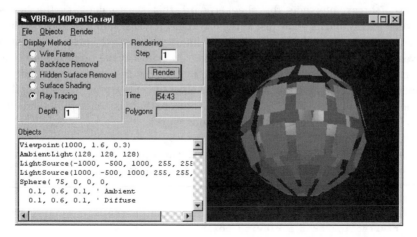

Figure 17.15   Program VBRay displaying 40 polygons and a sphere.

Figure 17.15 shows program VBRay displaying a scene containing 40 RayPolygon objects surrounding a sphere.

Checkerboards

The RayDisk and RayPolygon classes represent shapes that lie in a plane. To see if a ray intersects their shapes, these classes first find the intersection between the ray and their planes. They then use different methods to decide whether the point on the plane lies within their shapes.

You can extend this to manage other, possibly more complex, planar shapes. For example, you could use a similar technique to implement concentric rings or multiple polygons on the same plane.

The RayCheckerboard class manages a checkerboard pattern. You define a checkerboard with the point at the corner of the checkerboard and two vectors used to generate its rectangular areas. The point and vectors define a plane much as a point and normal vector do. If the point has coordinates (px, py, pz), and the vectors are <v1x, v1y, v1z> and <v2x, v2y, v2z>, you can find the points on the plane using the parametric equations:

```
X(t, u) = px + i * v1x + j * v2x
Y(t, u) = py + i * v1y + j * v2y
Z(t, u) = pz + i * v1z + j * v2z
```

where the values i and j vary over the real numbers.

The RayCheckerboard class also takes two parameters, NumSquares1 and Num-Squares2, that tell it how to restrict the area on this plane. To find the corners of the checkerboard squares, the class uses integer values for i and j where:

```
0 <= i <= NumSquares1
0 <= j <= NumSquares2
```

To see if a ray intersects the checkerboard, this class calculates the intersection between the ray and its plane just as the RayPlane, RayDisk, and RayPolygon classes do. It then plugs the coordinates of the point of intersection into the previous equations and solves for the values i and j. If those values indicate that the point lies on one of the object's rectangular areas, the FindT function returns the parameter t indicating the point's distance along the ray. If the i and j values indicate the point does not lie on one of the object's squares, FindT returns -1 to indicate there is no useful intersection. The following code shows how the FindT function works.

```
' Return the value T for the point of intersection
' between the vector from point (px, py, pz) in
' the direction <vx, vy, vz>.
'
' direct_calculation is true if we are finding the
' intersection from a viewing position ray. It is
' false if we are finding a reflected intersection
' or a shadow feeler.
Public Function RayTraceable_FindT( _
    ByVal direct_calculation As Boolean, _
    ByVal px As Single, ByVal py As Single, _
    ByVal pz As Single, ByVal Vx As Single, _
    ByVal Vy As Single, ByVal Vz As Single) As Single
Dim A As Single
Dim B As Single
Dim C As Single
Dim D As Single
Dim Nx As Single
Dim Ny As Single
Dim Nz As Single
Dim denom As Single
Dim t As Single
Dim Cx As Single
Dim Cy As Single
Dim Cz As Single
Dim dx As Single
Dim dy As Single
Dim dz As Single
Dim X As Single
Dim Y As Single
Dim Z As Single
Dim v1x As Single
Dim v1y As Single
Dim v1z As Single
Dim v2x As Single
Dim v2y As Single
Dim v2z As Single
Dim i As Single
Dim j As Single

    ' See if we have been culled.
    If direct_calculation And DoneOnThisScanline Then
```

```
        RayTraceable_FindT = -1
        Exit Function
End If


' Find the unit normal at this point.
GetUnitNormal Nx, Ny, Nz


' Compute the plane's parameters.
A = Nx
B = Ny
C = Nz
D = -(Nx * Point1.Trans(1) + _
      Ny * Point1.Trans(2) + _
      Nz * Point1.Trans(3))


' If the denominator = 0, the ray is parallel
' to the plane so there's no intersection.
denom = A * Vx + B * Vy + C * Vz
If denom = 0 Then
    RayTraceable_FindT = -1
    Exit Function
End If


' Solve for t.
t = -(A * px + B * py + C * pz + D) / denom


' If there is no positive t value, there's no
' intersection in this direction.
If t < 0.01 Then
    RayTraceable_FindT = -1
    Exit Function
End If


' Get the point of intersection with the plane.
X = px + t * Vx
Y = py + t * Vy
Z = pz + t * Vz


' Get the square vectors.
px = Point1.Trans(1)
py = Point1.Trans(2)
pz = Point1.Trans(3)
v1x = Point2.Trans(1) - px
v1y = Point2.Trans(2) - py
v1z = Point2.Trans(3) - pz
v2x = Point3.Trans(1) - px
v2y = Point3.Trans(2) - py
v2z = Point3.Trans(3) - pz


' Get the i and j values for this point.
If (Abs(v1x) > 0.001) And _
    (Abs(v1y * v2x - v2y * v1x) > 0.001) _
```

```
        Then
            j = (v1y * (X - px) + v1x * (py - Y)) / _
                (v1y * v2x - v2y * v1x)
            i = (X - px - v2x * j) / v1x
        ElseIf (Abs(v1y) > 0.001) And _
            (Abs(v1z * v2y - v2z * v1y) > 0.001) _
        Then
            j = (v1z * (Y - py) + v1y * (pz - Z)) / _
                (v1z * v2y - v2z * v1y)
            i = (Y - py - v2y * j) / v1y
        Else
            j = (v1x * (Z - pz) + v1z * (px - X)) / _
                (v1x * v2z - v2x * v1z)
            i = (Z - pz - v2z * j) / v1z
        End If

        ' See if the point is ok.
        If (i < 0) Or (j < 0) Or _
            (i > NumSquares1) Or (j > NumSquares2) _
        Then
            ' Not on the area of interest.
            RayTraceable_FindT = -1
            Exit Function
        ElseIf (Int(i) + Int(j)) Mod 2 <> 0 Then
            ' Not on a drawn square.
            RayTraceable_FindT = -1
            Exit Function
        Else
            ' We had a hit.
            If direct_calculation Then HadHit = True

            RayTraceable_FindT = t
        End If
    End Function
```

Figure 17.16 shows program VBRay displaying a sphere surrounded by six RayChecker-board objects. With a little work, you could produce a similar image using RayPolygon objects instead of RayCheckerboard objects. That would require 78 separate polygons instead of 6 checkerboards so it would slow the program greatly.

This method of mapping a point's (x, y, z) coordinates into (i, j) coordinates on the plane is similar to texture mapping described later in this chapter. In texture mapping, the transformed coordinates are used to decide what color to make the pixel rather than to decide whether the point lies on the object.

Cylinders

The round cylinders considered here consist of all the points that are a fixed distance from a line called the cylinder's *axis*. You can define a cylinder by specifying its radius and two points along its axis. If you want the cylinder to have a finite length, the two

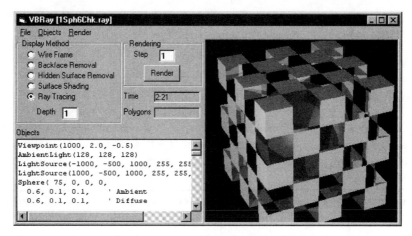

Figure 17.16 A sphere surrounded by RayCheckerboard objects.

points you specify can lie at the ends of the cylinder. Figure 17.17 shows a finite cylinder specified by the points P_1 and P_2.

If $P_1 = (x1, y1, z1)$ and $P_2 = (x2, y2, z2)$, you can write the parametric equations for a cylinder's axis as:

```
X(u) = x1 + Wx * u
Y(u) = y1 + Wy * u
Z(u) = z1 + Wy * u
```

where:

```
Wx = x2 - x1
Wy = y2 - y1
Wz = z2 - z1
0 <= u <= 1
```

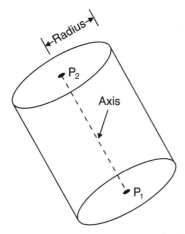

Figure 17.17 A cylinder.

Now suppose you have a ray that passes through the point (px, py, pz) in the direction of the vector <Vx, Vy, Vz>. The parametric equations for this ray are:

```
X(t) = px + Vx * t
Y(t) = py + Vy * t
Z(t) = pz + Vy * t
```

Suppose H is a point of intersection between the ray and the cylinder. The shortest distance from the cylinder's axis to the point H follows a vector R perpendicular to the axis as shown in Figure 17.18. The point I in Figure 17.18 marks the end of the vector R.

Because the cylinder's axis is parallel to the vector W, the vectors W and R are perpendicular, so the dot product $W \cdot R$ must be zero.

```
W · R= Wx * Rx + Wy * Ry + Wz * Rz
     = Wx * (Hx - Ix) + Wy * (Hy - Iy) + Wz * (Hz - Iz)
```

The point H lies along the ray, so the parametric equations for the ray must generate the point H. In other words, for some value of t, Hx = px + Vx * t, Hy = py + Vy * t, and Hz = pz + Vz * t.

Similarly, the point I lies along the cylinder's axis, so the parametric equations for the axis must generate the point I. For some value of u, Ix = x1 + Wx * u, and so forth.

Substituting the parametric equations for the coordinates of the points H and I into the equation for the dot product gives:

```
W · R= Wx * ((px + Vx * t) - (x1 + Wx * u)) +
       Wy * ((py + Vy * t) - (y1 + Wy * u)) +
       Wz * ((pz + Vz * t) - (z1 + Wz * u))
```

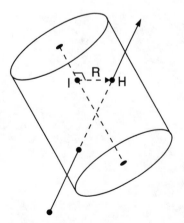

Figure 17.18   A ray intersecting a cylinder in two places.

If you multiply this out and group the t and u terms, you get:

```
V · R= u * (-Wx² - Wy² - Wz²) +
        t * (Wx * Vx + Wy * Vy + Wz * Vz) +
        Wx * (px - x1) + Wy * (py - y1) + Wz * (pz - z1)
```

Because the dot product should be equal to zero, you can set this equation equal to zero and solve for the parameter u. With some rearranging and a couple of substitutions, the equation becomes:

```
u = A * t + B
```

where:

```
A = (Wx * Vx + Wy * Vy + Wz * Vz) / (Wx² + Wy² + Wz²)
B = (Wx * (px - x1) + Wy * (py - y1) + Wz * (pz - z1)) /
       (Wx² + Wy² + Wz²)
```

This gives you an equation for u in terms of t. The values of A and B are complicated, but they are still only constants. Their values depend on the geometry of the cylinder and the ray.

Because this equation contains two unknown values u and t, it does not hold enough information for you to solve for both values. You need another equation relating u and t. You can get one by noting that the length of vector R must equal the radius of the cylinder. Equivalently, the square of the length of vector R must equal the square of the radius.

```
Radius² = (Hx - Ix)² + (Hy - Iy)² +(Hz - Iz)²
```

Substituting the parametric values for the points H and I as before gives:

```
Radius² =    ((px + Vx * t) - (x1 + Wx * u))² +
        ((py + Vy * t) - (y1 + Wy * u))² +
        ((pz + Vz * t) - (z1 + Wz * u))²
```

Replacing the parameter u with the equation describing u in terms of t, this becomes:

```
Radius²       =       (px + Vx * t - x1 - Wx * (A * t + B))²
        (py + Vy * t - y1 - Wy * (A * t + B))² +
        (pz + Vz * t - z1 - Wz * (A * t + B))²
  =     (t * (Vx - Wx * A) + (px - x1 - Wx * B))² +
        (t * (Vy - Wy * A) + (py - y1 - Wy * B))² +
        (t * (Vz - Wz * A) + (pz - z1 - Wz * B))² +
```

You can make this equation easier to manage by making the following substitutions.

```
Cx = Vx - Wx * A
Cy = Vy - Wy * A
Cz = Vz - Wz * A
```

```
Dx = px - x1 - Wx * B
Dy = py - y1 - Wy * B
Dz = pz - z1 - Wz * B
```

Then subtracting Radius^2 from both sides of the equation gives:

```
0    = (t * Cx + Dx)² + (t * Cy + Dy)² + (t * Cz + Dz)² - Radius²
     = t² * (Cx² + Cy² + Cz²) +
       t * 2 * (Cx * Dx + Cy * Dy + Cz * Dz) +
       (Dx² + Dy² + Dz² - Radius²)
```

You can simplify this again by making one final set of substitutions.

```
t² * A1 + t * B1 + C1 = 0
```

where:

```
A1 = Cx² + Cy² + Cz²
B1 = 2 * (Cx * Dx + Cy * Dy + Cz * Dz)
C1 = Dx² + Dy² + Dz² - Radius²
```

Finally, you can use the quadratic formula to solve this equation for t.

```
t = (-B1 ± Sqr(B1² - 4 * A1 * C1)) / 2 / A1
```

When you enter the values for A1, B1, and C1, you get one of three possible results. First, if $B1^2 - 4 * A1 * C1 < 0$, the square root has no real solutions. In this case, the ray does not intersect the cylinder in real, three-dimensional space.

Second, if $B1^2 - 4 * A1 * C1 = 0$, the equation has a single solution t = -B1/2/A1. In this case the ray is tangent to the cylinder, meeting it at a single point.

Finally, if $B1^2 - 4 * A1 * C1 > 0$, the equation gives two possible values for t. Values less than zero represent points that lie behind the point at which the ray originates. These intersections are not interesting to a ray-tracing program. Larger values for t represent points further from the beginning of the ray than the points represented by smaller values. Thus, the position on the cylinder closest to the point (px, py, pz) in the direction of the vector <Vx, Vy, Vz> corresponds to the smaller positive value of t.

Once you have determined t, you can use that value in the parametric equations for the ray to determine H, the actual point of intersection.

You can also use the value of t and the equation u = A * t + B to solve for the corresponding value of u. Then, using this value and the parametric equations for the cylinder's axis, you can find the point I. Finally, from points H and I you can find the vector R. This vector is normal to the cylinder's surface at the point H. You can use it as the surface normal when you calculate the color of the pixel in the HitColor subroutine.

In many programs, you will want to use a cylinder of finite length. In that case, you do not want to display intersections that occur beyond the ends of the cylinder. To detect these intersections, check the value of the parameter u corresponding to the intersection. Because the vector W is created with two points P_1 and P_2 that lie on the ends of the cylinder, u is between 0.0 and 1.0 if the corresponding point I in Figure 17.18 lies within the cylinder. If u < 0.0 or u > 1.0, the point of intersection is not on the finite portion of the cylinder, so you can ignore it.

This method does nothing to handle the ends of the cylinder. If you want the cylinder to be solid, create two RayDisk objects to cap the ends.

If you want the cylinder to be hollow so that you can look into its interior, you need to modify the intersection routine to examine both values of t. If the value closer to the center of projection lies outside the finite part of the cylinder, you need to consider the other value for t. If that value lies on the finite cylinder, the ray is reaching it through the inside of the cylinder, and it should be visible.

The RayCylinder class used by program VRay manages finite cylinders that are not hollow. The following code shows how the FindT function locates the cylinder's point of intersection with a ray.

```
' Return the value T for the point of intersection
' between the vector from point (px, py, pz) in
' the direction <wx, wy, wz>.
'
' direct_calculation is true if we are finding the
' intersection from a viewing position ray. It is
' false if we are finding a reflected intersection
' or a shadow feeler.
Public Function RayTraceable_FindT( _
    ByVal direct_calculation As Boolean, ByVal px As Single, _
    ByVal py As Single, ByVal pz As Single, _
    ByVal Vx As Single, ByVal Vy As Single, _
    ByVal Vz As Single) As Single
Dim x1 As Single
Dim y1 As Single
Dim z1 As Single
Dim Wx As Single
Dim Wy As Single
Dim Wz As Single
Dim w_len_squared As Single
Dim WdotV As Single
Dim A As Single
Dim B As Single
Dim Cx As Single
Dim Cy As Single
Dim Cz As Single
Dim dx As Single
Dim dy As Single
Dim dz As Single
Dim A1 As Single
Dim b1 As Single
Dim C1 As Single
```

```
Dim B24AC As Single
Dim t1 As Single
Dim t2 As Single

    ' Find the axis vector.
    Wx = Point2.Trans(1) - Point1.Trans(1)
    Wy = Point2.Trans(2) - Point1.Trans(2)
    Wz = Point2.Trans(3) - Point1.Trans(3)

    ' Find A and B for u = A * t + B.
    w_len_squared = Wx * Wx + Wy * Wy + Wz * Wz
    WdotV = Wx * Vx + Wy * Vy + Wz * Vz
    A = WdotV / w_len_squared

    x1 = Point1.Trans(1)
    y1 = Point1.Trans(2)
    z1 = Point1.Trans(3)
    B = (Wx * (px - x1) + _
        Wy * (py - y1) + _
        Wz * (pz - z1)) / w_len_squared

    ' Solve for t.
    Cx = Vx - Wx * A
    Cy = Vy - Wy * A
    Cz = Vz - Wz * A
    dx = px - x1 - Wx * B
    dy = py - y1 - Wy * B
    dz = pz - z1 - Wz * B
    A1 = Cx * Cx + Cy * Cy + Cz * Cz
    b1 = 2 * (Cx * dx + Cy * dy + Cz * dz)
    C1 = dx * dx + dy * dy + dz * dz - Radius * Radius

    ' Solve the quadratic A1*t^2 + B1*t + C1 = 0.
    B24AC = b1 * b1 - 4 * A1 * C1
    If B24AC < 0 Then
        RayTraceable_FindT = -1
        Exit Function
    ElseIf B24AC = 0 Then
        t1 = -b1 / 2 / A1
    Else
        B24AC = Sqr(B24AC)
        t1 = (-b1 + B24AC) / 2 / A1
        t2 = (-b1 - B24AC) / 2 / A1
        ' Use only positive t values.
        If t1 < 0.02 Then t1 = t2
        If t2 < 0.02 Then t2 = t1
        ' Use the smaller t value.
        If t1 > t2 Then t1 = t2
    End If

    ' If there is no positive t value, there's no
    ' intersection in this direction.
```

```
      If t1 < 0.02 Then
          RayTraceable_FindT = -1
          Exit Function
      End If


      ' See where on the cylinder this point is.
      HitU = t1 * A + B


      ' If this is not between Point1 and Point2,
      ' ignore it.
      If HitU < 0 Or HitU > 1 Then
          RayTraceable_FindT = -1
      Else
          RayTraceable_FindT = t1
      End If
  End Function
```

The FindHitColor function for cylinders is similar to the corresponding functions for other objects. The main difference is in how the function calculates the surface normal vector. For a cylinder, the function uses the values of t and u to find the points H and I as shown in Figure 17.18. The vector from point I to point H is normal to the surface at the point of intersection.

When it finds a point of intersection, function FindT saves the value of u in the module global variable HitU. Rather than recalculating the value u to find the normal vector, subroutine FindHitColor uses the value in HitU. It can then find the normal vector and pass it into the CalculateHitColor subroutine.

```
  ' Return the red, green, and blue components of
  ' the surface at the hit position.
  Public Sub RayTraceable_FindHitColor( _
      ByVal depth As Integer, Objects As Collection, _
      ByVal eye_x As Single, ByVal eye_y As Single, _
      ByVal eye_z As Single, ByVal px As Single, _
      ByVal py As Single, ByVal pz As Single, _
      ByRef R As Integer, ByRef G As Integer, _
      ByRef B As Integer)
  Dim Vx As Single
  Dim Vy As Single
  Dim Vz As Single
  Dim Nx As Single
  Dim Ny As Single
  Dim Nz As Single
  Dim n_len  As Single

      ' Find the unit normal at this point.
      Vx = Point2.Trans(1) - Point1.Trans(1)
      Vy = Point2.Trans(2) - Point1.Trans(2)
      Vz = Point2.Trans(3) - Point1.Trans(3)
      Nx = px - (Point1.Trans(1) + HitU * Vx)
      Ny = py - (Point1.Trans(2) + HitU * Vy)
```

```
        Nz = pz - (Point1.Trans(3) + HitU * Vz)
        n_len = Sqr(Nx * Nx + Ny * Ny + Nz * Nz)
        Nx = Nx / n_len
        Ny = Ny / n_len
        Nz = Nz / n_len

        ' Get the hit color.
        CalculateHitColor depth, Objects, Me, _
            eye_x, eye_y, eye_z, _
            px, py, pz, _
            Nx, Ny, Nz, _
            DiffuseKr, DiffuseKg, DiffuseKb, _
            AmbientKr, AmbientKg, AmbientKb, _
            SpecularK, SpecularN, _
            ReflectedKr, ReflectedKg, ReflectedKb, IsReflective, _
            TransmittedKr, TransmittedKg, TransmittedKb, TransN, _
            n1, n2, IsTransparent, R, G, B
    End Sub
```

Figure 17.19 shows program VBRay displaying six spheres and three cylinders.

Recursive Ray Tracing

Ray tracing as presented in the previous sections is quite useful. It does everything the hidden surface and shading algorithms described in earlier chapters do. It also performs smooth shading (as long as you can find equations for your objects), and it displays shadows. With only a little more work, you can make ray tracing model reflective and transparent surfaces, too.

The basic idea is to break the light transmitted at a point into local and global components. The local components are those that are caused locally at the point by ambient light and diffuse and specular reflection modified by shadowing. The global components

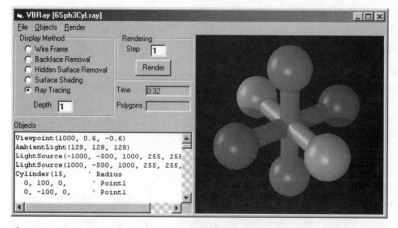

Figure 17.19 Six spheres and three cylinders.

are caused by light reaching the pixel from some other part of the scene. This includes light that reaches the point after reflecting off other objects and light that reaches the point by passing through a transparent surface. The following sections explain how to add the local and global terms you need to handle reflective and transparent objects.

Reflected Light

To compute the color of a pixel, calculate the local components directly. Then add in the global components. Because you know the viewing direction and the surface normal, you can calculate the direction from which reflected light would need to come if it were to hit the surface and reflect toward the viewpoint.

In Figure 17.20, V is the vector from the surface to the viewpoint, and N is the surface's normal vector at that point.

Using these two vectors V and N, you can calculate M, the reflection vector for the vector V. The calculation is similar to the calculation in Chapter 16, Shading Models, of the vector R that gives the direction of specular reflection. When those results are applied to this situation, the vector M is given by the equation:

```
M = 2 * N * (V · N) - V
```

For example, the X component of the vector M is:

```
Mx = 2 * Nx * (N · V) - Vx
```

Once you have found the vector M, you need to follow that vector until you intersect another object. The color at that point of intersection determines the color that reflects off the original object to the viewpoint.

At this point you can start to see the recursive nature of the algorithm. You begin with a ray starting at the original point of intersection. You need to trace this ray to find the color of the point where it intersects another object. This process is identical to that in the original problem in which you needed to follow a ray starting at the viewpoint to find the color of the point where that ray intersects an object.

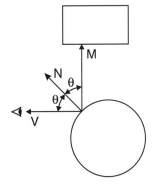

Figure 17.20   The vector M points in the direction of reflection.

If you write a function TraceRay to follow a ray and return the color at the point of its first intersection, you can describe the recursive ray tracing algorithm like this.

1. Find ray M in the reflection direction.
2. TraceRay = Local components (ambient, diffuse, specular) + k_r * TraceRay(M).

Here, k_r is a constant that represents the reflectiveness of the surface. If the surface is very reflective, k_r should be close to one. If the surface is not very reflective, k_r should be close to zero.

Adding this term to the lighting model gives:

$$I = I_a * k_a + \\ I_i * (k_d * (L \cdot N) + k_s * (R \cdot V)^n) * \\ (r_{min} + k_{dist}) / (r + k_{dist}) + \\ I_r * k_r$$

In this equation, I_r is the reflected component computed recursively.

The TraceRay function takes parameters that indicate the starting point and direction of a ray. It returns through parameters the red, green, and blue color components of the pixel where the ray intersects an object.

Once it has found the point of intersection between the ray and an object, TraceRay calls the object's FindHitColor routine to calculate the pixel's color. FindHitColor does little more than calculate the object's surface normal and then invoke the CalculateHit-Color subroutine. This is the subroutine that contains the color model information and that does all the interesting work.

The following code fragment shows the part of CalculateHitColor that deals with reflected light. You can see the complete source code on the CD-ROM, and you can learn more about the other parts of the shading model in Chapter 16, Shading Models.

When CalculateHitColor examines a reflective surface, it finds the mirror direction for the ray it is following. It then calls subroutine TraceRay to follow a new ray in that direction to find the reflected light's contribution. TraceRay calls FindHitColor, which calls CalculateHitColor, and the recursion starts all over again.

The depth parameter controls the depth of recursion. Each time CalculateHitColor calls TraceRay, it decreases depth. That guarantees that the recursion eventually stops when depth is zero.

```
' Return the red, green, and blue components of
' an object at a hit position (px, py, pz) with
' normal vector (nx, ny, nz).
Public Sub CalculateHitColor(ByVal depth As Integer, _
    Objects As Collection, ...)
        :
    ' *************
    ' * Reflected *
    ' *************
```

```
        If (depth > 1) And is_reflective Then
            ' Find the view mirror vector VM.
            vmx = 2 * Nx * VdotN - Vx
            vmy = 2 * Ny * VdotN - Vy
            vmz = 2 * Nz * VdotN - Vz

            ' Trace a ray from (px, py, pz) in the
            ' direction VM.
            TraceRay False, depth - 1, px, py, pz, _
                vmx, vmy, vmz, r_refl, g_refl, b_refl

            ' Multiply by the reflection coefficients.
            total_r = total_r + Krr * r_refl
            total_g = total_g + Krg * g_refl
            total_b = total_b + Krb * b_refl
        End If
            :
    End Sub
```

Figure 17.21 shows program VBRay displaying three spheres over a checkerboard. The middle sphere is green and very reflective. The checkerboard is also very reflective. You can easily see the reflections of all three spheres in the checkerboard and of the outer spheres in the middle sphere. If you look closely, you can see the reflections of the spheres in the checkerboard in the middle sphere, the reflection of the checkerboard off the middle sphere in the checkerboard, and other more complex reflections. The Depth text box in the program was set to 10 in this picture, so rays are traced through no more than 10 reflections.

Transparent Surfaces

Before examining the code for transparent surfaces, you need to understand some of the physics of light passing through a transparent object. The sections that follow discuss the details you need to know and describe how you can use them to draw transparent objects.

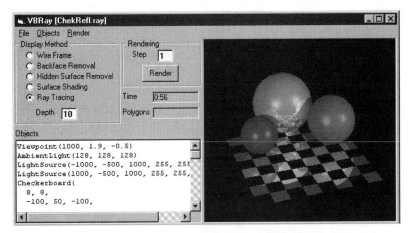

Figure 17.21   Three spheres over a reflective checkerboard.

Refraction

Light does not travel at the same speed in all substances. For instance, light travels faster through air or a vacuum than it does through water or glass. When light passes from one medium into another, its direction of travel changes. This change is called *refraction*. You can see refraction when you look at something through a curved lens, a prism, or a glass full of water.

The angle through which the light bends is determined by the speed of light in the substances the light is leaving and entering. Figure 17.22 shows a ray of light moving from air into a block of glass. The angles θ_1 and θ_2 are related to each other by the *indexes of refraction* of the two substances—in this case, air and glass.

The index of refraction of a substance is the ratio of the speed of light in vacuum to the speed of light in the substance.

```
Index of refraction = C_vacuum / C_substance
```

Table 17.1 lists the indexes of refraction for several common substances. You may find these numbers useful for characterizing objects in your ray-tracing programs. Of course, you are not restricted to these numbers. Using an unusually large index of refraction can sometimes produce interesting results.

If the index of refraction in one substance is n_1 and the index of refraction in the other is n_2, the angles in Figure 17.22 are related by Snell's law:

```
Sin(θ₁) / Sin(θ₂) = n₂ / n₁
```

This equation has some important consequences. If light passes from a substance with a high index of refraction into one with a lower index of refraction, then $n_1 > n_2$. In that case, if you replace θ_2 with 90 degrees in Snell's law, you can solve for θ_1.

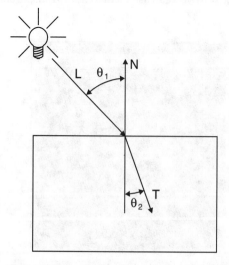

Figure 17.22   Refraction occurs when light passes from one substance into another.

Table 17.1 Indexes of Refraction for Common Substances

SUBSTANCE	INDEX OF REFRACTION
Vacuum	1.00 (by definition)
Air	1.00 (approximately)
Water	1.33
Ethyl Alcohol	1.36
Quartz	1.46
Glass	1.40 - 1.50 (various values)
Gelatin	1.53 (various values)

```
Sin(θ₁) = Sin(90) * n₂ / n₁
θ₁ = Arcsin(n₂ / n₁)
```

Because $n_1 > n_2$, the value of n_2/n_1 is less than one, so the arcsine exists. The angle θ_1 given by this equation is called the *critical angle*. When light strikes the boundary between the surfaces at this angle, it is refracted parallel to the boundary as shown in Figure 17.23.

If you increase the angle θ_1 beyond the critical angle, the light is reflected by the boundary as shown in Figure 17.24. This is called *internal reflection*. Internal reflection is the main reason fiber optic cable works. Light enters at the end of the cable core. As the light passes through the cable, it strikes the walls of the core making an angle greater than the critical angle with the walls' normals. This makes the light reflect back into the cable. Eventually, the light strikes the far end of the cable, making a fairly small angle with the normal there. Internal reflection does not occur, and the light leaves the cable. This process is illustrated in Figure 17.25.

You can compute the vector T in the direction of refraction using the equation:

```
T = L * n₁ / n₂ - (Cos(θ₂) - Cos(θ₁) * n₁ / n₂) * N
```

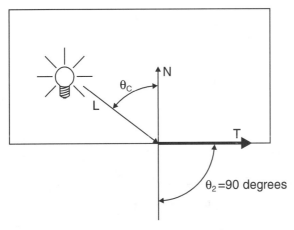

Figure 17.23 Light striking a surface at the critical angle refracts parallel to the surface.

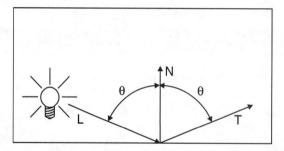

Figure 17.24 Light striking a surface at an angle greater than the critical angle is internally reflected.

For example, the X component of the vector T is:

```
Tₓ = Lₓ * n₁ / n₂ - (Cos(θ₂) - Cos(θ₁) * n₁ / n₂) * Nₓ
```

If N and L are unit vectors, then $Cos(\theta_1) = N \cdot L$. To find $Cos(\theta_2)$, you can use Snell's law, plus the fact that $Sin^2(\theta) + Cos^2(\theta) = 1$.

```
Sin(θ₁) / Sin(θ₂) = n₂ / n₁
Sin(θ₂) = Sin(θ₁) * n₁ / n₂
Sin²(θ₂) = (Sin(θ₁) * n₁ / n₂)² = Sin²(θ₁) * (n₁ / n₂)²
1 - Cos²(θ₂) = (1 - Cos²(θ₁)) * (n₁ / n₂)²
Cos²(θ₂) = 1 - (1 - Cos²(θ₁)) * (n₁ / n₂)²
Cos(θ₂) = Sqr(1 - (1 - Cos²(θ₁)) * (n₁ / n₂)²)
```

The following code fragment calculates the components of the vector T.

```
' Find the transmission vector T.
cos1 = Abs(NdotL)
n_ratio = N1 / N2
cos2 = Sqr(1 - (1 - cos1 * cos1) * n_ratio * n_ratio)
cos_factor = cos2 - cos1 * n_ratio
tx = -Lx * n_ratio - cos_factor * nx
ty = -Ly * n_ratio - cos_factor * ny
tz = -Lz * n_ratio - cos_factor * nz
```

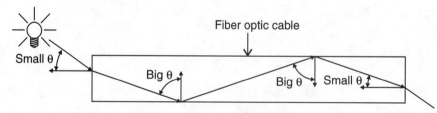

Figure 17.25 Light traveling through a fiber optic cable.

Directly Transmitted Light

Transparent surfaces add a little more complication to ray tracing than reflective ones. Transparent surfaces add not only to the global component a pixel's color but also to the local component.

The local contribution comes from light passing from the light source directly to an object and then through the object to the point. Figure 17.26 shows this situation. Usually, the viewpoint and light source are in the same substance. They both lie outside any objects in the scene's "air." This term is important, however, for rays that you trace recursively through transparent objects. Rays that originate inside transparent objects see this type of local contribution.

The vector L runs between the light source and the point of intersection. V runs from the intersection to the viewpoint. The vector T is a vector in the direction in which the light is refracted according to Snell's law.

Just as not all the specularly reflected light travels along the path of reflection, not all the refracted light travels along the vector T. You can model the light that actually reaches the viewpoint in a manner similar to the way you model specular reflection. You can set the amount of refracted light reaching the viewpoint to be some constant times the cosine of the angle ϕ raised to some power. You can select the constant and power to give you the sort of characteristics you want your object to have. If the vectors V and T are unit vectors, then $\mathrm{Cos}(\phi) = V \cdot T$, so you can let the direct reflected component for the light be:

```
I_i  *  k_t  *  (V  ·  T)^Nt
```

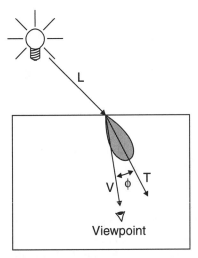

Figure 17.26   Not all transmitted light follows the direction of refraction.

The complete lighting model including directly transmitted light becomes:

```
I = I_a * k_a +
    I_i * (k_d * (L · N) + k_s * (R · V)^n) *
         (r_min + k_dist) / (r + k_dist) +
    I_r * k_r +
    I_i * k_t * (V · T)^Nt
```

Note that either the specular term or the direct transmitted term, but not both, can be nonzero. If the light source and viewpoint are on the same side of the surface, there is specular reflection. Because the light source and viewpoint are on the same side of the surface, any light that enters the object will not reach the viewpoint directly, so there can be no direct transmitted light.

Similarly if the light source and viewpoint lie on opposite sides of the surface, any light that is specularly reflected will not enter the object, so it cannot reach the viewpoint directly.

Indirectly Transmitted Light

The global component of transmitted light is indirectly transmitted. This is light that passes through a transparent object but does not originate directly at the light source. To compute the contribution due to this light, you need to follow a ray in the direction of refraction. When that ray strikes an object, use the color of that object to determine the contribution due to the ray. Adding a term for indirect transmission the lighting model becomes:

```
I = I_a * k_a +

    I_i * (k_d * (L · N) + k_s * (R · V)^n) *
         (r_min + k_dist) / (r + k_dist) +
    I_r * k_r +
    I_i * k_t * (V · T)^Nt +
    I_t * k_t
```

The constant k_t represents the transparency of the object. You can use the same value for both the direct and indirect transmitted components.

Transparent Surfaces in Visual Basic

To implement transparent objects in Visual Basic, you need to be able to determine the indexes of refraction before and after a light ray crosses a surface boundary. There are many ways you could keep track of the kinds of material through which a light ray passed. The approach taken here is one of the simpler options.

Each object has two indexes of refraction: N1 and N2. The value N1 is the index of refraction outside the object, and N2 is the index of refraction inside. Each object's Hit-Color subroutine uses the normal vector to determine whether the light ray is entering or leaving the object. If the normal vector points in more or less the same direction as the ray, the ray is leaving the object. If the normal vector and the ray meet at an angle greater than 90 degrees, the ray is entering the object.

If the light ray is leaving the object, the geometry of the situation is slightly different from that shown in the previous figures. In that case, all you need to do to make the equations work out is to switch the sign of $\cos(\theta)$. Because you compute this value using a dot product, $\cos(\theta)$ becomes $-(N \cdot V)$.

This method works quite well under normal circumstances in which most objects are surrounded by "air." It does not handle cases in which one transparent object partially overlaps another, however. When a light ray enters one of the objects, the use of N1 and N2 is correct. If the ray then passes from the first object into the second, the values of N1 and N2 for the second object are probably wrong.

For example, suppose your scene includes a glass cylinder overlapping a glass sphere. You should set N1 = 1.0 (air) and N2 = 1.4 (glass) for both objects. If a light ray crosses through the cylinder directly into the sphere, there should be no refraction. Because both objects are made of glass, the ray should pass through without changing direction. Because N1 = 1.0 and N2 = 1.4 for the sphere, however, the ray will be incorrectly refracted.

For many scenes, this restriction is not too great a burden. Even if you do create overlapped objects like this, the resulting reflections and refractions are usually complicated enough that it is difficult to notice that the image is not exactly as it should be. If you really want the calculations to be correct, modify this simple method for computing refraction so that the ray tracing routine always knows what kind of substance it is passing through and what kind of substance it is entering.

The following code shows the parts of the CalculateHitColor subroutine that deal with transmitted light.

```
' Return the red, green, and blue components of
' an object at a hit position (px, py, pz) with
' normal vector (nx, ny, nz).
Public Sub CalculateHitColor(ByVal depth As Integer, _
    Objects As Collection, ...)
        :
    ' Consider each light source.
    For Each light_source In LightSources
          :
        ' **********************
        ' * Direct Transmitted *
        ' **********************
        ' See if the light and viewpoint are on
        ' opposite sides of the surface and if we
        ' are not in shadow.
        If is_transparent Then
            ' Find LT, the light transmission vector.
            cos1 = Abs(LdotN)
            n1_over_n2 = n1 / n2
            cos2 = Sqr(1 - (1 - cos1 * cos1) * n1_over_n2 * _
                n1_over_n2)
            ' Note that the incident vector I = -L.
            normal_factor = cos2 - n1_over_n2 * cos1
            ltx = -n1_over_n2 * nlx - normal_factor * Nx
```

```
            lty = -n1_over_n2 * nly - normal_factor * Ny
            ltz = -n1_over_n2 * nlz - normal_factor * Nz

            ' Calculate V dot LT.
            VdotLT = Vx * ltx + Vy * lty + Vz * ltz

            ' See if V and LT point in generally
            ' the same direction.
            If VdotLT > 0 Then
                ' Calculate V dot LT to the TransN.
                transmitted_factor = VdotLT ^ TransN

                ' Add the direct transmitted component.
                total_r = total_r + Ktr * light_source.Ir * _
                    transmitted_factor
                total_g = total_g + Ktg * light_source.Ig * _
                    transmitted_factor
                total_b = total_b + Ktb * light_source.Ib * _
                    transmitted_factor
            End If
        End If
    Next light_source
        :
    ' *************************
    ' * Indirectly Transmitted *
    ' *************************
    ' See if the surface is transparent.
    If (depth > 1) And is_transparent Then
        ' Find VT, the viewing transmission vector.
        cos1 = Abs(VdotN)
        n1_over_n2 = n1 / n2
        cos2 = Sqr(1 - (1 - cos1 * cos1) * n1_over_n2 * _
            n1_over_n2)
        ' Note that the incident vector I = -V.
        normal_factor = cos2 - n1_over_n2 * cos1
        vtx = -n1_over_n2 * Vx - normal_factor * Nx
        vty = -n1_over_n2 * Vy - normal_factor * Ny
        vtz = -n1_over_n2 * Vz - normal_factor * Nz

        TraceRay False, depth - 1, target_object, _
            px, py, pz, vtx, vty, vtz, _
            r_tran, g_tran, b_tran

        ' Add the indirectly transmitted components.
        total_r = total_r + Ktr * r_tran
        total_g = total_g + Ktg * g_tran
        total_b = total_b + Ktb * b_tran
    End If
        :
End Sub
```

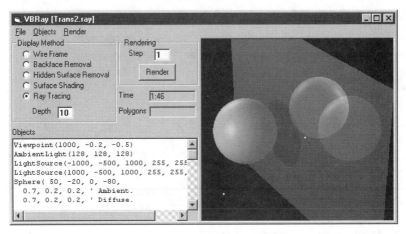

Figure 17.27 Side view of two spheres and a partially reflective and transparent polygon.

Figure 17.27 shows program VBRay displaying two spheres and a polygon. The polygon is partially reflective and partially transparent, so it shows a reflected image of one sphere and a transmitted image of the other. Figure 17.28 shows the same objects from above so that you can see their relationship.

Figure 17.29 shows program VBRay displaying a transparent sphere in front of two other spheres and a polygon.

The previous code works well for closed objects like the sphere shown in Figure 17.29. Flat objects such as polygons and disks, however, can be used in one of two ways. First, you may want to use the object as if it were a thin piece of glass or metal. This is the way the earlier sections in this chapter use these objects.

A light ray passing through a thin piece of glass is bent as it enters the glass, and then it is bent by an opposite amount as it leaves the glass a short while later. The images of objects behind the glass are shifted slightly, but they are not distorted. You can make a disk or polygon object ignore the minor shift in the transmitted light rays by setting the

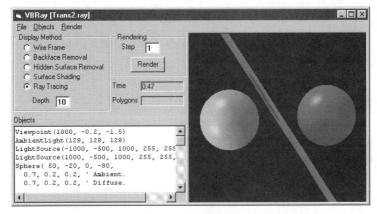

Figure 17.28 Top view of two spheres and a partially reflective and transparent polygon.

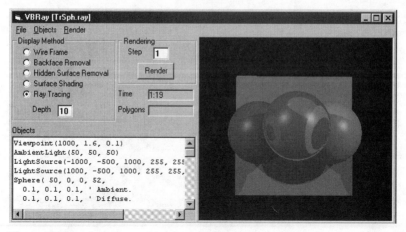

Figure 17.29 A transparent sphere in front of two other spheres and a polygon.

object's two indexes of refraction N1 and N2 to the same value. Light rays then enter and leave the object, moving in the same direction.

These flat objects ensure that the light travels through them normally by adjusting their surface normals if necessary. In the FindHitColor subroutine, these objects determine whether their normal points toward the center of projection. If it does not, the routine reverses the normal's components so that it does. That gives these objects the same color when they are viewed from either side.

The second way you might use one of these flat objects is as one face of a closed solid like a cube or closed-ended cylinder. In that case you do not want to ignore refraction as light rays pass through the object.

To make flat objects work as the faces of solids, you need to orient them so that the program knows when it is entering and when it is leaving the solid. These objects should not reverse their normals to point toward the center of projection. Then the program can use the normal to tell when it is entering and exiting an object.

The RayFace class implements this feature. It is identical to the RayPolygon class, except it does not change its normal in its FindHitColor subroutine.

Figure 17.30 shows program VBRay displaying a sphere and a transparent prism made up of five RayFace objects.

Assumptions

As is the case with all lighting models, the model used by program VBRay is only an approximation of the true physics of lighting. This model has been adjusted until it produces a fairly interesting and realistic picture under a variety of circumstances, but it is still just an approximation.

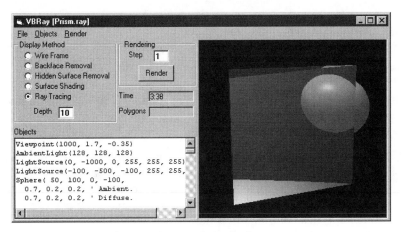

Figure 17.30   A sphere and a transparent prism.

A light source sends an infinite number of light rays into a scene. Each time one of those rays strikes an object, it sends out an infinite number of other rays in new directions. Many of the new rays follow the angle of reflection closely. Many more follow the path of refraction. Still others head out in nearly every direction, following paths of diffuse reflection or diffuse refraction. Because a computer cannot follow an infinite number of rays, ray-tracing algorithms follow only those rays that are considered the most important. In some cases, the algorithm misses other important rays.

For example, to decide whether a point is shadowed, the program traces a ray from he point back toward each light source. If the ray intersects an object, the program considers the point in the object's shadow. If the object is transparent, however, light should pass through it. Depending on the shape of the object, it may not shadow the point.

A transparent object may also refract light to create a bright spot on some object behind it. Unless the mirror direction at that spot just happens to point back toward the bright parts of the object, the program will not find it.

Similarly, the program misses some of the effects of reflective objects. A shiny surface may reflect light into an object and make it brighter. Unless the object's mirror direction just happens to point back toward the shiny surface, the program will miss this.

This model makes another approximation that is not quite as limiting when it assumes that light at all frequencies travels at the same speed through any given substance. In fact, the index of refraction for different wavelengths of light is different. This is why prisms and rainbows break light into colors. When the light enters a prism, the different wavelengths of light are bent by slightly different amounts because their indexes of refraction differ slightly. Because different wavelengths are bent by different amounts, they leave the prism heading in different directions, and you can see the separated colors. Assuming the indexes of refraction for all wavelengths are the same does not make images appear unnatural, but it does mean your programs cannot easily produce a rainbow.

Adaptive Depth Control

Program VBRay recursively follows a ray until either it does not intersect any objects in the scene or the ray-tracing routines reach a maximum depth of recursion. The program also stops following a ray if it can have no contribution to the color of the pixel whose value is being computed. For example, the program will not follow a refractive ray passing through a totally nontransparent object.

It will, however, follow a ray through a surface that is almost but not quite opaque. Each time a light ray reflects off a surface or passes through a transparent object, the possible contribution by the ray grows a bit smaller. The contribution due to a reflected ray, for example, is the value of the pixel where the ray intersects an object times the constant k_r. If $k_r = 0.1$, this contribution is fairly small. If the ray then reflects off another object with $k_r = 0.1$, the new ray's contribution will be only $0.1 * 0.1 = 0.01$ times the value of the pixel where the new ray intersects an object. After several reflections like this, the contribution due to the new light rays is undetectably small.

Instead of making your program run to some predefined depth of recursion, you can make it follow a light ray until the maximum contribution possible falls below some lower limit. When a ray the program is following cannot contribute significantly, the program should stop following it.

The simplest way to keep track of a ray's contribution is to change the depth parameter into the maximum contribution possible for a ray. Because the greatest value the red, green, and blue components of a ray's contribution can possibly have is 255, set the depth to 255 in your first call to the TraceRay subroutine.

Before you recursively invoke the TraceRay routine, reduce the depth parameter by a factor of the appropriate constant. If the new depth is less than one, the ray cannot contribute much to the original pixel's color, so you can ignore the ray. For example, the following code shows how you can update and check the depth parameter before following a reflective ray.

```
factor = Krr
If Krg > factor Then factor = Krg
If Krb > factor Then factor = Krb
new_depth = depth * factor
If new_depth > 0 Then _
    TraceRay False, new_depth, target_object, _
        px, py, pz, vmx, vmy, vmz, _
        r_refl, g_refl, b_refl
```

With this new system in place, you can also reduce the value of the depth parameter as light passes through partially transparent objects. You can assign each object that is at least partially transparent a transparency coefficient. Then reduce the value of the depth parameter by this amount for every unit of distance a ray travels through the object. This makes a light ray weaker after it passes a long distance through a murky, translucent object.

Similarly, you can reduce the value of the depth parameter as rays pass through empty space. This is similar to the way the lighting model reduces diffuse and specular reflection as objects move farther from the light source.

Texture Mapping

The shading models used by ray-tracing programs create images that are quite realistic, but they are a bit too perfect to feel true to life. Light reflects off surfaces perfectly evenly. Shades of color blend with perfect smoothness as a surface curves away from the viewing position. Colors are often too pure to seem natural.

Texture mapping attempts to make ray-traced objects appear more realistic by modifying the ways their surfaces are drawn. They add images, texture, and uneven shading to the otherwise mathematically perfect ray-traced objects.

There are many different texture mapping algorithms, some of which are extremely complex. This chapter describes three of the simpler techniques: normal perturbation, environment mapping, and special environment mapping. They provide remarkable results with surprisingly simple code.

Normal Perturbation

After a ray-tracing program intersects a ray with a solid, it calculates the color of the point of intersection. The shading model uses a number of parameters to determine the point's color including the viewing position, the position of the light sources and other objects, and the surface's normal vector at that point. You can give an object a rough texture by simply changing its surface normal vectors by small random amounts.

The RayBumpySphere class demonstrates this technique. The following code shows how this object's FindHitColor function perturbs its normal vector. First it finds the sphere's surface normal as usual. It then adds a small random value to the vector's X, Y, and Z components. The value Bumpiness is a property of the object and should be fairly small. To randomize the normal vector, the program adds a random value between 0 and Bumpiness to the vector's X, Y, and Z components. The normal vector has length 1 when the random amounts are added, so setting Bumpiness to 0.2 or 0.4 produces a reasonably large effect.

After randomizing the vector's components, FindHitColor renormalizes the vector so that it again has length 1. It then calls the CalculateHitColor subroutine as usual passing it this modified vector.

```
' Find the unit normal at this point.
Nx = px - Center.Trans(1)
Ny = py - Center.Trans(2)
Nz = pz - Center.Trans(3)
n_len = Sqr(Nx * Nx + Ny * Ny + Nz * Nz)
Nx = Nx / n_len
Ny = Ny / n_len
Nz = Nz / n_len
```

```
' Randomize the normal a little bit and
' renormalize.
Nx = Nx + Rnd * Bumpiness
Ny = Ny + Rnd * Bumpiness
Nz = Nz + Rnd * Bumpiness
n_len = Sqr(Nx * Nx + Ny * Ny + Nz * Nz)
Nx = Nx / n_len
Ny = Ny / n_len
Nz = Nz / n_len
```

The result is a surface that looks more like the textured plastic and metal commonly used to make computers than the perfectly smooth objects produced by the standard shading model. Figure 17.31 shows a sphere produced with this technique.

This simple method has a couple of drawbacks. First, each pixel is randomized independently. That gives the surface a texture on a very fine scale. Many real surfaces are more similar to the fractal surfaces described in Chapter 14, Surfaces. They have big bumps that contain smaller bumps that contain smaller bumps. The technique demonstrated by the RayBumpySphere class produces very small bumps of perfectly even size.

Another drawback to this method is that it randomizes the surface normals randomly. In other words, if you generate the same image again from a slightly different viewpoint or from a slightly different distance, all the normals are perturbed in a different way. If you generate only individual images, that is not a problem. If you try to run them together as an animation, however, the texture on the surface moves around. The image seems to sparkle. To prevent this, the surface needs to generate the same random perturbations for a particular point on the surface, no matter how it is viewed.

Environment Mapping

Environment mapping takes an image and maps it onto a surface. You can use some of the same techniques described in Chapter 7, Area Processes, to map pixels from the

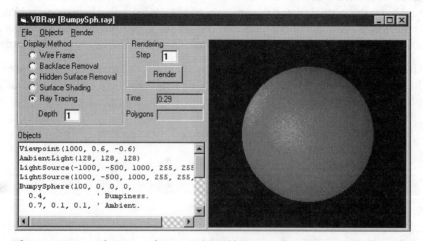

Figure 17.31 A bumpy sphere produced by normal vector perturbation.

image to the surface. Write a function that maps points on the surface back to points in the image. The point in the image will probably not fall exactly on one of the image's pixels, so use bilinear interpolation to find the best color to use.

These are the same steps described in Chapter 7 for stretching, shrinking, and warping images. The only tricky part is creating the function that maps points on the surface to points on the image.

Rectangles are among the easiest shapes to map. The program finds the coordinates of the point in the rectangle's frame of reference. It can then map those coordinates onto a rectangular image.

The RayCheckerboard class described earlier already maps a point into its own coordinate system to determine whether the point lies on one of its rectangular areas. This object is defined by a point at the corner of its first square and two vectors that define the edges of that square. To map a point, the object converts the coordinates of the point into multiples of these two vectors. For example, the point with checkerboard coordinates (1, 1) is at the opposite corner in the first square.

The RayMappedCheckerboard uses this same technique. To find a point's hit color, it uses these multiples to map the point to the object's image. For instance, if the point has checkerboard coordinates (0.5, 0.75), the FindHitColor function maps it to a position halfway through the image from right to left and three-quarters of the way through the image from top to bottom.

Once it has found a color for the point on the surface, the program can use that value to determine the surface's ambient and diffuse reflection parameters for that point. For example, suppose the color has red component 127. Since that is half of the maximum possible value 255, the program can set the object's red ambient and diffuse reflection coefficients to 0.5 at that point.

The RayMappedCheckerboard class uses this method. It also has its own ambient and diffuse reflection coefficients that it combines with the base values provided by the image.

Figure 17.32 shows three RayMappedCheckerboard objects each displaying a single square each. The objects' ambient and diffuse coefficients are all 1.0 and the light sources are white, so the results match the colors in the original images closely.

Special Environment Mapping

The basic environment mapping technique described in the previous section uses an image to determine the base color value for points on a surface. Similarly, you can use the pixels in an image to determine other characteristics of the point.

For example, the program could calculate the point's base color as before using an image. Then if the base color is black, the program can make the object transparent at that point. This lets objects behind the point show through.

The RayHoledCheckerboard class demonstrates this approach. It maps the points on its surface using an image just as the RayMappedCheckerboard class does. When it finds a

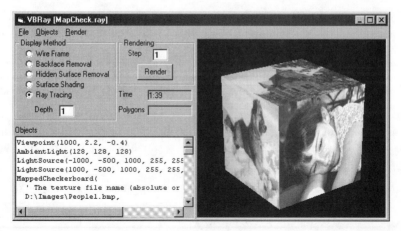

Figure 17.32   Environment mapping three pictures onto RayMappedCheckerboard objects.

point that should be black, however, it sets the object's transmission coefficients to 1.0, making the object perfectly transparent.

Figure 17.33 shows a sphere and a RayHoledCheckerboard object mapped with an image of some text. The image is black except where the text lies, so it is mostly transparent.

This technique produces some interesting results, but it has a major drawback. Most notably, the entire checkerboard object shadows other objects. If the light sources in Figure 17.33 were adjusted so the checkerboard shadowed the sphere, you would see a rectangular shadow, not one shaped like the text.

One way to fix this problem would be to modify the object's FindT function so that it, too, considered the image when determining whether a ray intersected the checkerboard. Then it would shadow other objects only where it was actually drawn.

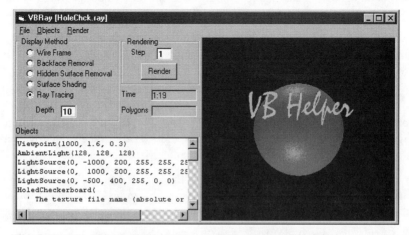

Figure 17.33   Using an image map to determine transparency.

Summary

Ray tracing is nearly the end of the quest for visual realism. Recursive ray tracing lets you produce amazingly realistic images. They may look somewhat artificial if they display only spheres, cylinders, and polygons, but they can look almost like photographs.

Ray tracing is a complex subject and there are many other techniques you can apply to your programs. Advanced graphics researchers have developed techniques for simulating fire, clouds, hair, and many other interesting phenomena.

Ray tracing is not quite the end of the road in producing realistic images. A newer technique called radiosity produces some of the most photorealistic images ever generated by computers. It uses sophisticated area mapping techniques to account for diffuse light reflecting off of objects onto other nearby objects.

Advanced ray tracing techniques and radiosity are much more complicated and time-consuming than the techniques described here. For more information on these topics, consult the latest graphics research literature.

PART SIX

Beyond Three Dimensions

P art Six covers two major topics. Chapter 18, Higher-Dimensional Transformations, shows methods for viewing higher-dimensional data. It explains how to use animation to display four-dimensional surfaces. It also extends the transformations covered in previous chapters to higher dimensions.

Chapter 19, Mathematical Tools, describes some useful mathematical formulas. It summarizes the standard transformation matrices in two, three, and four dimensions.

CHAPTER 18

Higher-Dimensional Transformations

A computer monitor has only two dimensions: width and height. It cannot directly display three-dimensional objects. Before you can view a picture of three-dimensional objects on your screen, you must transform the objects into a two-dimensional form. You can do this using one of the projection techniques described in Chapter 13, Three-Dimensional Transformations. These include orthographic, oblique, and perspective projection. You can also use the ray-tracing techniques described in Chapter 17, Ray Tracing, to calculate a projection for each of the pixels on the screen.

Viewing higher-dimensional objects is the same in principle. Before you can view a four-dimensional object on your computer, you need to transform the four-dimensional information into a two-dimensional form. There are two main ways you can do this: *temporal projection* and *spatial projection*.

Temporal Projection

You can remove one dimension from your data by converting it into a time dimension. First, create a series of images corresponding to different values for the dimension you want to remove. Then play the images back as an animation with the timing of the images replacing the removed dimension.

For instance, suppose you have a mathematical model that described stock market prices as a function of two variables U and I representing the unemployment rate and the rate of inflation, respectively. This model would be a function of two dimensions: one representing unemployment rate and one representing inflation rate. You could use the techniques described in Chapter 14, Surfaces, to display the corresponding three-dimensional surface.

Now suppose you have a more complicated model that predicts market prices in terms of unemployment rate, rate of inflation, and M, the number of months until the next presidential election. Now market price is a function of three dimensions. The surface this function defines is a four-dimensional surface. One way you could display the surface would be to convert the M dimension into a temporal dimension.

You would start by selecting various values for M, perhaps M = 0, 1, 2, ..., 47 months. If you set M equal to one of these values, the model then describes stock market prices in terms of only the remaining variables U and I. Holding M fixed, you can create a two-dimensional projection of the resulting three-dimensional surface. When you have created projections for each value of M, you can display the images in order as an animated sequence.

Looking at individual images, you might notice trends in the two variables U and I. For instance, you might find that market prices are lower when the unemployment rate U is large. As you watched the animation, you might notice trends that depend on the value of M. You might find that stock prices fall for most values of U and I at the beginning of the animation (when M is small—just before an election), and that prices rise near the end of the animation (when M is large—just after an election).

You could just as easily select U or I as the temporal variable instead of M. For example, you could select various values for the unemployment rate and then create images of the resulting three-dimensional surfaces. You could then display the results in an animation. As you watch this animation, you might learn that stock prices generally fall as the animation progresses and the unemployment rate decreases.

By making different variables temporal, you may be able to visualize different aspects of your data. Which gives the best result depends on your particular problem. You will probably need to run separate animations using each variable as a temporal variable to be sure you have had a chance to spot all the obvious trends in the data.

Temporal projection works well for simple surfaces in four dimensions, but it is hard to generalize for higher dimensions. Suppose you extended the model described in the previous section so that it included as a variable H, the number of housing starts in the previous month. The model is now a function of four variables producing a surface in five dimensions.

You could pick a variable, perhaps M, to use as a temporal variable. Then for various values of M, you would display the resulting four-dimensional surface. To do that, you would need to make another variable, say H, temporal as well. If you used 48 different values for the variable M and 20 for the variable H, you would create a total of 48 animated sequences, each containing 20 frames.

Viewing 48 separate animation sequences and looking for trends can be quite difficult. You may not notice that there is a slow rise in stock market prices during the 17th frame of each animation sequence. Replaying the images as 20 sequences containing 48 frames each might make that trend more obvious, but it would probably obscure others. Only by examining the images in both ways and by converting other combinations of the four variables U, I, M, and H into temporal variables can you hope to see most of the obvious data trends.

Example program Temporal uses this technique to display a graph of the four-dimensional surface defined by the equation:

```
y(x, z, t) = 0.25 * Cos(3 * Sqr(x² + z²) - t)
```

When you click the Create Images button, the program generates 20 images corresponding to values of the temporal variable t between $\pi/10$ and $2 * \pi$. Once you have created the images, click the play Images button to make the program animate them. The program repeatedly cycles through the images until you click the button again.

Spatial Projection

An alternative method for displaying objects in higher dimensions is to project them into lower dimensions. Just as you can use a parallel or perspective projection to display a three-dimensional object on a two-dimensional screen, you can use a projection to convert higher-dimensional data into lower-dimensional data.

For example, you could perform a simple parallel projection from any number of dimensions onto the X-Y plane by simply ignoring the coordinate values for all the other coordinate axes. The point (a, b, c, d, e, ...) is projected to the point (a, b). As is the case in two dimensions, you can make different translations and rotations before you perform the projection, so you can view objects from different directions.

Rather than projecting directly from four or more dimensions down to two, you can first project your objects into three dimensions. Once you have converted your data into three-dimensional objects, you can view the objects using different three-dimensional projections. This approach usually allows you to develop more intuition about the structure of the object in three dimensions. Using that intuition, you can try to build a feeling for the higher-dimensional nature of the objects. Figure 18.1 shows this strategy schematically.

Four-Dimensional Transformations

The sections that follow describe the most useful four-dimensional transformations. Some, like translation and scaling, are straightforward extensions of three-dimensional transformations. Others, like rotation and perspective projection, are a little more confusing. These more complicated transformations are described mathematically and by

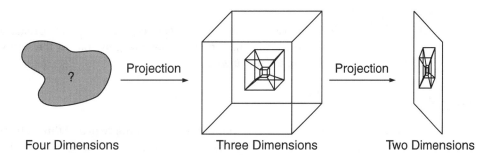

Four Dimensions   Three Dimensions   Two Dimensions

Figure 18.1   Projecting a many-dimensional object into three dimensions and then into two dimensions.

analogy. It is usually easier to understand the more complicated transformations in terms of how they relate to their lower-dimensional counterparts. Once you have mastered two-, three-, and four-dimensional transformations, you will be able to extend them to even higher dimensions.

Homogeneous Coordinates

The most obvious difference between three- and four-dimensional objects is that four-dimensional objects have an extra coordinate. In the rest of this chapter, the fourth coordinate axis is called the W axis. To allow the X, Y, and Z coordinates of a point to retain their usual three-dimensional meanings, the W coordinate of a point is written last as in (x, y, z, w).

As is the case in two and three dimensions, you can manipulate four-dimensional points and transformations most conveniently if you use homogeneous coordinates. All you need to do is add an extra scale factor to the representation of a point in four dimensions. For example, the point (a, b, c, d) is written in homogeneous coordinates as [a * S, b * S, c * S, d * S, S]. You can normalize a point by dividing it by the scale factor S. The usual representation for the point (a, b, c, d) is [a, b, c, d, 1].

As is the case in two and three dimensions, homogeneous coordinates allow you to write many useful four-dimensional transformations as matrices. You can represent translation, scaling, rotation, and projection using matrices. To apply one of these transformations to a point, multiply the point's vector by the corresponding transformation matrix. As before, you can combine transformation matrices by multiplying them to represent complex combinations of translation, scaling, rotation, and projection in a single matrix.

If you apply the four-dimensional identity transformation to any point, that point's coordinates are left unchanged. The matrix representing the four-dimensional identity transformation is:

$$\begin{vmatrix} 1 & 0 & 0 & 0 & 0 \\ 0 & 1 & 0 & 0 & 0 \\ 0 & 0 & 1 & 0 & 0 \\ 0 & 0 & 0 & 1 & 0 \\ 0 & 0 & 0 & 0 & 1 \end{vmatrix}$$

The identity matrix is the basis of many of the more complicated transformations. For instance, you can build a transformation matrix by changing four of the terms in the identity matrix and leaving the rest unchanged.

Translation

Translation in four dimensions is a simple extension of the two- and three-dimensional cases. The transformation matrix representing translation by Tx, Ty, Tz, and Tw in the X, Y, Z, and W directions is:

$$\begin{vmatrix} 1 & 0 & 0 & 0 & 0 \\ 0 & 1 & 0 & 0 & 0 \\ 0 & 0 & 1 & 0 & 0 \\ 0 & 0 & 0 & 1 & 0 \\ Tx & Ty & Tz & Tw & 1 \end{vmatrix}$$

When you multiply this matrix by a generic point [x, y, z, w, 1], the result is [x + Tx, y + Ty, z + Tz, w + Tw, 1], as it should be.

Scaling

Four-dimensional scaling is also a simple extension of the two- and three-dimensional operations. The transformation matrix representing scaling by factors of Sx, Sy, Sz, and Sw in the X, Y, Z, and W directions is:

$$\begin{vmatrix} Sx & 0 & 0 & 0 & 0 \\ 0 & Sy & 0 & 0 & 0 \\ 0 & 0 & Sz & 0 & 0 \\ 0 & 0 & 0 & Sw & 0 \\ 0 & 0 & 0 & 0 & 1 \end{vmatrix}$$

When you multiply this matrix by the point [x, y, z, w, 1], the result is [x * Sx, y * Sy, z * Sz, w * Sw, 1].

Reflection

In two dimensions, you can reflect a point across a line. In the simplest reflections, that line is either the X or Y coordinate axis. For example, to reflect a point across the X axis, leave the point's X coordinate unchanged and reverse the sign of its Y coordinate. You can use translations and rotations to reflect a point across a line other than one of the coordinate axes.

In three dimensions, you can reflect a point across a plane. In the simplest reflections, that plane is one of the X-Y, X-Z, or Y-Z coordinate planes. For example, to reflect a point across the X-Y plane, leave the point's X and Y coordinates unchanged and reverse the sign of its Z coordinate. You can use translations and rotations to reflect a point across a plane other than one of the coordinate planes.

In four dimensions, you can reflect a point across a three-dimensional space. In the simplest reflections, that space is one of the four coordinate spaces: X-Y-Z, X-Y-W, X-Z-W, or Y-Z-W. For example, to reflect a point across the Y-Z-W space, leave the point's Y, Z, and W coordinates unchanged and reverse the sign of its X coordinate. The transformation matrix that represents this reflection is shown below.

$$\begin{vmatrix} -1 & 0 & 0 & 0 & 0 \\ 0 & 1 & 0 & 0 & 0 \\ 0 & 0 & 1 & 0 & 0 \\ 0 & 0 & 0 & 1 & 0 \\ 0 & 0 & 0 & 0 & 1 \end{vmatrix}$$

In a manner analogous to the case of two and three dimensions, you can use translations and rotations to reflect a point across a space other than one of the four coordinate spaces.

Similarly, in an even higher N-dimensional space, you can reflect a point across an N −1-dimensional space. To make a matrix for reflecting across a coordinate space, change one of the 1's in the identity matrix's diagonal to −1. Modify one of the first entries, leaving the scaling value in the lower-right corner unchanged.

Rotation

In two dimensions, you can rotate a point around another point. In the simplest form of rotation, the point of rotation is the origin. You can use a single translation to rotate around a point other than the origin.

In three dimensions, you can rotate a point around a line called the *axis of rotation*. In the simplest of these rotations, the axis of rotation is one of the X, Y, or Z coordinate axes. When you rotate a point around a coordinate axis, the corresponding coordinate for the point does not change, but the others do.

For example, when you rotate a point around the X axis, the point's X coordinate stays the same while its Y and Z coordinates change. The Y and Z coordinates are changed exactly as the coordinates of the point's projection onto the Y-Z plane would have been changed if the projected point were rotated around the origin. In that sense, a three-dimensional rotation around a coordinate axis is the same as a two-dimensional rotation in the coordinate plane perpendicular to the axis.

The fact that a point's X coordinate does not change is reflected in the transformation matrix. The first row and column, which correspond to the X coordinate, are the same as those in the identity matrix. The rows and columns corresponding to the Y and Z axes are not.

$$\begin{vmatrix} 1 & 0 & 0 & 0 \\ 0 & \cos(\theta) & \sin(\theta) & 0 \\ 0 & -\sin(\theta) & \cos(\theta) & 0 \\ 0 & 0 & 0 & 1 \end{vmatrix}$$

You can use translations and rotations to rotate a point around a line other than one of the coordinate axes.

In four dimensions, you rotate a point around a plane! In the simplest kinds of rotation, the plane of rotation is one of the six coordinate planes: X-Y, X-Z, X-W, Y-Z, Y-W, or Z-W. When you rotate a point around a coordinate plane, the corresponding coordinates for the point do not change, and the others do. For example, when you rotate a point around the X-Z plane, the point's X and Z coordinates remain unchanged while its Y and W coordinates are modified. The Y and W coordinates are changed exactly as they would be during a rotation around the origin in the two-dimensional Y-W plane.

The fact that a point's X and Z coordinates do not change is reflected in the four-dimensional transformation matrix. The first and third rows and columns, which correspond to the X and Z coordinates, are the same as those in the identity matrix. The other rows and columns are different.

$$
\begin{vmatrix}
1 & 0 & 0 & 0 & 0 \\
0 & \cos(\theta) & 0 & \sin(\theta) & 0 \\
0 & 0 & 1 & 0 & 0 \\
0 & -\sin(\theta) & 0 & \cos(\theta) & 0 \\
0 & 0 & 0 & 0 & 1
\end{vmatrix}
$$

You can use translations and rotations to rotate a point around a plane other than one of the six coordinate planes.

Inverse Transformations

Most of the four-dimensional inverse transformations are as easy to compute as are their two- and three-dimensional counterparts. To reverse a translation by distances Tx, Ty, Tz, and Tw, simply translate by distances -Tx, -Ty, -Tz, and -Tw. To reverse a scaling by amounts Sx, Sy, Sz, and Sw, scale by the inverses of those amounts: 1/Sx, 1/Sy, 1/Sz, and 1/Sw. To reverse a rotation through angle θ around a plane, rotate around that plane through angle $-\theta$.

Projections

As is the case in three dimensions, there are two major categories of projections in four dimensions: parallel and perspective. The following two sections describe the simplest of these projections. You can project in different directions from different centers of projection by using translations and rotations before you perform the projection.

Parallel Projections

Under the category of parallel projections, you could define all sorts of strange oblique projections similar to the three-dimensional cavalier and cabinet projections. These tend to confuse an already complicated situation, however. For that reason, this section describes only orthographic projections—parallel projections in which the projectors are perpendicular to the plane of projection.

In two dimensions, you can project a point onto a line. The simplest parallel projection would project a point parallel to one coordinate axis onto the other. For instance, you might project a point parallel to the Y axis onto the X axis. You could do this by simply ignoring the point's Y coordinate. Of course in computer graphics, you generally want to display images on a two-dimensional screen, so there is not much call for this sort of projection.

In three dimensions, you can project a point onto a plane. In the simplest parallel projections, you project a point parallel to one coordinate axis onto the plane defined by the other two. For instance, you might project a point parallel to the Z axis onto the X-Y plane. You can do this by simply ignoring the point's Z coordinate.

In three dimensions, you can also project a point onto a line. In the simplest form of this kind of projection, you would project a point parallel to two coordinate axes onto the third. For example, you could project a point parallel to the X and Z axes onto the Y axis. You can do this by simply ignoring the point's X and Z coordinates.

In four dimensions, you can project a point onto a three-dimensional space. In the simplest of these projections, you project a point parallel to one coordinate axis onto the space defined by the other three. For instance, you might project a point parallel to the W axis into X-Y-Z space. You can do this by simply ignoring the point's W coordinate.

Similarly, you can project a point from four dimensions down to two by ignoring two of the point's coordinates. You could go directly from four-dimensional space to the X-Y plane by ignoring the point's Z and W coordinates.

You could even project all the way from four-dimensional space down to one of the coordinate axes. This projection would probably not be very useful, however, because your computer's screen is two-dimensional.

You can use similar operations to project from higher-dimensional spaces into three or two dimensions. Just ignore the coordinates you do not want to use.

Example program Parallel uses this simple method to display projections for a four-dimensional cube. This cube, known as a *hypercube*, has corners at the 16 points with coordinates given by (±1, ±1, ±1, ±1).

Program Parallel projects the hypercube onto the X-Y plane by simply ignoring the Z and W coordinates of its points. Before performing the projection, the program rotates the cube in order around the X-W, Y-W, Z-W, X-Y, X-Z, and Y-Z planes. By entering amounts in radians by which the program should perform these rotations, you can view the hypercube from different directions. As you change the values, the program shows you the corresponding new view of the hypercube.

When you rotate a point around the X-W plane, neither its X nor W coordinates change. When you rotate a point around the X axis in three dimensions, its X coordinate does not change. If you ignore the W coordinate of the point, rotating the point around the X-W plane in four dimensions is equivalent to rotating it around the X axis in three dimensions.

That means a program like Parallel, which projects by ignoring the Z and W coordinates of points, will not show any difference between rotating a point around the X axis and rotating it around the X-W plane. Similarly, rotating a point around the Y-W plane looks just like rotating around the Y axis in two dimensions. Finally, rotating a point around the Z-W plane is equivalent to rotating around the Z axis in two dimensions. If you set the values for the rotations around the X-Y, X-Z, and Y-Z planes in program Parallel to zero, the transformations look just like normal rotations in three-dimensional space. In that case, the hypercube looks like a normal three-dimensional cube such as the one shown in Figure 18.2.

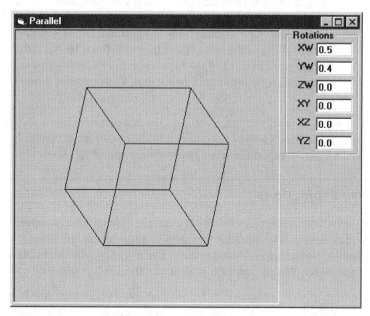

Figure 18.2   A hypercube rotated around only the X-W, Y-W, and Z-W planes looks like a normal three-dimensional cube.

If you rotate the hypercube around the X-Y, X-Z, and Y-Z planes, you get more interesting results as shown in Figure 18.3.

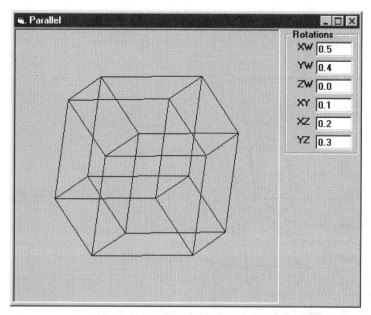

Figure 18.3   A more interesting projection of a hypercube.

You can get some idea of the nature of the hypercube if you think about its mathematics for a while. You can think of a hypercube as two cubes in three-dimensional subspaces, joined by connecting surfaces. One of these three-dimensional cubes is defined by all the hypercube's corners with W coordinate –1. The other is defined by the corners with W coordinate +1. Similarly, you can think of the hypercube as two three-dimensional cubes defined by the corners with X coordinate –1 or +1, with Y coordinate –1 or +1, or with Z coordinate –1 or +1.

Figure 18.4 shows another view of a hypercube. One of a pair of cubes is shown in bold. The edges connecting the two cubes are drawn in dashed lines. If you look closely in Figure 18.3 or 18.4, you can find the other pairs of corresponding cubes.

Perspective Projections

Perspective projection in four dimensions is a simple extension of perspective projection in three dimensions. The simplest perspective projections are along a coordinate axis into a three-dimensional coordinate space. For instance, you might place the center of projection on the W axis and then project into the X-Y-Z coordinate space.

The coordinates of points are scaled in four-dimensional projection much as they are in two-dimensional projection. Suppose you want to perform a perspective projection into the X-Y-Z coordinate space with center of projection at position $(0, 0, 0, d)$. If a point is located at (x, y, z, w), its projection has coordinates $(x * d/(d - w), y * d/(d - w), z * d/(d - w), 0)$. You can represent this transformation with the following matrix.

$$
\begin{vmatrix}
1 & 0 & 0 & 0 & 0 \\
0 & 1 & 0 & 0 & 0 \\
0 & 0 & 1 & 0 & 0 \\
0 & 0 & 0 & 0 & -1 / d \\
0 & 0 & 0 & 0 & 1
\end{vmatrix}
$$

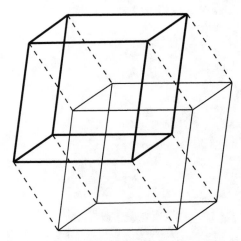

Figure 18.4   A hypercube is two cubes joined by connecting faces.

Example program Persp uses this projection matrix to display perspective views of a hypercube. The program first rotates the hypercube around the six coordinate planes using angles that you specify. It then applies a perspective projection to transform the hypercube into a three-dimensional object. Next it rotates the resulting object around the X, Y, and Z axes in three dimensions, again using angles you specify. This allows you to view the three-dimensional projection of the hypercube from different directions. Finally, the program performs a parallel projection into two dimensions by simply ignoring the points' Z coordinates.

Figure 18.5 shows a parallel projection of a perspective projection of a hypercube. The preprojection angles are all zero, so the hypercube was not rotated before the perspective projection down to three dimensions. The center of projection is located at (0, 0, 0, 3). After the hypercube was projected into three-dimensional space, it was rotated by 0.2 radians around the X axis and 0.1 radians around the Y axis.

You can still view the hypercube as two related three-dimensional cubes connected at the corners. In Figure 18.5, the inner and outer cubes are made up of the hypercube's corners where W = –1 and W = 1, respectively.

The inner cube is smaller because in four dimensions, it is farther from the center of projection at (0, 0, 0, 3). The points that make up the inner cube have W coordinates –1 while those in the outer cube have W coordinates +1.

If you rotate the hypercube before you project it from four dimensions into three, you can get strange results like those shown in Figure 18.6. In this picture, the hypercube was rotated through an angle of 0.8 radians around the X-Z plane before the perspective projection. If you look closely, you can still find pairs of three-dimensional cubes.

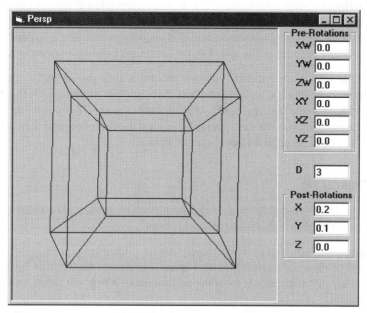

Figure 18.5 A parallel projection of a perspective projection of a hypercube.

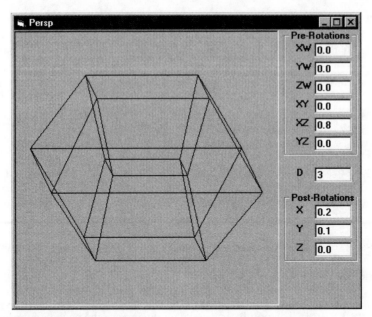

Figure 18.6   A hypercube that was rotated around the X-Z plane before projection into three-dimensional space.

Rotating a Hypercube

By rotating the hypercube before projecting it in program Persp, you can create strange pictures like the one shown in Figure 18.6. To try to understand rotation in the fourth dimension, you can write a program that performs similar rotations in small increments. Example program Animated presents animated sequences showing a hypercube being rotated around one or more of the X-Y, X-Z, or Y-Z planes before perspective projection.

Check the boxes for the coordinate planes around which you want the program to rotate the hypercube and click the Go button. For example, if you check the XY Plane box, the program rotates the hypercube around the X-Y plane. If you also check the YZ Plane box, the program rotates the hypercube around the X-Y plane and then around the Y-Z plane. Some of the combinations are quite strange.

Folding a Hypercube

Using paper, scissors, and glue, you can make a cube by folding up a collection of six squares. Figure 18.7 shows the steps you could take.

In a similar manner, you can create a hypercube by folding up a group of eight cubes. Start with eight cubes like those shown in Figure 18.8. Rotate each in turn by 90 degrees around the plane that separates it from the central cube. When you finish, you have created a hypercube.

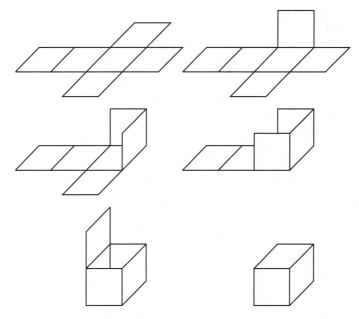

Figure 18.7   Folding up a cube.

Figure 18.9 shows the steps for folding up a hypercube. The bottom middle image in this figure shows the final cube folded only part of the way so that you can see how the last cube seems to disappear.

Example program Fold animates the hypercube folding process. It begins by creating eight cubes in X-Y-Z coordinate space. It then folds each into X-Y-Z-W space by rotating it around the appropriate plane.

In the first fold shown in Figure 18.9, the cube with the largest Y coordinates is folded. It is rotated around the plane that contains its bottom face—the face with the smallest Y coordinates. The corners defining this face are located at positions (–1, 1, 1, 0), (–1, 1, –1, 0), (1, 1, –1, 0), and (1, 1, 1, 0). The plane containing these points has Y = 1 and W = 0.

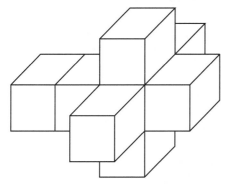

Figure 18.8   Eight cubes you can fold up to make a hypercube.

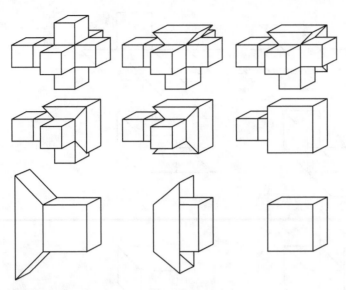

Figure 18.9 Folding up a hypercube.

You can convert this rotation into a simpler one by first translating the cube so that the plane of rotation coincides with the X-Z plane. You would first translate by distance −1 in the Y direction, rotate around the X-Z plane, and then translate by distance 1 in the Y direction.

Example program Fold uses the subroutine FoldYW to animate the process of rotating an object around a plane parallel to the X-Z plane. This routine takes as parameters the value of the Y and W coordinates of the plane. It translates the object so that the plane of rotation coincides with the X-Z plane, rotates the object, and then translates the object back.

```
' Animate folding this cube across the Y = y,
' W = w plane.
Private Sub FoldYW(ByVal col As Collection, _
    ByVal y As Single, ByVal W As Single, _
    ByVal theta As Single)
Dim cube As Polyline4d
Dim i As Single
Dim next_time As Long
Dim T1(1 To 5, 1 To 5) As Single
Dim r(1 To 5, 1 To 5) As Single
Dim T2(1 To 5, 1 To 5) As Single
Dim T1R(1 To 5, 1 To 5) As Single
Dim All(1 To 5, 1 To 5) As Single

    next_time = GetTickCount + MS_PER_FRAME

    ' Create the transformation matrices.
    m4Translate T1, 0, -y, 0, -W
```

```
m4Translate T2, 0, y, 0, W
m4XZRotate r, theta / FRAMES_PER_FOLD
m4MatMultiply T1R, T1, r
m4MatMultiply All, T1R, T2

For i = 1 To FRAMES_PER_FOLD
    If Not Running Then Exit Sub

        ' Rotate the cubes.
        For Each cube In col
            cube.Apply All
            cube.FixPoints
        Next cube

        ' Wait until it's time for the next image.
        WaitTill next_time
        next_time = GetTickCount + MS_PER_FRAME

        ' Display the picture.
        Draw picCanvas
    Next i
End Sub
```

Program Fold uses similar routines for rotating a cube around a plane parallel to the X-Y and Y-Z planes.

Most of the rotations used to fold up the hypercube are fairly easy to understand. In the second-to-last step, however, both of the two remaining cubes must be rotated together. Program Fold accomplishes this by placing both cubes in a collection, which it can then rotate as a single unit.

After the second-to-last cube is in position, the final cube has been rotated out of normal X-Y-Z coordinate space as shown in Figure 18.10. None of the points in this cube have W coordinates equal to zero. At this point, the corners of this cube with the smallest W coordinates are at locations $(-1, 1, -1, 2)$, $(-1, -1, -1, 2)$, $(-1, -1, 1, 2)$, and $(-1, 1, 1, 2)$. These points lie in the plane that is parallel to the Y-Z plane and has X = –1 and W = 2. To finish folding this last cube, the program uses subroutine FoldXW to rotate it around this plane.

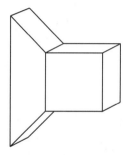

Figure 18.10   Before folding up the final cube.

The following Visual Basic code fragment folds up the cubes to create the hypercube. Code related to the projection that allows you to view the hypercube and code related to animation details have been omitted. The cubes are numbered as shown in Figure 18.11. Cube 3 sits in the middle between cubes 2 and 4.

```
' Fold up cube 5.
Set col = New Collection
col.Add TheCubes(5)
FoldYW col, 1, 0, PI / 2
If Not Running Then Exit Sub

' Fold up cube 6.
Set col = New Collection
col.Add TheCubes(6)
FoldZW col, -1, 0, -PI / 2
If Not Running Then Exit Sub

' Fold up cube 4.
Set col = New Collection
col.Add TheCubes(4)
FoldXW col, 1, 0, PI / 2
If Not Running Then Exit Sub

' Fold up cube 7.
Set col = New Collection
col.Add TheCubes(7)
FoldYW col, -1, 0, -PI / 2
If Not Running Then Exit Sub

' Fold up cube 8.
Set col = New Collection
col.Add TheCubes(8)
FoldZW col, 1, 0, PI / 2
If Not Running Then Exit Sub

' Fold up cubes 2 and 1 together.
Set col = New Collection
col.Add TheCubes(1)
col.Add TheCubes(2)
FoldXW col, -1, 0, -PI / 2
If Not Running Then Exit Sub

' Finish folding cube 1.
Set col = New Collection
col.Add TheCubes(1)
FoldXW col, -1, 2, -PI / 2
If Not Running Then Exit Sub
```

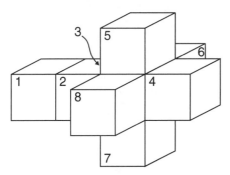

Figure 18.11   Cube numbering used by program Fold.

Summary

Higher-dimensional transformations allow you to examine objects that might otherwise be difficult to understand. By projecting values from four or more dimensions into two, you can gain some understanding of the data.

Temporal projection can be particularly useful for viewing four-dimensional data. By making a series of three-dimensional images while holding the fourth constant, you can create an animation that reveals trends in the data that might be extremely difficult to notice by looking at numeric data values.

CHAPTER 19

Mathematical Tools

Computer graphics is an extremely mathematics intensive topic. While you can understand the ideas behind many techniques with good intuition, actually implementing those techniques often requires some heavy-duty computation.

For example, the idea behind ray tracing is straightforward. Send a ray from the center of projection out through a pixel on the screen until it hits an object. Then calculate the color of the object at that point. Even though the idea is simple, the implementation can be extremely complex. The program must find the ray's components, calculate the point of intersection between the ray and various objects, find the surface normal at the point of intersection, and use fairly complex calculations to pick the right color.

This chapter reviews some of the mathematical operations used in this book. The sections that follow are intended as a refresher course and reference, not as a complete introductory math course. For more details, consult a mathematics text.

If you understand these concepts and do not need a review, by all means skim this chapter or skip it completely.

Vectors and Matrices

Vectors and matrices are extremely useful in computer graphics. They let you represent complex operations in a uniform way using homogeneous coordinates.

Vectors and matrices are used extensively in linear algebra, so if you want more information, look for a good linear algebra text. Linear algebra goes far beyond the simpler operations used by computer graphics, so the following sections barely hint at what you will find in a decent text.

Modules M3Ops.bas and M4Opos.bas contain routines that manipulate three- and four-dimensional transformation matrices respectively.

Vector Arithmetic

A point is represented by its coordinates in parentheses. The point with X coordinate 10, Y coordinate 37, and Z coordinate -9 in three-dimensional space is written (10, 37, –9). Points have a location but no size. You can think of them as being infinitely small.

A vector has a direction and a length. A vector is represented by components giving the vector's direction of movement written in pointed brackets. For example, <5, –20, 10> is a vector that represents the direction that moves 5 units in the X direction, –20 units in the Y direction, and 10 units in the Z direction.

You can visualize a vector as being an arrow with its tail at the origin and its head at the coordinates given by its components, but that is a little misleading. A vector has direction and length but no location. A vector is not positioned at any particular place in space.

Points and vectors have their own special arithmetic. If you add a vector to a point, you get another point. In Figure 19.1, the vector V is added to the point P to give the point P'.

Mathematically, you can add a vector to a point by adding the vector's components to the point's coordinates. If the point P has coordinates (px, py, pz) and the vector has components <vx, vy, vz>, the resulting point has coordinates (px + vx, py + vy, pz + vz).

By rearranging the equation P + V = P', you can get an equation for finding the vector between two points. The vector from point P to point P' is given by V = P' – P. Note that this is the opposite of the vector from point P' to the point P. These two vectors point in opposite directions.

To get the components of a vector between two points mathematically, subtract the corresponding coordinates as in <p'x - px, p'y - py, p'z - pz>.

Subtracting two points gives a vector, but adding two points does not give anything particularly useful.

A vector plus a vector gives another vector as shown in Figure 19.2. Keep in mind that the result is a vector, so it has direction and length but no location. Mathematically, you calculate the components of the result vector by adding the corresponding components of the two other vectors: < v1x + v2x, v1y + v2y , v1z + v2z>.

When you add two nonparallel vectors, the new vector lies in the same plane as the first two. In fact, if A and B are nonparallel vectors, C = i * A + j * B gives another vector in the same plane for any real values of i and j.

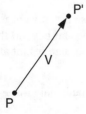

Figure 19.1   A point plus a vector equals a point.

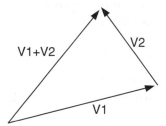

Figure 19.2   A vector plus a vector equals a vector.

Conversely, if C is a vector in the plane containing A and B, there is some i and j for which C = i * A + j * B. This gives you a way to generate points on a plane. Calculate vectors C for different values of i and j and add the resulting vectors to a point on the plane. The RayCheckerboard class described in Chapter 17, Ray Tracing, uses this technique.

Vector Length

The length of a vector V = <vx, vy, vz> is written |V| and is given by Sqr(vx * vx + vy * vy + vz * vz).

A vector V is *normalized* if |V| = 1. When you normalize a vector, you make its length 1 while keeping it pointed in its original direction. To normalize a vector, divide each of its components by the vector's length: <vx/|V|, vy/|V|, vz/|V|>.

Normalized vectors are particularly useful with dot products and cross products. The lengths of the vectors play a role in these calculations, and if the vectors have length 1, the calculations are simpler.

Dot Product

The dot product of two vectors A and B is written A · B and has value |A| * |B| * Cos(θ) where θ is the angle between the two vectors. Mathematically, you can calculate the dot product by multiplying the corresponding components of two vectors and adding the results:

```
A · B = ax * bx + ay * by + az * bz
```

This gives you method for calculating the cosine of the angle between two vectors:

```
Cos(θ) = (A · B)/(|A| * |B|)
```

If the vectors A and B are normalized, this simplifies to:

```
Cos(θ) = A · B
```

You can use this equation to determine whether two vectors are perpendicular, point in more or less the same direction, or point in opposite directions.

	< 0	$\cos(\theta) < 0$, so the vectors point in more or less opposite directions.
$A \cdot B$	= 0	$\cos(\theta) = 0$, so the vectors are perpendicular.
	> 0	$\cos(\theta) > 0$, so the vectors point in more or less the same direction.

If two vectors are parallel, the angle between them is zero, so:

```
A · B= |A| * |B| * Cos(0)
     = |A| * |B|
```

Projection of a Vector onto a Vector

You can use the dot product to find the projection of one vector onto another. Figure 19.3 shows the projection A' of the vector A onto the vector B. The definition of the cosine says:

```
Cos(θ) = |A'|/|A|
```

Solving for lA'l and replacing the cosine with the dot product gives:

```
|A'| = |A| * ((A · B)/(|A| * |B|))
     = (A · B)/|B|
```

The projection of A onto B is a vector in the same direction as B but that has the length $(A \cdot B)/|B|$. To find this vector, divide B by its length and then multiply by the desired length lA'l. This gives:

```
(B/|B|) * ((A · B)/|B|) = B * (A · B)/|B|2
```

For example, suppose A = <1, 1> and B = <3, 0> as shown in Figure 19.4. Then:

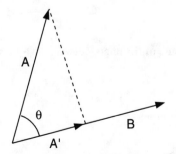

Figure 19.3 Projecting the vector A onto the vector B.

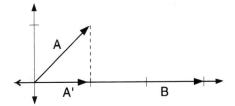

Figure 19.4 Projecting the vector <1, 1> onto the vector <3, 0>.

```
A' = B * (3 + 0)/3² = B/3 = <1, 0>
```

This agrees with Figure 19.4.

Cross Product

The cross product of two vectors A and B is written A × B and is another vector perpendicular to both A and B. It has length given by |A| * |B| * Sin(θ) where θ is the angle between the two vectors A and B.

Mathematically, the cross product between vectors A = <ax, ay, az> and B = <bx, by, bz> is given by:

```
<ay * bz - az * by, az * bx - ax * bz, ax * by - ay * bz>
```

If vectors A and B are not parallel, there are two directions perpendicular to them both. The vector given by the cross product has the direction determined by the right-hand rule. Visualize A and B starting at the origin. Hold your right hand so your fingers line up with vector A and curl toward vector B as shown in Figure 19.5. You may need to turn your hand upside down to make your fingers curl properly. When your fingers are properly aligned, your thumb points in the direction of the cross product vector.

If the vector <cx, cy, cz> is the cross product vector, <–cx, –cy, –cz> gives the other direction perpendicular to both A and B. If you spend some time visualizing the right-hand rule, you will find that A × B = –B × A.

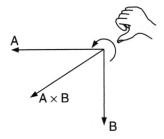

Figure 19.5 The right-hand rule gives the direction of the cross product vector.

Because the length of $A \times B = |A| * |B| * \sin(\theta)$, this gives you a method for calculating the sine of the angle between two vectors.

```
Sin(θ) = |A × B|/(|A| * |B|)
```

If A and B are normalized, this simplifies to:

```
Sin(θ) = |A × B|
```

Note also that $\sin^2(\theta) + \cos^2(\theta) = 1$, so

```
Sin(θ) = Sqr(1 - Cos²(θ))
```

Cross products are useful for finding vectors perpendicular to other vectors. For example, suppose A and B are two vectors in a plane. Then $A \times B$ gives a vector perpendicular to the plane.

For another example, suppose R is a vector from the center of a sphere to a point on the sphere. The cross product of this vector with any nonparallel vector gives a new vector A that is perpendicular to R. A is a vector in the plane tangent to the sphere at the end point of R. Now if you calculate $B = A \times R$, you get another vector in the tangent plane that is perpendicular to A and R. The vectors A and B define the sphere's tangent plane.

Matrix-Vector Multiplication

Matrix-vector multiplication uses only simple addition and multiplication, but there are so many operations, it can be a little confusing. When you multiply a vector by a matrix, the result is a new vector.

You can think of the matrix as a collection of vectors written vertically from top to bottom instead of horizontally from left to right. In that case, the components of the result vector are given by the dot products of the vector and the matrix's column vectors. For example, consider the following multiplication between vector V and matrix M.

```
              | m11 m12 m13 |
<vx, vy, vz> *| m21 m22 m23 |
              | m31 m32 m33 |
```

Written with the matrix represented by column vectors, this is:

```
              |m11| |m12| |m13|
<vx, vy, vz> *|m21| |m22| |m23|
              |m31| |m32| |m33|
```

The first column vector in the matrix is <m11, m21, m31>. The first entry in the result is the dot product between V and this column vector or vx * m11 + vy * m21 + vz * m31.

One trick you can use to keep track of the components during the calculation is to put your left index finger on the first component in V and your right index finger on the first entry in M. Multiply those items. Then move your left finger right one entry and your right finger down one row. Multiply those entries and add the result to the first value. Then move your fingers again. Continue until you reach the end of the vector and matrix.

Now start over with your right index finger on the matrix's second column. Keep going until you have used every column in the matrix.

Matrix-Matrix Multiplication

Matrix-matrix multiplication is just more of the same. When you multiply two matrices, the result is another matrix.

Consider the multiplication of two matrices M and N.

$$
\begin{vmatrix}
m11 & m12 & m13 \\
m21 & m22 & m23 \\
m31 & m32 & m33
\end{vmatrix}
*
\begin{vmatrix}
n11 & n12 & n13 \\
n21 & n22 & n23 \\
n31 & n32 & n33
\end{vmatrix}
$$

You can think of M as a collection of row vectors and N as a collection of column vectors.

```
<m11, m12, m13>   |n11|  |n12|  |n13|
<m21, m22, m23> * |n21|  |n22|  |n23|
<m31, m32, m33>   |n31|  |n32|  |n33|
```

The entry in row R column C in the result is the dot product between the row vector R in matrix M and the column vector C in matrix N. For example, the entry in row 2 column 3 of the result matrix is:

```
m21 * n13 + m22 * n23 + m23 * n33
```

You can use the same trick with your fingers that you can use for matrix-vector multiplication. Just repeat the process for each row in matrix M. (If this seems like counting on your fingers, don't worry about it. Everyone does it.)

Matrix multiplication is associative so:

```
M * N * O = (M * N) * O = M * (N * O)
```

This is important for computer graphics. It means you can combine a series of transformation matrices into a single matrix and then apply the whole thing all at once to a point instead of multiplying the point by the matrices one at a time.

On the other hand, matrix multiplication is not generally commutative.

```
M * N ≠ N * M
```

The order in which you apply two matrices is extremely important.

Transformation Matrices

The following sections list two-, three-, and four-dimensional transformation matrices. You can use them to manipulate points represented by homogeneous coordinates. These sections also include instructions for performing some of the more complicated combined operations such as rotation around an arbitrary line. The final section gives the formulas for converting from spherical to Cartesian coordinates.

Two-Dimensional Transformations

Translation by distances Tx and Ty:

$$\begin{vmatrix} 1 & 0 & 0 \\ 0 & 1 & 0 \\ Tx & Ty & 1 \end{vmatrix}$$

Scaling by scale factors Sx and Sy:

$$\begin{vmatrix} Sx & 0 & 0 \\ 0 & Sy & 0 \\ 0 & 0 & 1 \end{vmatrix}$$

Reflection across a coordinate axis:

ACROSS THE X AXIS

$$\begin{vmatrix} 1 & 0 & 0 \\ 0 & -1 & 0 \\ 0 & 0 & 1 \end{vmatrix}$$

ACROSS THE Y AXIS

$$\begin{vmatrix} -1 & 0 & 0 \\ 0 & 1 & 0 \\ 0 & 0 & 1 \end{vmatrix}$$

Rotation through angle θ around the origin:

$$\begin{vmatrix} \cos(\theta) & \sin(\theta) & 0 \\ -\sin(\theta) & \cos(\theta) & 0 \\ 0 & 0 & 1 \end{vmatrix}$$

Three-Dimensional Transformations

Translation by distances Tx, Ty, and Tz:

$$\begin{vmatrix} 1 & 0 & 0 & 0 \\ 0 & 1 & 0 & 0 \\ 0 & 0 & 1 & 0 \\ Tx & Ty & Tz & 1 \end{vmatrix}$$

Scaling by scale factors Sx, Sy, and Sz:

$$
\begin{vmatrix}
Sy & 0 & 0 & 0 \\
0 & Sx & 0 & 0 \\
0 & 0 & Sz & 0 \\
0 & 0 & 0 & 1
\end{vmatrix}
$$

Reflection across a coordinate plane:

ACROSS THE X-Y PLANE	ACROSS THE X-Z PLANE	ACROSS THE Y-Z PLANE
$\begin{vmatrix} 1 & 0 & 0 & 0 \\ 0 & 1 & 0 & 0 \\ 0 & 0 & -1 & 0 \\ 0 & 0 & 0 & 1 \end{vmatrix}$	$\begin{vmatrix} 1 & 0 & 0 & 0 \\ 0 & -1 & 0 & 0 \\ 0 & 0 & 1 & 0 \\ 0 & 0 & 0 & 1 \end{vmatrix}$	$\begin{vmatrix} -1 & 0 & 0 & 0 \\ 0 & 1 & 0 & 0 \\ 0 & 0 & 1 & 0 \\ 0 & 0 & 0 & 1 \end{vmatrix}$

Rotation through angle θ around an axis:

AROUND THE X AXIS	AROUND THE Y AXIS	AROUND THE Z AXIS
$\begin{vmatrix} 1 & 0 & 0 & 0 \\ 0 & \cos(q) & \sin(q) & 0 \\ 0 & -\sin(q) & \cos(q) & 0 \\ 0 & 0 & 0 & 1 \end{vmatrix}$	$\begin{vmatrix} \cos(q) & 0 & -\sin(q) & 0 \\ 0 & 1 & 0 & 0 \\ \sin(q) & 0 & \cos(q) & 0 \\ 0 & 0 & 0 & 1 \end{vmatrix}$	$\begin{vmatrix} \cos(q) & \sin(q) & 0 & 0 \\ -\sin(q) & \cos(q) & 0 & 0 \\ 0 & 0 & 1 & 0 \\ 0 & 0 & 0 & 1 \end{vmatrix}$

Orthographic projection onto a coordinate plane:

FRONT VIEW (PROJECTING ALONG THE Z AXIS)	SIDE VIEW (PROJECTING ALONG THE X AXIS)	TOP VIEW (PROJECTING ALONG THE Y AXIS)
$\begin{vmatrix} 1 & 0 & 0 & 0 \\ 0 & 1 & 0 & 0 \\ 0 & 0 & 0 & 0 \\ 0 & 0 & 0 & 1 \end{vmatrix}$	$\begin{vmatrix} 0 & 0 & 0 & 0 \\ 0 & 1 & 0 & 0 \\ -1 & 0 & 0 & 0 \\ 0 & 0 & 0 & 1 \end{vmatrix}$	$\begin{vmatrix} 1 & 0 & 0 & 0 \\ 0 & 0 & 0 & 0 \\ 0 & -1 & 0 & 0 \\ 0 & 0 & 0 & 1 \end{vmatrix}$

Axonometric orthographic projections (the plane of projection is not a coordinate plane):

1. Translate the focus (Fx, Fy, Fz) to the origin.

2. Rotate the direction of projection into the Y-Z plane.

3. Rotate the direction of projection into the Y axis.

4. Project along the Y axis using a simple orthographic projection.

Oblique projection (projectors are not perpendicular to the plane of projection):

CAVALIER PROJECTION ONTO THE X-Y PLANE	CABINET PROJECTION ONTO THE X-Y PLANE
$\begin{vmatrix} 1 & 0 & 0 & 0 \\ 0 & 1 & 0 & 0 \\ -\cos(\theta) & -\sin(\theta) & 0 & 0 \\ 0 & 0 & 0 & 1 \end{vmatrix}$	$\begin{vmatrix} 1 & 0 & 0 & 0 \\ 0 & 1 & 0 & 0 \\ -\cos(\theta)/2 & -\sin(\theta)/2 & 0 & 0 \\ 0 & 0 & 0 & 1 \end{vmatrix}$

Perspective projection onto the X-Y plane with center of projection at (0, 0, d):

$$\begin{vmatrix} 1 & 0 & 0 & 0 \\ 0 & 1 & 0 & 0 \\ 0 & 0 & 0 & -1/d \\ 0 & 0 & 0 & 1 \end{vmatrix}$$

Reflection across an arbitrary plane:

1. Translate the plane so that it intersects the origin.
2. Rotate around the Z axis until the normal vector lies in the Y-Z plane.
3. Rotate around the X axis to make the normal vector lie along the Y axis.
4. Reflect across the X-Z plane.
5. Reverse the second rotation.
6. Reverse the first rotation.
7. Reverse the translation.

Rotation around an arbitrary line:

1. Translate the line to the origin.
2. Rotate around the Z axis until the line lies in the Y-Z plane.
3. Rotate around the X axis until the line lies along the Y axis.
4. Rotate around the Y axis.
5. Reverse the second rotation.
6. Reverse the first rotation.
7. Reverse the translation.

Projection onto an arbitrary plane:

1. Translate the focus to the origin.
2. Rotate around the Y axis to place the center of projection in the Y-Z plane.
3. Rotate around the X axis until the center of projection lies on the Z axis.
4. Project (parallel or perspective) along the Z axis onto the X-Y plane.

Projection onto an arbitrary plane with an UP vector:

1. Translate the focus to the origin.
2. Rotate around the Y axis to place the center of projection in the Y-Z plane.
3. Rotate around the X axis until the center of projection lies on the Z axis.
4. Rotate around the Z axis until the UP vector lies in the Y-Z plane.
5. Project (parallel or perspective) along the Z axis onto the X-Y plane.

Four-Dimensional Transformations

Translation by distances Tx, Ty, Tz, and Tw:

$$
\begin{vmatrix}
1 & 0 & 0 & 0 & 0 \\
0 & 1 & 0 & 0 & 0 \\
0 & 0 & 1 & 0 & 0 \\
0 & 0 & 0 & 1 & 0 \\
Tx & Ty & Tz & Tw & 1
\end{vmatrix}
$$

Scaling by scale factors Sx, Sy, Sz, and Sw:

$$
\begin{vmatrix}
Sy & 0 & 0 & 0 & 0 \\
0 & Sx & 0 & 0 & 0 \\
0 & 0 & Sz & 0 & 0 \\
0 & 0 & 0 & Sw & 0 \\
0 & 0 & 0 & 0 & 1
\end{vmatrix}
$$

Reflection across a coordinate space:

ACROSS X-Y-Z SPACE

$$
\begin{vmatrix}
1 & 0 & 0 & 0 & 0 \\
0 & 1 & 0 & 0 & 0 \\
0 & 0 & 1 & 0 & 0 \\
0 & 0 & 0 & -1 & 0 \\
0 & 0 & 0 & 0 & 1
\end{vmatrix}
$$

ACROSS X-Y-W SPACE

$$
\begin{vmatrix}
1 & 0 & 0 & 0 & 0 \\
0 & 1 & 0 & 0 & 0 \\
0 & 0 & -1 & 0 & 0 \\
0 & 0 & 0 & 1 & 0 \\
0 & 0 & 0 & 0 & 1
\end{vmatrix}
$$

ACROSS X-Z-W SPACE

$$
\begin{vmatrix}
1 & 0 & 0 & 0 & 0 \\
0 & -1 & 0 & 0 & 0 \\
0 & 0 & 1 & 0 & 0 \\
0 & 0 & 0 & 1 & 0 \\
0 & 0 & 0 & 0 & 1
\end{vmatrix}
$$

ACROSS Y-Z-W SPACE

$$
\begin{vmatrix}
-1 & 0 & 0 & 0 & 0 \\
0 & 1 & 0 & 0 & 0 \\
0 & 0 & 1 & 0 & 0 \\
0 & 0 & 0 & 1 & 0 \\
0 & 0 & 0 & 0 & 1
\end{vmatrix}
$$

Rotation through angle θ around a coordinate plane:

AROUND THE X-Y PLANE

$$
\begin{vmatrix}
1 & 0 & 0 & 0 & 0 \\
0 & 1 & 0 & 0 & 0 \\
0 & 0 & \cos(\theta) & \sin(\theta) & 0 \\
0 & 0 & -\sin(\theta) & \cos(\theta) & 0 \\
0 & 0 & 0 & 0 & 1
\end{vmatrix}
$$

AROUND THE X-Z PLANE

$$
\begin{vmatrix}
1 & 0 & 0 & 0 & 0 \\
0 & \cos(\theta) & 0 & \sin(\theta) & 0 \\
0 & 0 & 1 & 0 & 0 \\
0 & -\sin(\theta) & 0 & \cos(\theta) & 0 \\
0 & 0 & 0 & 0 & 1
\end{vmatrix}
$$

AROUND THE X-W PLANE

$$
\begin{vmatrix}
1 & 0 & 0 & 0 & 0 \\
0 & \cos(\theta) & \sin(\theta) & 0 & 0 \\
0 & -\sin(\theta) & \cos(\theta) & 0 & 0 \\
0 & 0 & 0 & 1 & 0 \\
0 & 0 & 0 & 0 & 1
\end{vmatrix}
$$

AROUND THE Y-Z PLANE

$$
\begin{vmatrix}
\cos(\theta) & 0 & 0 & \sin(\theta) & 0 \\
0 & 1 & 0 & 0 & 0 \\
0 & 0 & 1 & 0 & 0 \\
-\sin(\theta) & 0 & 0 & \cos(\theta) & 0 \\
0 & 0 & 0 & 0 & 1
\end{vmatrix}
$$

AROUND THE Y-W PLANE

$$\begin{vmatrix} \cos(\theta) & 0 & -\sin(\theta) & 0 & 0 \\ 0 & 1 & 0 & 0 & 0 \\ \sin(\theta) & 0 & \cos(\theta) & 0 & 0 \\ 0 & 1 & 0 & 0 & 0 \\ 0 & 0 & 0 & 0 & 1 \end{vmatrix}$$

AROUND THE Z-W PLANE

$$\begin{vmatrix} \cos(\theta) & \sin(\theta) & 0 & 0 & 0 \\ -\sin(\theta) & \cos(\theta) & 0 & 0 & 0 \\ 0 & 0 & 1 & 0 & 0 \\ 0 & 0 & 0 & 1 & 0 \\ 0 & 0 & 0 & 0 & 1 \end{vmatrix}$$

Orthographic projections:

PARALLEL TO THE W AXIS INTO X-Y-Z SPACE

$$\begin{vmatrix} 1 & 0 & 0 & 0 & 0 \\ 0 & 1 & 0 & 0 & 0 \\ 0 & 0 & 1 & 0 & 0 \\ 0 & 0 & 0 & 0 & 0 \\ 0 & 0 & 0 & 0 & 1 \end{vmatrix}$$

PARALLEL TO THE Z AXIS INTO X-Y-W SPACE

$$\begin{vmatrix} 1 & 0 & 0 & 0 & 0 \\ 0 & 1 & 0 & 0 & 0 \\ 0 & 0 & 0 & 0 & 0 \\ 0 & 0 & 0 & 1 & 0 \\ 0 & 0 & 0 & 0 & 1 \end{vmatrix}$$

PARALLEL TO THE Y AXIS INTO X-Z-W SPACE

$$\begin{vmatrix} 1 & 0 & 0 & 0 & 0 \\ 0 & 0 & 0 & 0 & 0 \\ 0 & 0 & 1 & 0 & 0 \\ 0 & 0 & 0 & 1 & 0 \\ 0 & 0 & 0 & 0 & 1 \end{vmatrix}$$

PARALLEL TO THE X AXIS INTO Y-Z-W SPACE

$$\begin{vmatrix} 0 & 0 & 0 & 0 & 0 \\ 0 & 1 & 0 & 0 & 0 \\ 0 & 0 & 1 & 0 & 0 \\ 0 & 0 & 0 & 1 & 0 \\ 0 & 0 & 0 & 0 & 1 \end{vmatrix}$$

Perspective projection into the X-Y-Z coordinate space with center of projection at (0, 0, 0, d):

$$\begin{vmatrix} 1 & 0 & 0 & 0 & 0 \\ 0 & 1 & 0 & 0 & 0 \\ 0 & 0 & 1 & 0 & 0 \\ 0 & 0 & 0 & 0 & -1/d \\ 0 & 0 & 0 & 0 & 1 \end{vmatrix}$$

Spherical Coordinates

Converting from spherical coordinates (R, ϕ, θ) to Cartesian coordinates (x, y, z):

```
y = R * Sin(φ)
x = R * Cos(φ) * Cos(θ)
z = R * Cos(φ) * Sin(θ)
```

Converting from Cartesian coordinates (x, y, z) to spherical coordinates (R, ϕ, θ):

```
R = Sqr(x² + y² + z²)
θ = arctangent(z/x)
φ = arctangent(y/Sqr(x² + z²))
```

Distances

This section contains formulas for calculating the distances between various objects. Module Distance.bas contains functions that return these distances. Example program Distance demonstrates these functions.

Point-to-Point

The distance between points A = (ax, ay, az) and B = (bx, by, bz) is written |AB|. This is the same as the length of the vector from A to B and is given by:

```
|<bx - ax, by - ay, bz - az>| =
Sqr((bx - ax)² + (by - ay)² + (bz - az)²)
```

Point-to-Line

Suppose a line passes through point C = (cx, cy, cz) in the direction of the vector V = <vx, vy, vz>. Now consider a point P = (px, py, pz) as shown in Figure 19.6.

A is the vector from point C to point P. A' is the projection of vector A along vector P. The section Projection of a Vector onto a Vector earlier in this chapter showed that:

```
|A'| = (A · V)/|V|
```

The shortest distance from point P to the line is along the vector A - A' perpendicular to the line. That means the shortest distance from P to the line is |A - A'|.

Then the Pythagorean theorem says:

```
|A - A'| = Sqr(|A|² - |A'|²)
         = Sqr(|A|² - ((A · V)/|V|)²)
```

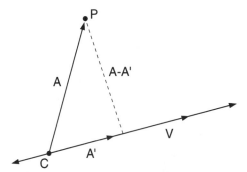

Figure 19.6 The shortest distance from point P to a line is along the vector A - A'.

This gives you a way to calculate the distance from the point to the line. For example, consider the point and line in Figure 19.7.

$C = (1, 1)$, $P = (1, 3)$, and $V = <2, 2>$. Then $A = P - C = <1 - 1, 3 - 1> = <0, 2>$. Plugging these values into the previous equation gives:

```
|A - A'| = Sqr(|A|² - ((A · V)/|V|)²)
         = Sqr(4 - ((0 * 2 + 2 * 2)/Sqr(8))²)
         = Sqr(4 - 2)
         = Sqr(2)
```

This agrees with Figure 19.7.

Point-to-Plane

Suppose C is a point on a plane with normal vector N and P is a point not on the plane. Let A be the vector from point C to point P. Then the shortest distance from point P to the plane is along A', the projection of vector A onto vector N as shown in Figure 19.8.

The section Projection of a Vector onto a Vector earlier in this chapter showed that:

```
|A'| = (A · N)/|N|
```

For a simple example, let $P = (0, 2, 0)$, $C = (0, 0, 0)$, and let the normal vector $N = <0, 1, 0>$. Then $A = <0, 2, 0>$ so:

```
|A'| = (0 * 0 + 2 * 1 + 0 * 0)/1
     = 2/1
     = 2
```

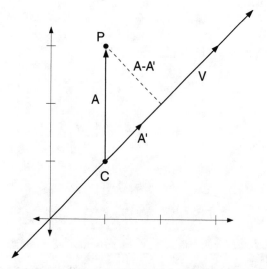

Figure 19.7   Finding the shortest distance between a point and a line.

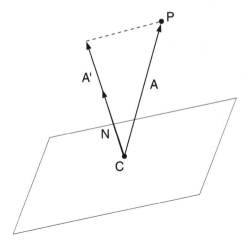

Figure 19.8   Finding the shortest distance between a point and a plane.

Line-to-Line

First, suppose the two lines are parallel. Then finding the distance between the lines is equivalent to finding the distance between any point on the first line and the second line. See the section Point-to-Line earlier in this chapter to see how to find this distance.

Now suppose the lines are not parallel. Then the lines are contained in two parallel planes, and the smallest distance between the lines is the same as the distance between the planes. Take the cross product of the vectors defining the lines to find a vector perpendicular to both lines and thus both planes. Now use the technique described in the previous section to find the distance between any point on one line with the other line's plane.

Suppose the lines are defined by the points P1 and P2, and vectors V1 and V2. Let A be the vector from point P1 to point P2. Then using the cross product and the previous section gives:

```
Distance = (A · N)/|N|
         = (A · (V1 × V2))/|V1 × V2|
```

This process is illustrated in Figure 19.9.

Plane-to-Plane

Two planes are parallel if they have the same normal vector. Obviously, if the planes are not parallel, the distance between them is zero because they intersect.

If two planes are parallel, you can pick any point on one plane and then use the techniques described in the earlier section Point-to-Plane to find the distance between that point and the other plane.

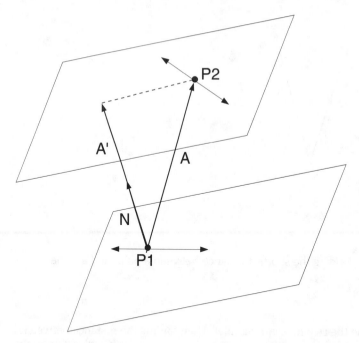

Figure 19.9   Finding the distance between two lines.

Platonic Solids

The Greek philosopher Plato (B.C. 427–347) classified the Platonic solids: tetrahedron, cube (or hexahedron), octahedron, dodecahedron, and icosahedron. These solids have several interesting properties. For example, they are the only regular three-dimensional solids.

The following sections describe other characteristics of the Platonic solids and explain how to find their vertices. Module Platonic.bas contains routines that generate the coordinates for the solids' vertices. Example program Solids, shown in Figure 19.10, uses

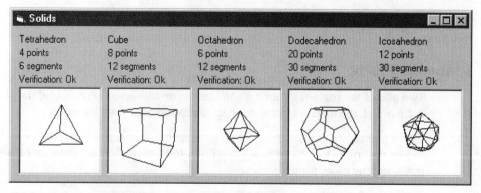

Figure 19.10   Program Solids computes and verifies vertex locations.

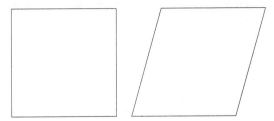

Figure 19.11   A regular polygon (left) and a polygon that is not regular (right).

these routines to create the Platonic solids. For each solid, it verifies that every vertex is the same distance from the origin and that each segment has the same length.

Regular Solids

A *regular polygon* is a two-dimensional shape in which all edges have the same length and the edges all make the same angles with respect to each other. Figure 19.11 shows two quadrilaterals. The one on the left is a square. It is a regular polygon because all its sides are the same length, and they all meet at 90 degree angles. The polygon on the right is a parallelogram and is not regular. While its sides all have the same length, they do not all meet at the same angles.

In a regular three-dimensional solid or polyhedron, all faces are regular polygons. The Platonic solids include the tetrahedron (4 faces), cube or hexahedron (6 faces), octahedron (8 faces), dodecahedron (12 faces), and the icosahedron (20 faces).

There are no other regular solids in three dimensions. You may have seen solids made up of more faces, all of which are identical. For example, some game stores sell 30-sided and even 100-sided dice. The faces of these solids are parallelograms, not regular polygons, so these are not regular solids.

Duals

The Platonic solids have some rather interesting *dual relationships*. To make the dual of a solid, place a vertex in the center of each of the solid's faces. Then connect each vertex to the vertices on the adjacent faces. For each of the Platonic solids, the result is another Platonic solid. Figure 19.12 shows a cube and its dual: an octahedron.

Figure 19.12   The dual of a cube is an octahedron.

The dual relationships are reflected in the numbers of faces and vertices of the different Platonic solids. For example, a cube has 6 faces and 8 vertices. Its dual, the octahedron, has 8 faces and 6 vertices. Table 19.1 lists the number of faces, vertices, and edges in the Platonic solids.

The number of faces, edges, and vertices are related to the shape and arrangement of the faces. Define the following values:

F = Total faces in the solid
E = Total edges in the solid
V = Total vertices in the solid
EF = Number of edges on each face
VF = Number of vertices on each face
SE = Number of faces that share each edge (always 2)
SV = Number of faces that share each vertex

Then:

```
E = F * EF/SE
V = F * VF/SV
```

For example, an icosahedron has 20 triangular faces with each vertex shared by 5 faces, so F = 20, EF = 3, VF = 3, SE = 2, and SV = 5. Plugging these numbers into the previous equations gives:

```
E = 20 * 3/2 = 30
V = 20 * 3/5 = 12
```

These values agree with Table 19.1.

Tetrahedron

A tetrahedron has four faces defined by equilateral triangles. In an equilateral triangle, the sides meet at 60-degree angles. Figure 19.13 shows a tetrahedron. The vertices are labeled A, B, C, and D.

Table 19.1   The Platonic Solids and Their Duals

SOLID	DUAL	FACES	VERTICES	EDGES
Tetrahedron	Tetrahedron	4	4	6
Cube	Octahedron	6	8	12
Octahedron	Cube	8	6	12
Dodecahedron	Icosahedron	12	20	30
Icosahedron	Dodecahedron	20	12	30

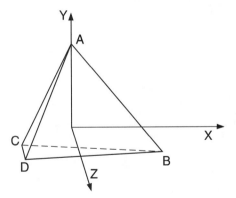

Figure 19.13   A tetrahedron.

In an equilateral triangle, the angles valeu values 30, 60, and 90 degrees and the sides have relative lengths of 1, 2, Sqr(3) as shown in Figure 19.14. These lengths are relative to each other. For example, if the short side has length 4, the other sides have lengths 4 * 2 and 4 * Sqr(3).

Consider a tetrahedron centered at the origin with one of the base vertices lying in the X-Y plane. Imagine looking at a tetrahedron centered at the origin from the top as shown in Figure 19.15. The lines from the origin to the tetrahedron's corners bisect the 60-degree angles that make up the solid's base. If the sides of the tetrahedron have length 2, Figure 19.15 shows the other important distances. This figure gives the X and Z coordinates of the tetrahedron's vertices.

Now imagine looking at the tetrahedron from the side as shown in Figure 19.16. Distance d1 is the height of the left face of the solid, so Figure 19.15 shows that d1 = Sqr(3). Figure 19.15 also shows that d2 = 1/Sqr(3), so the height of the tetrahedron H = Sqr(d1² − d2²) = Sqr(3 −1/3) = 2 * Sqr(2/3).

The last distance of importance is Ay, the Y coordinate of point A. Points A and B must be the same distance from the origin or, equivalently, the squares of the distances from these points to the origin must be the same.

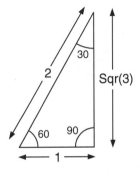

Figure 19.14   The 30-60-90 triangle has sides with relative lengths of 1, 2, Sqr(3).

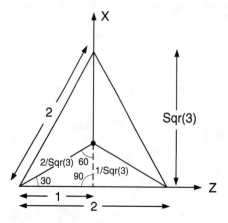

Figure 19.15 Top view of a tetrahedron.

Point A has coordinates (0, Ay, 0). Point B has coordinates ((Sqr(3) – 1/Sqr(3), Ay – 2 * Sqr(2/3), 0) = (2/Sqr(3), Ay – 2 * Sqr(2/3), 0). Setting the squares of distances equal gives:

```
Ay² = (2/Sqr(3))² + (Ay - 2 * Sqr(2/3))²
    = (4/3) + (Ay² - 2 * Ay * 2 * Sqr(2/3) + 4 * 2/3)
    = Ay² + 4 - 4 * Ay * Sqr(2/3)
```

Subtracting Ay^2 from both sides and solving for Ay gives:

```
Ay = 1/Sqr(2/3)
```

Using these results, you can write the coordinates for the tetrahedron's vertices. The coordinates are shown in Table 19.2.

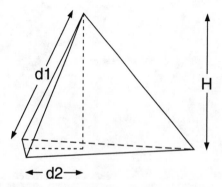

Figure 19.16 Side view of a tetrahedron.

Table 19.2   Tetrahedron Vertex Coordinates

VERTEX	X	Y	Z
A	0	1/Sqr(2/3)	0
B	Sqr(3) – 1/Sqr(3)	1/Sqr(2/3) – 2 * Sqr(2/3)	0
C	–1/Sqr(3)	1/Sqr(2/3) – 2 * Sqr(2/3)	–1
D	–1/Sqr(3)	1/Sqr(2/3) – 2 * Sqr(2/3)	1

Cube

The cube, shown in Figure 19.17, is much easier to understand than the tetrahedron. If you want the cube's sides to be 2 units long and you want the cube centered at the origin, the cube has the vertex coordinates shown in Table 19.3.

Table 19.3   Cube Vertex Coordinates

VERTEX	X	Y	Z
A	–1	1	–1
B	1	1	–1
C	1	1	1
D	–1	1	1
E	–1	–1	–1
F	1	–1	–1
G	1	–1	1
H	–1	–1	1

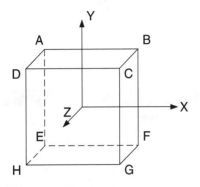

Figure 19.17   A cube.

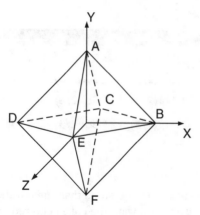

Figure 19.18 An octahedron.

Octahedron

The octahedron is also relatively straightforward. If you place the solid's vertices on the coordinate axes as shown in Figure 19.18, the points are located at the positions listed in Table 19.4. These coordinates define the dual of the cube described in the previous section.

Dodecahedron

Figure 19.19 shows a dodecahedron. Figure 19.20 shows the dodecahedron from the top. The figure assumes the side length is S. You can use this drawing to find the X and Z coordinates for the points on the top of the solid.

The first step in understanding this figure is to calculate the values of the labeled angles. Because there are five sides to this top face, $\theta_1 = 2 * \pi/5$. Angle θ_4 is half as big as θ_1, so $\theta_4 = \pi/5$.

The angle between the X and Z axes is $\pi/2$. Because that angle equals θ_2 plus θ_2, $\theta_1 + \theta_2 = \pi/2$, so:

```
θ₂ = π/2 - θ₁ = π/2 - 2 * π/5 = π/10
```

Table 19.4 Octahedron Vertex Coordinates

VERTEX	X	Y	Z
A	0	1	0
B	1	0	0
C	0	0	-1
D	-1	0	0
E	0	0	1
F	0	-1	0

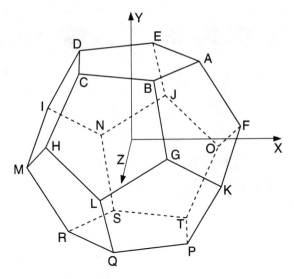

Figure 19.19   A dodecahedron.

Finally, $\theta_2 + \theta_3 = \theta_1$, so:

$$\theta_3 = \theta_1 - \theta_2 = 2 * \pi/5 - \pi/10 = 3 * \pi/10$$

Now that you have values for the angles, you can work on the X and Z coordinates. Note that all the segments running from the center of the pentagon to the vertices have the same length. The segment that ends at point A has length d1, so they all have length d1.

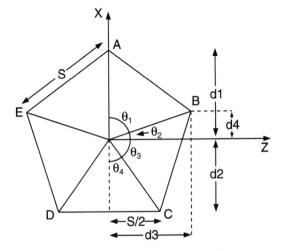

Figure 19.20   The top of a dodecahedron.

Table 19.5 Values from Figure 19.20

VARIABLE	VALUE
θ_1	$2 * \pi/5$
θ_2	$\pi/10$
3	$3 * /10$
4	$/5$
d1	$S/2/Sin(4)$
d2	$Cos(4) * d1$
d3	$Cos(2) * d1$
d4x	$Sin(\theta_2) * d1$

Using trigonometry in the triangle containing angle θ_4 gives $Sin(\theta_4) = (S/2)/d1$. Solving for d1 gives $d1 = S/2/Sin(\theta_4)$. Using this value, you can calculate the length of the other side of this triangle. $Cos(\theta_4) = d2/d1$ so $d2 = Cos(\theta_4) * d1$.

Similarly, using the triangle containing angle θ_2 gives $d3 = Cos(\theta_2) * d1$ and $d4 = Sin(\theta_2) * d1$.

Table 19.5 summarizes these values. Using these values and symmetry, you can find the X and Z coordinates of points A through E.

Figure 19.21 shows the complete dodecahedron from the top. This is a perspective transformation, so the bottom face is smaller than the top face. You can see from the alignment, however, that the bottom face is identical to the top face, except it has been rotated 180 degrees. Using this fact and the values in Table 19.5, you can find the X and Z coordinates for vertices P through T.

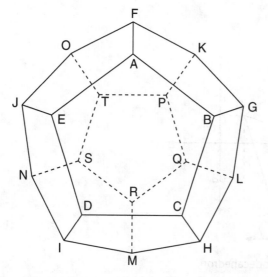

Figure 19.21 A complete dodecahedron viewed from the top.

Look again at Figures 19.19 and 19.20. These pictures show that the distance between points A and F is S and that the distance between points B and F is 2 * d3. Using the distance formula and squaring these values gives the equations:

```
|AF|² = S² = (Ax - Fx)² + (Ay - Fy)² + (Az - Fz)²
|BF|² = (2 * d3)² = (Bx - Fx)² + (By - Fy)² + (Bz - Fz)²
```

Figures 19.19 and 19.20 show that Az = Fz = 0, Ax = d1, Bx = d4, Bz = d3, and Ay = By. Let d5 = Ay - Fy be the difference between Ay and Fy. Then these equations become:

```
S²        = (d1 - Fx)² + d5²
(2 * d3)² = (d4 - Fx)² + d5² + d3²
```

Subtracting the second equation from the first gives:

```
S² - (2 * d3)² = (d1 - Fx)² - (d4 - Fx)² - d3²
               = (d1² - 2 * d1 * Fx + Fx²) -
                 (d4² - 2 * d4 * Fx + Fx²) - d3²
               = Fx * 2 * (d4 - d1) + (d1² - d4² - d3²)
```

Using the values in Table 19.5, you can calculate D1, D4, and Bz. That means this equation contains only one unknown value: Fx. Solving for Fx gives:

```
Fx = [S² - (2 * d3)² - (d1² - d4² - d3²)]/[2 * (d4 - d1)]
```

This is a bit messy, but it is a value that you can compute.

Adding the two equations for the distances |AF| and |BF| gives:

```
S² + (2 * d3)² = (d1 - Fx)² + 2 * d5² + (d4 - Fx)² + d3²
```

If you solve this for d5, you get:

```
d5 = Sqr((S² + (2 * d3)² - (d1 - Fx)² - (d4 - Fx)² - d3²)/2)
```

This is another messy expression, but at this point, all of these values are known.

If you look closely at Figure 19.21, you will see that points F, G, H, I, and J form a pentagon similar to the one in Figure 19.20. The only difference is the distance from the center of the pentagon to the vertices. For points F through J, this distance is Fx, the X coordinate of vertex F. Using this fact and trigonometry similar to that displayed in Figure 19.20, you can find the X and Z coordinates for points F through J.

Using symmetry, you can find the X and Z coordinates for points K through O.

The only remaining values to find are the points' Y coordinates. Points A and F must be the same distance from the origin so:

```
Ax² + Ay² + Az² = Fx² + Fy² + Fz²
```

Table 19.6 Intermediate Values for the Dodecahedron

VARIABLE	VALUE
Fx	$(S^2 - (2 * d3)^2 - (d1^2 - d4^2 - d3^2))/2/(d4 - d1)$
d5	$Sqr((S^2 + (2 * d3)^2 - (d1 - Fx)^2 - (d4 - Fx)^2 - d3^2)/2)$
Fy	$(Fx^2 - d1^2 - d5^2)/(2 * d5)$
Ay	$d5 + Fy$

The earlier calculations obtained a value for d5 = Ay − Fy. Substituting Fz = 0, Ax = d1, Az = 0, and Ay = d5 + Fy into this equation gives:

```
d1² + (d5 + Fy)² = Fx² + Fy²
```

The value Fx is known at this point, so you can solve this equation for the one remaining unknown value Fy:

```
d1² + d5² + 2 * d5 * Fy + Fy² = Fx² + Fy²
2 * d5 * Fy = Fx² - d1² - d5²
Fy = (Fx² - d1² - d5²)/(2 * d5)
```

From these values and symmetry, you can calculate all the vertex coordinates for the dodecahedron. Table 19.6 shows the remaining intermediate variables used to find the points' coordinates. Table 19.7 shows the vertex coordinates for the dodecahedron.

Table 19.7 Dodecahedron Vertex Coordinates

VERTEX	X	Y	Z
A	d1	Ay	0
B	d4	Ay	d3
C	−d2	Ay	S/2
D	−d2	Ay	−S/2
E	d4	Ay	−d3
F	Fx	Fy	0
G	Fx * Sin(theta2)	Fy	Fx * Cos(theta2)
H	−Fx * Sin(theta3)	Fy	Fx * Cos(theta3)
I	−Fx * Sin(theta3)	Fy	−Fx * Cos(theta3)
J	Fx * Sin(theta2)	Fy	−Fx * Cos(theta2)
K	Fx * Sin(theta3)	−Fy	Fx * Cos(theta3)
L	−Fx * Sin(theta2)	−Fy	Fx * Cos(theta2)
M	−Fx	−Fy	0
N	−Fx * Sin(theta2)	−Fy	−Fx * Cos(theta2)

Table 19.7 *(Continued)*

VERTEX	X	Y	Z
O	Fx * Sin(theta3)	−Fy	−Fx * Cos(theta3)
P	d2	−Ay	S/2
Q	−d4	−Ay	d3
R	−d1	−Ay	0
S	−d4	−Ay	−d3
T	d2	−Ay	−S/2

Icosahedron

Figure 19.22 shows an icosahedron. One way you could find the coordinates of the vertices of an icosahedron is to use a dodecahedron. Because these solids are duals, the center points of the faces of a dodecahedron give the vertices for an icosahedron. It is not too hard to find these coordinates directly, however, particularly since most of the calculations follow immediately from the previous section.

Figure 19.23 shows parts of an icosahedron from the top. This picture shows only vertices B though K and some of the edges connecting them. The edges shown define two pentagons of constant Y value. The points B through F have the same Y value, and the points G through K have the same Y value.

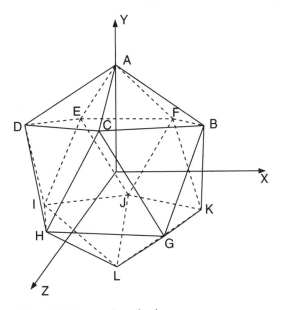

Figure 19.22 An icosahedron.

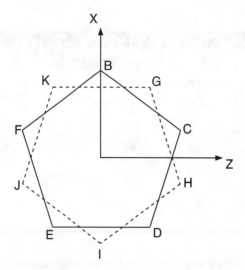

Figure 19.23   Top view of part of an icosahedron.

Figure 19.20 shows the geometry of these pentagons. Using that picture and the results of the previous section gives you all the X and Z coordinates for points B though K. Points A and L have X and Z coordinates equal to 0 since they lie on the Y axis.

The only values that you still need to calculate are the Y coordinates Ay and By of points A and B. Then points C through F have Y coordinate By, points G through K have Y coordinate -By, and point L has Y coordinate –Ay.

First, consider the five faces that contain point A as shown in Figure 19.24. The length of the edges is defined to be S, and the distance d1 is given by Figure 19.20. Then you can calculate d6:

```
d6 = Sqr(S² - d1²)
```

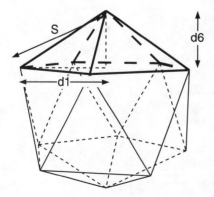

Figure 19.24   The top five faces in an icosahedron.

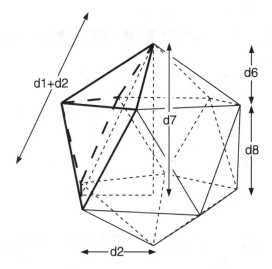

Figure 19.25 The five faces containing point D.

Now consider the five faces that contain point D as shown in Figure 19.25. The diagonal segment runs from the bottom to the top of the pentagon containing the points A, C, H, I, and E. Figure 19.20 shows that the length of this segment is d1 + d2.

Considering the top view of the icosahedron, Figure 19.20 also shows that the horizontal distance from the bottom of this pentagon to the center of the solid is d2. You can use these facts to find the vertical height of this pentagon:

```
d7 = Sqr((d1 + d2)² - d2²)
```

Once you know the values d6 and d7, you can calculate d8 = d7 − d6. Since the solid is centered vertically at the origin, By = d8/2. Then Ay = By + d6.

Table 19.8 lists the intermediate values used to calculate the coordinates of the icosahedron's vertices. The values θ_1 through θ_4 and d1 through d4 come from Figure 19.20. Table 19.9 shows the vertex coordinates for the icosahedron.

Table 19.8 Intermediate Values for the Icosahedron

VARIABLE	VALUE
θ_1	2 * π/5
θ_2	π/10
3	3 * /10
4	/5
d1	S/2/Sin(4)
d2	Cos(4) * d1

Continues

Table 19.8 Intermediate Values for the Icosahedron *(Continued)*

VARIABLE	VALUE
d3	Cos(2) * d1
d4	Sin(2) * d1
d6	Sqr(S2 – d12)
d7	Sqr((d1 + d2)2 – d22)
d8	d7 - d6
By	d8/2
Ay	By + d6

Table 19.9 Icosahedron Vertex Coordinates

VERTEX	X	Y	Z
A	0	Ay	0
B	d1	By	0
C	d4	By	d3
D	–d2	By	S/2
E	–d2	By	–S/2
F	d4	By	–d3
G	d2	–By	S/2
H	–d4	–By	d3
I	–d1	–By	0
J	–d4	–By	–d3
K	d2	–By	–S/2
L	0	–Ay	0

Summary

This chapter describes some of the mathematics used throughout this book. There are certainly other interesting three-dimensional solids you can build. For example, some of the programs in the book display stellate polyhedra. To make a stellate polyhedron, replace each face of a normal polyhedron with a pyramid that has the original face as its base.

For more information on constructing solids, find a good geometry text. To learn more about vectors and matrices, consult a linear algebra book. For more information on calculating distances and building surfaces, look for an analytic geometry book. Analytic geometry is often paired with calculus, so you may end up with a book on both. If you get books on all of these subjects, you will have a reasonably powerful library of useful mathematics.

To use this CD-ROM, your system must meet the following requirements:

A machine reasonably capable of running Visual Basic. Programs will run faster on machines with faster processors and more memory.

Hard drive space: To copy all the new source code down to your hard drive, 79 MB. To copy all CD-ROM materials, 265 MB. You can also load programs and files directly from the CD-ROM without copying them to your hard drive.

Peripherals: CD-ROM drive.